S0-BIQ-370

Wiley
CMAexcel Learning System
Exam Review 2015

About IMA® (Institute of Management Accountants)

IMA®, the association of accountants and financial professionals in business, is one of the largest and most respected associations focused exclusively on advancing the management accounting profession. Globally, IMA supports the profession through research, the CMA® (Certified Management Accountant) program, continuing education, networking, and advocacy of the highest ethical business practices. IMA has a global network of more than 65,000 members in 120 countries and 300 local chapter communities. IMA provides localized services through its offices in Montvale, NJ, USA; Zurich, Switzerland; Dubai, UAE; and Beijing, China. For more information about IMA, please visit www.imanet.org.

Wiley CMAexcel Learning System Exam Review 2015

Self-Study Guide

Part 2: Financial Decision Making

The Association of Accountants and Financial Professionals in Business®

Cover Design by: David Riedy

Cover image: © iStock.com/turtleteeth

Copyright © 2014 by Institute of Management Accountants. All rights reserved.

Published by John Wiley & Sons, Inc., Hoboken, New Jersey.

Published simultaneously in Canada.

These materials are copyrighted and may not be reproduced in any form or used in any way to create derivative works. Any reproduction, reuse, or distribution of CMA Learning System® materials without prior written permission from the Institute of Management Accountants (IMA) is illegal and a material violation of the *IMA Statement of Ethical Professional Practice.*

Any Certified Management Accountant (CMA) or CMA candidate who reproduces, reuses, or distributes CMA Learning System® materials or content in any form without prior authorization from IMA is subject to legal action and will be reported to the Institute of Certified Management Accountants (ICMA) and immediately expelled from the IMA and CMA program.

It is your responsibility to ensure that any CMA exam review materials that you are using have been provided to you through authorized channels or personnel. If you are in doubt about the authenticity of your materials or question the means by which they have been provided to you, contact IMA customer service at (800) 638-4427 in the U.S. or +1 (201) 573-9000.

This material is designed for learning purposes and is distributed with the understanding that the publisher and authors are not offering legal or professional services.

No part of this publication may be reproduced, stored in a retrieval system, or transmitted in any form or by any means, electronic, mechanical, photocopying, recording, scanning, or otherwise, except as permitted under Section 107 or 108 of the 1976 United States Copyright Act, without either the prior written permission of the Publisher, or authorization through payment of the appropriate per-copy fee to the Copyright Clearance Center, Inc., 222 Rosewood Drive, Danvers, MA 01923, (978) 750-8400, fax (978) 646-8600, or on the Web at www.copyright.com. Requests to the Publisher for permission should be addressed to the Permissions Department, John Wiley & Sons, Inc., 111 River Street, Hoboken, NJ 07030, (201) 748-6011, fax (201) 748-6008, or online at www.wiley.com/go/permissions.

Limit of Liability/Disclaimer of Warranty: While the publisher and author have used their best efforts in preparing this book, they make no representations or warranties with respect to the accuracy or completeness of the contents of this book and specifically disclaim any implied warranties of merchantability or fitness for a particular purpose. No warranty may be created or extended by sales representatives or written sales materials. The advice and strategies contained herein may not be suitable for your situation. You should consult with a professional where appropriate. Neither the publisher nor author shall be liable for any loss of profit or any other commercial damages, including but not limited to special, incidental, consequential, or other damages.

For general information on our other products and services or for technical support, please contact our Customer Care Department within the United States at (800) 762-2974, outside the United States at (317) 572-3993 or fax (317) 572-4002.

Wiley also publishes its books in a variety of electronic formats. Some content that appears in print may not be available in electronic books. For more information about Wiley products, visit our web site at www.wiley.com.

Library of Congress Cataloging-in-Publication Data

Wiley CMAexcel exam review learning system.

    v. cm.

    Contents: pt. 1. Financial reporting, planning, performance, and control—pt. 2. Financial decision making.

    Includes bibliographical references and index.

    ISBN 978-1-118-95616-8 (Part 1, 1-year access)

    ISBN 978-1-118-95618-2 (Part 2, 1-year access)

    ISBN 978-1-118-99529-7 (Part 1, 2-year access)

    ISBN 978-1-118-99533-4 (Part 2, 2-year access)

    ISBN 978-1-118-95615-1 (Part 1, no pin)

    ISBN 978-1-118-95617-5 (Part 2, no pin)

    ISBN 978-1-118-95624-3 (Part 1 + OIR, 1-year access)

    ISBN 978-1-118-95625-0 (Part 2 + OIR, 1-year access)

    ISBN 978-1-118-99535-8 (Part 1 + OIR, 2-year access)

    ISBN 978-1-118-99542-6 (Part 2 + OIR, 2-year access)

       1. Accounting—Examinations—Study guides. 2. Accounting—Examinations, questions, etc. I. Title: Wiley Certified Management Accountant exam review learning system. II. Title: CMA exam review learning system.

    HF5661.W499   2014

    657.076—dc23

                                         2012022854

Printed in the United States of America

10 9 8 7 6 5 4 3 2 1

Contents

Essay Exam Support Materials   **509**

Answers to Section Practice Questions   **629**

Acknowledgments of Subject Matter Experts

The Wiley CMAexcel Learning System (WCMALS) content is written to help explain the concepts and calculations from the Certified Management Accountant (CMA) exam Learning Outcome Statements (LOS) published by the Institute of Certified Management Accountants (ICMA).

IMA would like to acknowledge the team of subject matter experts who worked together in conjunction with IMA staff to produce this version of the WCMALS.

Lynn Clements, DBA, CMA, CFM, CPA, Cr. FA, CFE, is a professor of accounting at Florida Southern College in Lakeland, Florida. She earned her Ph.D. in business administration with an accounting concentration from Nova Southeastern University. Clements has been a member of the Institute of Management Accountants since 1990. She has published many research articles and regularly teaches continuing professional education courses to the accounting community.

Saurav Dutta, CMA, is an associate professor and former chair of the Accounting Department at the State University of New York at Albany. Dutta is the author of some 20 research articles published in various academic journals. He received his Ph.D. in accounting from the University of Kansas and is also the recipient of the Robert Beyer Silver Medal for securing the second highest total score in a CMA examination.

Tony Griffin, CMA, is the accounting manager for Dayton Aerospace, Inc., a senior management consulting firm specializing in defense acquisition and logistics support to government and industry customers. Griffin has been actively involved in supporting the IMA and the CMA certification by serving as president of his local IMA chapter and by organizing and leading CMA review courses in the Dayton, Ohio, area.

Karen L. Jett, CMA, is a consultant specializing in values-based organizational development and ethics training. Prior to starting her own business (Jett Excellence), she acquired over two decades of experience working in privately held companies and holds a degree in accounting from Temple University (Philadelphia, PA). Jett is author of *Grow Your People, Grow Your Business* (Mira Digital, 2008) and Questioning Ethics, an innovative ethics training system designed specifically for smaller businesses. She has taught the CMA Review Courses for many years, both as an adjunct professor at Villanova University (Villanova, PA) and directly to corporate clients.

Jan Kooiman, CMA, holds a doctorate in business economics from the University of Amsterdam. He worked for an accounting and audit firm before stepping into the professional world as chief financial officer and board member of an international company. Kooiman is a qualified transactional Six Sigma Black Belt and Trainer and is adjunct professor of finance, business, and wccounting at the Webster and Leiden University in the Netherlands, teaching MBA Finance and Management Accounting. He is also the program manager and instructor of the CMA program at the World Trade Center Amsterdam.

Lou Petro, CMA, CPA, CGMA, CIA, CCP, CISA, CFE, CFM, PE, is a senior manager with a major fraud investigation firm and a former consultant and auditor. Petro specializes in fraud deterrence and investigation, corporate governance, bankruptcy, information systems auditing, production and inventory controls, internal controls, and cost and managerial accounting. He has also taught auditing, systems, accounting, and finance courses at colleges and universities in Michigan and Ontario.

Tara Shawver, DBA, CMA, is an associate professor of accounting at King's College (Wilkes-Barre, PA). She earned her Ph.D. in business administration with an accounting concentration from Nova Southeastern University. Shawver has been an active member of the Institute of Management Accountants since 2003. She is an active volunteer with the IMA, serving as president of the Pennsylvania Northeast Chapter. She has published many research articles and frequently presents at IMA's Annual Conference and Exhibition and the American Accounting Association.

Siaw-Peng Wan, CFA, is a professor of finance and the MBA program director at Elmhurst College (Elmhurst, IL). He received his Ph.D. in economics from the University of Illinois at Urbana-Champaign, and he recently became a CFA charter holder. His most recent articles on online investing and banking have appeared in *The Internet Encyclopedia* and *The Handbook of Information Security*. Wan has taught CMA Review Courses at Northern Illinois University since 2004.

Candidate Study Information

CMA Certification from ICMA

The Certified Management Accountant (CMA) certification provides accountants and financial professionals with an objective measure of knowledge and competence in the field of management accounting. The CMA designation is recognized globally as an invaluable credential for professional accountancy advancement inside organizations and for broadening professional skills and perspectives.

The two-part CMA exam is designed to develop and measure critical-thinking and decision-making skills and to meet these objectives:

- To establish management accounting and financial management as recognized professions by identifying the role of the professional, the underlying body of knowledge, and a course of study by which such knowledge is acquired.
- To encourage higher educational standards in the management accounting and financial management fields.
- To establish an objective measure of an individual's knowledge and competence in the fields of management accounting and financial management.
- To encourage continued professional development.

Individuals earning the CMA designation benefit by being able to:

- Communicate their broad business competency and strategic financial mastery.
- Obtain contemporary professional knowledge and develop skills and abilities that are valued by successful businesses.
- Convey their commitment to an exemplary standard of excellence that is grounded on a strong ethical foundation and lifelong learning.
- Enhance their career development, salary qualifications, and professional promotion opportunities.

The CMA certification is granted exclusively by the Institute of Certified Management Accountants (ICMA).

CMA Learning Outcome Statements (LOS)

The Certified Management Accountant exam is based on a series of Learning Outcome Statements (LOS) developed by the Institute of Certified Management Accountants (ICMA). The LOS describes the knowledge and skills that make up the CMA body of knowledge, broken down by part, section, and topic. The Wiley CMAexcel Learning System (WCMALS) supports the LOS by addressing the subjects they cover. Candidates should use the LOS to ensure they can address the concepts in different ways or through a variety of question scenarios. Candidates should also be prepared to perform calculations referred to in the LOS in total or by providing missing components of a calculation. The LOS should not be used as proxies for exact exam questions; they should be used as a guide for studying and learning the content that will be covered on the exam.

A copy of the ICMA Learning Outcome Statements is included in Appendix B at the end of this book. Candidates are also encouraged to visit the IMA website to find other exam-related information at www.imanet.org.

CMA Exam Format

The content tested on the CMA exams is at an advanced level—which means that the passing standard is set for mastery, not minimum competence. Thus, there will be test questions for all major topics that require the candidate to synthesize information, evaluate a situation, and make recommendations. Other questions will test subject comprehension and analysis. However, compared to previous versions, this CMA exam will have an increased emphasis on the higher-level questions.

The content is based on a series of LOS that define the competencies and capabilities expected of a management accountant.

There are two exams, taken separately: Part 1: Financial Reporting, Planning, Performance, and Control, and Part 2: Financial Decision Making. Each exam is four hours in length and includes multiple-choice and essay questions. One hundred multiple-choice questions are presented first, followed by two essay questions. All of these questions—multiple-choice and essay—can address any of the LOS for the respective exam part. Therefore, your study plan should include learning the content of the part as well as practicing how to answer multiple-choice and essay questions against that content. The study plan tips and the final section of this WCMALS book contains important information to help you learn how to approach the different types of questions.

Note on Candidate Assumed Knowledge

The CMA exam content is based on a set of assumed baseline knowledge that candidates are expected to have. Assumed knowledge includes economics, basic statistics, and financial accounting. Examples of how this assumed knowledge might be tested in the exam include:

- How to calculate marginal revenue and costs as well as understand the relevance of market structures when determining prices
- How to calculate variance when managing financial risk
- How to construct a cash flow statement as part of an analysis of transactions and assess the impact of the transactions on the financial statements

Please note that prior courses in accounting and finance are highly recommended to ensure this knowledge competency when preparing for the exam.

Overall Expectations for the CMA Candidates

Completing the CMA exams requires a high level of commitment and dedication of up to 150 hours of study for each part of the CMA exam. Completing the two-part exam is a serious investment that will reap many rewards, helping you to build a solid foundation for your career, distinguish yourself from other accountants, and enhance your career in ways that will pay dividends for a lifetime.

Your success in completing these exams will rest heavily on your ability to create a solid study plan and to execute that plan. IMA offers many resources, tools, and programs to support you during this process—the exam content specifications, assessment tools to identify the content areas you need to study most, comprehensive study tools such as the Online Test Bank, classroom programs, and online intensive review courses. We encourage you to register as a CMA candidate as soon as you begin the program to maximize your access to these resources and tools and to draw on these benefits with rigor and discipline that best supports your unique study needs. We also suggest candidates seek other sources if further knowledge is needed to augment knowledge and understanding of the ICMA LOS.

For more information about the CMA certification, the CMA exams, or the exam preparation resources offered through IMA, visit www.imanet.org.

Updates and Errata Notification

Please be advised that our materials are designed to provide thorough and accurate content with a high level of attention to quality. From time to time there may be clarifications, corrections, or updates that are captured in an Updates and Errata Notification.

To ensure you are kept abreast of changes, this notification will be available on Wiley's CMAexcel update and errata page. You may review these documents by going to www.wiley.com/go/cmaerrata2015

How to Use the Wiley CMAexcel Learning System

This product is based on the CMA body of knowledge developed by the Institute of Certified Management Accountants (ICMA). This material is designed for learning purposes and is distributed with the understanding that the publisher and authors are not offering legal or professional services. Although the text is based on the body of knowledge tested by the CMA exam and the published Learning Outcome Statements (LOS) covering the two-part exams, Wiley CMAexcel Learning System (WCMALS) program developers do not have access to the current bank of exam questions. It is critical that candidates understand all LOS published by the ICMA, learn all concepts and calculations related to those statements, and have a solid grasp of how to approach the multiple-choice and essay exams in the CMA program.

Some exam preparation tools provide an overview of key topics; others are intended to help you practice one specific aspect of the exams such as the questions. The WCMALS is designed as a comprehensive exam preparation tool to help you study the content from the exam LOS, learn how to write the CMA exams, and practice answering exam-type questions.

Study the Book Content

The **table of contents** is set up using the CMA exam content specifications established by ICMA. Each section, topic, and subtopic is named according to the content specifications and the **Learning Outcome Statements (LOS)** written to correspond to these specifications. As you go through each section and major topic, refer to the related LOS found in Appendix B. Then review the CMALS book content to help learn the concepts and formulas covered in the LOS.

The **Learning Outcome Statements Overviews** provide a quick reference to the LOS as well as key points to remember within them. These sections should not replace the in-depth discussion of the material that is in this book. However, these overviews do serve as a refresher on what has been learned and can be used as a tool to reinforce the knowledge that you have obtained.

The **knowledge checks** are designed to be quick checks to verify that you understand and remember the content just covered by presenting questions and correct answers. The answers refer to the appropriate sections in the book for you to review the content and find the answer yourself.

The **practice questions** are a sampling of the type of exam questions you will encounter on the exam and are considered complex and may involve extensive written and/or calculation responses. Use these questions to begin applying what you have learned, recognizing there is a much larger sample of practice questions available in the Online Test Bank (described in the next section).

The WCMALS also contains a **bibliography and references** in case you need to find more detailed content on an LOS. We encourage you to use published academic sources. While information can be found online, we discourage the use of open-source, unedited sites such as Wikipedia.

Suggested Study Process Using the WCMALS

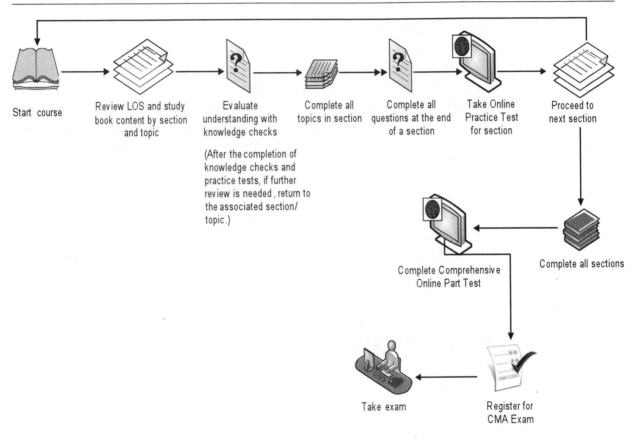

Start course

Review LOS and study book content by section and topic

Evaluate understanding with knowledge checks

(After the completion of knowledge checks and practice tests, if further review is needed, return to the associated section/topic.)

Complete all topics in section

Complete all questions at the end of a section

Take Online Practice Test for section

Proceed to next section

Complete all sections

Complete Comprehensive Online Part Test

Register for CMA Exam

Take exam

WCMALS Book Features

The WCMALS books use a number of features to draw your attention to certain types of content:

Key terms are **bolded** where they appear in the text with their definition, to allow you to quickly scan through and study them.

 Key formulas are indicated with this icon. Be sure you understand these formulas and practice applying them.

Knowledge checks at the end of each topic are review questions that let you check your understanding of the content just read. (They are not representative of the type of questions that appear on the exam.)

 Study tips offer ideas and strategies for studying and preparing for the exam.

 Practice questions are examples of actual exam questions. Presented at the end of each section, these questions help you solidify your learning of that section and apply it to the type of questions that appear on the exam.

Online Test Bank

Included with your purchase of the Wiley CMAexcel Learning System Part 2 book is an Online Test Bank made available to you through www.wileycma.com. This test bank includes **six section-specific tests** that randomize questions from a selected section only. The course also includes **a comprehensive Part 2 test** that emulates the percentage weighting of each section on the actual Part 2 exam. All questions are drawn from a bank of more than 780 questions, so that each time you repeat the test, you will receive a different set of questions covering all the topics in the section. All the multiple-choice questions provide feedback in response to your answers. Your scores will be recorded so that you can track your progress over time.

It is suggested that you integrate the Online Test Bank throughout your study program instead of leaving them until the end. The section-specific tests are designed for you to practice questions related to the section content—read and learn a section and then practice the online questions related to the section. This also will help you identify if further study of the section content is required before moving to the next section.

The comprehensive Part 2 test is designed to help you simulate taking the actual CMA exam. Try the comprehensive Part 2 test after you have studied all the Part 2 content. You can take this exam multiple times. Each time you will receive a different combination of questions. It is recommended that you set up your own exam simulation—set aside four hours in a room without interruption, do not have any reference books open, and work through the comprehensive part exam as if you were taking the real exam. This will prepare you for the exam setting and give you a good idea of how ready you are.

In addition, sample essay questions are provided that simulate the testing environment. The correct answer is provided which will enable you to self-score your answer.

You are strongly encouraged to make full use of all online practice and review features as part of your study efforts. Please note that these features are subscription based and available only for a specific number of months from the time of registration.

Learn to Write the CMA Exam

The four-hour CMA exam will test your understanding of each part's content using both multiple-choice and essay questions. This means you must learn to write two types of tests in one sitting. The WCMALS books contain tips, instruction, and examples to help you learn to write an essay exam. Be sure to study the Essay Exam Support Materials section so that in addition to practicing with the Online Test Bank, you also learn to respond to the part content in essay format.

Create a Study Plan

Each part of the two-part CMA exam uses a combination of a multiple-choice format and an essay format to test your understanding of the part concepts, terms, and calculations. Creating a study plan is an essential ingredient to planning a path to success. Managing your plan is critical to achieving success. The next tips and tactics are included to help you prepare and manage your study plan.

Study Tips

There are many ways to study, and the plan you create will depend on things such as your lifestyle (when and how you can schedule study time), your learning style, how familiar you are with the content, and how practiced you are at writing a formal exam. Only you can assess these factors and create a plan that will work for you. Some suggestions that other exam candidates have found helpful follow.

- Schedule regular study times and stay on schedule.
- Avoid cramming by breaking your study times into small segments. For example, you may want to work intensely for 45 minutes with no interruptions, followed by a 15-minute break during which time you do something different. You may want to leave the room, have a conversation, or exercise.
- When reading, highlight key ideas, especially unfamiliar ones. Reread later to ensure comprehension.
- Pay particular attention to the terms and equations highlighted in this book, and be sure to learn the acronyms in the CMA body of knowledge.
- Create personal mnemonics to help you memorize key information. For example, CCIC to remember the four ethical standards: Competence, Confidentiality, Integrity, and Credibility.
- Create study aids such as flash cards.
- Use index cards, and write a question on one side and the answer on the other. This helps reinforce the learning because you are writing the information as well as reading it. Examples: What is _____? List the five parts of _____.
- In particular, make flash cards of topics and issues that are unfamiliar to you, key terms and formulas, and anything you highlighted while reading.
- Keep some cards with you at all times to review when you have time, such as in an elevator, while waiting for an appointment, and so on.

- Use a flash card partner. This person does not need to understand accounting. He or she only needs the patience to sit with you and read the questions off the flash card.
- As test time approaches, start to eliminate the questions you can easily answer from your stack so you can concentrate on the more challenging topics and terms.
- If particular topics are difficult, tap into other resources such as the Internet, library, accountant colleagues, or professors, to augment your understanding.
- Use your study plan—treat it as a living document and update it as you learn more about what you need to do to prepare for the exam.
- Use the knowledge checks in the book to assess how well you understand the content you just completed.
- Use the Online Test Bank to test your pability to answer multiple-choice practice questions on each section's content as you finish it. After completing the first 40 questions presented, review areas in the book that you were weak on in the practice test. Then try the section test again.
- Be sure to learn how to take a multiple-choice question exam—there are many online resources with tips and guidance that relate to answering multiple-choice exams.
  - Make an attempt to answer all questions. There is no penalty for an incorrect answer—if you don't try, even when you are uncertain, you eliminate the potential of getting a correct answer.
  - Create your own "simulated" multiple-choice trial exam using the full part Online Practice Test.
- Learn to write an effective essay answer.
  - Use the Essay Exam Support Materials section of this book. This content shows a sample grading guide and includes a sample of a good, a better, and a best answer in addition to some helpful tips for writing an essay answer.
  - Learn how points are awarded for an essay answer so that you can ensure you get the most points possible for your answers, even when you are very challenged by a question.
  - Practice essay responses using the questions in the WCMALS book as well as the Online Test Bank.
- Be sure to access the Online Test Bank and its Essay Questions until you are comfortable with the content.

Ensure you are both well rested and physically prepared for the exam day as each exam is four hours in length with no break for meals. Learning how to answer a multiple-choice and essay exam and being mentally and physically prepared can improve your grade significantly. Know the content and be prepared to deal with challenges with a focused, confident, and flexible attitude.

Introduction

Welcome to Part 2: Financial Decision Making of the Wiley CMAexcel Learning System.

This Part 2 *Self-Study Guide* is composed of five sections:

Section A: Financial Statement Analysis focuses on important ratios and other analytical tools used to evaluate an organization's financial health, including coverage of special issues, such as foreign currency fluctuations, off-balance sheet financing, U.S. GAAP versus IFRS, and fair value accounting.

Section B: Corporate Finance examines key concepts in corporate finance, including risk and return, working capital management, raising capital, corporate restructuring, and international finance issues.

Section C: Decision Analysis reviews fundamental information about the decision-making process, including relevant cost analysis, cost/volume/profit analysis, pricing concepts, and marginal analysis. It also addresses the assessment and management of risk—risk identification and exposure, and risk mitigation strategies.

Section D: Risk Management focuses on enterprise risk management (ERM). ERM provides a comprehensive approach to risk identification, assessment, and response.

Section E: Investment Decisions begins with an overview of the capital budgeting process and then reviews principles used to evaluate investment alternatives—discounted cash flow analysis, payback and discounted payback, ranking investment projects, and risk analsyis.

Section F: Professional Ethics focuses on ethical considerations for the organization, with discussion of the provisions of the U.S. Foreign Corrupt Practices Act and IMA's Statements of Management Accounting, *Values and Ethics: From Inception to Practice*. In addition, this section presents the *IMA Statement of Ethical Professional Practice* in the context of the ethical demands an individual will face within an organization.

Financial Statement Analysis

While financial statements summarize the past performance of an organization, they also can provide users with valuable insights into future performance. Financial statement analysis is performed by stockholders and creditors and is also an important tool for management accountants and financial analysts to use to better understand their company's competitive position.

Financial statements can be analyzed to identify trends in key financial data, compare financial performance across companies, and calculate financial ratios that can be used to assess a company's current performance as well as its prospects for the future. In addition, the management accountant should be familiar with the analytical techniques used by external investors to evaluate their company.

This section focuses on important ratios and other analytical tools used to evaluate an organization's financial health, including coverage of special issues, such as foreign currency fluctuations, off-balance sheet financing, fair value accounting, and U.S. generally accepted accounting principles (GAAP) versus International Financial Reporting Standards (IFRSs).

Learning Outcome Statements Overview: Financial Statement Analysis

Section A.1. Basic Financial Statement Analysis

A. For the balance sheet and income statement, prepare and analyze common-size financial statements; that is, calculate percentage of assets and sales, respectively; also called vertical analysis.
   a. Common-size statements recast all items in a particular financial statement as a percentage of a selected (usually the largest and most important) item on the statement.
   b. A base amount (generally total assets on the balance sheet and net sales on the income statement) is valued at 100%, and the elements within the statement are expressed as a percentage of the base amount.
B. For the balance sheet and income statement, prepare a comparative financial statement horizontal analysis; that is, calculate trend year over year for every item on the financial statement compared to base year.
   a. Horizontal common-size statements compare key financial statement (income statement or balance sheet) values and relationships for the same company over a period of years.
C. Calculate the growth rate of individual line items on the balance sheet and income statement.
   a. Growth rates for individual items are calculated by looking at the difference between the Year 2 amount and the Year 1 amount divided by the Year 1 (base) amount and converted to a percentage.

Section A.2. Financial Ratios

The candidate should be able to:

Liquidity

A. Calculate and interpret the current ratio, the quick (acid test) ratio, the cash ratio, the cash flow ratio, and the net working capital ratio.

a. Current ratio—Measures the degree to which current assets cover current liabilities.

$$\text{Current Ratio} = \frac{\text{Current Assets}}{\text{Current Liabilities}}$$

b. Quick (acid-test) ratio—Examines liquidity from a more immediate aspect than does the current ratio by eliminating inventory from current assets.

$$\frac{\text{Quick}}{\text{(Acid-Test) Ratio}} = \frac{\text{Cash} + \text{Marketable Securities} + \text{Accounts Receivable}}{\text{Current Liabilities}}$$

c. Cash ratio—Compares only cash and marketable securities to current liabilities, eliminating receivables and inventory from the asset portion.

$$\text{Cash Ratio} = \frac{\text{Cash} + \text{Marketable Securities}}{\text{Current Liabilities}}$$

d. Cash flow ratio—Measures a firm's ability to meet its debt obligations with cash generated in the normal course of business.

$$\text{Cash Flow Ratio} = \frac{\text{Operating Cash Flow}}{\text{Current Liabilities}}$$

B. Explain how changes in one or more of the elements of current assets, current liabilities, or unit sales can change the liquidity ratios and calculate that impact. [See Topic 2: Financial Ratios (in book).]

C. Demonstrate an understanding of the liquidity of current liabilities.

    a. Liquidity is a relative measure of the proximity of the asset or liabilities to cash (i.e., how soon the asset or liability will be converted to cash). On the balance sheet, liabilities are ordered in order of liquidity. The soonest to be paid off is listed first.

Leverage

D. Define solvency.

    a. Solvency is the degree to which the current assets of an organization exceed the current liabilities of the organization.

E. Define operating leverage and financial leverage.

    a. Operating leverage—The existence of fixed operating costs in operations. Measure of how revenue growth translates into growth in EBIT.

    b. Financial leverage—Raising capital through debt rather than equity. Measures the amount of fixed costs (interest and preferred stock dividends) included in the financing structure of a company.

F. Calculate degree of operating leverage and degree of financial leverage.

    a. Degree of operating leverage (DOL):

$$\text{DOL} = \frac{\%\ \text{Change in EBIT}}{\%\ \text{Change in Sales}}$$

or

$$= \frac{\text{Contribution Margin}}{\text{EBIT}}$$

    b. Degree of financial leverage (DFL):

$$\text{DFL} = \frac{\%\ \text{Change in Net Income}}{\%\ \text{Change in Earnings Before Interest and Taxes (EBIT)}}$$

or

$$= \frac{\text{EBIT}}{\text{Earnings Before Taxes (EBIT)}}$$

G. Demonstrate an understanding of the effect on the capital structure and solvency of a company with a change in the composition of debt vs. equity by calculating leverage ratios. [See Topic 2: Financial Ratios (in book).]

H. Calculate and interpret the financial leverage ratio, and determine the effect of a given change in capital structure on this ratio.

    a. Financial leverage ratio—Measures the ratio of the composition how assets are financed in a company. A ratio of 2.0 indicates that liabilities and equity are equal. A ratio less than 2.0 indicates that equity is larger than liabilities. A ratio greater than 2.0 indicates that liabilities are larger than equity.

$$\text{Financial Leverage Ratio} = \frac{\text{Assets}}{\text{Equity}}$$

I. Calculate and interpret the following ratios: total debt to total capital, debt to equity, long-term debt to equity, and debt to total assets.

    a. Total debt to total capital—Measures the proportion of debt compared to the total capital of a corporation.

$$\text{Total Debt to Total Capital Ratio} = \frac{\text{Current Liabilities + Long-Term Liabilities}}{\text{Total Debt + Total Equity}}$$

    b. Debt to equity—Measures the firm's ability to pay long-term debt and how well long-term creditors are protected.

$$\text{Debt to Equity Ratio} = \frac{\text{Total Debt}}{\text{Equity}}$$

  c. Long-term debt to equity—Compares long-term debt only to shareholders' equity.

$$\text{Long-Term Debt to Total Capital Ratio} = \frac{\text{Total Debt} - \text{Current Liabilities}}{\text{Equity}}$$

  d. Debt to total assets—measures the proportion of assets financed through debt.

$$\text{Debt to Total Assets Ratio} = \frac{\text{Total Debt}}{\text{Total Assets}}$$

J. Define, calculate and interpret the following ratios: fixed charge coverage (earnings to fixed charges), interest coverage (times interest earned), and cash flow to fixed charges.

  a. Fixed charge coverage (earnings to fixed charges)—Measures a company's ability to satisfy fixed financing expenses.

$$\text{Fixed Charge Coverage} = \frac{\text{Earnings Before Fixed Charges and Taxes}}{\text{Fixed Charges}}$$

Note: Fixed charges include interest, required principal repayment, and leases.

  b. Interest coverage (times interest earned ratio)—Measures a firm's ability to pay interest through its operations.

$$\frac{\text{Interest Covered}}{\text{(Times Interest Earned Ratio)}} = \frac{\text{Earnings Before Interest and Taxes (EBIT)}}{\text{Interest Expense}}$$

Note: Fixed charges include interest, required principal repayment, and leases.

  c. Cash flow to fixed charges—Measures a firm's ability to satisfy fixed charges, such as interest and leases, from the cash flow generated through the normal operations of the business.

$$\frac{\text{Cash Flow to Fixed}}{\text{Charges Ratio}} = \frac{\text{Cash from Ops.} + \text{Fixed Charges}}{\text{Fixed Charges}}$$

Note: Cash from operations is after-tax.

K. Discuss how capital structure decisions affect the risk profile of a firm.

  a. Higher debt in the capital structure of a company creates higher fixed costs for interest and principal payments and increases the company's risk. This creates a higher bankruptcy risk, which translates into higher interest rates charged by its creditors.

Activity

L. Calculate and interpret accounts receivable turnover, inventory turnover and accounts payables turnover.

a. Accounts receivable turnover—Measures the average number of times that receivables from sales are collected during a year.

$$\text{Accounts Receivable Turnover Ratio} = \frac{\text{Credit Sales}}{\text{Average Gross Accounts Receivables}}$$

b. Inventory turnover—Measures the average number of times that inventory was sold during a year.

$$\text{Inventory Turnover Ratio} = \frac{\text{Cost of Goods Sold}}{\text{Average Inventory}}$$

c. Accounts payables turnover—measures the average number of times that payables are paid during a year.

$$\text{Accounts Payable Turnover Ratio} = \frac{\text{Credit Purchases}}{\text{Average Accounts Payable}}$$

M. Calculate and interpret days sales outstanding in receivables, days sales in inventory, and days purchases in accounts payable.

a. Days sales outstanding in receivables

$$\text{Day's Sales in Receivables} = \frac{\text{Average Accounts Receivable}}{(\text{Credit Sales}/365)}$$

or

$$= \frac{365}{\text{Accounts Receivable Turnover}}$$

b. Days sales in inventory

$$\text{Day's Sales in Inventory} = \frac{\text{Average Inventory}}{\text{Cost of Sales}/365}$$

or

$$= \frac{365}{\text{Inventory Turnover}}$$

c. Days purchases in payables

$$\text{Day's Purchases in Payables} = \frac{\text{Average Payables}}{(\text{Purchases}/365)}$$

or

$$= \frac{365}{\text{Payables Turnover}}$$

N. Define and calculate the operating cycle and cash cycle of a firm.
  a. Operating cycle—The time elapsed between when goods are acquired and when cash is received from the sale of the goods.

$$\text{Operating Cycle} = \text{Day's Sales in Account Receivable} + \text{Day's Sales in Inventory}$$

O. Calculate and interpret total assets turnover and fixed asset turnover.
  a. Total assets turnover—Measures the amount of sales for every dollar of a company's assets.

$$\text{Total Asset Turnover Ratio} = \text{Sales} / \text{Average Total Assets}$$

  b. Fixed asset turnover—measures the amount of sales for every dollar of fixed assets in the company.

$$\text{Fixed Asset Turnover Ratio} = \text{Sales} / \text{Average Net Plant, Property, and Equipment}$$

Profitability

P. Calculate and interpret gross profit margin percentage, operating profit margin percentage, net profit margin percentage and earnings before interest, taxes, depreciation, and amortization (EBITDA) margin percentage.
  a. Gross profit margin percentage—Measures gross profit (sales minus cost of sales) as a percentage of sales.

$$\text{Gross Profit Margin Precentage} = \frac{\text{Gross Profit}}{\text{Sales}}$$

  b. Operating profit margin—Ratio of operating profit (EBIT) to sales.

$$\text{Operating Profit Margin Percentage} = \frac{\text{Operating Income}}{\text{Sales}}$$

  c. Net profit margin percentage—net income as a percentage of sales.

$$\text{Net Profit Margin Percentage} = \frac{\text{Net Income}}{\text{Sales}}$$

    d. EBITDA margin percentage—EBITDA as a percentage of sales.

$$\text{EBITDA Margin} = \frac{\text{EBITDA}}{\text{Sales}}$$

Q. Calculate and interpret return on assets (ROA) and return on equity (ROE).
    a. ROA—Indicates how a company is using its assets to generate earnings. Measures the amount of net income returned as a percentage of total assets.

$$\text{Return on Assets} = \frac{\text{Net Income}}{\text{Average Total Assets}}$$

    b. ROE—Amount of net income returned as a percentage of shareholders equity.

$$\text{Return on Equity} = \frac{\text{Net Income}}{\text{Average Equity}}$$

Market

R. Calculate and interpret the market/book ratio, the price/earnings ratio and price to EBITDA ratio.
    a. Market/book ratio—Measures the value of a company by comparing the company's current stock price to its book value.

$$\text{Market-to-Book Ratio} = \frac{\text{Current Stock Price}}{\text{Book Value per Share}}$$

    b. Price/earnings (P/E) ratio—Measures the relationship between a company's share price and its earnings per share.

$$\text{P/E Ratio} = \frac{\text{Market Price per Share}}{\text{EPS}}$$

    c. Price to EBITDA ratio—Measures the relationship between a company's share price and its EBITDA per share.

$$\text{Price to EBITDA Ratio} = \frac{\text{Market Price per Share}}{\text{EBITDA per Share}}$$

S. Calculate and interpret book value per share.
    a. Measure the amount of money a shareholder would get per share if the company were to liquidate all assets at current book values and satisfy all liabilities at book value.

$$\text{Book Value per Share} = \frac{\text{Total Stockholders' Equity} - \text{Preferred Equity}}{\text{Number of Common Shares Outstanding}}$$

T. Identify and explain the limitations of book value per share.

  a. Book value per share does not provide an accurate picture of what a shareholder would receive upon liquidation since it is probable that a company would sell its assets at current book values. Market values would be a better indication of how much a shareholder would receive upon liquidation.

U. Calculate and interpret basic and diluted earnings per share.

  a. Basic earnings per share—Expresses net income on a per-share basis. Portion of a company's profit for each outstanding share of common stock.

$$\text{Basic EPS} = \frac{\text{Net Income} - \text{Preferred Dividends}}{\begin{array}{c}\text{Weighted Average Number of}\\\text{Common Shares Outstanding}\end{array}}$$

Note that the number of shares outstanding is weighted by the number of months shares are outstanding.

  b. Diluted earnings per share—Measure to compute net income on a per-share basis if all convertible securities were exercised. Convertible securities include convertible preferred stock, convertible bonds, stock options, and warrants.

$$\text{Diluted EPS} = \frac{\text{Net Income} - \text{Preferred Dividends}}{\begin{array}{c}\text{Diluted Weighted Average Number}\\\text{of Common Shares Outstanding}\end{array}}$$

Diluted EPS adjusts common shares by adding shares that may be issued for convertible securities and options.

V. Calculate and interpret earnings yield, dividend yield, dividend payout ratio and shareholder return.

  a. Earnings yield—Inverse of the P/E ratio. Estimates the interest rate that may be earned from holding a stock, assuming earnings stay the same.

$$\text{Earnings Yield} = \frac{\text{Earnings per Share}}{\text{Market Price per Share}}$$

  b. Dividend yield—Measure of the cash return realized by the investor, against the current market value of the stock, by the payout of the dividend.

$$\text{Dividend Yield} = \frac{\text{Annual Dividends per Share}}{\text{Market Price per Share}}$$

   c. Dividend payout ratio—Measures the percentage of earnings paid to shareholders in dividends.

$$\text{Dividend Payout Ratio} = \frac{\text{Common Dividend}}{\text{Earnings Available to Common Shareholders}}$$

General

W. Identify the limitations of ratio analysis.

   a. Users of financial statements often place too much emphasis on summary indicators and key ratios, such as the current ratio or the earnings per share amount. No single ratio or measure can capture all relevant or important information about a particular company. The calculation of various ratios is merely the starting point.

X. Demonstrate a familiarity with the sources of financial information about public companies and industry ratio averages.

   a. Annual reports include many financial and nonfinancial disclosures and information that can be used to calculate ratios and assess profitability, performance, liquidity, and solvency.

Y. Evaluate the financial strengths and performance of an entity based on multiple ratios.

   a. Stakeholders can use the ratios noted above to compare industry averages in order to make informed decisions.

Section A.3. Profitability Analysis

A. Demonstrate an understanding of the factors that contribute to inconsistent definitions of "equity," "assets," and "return" when using ROA and ROE.

There are a myriad of ways to assess return on investment (ROI), depending on who is doing the calculation and what the objective is. Many of the differences have to do with the definition of equity, assets, and return. **Note: While there may be various approaches to calculating ROI, ROA, and ROE, the formulas listed in this text are the ones that are tested on the CMA exam.**

   a. Equity—Some analysts use total stockholder's equity as the denominator in ROE while other exclude preferred stock since they are not entitled to the total returns of the business.

   b. Assets—Some analysts modify total assets from the denominator to exclude unproductive assets or adjust accumulated depreciation to get a better number for the amount invested in the business.

   c. Return—Some analysts use net income as the numerator while others use EBITDA, net income less preferred dividends, or other measures of income.

B. Determine the effect on return on total assets of a change in one or more elements of the financial statements.

a. A higher ROA (compared to the previous year) could result from increased net income, a lower asset value, or both. All other things being equal, any increase in net income will increase ROA, and any increase in total assets will lower ROA.

C. Identify factors to be considered in measuring income, including estimates, accounting methods, disclosure incentives, and the different needs of users.

   a. Many different factors may affect the ratios of a company that need to be considered when doing ratio analysis. See Topic 3: Profitability Analysis for more detail.

D. Explain the importance of the source, stability, and trend of sales and revenue.

   a. Analysts, investors, and creditors all need to determine whether revenue represents the stable trend of a growing business or an unusual or one-time event. They also need to be aware of where the revenue is coming from and if it is recorded accurately. It is also essential to understand trends in the industry for consumer preferences, level of competition, and other factors that may affect revenue in the future.

E. Demonstrate an understanding of the relationship between revenue and receivables and between revenue and inventory.

   a. Revenue and receivables relationship—Noncash revenue (sales) is recorded as accounts receivables (A/R). Thus, the implicit assumption behind accounts receivable is that revenue must have been earned to be recognized. If a company inappropriately recognizes revenue early, net income is overstated and current assets on the balance sheet are overstated. Further, an increase in receivables without a corresponding increase in sales may signal problems with collections from customers.

   b. Revenue and inventory relationship—Because merchandising and manufacturing primarily earn revenue through sales of merchandise, the increase in revenue should correspond to an increase in inventory. However, an increase in inventory balance without a corresponding increase in sales may signal problems with inventory management.

F. Determine and analyze the effect on revenue of changes in revenue recognition and measurement methods. [See Topic 3: Profitability Analysis (in book) for more detail.]

G. Analyze cost of sales by calculating and interpreting the gross profit margin.

   a. The gross profit margin percentage is a measurement of gross profit (sales minus cost of sales) as a percentage of sales.

$$\text{Gross Profit Margin Precentage} = \frac{\text{Sales} - \text{Cost of Sales}}{\text{Sales}}$$

H. Distinguish between gross profit margin, operating profit margin and net profit margin and analyze the effects of changes in the components of each. [See Section A.2. Financial Ratios (in book).]

enables the firm to borrow cash without showing the corresponding liability.

   iv. Joint ventures—Business entities that aere owned, operated, and jointly controlled by a small group of investors with a specific business purpose. Sometimes a corporation is a partner in a venture, which allows it to be active in management and involved in decision making but not report the venture on the financial statement of the corporation.

2. Explain why companies use off-balance sheet financing.
   i. By not showing the asset and corresponding liability, companies improve their ratios. Lower assets can increase ROA, while lower liabilities can decrease debt-to-equity ratio. Not reporting liabilities can also increase the perceived risk of the entity for debt and equity financing sources.

3. Calculate the impact of off-balance sheet financing on the debt-to-equity ratio.
   i. If a company reports total assets of $1,000,000, liabilities of $200,000, and equity of $800,000, debt-to-equity ratio would be .25 ($200,000 / 800,000). Assume that company entered into an operating lease for an asset with a fair market value of $200,000, and it was not required to report the asset and related liability on the financial statements. The true assets of the company are $1,200,000 with liabilities of $400,000 and equity of $800,000. The adjust debt-to-equity ratio would be .50 ($400,000 / 800,000).

D. Describe how to adjust financial statements for changes in accounting treatments (principles, estimates, and errors) and how these adjustments impact financial ratios.
   a. Change in accounting principle—Change from one generally accepted accounting principle to another. Comparative financial statements are recast to reflect the changes. The cumulative effect (net of tax) of the change is reported as a prior-period adjustment in the earliest period reported. The accounting records are adjusted to reflect the cumulative effect (net of the change) as of the beginning of the current period. The change and its effects on income and balance sheet amounts are disclosed in the notes to the financial statements.
   b. Change in accounting estimate—Revision of an estimate because of new information or new experience. Changes in accounting estimates are handled on a prospective basis.
   c. Correction of an error—Correction of an error caused by a transaction being recorded incorrectly or not at all. The error correction must be handled as a prior-period adjustment to the earliest period reported in the financial statements.

E. Distinguish between book value and market value, and distinguish between accounting profit and economic profit.
   i. Book value versus market value—Companies are required to disclose which assets and liabilities have been adjusted to fair value and which hierarchy (Levels 1–3) is used to determine the value.
      • Economic profit—Profit, as an economic term, is the measure of the resources generated by the firm in excess of the resources consumed over the life of the firm. At any given time, the economic profits of the firm

are the net present value of its earnings over its lifetime. Another way to look at it is the excess of return over the return of a similar risk investment using the same resources.

- Accounting profit—The measurement of accounting profit is based on accrual accounting. The measurement of resources generated and consumed follows the rules set by GAAP (or net income).

F. Identify the determinants and indicators of earnings quality, and explain why they are important.

   i. Earnings quality pertains to the validity and veracity of the reported information—Earnings quality factors are:

- Selection of accounting principles.
- Off-balance sheet financing and its effect on the financials.
- Provision for maintenance of assets and future earnings power.
- Effect of economic forces on earnings.

Basic Financial Statement Analysis

I N ORDER TO EVALUATE COMPANIES, financial analysts examine financial statements in different ways; they may create variants of financial statements, such as common-size statements, and consider other issues that may affect the company's performance. Moreover, a financial analyst is expected to be able to prepare base-year statements to enable trend analysis and review the growth rates of the various elements of the financial statement.

READ the Learning Outcome Statements (LOS) for this topic as found in Appendix B and then study the concepts and calculations presented here to be sure you understand the content you could be tested on in the CMA exam.

Common-Size Statements

Common-size statements recast all items in a particular financial statement as a percentage of a selected (usually the largest and most important) item on the statement. These statements can be used to:

- Compare elements in a single year's financial statements.
- Analyze trends across a number of years for one business.
- Compare businesses of differing sizes within an industry (such as Wal-Mart to Target).
- Compare the company's performance and position with an industry average.

Common-size statements are useful when comparing businesses of different sizes because the financial statements of a variety of companies can be recast into the uniform common-size format regardless of the size of individual elements. The analyst must use judgment to resolve the issue of actual comparability between individual companies in different industries where common-size statements reflect the fundamental differences in conducting business in these industries.

Investments are the most significant account for companies in the financial industry, but this account is small or nonexistent for retailers. The business model of financial companies, and in particular investment banks, is to hold investments that yield a high return. Therefore, it is not surprising that investments are about 70% of the total assets. Leaders in the pharmaceutical and computer industries have investments in smaller companies in their respective industries, though the investment amount comprises a much smaller proportion of their total assets than for financial companies.

It is interesting to note that the retailer and the pharmaceutical company have a significant proportion of their assets in plant, property, and equipment. This signifies that retailers own most of their stores rather than leasing them. Similarly, the pharmaceutical companies have a significant proportion of their assets tied up in their means of production (plant and equipment). The investment in plant, property, and equipment is minuscule for the financial institution, primarily because its assets are mostly composed of investments, and they do not require manufacturing plants or machinery and equipment to function. Normally, traditional manufacturers have a significant proportion of their assets in plant, property, and equipment. However, in recent times with the advent of lean manufacturing, the proportion of plant, property, and equipment in relation to total assets is decreasing for manufacturers. This is signified by the relatively low amount of plant, property, and equipment account for the computer manufacturer (e.g., Dell Computers).

The common sizing of liabilities and equities provides some interesting insights as to how these companies are financed. While the manufacturing and pharmaceutical companies obtain approximately equal financing through debt and equity (equity being 46% for the manufacturer and 48% for the pharmaceutical), the retailer and the financial institution obtain most of their financing through debt. The retailer obtains approximately a quarter of its financing from equity whereas the financial institution obtains only 5% of its financing from equity holders.

Additionally, the financial institution obtains most of its financing—approximately three-quarters—from short-term obligations, consisting primarily of deposits in accounts that could be withdrawn at the customer's discretion at any time.

The short-term obligation for the retailer in terms of accounts payable is approximately a third of the total assets, which represents payments due to suppliers of its merchandise. An interesting insight could be gained by comparing the amount of inventory to the amount of accounts payable. In this case, they are approximately the same, implying that the retailer is, on average, able to sell the merchandise around the same time as when the supplier payment is due. The concept is formally referred to as comparing inventory turnover to accounts payable turnover.

Similar inferences can be drawn through common sizing of the income statement. Different industries have different cost structures and profit margins. Comparing the various categories of common-size expenses—such as cost of sales, research and development (R&D) expense, advertising expenses, and general overhead—provide validation of the differing business models across industries. For example, a retailer has a higher proportion of cost of sales than a pharmaceutical company, which traditionally has a very small cost of sales relative to its total sales, signifying a high profit margin. Similarly, while the R&D expenses for a pharmaceutical company are high, they are nonexistent for a retailer.

Such analysis and ability to draw inferences is critical in conducting common-size analysis. The mechanical aspect of developing common-size statements is of limited usefulness unless the analyst is able to make inferences and identify issues of concern based on the expectations formed through experience and knowledge.

Horizontal Common-Size Statements

A **horizontal common-size statement**, also called a **variation analysis** or **trend analysis**, compares key financial statement values and relationships for the same company over a period of years. The increase or decrease in each of the major accounts is shown as a percentage of the base-year amount and hence is sometimes referred to as the base-year financials. As illustrated in Figure 2A-4, such an analysis sets the base year at a value of 100% and then shows subsequent years in relation to increases or decreases over the base year.

Figure 2A-4 Horizontal Common-Size Statement (Variation or Trend Analysis)

	Year 0	Year 1	Year 2	Year 3	Year 4
Sales	$200,000	$210,000	$250,000	$260,000	$300,000
Base-year multiplier	100%	105%	125%	130%	150%
Cost of sales	$100,000	$110,000	$130,000	$150,000	$160,000
Base-year multiplier	100%	110%	130%	150%	160%

Note in Figure 2A-4 how cost of sales is growing faster than sales. This can be inferred through a simple computation of percentage growth in cost of sales and comparing it to the percentage growth in sales. Horizontal or trend analysis helps the analyst examine relationships to detect strengths and weaknesses. In this example, management needs to focus on controlling costs. This analysis can reveal trends in the direction, rate, and volume of change. Further analysis also can examine trends in related areas, such as a disparity between an increase in sales and a proportionately greater increase in receivables. Changes can be divided between year-to-year changes and longer-term trends.

By reading across each row—the horizontal analysis—one can quickly spot any unusual change in a particular account from the previous year. Any large changes or a reversal of a trend (a decrease after years of increases) signals issues that have to be further investigated and analyzed. The horizontal analysis provides an initial and quick overview of the financial statements, but it is by no means the final step of a thorough analysis. The purpose of horizontal analysis is primarily attention directing, in that it quickly and efficiently directs attention to the accounts that require further investigation.

The analyst must use caution in interpreting results using horizontal common-size statements. Changes between years can be expressed in actual dollar amounts but are much more commonly expressed as percentages. When using percentages, the analyst must keep in mind the size of the basis for comparison. For example, a 400% increase in net income might sound remarkable until you learn that last year's income was $1,000.

Also, expressing change as a percentage loses meaning when the base is zero or below or the new value is zero. For example, if a company's net income in year 1 has a negative value and in year 2 has a positive value, there is no way to express the change as a percentage. In a case such as this, a comparison must be made by examining the raw numbers.

Another use of horizontal analysis is in cost control. Often companies that are experiencing sales growth tend to disregard controlling expenses. As a result, fixed expenses, which consist of overhead and other indirect expenses, may rise due to a lax management approach. Horizontal analysis can identify the fixed expenses that are increasing over time as sales are increasing. While it is possible that the increase in fixed expenses is justified due to inflation or growth of operations and facilities, an investigation could identify wastage or overconsumption of these resources and provide a means to increase profitability by limiting these expenses.

If changes between years are expressed in actual dollar amounts, the analyst also must bear in mind the relative conditions with which the firm started. For example, an increase in sales of $100,000 in a year has a different meaning for a company that began with sales of $10,000 than it does for a company that began with sales of $2,000,000.

Data across a number of years also can be presented as averages. This method mitigates the effect of unusual fluctuation in data for specific years. That is, a rolling average over two or three years could be used as input to the horizontal analysis. In that way, an unusual year that affects multiple averages and trends could be spotted even when large variations in data are present.

Knowledge Check:
Basic Financial Statements

The next questions are intended to help you check your understanding and recall of the material presented in this topic. They do not represent the type of questions that appear on the CMA exam.

Directions: Answer each question in the space provided. Correct answers and section references appear after the knowledge check questions.

1. In a common-size balance sheet, the inventory account as a percentage of total assets is expected to be highest for companies in

   ☐ **a.** the finance industry, such as Citibank.

   ☐ **b.** the airline industry, such as United Airlines.

   ☐ **c.** the retailing industry, such as Wal-Mart.

   ☐ **d.** the pharmaceutical industry, such as Pfizer.

2. Which of the following statements regarding common-size statements is true?

   ☐ **a.** Common-size statements for two companies, with both showing a 100% increase in profits, show that both companies would make equally attractive investments.

   ☐ **b.** Horizontal common-size statements can be made only for companies with at least 10 years of operational data.

   ☐ **c.** Common-size statements can be used to compare companies of different sizes.

   ☐ **d.** All of the above are true.

Knowledge Check Answers:
Basic Financial Statement Analysis

1. In a common-size balance sheet, the inventory account as a percentage of total assets is expected to be highest for companies in [See **Vertical Common-Size Statements.**]

    ☐ **a.** the finance industry, such as Citibank.

    ☐ **b.** the airline industry, such as United Airlines.

    ☑ **c.** the retailing industry, such as Wal-Mart.

    ☐ **d.** the pharmaceutical industry, such as Pfizer.

2. Which of the following statements regarding common-size statements is true? [See **Common-Size Statements.**]

    ☐ **a.** Common-size statements for two companies, with both showing a 100% increase in profits, show that both companies would make equally attractive investments.

    ☐ **b.** Horizontal common-size statements can be made only for companies with at least 10 years of operational data.

    ☑ **c.** Common-size statements can be used to compare companies of different sizes.

    ☐ **d.** All of the above are true.

Financial Ratios

A RATIO IS A COMPARATIVE RELATIONSHIP between two (or more) financial statement amounts. Ratios provide incremental information about the financial health of the company beyond the raw amounts presented in the financial statements. Financial ratios are commonly used for three types of inferences: inferences on liquidity, solvency, and operations; inferences on capital structure; and inferences on profitability.

READ the Learning Outcome Statements (LOS) for this topic as found in Appendix B and then study the concepts and calculations presented here to be sure you understand the content you could be tested on in the CMA exam.

Liquidity/Solvency Ratios

Liquidity is a relative measure of the proximity of current assets and current liabilities to cash and is an indication of company's ability to meet its short-term obligations. Since most of the liabilities of a company (except unearned revenue) are paid in cash, a good measure of this ability is how rapidly a company can convert its other assets into cash, if the need arises. Financial analysts focus on short-term, medium-term, and long-term liquidity, given the time horizon of when the debt has to be paid. When the time horizon is short, only a few types of assets can be converted quickly to cash; hence only those are used in computing the short-term liquidity ratios. As the time horizon increases, more and more assets can be sold and converted to cash; hence those are incorporated in the computation of medium- and long-term liquidity.

Solvency is the ability of a company to meet its long-term obligations or the company's ability to meet its long-term fixed expenses and to meet long-term expansion and growth. In essence, it measures the extent to which a company has enough assets to cover its liabilities. Solvency often is confused with liquidity, but it is not the same thing. Various account combinations, primarily ratios, are used to measure both liquidity and solvency, and some of these key ratios are illustrated throughout this topic.

Working Capital Analysis

Working capital is a measure of a company's ability in the short run to pay its obligations. It looks at short-term financial health. Working capital is calculated as shown:

$$\text{Net Working Capital} = \text{Current Assets} - \text{Current Liabilities}$$

Current assets are defined as cash or other liquid investments, such as inventory and accounts receivable (A/R), that can be converted to cash within a year. **Current liabilities** are obligations that will be paid within a year, such as accounts payables and notes and interest payables. A positive value of working capital indicates that there are enough current assets to cover current obligations. Current measures of working capital can be compared to previous measures to determine if there has been a change that should cause concern.

To examine working capital, we compare two companies:

- AEW, Inc. has $1,000,000 in current assets and $500,000 in current liabilities. AEW's working capital is $500,000 ($1,000,000 current assets − $500,000 current liabilities).
- KF, Inc. has $20,000,000 in current assets and $19,500,000 in current liabilities. KF's working capital is also $500,000 ($20,000,000 current assets − $19,500,000 current liabilities).

Obviously, there is a difference between working capital of $500,000 for AEW, with $1,000,000 in current assets, and KF, with $20,000,000 in current assets. In order to understand what working capital of $500,000 means for a company's liquidity, the analyst should study these ratios to examine relationships between current assets and current liabilities: current ratio, quick (acid-test) ratio, and cash ratio.

Current Ratio

The **current ratio** measures the degree to which current assets cover current liabilities. A higher ratio indicates greater ability to pay current liabilities with current assets, thus greater liquidity.

$$\text{Current Ratio} = \frac{\text{Current Assets}}{\text{Current Liabilities}}$$

Using the numbers from the example:

- AEW has a current ratio of 2 ($1,000,000 / $500,000). AEW has sufficient current assets to pay its current liabilities twice.
- KF's current ratio is 1.026 ($20,000,000 / $19,500,000); KF has sufficient current assets to pay current liabilities only once.

AEW and KF have the same working capital, but AEW is better positioned against uncertainty if it is not able to obtain additional assets (via sales) in the near-term future. KF must generate additional current assets before the next cycle of debt obligations is due. It appears that AEW is more liquid than KF.

There are limitations to using the current ratio to assess liquidity. Because cash is the only acceptable means of payment, it is important to consider the composition of current assets and determine whether those listed as current assets can be converted to cash readily.

For example, if prepaid expenses compose most of the current assets, the current ratio overstates the liquidity of the company because the prepaid expenses cannot be converted to cash to settle the liabilities.

Further, the current ratio cannot predict or indicate patterns of future cash flows, nor can it measure the adequacy of future liquidity. For example, if there is a significant amount of A/R from one customer and that customer files for bankruptcy, there would be significant delay in receiving the payment. Even though the current ratio is high because of the receivables, the debt-paying ability of the company is compromised due to the noncollection of a significant receivable.

The current ratio examines only the current relationship between current assets and current liabilities. Problems with liquidity will affect other aspects of the company's financial situation and ultimately may affect the company's ability to pay long-term obligations (solvency) or use its assets efficiently (operating activity). Traditionally, for a company in the manufacturing industry, a current ratio of 2.0 or above is considered healthy. However, in the current economic environment of e-business, a lower current ratio is acceptable.

Quick (Acid-Test) Ratio

The **quick ratio**, or **acid-test ratio**, examines liquidity from a more immediate aspect than does the current ratio by eliminating inventory from current assets. The quick ratio removes inventory because it turns over at a slower rate than receivables or cash and assumes that the company will be able to sell the items to a customer and collect cash. Although there are a few different ways to compute the quick (acid-test) ratio (by making adjustments to the numerator), the formula listed next is the one that is used on the CMA exam.

$$\text{Quick (Acid-Test) Ratio} = \frac{\text{Cash + Marketable Securities + Accounts Receivable}}{\text{Current Liabilities}}$$

Current assets include cash equivalents and marketable securities. Cash equivalents include money in petty cash, checking accounts, savings accounts, and the like. Marketable securities are highly liquid short-term investments, which generally can become cash in a very short time (several minutes). A usual guideline for a reasonable quick ratio is 1 or greater, but this may vary by industry. The quick ratio, like all ratios, should be judged by comparing it to the firm's past values for the ratio and to the values for similar companies and industry averages. Although the quick ratio is a strong indicator of short-term solvency, it is not perfect. In reality, qualitative information, such as credit terms with suppliers and customers, is useful indicator of short-term solvency.

The current ratio, quick ratio, and working capital calculations are by far the most common liquidity measures; however, several other ratios give analysts further information. Among these are the cash ratio and the cash flow ratio.

Cash Ratio

The **cash ratio** analyzes liquidity in a more conservative manner than the quick ratio, by looking at a company's immediate liquidity. The cash ratio compares only cash and marketable securities to current liabilities, eliminating receivables and inventory from the asset portion. When using this formula, cash and cash equivalents are used for the term cash in the numerator, as shown next

$$\text{Cash Ratio} = \frac{\text{Cash} + \text{Marketable Securities}}{\text{Current Liabilities}}$$

To apply the cash ratio to AEW's and KF's financial information:

Of its $1,000,000 in current assets, AEW has $250,000 in cash and $300,000 in marketable securities. The remaining current assets include receivables and inventory. AEW's cash ratio is calculated as shown:

$$\text{AEW Cash Ratio} = \frac{\$250,000 + \$300,000}{\$500,000} = \frac{\$550,000}{\$500,000} = 1.1$$

KF's cash and cash receivables total $2,000,000, and its marketable securities total $9,000,000. Remaining current assets represent receivables and inventory. KF's cash ratio is calculated as shown:

$$\text{KF Cash Ratio} = \frac{\$2,000,000 + \$9,000,000}{\$19,500,000} = \frac{\$11,000,000}{\$19,500,000} = 0.564$$

A firm generally is not expected to have enough cash equivalents and marketable securities to cover current liabilities. Although this limits the usefulness of the cash ratio, the ratio is helpful for companies that have slow inventory turnover or slow collection of receivables. A cash ratio that is too high may indicate that a company is not using its resources productively in its operations. A cash ratio that is too low, however, could indicate a problem with meeting current liabilities. Another limitation of the cash ratio is that it contains marketable securities, and those may have to be liquidated to pay the debt. As the value of marketable securities is volatile (changes day to day), this ratio (computed based on year-end prices), may not be valid over a longer time horizon.

Cash Flow Ratio

The **cash flow ratio**, shown next, measures a firm's ability to meet its debt obligations with cash generated in the normal course of business.

$$\text{Cash Flow Ratio} = \frac{\text{Operating Cash Flow}}{\text{Current Liabilities}}$$

Higher ratios of operating cash flow to liabilities indicate a higher likelihood that the firm will be able to meet its obligations with cash generated from normal business operations. This ratio measures the ability of the company to meet its short-term obligations based on cash generated in the normal course of business. A deteriorating cash flow ratio, over time, indicates impending liquidity problems.

Sensitivity Analysis on Liquidity Ratios

In analyzing the ratios, it is important to gauge how sensitive these ratios are to changes in their components. An increase in the numerator of a ratio will increase the value of the ratio, whereas an increase in the denominator of a ratio will reduce the value of the ratio, and vice versa. Since a higher number is preferable for these ratios, a decrease in the numerator or an increase in the denominator adversely affects the ratio and inferences made.

Thus, an increase in liabilities would adversely affect the ratio, whereas an increase in current assets or cash flows (the term in the numerator) would improve the ratios. The amount of increase or decrease in a particular ratio depends on the value of the ratio.

It should be noted that an equal increase in both the numerator and the denominator of the ratio would worsen the ratio, if the ratio is greater than 1. Similarly, an equal decrease in both the numerator and denominator would improve a ratio that is greater than 1.

Sometimes companies use this mathematical fact to improve the appearance of the liquidity ratios. As an example, paying off current liabilities right before the balance sheet date would improve the current and the quick ratios.

For example: Company Q has current assets of $1,000,000 and current liabilities of $600,000 yielding a current ratio of 1.67.

$$\text{Current Ratio} = \frac{\text{Current Assets}}{\text{Current Liabilities}}$$

$$\text{Current Ratio} = \$1,000,000 / \$600,000$$
$$= 1.67$$

If the company were to pay off $200,000 of current liabilities just prior to preparing its financials, the current assets will reduce to $800,000 and the current liabilities will reduce to $400,000, improving the current ratio to 2.0.

$$\text{Current Ratio} = [\$1,000,000 - \$200,000 / [\$600,000 - \$200,000]$$
$$= \$800,000 / \$400,000$$
$$= 2.0$$

It is important to note that when companies engage in such activities for the sole purpose of improving the financial ratios, it is called **window dressing**, and the behavior may be ethically questionable.

Capital Structure Analysis

In addition to assessing a firm's ability to meet its short-term obligation, it is important to evaluate its ability to pay long-term debts as they mature. Doing this requires comparing the amount of long-term obligations and the company's ability to generate cash in the long term. This ability is greatly affected by the amount of long-term debt the company has in relation to equity.

Capital structure is the mix of long-term debt, on which interest and principal payments must be made, and equity, in the form of common and preferred stock, which the firm uses to finance operations. The capital structure affects both the risk and returns of the firm and is directly related to leverage.

Financial leverage is the use of debt (fixed cost funds) to increase returns to owners (stockholders). Debt that is too low may result in a company not being able to take full advantage of opportunities. Debt that is too high may affect the company's ability to weather difficult economic times and continue to pay its obligations as debt or interest payments come due. There is no standard guideline or optimal leverage number; it varies by industry and firm.

Firms have a mix of debt and equity financing. Debt holders, including financial institutions and corporate bond investors, are often, but not always, promised a return based on the stated interest rate for the debt. There are costs associated with issuing debt and equity. (Debt is usually cheaper but will increase as the firm's ratio of debt to equity increases.) Most companies maintain a balance of debt and equity based on the cost of capital for each and the level of risk they wish to maintain.

Debt as Leverage

A company uses leverage in two ways: financial and operating.

Financial leverage is raising capital through debt rather than equity. While debt holders are entitled to interest, the owners share the earnings of the company. Hence, when a company can earn a higher rate of return on its invested capital through its operations than the interest rate on its debt, it could increase the return for its investors by financing the growth of company operations through borrowed capital.

Operating leverage is the existence of fixed operating costs. Because these costs are fixed, the higher the percentage of operating leverage, the greater the effect changes in sales revenues have on operating income.

The focus on leverage in this section is on financial leverage. The cost of financial leverage is interest costs, which must be paid regardless of sales.

Degree of Operating Leverage

Business risk is often measured by the degree of operating leverage (DOL). DOL is defined as the percentage change in operating income given a percentage change in sales. It is caused by the organization's cost structure (the relationship of fixed and variable costs). It is calculated by:

$$DOL = \frac{\% \text{ change in EBIT}}{\% \text{ change in sales}}$$

or

$$\frac{CM}{EBIT}$$

Contribution margin (CM) is calculated by taking sales less all variable costs. EBIT equals CM less fixed costs.

For example: If a company has sales of $500,000, variable costs of $250,000, and fixed costs of $125,000, its DOL is calculated as shown:

$$DOL = CM/EBIT = (\$500,000 - \$250,000)/(\$500,000 - \$250,000 - \$125,000)$$
$$DOL = \$250,000/\$125,000 = 2$$

A DOL of 2 implies that every 1% increase in sales will result in a 2% (2 × 1%) increase in EBIT. Also, every 1% decrease in sales will result in a 2% (2 × 1%) decrease in EBIT. Companies with a high DOL often have a high degree of business risk. For example, a manufacturing company with excess capacity and high DOL will increase net income with one additional sale. That opportunity for high variability in net income is defined as increased business risk

Degree of Financial Leverage

Financial risk is often measured by the degree of financial leverage (DFL). DFL is defined as the percentage change in net income (NI) divided by the percentage change in EBIT or as the ratio of EBIT divided by EBT. Financial leverage increases by increasing the balance between tax-deductible debt payments (interest) relative to nondeductible equity payments (dividends). Increasing DFL will increase net income but exposes the company to a higher risk of default on the debt instruments, which increases financial risk.

DFL is calculated by:

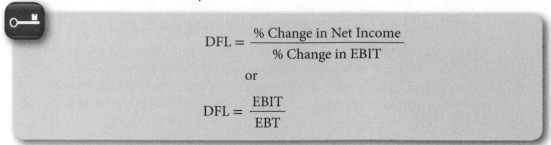

$$DFL = \frac{\% \text{ Change in Net Income}}{\% \text{ Change in EBIT}}$$

or

$$DFL = \frac{EBIT}{EBT}$$

Assume that the company used in the DOL example has interest payments of \$25,000. Its DFL is calculated as:

$$DFL = \$125,000/(\$125,000 - \$25,000)$$
$$DFL = \$125,000/\$100,000 = 1.25$$

A DFL of 1.25 implies that every 1% increase in EBIT will result in a 1.25% (1.25 × 1%) increase in NI. Also, every 1% decrease in EBIT will result in a 1.25% (1.25 × 1%) decrease in NI.

Degree of Total Leverage

The combination of business and financial risk, called the degree of total leverage (DTL), is the product of operating and financial leverage.

$$DTL = DOL \times DFL$$

The DTL for the example just presented is 2.5 and is calculated as:

$$DTL = (DOL \text{ of } 2) \times (DFL \text{ of } 1.25) = 2.5$$

A DTL of 2.5 implies that every 1% increase in sales will result in a 2.5% (2.5 × 1%) increase in NI. Also, every 1% decrease in sales will result in a 2.5% (2.5 × 1%) decrease in NI.

Financial Leverage Ratio

On the CMA exam, the **financial leverage ratio** is computed as:

$$\text{Financial Leverage Ratio} = \frac{\text{Assets}}{\text{Equity}}$$

A higher ratio implies that the assets of the company are financed primarily through debt. A financial leverage ratio of 2.0 reflects that the liabilities of the company are equal to the equity. A ratio of greater than 2.0 implies that liabilities are larger than equity; a ratio of less than 2.0 implies higher equity than the liabilities of the company.

Financial leverage has a magnifying effect on earnings. When the earnings are positive, a marginal percentage change in revenue translates to a greater percentage change on earnings per share or on return on equity measures.

Correspondingly, however, as debt represents fixed costs, leverage also has a magnifying effect on losses. If the financial leverage ratio, for example, is 3.0 and the company experiences a loss, it will experience a greater percentage loss in net income than the percentage decline in revenue. An increase in the financial leverage ratio, therefore, represents not only increased opportunity for leveraging returns but also an increased risk of magnifying any losses and of the company's inability to meet long-term debt. In summary, the potential loss or profit being magnified belongs to the stockholder. So if a firm is profitable, the benefit realized from a high net income with a high financial leverage ratio goes to stockholders.

If fixed assets to stockholders' equity ratio is more than 1, it means that stockholders' equity is less than the fixed assets and the company is using debt to finance a portion of fixed assets. If the ratio is less than 1, it means that stockholders' equity is more than the fixed assets and the stockholders' equity is financing not only the fixed assets but also a part of the working capital. Different industries have different norms. Generally a ratio of 0.60 to 0.70 (or 60% to 70%, if expressed in percentage) is considered satisfactory for most industrial undertakings. (Source: http://www.accountingformanagement.org/)

Ratio Analysis on Debt/Liabilities

Analysts can examine capital structure by comparing debt to assets (asset-based analysis) or to equity (equity-based analysis). Various stakeholders evaluate capital structure ratios (also known as leverage ratios) in different ways. For example, creditors or potential creditors wish to see low debt ratios, whereas stockholders and managers seek optimal debt levels, using as much debt in a firm's capital structure as can be managed effectively. Optimal debt ratios vary by industry. Firms in noncyclical industries, for example, tend to have higher debt ratios than those in cyclical industries. When performing cross-sectional analysis, therefore, one should compare only firms in the same industries.

The three primary ratios used to measure leverage are debt to total assets ratio, debt to equity ratio, and times interest earned (interest coverage) ratio.

Total Debt to Total Capital Ratio

The **total debt to total capital ratio**, shown next, measures the proportion of debt compared to the total capital of a corporation. It is a measurement of the financial leverage of a corporation.

$$\text{Total Debt to Total Capital Ratio} = \frac{\text{Current Liabilities} + \text{Long-Term Liabilities}}{\text{Total Debt} + \text{Total Equity}}$$

Companies can finance their operations through either debt or equity. This ratio provides an understanding of how a company is financing its operations and provides insights into the financial strength of the company. The higher the ratio, the higher the debt being used to finance the operations of the company. Comparing this ratio to that of the industry, a higher ratio typically means financial weakness, weighing financially on the company, and increasing the default risk.

Debt to Equity Ratio

The **debt to equity ratio**, shown next, also measures the firm's ability to pay long-term debt and how well long-term creditors are protected. It measures the relationship of debt to equity when financing asset purchases. For example, a debt to equity ratio of 2 indicates that a firm historically has paid two parts debt to one part equity when financing asset purchases. The lower the ratio, the less reliant the company is on debt.

$$\text{Debt to Equity Ratio} = \frac{\text{Total Debt}}{\text{Equity}}$$

The debt to equity ratio can be compared to previous years' records for the same company. It also can be compared to competitors' and industry averages. A higher ratio indicates that the firm is highly leveraged, and there is a higher risk of bankruptcy.

Long-Term Debt to Equity Ratio

The **long-term debt to equity ratio**, shown next, compares long-term debt only to shareholders' equity.

$$\text{Long-Term Debt to Equity Ratio} = \frac{\text{Total Debt} - \text{Current Liabilities}}{\text{Equity}}$$

A company with a low long-term debt to equity ratio has the ability to raise debt capital if it is needed. Its fixed financing costs are lower because there are lower interest payments; however, the firm's return on capital probably will be lower because it is not using debt to its full capacity.

Debt to Total Assets Ratio

The **debt to total assets ratio**, shown next, measures the proportion of assets financed through debt.

$$\text{Debt to Total Assets Ratio} = \frac{\text{Total Debt}}{\text{Total Assets}}$$

This ratio shows the percentage of assets financed by creditors and indicates how well creditors are protected in case the company becomes insolvent.

A lower debt to total assets ratio indicates a better position for creditors, because the company has enough assets to cover long-term debt obligations. A higher ratio, which indicates that creditors are not well protected, may make it more difficult and expensive for the company to issue additional debt securities.

An unusually low debt to total assets ratio is also problematic, because debt may be a cheap source of capital to finance growth. However, very successful companies—for example, Microsoft—do not have much debt, primarily because they generate so much cash from their operation.

Fixed-Charge Coverage Ratio

The **fixed-charge coverage ratio** measures a company's ability to satisfy fixed financing expenses, such as interest and leases. The fixed-charge coverage ratio is calculated as shown:

$$\text{Fixed Charge Coverage} = \frac{\text{Earnings Before Fixed Charges and Taxes}}{\text{Fixed Charges}}$$

Note: Fixed charges include interest, required principal repayment, and leases. Earnings before fixed charges and taxes are equal to the earnings before interest and taxes + fixed charges.

Times Interest Earned (Interest Coverage) Ratio

The **times interest earned ratio**, shown next, measures a firm's ability to pay interest through its operations.

$$\text{Times Interest Earned Ratio} = \frac{\text{Earnings Before Interest and Taxes (EBIT)}}{\text{Interest Expense}}$$

If the ratio is sufficiently high, the firm should be able to meet its interest obligations. When combined with the debt ratio, the times interest earned ratio gives an analyst a strong indication of a firm's ability to manage debt effectively—or, in other words, to remain solvent.

The combination of a high debt ratio and low times interest earned ratio (when compared to industry averages) is a signal of poor solvency. If, however, a firm has a slightly higher debt ratio along with a higher times interest earned ratio, an analyst should have less worry. Again, debt is a cheap form of capital, and a firm should seek an optimal level of debt, even if the industry average is less.

Cash Flow to Fixed Charges Ratio

The **cash flow to fixed charges ratio** measures a firm's ability to satisfy fixed charges, such as interest and leases from the cash flow generated through the normal operations of the business. The cash flow to fixed charges ratio is computed as shown:

$$\text{Cash Flow to Fixed Charges Ratio} = \frac{(\text{Cash from Ops.} + \text{Fixed Charges} + \text{Tax Payments})}{\text{Fixed Charges}}$$

Note: Cash from operations is after tax. Fixed charges include interest, required principal repayment, and leases.

Capital Structure and Risk

Increases in debt create higher fixed costs for interest and principal payments. Considering the ratios of capital structure, it results in a higher debt to equity ratio and, therefore, a less favorable position for long-term debt-paying ability. Decreases in equity, as a result of redemption of stock or losses from operations, also would result in a higher debt to equity ratio and higher risk for the company's ability to pay long-term debt. Increases in equity, such as those from profits, without corresponding increases in debt would lower the debt to equity ratio, increasing the company's position for long-term debt-paying ability.

Capital structure of a firm is related to the "risk" of the firm, particularly bankruptcy risk. An increase in the amount of debt worsens the capital structure, increasing the possibility of bankruptcy. This is because higher debt means higher interest payments and payment of the principal, requiring a higher amount of cash flows to meet these obligations. Any strain on the cash flow is more dangerous for firms with higher debt because they still have to meet the debt payments. Failure to do so could result in bankruptcy.

This higher bankruptcy risk faced by the firm translates into higher interest rates charged by its creditors. This is referred to as the "cost of capital" for the firm. Management tries to reduce the cost of capital to increase the financial leverage of the firm. Thus, management takes much care to manage the capital structure and its disclosure because of the direct impact it has on the cost of capital and thus on the profitability of the firm.

Off-Balance Sheet Financing

Off-balance sheet financing is a form of financing in which large capital expenditures are kept off an organization's balance sheet through various classification methods. Organizations often use off-balance sheet financing to keep their debt to equity and leverage ratios low, especially if the inclusion of a large expenditures would violate debt covenants. Four of the common techniques employed to achieve off-balance sheet financing are: factoring of A/Rs, special-purpose entities, leases, and joint ventures.

Factoring of Accounts Receivables

Some firms, in attempt to raise cash, borrow using A/R as collateral. This is called **factoring of accounts receivable** and is done to avoid recording a payable or a liability. Doing this enables the firm to borrow cash without showing the corresponding liability; hence such transaction is called "off-balance sheet financing."

Special-Purpose Entities

Many firms create special-purpose entities (SPEs) for a "special," sometimes undisclosed, business purpose. For example, SPEs may be created to facilitate leasing activities, loan securitizations, R&D activities, or trading in financial derivatives. This business technique was extensively used by Enron Corporation as a vehicle to set up energy futures trading and other related business ventures. Because these were created as "separate" entities from the parent corporation, the financials and business transactions of these SPEs were not consolidated with that of the parent. By excluding such ventures from consolidation, Enron was able to keep billions of dollars of debt off its balance sheet, hiding significant business risk from investors and creditors.

Leases

Firms usually use leases to get use of an asset without having to show it on the balance sheet as an asset and the corresponding liability. If the firm were to purchase the asset, it might have to use cash, thus converting short-term assets into long-term assets and worsening short-term liquidity ratio. Purchasing the asset on credit would increase the firm's accounts payables, again worsening its short-term liquidity ratios. If the firm were to use long-term financing to purchase, it would worsen the debt to equity or other solvency ratios.

To avoid any of these adverse consequences on the balance sheet, firms sometimes lease the asset. Generally accepted accounting principles require that a determination be made on whether the lease is an operating lease or a capital lease. When the lease meets one of the four conditions established for capital leases, the lease payments are accounted for as a long-term liability.

However, sometimes firms are able to structure a lease so as not to meet any of the four conditions. It can then classify the lease as an operating lease. With an operating lease, the firm is able to obtain the use of the asset without having to record its obligation to pay, thus obtaining off-balance sheet financing.

Joint Ventures

A joint venture is a business entity that is owned, operated, and jointly controlled by a small group of investors with a specific business purpose. Sometimes a corporation is a partner in a venture, which allows it to be active in management and involved in decision making but not report the venture on the financial statement of the corporation. An investment in a corporate joint venture that exceeds 50% of the venture's outstanding shares must be treated as a subsidiary investment, leading to consolidation in the financial statement. However, firms sometimes are careful to hold less than 50% (say 48.5%) of outstanding shares to avoid such consolidation—providing off-balance sheet financing.

Operating Activity Analysis

Another way to analyze liquidity is to focus on the management of key current assets, namely inventory and A/R. A manager successfully managing inventory and collecting A/R in a timely manner also will be improving liquidity. Operating activity analysis is done over a period of an operating cycle—the time elapsed between when goods are acquired and when cash is received from the sale of the goods.

Accounts Receivable Turnover Ratio

The **A/R turnover ratio** measures the average number of times that receivables from sales are collected during a year.

$$\text{Accounts Receivable Turnover Ratio} = \frac{\text{Credit Sales}}{\text{Average Gross Accounts Receivables}}$$

An underlying assumption of this ratio is that sales occur evenly throughout the year, hence average A/R can be estimated using the average of beginning and ending A/R balances. When sales are seasonal, or uneven, the beginning and ending balances may not be representative of the average A/R balance. This is one of the reasons that most retailers have a fiscal year ending on January 31 and not December 31, because the sales in that industry are seasonal.

A/R turnover also can be analyzed in days instead of times per year. There are two conventions used for number of days in a year—360 and 365. When performing calculations, be consistent and state your assumptions. **Note:** The CMA exam uses the 365-day convention in all formulas requiring an assumption for the number of days in a year.

Days' sales in receivables (also known as average collection period) measures the liquidity of receivables. An internal analyst compares days' sales in receivables with the company's credit terms to determine how efficiently the company manages its receivables. If a company's credit term is 30 days, days' sales in receivables should not be substantially over 30 days. If significant differences are found, attention should be focused on collections policies. As is the case with many ratios, the analyst should examine extreme values in days' sales in receivables. For example, a firm with exceptionally low days' sales in receivables may have excessively tight credit policies that can result in lost sales.

$$\text{Days' Sales in Receivables} = \frac{\text{Average Accounts Receivable}}{(\text{Annual Credit Sales}/365)}$$

$$\text{or}$$

$$= \frac{365}{\text{Accounts Receivable Turnover}}$$

The internal analyst also must make a distinction between cash sales and credit sales; only credit sales should be included in these ratios. Further, **days' sales in receivables** is not relevant for primarily cash businesses, such as fast food restaurants. If cash sales are included, liquidity will be overstated. An increase in the amount of time it takes to turn over receivables indicates deteriorating liquidity. Note that sometimes the days' sales in receivables is calculated using ending values of A/R instead of average receivables as shown. However, the formula just shown is the one that is tested on the CMA exam.

Inventory Turnover Ratio

The **inventory turnover ratio** measures the average number of times that inventory was sold during a year. Inventory is one of the most significant assets in determining liquidity, because the inventory account often is more than half of the total current assets. The inventory of a retailer is the merchandise available for sale. In a manufacturing environment, inventory includes raw materials, work in process, and finished goods. Only the finished goods inventory (if a number is separately available) should be used in computing this ratio.

As with A/R, inventory turnover can be calculated as times per year or as number of days of turnover, as shown next.

$$\text{Inventory Turnover Ratio} = \frac{\text{Cost of Goods Sold}}{\text{Average Inventory}}$$

$$\text{Days' Sales in Inventory} = \frac{\text{Average Inventory}}{(\text{Cost of Sales}/365)}$$

$$\text{or}$$

$$= \frac{365}{\text{Inventory Turnover}}$$

If sales are fairly constant, a lower number of days or a greater number of turnovers of inventory indicates better inventory control and stronger liquidity. Generally, successful companies are those that are able to keep their inventory low with high turnovers while still meeting customer orders on a timely basis. With recent adoption of just-in-time inventory policies and an efficient supply chain management, the inventory turnover ratio has increased.

$$\text{Operating Cycle} = \text{Day's Sales in Receivables} + \text{Day's Sales in Inventory}$$

The operating cycle indicates how quickly the company will receive cash once inventory is acquired or a product is manufactured (this depends on the type of business). A shorter operating cycle translates into improved liquidity.

Other Turnover Ratios

Even though the inventory and receivable turnovers are common and widely used, other turnover ratios may be useful in certain industries. These are the **total asset turnover ratio** and **fixed asset turnover ratio**. For these, total sales are divided by either average total assets or average fixed assets to obtain the turnover ratio.

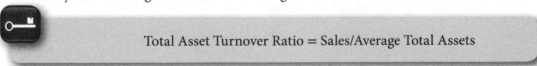

$$\text{Total Asset Turnover Ratio} = \text{Sales}/\text{Average Total Assets}$$

$$\text{Fixed Asset Turnover Ratio} = \text{Sales/Average Net Plant, Property, and Equipment}$$

In capital-intensive industries with significant investments in fixed assets, it may be useful to determine the relationship between sales and the investment in fixed or total assets.

Measuring the Ability to Pay

Any judgment regarding payment of current liabilities should be made in light of the degree of urgency of payment. Several measurements can be made to assess the company's policy in paying off current liabilities. Such analysis could be used by new suppliers to assess the timeliness and creditworthiness of the company.

Days' Purchases in Accounts Payables

Measurement of days' purchases in accounts payables usually indicates the payment terms that the company has with its suppliers, assuming that the company is not in default on its payments.

$$\text{Days' Purchases in Accounts Payables} = \frac{\text{Average Accounts Payables}}{\text{Credit (Purchase/365)}}$$

$$\text{or}$$

$$= \frac{365}{\text{Payables Turnover}}$$

Outside analysts may find it impossible to determine credit purchases. A reasonable approximation is to substitute total purchases instead of credit purchases. Total purchases can be determined by adjusting the cost of goods sold by the changes in inventory balance. A large ratio would indicate that the company either has good relationship with its suppliers and enjoys liberal payment plan or is delinquent in making payments. Further investigation of the credit terms with its major suppliers would provide a reasonable assessment of which of these is true for a particular situation. A larger number than the firm's credit terms would indicate past-due obligations.

The formula also uses average accounts payables, which is the current year plus the prior year ending accounts payables divided by 2 (assuming even purchasing patterns throughout the year). However, sometimes this formula is calculated simply using ending accounts payables.

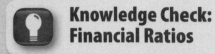

Knowledge Check: Financial Ratios

The next questions are intended to help you check your understanding and recall of the material presented in this topic. They do not represent the type of questions that appear on the CMA exam.

Directions: Answer each question in the space provided. Correct answers and section references appear after the knowledge check questions.

Use the next financial statements for XYC Company to answer questions 1 through 9.

XYC Company Balance Sheet		
	December 31, Y2	**December 31, Y1**
ASSETS		
Current assets:		
Cash and short-term investments	$24,628	$36,125
Trade receivables, net of $30K allowance	429,949	385,273
Other receivables	18,941	15,210
Note receivable—related party	80,532	
Inventory	252,567	215,619
Prepaid insurance	7,500	7,500
Total current assets	**$814,117**	**$659,727**
Fixed assets:		
Property and equipment	209,330	209,300
Less accumulated depreciation	(75,332)	(63,402)
Net fixed assets	**133,998**	**145,898**
TOTAL ASSETS	**$948,115**	**$805,625**
LIABILITIES AND EQUITY		
Current liabilities:		
Accounts payables	$175,321	$165,200
Accrued expenses	2,500	1,200
Current portion of long-term debt	36,000	36,000
Line of credit	145,000	111,993
Total current liabilities	**$358,821**	**$314,393**
Long-term debt:	**117,343**	**120,000**
Total current and long-term liabilities	**$476,164**	**$434,393**
Shareholders' equity:		
Common stock, $1 par value	$100,000	$100,000
Additional paid-in capital	50,000	50,000
Retained earnings	321,951	221,232
Total shareholders' equity	**$471,951**	**$371,232**
TOTAL LIABILITIES AND SHAREHOLDERS' EQUITY	**$948,115**	**$805,625**

Note: Y1 and Y2 dividends per share $1 paid $.25 per quarter; 100,000 shares of common stock outstanding.

XYC Company Income Statement

	YTD Actual	
	December 31, Y2	**December 31, Y1**
INCOME		
Sales, net	**$1,986,456**	**$1,822,326**
Less:		
Cost of goods sold	1,187,652	1,020,503
GROSS PROFIT	**$ 798,804**	**$ 801,823**
Operating expenses:		
Operating expenses, combined	$ 556,732	$ 546,698
Total operating expenses	**$ 556,732**	**$ 546,698**
Operating income (loss)	**$ 242,072**	**$ 255,125**
Other income (expense):		
Interest expense	($16,453)	($16,523)
Other income (expense)	(2,600)	(1,900)
Income taxes	(22,300)	(23,646)
Total other income (expense)	**(41,353)**	**(42,069)**
NET INCOME (LOSS)	**$200,719**	**$213,056**

1. What is XYC Company's working capital for Y2 and for Y1? _____

2. What is XYC Company's current ratio for Y2 and for Y1? _____

3. What is XYC Company's acid-test ratio for Y2 and for Y1? _____

4. What is XYC Company's cash ratio for Y2 and for Y1? _____

5. What is XYC Company's debt to total assets ratio for Y2 and for Y1?
    _____

6. What is XYC Company's debt to equity ratio for Y2 and for Y1? _____

7. What is XYC Company's times interest earned ratio for Y2 and for Y1? _____

8. What is XYC Company's financial leverage ratio for Y2? _____

9. What is XYC Company's fixed assets to equity capital ratio for Y2 and for Y1?
    _____

Use the following information to answer questions 10 and 11:

XZ Company has $1,000,000 in net sales in the accounting period. Assume that all sales are credit sales. Its cost of goods sold is $500,000, its average inventory is $100,000, and its accounts payables are $150,000. Its terms of credit are 30 days, and its average receivables from sales are $100,000.

10. Calculate XZ Company's inventory turnover ratio. _____

11. Calculate XZ Company's accounts receivable turnover ratio. _____

12. Assume that in year 1, a company has sales of $500,000, variable costs of $300,000, and fixed costs of $100,000. What is its degree of operating leverage (DOL)?

☐ **a.** 2.0

☐ **b.** 1.25

☐ **c.** 2.5

☐ **d.** 2.08

13. Assuming that the company in question 12 has interest payments of $20,000, what is the company's degree of financial leverage (DFL)?

☐ **a.** 2.0

☐ **b.** 1.25

☐ **c.** 2.5

☐ **d.** 2.08

14. Using the data in questions 12 and 13, what is the company's degree of total leverage (DTL)?

☐ **a.** 5.0

☐ **b.** 1.25

☐ **c.** 2.5

☐ **d.** 2.08

Knowledge Check Answers: Financial Ratios

1. XYC's working capital for Y2 is $455,296 ($814,117 − $358,821); its working capital for Y1 is $345,334 ($659,727 − $314,393). [**See Working Capital Analysis.**]

2. XYC's current ratio for Y2 is 2.269 ($814,117 ÷ $358,821); its current ratio for Y1 is 2.098 ($659,727 ÷ $314,393). [**See Current Ratio.**]

3. XYC's acid-test ratio for Y2 is 1.54; its acid-test ratio for Y1 is 1.39. [**See Quick (Acid-Test) Ratio.**]

$$Y_2 = \frac{\$24,628 + \$429,949 + \$18,941 + \$80,532}{\$358,821} \qquad Y_1 = \frac{\$36,125 + \$385,273 + \$15,210}{\$314,393}$$

4. XYC's cash ratio for Y2 is .069 ($24,628 ÷ $358,821); its cash ratio for Y1 is .115 ($36,125 ÷ $314,393). [**See Cash Ratio.**]

5. The debt to total assets ratio for Y2 is .502 ($476,164 ÷ $948,115); the debt ratio for Y1 is .539 ($434,393 ÷ $805,625). [**See Ratio Analysis on Debt/Liabilities.**]

6. The debt to equity ratio for Y2 is 1.009 ($476,164 ÷ $471,951); the debt to equity ratio for Y1 is 1.17 ($434,393 ÷ $371,232). [**See Debt to Equity Ratio.**]

7. The times interest earned ratio for Y2 is 14.555; the times interest earned ratio for Y1 is 15.326. [**See Times Interest Earned (Interest Coverage) Ratio.**]

$$Y_2: \frac{\$200,719 + 16,453 \,(\text{Interest}) + 22,300 \,(\text{Taxes})}{\$16,453} = \frac{\$239,472}{\$16,453}$$

$$Y_1: \frac{\$213,056 + 16,523 \,(\text{Interest}) + 23,646 \,(\text{Taxes})}{\$16,523} = \frac{\$253,225}{\$16,523}$$

8. The financial leverage ratio for Y2 is 2.008. Financial leverage is calculated by taking total assets and dividing by total equity. Total assets in Y2 is $948,115. Total equity in Y2 is $471,951. Therefore, $948,115 / $471,951 equals 2.008. [**See Financial Leverage Ratio.**]

9. The fixed assets to equity capital ratio for Y2 is .284 ($133,998 ÷ $471,951); the fixed assets to equity capital ratio for Y1 is .393 ($145,898 ÷ $371,232). [**See Financial Leverage Ratio.**]

10. XZ's inventory turnover ratio is 5 ($500,000 ÷ $100,000). [**See Inventory Turnover Ratio.**]

11. XZ's accounts receivable turnover ratio is 10 ($1,000,000 ÷ $100,000). [**See Accounts Receivable Turnover Ratio.**]

12. Assume that in year 1, a company has sales of $500,000, variable costs of $300,000, and fixed costs of $100,000. What is its degree of operating leverage (DOL)? [**See *Degree of Operating Leverage.***]

    ☑ **b.** 2.0

    ☐ **b.** 1.25

    ☐ **c.** 2.5

    ☐ **d.** 2.08

    > *Explanation:* **DOL = CM/OI = (Sales – Variable Costs) / (Sales – Variable Costs – Fixed Costs) = ($500,000 – $300,000) / ($500,000 – $300,000 – $100,000) = $200,000 / $100,000 = 2.0**

13. Assuming that the company in question 12 has interest payments of $20,000, what is the company's degree of financial leverage (DFL)? [**See *Degree of Financial Leverage.***]

    ☐ **a.** 2.0

    ☑ **b.** 1.25

    ☐ **c.** 2.5

    ☐ **d.** 2.08

    > *Explanation:* **DFL = EBIT / EBT =S $100,000 / ($100,000 – $20,000) = 1.25**

14. Using the data in questions 12 and 13, what is the company's degree of total leverage (DTL)? [**See *Degree of Total Leverage.***]

    ☐ **a.** 5.0

    ☐ **b.** 1.25

    ☑ **c.** 2.5

    ☐ **d.** 2.08

    > *Explanation:* **DTL = DOL × DFL = 2.0 × 1.25 = 2.5**

Profitability Analysis

Profitability is a firm's ability to generate earnings over a period of time with a given set of resources. It is analyzed by examining the elements of revenues, the cost of sales, and operating and other expenses.

There are a number of ways an investor can look at return on his or her investment. Some returns involve the price of the stock as it trades in the securities markets. Although there are actions a company can take to make its stock more attractive to investors, return on market price depends on when each investor purchases and sells the stock. Thus, the analyst of a company's financial and operating performance cannot make this calculation for the individual investor. An analyst, can, however, examine how the investor's contribution to the company performed on a per-share basis. This can be done by measuring earnings per share and the dividend yield.

READ the Learning Outcome Statements (LOS) for this topic as found in Appendix B and then study the concepts and calculations presented here to be sure you understand the content you could be tested on in the CMA exam.

Earnings per Share

Earnings per share (EPS) is an important measure investors use to determine whether to purchase a security. It is used as a basis for comparison in the price earnings and earnings yield ratios.

EPS expresses net income on a per-share basis. Notice in the formula that preferred dividends are subtracted from net income because preferred dividends take priority in payout and are therefore not available to common shareholders.

$$\text{Earnings per Common Share} = \frac{\text{Net Income} - \text{Preferred Dividends}}{\text{Weighted Average Number of Common Shares Outstanding}}$$

For example: If Company Q has $1,000,000 in net income and an average of 1,000,000 shares of common stock outstanding, it has generated $1 in earnings per share.

That is the simplest case. If the number of shares outstanding fluctuates during the year, the weighted average requires a calculation based on the fraction of the year each share was outstanding.

For example: To take a slightly more complicated case, if there were 800,000 shares outstanding from Jan. through June and 1,200,000 shares outstanding between July and Dec., the weighted average would be calculated as shown next:

$$800{,}000 \text{ Shares (Jan.} - \text{June)} \times 6 \text{ Months} / 12 \text{ Months} = 400{,}000 \text{ Shares}$$

$$1{,}200{,}000 \text{ Shares (July} - \text{Dec.)} \times 6 / 12 = 600{,}000 \text{ Shares}$$

$$\text{Weighted Average Shares Outstanding (Jan.} - \text{Dec.)} = 400{,}000 \text{ Shares} + 600{,}000 \text{ Shares}$$
$$= 1{,}000{,}000 \text{ Shares}$$

Diluted Earnings per Share

Calculating earnings per share of common stock outstanding becomes more complicated if the various factors that may dilute the EPS by spreading the earnings over other types of stock-related securities are considered. These include, most notably, stock options, warrants, and some convertible bonds and preferred stocks.

For example: At some time during the year Company Q declares a convertible bond issue into 100,000 shares of new common stock. Now there are 1,100,000 shares outstanding—but no new earnings. The previous stockholders are sharing the company's earnings with 10% more stockholders.

Similar situations can occur when certain options or warrants are exercised or when the company declares a stock dividend (but in that case, the current shareholders get a prorated allocation to prevent dilution of their investment).

To accommodate these related securities, the calculation adds two items to the denominator:

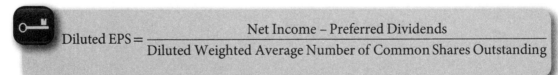

$$\text{Diluted EPS} = \frac{\text{Net Income} - \text{Preferred Dividends}}{\text{Diluted Weighted Average Number of Common Shares Outstanding}}$$

Diluted EPS adjusts common shares by adding shares that may be issued for convertible securities and options.

For example: Company CBA has net income for the year of $50,000,000 and pays out $5,000,000 in dividends on its preferred stock. On January 1, it has 2,000,000 shares of common stock outstanding; it issues another 2,000,000 on April 1 and a final 1,000,000 on August 1. There is an outstanding stock option for 50,000 shares and a "fully diluted" $1,000,000 convertible bond issue (with a yield when it was issued of more than two-thirds of the average yield on AA corporate bonds at that time). Assume that each $1,000 bond is convertible into 1,000 shares.

Its weighted average common stock outstanding is calculated as shown:

Weighted Average Common Stock Outstanding
$$= (2,000,000 \times 3/12) + (4,000,000 \times 4/12 + (5,000,000 \times 5/12)$$
$$= 3,920,000 \text{ Shares}$$

In addition to the stock and the option on 50,000 shares, there are 1,000 convertible bonds outstanding ($1,000,000 in bonds worth $1,000 each). These bonds could be exchanged for 1,000 shares of stock for each $1,000 worth of bonds, adding 1,000,000 shares of common stock to the outstanding amount and saving the firm the amount of after-tax interest that would have been payable to the bondholders. Because the shares of stock underlying those bonds appear in the denominator as if the bonds had been sold, the numerator has to add in the amount that would be saved on interest by the conversion of bonds into stock. Assuming that the bonds have a coupon rate of 5% and would have matured in one year from the date of conversion, the firm would save $30,000 ($50,000 minus taxes paid at a 40% rate).

Putting the weighted average common stock, option, and convertible bonds outstanding into the equation as the divisor under net income minus preferred dividends plus interest payable on outstanding convertible bonds, we get:

$$\text{Fully Diluted EPS} = \frac{\$50,000,000 - \$5,000,000 + \$30,000}{\$3,920,000 + \$50,000 + \$1,000,000}$$

$$= \$9.06 \text{ per Fully Diluted Share}$$

EPS is commonly used by investors as a measure of a company's success. A higher EPS relative to other companies may well translate into a solid ROI through dividends, price gains, or both. If EPS rises over successive accounting periods, creditors and investors look favorably on the company, and management is assured that its policies are succeeding. If EPS begins falling, the reverse is true. The firm begins to look like a bad investment and a credit risk. Management needs to review its products or services against the competition, revisit its goals, and scrutinize operations to improve efficiency before dwindling EPS share lead to bankruptcy.

Dividend Payout Ratio

The **dividend payout ratio** is a near complement to the percentage of shareholders' equity. However, it considers EPS on a fully diluted basis, which is a more conservative measure than comparing earnings against currently outstanding shares of common stock only.

$$\text{Dividend Payout Ratio} = \frac{\text{Common Dividend}}{\text{Earnings Available to Common Shareholders}}$$

Dividend Yield

The **dividend yield**, shown next, is a measure of the cash return realized by the investor, against the current market value of the stock, by the payout of the dividend. This ratio is helpful to investors seeking income from their securities investments.

$$\text{Dividend Yield} = \frac{\text{Annual Dividends per Share}}{\text{Market Price per Share}}$$

Because some companies hold earnings to generate growth (growth stocks) whereas others pay out a majority of earnings in the form of dividends (income stocks) and the market price of common stock trades according to factors in the investment market, no generalization can be made about an appropriate dividend yield on a share of common stock.

Sustainable Equity Growth

Although some companies fail because of ever-declining revenues, companies also fail by attempting to grow too fast. Many small businesses, in particular, go under because they take on a contract with deadlines that cannot be met with their current staff, equipment, capital, and expertise. The **sustainable growth ratio** indicates the maximum earnings growth a firm can have without resorting to other means of financing.

The key to sustainable growth is retaining sufficient earnings to reinvest in growth rather than paying out too much in earnings as dividends. This can be calculated as 1 minus the dividend payout ratio multiplied by return on equity (ROE).

$$\text{Sustainable Growth Rate} = (1 - \text{Dividend Payout Ratio}) \times \text{ROE}$$

If the firm pays out dividends at a rate of 30% of earnings, for example, it retains the other 70% (1 – 30% = 70%). The resulting increase in shareholders' equity will also earn a rate of return and can continue to generate growth in earnings. Ability to take on debt grows as shareholders' equity grows, allowing more borrowing without dangerous changes to the ratio of debt to total assets or debt to equity. If a firm grows at a rate greater than its sustainable growth rate, it will need additional capital from debt or equity. Unfortunately, not all firms can access the money needed to survive in that situation.

Return on Capital Investment

An important question concerning calculations of invested capital is: How well did the company do with the capital it had to work with? **Return on investment (ROI)** and **return on assets (ROA)** are measures of a business's efficiency in using its assets to create profits. The analyst compares ROI to alternative uses of the invested capital as well as the return realized by similar businesses. A relationship exists between risk and reward of investments. An investment can yield a small return, such as interest on U.S. Treasury securities, with virtually no risk (known as the riskless rate of return). Riskier investments (those with more volatile returns) require higher returns in order to justify the higher risk. ROI measures relate the reward (income) to the amount of capital used to generate income (investment).

Components of Return on Capital Investment

The previous section explored ratios related to capital structure—the relative amounts of debt and equity that firms use to build and operate a business. Liquidity and solvency analysis deal with a firm's ability to meet its obligation to creditors.

There is another important stakeholder for the firm: the owner or the shareholder. The owner is entitled to the residual of the firm, which is the excess of what the company earns after settling all its obligations, which is commonly known as the profit or income. Hence, the analysis of how well the firm is meeting the needs of the owner is significant. Many measures exist to perform the analysis. One common way is to focus on the ROI to measure how productively the firm employs its debt and equity. Various measures of profitability indicate how effectively and efficiently management is employing the resources available to them to generate excess for the owners.

There are myriad ways to assess ROI and at least three ways to name it:

1. ROI is, simply, return on investment— essentially the degree of profit in relation to the capital deployed by the business.
2. ROA is return on assets—essentially the same set of factors as ROI (although calculations may vary the individual factors).
3. ROE is return on equity—essentially the degree of profit in relation to equity, which is less than total investment or total assets because it leaves leverage (debt) out of the picture.

While considering which measure is most applicable, a fundamental issue is: Return to whom? The response to the "whom" determines which of the measures is most informative. For example, when the "whom" are all stakeholders, the appropriate measures are the total assets or total invested capital. When focusing on the owners, however, the applicable measure would be the ROE.

Definitions of Invested Capital

Defining *invested capital* presents difficulties for the analyst, because there are differing views on how the elements of assets and profits should be defined. Invested capital (used in ROA or return on invested capital) can be defined as all assets, modified investment basis, or shareholders' equity only.

Analysts who use the modified investment basis to calculate ROI or ROA believe that some components can skew the results. These analysts remove elements from total assets or make determinations of whether to use book value or market value for certain assets. The next elements of financial statements may be modified or not included in the investment base, depending on the analyst's preference:

- **Unproductive assets.** Unproductive assets include such items as an idle plant, surplus inventories, and intangible assets.
- **Depreciable assets.** Assets that can be depreciated, such as buildings and equipment, will carry lower values on the books as they are depreciated, resulting in higher ROI against the same earnings.
- **Preferred shareholders' book value.** Some analysts exclude preferred shareholders' book value because, during liquidation, preferred shareholders are entitled only to the book value of the preferred shares, not to the total returns of the business.

Since the value of assets changes over the course of the year, the appropriate measure may be the beginning, ending, or the average. The choice varies widely; however, when the absolute value of the assets is large relative to the changes in assets, the choice usually does not lead to material difference in the ratio. Usually, though, most analysts average the value of the assets over the period—that is, the average of the beginning and the ending value. Note that while there may be various approaches to calculating ROI, ROA, and ROE, the formulas listed in this text are the ones that are tested on the CMA exam.

Profitability Analysis

The numerator of the return ratio is some measure of earnings or profits. The measure selected for the numerator should match the investment base in the denominator. For example, if total assets are used in the denominator, the income to all providers of the capital ought to be included in the numerator, which includes interest. Thus, interest usually is added back to the net income when computing the ROA. This leads to a popular measure known as **earnings before interest, taxes, depreciation, and amortization (EBITDA).**

When return on common equity capital is computed, net income after deductions for interest and preferred dividends is used. The final ROI always must reflect all applicable costs and expenses, including income taxes, particularly when the return on shareholders' equity is computed. Profit, or "the profit motive," is realized when an organization is generating more resources than it consumes during the course of a year. That is, profit is the amount by which revenue from sales exceeds the costs required to achieve those sales. And the profit margin is the percentage of revenues represented by that excess of revenues over costs. Revenues and costs, however, are measured by diverse criteria.

Profit margins commonly are calculated using one of three different profit measures:

1. **Gross profit**, which equals net sales revenue minus the cost of goods sold (COGS).
2. **Operating income**, which equals gross profit minus various administrative expenses, not including interest or taxes (because they are not part of

operations). Operating income is sometimes called earnings before interest and taxes (EBIT).

3. **Net income**, which reduces revenues by all expenses—cost of goods, operating expenses, and interest and taxes.

The discussion that follows looks at the profit margin calculations that relate each of these to net sales, which is all the money actually received from selling a product or service. Net sales are calculated by taking revenue minus discounts, allowances, and refunds on returned items.

Cost of sales analysis is a key to analysis of a business's profitability. The COGS (the beginning inventory valuation in an accounting period plus net purchases minus the ending inventory valuation) represents a large expense for merchandising and manufacturing businesses. Changes in the COGS in such industries have a large impact on profits. The COGS as a percentage of sales revenue is the single most significant cost category.

The gross profit margin percentage is a measurement of gross profit (sales minus cost of sales) as a percentage of sales:

$$\text{Gross Profit Margin} = \text{Sales} - \text{Cost of Sales}$$

$$\text{Gross Profit Margin Percentage} = \frac{\text{Sales} - \text{Cost of Sales}}{\text{Sales}} = \frac{\text{Gross Profit}}{\text{Sales}}$$

For example: Consider Company A, which realizes $10,000,000 in sales, with a COGS of $4,500,000 and gross profit of $5,500,000. That $5,500,000 represents 55% of net sales ($5,500,000 / $10,000,000 = 55%). Thus, Company A's gross profit margin for the period is 55%.

As with all financial ratios, the gross margin derives its meaning by comparison to performance of the company in past years as well as by comparison to industry averages. One of the things an analyst looks for is the trend of the gross profit margin: Is it increasing, decreasing, or remaining steady? An increase in gross profit margin indicates that the firm is doing a better job of managing the cost of sales, while a decrease would indicate that the cost of sales is increasing.

The analyst must also look for reasons that explain changes. Here are some reasons that gross profit margin may decrease:

- Sales prices have not increased at the same rate as the change in inventory costs.
- Sales prices have declined due to competition.
- The mix of products sold has changed to more products with lower profit margins.
- Inventory is being stolen. (If this is the case, the cost of goods will be higher against the same sales.)

Return on Assets

Calculation of ROA in its simplest form, as shown next, uses net income and the value of all assets. As noted, ROA is essentially the same set of factors as ROI, although calculations may mix and match the factors differently.

$$\text{Return on Assets (ROA)} = \frac{\text{Net Income}}{\text{Average Total Assets}}$$

Net income is the bottom line of the income statement. It includes, in other words, revenue from sales reduced by all expenses: COGS, operating expenses, other expenses (offset by other income), provision for income taxes, loss (or income) from discontinued operations (net of tax), extraordinary items (net of tax), and even the effects of changes in accounting principles (also net of tax). Other measures of profit, which are described next in the DuPont Model section, exclude some of those costs.

Average total assets are calculated as the sum of assets at the beginning and ending of the period divided by 2.

ROA may be the most frequently cited measure of the success of firms. Along with ROE, ROA can be used to rank firms in the same industry; the higher the ratio, the greater the firm's success in making its total assets productive. As income rises and total asset value stays the same, the ratio, too, increases—and the firm looks more successful. If, however, the firm increases the amount of its assets, the ratio will decline unless profits go up proportionally.

The ROA has two components: return on sales and the asset turnover ratio. Return on sales is a profitability measure, and the asset turnover ratio is an operational measure. The two can be multiplied to yield the ROA.

Separating ROA into these two components simplifies the analysis of the change in return on asset measure from one period to the next. Was the return on asset decrease due to a reduction of profit margin (return on sales) or because of employing a larger asset base (decrease in asset turnover ratio)? When a firm replaces its depreciated assets with brand-new ones, the asset base increases without necessarily increasing sales; this causes the asset turnover ratio to decrease, resulting in a lower ROA. However, since normal replacement of worn-out assets is a normal course of business, such decreases in ROA need not cause concern. This concept is developed more fully in the DuPont model.

DuPont Model for ROA

The **DuPont model** breaks apart the formula for ROA just cited and calculates ROA by multiplying the net profit margin by asset turnover. Those two components are implied by the simpler formula given earlier but are not separately visible in it. There is also a revised version of the model that focuses more on ROE than ROA. We will look at the version for ROA first and then at the modified model that calculates ROE.

Here's how the DuPont model turns ROA measured as net income divided by total assets into profit margin times asset turnover. Sales are inserted into the equation as shown:

$$ROA = \frac{\text{Net Income}}{\text{Average Total Assets}} = \frac{\text{Net Income}}{\text{Sales}} \times \frac{\text{Sales}}{\text{Average Total Assets}}$$

ROA is composed of two components: net profit margin and total asset turnover:

Net Profit Margin = Net Income / Sales

Total Asset Turnover = Sales / Average Total Assets

Therefore:

ROA = Net Profit Margin × Total Asset Turnover

Net income divided by sales is the net profit margin. And sales divided by average total assets is total asset turnover. Note that net income divided by sales is also called net profit margin. Sales divided by average total assets is also called total asset turnover.

For example: If Company A has total assets of $1,000,000 and net income of $200,000, its ROA, calculated the simpler way, is 20%: ($200,000 / $1,000,000 = 20%). Assuming sales of $2,000,000 and calculating by the DuPont method produces the same result:

Net Profit Margin = Net Income / Sales
= $200,000 / $2,000,000
= 10%

Total Asset Turnover = Sales / Total Asset
= $2,000,000/$1,000,000
= 2 Times

ROA = Net Profit Margin × Total Asset Turnover
= 10% × 2 Times
= 20%

When analyzing ROA, it is useful to look at both profit margin and total asset turnover. Profit margin tells how much money the firm is earning in relation to revenues, that is, how well management did at controlling costs during the accounting period. Asset turnover is the ratio of annual sales to the asset base; it shows how well management did at using assets efficiently.

For example: If there are two companies with a 10% profit margin and total assets of $1,000,000, the one with higher sales per year will be more attractive.

Turnover (efficient asset usage), in other words, magnifies the value of a given profit margin and thus is an essential point of focus.

It is also true that a high profit margin (asset turnover) can at least partially mask problems with turnover (profits). That is why management would want to watch both the profit margin and the turnover carefully rather than looking at only the ROA calculated by the simpler formula.

If ROA weakens (the ratio goes down), management might consider any of these actions:

- Cut expenses by improving productivity through automation or reducing discretionary spending, thus increasing net profit.
- Reduce assets by improving inventory control, for example, or speeding up receivables (without reducing sales).
- Boost sales while maintaining the profit margin and level of assets.

Both profitability and asset utilization determine the return realized on a company's assets. Financial leverage shows the extent of the use of leverage to magnify returns.

A higher ROA value indicates a more efficient use of assets to generate profits. A higher ROA (compared to the previous year) could result from increased net income, a lower asset value, or both. For example, if assets are lower in the second year of comparison yet income remains the same (the denominator is a lower value), the ROA ratio would increase. Conversely, if net income decreases, assets increase, or both, the ROA ratio would decrease, indicating a less efficient use of assets to generate profits.

Calculating Return on Common Equity

ROE measures the return made on the common shareholders' equity rather than return on total assets.

$$ROE = \frac{\text{Net Income}}{\text{Average Equity}}$$

Because ROE focuses on the return to the common shareholder, the denominator is no longer average total assets but equity. Usually shareholders' equity includes the book value of common shares outstanding (including paid-in capital from common stock) plus retained earnings. (It excludes treasury stock, which is being held by the company instead of shareholders.) For simplicity, shareholders' equity is equal to total assets minus total liabilities if there is no preferred stock issued.

The net income is the income available to common shareholders after deduction of all payments to bondholders and preferred shareholders. (Bond interest and preferred dividends are paid before dividends on common stock. That is one of the meanings of "preferred" in preferred stock.) If a firm is successful, ROE should be greater than the cost of equity capital. Moreover, ROE provides a means of comparing the investment opportunities in different companies. Higher ROE ratios suggest better returns for common stockholders.

DuPont Model for ROE

The DuPont model breaks apart the formula for ROE cited earlier and calculates ROE by multiplying the company's tax burden (Net Profit ÷ Pretax Profit), the company's interest burden (Pretax Profit ÷ EBIT), the company's operating profit margin (EBIT ÷ Sales), the company's asset turnover (Sales ÷ Assets), and the company's leverage ratio (Assets ÷ Equity) as shown:

$$\text{ROE} = \frac{\text{Net Profit}}{\text{Pretax Profit}} \times \frac{\text{Pretax Profit}}{\text{EBIT}} \times \frac{\text{EBIT}}{\text{Sales}} \times \frac{\text{Sales}}{\text{Assets}} \times \frac{\text{Assets}}{\text{Equity}}$$

Recall the standard ROE calculation:

$$\text{ROE} = \text{Net Income} / \text{Average Equity}$$

ROE can also be calculated as shown:

$$\text{ROE} = (\text{Net Income} / \text{Average Total Assets})$$
$$\times (\text{Average Total Assets}) / \text{Average Equity}$$

$$\text{ROE} = \text{ROA} \times \text{Financial Leverage}$$

The relationship of average total assets to average stockholders' equity is called the equity multiplier (or, more simply, financial leverage) because of its power to boost return to stockholders without requiring more equity. If the firm in our example had 45% of its assets in stock and 55% in debt, for example, the **financial leverage ratio** would be calculated this way:

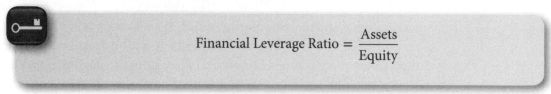

$$\text{Financial Leverage Ratio} = \frac{\text{Assets}}{\text{Equity}}$$

$$\text{Financial Leverage Ratio} = \$1,000,000 / \$450,000 = 2.22$$

The ROE would then become:

$$\text{ROE} = \text{ROA} \times \text{Financial Leverage} = 20\% \times 2.22 = 44.4\%$$

If the firm's assets were composed 100% of common equity, the ROA and ROE would be the same. (The multiplier would become 1.) But when all the ROA goes to stockholders, who contribute only 45% of the capital, the ROE goes above the 20% ROA. The company, in this instance, is using leverage productively.

Financial leverage also is referred to as the equity multiplier. That is, it is the factor by which return on equity grows faster than the ROA, for a small increase in profitability. From the shareholders' point of view, return on equity increases as the firm borrows more money (as long as the money is used effectively and earns an income greater than the interest costs) rather than raising cash through issuance of more shares. Financial leverage can be used effectively by borrowing capital, either short term or long term, and earning a return that is higher than the corresponding interest cost.

Another way of saying the same thing is that increased leverage increases ROE, to the benefit of shareholders, without necessarily increasing ROA. To be productive for the firm, then, the increased leverage needs to be accompanied by positive ROA. It is up to financial managers to determine the best mix of debt and equity to keep the company competitive in the marketplace and attractive to shareholders and creditors.

An alternative, and a more thorough, method of computing the financial leverage is by listing all sources of capital, various form of debt, preferred stock, and common stock. Then the amount paid to each one of those stakeholders in terms of interest, preferred dividends, and so on, is added together. Short-term liabilities, such as accounts payable and unearned revenue, are not included because they represent interest-free loans. The cost of capital then can be computed by dividing the amount paid to a particular source of capital by the amount of capital provided by that source. When the financial leverage is being used appropriately, the common shareholder earns the highest rate of return.

This is an indicator that management is effective in raising capital for its operation and maximizing the returns to the owners/shareholders.

Revenue Analysis

Revenue is an indicator of resources generated by a business from its customers through its operations. Fundamentally, a company exists to provide goods or services to a customer and generate more resources than it expends in providing the good or service. Lenders and owners provide capital to the business because they believe in the business model that the firm would be able to, in the long run, provide some good/service to customers at a price higher than what is required to provide that service. Accountants must be careful to recognize revenue as it is one of the fundamental measures in the financial statement. Remember that revenue is used as the base for common-sizing the income statement.

In the accrual basis of accounting, revenues are recognized when earned, and the revenue recognition principle involves two factors: substantial performance of service and reasonable estimate of income. Revenue can be recorded when both of these conditions are met. In the normal course of business, the two conditions are met at the point of sale. However, there are exceptions. Sometimes revenue is earned uniformly and continuously over time. In these cases, the earnings process takes place with the passage of time. Rent revenue, interest revenue, and revenue for insurance companies are example of such processes. Thus, recognition of revenue at the time of sale of an insurance policy would be incorrect. Instead, the revenue has to be recognized with the passage of time or at the expiry of the policy.

An analyst must evaluate carefully whether the timing of revenue recognition is appropriate, given the nature of the business. Early recognition of revenue would lead to higher reported income and better profitability as well as liquidity ratios. In order to ascertain whether revenue recognition policies are acceptable, the analysis must consider how the company "earns" revenue—that is, what constitutes the "earnings" process and what constitutes substantial performance of service for the firm. The definition will vary across firms depending on their business models.

Sources of Revenue

For financial statements to present the profits of the company accurately, accountants must recognize revenues at the appropriate times. Consider, for example, a firm that, at the end of the year, believes that it will complete a large contract and receive payment in the near future. If the firm places the revenues in its books and later the sale is not completed, income would be overstated in one year and understated (due to the correction) in the next. To avoid this type of misleading reporting, accountants have adopted these rules regarding the recognition of revenues:

- Activities for creation of revenue must be substantially complete.
- The risk of ownership must have been effectively passed on to the buyer.
- The revenue must be able to be measured or estimated with substantial accuracy.
- The revenue recognized normally must result either in an increase in cash, receivables, or other asset or a decrease in a liability.
- Business transactions must be at arm's length, with independent parties. In other words, a business cannot sell to an affiliate or subsidiary and call it a sale.

These rules are subject to interpretation and exceptions, such as recognition revenue from installment sales, long-term contracts, and other issues.

Revenue Trends and Stability

Analysts, investors, and creditors all need to determine whether revenue represents the stable trend of a growing business or an unusual or one-time event. Sales indexes of various product lines can be correlated and compared to composite industry figures or to product sales trends of specific competitors. Important considerations bearing on the quality and stability of the sales and revenues trend include those listed next.

- Elasticity of demand for products (how consumers respond to a change in the price of a product)
- Ability of the business to anticipate demand trends by the introduction of new products and services

- Level of competition
- Degree of customer concentration and dependence on a single industry or a single customer, such as for government contractors
- Degree of dependence on relatively few leading sales associates
- Degree of geographical diversification of markets

Interrelationships Among Revenue, Inventory, and Receivables

Noncash revenue (sales) is recorded as accounts receivable. Thus, the implicit assumption behind accounts receivable is that revenue must have been earned to be recognized. If a company inappropriately recognizes revenue early, net income is overstated and current assets on the balance sheet are overstated. Inappropriately recognizing revenues after they are earned will understate net income and current assets. Further, an increase in receivables without a corresponding increase in sales may signal problems with collections from customers.

Because merchandising and manufacturing primarily earn revenue through sales of merchandise, the increase in revenue should correspond to an increase in inventory. However, an increase in inventory balance without a corresponding increase in sales may signal problems with inventory management. Again, the application of ratios (such as inventory turnover) may highlight potential problems.

Income Measurement Analysis

There is no absolute measure of "real earnings." The income and expenses presented in the income statement are subject to a variety of judgments and accounting methods.

Income is measured for a number of reasons, including to:

- Determine what income can be relied on for purposes of income forecasting.
- Determine how stable the major elements of income are.
- Measure the earnings power of the business.

An analysis must determine the net income, which is relevant to the business and to the different needs of users.

These factors need to be considered in measuring income:

- Estimates
- Accounting methods
- Disclosure of incentives
- Different needs of users

Estimates

The determination of income depends on estimates regarding future events and their outcomes. For publicly traded companies, management makes the estimates, which the auditors verify for reasonableness. The estimates and assumptions could affect the measurement of income significantly. For example, the estimate of useful life for depreciable assets affects the depreciation expense and thereby the reported income. A generous estimate of longer useful life reduces depreciation expense, thereby increasing income.

Accounting Methods

It is important to understand and assess the implications that the use of one accounting principle as opposed to another (such as straight-line versus accelerated depreciation) has on the firm's measurement of income as well as how it compares to other businesses. The accounting methods are chosen at the discretion of management, and the auditor's role is to ensure that the method selected is one of the many generally accepted accounting methods and that its use has been consistent over years. Auditors are responsible for understanding the effect of these methods on reported income and other financial statement measures, including how they affect the computation of ratios.

For example, two commonly used methods of inventory valuation are first-in, first-out (FIFO) and last-in, first-out (LIFO). For the same underlying economic event, use of LIFO, under certain assumptions of increasing inventory units and prices, yields lower income than the FIFO inventory valuation method. Thus, a firm using LIFO would report lower income and lower inventory value than a similar firm using FIFO inventory valuation method. Lower income and lower assets both affect the computation of the return of asset ratio. An analyst is required to consider such effects of accounting policy choices on various financial ratios. The CMA exam tests the ability to evaluate and deduce the effects of various accounting choices on common ratios.

Disclosure Incentives

The degree of informative disclosure about the results of operations and the asset base of segments of a business can vary widely. Full disclosure would call for providing detailed income statements for each significant segment. This is rarely found in practice because of the difficulty of obtaining such breakdowns internally and management's reluctance to divulge information that could harm the business's competitive position.

The more information a company discloses, the better its position will be understood, and as a result, the stock price will more correctly reflect its fair value. However, because it is not always in the best interest of management to disclose information that might be used by competitors, the level of disclosure may be tempered, even at the expense of undervaluation in the equity market.

Different Needs of Users

Users of financial statement analysis often have different needs. For example, the investing public is interested in analysis of the financial position of the business and its ability to earn future profits. Investors use an analysis of past trends and the current position to project the future prospects of the business.

Creditors obtain limited return from extending credit and tend to judge conservatively. Creditors risk loss of capital loaned and so look for the firm's ability to repay both short- and long-term debt. Suppliers extend credit and must weigh their risk of loss of income if not paid for merchandise. If, for example, a supplier sells a product with a 10% markup, it would need to sell ten of the product items to make up for the loss on one not paid for.

Management analyzes data from the viewpoints of both investors and creditors. Management is concerned about the current position to meet obligations and future earnings prospects. Union representatives analyze financial statements for the firm's ability to grant increases in wages and fringe benefits. Government is interested in financial statements and the health of businesses for tax and regulatory purposes.

Limitations of Ratio Analysis

Users of financial statements often place too much emphasis on summary indicators and key ratios, such as the current ratio or the EPS amount. No single ratio, or measure, is capable of capturing all relevant or important information about a particular company. The calculation of various ratios is merely the starting point. Analysis requires thinking about these ratios, forming expectations, and understanding the reasons of variances from those expectations. There is no overarching rule of what a ratio ought to be, and it depends on the particular industry as well as the business model.

The next step of analysis after computing ratios is to create benchmarks of what these ratios are expected to be. The benchmarks could be determined based on past financial information about the company or by using the financials of other companies in the same industry. Comparison with the industry standard would indicate whether a particular ratio of a company is normal for companies in that industry. Abnormal ratios or trends have to be further investigated.

Additionally, many financial statements contain information on nonoperating items, such as extraordinary losses or effects of discontinued operations. When these items exist, a judgment must be made as to whether to include their effects while making comparison to the benchmark. If these items are truly one-time aberrations and not the norm for the company or the industry, it is more meaningful to ignore the effects of these items on the financials and ratios.

Ratios mean nothing without some means of comparison: past ratios of the same business, a predetermined standard, or ratios of other companies in the same industry. Numbers within the financial statements must be interpreted based on an understanding of the accounting principles employed by the business.

For a ratio to make sense, there must be a relationship between the two accounts used in the ratio—for example, there is no relationship between shipping costs and marketable securities. The validity of ratios also depends on the validity of the numbers used in the calculations. If the business's accounting system cannot be relied on to produce reliable figures, ratios are also unreliable.

Ratios require careful interpretation, because factors affecting the numerator may correlate with those affecting the denominator. For example, it is possible to improve the ratio of operating expense to sales by reducing costs of sales. However, if reducing sales costs, such as marketing, consequently results in a loss of sales or share of market, the seeming improvement in profitability may, in fact, have an overall detrimental effect on the future earnings potential of the business.

In addition to understanding internal factors that affect ratios, it is essential to understand the status of external conditions, such as business conditions and industry position. Other limitations of ratio analysis are listed next.

- Uses of different accounting methods (depreciation, inventory valuation method, etc.) make comparability difficult.
- Seasonal fluctuations should be considered.
- Analyzing conglomerates is difficult because of lack of comparability (across firms).

The possibility that the firm has engaged in window dressing also can present a challenge. An internal accountant may be motivated to increase net income and to use decisions at his or her discretion (depreciation, etc.) to affect the results of the firm's financial statements.

Financial statements are a result of applying various accounting treatments and making various estimates. For example, depreciation expense is determined based on an estimate of useful life and a choice of the depreciation method: straight line or double declining balance. Thus, the numbers on the financial statement and thereby the ratios computed using those numbers are greatly affected by these estimates and accounting policy choices.

In making comparisons across companies, it is important to consider whether the accounting estimates are similar and whether the accounting method used is identical. Such information usually is available in the footnotes to the financials and should be incorporated in the analysis of the financials. For example, the choice of inventory valuation method, FIFO or LIFO, could have significant impact on the value of inventory and cost of sales and thereby could affect ratios such as the current ratio or the gross profit margin.

Changes in accounting methods, such as a change in depreciation method, also have an impact on the ratios. Such changes make comparisons of the ratios or the trends over time more difficult. Prior to conducting a trend analysis or time-series analysis, it is necessary to ensure that there were no significant accounting policy changes during that time period. Information on significant accounting method or policy change is addressed in the management discussion and analysis section of the financial statement, and its impact on various accounts explicitly discussed in the footnotes to the financials.

Knowledge Check: Profitability Analysis

The next questions are intended to help you check your understanding and recall of the material presented in this topic. They do not represent the type of questions that appear on the CMA exam.

Directions: Answer each question in the space provided. Correct answers and section references follow these questions.

1. Which of the following statements is false?

   ☐ **a.** Unproductive assets are assets that currently are not being utilized.

   ☐ **b.** Depreciable assets result in lower ROI.

   ☐ **c.** Current liabilities are not included in total liabilities for purposes of defining invested capital.

   ☐ **d.** Preferred shareholders' book value usually is excluded from shareholders' book value.

Use the following financial statements for XYC Company to answer questions 2 and 3

XYC Company Balance Sheet		
	December 31, Y2	December 31, Y1
ASSETS		
Current assets:		
Cash and short-term investments	$24,628	$36,125
Trade receivables, net of $30K allowance	429,949	385,273
Other receivables	18,941	15,210
Note receivable—related party	80,532	
Inventory	252,567	215,619
Prepaid insurance	7,500	7,500
Total current assets	**$814,117**	**$659,727**
Fixed assets:		
Property and equipment	209,330	209,300
Less accumulated depreciation	(75,332)	(63,402)
Net fixed assets	**133,998**	**145,898**
TOTAL ASSETS	**$948,115**	**$805,625**
LIABILITIES AND EQUITY		
Current liabilities:		
Accounts payable	$175,321	$165,200
Accrued expenses	2,500	1,200
Current portion of long-term debt	36,000	36,000
Line of credit	145,000	111,993

Total current liabilities	$358,821	$314,393
Long-term debt:	117,343	120,000
Total current and long-term liabilities	$476,164	$434,393
Shareholders' equity:		
Common stock, $1 par value	$100,000	$100,000
Additional paid-in capital	50,000	50,000
Retained earnings	321,951	221,232
Total shareholders' equity	$471,951	$371,232
TOTAL LIABILITIES AND SHAREHOLDERS' EQUITY	$948,115	$805,625

Note: Y1 and Y2 dividends per share $1 paid $.25 per quarter; 100,000 shares of common stock outstanding.

XYC Company Income Statement		
	YTD Actual	
	December 31, Y2	**December 31, Y1**
INCOME		
SALES, NET	$1,986,456	$1,822,326
Less:		
Cost of goods sold	1,187,652	1,020,503
GROSS PROFIT	$798,804	$ 801,823
Operating expenses:		
Operating expenses, combined	$556,732	$546,698
Total operating expenses	$556,732	$546,698
Operating income (loss)	$242,072	$255,125
Other income (expense):		
Interest expense	($16,453)	($16,523)
Other income (expense)	(2,600)	(1,900)
Income taxes	(22,300)	(23,646)
Total other income (expense)	(41,353)	(42,069)
NET INCOME (LOSS)	$200,719	$213,056

2. What is XYC Company's ROA for Y2 and Y1? (Use year-end assets for calculations.)

3. What is XYC Company's ROE for Y2 and Y1? _____

4. All of the following are possible needs of users of financial statements **except:**

☐ **a.** The investing public needs to know what the company will make in the next fiscal year.

☐ **b.** Credit grantors need assurances about the company's ability to repay obligations.

☐ **c.** Suppliers need assurances that the company will pay for products or materials the supplier sells it on credit.

☐ **d.** Management needs to know about the company's ability to pay obligations and the prospects for future earnings.

5. Which of the following statements is true?

☐ **a.** Revenue is sales minus cost of sales.

☐ **b.** A company that discloses more in its financial statements will provide investors with more information to assess the fair value of the stock's price.

☐ **c.** Revenue can be recognized when a business sells inventory to a subsidiary with a buy-back guarantee contract.

☐ **d.** An increase in receivables with a corresponding increase in sales indicates trouble with collections.

6. Which of the following statements is true?

☐ **a.** Depreciation expenses are write-offs of already purchased fixed assets and do not affect the bottom line.

☐ **b.** After a year of negative income, a company should use percentages in variation analysis, because this helps clarify the trend of income.

☐ **c.** The operating cash flow to income ratio requires information from the statements of shareholders' equity to be calculated.

☐ **d.** Trend analysis or variation analysis help analysts compare performance from year to year.

Knowledge Check Answers: Profitability Analysis

1. Which of the following statements is false? [See *Definitions of Invested Capital.*]

    ☐ **a.** Unproductive assets are assets that currently are not being utilized.

    ☑ **b.** Depreciable assets result in lower ROI.

    ☐ **c.** Current liabilities are not included in total liabilities for purposes of defining invested capital.

    ☐ **d.** Preferred shareholders' book value usually is excluded from shareholders' book value.

2. The ROA for Y2 is .212 ($200,719 / $948,115); the ROA for Y1 is .265 ($213,056 / $805,625). [See *Return on Assets.*]

3. The ROE for Y2 is .425 ($200,719 / $471,951); the ROE for Y1 is .574 ($213,056 / $371,232). [See *Calculating Return on Common Equity.*]

4. All of the following are possible needs of users of financial statements except: [See *Limitations of Ratio Analysis.*]

    ☑ **a.** The investing public needs to know what the company will make in the next fiscal year.

    ☐ **b.** Credit grantors need assurances about the company's ability to repay obligations.

    ☐ **c.** Suppliers need assurances that the company will pay for products or materials the supplier sells it on credit.

    ☐ **d.** Management needs to know about the company's ability to pay obligations and the prospects for future earnings.

    Financial statements cannot tell investors what the profits will be in the next year.

5. Which of the following statements is true? [See *Disclosure Incentives.*]

    ☐ **a.** Revenue is sales minus cost of sales.

    ☑ **b.** A company that discloses more in its financial statements will provide investors with more information to assess the fair value of the stock's price.

    ☐ **c.** Revenue can be recognized when a business sells inventory to a subsidiary with a buy-back guarantee contract.

☐ **d.** An increase in receivables with a corresponding increase in sales indicates trouble with collections.

6. Which of the following statements is true? [**See** *Limitations of Ratio Analysis.*]

☐ **a.** Depreciation expenses are write-offs of already purchased fixed assets and do not affect the bottom line.

☐ **b.** After a year of negative income, a company should use percentages in variation analysis, because this helps clarify the trend of income.

☐ **c.** The operating cash flow to income ratio requires information from the statements of shareholders' equity to be calculated.

☑ **d.** Trend analysis or variation analysis help analysts compare performance from year to year.

Special Issues

THIS SECTION PRESENTS SEVERAL THEORETICAL and contemporary issues affecting accounting practice. Fundamentally, accounting income purports to measure economic profitability; however, there are differences in measurement, and it is important for the management accountant or financial analyst to understand those differences. Such differences in accounting measurement lead to a divergence in the accounting value and the economic value of the firm (measured through share prices). Furthermore, economic complexities, such as inflation and foreign currency transactions, affect financial reporting and are discussed in this section. Recently, the International Accounting Standards Board and the Financial Accounting Standards Board have been working jointly to harmonize U.S. generally accepted accounting principles with the international standards, and the adoption of international standards by the U.S. companies may become more prevalent. The section provides an overview of the international standards for some of the key financial accounting topics.

 READ the Learning Outcome Statements (LOS) for this topic as found in Appendix B and then study the concepts and calculations presented here to be sure you understand the content you could be tested on in the CMA exam.

Economic Profit and Accounting Profits

Profit, as an economic term, is the measure of the resources generated by the firm in excess of the resources consumed over the life of the firm. At any given time, the economic profits of the firm are the net present value of its earnings over its lifetime. However, this is not what gets measured as accounting income or accounting profit. The measurement of accounting profit is based on accrual accounting. The measurement of resources generated and consumed follow the rules set by generally accepted accounting principles (GAAP).

The conflict between accounting profit and economic profit arises because earning income is a process that takes place over a period of time rather than at any one point of time. For example, "earning" of an economic profit takes place not only at the time of sale but also at the time of manufacturing, time of shipping and displaying, and so on. However, accounting requires measuring the generation of resources at artificial points of time (December 31 for most corporations). As a result, approximations are needed because the earning process does not end on that day. The methods to determine these approximations or estimates are based on U.S. GAAP in the United States.

The need to report on a periodic and ongoing basis, even though the business is continuing, leads to the need to make such approximations, causing the economic profit to be different from the accounting profit. The objective of financial accounting is not to make the accounting profit close to the economic profit but to provide a reasonable basis to infer the economic profit from the reported accounting profits.

Accounting Changes and Error Corrections

Financial statements must reflect the results of:

- Changes in accounting principle.
- Changes in estimates.
- Changes in reporting entities.
- Error corrections.

Changes in accounting principle occur as a result of new rules issued by the FASB or because management has elected to change from one GAAP method to another GAAP method, where a choice is allowed. An example would be a company changing from the weighted average cost method for valuing inventory to the FIFO method. Note that changing from a cash-based method to a GAAP method is not considered a change in accounting principle as the cash-based method is not GAAP. This type of change would be considered an error correction (further discussed below) and would be treated as such. Further note that a change in depreciation method (e.g., changing from the straight-line method to the double-declining balance method) is not considered a change in accounting principle. Instead, it is considered a "change in accounting estimate effected by a change in principle." It is, therefore, treated as a change in estimate and accounted for in a similar manner as a change in estimate (further discussed below).

Changes in estimate involve the change in an estimated financial statement amount based on new information or experience. This might include, for instance, changing the bad debt percentage of sales estimate from 2% to 3% or changing the useful life of an asset from five to seven years.

Changes in reporting entities include changes that result in the financial statements representing a different entity. Some examples include presenting consolidated statements in place of individual statements, a change in subsidiaries, or a change in the use of the equity method for an investment.

A correction of an error occurs when a material error is made in a prior period's financial statements and requires an adjustment to restate the financial statements so that, cumulatively, they reflect an accurate retained earnings balance.

Accounting Issues and Impact

Under ASC Topic 250, *Accounting Changes and Error Corrections* (formerly covered in FASB Statement No. 154), changes in accounting principle require retrospective application. This approach requires restatement of prior period financial statements to incorporate the effect of the new principle "as if" it had been used in prior periods. Beginning retained earnings of the earliest period presented is adjusted to reflect the effect of this change on all prior periods not presented.

Changes in estimates require prospective application, meaning that the financial statements are not restated but rather the change is reported in the current period and in future periods only.

Changes in reporting entities also require retrospective application similar to changes in accounting principle. Prior-period financial statements are reflected to show the financial information for the new reporting entity as if they entity had existed in that form all along. Cumulative earnings differences are reported through beginning retained earnings as of the beginning of the first period presented.

Errors made that affect the income or loss reporting in prior periods are corrected by adjusting the beginning balance of retained earnings. When financial statements of prior years are being reported on a comparative basis, they are restated to correct amounts. The effect of the error on earlier periods is presented as an adjustment of beginning retained earnings for the earliest period presented.

Earnings Quality

Reported business income, as measured by the accounting process, is not an absolute truth but is a result of many assumptions used and the accounting principles applied. Changing the assumptions or changing the accounting principle employed could change the reported income drastically. Complicating reporting of earnings in accrual accounting is the fact that a cash expenditure can affect numerous accounting periods, and it may take a number of periods before a transaction results in the collection of all amounts due. Investors, as a result, are very much interested in earnings quality.

Earnings quality pertains to the validity and veracity of the reported information. Analysis of earnings quality identifies the results of management choices on financial statements and judges management's motivations, propensities, and attitudes. The basic factors of earnings quality are listed next.

- Selection of accounting principles
- Off-balance sheet financing and its effect on the financials
- Provision for maintenance of assets and future earnings power
- Effect of economic forces on earnings

Selection of Accounting Principles

Management and accountants have discretion in choosing from among accepted accounting principles. A company can tend to be liberal or conservative in its accounting methods. Conservative accounting is less likely to overstate earnings, so the quality of earnings is higher. The last-in, first-out (LIFO) inventory valuation method is considered conservative during times of rising prices (earnings are lower and assets are valued lower). However, excessive conservatism may result in lack of reporting integrity over the long run and is not desirable. The analyst can examine the selection of accounting principles to determine their effects on the financial health and reporting of the company.

Off-Balance Sheet Financing and Its Effect on the Financials

The term *off-balance sheet financing* is used to denote various types of transactions through which a firm can use a resource without showing either the asset or the corresponding liability on the balance sheet. Firms structure certain transactions in such way to improve the appearance of the balance sheet by improving debt to equity ratio and debt to total asset ratio. By lowering these ratios, firms effectively reduce the cost of capital and thereby the corresponding interest expense. Although some of these methods are within the permissible domain under Financial Accounting Standards Board (FASB) standards, some may get eliminated under the International Financial Reporting Standards (IFRS) regulations.

Provision for Maintenance of Assets and Future Earnings Power

Management can put off discretionary expenses, such as repairs and maintenance, to show higher earnings. However, if necessary maintenance and repairs are neglected for the short-term reason of showing higher profits, premature deterioration of assets may have a negative effect on earnings in the long run.

Other discretionary expenses, which have little effect in the short run if put off but great effect in the long run, include advertising and research and development (R&D) costs. It should be noted, however, that R&D costs must be examined carefully, as they do not always produce results that increase corporate profits.

Effect of Economic Forces on Earnings

The effects of cyclical and other economic forces on earnings are not a primary result of management decisions. However, skillful management can minimize the effects of business cycles on the stability of sources and variability of earnings. Earnings variability is undesirable. Thus, higher variability of earnings indicates lower quality of earnings.

Earnings Persistence

Earnings persistence is a measure of how well current earnings predict future earnings. The trend of income generally is considered more important than the size. Earnings that fluctuate up and down with business cycles are less desirable than earnings that display a larger degree of stability, or persistence, over the business cycle. Earnings that display a steady growth trend are most desirable.

Earnings may show fluctuations from year to year that are due not to income from operations but to other unusual and extraordinary income and expenses. In order to isolate the effect of extraordinary income or expenses, financial analysts recast and adjust income statements to show persistent earnings over a number of years for a company.

Recast Income Statement

Financial analysts recast the published income statements to separate out the stable, normal, and continuing elements from those elements that are random, erratic, unusual, or nonrecurring and warrant separate analytical treatment or consideration. Recasting identifies elements included in the income statement of a given period that should more properly be included in the operating results of one or more prior reporting periods.

In recasting, items such as discretionary expenses and gains or losses due to changes in accounting principles are identified. These items must be separated from the normal flow of the income statement net of taxes, with the effect of taxes on the less-usual events shown separately. The bottom line of the recast income statement remains the same as reported net income. Taxes on a recast income statement are computed at the statutory rate, deducting tax benefits for such things as tax credits, capital gains, tax-free income, or foreign taxes.

Figure 2A-5 shows an original income statement; Figure 2A-6 shows the recast income statement.

Figure 2A-5 Income Statement for ABC Corporation

	(in thousands of dollars)				
	Year 5	Year 4	Year 3	Year 2	Year 1
Revenues:					
Services	$410	$255	$250	$230	$100
Products	895	700	750	600	550
Other	195	180	150	50	50
Total revenues	$1,500	$1,135	$1,150	$880	$700
Expenses:					
Salaries	$950	$780	$790	$620	$550
Other	150	120	120	90	80
Interest	50	40	40	30	10
Taxes	330	158	140	112	35
Total expenses:	$1,480	$1,098	$1,090	$852	$675
Net income from continuing operations:	$20	$37	$60	$28	$25
Income (loss) from discontinued operations		(1)	(7)	(1)	1
Income before cumulative effect of accounting change	$20	$36	$53	$27	$26
Cumulative effect on prior years of accounting change		(16)			
Net income:	**$20**	**$20**	**$53**	**$27**	**$26**

Figure 2A-6 Recast Income Statement for ABC Corporation

	(in thousands of dollars)				
	Year 5	**Year 4**	**Year 3**	**Year 2**	**Year 1**
Revenues:	$1,500	$1,135	$1,150	$ 880	$ 700
Costs and expenses:					
Cost of sales	810	646	645	522	417
Selling, general, administration	400	240	220	180	150
Maintenance and repairs	100	50	30	25	15
Advertising	50	40	50	30	30
Research and development	25	10	25	25	25
Amortization	40	40	30	30	20
Interest expense	50	40	50	30	10
Total costs and expenses	1,475	1,066	1,050	842	667
Income before taxes	25	69	100	38	33
Income taxes	(9)	(24)	(35)	(13)	(12)
Income from continuing operations	16	45	65	25	21
Benefit for income at capital gains rate	2	1	2	2	2
Investment tax credit	2	0.5	1	1	1
State income taxes	(2)	(8)	(10)	(3)	(2)
Tax benefit from state income taxes	1	0.5	0.5	0.5	0.5
Other tax adjustments—net	0.5	(1)	1	0.5	0.5
Net income of unconsolidated finance subsidiaries	0.5	(1)	0.5	2	2
Income (loss) from discontinued operations		(1)	(7)	(1)	1
Cumulative effect on prior years of accounting changes		(16)			
Net income as reported:	**$20**	**$20**	**$53**	**$27**	**$26**

Note that the net income, on the bottom line of each statement, is the same. Certain items, such as tax adjustments and income or loss from subsidiaries, have been pulled out from the flow of operating expenses. In addition, the expenses have been recorded into different categories from those on the initial income statement so they can be analyzed separately for their effects on the company's financial position.

Book Value per Share

Book value is the amount of money that would be available to shareholders if an organization's assets were sold at their balance sheet value and all liabilities were paid. Book value per share is calculated by subtracting all liabilities from all assets, then dividing it by the total number of outstanding shares (or equivalents). If an organization's calculated book value per share is higher than the current stock price, the organization may be undervalued; if an organization's stock price is substantially higher than the book value per share, it may be overvalued and prone to corrections. A major limitation with book value is that it may be difficult to value assets accurately. A variety of legitimate accounting techniques for measuring assets may result in different valuations. Further, it may be unrealistic to assume that the value of an asset on the balance sheet equals the value an organization would receive if the asset were sold.

In determining book value per share, the value of the preferred shareholders' equity (its par value) is deducted from total equity because preferred shareholders have priority in liquidation; thus, the par value of preferred stock would not be available to holders of common stock. Preferred stock is at the call price if one exists and is reduced by any preferred stock dividends in arrears.

$$\text{Book Value per Share} = \frac{\text{Total Stockholders' Equity} - \text{Preferred Equity}}{\text{Number of Common Shares Outstanding}}$$

For example: Company Q with $10,000,000 in shareholders' equity, $500,000 par value of preferred stock, and 9 million shares of common stock outstanding would compute the book value per share in this way:

$$\text{Book Value per Share} = \frac{\$10,000,000 - \$500,000}{9,000,000} = \frac{\$9,500,000}{9,000,000} = \$1.06$$

This measure is used in conjunction with the market value of the share, or price per share, to determine the premium the market places on the future potential of the company.

Market to Book Value Ratio

The **market to book value ratio** compares the current book value of each share of common stock to its current market value.

$$\text{Market to Book Ratio} = \text{Current Stock Price} / \text{Book Value per Share}$$

Price/Earnings P/E Ratio

The **price/earnings (P/E) ratio** compares the market price of the stock to earnings per share:

$$\text{Price Earnings Ratio} = \text{Market Price per Share} / \text{Earnings per Share}$$

The P/E ratio is expressed as a multiple of earnings per share (EPS). Investors consider the P/E ratio when choosing an acceptable investment; P/E ratios vary by industry. Businesses in high-growth industries generally have high P/E ratios. Managers like to see high P/E ratios because it indicates strong market confidence.

Earnings Yield

The earnings yield is the inverse of the P/E ratio. It represents the income-producing power of $1 invested in common stock (at its current price):

Earnings Yield = EPS / Current Market Price per Common Share

Analysis also can be made regarding the percentage of earnings retained for future growth and the percentage of earnings paid out as dividends to common shareholders.

Effects of Changing Prices and Inflation

Inflation, or an increase in prices over time, is an important consideration in analyzing financial statements. These statements are based on historical costs (usually) and are not adjusted for the effects of increasing prices. Typically, the sales revenue of a company increases over the year. However, that does not necessarily mean that the company's business is growing in real terms. For example, an increase in total sales from $200,000 in one year to $210,000 the next year could be due to increase in the sales volume or an increase in the sales price. If it is the latter, and the company raised the selling price by 5% when the economy-wide inflation was 8%, it is a good sign. In fact, it signifies a drop in the "real" economic price and did not even result in a higher sales volume.

Fortunately, inflation has been relatively subdued in the United States in the past several years. Thus, the factors and concerns just mentioned are not that important in the United States or most Western European countries. However, these concerns could be of significant importance to highly inflationary economies, such as in Latin America. During the late 1970s, United States economy was highly inflationary. As a response, the FASB required a separate note in the financial statement to calculate the effects of inflation. This requirement was discontinued in the mid-1980s when the inflation had subsided and the profession was of the opinion that the marginal cost of providing the additional information exceeded the marginal benefit, given low inflation. In future, however, such a requirement could be reinstated in periods of high inflation when the marginal benefit of such information to the users of the financial statements exceeds the marginal cost to the company.

Through horizontal (or trend) analysis, the effects of inflation could be incorporated by calculating the rates in terms of a base-year dollar value. That is, if the inflation is, say, 10%, the sales amounts in successive years is divided by a factor of 1.1, 1.21, and so on.

For example: Assume the base year to be 2010 and sales were $300,000. In successive years 2011 and 2012, the sales were $320,000 and $350,000. Thus, the sales growth in absolute dollars was 6.67% ($20,000 / $300,000) in 2011 and 9.375% ($30,000 / $320,000) in 2012. However, in terms of base-year dollars, these sales would be recast as $290,909 ($320,000 / 1.1) and $289,256 ($350,000 / 1.21), which actually reflects a decline in sales over the two years.

Fair Value Standards

FASB Accounting Standards Codification (ASC) Topic 820, *Fair Value Measurements and Disclosures* (formerly FAS No. 157, *Fair Value Measurements*), defines *fair value* and establishes a framework for measuring fair value uniformly for various accounts and accounting treatments. A fair value measurement assumes that the asset or liability is exchanged in an orderly transaction between market participants on the measurement date. When a principal market exists, the price at that market is the fair value. However, in situations where a principal market does not exist, the price at the "most advantageous" market would be used to determine the fair value if there are multiple markets for the asset or the liability. Additionally, a fair value measurement assumes the highest and best use of the asset by market participants. In broad terms, the phrase *highest and best use* refers to use of an asset that would maximize the value of the asset. Best use is determined based on the use of the asset by market participants even if the intended use is different. For example, if a land in prime residential neighborhood is acquired to build a warehouse, the fair value of the land would be the value if it were used for residential purposes.

In order to determine fair value, three approaches are suggested: **market approach, income approach**, and **cost approach**. The market approach uses prices generated by transactions involving identical or comparable assets. The income approach uses valuation techniques to convert future amounts to a single discounted present amount. The cost approach is based on the replacement value of the asset (i.e., the amount required to replace the asset).

To increase consistency and comparability in fair value measurements, a fair value hierarchy is created to prioritize the inputs to valuation techniques to determine the fair value. This hierarchy gives the highest priority to quoted prices in active markets (Level 1) and lowest priority to unobservable inputs (Level 3). In the intermediate, the input could be determined indirectly from the values of related assets, which have quoted prices in active markets (Level 2). The disclosure in the financial statement has to include the classification of assets into these three categories.

Using fair value in financial reporting, as opposed to cost-based reporting, provides more current information about the valuation of assets in comparison to using historical cost. Many financial institutions and investors rely on fair values to make decisions that involve financial assets and liabilities. In many cases, fair value represents the market's expectations about expected future cash flows that may be derived from such assets or liabilities. Fair value makes it possible to compare financial instruments (assets or liabilities) that embody the same economic characteristics, regardless of when they were issued or purchased, when making decisions to buy, hold, or sell those financial instruments. The disadvantages of using fair value include increased volatility in the value of the asset and uncertainty as to the reliability of estimates related to the flexibility in the estimate of the fair value of those instruments.

In May 2011 the International Accounting Standards Board issued IFRS No. 13, *Fair Value Measurement*. IFRS No. 13 defines fair value and replaces the requirement contained in individual standards. This new guidance establishes a single source framework for fair value measurement, as well as required fair value measurement disclosures.

Accounting for Foreign Currency Transactions and Financial Statements

The exposure of U.S. corporations to foreign currency (FC) has rapidly expanded, and currently U.S. companies' purchases and sales abroad amount to approximately $4 trillion per year. For some companies, almost 70% of their revenues are realized abroad, in foreign currency. Conducting business abroad poses multiple accounting challenges; primary problems include these seven:

1. Accounting for sales made abroad and denominated in FC
2. Accounting for purchases made abroad and denominated in FC
3. Accounting for assets held abroad, the value of which is denominated in FC
4. Accounting for liabilities held abroad, the value of which is denominated in FC
5. Accounting for a foreign subsidiary that has to be consolidated in a U.S. corporation's financial statements
6. Accounting for intercompany transactions with a foreign subsidiary
7. Hedging in foreign currency to mitigate exposure to fluctuations in foreign currency

Of these concepts, the ones relevant for the CMA exam are the first five and are covered in this section.

When U.S. corporations conduct business abroad (buying or selling of goods), these transactions usually are denominated in the currency of the place where the transaction takes place. For example, prices at McDonald's in New York City are denominated in U.S. dollars (USD), but prices at McDonald's in Mexico City are denominated in pesos and those in London are denominated in British pounds. Thus, a business may have multiple transactions in various foreign currencies during the course of a year. However, when preparing the financials, all of those transactions have to be converted to USD because the reporting currency for a U.S. company listed on any of the U.S. stock exchanges is USD.

Similarly, assets and liabilities of the company may be denominated in foreign currency and ultimately would get settled in that currency. However, for reporting purposes, the equivalent amount has to be shown in USD. FASB Accounting Standards Codification (ASC) Topic 830, *Foreign Currency Matters* (formerly FAS No. 52, *Foreign Currency Translation*, which was issued in 1981), provides guidance on these issues.

An exchange rate is the purchase price of one unit of a currency in terms of the other. Exchange rates are quoted either directly (i.e., number of units of the domestic currency (i.e., the USD) that can be converted into one unit of foreign currency (i.e., the euro) or indirectly (the number of foreign currency units (i.e., euros) that one unit of the domestic currency (i.e., USD) can be converted into. For example, a direct quote of USD for one euro of $1.40 (presented as $1.40 = €1) means that $1.40 could be exchanged (purchased or sold) for one euro. This quote can also be stated indirectly as $1 = €.714286, meaning that one USD can be exchanged (purchased or sold) for .714286 euros. Note that an exchange rate quoted "indirectly" is simply the reciprocal of the direct exchange quote.

The exchange rates may be fixed by a government unit or allowed to fluctuate based on demand and supply of a particular currency. The terminology related to these fluctuations is called weakening or strengthening of the currency. A currency falls, or weakens, relative to another currency if it takes more of that currency to purchase one unit of the other currency. A currency rises, or strengthens, if it takes fewer units of that currency to purchase one unit of the other currency.

The most common types of FC transactions are imports and exports of goods and services. An export of goods by a U.S. company to a German customer would be considered an FC transaction if the sale is denominated in the foreign currency (i.e., euros). This transaction will have to be translated to into USD using the euro/USD exchange rate on a specified date. Similarly an import of goods from a Canadian company by a U.S. business would be considered an FC transaction if the purchase was denominated in Canadian dollars. ASC Topic 830 stipulates two requirements for foreign currency transactions:

1. At the date of transaction, each asset, liability, revenue, expense, gain, or loss arising from the transaction shall be measured and recorded in the functional currency (usually the reporting currency) using the exchange rate in effect on that date.
2. At each balance sheet date, recorded balances (receivables and/or payables) shall be adjusted to reflect the exchange rate on the balance sheet date. Recorded balances (receivables and/or payables) may also required further adjustment on the payment date, if the exchange rate has changed from the balance sheet date to the payment date.

An FC transaction (purchase or sale) whose exchange rate is quoted directly is translated into USD by multiplying the foreign currency units by the exchange rate in effect on the specified date of translation (i.e., the date of sale or purchase, balance sheet date, payment date). Conversely, an FC transaction (purchase or sale) whose exchange rate is quoted indirectly is translated into USD by dividing the foreign currency units by the exchange rate on the specified date of translation.

Sales Denominated in Foreign Currency

When a U.S. company sells products abroad, the first requirement of ASC Topic 830 is that the transaction and any resulting accounts (i.e., sales, receivables) must be translated into USD using the exchange rate on that date. Further, if the sale was on credit, the A/R balance on the balance sheet would have to be converted to USD using the exchange rate in effect on the balance sheet date.

For example: Suppose on December 16, the Trading Company sold merchandise to a German company for €20,000, when the (indirect) spot rate for euros was $0.660. The balance sheet was prepared on December 31, when the indirect spot rate was $0.665. Trading Company collected the amount (in euros) on January 31 when the indirect spot rate was $0.6725. The journal entries that would be recorded on each of these dates are as follows:

December 16:

Accounts Receivable	30,303	
Revenue		30,303

Calculation: (€20,000/$0.660 = $30,303)

Note: The indirect exchange rate can be converted into a direct exchange rate by dividing the $0.660 into 1. The resulting quotient (i.e., 1.515152) can then be multiplied by the €20,000 to derive the same USD equivalent.

December 31:

Exchange Loss	228	
Accounts Receivable		228

Calculation: [(1/$0.665) − (1/$0.660)] × (€20,000) = ($228)

January 31:

Cash	29,740	
Exchange Loss	335	
Accounts Receivable		30,075

Calculations: [(€20,000 × (1/$0.6725) = $29,740) (USD received on January 31)]; ($29,740 − $30,075 (USD A/R balance at December 31)) = ($335)

In the December 31 financial statements, the transaction would result in the following balances:

Revenue	$30,303
Accounts Receivable	30,075
Exchange Loss	($228)

Purchases in Foreign Currency

Similarly, when a purchase is made abroad, the first requirement is to record FC transactions at the spot rate (exchange rate) in effect at the transaction date. The unit of measurement is changed from the foreign currency to USD. If the accounts payable (A/P) (in foreign currency) remains unpaid on the balance sheet date, it has to be converted using the exchange rate in effect on the balance sheet date, and any resulting exchange gain or loss has to be recorded.

For example: Assume that a U.S.-domiciled company purchases inventory from a Canadian supplier for 10,000 Canadian dollars. The spot rate (quoted directly) in effect on the date of purchase is $0.70 = C$1. The U.S. Company records the transaction as shown:

Inventory	7,000	
Account Payable		7,000
Calculation: (C$10,000 × 0.70 = $7,000)		

If the account payable has not been settled on December 31 (the balance sheet date), when the spot rate is $0.69, the following adjustment would be made:

Accounts Payable	100	
Exchange Gain		100
Calculation: [(0.70−0.69)(C$10,000) = $100]		

Effects on Financial Ratios

When sales are denominated in FC, it results in accounts receivables denominated in FC. If the dollar subsequently weakens with respect to the FC, an exchange gain is recorded on the balance sheet date and the A/R balance becomes larger, thus favorably affecting the short-term liquidity ratios. If the dollar strengthens with respect to the FC, an exchange loss is recorded on the balance sheet date and the A/R balance becomes smaller, thus unfavorably affecting short-term liquidity ratios.

Similarly, when a purchase is denominated in FC, it results in A/P denominated in FC. If the dollar subsequently weakens with respect to the FC, an exchange loss is recorded on the balance sheet date and the A/P balance becomes larger, thus unfavorably affecting short-term liquidity ratios. If the dollar strengthens with respect to the FC, an exchange gain is recorded on the balance sheet date and the A/P balance becomes smaller, thus favorably affecting short-term liquidity ratios.

To mitigate these effects of fluctuations in FC, companies sometimes hedge their exposure through purchase of forward contracts or options. Such hedges are called "cash flow hedges" for accounting purposes.

Accounting for Financial Statements of Foreign Subsidiaries

When a foreign subsidiary does not keep its records in the parent's currency (also known as the "reporting currency"), the subsidiary's financial statements must be translated into the parent's reporting currency prior to consolidation. ASC Topic 830 governs the accounting principles used in converting or "translating" the financials of a foreign subsidiary into the reporting currency (i.e. USD).

Functional currency

Choosing the appropriate method for translating subsidiaries' foreign currency financial statements depends upon what an entity's **functional currency** is. ASC Topic 830, Foreign Currency Matters (formerly addressed in FASB Statement No. 52), defines the functional currency as the currency of the primary economic environment in which the subsidiary operates. The subsidiary's local currency would be its functional currency if its operations are relatively self-contained and integrated within a particular country. On the other hand, the parent's currency would be the functional currency if the operations of the branch or subsidiary are essentially an extension of the parent company's operations.

Determining which currency is the functional currency would depend on factors such as where the subsidiary's sales market is, how its sales prices are determined, where its expenses are incurred, its sources of financing, and the extent of intercompany transactions. Self-contained operations would typically have their sales, purchases, and financing denominated in their local currency and would have few intercompany transactions. On the other hand, integral operations would typically have their sales, purchases, and financing denominated in the parent's currency and would have a number of intercompany transactions.

If a subsidiary operates in a hyperinflationary environment (one with inflation of 100% or more over a three-year period), the parent's currency is always the functional currency.

Currency translation methods

ASC Topic 830 permits two different methods for converting the financial statements of foreign subsidiaries into USD, based on the foreign subsidiary's functional currency.

When the parent's currency is the functional currency, the statements of the branch or subsidiary are remeasured into the parent's currency using the **temporal method**. However, when the subsidiary's local currency is the functional currency, the statements are translated using the **current rate method**. When the subsidiary uses its local currency but this currency is not the functional currency or the parent's reporting currency, then the statements must first be **remeasured** to the functional currency and then translated to the parent's reporting currency.

Typically, there are three steps in consolidating a foreign subsidiary:

1. Modify the foreign financials so they conform to U.S. GAAP. *Doing this may require numerous modifications.*
2. Remeasure the trial balance into the functional currency. *This step is needed only when the currency used to maintain the financial records is not the functional currency.*
3. Translate the financials from the functional currency into the reporting currency. *This step is needed only when the functional currency is not the reporting currency.*

Thus, the conversion process may apply either the temporal method or the current rate method individually, or it may apply the temporal method followed by the current rate method.

Remeasurement Using the Temporal Method

Under the temporal method, also known as the monetary/nonmonetary method, nonmonetary balances (all balance sheet items other than cash, claims to cash, and cash obligations) are translated using historical exchange rates, and the expenses associated with them should be translated at the historical exchange rate in effect when the item was recorded originally.

These nonmonetary accounts include:

Investments carried at cost.

Inventories carried at cost and cost of goods sold.

Prepaid expenses such as rent, insurance, and advertising.

PP&E and depreciation expense.

Intangible assets and amortization expense.

Deferred charges and credits.

Deferred revenue.

Paid-in capital accounts.

Monetary assets and liabilities (cash, receivables, and payables) and other assets and liabilities measured at current values (market values or discounted cash flows) are translated at the current exchange rate on the balance sheet date. Income statement accounts other than those just mentioned are translated using the average exchange rate for the current year (quarter or month) for simplicity. In the temporal method, translation gains and losses are reported in income.

The example in Figure 2A-7 shows a remeasurement from euros to U.S. dollars, the branch's functional currency. As indicated, accounts have been translated using either the current rate on the balance sheet date, the historical exchange rate, or the average rate for the year. The home office account, which represents equity, is not remeasured; rather, the beginning balance in dollars is carried forward.

Translation Using the Current Rate Method

In the current rate method, all assets and liabilities are translated using the current exchange rate on the balance sheet date. Paid-in capital accounts are translated using the historic rate. For simplicity, ASC Topic 830 requires translation of income statement accounts based on the average rate for the current year (although some accountants would argue for using the end-of-year rate on the income statement as well as the balance sheet). Translation gains and losses are not shown in net income but are reported as a component of other comprehensive income.

Figure 2A-7 Remeasurement Using the Temporal Method

Bounce Sporting Goods Company
Remeasurement of European Branch Trial Balance to U.S. Dollars
December 31, Year 1

	Balance (euros) debit (credit)	Exchange Rates	Balance (U.S. dollars) debit (credit)
Cash	€19,950	$0.24*	$4,788
Trade accounts receivable	352,800	0.24*	84,672
Inventories	157,500	0.21†	33,075
Home office	(432,250)		(78,400)
Sales	(700,000)	0.225‡	(157,500)
Cost of goods sold	472,500	0.21†	99,225
Operating expenses	129,500	0.225‡	29,138
Subtotals	€0		$14,998
Transaction gain	0		(14,998)
Totals	€0		$0

*Current rate (on December 31, Year 1) = .24.

†Applicable historical rate.

‡Average exchange rate for the year.

An example of a translation worksheet from euros to U.S. dollars appears in Figure 2A-8. Use of the current, average, or historical exchange rate is indicated. The retained earnings balance is not translated; rather, the dollar amount of beginning retained earnings from the prior year would be carried forward. Ending retained earnings would be the sum of this beginning balance, plus the translated income amount, less any dividends declared during the year.

Financial Statement Presentation and Disclosure Requirements for Foreign Currency

The income statement or notes should list the aggregate gains or losses from foreign entities over the accounting period. Changes in cumulative translation adjustments for the period also must be disclosed in a separate statement, a note, or the statement of stockholders' equity. Details of translation adjustments include the beginning and ending amounts of cumulative translation adjustments, aggregate adjustments, hedges of net investments, long-term intercompany transactions, income taxes allocated to translation adjustments, and decreases from liquidating a foreign investment.

After the financials have been converted into the parent's reporting currency (USD), the parent company prepares the worksheet eliminations to consolidate the foreign subsidiary and the parent company.

Figure 2A-8 Translation Using the Current Rate Method (Subsidiary Financial Statements) to Reporting Currency from Functional Currency

Bounce International Germany

Translation of Financial Statements to U.S. Dollars

For Year Ended August 31, Year 2

	German Euros	Exchange Rate	U.S. Dollars
Income Statement			
Net sales	€206,400	$0.515*	$106,296
Other revenue	51,600	0.515*	26,574
Total revenue	€258,000		$132,870
Cost of goods sold	€154,800	0.515*	$79,722
Operating expenses and income taxes	82,560	0.515*	42,518
Total costs and expenses	€237,360		$122,240
Net income	€20,640		$10,630
Balance Sheet			
Cash	€8,600	$0.49†	$4,214
Trade accounts receivable (net)	34,400	0.49†	16,856
Inventories	154,800	0.49†	75,852
Short-term prepayments	3,440	0.49†	1,686
Plant assets (net)	275,200	0.49†	134,848
Intangible assets (net)	17,200	0.49†	8,428
Total assets	€493,640		$241,884
Notes payable	€17,200	$0.49†	$8,428
Trade accounts payable	25,800	0.49†	12,642
Common stock	430,000	0.54‡	232,200
Retained earnings	20,640		11,146
Cumulative translation adjustments			(22,532)
Total liabilities and stockholders' equity	€493,640		$241,884

*Average for year ended December 31, Year 2.

†Current rate (on December 31, Year 2).

‡Historical rate (on December 31, Year 1, date of X Corporation's investment).

Knowledge Check: Special Issues

The next questions are intended to help you check your understanding and recall of the material presented in this topic. They do not represent the type of questions that appear on the CMA exam.

Directions: Answer each question in the space provided. Correct answers and section references follow these questions.

1. To consolidate a German subsidiary of an U.S. company for which the functional currency is euro, the process includes:

   ☐ **a.** translation of the financials.

   ☐ **b.** remeasurement of the financials.

   ☐ **c.** first remeasurement, then translation of the financials.

   ☐ **d.** first translation, then remeasurement of the financials.

2. Fair value standards require measurement of fair value of an asset by using

   ☐ **a.** the commonly available price in the primary use of the asset.

   ☐ **b.** the average of the prices in all available markets for the asset.

   ☐ **c.** the price in the most advantageous market.

   ☐ **d.** the price in the most conservative market (worst use).

3. IFRS Standards disallow the use of which kind of inventory valuation method?

   ☐ **a.** First-in, first-out

   ☐ **b.** Weighted average

   ☐ **c.** Specific identification

   ☐ **d.** Last-in, first-out

4. Lester Company's comparative balance sheets showed total assets to be $1,500,000 and total liabilities of $900,000 on December 31, 2012. It has 250,000 shares outstanding. The shares are trading at $12 per share. What is the market to book value for Lester?

   ☐ **a.** 0.2

   ☐ **b.** 2

   ☐ **c.** 5

   ☐ **d.** Cannot be determined.

5. Name some of the variables affecting the quality of earnings.

   a. _____

   b. _____

c.   _____

d.   _____

e.   _____

Knowledge Check Answers: Special Issues

1. To consolidate a German subsidiary of an U.S. company for which the functional currency is euro, the process includes: [**See *Accounting for Foreign Subsidiaries*.**]

   ☑ **a.**   translation of the financials.

   ☐ **b.**   remeasurement of the financials.

   ☐ **c.**   first remeasurement, then translation of the financials.

   ☐ **d.**   first translation, then remeasurement of the financials.

2. Fair value standards require measurement of fair value of an asset by using: [**See *Fair Value Standards*.**]

   ☐ **a.**   the commonly available price in the primary use of the asset.

   ☐ **b.**   average of the prices in all available markets for the asset.

   ☑ **c.**   the price in the most advantageous market.

   ☐ **d.**   the price in the most conservative market (worst use).

3. IFRS Standards disallow the use of which kind of inventory valuation method? [**See *Inventory*.**]

   ☐ **a.**   First-in, first-out

   ☐ **b.**   Weighted average

   ☐ **c.**   Specific identification

   ☑ **d.**   Last-in, first-out

4. Lester Company's comparative balance sheets showed total assets to be $1,500,000 and total liability of $900,000 on December 31, 2012. It has 250,000 shares outstanding. The shares are trading at $12 per share. What is the market to book value for Lester? [**See *Market to Book Value Ratio*.**]

   ☐ **a.**   0.2

   ☐ **b.**   2

   ☑ **c.**   5

   ☐ **d.**   Cannot be determined.

   Equity or Book value = $600,000

   Market value = 250,000 × 12

5. Name some of the variables affecting the quality of earnings. [**See *Earnings Quality.***]

    a. **Choice of accounting methods**

    b. **Accounting estimates**

    c. **Effects of inflation**

    d. **Off-balance sheet financing**

    e. **Maintenance of assets and future earning**

Directions: This sampling of questions is designed to emulate actual exam questions. Read each question and write your response on another sheet of paper. See the "Answers to Section Practice Questions" section at the end of this book to assess your response. Validate or improve the answer you wrote. For a more robust selection of practice questions, access the **Online Test Bank** at www.wileycma.com.

Question 2A1-AT01

Topic: Basic Financial Statement Analysis

Gordon has had the following financial results for the last four years:

	Year 1	Year 2	Year 3	Year 4
Sales	$1,250,000	$1,300,000	$1,359,000	$1,400,000
Cost of goods sold	750,000	785,000	825,000	850,000
Gross profit	$ 500,000	$ 515,000	$ 534,000	$ 550,000
Inflation factor	1.00	1.03	1.07	1.10

Gordon has analyzed these results using vertical common-size analysis to determine trends. The performance of Gordon can **best** be characterized by which one of the following statements?

- ☐ **a.** The common-size gross profit percentage has decreased as a result of an increasing common-size trend in cost of goods sold.

- ☐ **b.** The common-size trend in sales is increasing and is resulting in an increasing trend in the common-size gross profit margin.

- ☐ **c.** The common-size trend in cost of goods sold is decreasing, which is resulting in an increasing trend in the common-size gross profit margin.

- ☐ **d.** The increased trend in the common-size gross profit percentage is the result of both the increasing trend in sales and the decreasing trend in cost of goods sold.

Question 2A1-AT02

Topic: Basic Financial Statement Analysis

In assessing the financial prospects for a firm, financial analysts use various techniques. An example of vertical, common-size analysis is

- ☐ **a.** an assessment of the relative stability of a firm's level of vertical integration.

- ☐ **b.** a comparison in financial ratio form between two or more firms in the same industry.

    ☐ **c.** advertising expense is 2% of sales.

    ☐ **d.** comparison in financial form between two or more firms in different industries.

Question 2A1-AT03

Topic: Basic Financial Statement Analysis

When preparing common-size statements, items on the balance sheet are generally stated as a percentage of _____ and items on the income statement are generally stated as a percentage of _____.

    ☐ **a.** total assets; net sales

    ☐ **b.** total shareholders' equity; net income

    ☐ **c.** total assets; net income

    ☐ **d.** total shareholders' equity; net sales

Question 2A1-LS01

Topic: Basic Financial Statement Analysis

Which of the following statements is **true** regarding common-size statements?

    ☐ **a.** Common-size statements can be used to compare companies of different sizes.

    ☐ **b.** Common-size statements indexed over two years for two companies, with both showing a 10% increase in profits, show that both companies would make equally attractive investments.

    ☐ **c.** Horizontal common-size statements can be made only for companies with at least ten years of operational data.

    ☐ **d.** All of the above.

Question 2A1-LS02

Topic: Basic Financial Statement Analysis

A common-size statement is helpful

    ☐ **a.** for figuring out how assets are allocated.

    ☐ **b.** for determining the next investment the company should make.

    ☐ **c.** for considering whether to buy or sell assets.

    ☐ **d.** in comparing companies of different sizes.

Question 2A2-CQ01

Topic: Financial Ratios

Broomall Corporation has decided to include certain financial ratios in its year-end annual report to shareholders. Selected information relating to its most recent fiscal year is provided next.

Cash	$ 10,000
Accounts receivable	20,000
Prepaid expenses	8,000
Inventory	30,000
Available-for-sale securities	
At cost	9,000
Fair value at year-end	12,000
Accounts payable	15,000
Notes payable (due in 90 days)	25,000
Bonds payable (due in 10 years)	35,000
Net credit sales for year	220,000
Cost of goods sold	140,000

Broomall's working capital at year-end is

- ☐ **a.** $40,000.
- ☐ **b.** $37,000.
- ☐ **c.** $28,000.
- ☐ **d.** $10,000.

Question 2A2-CQ02

Topic: Financial Ratios

Birch Products Inc. has the following current assets:

Cash	$ 250,000
Marketable securities	100,000
Accounts receivable	800,000
Inventories	1,450,000
Total current assets	$2,600,000

If Birch's current liabilities are $1,300,000, the firm's

- ☐ **a.** current ratio will decrease if a payment of $100,000 cash is used to pay $100,000 of accounts payable.
- ☐ **b.** current ratio will not change if a payment of $100,000 cash is used to pay $100,000 of accounts payable.
- ☐ **c.** quick ratio will decrease if a payment of $100,000 cash is used to purchase inventory.
- ☐ **d.** quick ratio will not change if a payment of $100,000 cash is used to purchase inventory.

Question 2A2-CQ08

Topic: Financial Ratios

Lowell Corporation has decided to include certain financial ratios in its year-end annual report to shareholders. Selected information relating to its most recent fiscal year is provided next.

Cash	$ 10,000
Accounts receivable (end of year)	20,000
Accounts receivable (beginning of year)	24,000
Inventory (end of year)	30,000
Inventory (beginning of year)	26,000
Notes payable (due in 90 days)	25,000
Bonds payable (due in 10 years)	35,000
Net credit sales for year	220,000
Cost of goods sold	140,000

Using a 365-day year, compute Lowell's accounts receivable turnover in days.

☐ **a.** 26.1 days

☐ **b.** 33.2 days

☐ **c.** 36.5 days

☐ **d.** 39.8 days

Question 2A2-CQ14

Topic: Financial Ratios

Cornwall Corporation's net accounts receivable were $68,000 and $47,000 at the beginning and end of the year, respectively. Cornwall's condensed income statement is shown next.

Sales	$900,000
Cost of goods sold	527,000
Operating expenses	175,000
Operating income	198,000
Income tax	79,000
Net income	$119,000

Cornwall's average number of days' sales in accounts receivable (using a 365-day year) is

☐ **a.** 8 days.

☐ **b.** 13 days.

☐ **c.** 19 days.

☐ **d.** 23 days.

Question 2A2-CQ21

Topic: Financial Ratios

Marble Savings Bank has received loan applications from three companies in the auto parts manufacturing business and currently has the funds to grant only one of these requests. Specific data, shown next, have been selected from these applications for review and comparison with industry averages.

	Bailey	Nutron	Sonex	Industry
Total sales (millions)	$4.27	$3.91	$4.86	$4.30
Net profit margin	9.55%	9.85%	10.05%	9.65%
Current ratio	1.82	2.02	1.96	1.95
Return on assets	12.0%	12.6%	11.4%	12.4%
Debt/equity ratio	52.5%	44.6%	49.6%	48.3%
Financial leverage	1.30	1.02	1.56	1.33

Based on this information, select the strategy that should be the **most** beneficial to Marble Savings.

- ☐ **a.** Marble Savings Bank should not grant any loans as none of these companies represents a good credit risk.

- ☐ **b.** Grant the loan to Bailey as all the company's data approximate the industry average.

- ☐ **c.** Grant the loan to Nutron as both the debt to equity ratio and degree of financial leverage are below the industry average.

- ☐ **d.** Grant the loan to Sonex as the company has the highest net profit margin and degree of financial leverage.

Question 2A2-CQ29

Topic: Financial Ratios

The following information concerning Arnold Company's common stock was included in the company's financial reports for the last two years.

	Year 2	Year 1
Market price per share on December 31	$60	$50
Par value per share	10	10
Earnings per share	3	3
Dividends per share	1	1
Book value per share on December 31	36	34

Based on the price/earnings information, investors would **most likely** consider Arnold's common stock to

- ☐ **a.** be overvalued at the end of year 2.

- ☐ **b.** indicate inferior investment decisions by management in year 2.

- ☐ **c.** show a positive trend in growth opportunities in year 2 compared to year 1.

- ☐ **d.** show a decline in growth opportunities in year 2 compared to year 1.

Question 2A2-CQ30

Topic: Financial Ratios

Devlin Inc. has 250,000 shares of $10 par value common stock outstanding. For the current year, Devlin paid a cash dividend of $3.50 per share and had earnings per share of $4.80. The market price of Devlin's stock is $34 per share. Devlin's price/earnings ratio is

- ☐ **a.** 2.08.
- ☐ **b.** 2.85.
- ☐ **c.** 7.08.
- ☐ **d.** 9.71.

Question 2A3-CQ01

Topic: Profitability Analysis

For the year just ended, Beechwood Corporation had income from operations of $198,000 and net income of $96,000. Additional financial information is given next.

	January 1	December 31
7% bonds payable	$95,000	$77,000
Common stock ($10 par value)	300,000	300,000
Reserve for bond retirement	12,000	28,000
Retained earnings	155,000	206,000

Beechwood has no other equity issues outstanding. Beechwood's return on shareholders' equity for the year just ended is

- ☐ **a.** 19.2%.
- ☐ **b.** 19.9%.
- ☐ **c.** 32.0%.
- ☐ **d.** 39.5%.

Question 2A3-AT01

Topic: Profitability Analysis

For a given level of sales and holding all other financial statement items constant, a company's return on equity (ROE) will

- ☐ **a.** decrease as its total assets increase.
- ☐ **b.** increase as its debt ratio decreases.
- ☐ **c.** decrease as its cost of goods sold as a percentage of sales decrease.
- ☐ **d.** increase as its equity increases.

Question 2A3-LS01

Topic: Profitability Analysis

BDU Company has net income of $500,000 and average assets of $2,000,000 for the current year. If its asset turnover is 1.25 times, what is its profit margin?

- ☐ **a.** 0.25
- ☐ **b.** 0.31
- ☐ **c.** 0.36
- ☐ **d.** 0.2

Question 2A3-LS05

Topic: Profitability Analysis

Which of the following must be considered in measuring income?

I. Estimates regarding future events

II. Accounting methods used by the company

III. The degree of informative disclosure about results of operations

IV. Different needs of users

- ☐ **a.** I and II only
- ☐ **b.** II and III only
- ☐ **c.** I, II, III, and IV
- ☐ **d.** I, II, and IV only

Question 2A3-LS09

Topic: Profitability Analysis

In the last fiscal year, LMO Company had net sales of $7,000,000, a gross profit margin of 40%, and a net profit margin of 10%. What is its cost of goods sold?

- ☐ **a.** $4,200,000
- ☐ **b.** $6,300,000
- ☐ **c.** $2,800,000
- ☐ **d.** $700,000

Question 2A3-LS10

Topic: Profitability Analysis

An increase in the gross profit margin for a merchandising firm indicates that the firm

- ☐ **a.** is increasing its revenues.
- ☐ **b.** is decreasing its fixed costs.
- ☐ **c.** is doing a better job of managing cost of sales.
- ☐ **d.** has been managing its quality control better, which results in fewer returns.

Question 2A3-LS11

Topic: Profitability Analysis

Earnings power is

- ☐ **a.** the company's ability to turn liabilities into income-generating activities.
- ☐ **b.** a forecasting tool that anticipates probable future conditions instead of making the assumption of a continued trend.
- ☐ **c.** a mathematical calculation based on past earnings that can absolutely predict future earnings.
- ☐ **d.** the best possible estimate of the average business earnings of a number of years.

Question 2A4-LS01

Topic: Special Issues

Which of the following are elements of earnings quality?

I. Management's discretion in choosing from among accepted accounting principles

II. Management compensation in relation to net earnings

III. The degree to which assets are maintained

IV. The effect of cyclical and other economic forces on the stability of earnings

- ☐ **a.** I, III, and IV only
- ☐ **b.** I and III only
- ☐ **c.** II and IV only
- ☐ **d.** I, II, III, and IV

Question 2A4-LS02

Topic: Special Issues

Which of the following statements is true?

- ☐ **a.** Economic profits are accounting profits minus explicit costs.
- ☐ **b.** Economic profits are accounting profits minus implicit costs.
- ☐ **c.** Accounting profits are economic profits minus implicit costs.
- ☐ **d.** Accounting profits are economic profits minus explicit costs.

Question 2A4-LS03

Topic: Special Issues

Which of the following statements is **true**?

☐ **a.** Financial statements need not make adjustments for inflation, as earnings automatically reflect the higher prices.

☐ **b.** Financial statements generally make adjustments for inflation, so earnings may be clearly represented over time.

☐ **c.** Financial statements make adjustments for inflation every year and state the inflation rate for the year in the footnotes of the annual report.

☐ **d.** Financial statements generally do not make adjustments for inflation, so earnings may be significantly compounded over time.

Question 2A4-LS04

Topic: Special Issues

A European company provides annual reports for U.S. investors purchasing ADRs of the company's stock in the United States. The company reports €1,500,000 net income. The exchange rate between the euro and the U.S. dollar is €1.19/$1. Which of the following statements is true?

☐ **a.** Annual statements sent to U.S. investors will show net income as €1,500,000.

☐ **b.** Annual statements sent to U.S. investors will show net income as $1,260,504.

☐ **c.** Annual statements sent to U.S. investors will show net income as $1,785,000.

☐ **d.** Annual statements sent to U.S. investors will show net income as $1,500,000.

 To further assess your understanding of the concepts and calculations covered in Part 2, Section A: Financial Statement Analysis, practice with the **Online Test Bank** for this section. **REMINDER:** See the "Answers to Section Practice Questions" section at the end of this book.

Corporate Finance

Corporate finance is a cornerstone in advancing core business goals and achieving strategic objectives. For-profit businesses, not-for-profit institutions, and public entities all must make expenditures to cover a wide variety of costs. All investments—both short and long term—must support organizational core competencies. Simply stated, corporate finances must support organizational strategies and ensure that any short-term obstacles do not disrupt long-term strategies.

Organizations may choose from several types of financial instruments. Management accountants often are called on to evaluate the appropriateness of the instruments for an organization. To do so, they need to understand the general uses of the different instruments and the economic risks and benefits of owning or issuing them. They also must ensure that the organization can earn a sufficient rate of return from the investments chosen to cover the costs of generating funds.

Prudent investment decisions help to ensure the financial soundness of any firm. For publicly traded corporations in particular, financial stability and value creation induce investors to purchase the firm's stocks, bonds, and securities.

This section examines key concepts in corporate finance, ranging from basic risk and return concepts to international finance issues. The section covers these topics:

- Risk and return
- Long-term financial management
- Raising capital
- Working capital management
- Corporate restructuring
- International finance

Management accountants provide valuable assistance in all of these areas.

Learning Outcome Statements Overview: Corporate Finance

Section B.1. Risk and Return

A. Calculate rates of return.

   a. At the simplest level, a return is calculated as the cash payments received (such as dividends or interest), plus the change in market price (appreciation or loss in price), divided by the beginning price of the security. The formula for rate of return is:

$$R = \frac{(P_t - P_{t-1}) + D_t}{P_{t-1}}$$

   where
   R = rate of return (holding period return)
   P = stock price at the end of the period
   t = time period
   P_{t-1} = stock price at the beginning of the period
   D_t = cash dividend at the end of the time period

B. Identify and demonstrate an understanding of systematic (market) risk and unsystematic (company) risk.

   a. Systematic (market) risk—Risk associated with changes in return based on the market as a whole. Systematic risk is common to an entire class of investments because of unavoidable national or global economic changes.

   b. Unsystematic (company) risk—Risk that is independent of economic, political, or other factors or general market movements. It is associated with a specific company or industry.

C. Identify and demonstrate an understanding of credit risk, foreign exchange risk, interest rate risk, market risk, industry risk and political risk.

   a. Credit risk—Investor's risk that the borrower will not make payments as promised (also called "default risk").

   b. Foreign exchange risk—The risk that there will be a change in the exchange rate of one currency in relation to another (also called "currency risk").

   c. Interest rate risk—The risk that the market rate of interest will vary, affecting the value of an interest-bearing asset.
   d. Market risk—The risk that a portfolio will decrease due to changes in market risk factors, including stock prices, interest rates, foreign exchange rates, and commodity prices.
   e. Industry risk—The combined set of risks particular to an industry.
   f. Political risk—The risk that political decisions may complicate the operations and profitability of business.
D. Demonstrate an understanding of the relationship between risk and return.
   a. Risk is an important consideration in making financial decisions. Under rational market conditions, those investments with greater expected risk should provide a higher expected rate of return than investments with lower risk.
E. Distinguish between individual security risk and portfolio risk.
   a. The formulas for expected return, standard deviation, and coefficient of variation are used to assess the risk of an individual security. Calculations used to assess the risk of a portfolio are more complicated than the standard deviation and the variance of a single investment. Covariance and correlation are useful measure of portfolio risk. [See Topic 1: Risk and Return (in book) for more information.]
F. Demonstrate an understanding of diversification.
   a. *Diversification* refers to holding a wide range of different investments in a portfolio. The primary goal of diversification is to reduce the variability (or risk) of a portfolio. It is the don't-put-all-your-eggs-in-one-basket theory.
G. Define beta, and explain how a change in beta impacts a security's price.
   a. Beta (β) describes an investment's sensitivity to market movements. It is a quantitative measure of the volatility of a given investment relative to the overall market. Specifically, beta indicates the amount that investors expect an investment price to change for each additional 1% change in the market. The higher the beta of a stock (over 1.0), the more sensitive, or volatile, it is to overall market movements. The more volatile a stock is, the higher the perceived level of risk.
H. Demonstrate an understanding of the capital asset pricing model (CAPM), and calculate the expected risk-adjusted returns using CAPM.
   a. Capital asset pricing model (CAPM)—An economic model for valuing a portfolio by relating risk and expected return. The idea behind the CAPM is that investors demand an additional expected return (also known as risk premium) when asked to accept additional risk above that found in a risk-free asset (e.g., Treasury bills).

$$K_e = R_f + \beta (K_m - R_f)$$

where
K_e = required rate of return
R_f = risk free rate such as the return on UST bill or T-bonds
β = beta coefficient for the company
K_m = return on a market portfolio

b. Degree of operating leverage (DOL)—The percentage change in operating income given a percentage change in sales. It is caused by the organization's cost structure (the relationship of fixed and variable costs). It is calculated by:

$$DOL = \frac{\text{Contribution Margin}}{\text{Operating Income}}$$

I. Explain how operating leverage can increase return and business risk concurrently.

    a. Companies with a high DOL often have a high degree of business risk. For example, a manufacturing company with excess capacity and high DOL will increase net income with one additional sale. That opportunity for high variability in net income is defined as increased business risk.

J. Describe and calculate financial risk.

    a. Financial risk—The risk associated with any form of financing. A company's two most common forms of financing are debt and equity (stock). Debt financing increases the variability of earnings before taxes (but after interest). Financial risk is often measured by the degree of financial leverage (DFL).

    b. Degree of financial leverage (DFL)—The percentage change in earnings per share (EPS) given a percentage change in operating income. It is calculated by:

$$DFL = \frac{\text{\% Change in Net Income}}{\text{\% Change in EBIT}}$$

$$\text{or}$$

$$= \frac{\text{EBIT}}{\text{EBT}}$$

K. Explain how financial leverage can increase return and financial risk concurrently.

    a. Increasing DFL will increase net income but exposes the company to a higher risk of default on the debt instruments, which increases financial risk.

L. Explain how portfolio theory can be used to decrease the financial risk of a business.

    a. Portfolio management (or portfolio theory) is a decision approach that permits an investor or manager to classify, estimate, and control risks and returns. Portfolio theory involves identifying financial instruments, evaluating each instrument's risks and returns, and selecting the mix of investments that will diversify the risks in order to achieve the highest aggregate return.

M. Demonstrate an understanding of how individual business activities can affect the business's portfolio risk.

Section B.2. Long-Term Financial Management

A. Describe the term structure of interest rates, and explain why it changes over time.

    a. Term structure of interest—The relationship between an interest rate and the time to maturity. As the time to maturity increases, the risk of that security increases because there is greater risk of uncertainty and default. Since investors expect increased returns when risk increases, the interest rate is usually greater as the time to maturity is extended.

B. Define and identify the characteristics of common stock and preferred stock.

    a. Common stock—Provides equity ownership in a corporation. The owner of common stock is entitled to their share of the assets and earnings of the corporation. Characteristics of common stock include:

- Subordinate to all debt holders and preferred stockholders
- No maturity date
- No guarantee of return
- Common stock gives voting rights to holders
- Preemptive rights—allows current shareholders to maintain proportional ownership should the company issue more stock

    b. Preferred stock—Hybrid between bonds and common stock. Provides partial ownership in a corporation but generally offers a fixed dividend. Characteristics of preferred stock include:

- Holders generally receive a fixed dividend on their investment.
- Holders usually do not have voting rights.
- Dividends not paid can accumulate to future periods
- Usually have a stated call, or redemption, price.
- Usually have convertible features where holders can convert to common stock.

C. Identify and describe the basic features of a bond such as maturity, par value, coupon rate, provisions for redeeming, conversion provisions, covenants, options granted to the issuer or investor, indentures, and restrictions.

    a. Maturity—The date to which the principal amount of the bond is to be repaid.

    b. Par value—The principal amount of the bond due at maturity (face amount).

    c. Coupon rate—The interest rate on a bond, expressed as a percentage of the bond's face/par value.

    d. Provisions for redeeming—Bonds can have features to liquidate before the date of maturity at the option of the issuer or holder.

        i. Callable bonds—Bonds can be called by the issuer at a specified rate before the maturity date of the bond.

    e. Conversion provisions—Convertible bonds can be converted, at the option of the holder, to common stock of the company at a specified amount before the maturity date of the bond.

    f. Covenants—Set limits on certain actions the company might be taking during the term of the agreement. They can limit the borrower from paying too much dividends, pledging assets (negative covenants). They can also require the company to maintain certain ratios (positive covenants)

g. Options granted to the issuer or investor—Generally are callability and conversion features mentioned above.

h. Indenture—Legal document that details the mechanics of the bond issuer, security features, covenants, etc.

D. Identify and evaluate debt issuance or refinancing strategies.

a. The cost of debt is measured by the interest rate required to be paid. The interest rate is affected by the perceived risk of default determined by the profitability, liquidity, and solvency of the company. Other factors, such as collateral pledged, time to maturity, and industry in which the company operates, have an effect on the interest rate as well. There are numerous strategies to reduce the perceived risk of the company in order to lower the cost of debt. As the perceived risk of a company is reduced, there are options to refinance prior debt with new, lower-cost funds. Conversion strategies and callable bonds are among those strategies.

E. Value bonds, common stock, and preferred stock using discounted cash flow methods.

a. Bond—The value of a bond is the sum of its discounted cash flows. The discount rate used is the market rate of interest. The formula is:

$$V_b = I\,(\text{PVIFA}_{k,n}) + F(\text{PVIF}_{k,n})$$

where

V_b = value of the bond
I = interest in each time period calculated at the coupon on rate of interest
PVIFA = PV interest factor annuity
k = discount rate market rate of interest
n = number of periods
F = principal or face value of the bond
PVIF = PV interest factor

b. Common stock and preferred—There are various methods to value common stock and preferred stock. Similar to valuing bonds, these methods attempt to calculate the sum of the discounted cash flows. The most common are the basic dividend discount model, the zero dividend growth model, the constant dividend growth model, and the variable dividend growth model. The two most common used in the CMA exam are detailed next.

i. Basic dividend discount model

$$V_s = \sum_{\infty}^{t=1} \frac{D_t}{(1+k_s)}$$

where
V_s = intrinsic value of a share of common stock
D_t = expected dividends per share on the common stock in period t
k_s = investor's required rate of return on the common stock (cost of equity)

ii. Constant dividend growth model

$$V_s = \sum_{\infty}^{t=1} \frac{D_0(1+g)^t}{(1+k_s)^t}$$

where

D_o = dividends per share on the common stock in the current period

g = constant dividend growth rate

k_s = investor's required rate of return on the common stock (cost of equity)

t = time period

F. Demonstrate an understanding of duration as a measure of bond interest rate sensitivity.

　　a. A bond's coupon rate never changes (except with step-up bonds), but inflation and changes in market interest rates affect the value of a bond. Since the coupon rate doesn't change, an increase in the market interest rate reduces the value of the bond. The longer the duration of the bond, the more sensitive it will be to interest rate fluctuations.

G. Explain how income taxes impact financing decisions.

　　a. Debt has tax advantages at the corporate level because interest payments reduce the firm's taxable income whereas dividends and share repurchases do not. As a result, the after-tax cost of debt is less than the stated interest rate on the note. The same is not true with dividend payments on common and preferred stock since they are not deductible by the corporation.

H. Define and demonstrate an understanding of derivatives and their uses.

　　a. Derivative—A financial instrument whose characteristics and value are derived from the underlying price or value of some other, more basic financial instrument. Corporations do not use derivatives to raise money but buy or sell them to protect against adverse changes in market factors. For example, a corporation might use a derivative to manage the risk associated with an underlying investment and protect against fluctuations in its value.

I. Identify and describe the basic features of futures and forwards.

　　a. Futures—A forward-based contract that is conceptually similar to a forward contract but different in execution. The basic difference is that unlike forwards (which are often privately negotiated by an intermediary), futures are standardized contracts traded on organized exchanges.

　　b. Forwards—A forward contract is a customized agreement between two parties to buy or sell a specific amount of an asset at a future date for a set price.

J. Distinguish a long position from a short position.

　　a. Long position—Gains value when the underlying asset price rises and loses value when the asset price falls.

　　b. Short position—Gains value when the underlying asset price falls and loses value when the asset price rises.

K. Define options and distinguish between a call and a put by identifying the characteristics of each.

　a. *Options*—A contract between two parties wherein the purchaser of the contract has the right (but not the obligation) to buy or sell a given amount of an underlying asset.

　　i. Call option—A type of option contract giving the owner the right (but not the obligation) to buy the underlying asset from the writer at a fixed price during the specified time period.

　　ii. Put option—A type of option contract giving the owner the right (but not the obligation) to sell to the writer the underlying asset at a fixed price during the specified time period.

L. Define exercise price, strike price, option premium and intrinsic value.

　a. Exercise price (or strike price)—Refers to the fixed price of the contract.

　b. Option premium—The initial purchase price of the option; it is usually stated on a per-unit basis. The writer (seller) of an option contract receives an up-front premium from the buyer (owner) of the contract.

　c. Intrinsic value—A measure of the theoretical value of an asset.

M. Demonstrate an understanding of the interrelationship of the variables that comprise the value of an option; for example, relation between exercise price and strike price, and value of call.

　a. An option is referred to as "at the money" if the underlying asset price equals the strike price. For example, the owner has option to purchase stock at $15 per share (exercise price). When the stock is valued at $15 per share, the option is at the money.

　b. An option is referred to as "in the money" if the underlying asset price is greater than the strike price. Using the same numbers above, if the underlying asset is valued above $15 per share, the option is in the money.

　c. An option is referred to as "out of the money" if the underlying asset price is less than the strike price. Using the same numbers above, if the underlying asset is valued below $15 per share, the option is out of the money.

N. Define swaps for interest rate and foreign currency.

　a. Swap—A private agreement between two parties (called "counterparties") to exchange (or swap) future cash payments. The simplest type of interest swap, called a "plain vanilla interest rate swap," involves trading fixed interest rate payments for floating-rate payments:

　　• Party A agrees to pay Party B a series of future payments that are equal to a *predetermined fixed interest rate* multiplied by the notational principal.

　　• Party B agrees to pay Party A a series of future payments that are equal to a *floating interest rate* multiplied by the same notational principal.

O. Define and identify characteristics of other sources of long-term financing, such as leases, convertible securities, warrants, and retained earnings.

　a. Other forms of long-term financing available to companies include leases, convertible securities, and warrants. [See Figure 2B-13 in Topic 2: Long-Term Financial Management (in book) for more detail.]

P. Demonstrate an understanding of the relationship among inflation, interest rates, and the prices of financial instruments.

   a. Inflation reduces the return on a financial instrument as the purchasing power of the dollar is reduced. The longer the time to maturity of a financial instrument, the more effect inflation will have on the returns. Therefore, as inflation increases, the value of financial instrument will decrease.

Q. Define the cost of capital and demonstrate an understanding of its applications in capital structure decisions.

   a. Cost of capital—A composite of the costs of various sources of funds comprising a firm's capital structure (i.e., interest rate on debt, required return on preferred stock and common stock). It represents the minimum rate of return that must be earned on new investments so that shareholders' interests won't be diluted.

   b. A corporation's management team is charged with ensuring efficiency and profitability from assets as well as minimizing the cost of the funds that the firm incurs from investments. In fulfilling this fiduciary responsibility, management makes various financing decisions that affect the firm's capital structure.

R. Determine the weighted average (historical) cost of capital and the cost of its individual components.

   a. The cost of capital is found by determining costs for the individual types of capital (debt and equity) and then multiplying each component cost by its proportion in the firm's total capital structure. The formula is:

$$K_a = p_1 k_1 + p_2 k_2 + \ldots p_n k_n$$

where

     K_a = cost of capital (expressed as a percentage)
     p = proportion that element comprises of the total capital structure
     k = cost of an element in the capital structure
   $1, 2, n$ = different types of financing (each with its own cost and proportion in the capital structure)

   b. Calculating cost of debt—The after-tax cost of debt is lower than the stated interest rate since interest payments are tax deductible. Cost of debt to the company is calculated by taking the interest rate times 1 minus the firm's tax rate:

After-Tax Cost of Debt = kd $(1 - t)$
kd = Before-Tax Cost of Debt
t = Firm's Marginal Tax Rate

   c. Calculating cost of preferred stock—The cost associated with preferred stock is a function of the dividend paid (if any) to shareholders and flotation costs.

$$k_p = \frac{D_p}{P_p - F}$$

where

k_p = component cost of preferred stock
D_p = preferred stock dividend
P_p = the current price per share (current or prospective cost)
F = flotation costs as a dollar amount

d. Calculation cost of common equity—Common equity is comprised of common stock, paid-in capital, and retained earnings. There is more than one way to compute cost of common equity, such as the historical rate of return, dividend growth model, and CAPM. All of these are described more fully in Topic 2: Long-Term Financial Management (in book).

i. Dividend growth model formula:

$$k_s = \frac{D_1}{P_0} + g$$

where

k_s = cost of internal equity capital
D_1 = dividend per share at the time
P_0 = market price per share at the time
g = expected dividend growth rate

ii. CAPM formula:

$$K_s = R_f + \beta (K_m - R_f)$$

where

K_s = cost of internal equity capital
R_f = risk free rate (e g., the rate on T-bonds or a 30 day T-bill)
β = stock's beta estimate (obtained from a brokerage firm or investment advisory service, or calculated by the firm)
k_m = estimate of the return on the market as a whole or on an average stock value

S. Calculate the marginal cost of capital.
   a. Marginal cost of capital (MCC)—The last dollar of new capital that the firm raises. There are five steps to develop an MCC schedule:
      1. Determine the appropriate weights of the new financing.
      2. Calculate the component cost of capital associated with each amount of capital raised.
      3. Calculate the range of total new financing at which the cost of the new components increases.
      4. Calculate the MCC for each range of total new financing.
      5. Plot an MCC schedule.
      [See Topic 2: Long-Term Financial Management (in book) for more detailed analysis.]

T. Explain the importance of using marginal cost as opposed to historical cost.
   a. Companies are limited in the amount of funds available for investments since market investors evaluate the financial merits of different companies,

compare them, and determine reasonable limits for individual companies beyond which investors will not make funds readily available. As capital needs increase in a company, typically the cost of that capital must increase to account for increased risk. As such, it is important to use the marginal cost of capital as opposed to historical cost of capital when determining cost of new capital.

U. Demonstrate an understanding of the use of the cost of capital in capital investment decisions.

  a. Since management has a fiduciary responsibility to maximize shareholder return, it is charged with choosing investments that will not dilute shareholders' return. Therefore, management must choose investments that will generate returns greater than the company's cost of capital.

V. Demonstrate an understanding of how income taxes impact capital structure and capital investment decisions.

  a. Debt has tax advantages at the corporate level because interest payments reduce the firm's taxable income whereas dividends and share repurchases do not. As a result, the after-tax cost of debt is less than the stated interest rate on the note. The same is not true with dividend payments on common and preferred stock since they are not deductible by the corporation. Debt, at the right levels, carries a much lower after-tax cost than that of equity and should be used in the capital structure to reduce the company's overall cost of capital.

W. Use the constant growth dividend discount model to value stock, and demonstrate an understanding of the two-stage dividend discount model.

  a. Using the constant dividend growth model, the value of a common stock is calculated from the dividend growth model formula shown in LOS R earlier. The price is the next dividend divided by the cost of common stock equity minus the dividend growth rate $[P = D/(ks - g)$.

  b. The two-stage dividend growth model looks at a situation where there is a change in the dividend growth rate. For example, suppose a stock pays a current dividend of $2 per year and the expected growth rate in the dividend is expected to be 20% for the next three years. The growth rate after that is expected to be 7% in perpetuity. Assuming the required rate of return on the stock, the current price of the stock would be $36.93. The price is computed by the following formula:

$$P = 2.40/1.15 + 2.88/(1.15)(1.15) + 3.456/(1.15)(1.15)(1.15) + P3/(1.15)(1.15)$$
$$(1.15)P3 = 3.456(1.07)/(.15 - .07) = \$3.69792.$$

X. Demonstrate an understanding of relative or comparable valuation methods, such as price/earnings (P/E) ratios, market/book ratios, and the price/sales ratios.

  a. Relative or comparative valuation models are nonconceptually sound value estimation models used a surrogates for the conceptually sound DCF models.

  b. The P/E model estimates the price of a stock as either the previous year EPS or the expected EPS for the current year times an expected P/E ratio. For example, if last year's EPS was \$5 and the expected P/E ratio is 7, the price of the stock would be \$35 (5 times 7).

c. The market (or price) to book ratio estimates the price of the stock as a multiple of its book value per share. Common multiples are in the 5 to 7 range.

d. The price to sales ratio estimates the price of the stock as a multiple of the sales per share of stock. Multiples vary widely depending on the industry.

Section B.3. Raising Capital

A. Identify the characteristics of the different types of financial markets and exchanges.
   a. Capital market—Market in which individuals and institutions trade financial securities.
   b. Stock market—Market that allows investors to buy and sell shares in publicly traded companies. Split into the primary market (where new issues are first offered) and the secondary market (where trading continues after first issue).
   c. Bond market—Market that allows investors to buy and sell corporate, municipal, and government debt investments.
   d. Money market—Market where highly liquid, short-term securities are traded.
B. Demonstrate an understanding of the concept of market efficiency, including the strong form, semistrong form, and weak form of market efficiency.
   a. Market efficiency—Refers to the degree to which stock prices reflect all available information for that security. The efficient market hypothesis has three forms:
      i. Strong form—All information (public or private) is incorporated in a security price. Therefore, it is not possible for insiders to earn abnormal profits.
      ii. Semistrong form—All publicly available information (no private information) is incorporated in a security price. Therefore, abnormal returns from insider trading are possible.
      iii. Weak form—Security prices reflect all recent price movements only. Therefore, technical analysis will not provide a basis for abnormal returns.
C. Describe the role of the credit rating agencies.
   a. Credit rating agencies assign a rating to each debt security based on creditworthiness of the company or government issuing the security. That rating then is used to determine the market rate of interest on the debt security.
D. Demonstrate an understanding of the roles of investment banks, including underwriting, advice, and trading.
   a. Investment banks are financial institutions that assist companies and governments in issuing securities for the purpose of raising capital. The services of an investment bank include providing advice, selling securities, and underwriting. An underwriter bears some or all of the risks of selling and holding the securities in exchange for a premium.

E. Define initial public offerings (IPOs).

    a. Initial public offering—The first sale of stock by a private company to the public.

F. Define subsequent/secondary offerings.

    a. Subsequent/secondary offerings—The issuance of new stock for public sale from a company that has already made on IPO.

G. Describe lease financing, explain its benefits and disadvantages, and calculate the net advantage to leasing using discounted cash flow concepts.

    a. Lease financing—A contract that allows for the use of an asset but not the ownership or title to that asset. Payments are made as monthly rental payments. If lease financing is structured correctly, the asset and related liability can be left off the balance sheet to improve financial ratios. [See Section E, Topic 2: Discounted Cash Flow Analysis (in book) for details on computing net advantage.]

H. Define the different types of dividends, including cash dividends, stock dividends, and stock splits.

    a. Cash dividends—Dividends paid in the form of cash, usually a check.

    b. Stock dividends—Dividends paid in the form of additional stock. Allow a corporation to conserve cash for investment purposes while still rewarding investors.

    c. Stock splits—Involve the issuance of new stock shares to replace existing shares. A two-for-one stock split, for example, involves replacing each existing share with two new shares.

I. Identify and discuss the factors that influence the dividend policy of a firm.

    a. The issue in dividend policy is how much the corporation should return to shareholders versus how much should be reinvested in the business. The factors that influence the policy are: shareholder preferences, liquidity, solvency, borrowing capacity, earnings stability, growth opportunities, inflation, capital impairment restrictions, restrictive covenants, and taxes.

J. Demonstrate an understanding of the dividend payment process for both common and preferred stock.

    a. There are four relevant dates to the dividend payment process: declaration date, payment date, record date, and ex-dividend date.

        i. Declaration date—States that the company declares a dividend today payable on a set date to shareholders of record on a date between the declaration date and the payment date.

        ii. Payment date—The date the dividend is actually paid.

        iii. Record date—Date between the declaration date and the payment date that provides the current holders with a right to receive the dividend.

        iv. Ex-dividend date—A date set by the stock exchange handling the stock that allows the exchange time to record ownership changes.

K. Define share repurchase, and explain why a firm would repurchase its stock.

    a. Share repurchase—Corporations buying back their own stocks (treasury stock). Companies may do this in order to provide shares for stock ownership plans, employee retirement plans, mergers and acquisitions, or stock options and warrants. They also may purchase their own shares to control the share price or to go private.

L. Define insider trading, and explain why it is illegal.

    a. Insider trading—Involves directors and management of a corporation buying or selling the corporation's securities to gain an advantage over investors who are not privy to the information.

Section B.4. Working Capital Management

Working Capital

A. Define working capital and identify its components.

    a. Working capital—Generally refers to the funds a company holds in current (short-term) asset accounts. Net working capital refers specifically to the difference between a firm's *current assets* and its *current liabilities*. The basic components of an organization's working capital are cash, marketable securities, accounts receivable, and inventory.

B. Calculate net working capital.

    a. Net working capital (or just plain working capital) is calculated as current assets less current liabilities.

C. Explain the benefit of short-term financial forecasts in the management of working capital.

    a. Short-term financial forecasts are essential in understanding the working capital needs of a company. Short-term financial forecasts can alleviate costs of holding onto excess cash and inventories when it may not be necessary and can provide information about potential working capital deficits. The forecast allows management to determine the structure of its working capital based on short-term needs.

Cash

D. Identify and describe factors influencing the levels of cash.

    a. Liquidity requirements and a firm's profitability and risk policies are the primary determinants of its cash levels.

        i. Liquidity—Refers to the ability to convert assets into cash quickly without incurring loss. A business needs to monitor net working capital to cover the imbalances of cash inflows and outflows and to ensure sufficient liquidity.

        ii. Profitability and risk policies—Profitability typically varies inversely with liquidity. A firm must determine the optimal levels of investment in current assets as well as the appropriate mix of short- and long-term financing necessary to support liquidity requirements.

E. Identify and explain the three motives for holding cash.

    a. Transactions motive—A firm must have sufficient cash reserves or near-cash reserves to meet financial payments arising from ordinary business operations (e.g., small purchases, employee compensation, taxes, and dividends).

    b. Precautionary motive—Holding cash to provide a buffer for unexpected cash needs.

    c. Speculative motive—Involves the use of surplus liquid reserves to take advantage of short-term investments or other temporary situations that may arise.

F. Prepare forecasts of future cash flows.

    a. Forecast of future cash flows involves obtaining details of cash receipts and disbursements for a specified time period to gain an understanding of possible cash needs or surpluses. Preparing an accurate forecast can substantially improve liquidity and increase profitability. [See Topic 4: Working Capital Management (in book) for more detail on preparing a forecast.]

G. Identify methods of speeding up cash collections.

    a. Firms generally attempt to speed up cash collections by reducing collection float. Collection float is the time interval between when the maker mails a check and when the funds are available for the receiving firm to use. Companies can use these methods to help reduce collection float:

        i. Lockbox system—An arrangement between a firm and a banking institution in which all deposits are received directly by the bank and immediately deposited into the firm's account.

        ii. Electronic payment system—facilitates a payment or a transfer in an electronic format.

        iii. Automated clearing house (ACH)—Provides an electronic alternative to checks. Payment information is processed and settled electronically.

        iv. Concentration banking system—Systematically transfers deposits received from field banks and/or lockbox banks to the firm's disbursement bank to create a centralized inventory of liquid reserves held as cash or for short-term credit or investment transactions.

H. Calculate the net benefit of a lockbox system.

    a. See Figure 2B-20 in Topic 4: Working Capital Management (in book) for a computation of net benefit of a lockbox system.

I. Define concentration banking.

    a. Concentration banking system—Systematically transfers deposits received from field banks and/or lockbox banks to the firm's disbursement bank to create a centralized inventory of liquid reserves held as cash or for short-term credit or investment transactions.

J. Demonstrate an understanding of compensating balances.

    a. Compensating balance—A non-interest-bearing deposit maintained in the company's deposit accounts at the bank for account service charges, lines of credit, or investments. Banks may require these balances in order to reduce default exposure on loans and lines of credit.

K. Identify methods of slowing down disbursements.

    a. Companies generally attempt to slow down disbursements by increasing disbursement float. To do so, companies can use the next approaches:

    i. Centralized payables—Payments are made through a single account (usually headquarters or a centralized processing center). Centralizing the payment function provides greater assurance that checks and funds will be disbursed when desired than with a decentralized payables system, where the likelihood of excess balances is greater.

    ii. Payable through draft (PTD)—A payment instrument that is drawn against the maker, not the maker's bank. Using a PTD delays the time the firm has to have funds available and allows it to maintain smaller bank balances.

L. Demonstrate an understanding of disbursement float.

    a. See item K above for detail on disbursement float.

Marketable Securities

M. Identify and describe reasons for holding marketable securities.

    a. Marketable securities are investments that mature in a year or less. Holding too much cash idle in bank accounts not only incurs maintenance costs but also results in a loss of potential interest income. That is why companies hold a short-term investment portfolio of interest-earning marketable securities. Specifically, companies invest in marketable securities to reserve liquidity, manage controllable outflows, and generate income.

N. Define the different types of marketable securities, including money market instruments, T-bills, Treasury notes, Treasury bonds, repurchase agreements, Federal agency securities, bankers' acceptances, commercial paper, negotiable CDs, Eurodollar CDs, and other marketable securities.

    a. Money market instrument—Short-term debt securities that mature in one year or less. Major issuers of money market securities are the U.S. government, foreign government securities dealers, commercial paper (CP) dealers, bankers' acceptance (BA) dealers, and other money market brokers specializing in short-term instruments.

    b. Treasury bills (T-bills)—Obligations of the U.S. Treasury backed by the full faith and credit of the U.S. government. T-bills do not bear interest. They are sold at a discount and mature to face value in *one year or less.*

    c. Treasury notes (T-notes)—Obligations of the U.S. Treasury backed by the full faith and credit of the U.S. government. T-notes bear interest semiannually and mature within *one to ten years.*

    d. Treasury bonds—Obligations of the U.S. Treasury backed by the full faith and credit of the U.S. government. T-bonds bear interest semiannually and have maturities *longer than ten years.*

    e. Repurchase agreements—Agreements to purchase a security from another party, usually a bank or security dealer, who agrees to buy it back at a specified date for a fixed price.

    f. Federal agency securities—Interest-bearing securities usually offered and redeemed at face value. Generally not backed by the full faith and credit of the U.S. government but still considered relatively safe investments and free of default risk.

g. Bankers' acceptances (BAs)—Essentially time drafts that result from commercial trade financing; frequently involve international transactions. BAs involve letters of credit "accepted" by a bank; typically implies the BA is backed by that bank.

h. Commercial paper—Unsecured short-term loan issued by a corporation. Maturity ranges from 1 to 270 days.

i. Negotiable certificates of deposit (CDs)—Interest-bearing deposits issued by banks or saving and loan institutions that can be traded in money markets; generally sold at face value in denominations of $1 million.

j. Eurodollar CDs—Typically nonnegotiable dollar-denominated time deposits held by banks outside the United States (although not necessarily in Europe); not subject to U.S. banking regulations.

O. Evaluate the trade-offs among the variables in marketable security selections, including safety, marketability, yield, maturity, and taxability.

a. Safety—Although a certain degree of risk is inherent in any investment, a firm must assess the specific risk associated with a security and weigh that risk against the potential for financial returns (or losses).

b. Marketability—Refers to the owner's ability to sell the security in large volumes relatively quickly without a substantial price concession.

c. Yield—A security's yield (return) is related to its interest rate. The safer the investment, the lower the yield. The shorter the time to maturity, generally the lower the yield.

d. Maturity—The "time to maturity" refers to the life of the security. The longer the maturity, generally the higher the yield but the less liquid the investment is.

e. Taxability—A company should evaluate the tax implications of the security. A firm's effective tax rate will determine the advantage of tax-exempt alternatives and the after-tax rate from taxable investments.

P. Demonstrate an understanding of the risk and return trade-off.

a. Risk is an important consideration in making financial decisions. Under rational market conditions, those investments with greater expected risk should provide a higher expected rate of return than investments with lower risk.

Accounts Receivable

Q. Identify the factors influencing the level of receivables.

a. As with other current assets, A/R have profitability and risk trade-offs. Extending credit may stimulate sales and profits. But a company incurs costs for carrying receivables and runs the risk of potential bad-debt losses.

R. Demonstrate an understanding of the impact of changes in credit terms or collection policies on accounts receivable, working capital and sales volume.

a. Credit terms stipulate the form and timing of payment extended to a customer for the receipt of goods and services as well as the discount terms (if any). Changing credit terms can increase the investment in receivables but also can increase the sales volume.

    b. Credit and collection policies involve an assessment of the creditworthiness of the buyer, the credit terms extended, and the level of collection procedures required. In the absence of credit standards, sales revenues and contribution margins are maximized but often are offset by large bad-debt losses, collection costs, and high costs from carrying very large receivables. With tighter credit standards, sales revenues and contribution margins decline but so do the average collection period, bad-debt losses, and receivable carrying costs.

S. Define default risk.

    a. Default risk—The risk that a company (or an individual) will not be able to pay interest or principal on debt obligations.

T. Identify and explain the factors involved in determining an optimal credit policy.

    a. In the absence of credit standards, sales revenues and contribution margins are maximized but often are offset by large bad-debt losses, collection costs, and high costs from carrying very large receivables. With tighter credit standards, sales revenues and contribution margins decline but so do the average collection period, bad-debt losses, and receivable carrying costs.

Inventory

U. Define lead time and safety stock; identify reasons for carrying inventory and the factors influencing its level.

    a. Lead time—Time between placing an order and getting the units in stock and ready for use.

    b. Safety stock—Generally refers to a quantity of stock planned and held in inventory to protect against fluctuations in supply and demand or as protection against production forecast errors and/or short-term changes in backlog.

    c. Inventories are carried to compensate for the variability between the supply of an item and the demand for it. Inventory control involves balancing conflicting costs—balancing the cost of holding sufficient stock to provide a specified level of customer service with the cost of purchasing the inventory. The point at which those costs intersect provides answers to many inventory control issues, such as what to keep in stock, when orders should be placed, how much should be ordered, and so on.

V. Identify and calculate the costs related to inventory, including carrying costs, ordering costs, and shortage (stock-out) costs.

    a. Carrying costs—The marginal costs of carrying the inventory. They include marginal storage and handling costs, obsolescence and deterioration costs, insurance, taxes, and the cost of the funds invested in inventories.

    b. Ordering costs—The marginal costs of placing a purchase or production order. They are the marginal cost of computer time to prepare orders and the cost of the supplies used to generate an order.

    c. Shortage (stock-out) costs—The costs of losing a sale because insufficient inventory is on hand when needed.

W. Explain how a just-in-time (JIT) inventory management system helps manage inventory.

   a. The primary purpose of JIT is to eliminate raw material and purchased parts, finished goods, and work-in-process inventories, which would eliminate the need for inventory management and replace it with procurement management for raw materials and purchased parts, shipping management for finished goods, and throughput management for work-in-process.

X. Identify the interaction between high inventory turnover and high gross margin (calculation not required).

   a. High inventory turnover reduces the size of the inventory and the consequent carrying cost of the inventory. The reduction in carrying costs should reduce cost of goods sold and increase gross margin. Gross margin is net sales less cost of goods sold.

Y. Demonstrate an understanding of Economic Order Quantity (EOQ) and how a change in one variable would affect the EOQ (calculation not required).

   a. Economic order quantity (EOQ) represents the optimum order size—the quantity of a regularly ordered item to be purchased at a point in time that results in minimum total cost. As demonstrated by the formula above, as marginal cost per order and total units demanded increase, the EOQ will increase. As the cost of carrying the inventory increases, the EOQ will decrease.

Short-Term Credit and Working Capital Cost Management

Z. Demonstrate an understanding of how risk affects a firm's approach to its current asset financing policy (aggressive, conservative, etc.).

   a. An aggressive working capital management policy focuses on high profitability potential, despite the cost of high risk and low liquidity. Aggressive asset management results in capital being minimized in current assets versus long-term investments. Aggressive financing policies include higher levels of lower-cost short-term debt and less long-term capital investments.

   b. A conservative working capital management policy focuses on low-risk, low-return working capital investment and financing. A conservative policy places a greater proportion of capital in liquid assets but at the sacrifice of some profitability.

AA. Identify and describe the different types of short-term credit, including trade credit, short-term bank loans, commercial paper, lines of credit, and bankers' acceptances.

   a. Trade credit—A source of short-term financing created when a supplier grants credit terms to customers on purchases.

   b. Unsecured short-term bank loan—A form of bank credit that is not backed by a pledge of specific collateral or assets. Such loans are made based on the financial soundness and creditworthiness of the borrower.

   c. Secured short-term bank loan—A form of credit based on the pledging of an asset for collateral.

    d. Commercial paper—An unsecured promissory note issued by a corporation. Commercial paper is sold at a discount from par value and is backed by a promise of the corporation to buy back the paper at maturity by paying par value.

    e. Line of credit—An agreement allowing a firm to borrow up to a specified limit during a particular time period. The borrower has access to the credit amount but pays interest only on actual borrowing.

    f. Bankers' acceptance (BA)—A negotiable short-term instrument used primarily to finance the import and export of goods.

BB. Estimate the annual cost and effective annual interest rate of not taking a cash discount.

    a. The formula for determining the opportunity cost of giving up a discount computed at an annual rate (of 365 days) is:

$$EID = \frac{DR}{1 - DR} \times \frac{365}{N - DP}$$

where
EID = effective rate of interest for forgoing the trade credit discount
DR = discount rate
N = net payment period
DP = discount period

CC. Calculate the effective annual interest rate of a bank loan with a compensating balance requirement and/or a commitment fee.

    a. The formula for effective annual rate of interest for a loan with a compensating balance or commitment fee is:

$$EI = \left(\frac{PR + CF}{1 - CB}\right)\left(\frac{365}{N - DP}\right)$$

where
EI = effective rate of interest
PR = principal interest charge (%)
CF = commitment fee (%)
CB = compensating balance (%)
M = loan length in days

DD. Demonstrate an understanding of factoring accounts receivable and calculate the cost of factoring.

    a. Factoring is the sale or transfer of A/R in a secured short-term loan to a third party (factor). To compute the cost of factoring, you must take into account the total service charges as well as the interest charged on the short-term loan. You can then annualize the cost of the funds available for use to determine the effective interest rate.

EE. Explain the maturity matching or hedging approach to financing.

    a. Maturity matching—A working capital management approach that hedges risk by matching the maturities of the company's assets and liabilities.

Thus, the company attempts to finance short-term projects with short-term financing and long-term projects with long-term assets.

    b. Hedging—A method of reducing exposures to adverse fluctuations in prices, interest rates, or foreign exchange rates. Companies hedge an investment by taking an offsetting position in a second investment instrument.

FF. Demonstrate an understanding of the factors involved in managing the costs of working capital.

    a. All of the factors described above need to be taken into consideration for effective management of working capital. [For more detail, read Topic 4: Working Capital Management (in book).]

General

GG. Recommend a strategy for managing current assets that would fulfill a given objective.

    a. After reviewing the items above, you should be able to assess and evaluate a given objective and recommend a strategy for effective working capital management. [For more detail, read Topic 4: Working Capital Management (in book).]

Section B.5. Corporate Restructuring

A. Demonstrate an understanding of mergers, acquisitions, and leveraged buyouts.

    a. Mergers—Combination of two or more companies where all but one legally ceases to exist. The survivor continues under its existing name.

    b. Acquisitions—Actions in which a company buys a target company's ownership and assumes control of that company.

    c. Leveraged buyouts—Mergers that occur when a buyer of a company borrows a major portion of the purchase price using the purchased assets as collateral for the borrowings.

B. Identify defenses against takeovers (e.g., golden parachute, leveraged recapitalization, poison pill [shareholders' rights plan], staggered board of directors, fair price, voting rights plan, white knight).

    a. Some of the most common tactics to avoid takeovers are:

- Staggering terms—A company can stagger the terms of board of directors instead of all of them coming up for election at the same time.
- Golden parachutes—Provide for exorbitant pay and benefits if the company is taken over or goes through a merger.
- Supermajority vote—Corporate charter requires a supermajority (such as 80%) of the shareholders instead of 51% in order to approve takeover.
- Poison pills—Securities that have value only when an unfriendly bidder obtains control of a certain percentage of the target's shares.
- White knight—Involves the target finding a friendlier buyer with which to merge.
- Pac-Man—A role reversal in which the target company attempts to buy out the so-called hostile buyer.

C. Identify and describe divestiture concepts such as spin-offs, split-ups, equity carve-outs, and tracking stock.

   a. Spin-offs—The parent company distributes stock in a subsidiary to the shareholders of the parent company on a pro rata basis. The subsidiary then becomes a separate corporation.

   b. Split-ups—A single company splits into two or more separately run companies. Shares of the original company are exchanged for shares in each of the new companies.

   c. Equity carve-outs—The common stock of the subsidiary is sold directly to the public rather than being distributed to the parent's shareholders. Usually the parent maintains a controlling interest in the subsidiary during the equity carve-out.

   d. Tracking stocks—Common stocks issued by a parent company to track the performance of a particular strategic business unit (SBU).

D. Evaluate key factors in a company's financial situation and determine if a restructuring would be beneficial to the shareholders.

   a. A corporation engages in mergers and acquisitions to maximize shareholder wealth. Some reasons a company might engage in restructuring are:
   - To obtain another company's assets, skills, or technology.
   - To achieve economies of scale.
   - To obtain resources.
   - To obtain customers.
   - To grow faster than internally possible.
   - To diversify.
   - To be able to use net operating loss carryforwards.

E. Validate possible synergies in targeted mergers and acquisitions.

   a. The benefits of restructuring just listed are possible synergies that would allow the postmerger corporation to be worth more than the sum of the individual unmerged corporations.

F. Define bankruptcy.

   a. Bankruptcy—Legal status of a person or entity that cannot repay the debts it owes to creditors. A corporation may file bankruptcy under Chapter 11 or Chapter 7.
   - Chapter 11—Provides a debtor company the opportunity to restructure its business. A variety of actions may be used, such as restructuring of existing loans, acquisition of new financing with priority of company earnings, rejection of specific contracts, and the cancellation of certain contracts.
   - Chapter 7—Involves a corporate liquidation. The creditors select a trustee who liquidates the business and pays the creditors according to the priority of claims set forth in Chapter 7.

G. Differentiate between reorganization and liquidation.

   a. Reorganization—Involved with a Chapter 11 bankruptcy in which terms of obligations are modified and the company continues to operate.

   b. Liquidation—Involved with a Chapter 7 bankruptcy in which company ceases to operate, assets are liquidated, and debts are satisfied in the order listed above.

H. Evaluate a proposed business combination and make a recommendation based on both quantitative and qualitative considerations.

    a. Quantitative models used to evaluate a proposed business combination include the DCF model discussed as well as the following:

- Relative price to earnings (P/E) ratio (most common)
- Market (price per share) to book (book value per share) ratio
- Market price to sales ratio
- Revenue multiple
- Earnings multiple

Earnings may be EBIT (earnings before interest and taxes), EBT (earnings before taxes), EAT (earnings after taxes or net income), or EBITDA (earnings before interest, taxes, depreciation, and amortization).

    b. The use of earnings-based or revenue multipliers requires qualitative considerations among which are earnings quality, earnings persistence, earnings power, and nonrecurring factors or extraordinary items. Earnings quality or closeness to operating cash flow is affected by the choice of accounting principles, accounting estimates, the provision for future earnings through research and development, quality control, maintenance, advertising and promotion, and human resource development, and the company's sensitivity to business cycles. Earnings persistence is a measure of how well current earnings can predict future earnings. Earnings power is the best possible estimate of average earnings over a period of time.

Section B.6. International Finance

A. Demonstrate an understanding of foreign currencies and how foreign currency affects the prices of goods and services.

    a. A flexible or floating exchange rate is a system wherein the exchange rates for currencies are determined by market supply and demand, just as are the prices of other financial assets, such as stocks and bonds. Thus, the value of the currency floats according to market action.

    b. When a currency appreciates in value, it has more buying power in relation to another specific currency; when it depreciates in value, it has less buying power in relation to other specific currencies. As a result of appreciation, a currency will buy more units of another currency; therefore, the holder of the currency can buy more goods than before.

B. Identify the variables that affect exchange rates.

    a. Currencies float in relation to each other. The exchange rate is determined as a trading relationship between two currencies and is affected by:

        i. Differences in inflation rates.

        ii. Differences in interest rates.

        iii. Current-account deficits.

        iv. Level of public debt.

        v. Ratio of exports to imports.

        vi. Political and economic stability.

C. Calculate whether a currency has depreciated or appreciated against another currency over a period of time, and evaluate the impact of the change.

a. Suppose that Italy is exporting product A to the United States for €50 and the United States is exporting product B to Italy for $50. If the exchange rate ($/€) is 1.25:

The relative price of product A for U.S. consumers is

$$1.25(\$/€) \times €50 = \$62.50$$

The relative price of product B for Italian consumers is

$$€ (1/1.25) = .8 (€/\$) \times \$50 = €40$$

If, two months later, the price of product A is still €50 in Italy but has fallen to $60 (from $62.50) in the United States, we can conclude that the dollar has risen in value (appreciated) relative to the euro. Correspondingly, the euro has fallen relative to the dollar, and product B, still at $50 in the United States, will now cost a European buyer €41.67. We can calculate the exchange rate based on the real versus relative price as shown:

$$\$60/€50 = 1.2 \; (\$/€)$$

$$€41.67/\$50 = .8334 \; (€/\$)$$

D. Demonstrate how currency futures, currency swaps, and currency options can be used to manage exchange rate risk.

a. Companies can use the next tools to hedge risk with a transaction denominated in a foreign currency. These tools allow for earnings stability when doing business in different currencies.

i. Currency futures—Contracts to exchange a number of foreign currency units for another at a specific date for a specific price (exchange rate).

ii. Currency options—Provide the option (but not the requirement) to make the same type of exchange as a currency future.

iii. Currency swaps—Two parties agree to exchange the principal and interest aspects of a loan in one currency for equivalent aspects of another loan in a different currency.

E. Calculate the net profit/loss of cross-border transactions, and evaluate the impact of this net profit/loss.

a. Changes in exchange rates can change the reported value of a company's assets and liabilities on financial statements. When sales are denominated in a foreign currency (FC), accounts receivables are denominated in the FC. If the dollar subsequently weakens with respect to the FC, an exchange gain is recorded on the balance sheet date and the accounts receivable (A/R) balance becomes larger, thus favorably affecting the short-term liquidity ratios. If the dollar strengthens with respect to the FC, an exchange loss is recorded on the balance sheet date and the A/R balance becomes smaller, thus unfavorably affecting short-term liquidity ratios. For example:

Assume that a U.S. business purchases inventory from a Canadian supplier for 10,000 Canadian dollars. The spot "direct" rate is 0.70 Canadian dollars to 1 USD. The U.S. importer records the transaction as shown:

Inventory	7,000	
Account Payable (FC)		7,000
Calculation: (C$10,000 × 0.70 = U.S.$7,000)		

If the account payable has not been settled on December 31, when the spot rate is $0.69, the adjustment is made as shown:

Accounts Payable (FC)	100	
Exchange Gain		100
Calculation: [(0.70 – 0.69)(C$10,000) = U.S.$100]		

F. Recommend methods of managing exchange rate risk, and calculate the net profit/loss of your strategy.

    a. See item D above for methods to manage exchange rate risk and item E for a computation of net profit/loss. [Also see Topic 6: International Finance (in book) for more detailed analysis.]

G. Identify and explain the benefits of international diversification.

    a. One of the risks of holding any financial asset is that it may prove to be unfavorable and decline in value. International investment that spans a number of countries is seen as a way of diversifying that risk. Much like diversification in an individual's portfolio, companies can expand internationally to reduce exposure to an economic downturn in its county of domicile.

H. Identify and explain common trade financing methods, including cross-border factoring, letters of credit, bankers' acceptances, forfaiting, and countertrade.

    a. Cross-border factoring—A factor is a financial institution that buys a firm's accounts receivable and collects on the accounts. Cross-border factoring occurs when there is a network of factors across borders.

    b. Letters of credit—Letters from a bank guaranteeing that a buyer's payment to a seller will be received on time and for the correct amount.

    c. Bankers' acceptances (BAs)—Forms of time drafts drawn to finance the export, import, domestic shipment, or storage of goods. A BA is accepted when a bank writes on the draft its agreement to pay it at maturity.

    d. Forfaiting—The purchase of receivables for goods or services from an exporter in order for the purchaser to obtain immediate cash without affecting the exporter's existing credit line.

    e. Countertrade—Exchanging goods or services for other goods or services (in whole or in part) rather than for money.

I. Demonstrate an understanding of how transfer pricing affects the effective worldwide tax rate.

a. Transfer pricing is the pricing of a product when selling from one part of a company to another. When the buyer and seller divisions are in different countries, the objective of transfer pricing is to minimize the company's effective worldwide income tax obligations. To accomplish this task, a company sets a high transfer price on goods shipped to a division in a country with relatively higher taxes and sets a low transfer price on goods shipped to a division in a country with relatively lower taxes.

Risk and Return

MANAGING THE FINANCES OF AN ORGANIZATION or making investments requires an understanding of risks and returns and their relationships. Since risk is variability in expected returns, this section begins with a discussion of rates of return.

This topic looks at risk and return relationships, portfolio theory, systematic and unsystematic risk, and the capital asset pricing model.

 READ the Learning Outcome Statements (LOS) for this topic as found in Appendix B and then study the concepts and calculations presented here to be sure you understand the content you could be tested on in the CMA exam.

Risk

In corporate finance, **risk** is the probability of not receiving the expected return from an investment. Risk implies a degree of uncertainty. Risk is measured by variability in returns; the greater the potential variability of returns, the riskier an investment. A one-year U.S. Treasury bill (T-bill) that provides a "guaranteed" rate of return on investment would be considered risk-free. The annual returns on shares of a stock or some other variable investment instrument are inherently riskier; the return may be much less than expected or, in the worst-case scenario, even less than the initial investment.

There are many types of risk, including:

- *Credit risk.* An investor's risk that the borrower will not make payments as promised (also called "default risk")
- *Foreign exchange risk.* The risk that there will be a change in the exchange rate of one currency in relation to another (also called "currency risk")
- *Interest rate risk.* The risk that the market rate of interest will vary, affecting the value of an interest-bearing asset
- *Market risk.* The risk that a portfolio will decrease due to changes in market risk factors, including stock prices, interest rates, foreign exchange rates, and commodity prices

- *Industry risk.* The combined set of risks particular to an industry
- *Political risk.* The risk that political decisions may complicate the operations and profitability of business

Calculating Rates of Return

Companies and investors assume risks to earn investment returns commensurate with the risks. A **return** (or **rate of return**) is the amount received on an investment from holding that investment for a period of time relative to the amount of the initial investment. Of course, not all returns end up as financial gains. The owner of a financial investment or asset may experience a loss over a given period of time. Returns reflect any change in market prices for the investment as well as interest or dividends received from the investment and usually are expressed as a percentage of the beginning market price of the investment.

At the simplest level, a return is calculated as the cash payments received (such as dividends or interest), plus the change in market price (appreciation or loss in price), divided by the beginning price of the security.

For example, the rate of return, also called the **holding period return (HPR)** for common stock over one period is:

$$R = \frac{(P_t - P_{t-1}) + D_t}{P_{t-1}}$$

where:

R = rate of return (holding period return)
P_t = stock price at the end of the period
t = time period
P_{t-1} = stock price at the beginning of the period
D_t = cash dividend at the end of the time period

For example: Assume that an investor buys a share of common stock for $20 exactly one year ago and the stock price rises to $22. During the period, the company pays a $2 cash dividend per share. What is the one-year rate of return for this stock?

- P_{t-1} (previous stock price) = $20
- P_t (current stock price) =$22
- D_t (cash dividend) = $2

$$R = \frac{(\$22 - \$20) + \$2}{\$20} = \frac{\$4}{\$20} = 0.20 \text{ or } 20\%$$

The time period (t) can be any length of time. In this case, t represents the HPR for the common stock for one year. Thus, the rate of return on common stock is 20%.

Risk and Return Relationship

Risk is an important consideration in making financial decisions. Under rational market conditions, those investments with greater expected risk should provide a higher expected rate of return than investments with lower risk.

Numerous studies of capital market history support the idea that returns to investors typically are a reflection of the risks they take. As an example, the next generalizations can be made about U.S. investment instruments (based on historical performance over long periods of time—typically several decades—so average rates of returns are not distorted by fluctuations of unusually high or low returns).

Risk and Returns from Treasury Bills

U.S. T-bills (U.S. government securities that mature in less than one year) are very safe securities. There is no risk of default. **Default risk** is the risk that a borrower will not pay the interest and/or principal on funds borrowed when they become due. Because of the short maturity period, the prices (while subject to inflation) are relatively stable. T-bills offer the most conservative rate of return.

Risk and Returns from Bonds

U.S. government bonds and corporate bonds have longer maturity periods than T-bills. They also have an additional dimension: Prices fluctuate as interest rates vary. Historically, bond prices rise when interest rates fall and fall when interest rates rise.

Thus, there is an inverse relation between the movement of bond prices and interest rates.

Similar to U.S. T-bills, government bonds have no risk of default. Corporate bonds do have a default risk. Over time, bond rates of return are higher than those of T-bills. On average, corporate bonds have slightly higher returns than government bonds.

Risk and Returns from Stocks

Stocks provide investments signifying an ownership position (called "equity") in a corporation. A stock investor also has a direct share in the risks of the enterprise.

On average, stock returns are significantly higher than the safe rates of return from T-bills or bonds. Stock investments in small U.S. firms historically outperform the returns from large U.S. firms. In addition, returns on common stocks are higher than returns on preferred stocks.

Risk and Return Attitudes

Evaluating the trade-offs between risk and return is a major component in the maximization of shareholder wealth.

Shareholder wealth is the market value of a company's common stock. It is also called the **market capitalization**. Shareholder wealth is calculated as the number of common shares outstanding times the market price per share (the price at which the firm's common stock trades for in the marketplace, such as the New York Stock Exchange).

Shareholder wealth maximization (SWM) refers to the maximization of shareholders' purchasing power. In an efficient market, SWM is the maximization of the current share price multiplied by the number of shares outstanding. It provides a convenient framework for evaluating both the timing and the risks associated with various investment and financing strategies and relies on cash flows as a measure of returns. From a financial perspective, SWM typically is assumed to be the major goal of a firm.

Certainty equivalent (CE) is a concept that describes the amount of cash an investor would have to receive to be indifferent between the payoff and a given gamble. It answers the question: What is the smallest certain payoff an investor would accept in exchange for a risky cash flow? A CE factor is used to convert a projected cash flow into a certain cash flow. General principles correlating the relationship of an investor's CE and the expected monetary value are summarized in Figure 2B-1.

Figure 2B-1 Certainty Equivalent and Attitudes Toward Risk

When the certainty equivalent is:		Then:
Less than expected value	→	Risk aversion (a risk adverse position) is present.
Equal to expected value	→	Risk indifference (a risk indifferent or neutral position) is present.
Greater than expected value	→	Risk preference (a risk seeking position) is present.

The term *risk aversion* refers to an investor's dislike of risk and need for a higher rate of return as an inducement to take on riskier investments. Thus, high-risk investments should offer an investor a higher expected return than low-risk investments. In other words, the greater the risk an investment poses, the higher the expected return needed to compensate an investor for buying and holding the investment. Conversely, an investor expects to earn lower expected returns for low-risk investments. Generally speaking, most investors are risk averse and seek higher returns for increasing risks.

There is no true or single measure of certainty in discussing investment returns. The concept of CE deals with expected returns; the actual return on the investment may vary. For example, the actual return on an investment classified as less risky could very well outperform the actual return on a risky investment.

Risk typically increases with time, as there is greater uncertainty and/or variability in forecasting for distant years.

Probability Distributions and Risk and Return

With the exception of risk-free Treasury securities, the actual rate of return often is described as a random variable subject to probability distribution. A **probability distribution** is a set of possible values that a random variable (e.g., an investment) can take and the likelihood that each will occur.

Three major descriptive statistical measures in a probability distribution are expected return, standard deviation, and coefficient of variation.

Expected Return

Expected return is the weighted average of the possible returns where the weights represent the probabilities of occurrence. It is a measure of central tendency of a probability distribution. The formula for expected return is:

$$\bar{R} = \sum_{i=1}^{n}(R_i)(P_i)$$

where:
  $\bar{R}$ = expected return
  n = total number of possibilities
  R_i = return for the ith possibility
  P_i = probability of that return occurring

Standard Deviation

Standard deviation is a statistical measure showing the variation or dispersion around the expected (most likely) return on an investment. It shows the distribution around the mean (average) and is computed as the square root of the variance.

The formula for standard deviation (σ) is:

$$\sigma = \sqrt{\sum_{i=1}^{n}(R_i - \bar{R})^2(P_i)}$$

In the equation, the deviations from the mean $(R_i - \bar{R})$ are squared to eliminate the problem of minus signs. Typically, the higher the standard deviation, the greater the variability of returns and the greater the total risk.

For example: Here is how an expected return and standard deviation of return would be computed given the probability distributions shown:

  σ = standard deviation
  n = total number of possibilities
  R_i = return for the ith time
  P_i = probability of that return occurring

Possible Return, R_i	Probability of Occurrence, P_i	Expected Return, $\bar{R}$ Calculation $(R_i)(P_i)$	Variance^2, Calculation $(R_i - \bar{R})^2 (P_i)$
−0.02	0.10	−0.002	$(-0.02 - 0.10)^2(0.10) = 0.00144$
0.05	0.20	0.010	$(0.05 - 0.10)^2(0.20) = 0.00050$
0.10	0.40	0.040	$(0.10 - 0.10)^2(0.40) = 0.00000$
0.15	0.20	0.030	$(0.15 - 0.10)^2(0.20) = 0.00050$
0.22	0.10	0.022	$(0.22 - 0.10)^2(0.10) = 0.00144$
	$\Sigma = 1.00$	$\Sigma = 0.10 = \bar{R}$	$\Sigma = 0.00388 = \sigma^2$

Standard deviation $= \sqrt{0.00388} = 0.06229$, or 6.229%

In this example:

- Distribution's variance = 0.00388
- Distribution's standard deviation = $\sqrt{0.00388}$
- Distribution's standard deviation = 0.06229, or 6.229%

Coefficient of Variation

Standard deviation can be misleading when comparing the risk or uncertainty of different investments if those investments are different sizes. Calculating the coefficient of variation helps to adjust for such size or scale differences.

Coefficient of variation (CV) provides a measure of relative risk. The CV is calculated by dividing the standard deviation by the mean of expected return.

$$CV = \frac{\sigma}{\bar{R}}$$

For example: Investment A and Investment B with normal probability distributions have these characteristics:

	Investment A	Investment B
Expected return, $\bar{R}$	0.06	0.18
Standard deviation, σ	0.04	0.06

Based on a comparison of the standard deviations for both investments, the larger of the two is Investment B (0.06), seemingly making it riskier than Investment A. However, Investment A has greater variation relative to the size of the expected return. To adjust for these differences, the CV provides a measure of risk per unit of expected return.

	Investment A	Investment B
CV	0.04/0.06 = 0.67	0.06/0.33 = 0.33

Using a measure of relative risk, Investment A with a CV of 0.67 is riskier than Investment B with a CV of 0.33. A higher CV indicates higher relative risk.

Risk and Return in a Portfolio Context

Investors rarely hold a single type of investment. Instead, they combine multiple investments in a portfolio. Simply defined, a **portfolio** is a mix of two or more assets. A portfolio may include any combination of cash, bonds, stocks, mutual funds, or other investments. The purpose of having a portfolio of investments rather than a single investment is to minimize risk.

Portfolio Risk

Risk and return in a portfolio context differ from risk and return concepts for a single investment. Calculations used to assess the risk of a portfolio are more complicated than the standard deviation and the variance of a single investment.

Covariance and correlation are useful portfolio measures. They are both statistical measures showing the degree to which two random variables (such as two investment returns in a portfolio) move together.

Covariance

Whereas variance measures how a single random variable moves with itself, **covariance** extends the concept, measuring how one random variable moves with another random variable. Covariance shows the way two different assets in a portfolio are expected to vary together—the way returns move relative to one another—rather than independently.

For example:

- The expected returns on a stock and a put option on the stock move in opposite directions and will have a negative covariance.
- The expected returns for two stocks in the same industry most likely would move in the same direction and have a positive covariance.
- The expected return of a stock paired with a riskless Treasury security would have zero covariance because the riskless asset's returns do not move, regardless of changes in the stock's returns.

As the number of assets in a portfolio grows, the covariance between various securities that have been paired becomes more important. The more different the movement between assets, the less portfolio risk.

The basic notation for covariance between random variables, x and y, is:

$$\text{Cov}_{x,y}$$

The covariance between two asset returns using expected outcomes is computed as:

$$\text{Cov}_{1,2} = \sum_{i=1}^{n} \left\{ P_i \left[R_{i,1} - E\left(\bar{R}_1\right) \right] \left[R_{i,2} - E\left(\bar{R}_2\right) \right] \right\}$$

where:

n = number of different securities in a portfolio
$R_{i,1}$ = return on asset 1 in state i
$R_{i,2}$ = return on asset 2 in state i
P_i = probability of state i occurring
$E(\bar{R}_1)$ = expected return on asset 1
$E(\bar{R}_2)$ = expected return on asset 2

For example: The next data on returns for two assets and their associated probabilities can be used to calculate the covariance between the two assets.

First, the expected return for each asset is computed as shown:

$$E(\bar{R}_1) = \sum_{t=1}^{n} P_i\, P_{i,1} \quad \begin{aligned} &= 0.25(0.06) + 0.50(0.16) + 0.25(0.26) \\ &= 0.015 + 0.080 + 0.065 = 0.160 \end{aligned}$$

$$E(\bar{R}_2) = \sum_{t=1}^{n} P_i\, P_{i,2} \quad \begin{aligned} &= 0.25(0.25) + 0.50(0.10) + 0.25(0.05) \\ &= 0.0625 + 0.0500 + 0.0125 = 0.125 \end{aligned}$$

P_i	$R_{i,1}$	$R_{i,2}$	$(R_{i,1}) - E(\bar{R}_1)$	$(R_{i,2}) - E(\bar{R}_2)$	$P_i[(\bar{R}_{i,1}) - E(\bar{R}_1)][(\bar{R}_{i,2}) - E(\bar{R}_2)]$
0.25	0.06	0.25	−0.100	0.125	−0.00313
0.50	0.16	0.10	0.00	−0.025	0.00000
0.25	0.26	0.05	+0.100	−0.075	−0.00188

$$\text{Cov}_{1,2} = \sum_{i=1}^{n} \left\{ P_i \left[R_{i,1} - E\left(\bar{R}_1\right) \right] \left[R_{i,2} - E\left(\bar{R}_2\right) \right] \right\} = -0.00501$$

Given the negative sign of the covariance, the returns on the two assets move in opposite directions.

The covariance calculation for a portfolio depends on the variance of individual securities and the correlations between all the pairs. A matrix of weighted correlations between every possible pair also must be constructed. Depending on the number of investments in a portfolio, there are potentially a very large number of possible combinations. Also, covariance values may range from negative infinity to positive infinity and are expressed in terms of square units.

Correlation

To simplify the interpretation of covariance, the covariance value is divided by the product of the random variable's standard deviations. The resulting value is the correlation coefficient (or correlation). The formula for the correlation of expected returns for two securities (1 and 2) is:

$$\text{Corr}_{1,2} = \frac{\text{Cov}_{1,2}}{\sigma_1 \sigma_2}, \text{ which implies } \text{Cov}_{1,2} = \text{Corr}_{1,2}\,\sigma_1\sigma_2$$

where:

σ_1 and σ_2 = standard deviations of a probability distribution of possible returns for the portfolio, security 1, and security 2, respectively

Key characteristics to understand about the correlation of the two random variables (in this example, assets 1 and 2) are:

- Correlation measures the strength of the linear relationship between two random variables.
- Correlation has no units.
- The correlation coefficient always lies in a range from −1.0 to +1.0. This is represented as:

$$-1 \le \text{Corr}_{1,2} \le +1$$

- A positive correlation means the securities move in the same direction. A +1.0 correlation means the random variables have perfect positive correlation. This means that a movement in one security results in an exact measurable positive movement in the other. This is represented as:

$$\text{Corr}_{1,2} = +1.0$$

- A negative correlation implies the securities move in the opposite direction.
- A −1.0 correlation means the random variables have perfect negative correlation. This means that a movement in one security results in an exact measurable negative movement in the other. This is represented as:

$$\text{Corr}_{1,2} = -1$$

- A 0 correlation means there is no linear relationship between the variables, indicating that prediction of R_1 cannot be made on the basis of R_2 using linear methods. This is represented as:

$$\text{Corr}_{1,2} = 0$$

Risk-adverse investors generally would want to diversify holdings to include securities that have less-than-perfect positive correlation.

For example:

$$\sigma_p = \sqrt{w_1^2 \sigma_1^2 + w_2^2 \sigma_2^2 + 2w_1 w_2 \text{Corr}_{1,2} \sigma_1 \sigma_2}$$

Assume a portfolio comprised of two investments with weights (w) of 40% and 60% and standard deviations of 0.05 and 0.09 respectively.

Now assume that the correlation coefficient is +1, 0, and −1. When the standard deviation of the portfolio, σ_p, is computed using these data, the results will show that the standard deviation of the portfolio is largest when the correlation coefficient is +1, declines when it is 0, and declines further when it is −1.

If $\text{Corr}_{1,2} = +1$, then $\sigma_p = \sqrt{(0.40)^2 (0.05)^2 + (0.60)^2 (0.09)^2 + 2(0.40)(0.60)(1)(0.05)(0.09)}$

$$= \sqrt{0.00040 + 0.00292 + 0.00216} = 0.074$$

If $\text{Corr}_{1,2} = 0$, then $\sigma_p = \sqrt{(0.40)^2 (0.05)^2 + (0.60)^2 (0.09)^2 + 2(0.40)(0.60)(0)(0.05)(0.09)}$

$$= \sqrt{0.00040 + 0.00292 + 0.0} = 0.058$$

If $\text{Corr}_{1,2} = -1$, then $\sigma_p = \sqrt{(0.40)^2 (0.05)^2 + (0.60)^2 (0.09)^2 + 2(0.40)(0.60)(-1)(0.05)(0.09)}$

$$= \sqrt{0.00040 + 0.00292 - 0.00216} = 0.034$$

As the example illustrates, the standard deviation of the portfolio decreases as the correlation coefficient goes from +1 to 0 to −1.

Portfolio Return

A portfolio rate of return is the weighted average of the expected returns of all the investments that make up that portfolio. The weights represent the proportions of each item in the portfolio; the sum of the weights must be equal to 100%.

The general formula for the expected rate of return for a portfolio is:

$$\bar{R}_p = \sum_{i=1}^{n} W_i \bar{R}_i$$

where:

$\bar{R}_p$ = expected return of a portfolio

n = number of different securities in the portfolio

W_i = proportion or weight of the total funds invested in the security

$\bar{R}_i$ = expected return for security i

A typical portfolio investment strategy is to construct an efficient portfolio (or optimal portfolio) that maximizes the rate of return for a given level of risk or minimizes risk for a given level of return.

For example: A two-asset portfolio with 40% in Asset A with an expected return of 12% and 60% in Asset B with an expected return of 18%. The rate of return on this portfolio would be:

$$\overline{R}_p = 0.40(12\%) + 0.60(18\%) = 4.8\% + 10.8\% = 15.6\%$$

Diversification

Diversification refers to holding a wide range of different investments in a portfolio. The primary goal of diversification is to reduce the variability (or risk) of a portfolio.

Diversification reduces portfolio risk as long as the different investments are unlikely to all move in the same direction in perfect tandem. (They are not perfectly positively correlated.) For example, having ten stocks in a portfolio all from the same industry tends to result in highly correlated returns. Thus, the performance of these companies typically would move up and down in value in a similar manner. Having fewer stocks in a portfolio representing different industries is more likely to show low correlation and low portfolio return variability. That is, the probability that individual stocks in different industries move up and down in value at the same time or at the same rate is low.

Figure 2B-2 is a conceptual illustration of the offsetting variability that portfolio diversification can provide.

Figure 2B-2 Diversification and Portfolio Risk

Well-conceived diversification reduces both the upside and downside potential in a portfolio and allows for more consistent performance under a wide range of economic conditions.

Systematic and Unsystematic Portfolio Risk

Extensive market research has examined the effect of diversification on portfolio risk when randomly selected investments are combined in weighted portfolios. As shown in Figure 2B-3, the level of portfolio risk reduction (standard deviation) is great at first and then tapers off as more investments are included in a portfolio.

Figure 2B-3 Portfolio Risk Reduction

In smaller portfolios, diversification can cut variability dramatically, but the improvement is much less significant as the portfolio grows in size with numerous investment holdings (typically 15 to 20 different investments).

A portfolio's total risk, as measured by its standard deviation, consists of two specific types of risk: systematic risk and unsystematic risk.

Systematic Risk

Systematic risk (also known as market risk, nondiversifiable risk, or unavoidable risk) is associated with changes in return based on the market as a whole. Systematic risk is common to an entire class of investments because of unavoidable national or global economic changes or other events that threaten the vast majority of (or all) businesses and impact large portions of the market. The value of investments usually declines across the board when investors are exposed to systematic market uncertainties. This is why, for example, stocks tend to move together in response to economy-wide or global perils.

Unsystematic Risk

Unsystematic risk (also known as unique risk, diversifiable risk, or avoidable risk) is independent of economic, political, or other factors or general market movements. It is associated with a specific company or industry.

Most estimates approximate that 60% to 75% of an individual stock's total risk (standard deviation) results from unsystematic risks. For example, a new product entry in an industry could make a company's product obsolete. Labor-management issues or a strike could negatively affect a company or an entire industry.

Most variability resulting from unsystematic risk is avoidable through diversification. For this reason, unsystematic risk sometimes is called "diversifiable risk." That is, holding a diversified portfolio reduces unsystematic risk because different portions of the market tend to perform differently at different times.

Figure 2B-4 shows how diversification can minimize unsystematic risk but cannot eliminate systematic risk.

Figure 2B-4 Systematic and Unsystematic Risk in a Portfolio

Unsystematic risk is extremely important when a portfolio has a limited number of investments. For a reasonable, well-diversified portfolio, systematic risk assumes much greater importance. That is why, for example, market changes (up or down) carry portfolios with them.

Market Risk and Beta

Because most investors diversify, risk is best judged in a portfolio context. An individual investment's contribution to the risk of a portfolio is a function of how that investment is most likely to be affected by a general market decline.

Beta (β) describes an investment's sensitivity to market movements. It is a quantitative measure of the volatility of a given investment relative to the overall market.

Specifically, beta indicates the amount that investors expect an investment price to change for each additional 1% change in the market.

- U.S. T-bills have a beta of 0; the return is fixed and unaffected by market changes.
- The average beta of all stocks is 1.0.
- Stocks with a beta greater than 1.0 are unusually sensitive to market movements; they are said to amplify overall market movements.
- Stocks with a beta less than 1.0 are less sensitive to market movements. They tend to move in the same direction as the market but not as far.

Another way of describing beta measures is that a beta above 1.0 is more volatile than the overall market; a beta below 1.0 is less volatile. A stock with a negative beta would move counter to the overall market.

Where systematic (market) risk is the primary determinant of risk in a well-diversified portfolio, the beta of an individual investment in that portfolio reflects

Knowledge Check:
Risk and Return

The next questions are intended to help you check your understanding and recall of the material presented in this topic. They do not represent the type of questions that appear on the CMA exam.

Directions: Answer each question in the space provided. Correct answers and section references appear after the knowledge check questions.

1. Suppose an investor buys a stock for $50 and sells it for $45 one year later. Assuming the stock pays a $4 dividend to the buyer, what is the holding period return on the stock?

   ☐ **a.** −10%

   ☐ **b.** +8%

   ☐ **c.** −2%

   ☐ **d.** None of the above

2. The standard deviation of a stock investment is best described as the

   ☐ **a.** variability of expected returns.

   ☐ **b.** sensitivity to market movements.

   ☐ **c.** trade-off between risk and return.

   ☐ **d.** variation around the mean return.

   For questions 3 through 5, match the following terms with their appropriate description.

   a. The amount of cash that would make an investor indifferent to risk at a point in time

   b. A benchmark for evaluating the relative merits of different portfolio items

   c. The degree to which two stock returns move together in a portfolio

3. _____ Correlation

4. _____ Security market line

5. _____ Certainty equivalent

6. A major benefit of portfolio diversification is

   ☐ **a.** reduced exposure to foreign exchange rates.

   ☐ **b.** minimization of unsystematic risk.

   ☐ **c.** reduction of systematic risk.

   ☐ **d.** a more favorable borrowing position.

7. Using the CAPM formula, calculate the required rate of return on a stock, assuming:

R_f = 7% (the risk-free rate on a U.S. Treasury security)

β = 0.75 (the beta coefficient for the company)

K_m = 13% (the return on the market portfolio)

☐ **a.** 13%

☐ **b.** 11.5%

☐ **c.** 9.5%

☐ **d.** 9%

Knowledge Check Answers: Risk and Return

1. Suppose an investor buys a stock for $50 and sells it for $45 one year later. Assuming the stock pays a $4 dividend to the buyer, what is the holding period return on the stock? [**See *Risk and Return Relationship.***]

   ☐ **a.** −10%

   ☐ **b.** +8%

   ☑ **c.** −2%

   ☐ **d.** None of the above

2. The standard deviation of a stock investment is best described as the [**See *Standard Deviation.***]

   ☐ **a.** variability of expected returns.

   ☐ **b.** sensitivity to market movements.

   ☐ **c.** c. trade-off between risk and return.

   ☑ **d.** d. variation around the mean return.

   For questions 3 through 5, match the following terms with their appropriate description.

   a. The amount of cash that would make an investor indifferent to risk at a point in time

   b. A benchmark for evaluating the relative merits of different portfolio items

   c. The degree to which two stock returns move together in a portfolio

3. __c__ Correlation

4. __b__ Security market line

5. __a__ Certainty equivalent

6. A major benefit of portfolio diversification is [**See *Unsystematic Risk.***]

   ☐ **a.** reduced exposure to foreign exchange rates.

   ☑ **b.** minimization of unsystematic risk.

   ☐ **c.** reduction of systematic risk.

   ☐ **d.** a more favorable borrowing position.

7. Using the CAPM formula, calculate the required rate of return on a stock, assuming:

   R_f = 7% (risk-free rate on a U.S. Treasury security)

   β = 0.75 (beta coefficient for the company)

   K_m = 13% (return on the market portfolio)

[See *Capital Asset Pricing Model*.]

- ☐ **a.**   13%
- ☑ **b.**   11.5%
- ☐ **c.**   9.5%
- ☐ **d.**   9.0%

$$K_e = R_f + \beta (K_m - R_f)$$
$$K_e = 7\% + 0.75 (13\% - 7\%)$$
$$K_e = 7\% + 0.75 (6\%)$$
$$K_e = 7\% + 4.5\%$$
$$K_e = 11.5\%$$

Long-Term Financial Management

A FINANCIAL INSTRUMENT EVIDENCES a transaction between two parties. It has monetary value or records a monetary transaction. For one party in the transaction, the financial instrument represents an investment; for the second party, the instrument is an obligation or liability.

This section covers risks and returns in investment and financing decisions, the various types of financial instruments (such as stocks, bonds, and derivatives), and the valuation of financial instruments.

In addition, this topic focuses on the details of the cost of capital, including the weighted average cost of capital, the cost of individual capital components, calculating the cost of capital, and the marginal cost of capital.

READ the Learning Outcome Statements (LOS) for this topic as found in Appendix B and then study the concepts and calculations presented here to be sure you understand the content you could be tested on in the CMA exam.

Risks and Returns in Investment and Financing Decisions

Individuals and organizations make decisions regarding investments in financial assets (e.g., stocks and bonds), tangible assets (e.g., plant and equipment), and intangible assets (e.g., patents and copyrights). The investment decisions discussed next relate to financial assets. Investment decisions related to other assets are discussed in Section D: Investment Decisions.

Organizations make investments in financial assets for different reasons including to:

- Ensure liquidity—to cover day-to-day cash obligations in a timely manner.
- Generate interest income for cash received for which there is no immediate use.

Financing involves obtaining the funding for an organization's assets. It allows a corporation to pursue long-term objectives through the obtaining of debt or equity capital.

Debt financing implies a legal liability or obligation of an organization to repay a creditor for borrowed funds by a specified date.

Equity financing represents selling an ownership claim in a company. Both debt and equity involve risk and return trade-offs:

- The cost of debt is represented by an interest rate; the interest paid is a tax-deductible expense.
- The value of equity is represented by a stock price or the net value of the company's assets. Dividends paid on equity are not tax-deductible.
- Whether a company finances assets through debt (e.g., types of loan agreements) or equity (preferred or common stock) is a key corporate financial issue.

Every company should have an investment and financing strategy in place. Figure 2B-6 summarizes basic aspects that investment and financing strategies should address.

Figure 2B-6 Basic Investing and Financing Considerations

Investment	Financing
• Corporate goals	• Debt versus equity financing
• Policies and guidelines	• Short- versus long-term financing
• Investment instrument selection and portfolio configuration	• Fixed versus floating rate interest payments
• Roles, responsibilities, and authority for investment activities	• Secured versus unsecured debt
• Financial controls	• On- versus off-balance sheet financing
• Performance measurement	• Tax considerations

An investment policy reflects an organization's tolerance for risk; the mix of debt and equity in borrowing determines a company's leverage and is closely linked to the firm's capital structure.

In financing, the financing mix should maximize firm value as measured by the company's common stock price multiplied by the number of common stock shares outstanding. Maximizing firm value requires the minimization of the firm's weighted average cost of capital (WACC). Potential risk can be reduced by matching the cash inflows of the assets being financed with the cash outflows used to finance the assets.

A company can reorganize the capital structure to maximize firm value by issuing additional debt, refinancing current debt at lower interest rates, and/or issuing stock.

Impact of Income Taxes on Financing Decisions

Many financing decisions rely heavily on tax effects. Generally speaking, debt has tax advantages at the corporate level because interest payments reduce the firm's taxable income (shielding it from federal and state taxes) whereas dividends and share repurchases do not. Interest tax shields associated with this financing approach tend to support increased leverage, provided a firm balances the tax benefits of debt against the costs of financial distress.

According to trade-off theory, optimal capital structure involves a trade-off between the benefit of debt due to the interest tax shelter and the costs of debt due to financial distress and agency costs. An **agency cost** is a direct or indirect expense that the principal bears as a result of having delegated authority to an agent. An **agent** is the person authorized to act on behalf of another (the principal) to perform some duty or service. **Financial distress** refers to any general weakening in a company's financial condition caused by issuing too much debt. Bankruptcy is the extreme case of financial distress. Various economic theories challenge this trade-off theory. At issue with this shielded income proposition is whether the tax deductibility of the interest payments associated with the borrowing affect the value of the firm.

Valuation

Valuation is the process that links risk and return to estimate the worth of an asset or a company. Understanding the concept of valuation requires a baseline understanding of value and related value concepts.

The term *value* has different meanings, depending on whether it is applied to an asset or a company. An asset generally is thought of as a financial asset—a monetary claim on an issuer, typically a paper asset such as a bond, common stock, or preferred stock.

Related value concepts are listed next.

- Going-concern value
- Liquidation value
- Liquidation value per share
- Book value
- Book value per share of common stock
- Market value
- Intrinsic value

Going-concern value refers to the value of a company as an operating entity. This value depends on the ability to generate future cash flows rather than balance sheet assets. It is sometimes referred to as value in use.

Liquidation value is the net amount of money that could be realized by selling the entity's assets after paying off the liabilities (debt). It is of utmost concern when an organization is facing bankruptcy.

Liquidation value per share is the actual amount per share of common stock that stockholders would receive if the entity sells all assets, pays all liabilities (included preferred stock), and divides the remaining money among the stockholders.

Book value is the value at which an asset is carried on a balance sheet. It is the accounting value of an asset, which is expressed as the cost of a fixed asset less its accumulated depreciation. The book value of a liability is its carrying value; for example, a bond is carried at face value plus premium or minus discount.

Book value per share of common stock refers to the ratio of stockholder equity to the number of common shares outstanding. Book value per share may have little relation to the liquidation value per share or the market value per share.

Market value is the market price at which investors buy or sell an asset at a given time. The key determinant of market value is supply and demand. The market value of a publicly traded security is its market price.

Intrinsic value is a measure of the theoretical value of an asset. Although not indicative of actual value, intrinsic value provides a basis for determining whether to buy or sell a financial asset when compared to its market value or price. Intrinsic value is also called **fundamental value**.

An asset's value is determined by the amounts and timing of the cash flows expected to be generated by the asset and the rate of return required by investors in the asset. The required rate of return is a function of the risk associated with the projected cash flows.

Measures of cash flow for security investments are:

- Annual dividends from common stock and preferred stock investments.
- Interest received from debt investments.
- Cash received upon the liquidation of investments.

Increased cash flows raise the price of an asset. If cash flows become more uncertain, the price of the asset will decline. In financial management, basic goals are to maintain or increase cash flows and to decrease risk. Attaining these goals supports the maximization of shareholder wealth.

Risk is challenging to estimate. Future cash flows must be discounted back to present cash flows at an appropriate rate of return to reflect risk. This is because the value of an asset (the price of an asset) is the present value (PV) of its future cash flows determined at the appropriate rate of return.

Subsequent content in this topic examines characteristics of various debt and equity instruments and their valuation.

Bonds

A **bond** is a debt instrument (a loan) issued for a period of more than one year. The investor acquiring a bond earns interest by lending money while the borrower (the issuer) gets needed capital (cash).

Bonds may be bought on a short-, medium-, and long-term basis. Although these distinctions may vary slightly, the general parameters are listed next:

- Short-term bonds: 2 to 5 years
- Medium-term (intermediate) bonds: 5 to 10 years
- Long-term bonds: 10 to 30 years

The relationship between an interest rate and the time to maturity is called the "yield curve" (or the "term structure of interest"). Investors expect increased returns with increased risks. Thus, the shape of a normal yield curve is upward sloping, and longer-term bonds normally pay returns (yields) higher than those of short-term bonds.

Issuers and Types of Bonds

There are many types of bonds, issued by several different sources. Common ones are listed in Figure 2B-7.

Figure 2B-7 Common Types of Bonds

Type	Description
Corporate bonds	Issued by large and small U.S. companies
	Used to finance growth, expansion, and other activities
Government bonds	Backed by the full faith and credit of the U.S. government
	Used to sustain government operations and pay interest on national debt
	Examples include U.S. Treasury bonds, Treasury notes, and savings bonds
Municipal bonds	Issued by various cities and states
	Used to pay for construction projects and other activities
Agency bonds	Issued by various federal, state, and local government agencies
	Examples include bonds issued by mortgage lenders (e.g., Ginnie Mae, Fannie Mae, and Freddie Mac) as well as other agency bonds issued to finance operations and raise money for special projects
International bonds	Marketed simultaneously in several countries, usually by London branches of international banks and security dealers

Bond Agreements

The written legal agreement among all parties involved in a bond issue is called an **indenture** (or deed of trust). An indenture defines the details of the bond issue, including:

- Terms and conditions of the bond issue
- The stated interest rate (often called the coupon rate)
- Maturity date
- Protective covenants (restrictions placed on the issuer such as maintaining certain financial ratios)
- Conditions defining default
- Subordination
- Sinking fund terms (payments made by the borrower to a separate custodial account; used to repay the debt at maturity and assure creditors that adequate funds are available)
- Collateral property to be pledged (if any)
- Designation and duties of the trustee

Covenants

Protective covenants set limits (restrictions) on certain actions the company might be taking during the term of the agreement. They are a particularly important feature in a bond indenture.

There are two types of covenants: negative and positive.

1. **Negative covenants** limit or prohibit the borrower from certain actions. Paying too much in dividends, pledging assets to other lenders, selling major assets, merging with another firm, and acquiring more long-term debt are all examples of actions that a negative covenant may address.
2. **Positive (affirmative) covenants** specify actions that the borrower promises to perform. Examples of positive covenants include maintaining certain ratios, preserving collateral in good condition, and making timely interest and principal payments. A failure to abide by positive covenants could place the bond issuer in default.

Bond Administration

Bonds are administered by a qualified trustee. The trustee is a third party chosen by the bond issuer to serve as the official representative of the bondholder. Individuals or institutions may serve as trustees; banks often administer bonds.

Trustee responsibilities include:

- Authenticating the bond issue's legality
- Ensuring that all contractual obligations are carried out
- Ensuring that sinking fund and interest payments are properly paid and applied
- Initiating appropriate actions if the borrower does not meet obligations
- Representing the bondholder in legal proceedings
- Administering redemption

The issuer of the bond compensates the trustee; the trustee's compensation is included in the costs of borrowing.

Bond Terminology

Generally speaking, a bond is a promise to pay a specified amount of interest over time and to repay principal at maturity.

Bond Principal

Principal (also known as par value, par, or face value) represents the dollar amount of the bond at the time it is issued. Par value is the amount the lender is repaid when the bond matures. Most bonds have a face value of $1,000.

Bond Interest

The interest rate stated on a bond is referred to as the coupon rate. A bond's **coupon rate** generally is comparable to what other bonds being issued at that time are paying.

Three common forms of coupon interest on bonds are:

1. *Fixed coupon rate.* Interest is paid consistently at the same rate.
2. *Floating coupon rate.* Interest varies based on economic changes.

3. *Zero coupon rate.* There are no ongoing interest payments (as the bond is sold at a deep discount and redeemed at full value as compound interest accrues to the par value).

Bonds are classified as fixed income securities if the coupon rate and the amount of bond payments are fixed at the time the bond is offered for sale. Traditionally, most bonds are sold with fixed coupon rates. This is a primary reason bonds generally are considered conservative investments and less risky than stocks and other types of investments with highly variable return rates.

After the initial issue (the sale of a bond), bonds are bought and sold through brokers in the **secondary market** (a secondhand market where a security can be traded after issuance), similar to the way stocks are traded. In the secondary market, a bond's price fluctuates with interest rates. If market interest rates fall, the bond price will rise. If market interest rates rise, the bond price will drop.

A bond's coupon rate is expressed as a percentage of the par value. Interest usually is paid semiannually (every six months). For example, if a semiannual bond has a 7% coupon, the issuer pays bondholders $35 (3.5%) every six months for every $1,000 par value bond that they hold.

A zero coupon bond is an exception. As the name implies, zero coupon bonds pay no interest. The face (par) value is paid at maturity.

The term *coupon* originated because bondholders traditionally received certificates specifying the terms of the bond with attached coupons that had to be physically detached and redeemed for cash when it was time to collect interest on the bond. The vast majority of newer bonds are issued electronically (similar to stock purchases). However, many coupon certificates still exist, as they have not yet reached maturity.

Bond Maturity

Bonds typically have a stated maturity. This is the final date on which the bond debt becomes due for payment and the obligation is settled. **Face** or **par value** is the value of a bond at maturity.

A bond often is bought and sold during its lifetime. Some types of bonds may be paid back (called) at an earlier date. At maturity, the bondholder receives the par value of the bond. A $1,000 bond is worth $1,000 at maturity (so long as the issuer does not default in payment).

Bond Ratings

A bond rating allows an investor to assess the general risks of buying a bond before making the actual purchase.

Bond issues often are rated by credit agencies based on numerous factors including:

- Current financial status of the issuer.
- Future financial prospects.
- Collateral (if any) securing the bond.

Moody's Investors Service and Standard & Poor's are two well-known credit rating services. A summary of their ratings and very general characteristics is provided in Figure 2B-8.

Figure 2B-8 Moody's and Standard & Poor's Bond Rating

Moody's	Standard & Poor's	
Aaa	AAA	
Aa	AA	Generally considered high-quality bonds
A	A	
Baa	BBB	
Ba	BB	Somewhat questionable; lack some of the high-quality characteristics
B	B	
Caa	CCC	Poor quality; danger of default
Ca	CC	
C	C	Junk bonds (highly speculative bonds with a greater-than-average chance of default)
—	D	

Some key points to understand about bond ratings are listed next.

- Bond ratings apply to the bond issue, not the company.
- U.S. Treasury bonds are rated AAA, because they are backed by the full faith and credit of the U.S. government.
- Ratings may be adjusted either up or down during the lifetime of a bond; a downgraded rating means that future issues will need to offer higher interest rates to attract buyers.
- Bonds with Aaa and AAA ratings are sold at the lowest rates of interest.
- Because of the default risk associated with junk bonds, they are higher-yield bonds.
- Junk bonds have a greater chance of defaulting, but in some circumstances they also may be an emerging entity and provide a highly profitable return.

Bond Yields

A bond's coupon rate never changes (except with step-up bonds), but inflation and changes in market interest rates affect the value of a bond.

Yields and Return

Current yield is the annual rate of return expressed as a percentage of the annual interest payment relative to the current price of the bond. A ten-year $1,000 bond paying 5% interest per annum earns $50 per year for ten years. If the current price of the bond is $1,250, the current yield would be about 4% ($50 / $1,250). The current yield is the same as the interest rate if the current price of the bond is at par.

Yield to maturity is the actual return on a bond from the time it is purchased to maturity, assuming that all payments received are reinvested at the same rate as the original bond's coupon rate. Yield to maturity considers:

- Interest over the life of the bond in relation to price.
- Purchase price in relation to par value (any gains and losses based on whether the bond was purchased above or below par).
- Any coupons or interest payments reinvested.

Inflation and Bond Real Returns

Inflation eats into the return of a bond. If a bond's return is more than the inflation rate, the bond produces a positive return. If the bond's return is less than the inflation rate, the bond produces a negative return. Consider the next examples.

- If a bond's return is 6% and inflation is 4%, the bond produces a 2% real return.
- If a bond's return is 6% and inflation is 8%, the bond produces a –2% real return.

Bond Duration

Yield-to-maturity calculations assume that all payments received are reinvested at the same rate as the original bond's coupon rate. However, bonds are subject to inflation. If interest rates fall, the interest payments and principal that bond investors receive will have to be reinvested at lower rates. Thus, bond investors face reinvestment risk when interest rates fall.

Duration gives an approximate sensitivity of bond/portfolio values to changes in yield to maturity. Thus, **bond duration** considers how the price of a bond changes in response to yield changes. The best interpretation of duration is the approximate percentage price changes for a 1% change in yield to maturity. Duration is an approximation of the price yield relation because the relation follows a curve, not a straight line.

Convexity is a measure of the curvature of how the price of a bond changes as the interest rate changes. Price changes in response to rising rates are smaller than price changes in response to falling rates.

A bond price-yield curve is shown in Figure 2B-9. Bond prices go up faster than they go down.

Figure 2B-9 Bond Price–Yield Curve

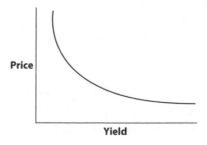

Bond duration is determined by a ratio of the percentage change in price to change in yield.

$$\text{Effective Duration} = \frac{(\text{Bond Price when Yields Fall} - \text{Bond Price when Yields Rise})}{2 \times (\text{Intial Price}) \times (\text{Change in Yield in Decimal Form})}$$

This is often expressed as:

$$\text{Duration} = \frac{V_- - V_+}{2V_0(\Delta y)}$$

where:

    V_- = bond value if the yield decreases by Δy

    V_+ = bond value if the yield increases by Δy

    V_0 = current bond price

    Δy = change yield used to get V_- and V_+, expressed in decimal form

Effective duration shows the average percentage price change for a 1% change in yield.

For example: Consider a ten-year, semiannual-pay bond with a 9% coupon that is currently priced $1,067.95 to yield 8%. If the yield declines by 50 basis points to 7.5%, the price of this bond will rise to $1,104.22. If the yield increases by 50 basis points to 8.5%, the price will fall to $1,033.24. Using the formula previously given, the effective duration of this bond would be:

$$\text{Effective Duration} = \frac{\$1,104.22 - \$1,033.24}{2\,(\$1067.95)\,(0.005)} = \frac{\$70.98}{10.6795} = 6.65$$

Thus, an effective duration of 6.65 means that a 1% change in yield produces an approximate change in the price of this bond of 6.65%.

Why is bond duration important? Understanding how much a bond will move in response to changing interest rates allows investors to buy, sell, or hold bonds according to how they think they will perform. Investors can use duration to compare bonds with different issue and maturity dates, coupon rates, and yields to maturity.

Some relationships involving bond duration are shown next. Holding other characteristics constant:

- A higher (lower) coupon means a lower (higher) duration.
- A longer (shorter) maturity means higher (lower) duration.
- A higher (lower) market yield means lower (higher) duration.

Bond Security

Bonds may be issued on a secured (asset-backed) or unsecured basis.

A **secured bond** is one that is backed by the collateral of a specific asset (e.g., inventories, real estate, or fixed assets) or revenues created from a specific project. A secured bond provides the investor with a lien against an asset in the event of default.

An **unsecured bond** (or **debenture**) is backed only by the good faith, integrity, and credit of the borrower and offers no specific collateral. When holding an unsecured bond, an investor has only a general claim but not against a specific asset. Because unsecured bonds have greater risk than secured bonds, they usually pay higher yields. Debentures may be subordinated or unsubordinated.

Bond Ranking and Liquidation

Bonds may be classified as equal, senior, or subordinated in relation to other debt obligations. These rankings affect priority in liquidation. If a bond issuer in default has both secured and unsecured bonds:

- Secured bondholders are paid off first.
- Unsubordinated debenture holders become general creditors and are paid off after the secured and priority debt holders are paid.
- Subordinated debenture holders are paid off after the general creditors.

Bond Valuation

The value of a bond is the sum of its discounted cash flows. The discount rate used is the market rate of interest. The market rate is also called the effective rate or the yield rate or the required rate of return. The steps to determine the value of a bond are:

- Calculate the PV of interest payments at the market rate.
- Calculate the PV of the face value at the market rate.
- Add the two PVs.

The next formula can be used to determine the value of a bond.

$$V_b = I\,(\text{PVIFA}_{k,\,n}) + F(\text{PVIF}_{k,\,n})$$

where:

V_b = value of the bond

I = interest in each time period (calculated at the coupon rate of interest)

PVIFA = PV interest factor annuity

k = discount rate (market rate of interest)

n = number of periods

F = principal or face value of the bond

PVIF = PV interest factor

For example: A company issued a 15-year annual pay bond that has five years before maturity. At issuance, the bond had a 10% coupon and a face value of $1,000. Investors require an 8% return on bonds of similar risk. The value of the bond is calculated as shown:

- Determine the annual interest (10% × $1,000 = $100).
- Use the PV annuity table in Appendix A to discount the annual interest of $100 at the required rate of 8% for five years.
- Use the PV tables in Appendix A to discount the face value of $1,000 at the required rate of 8% for five periods (years).
- Add the two PVs.

$$V_b = I(PVIFA_{k, n}) + F(PVIF_{k, n})$$
$$= \$100(3.9927) + \$1,000(0.6806)$$
$$= \$399.27 + \$680.60 = \$1079.87$$

The value of the bond is $1,079.87. This is the price an investor would pay for the bond. In this example, the bond value is above the face value. Because the discount rate is lower than the coupon rate, the bond sells at a premium. If the required rate was higher than the coupon rate, the bond would sell at a discount. If the required rate was equal to the coupon rate, the bond would sell at par (its face value).

If the bond had paid interest semiannually versus annually, some changes to the computation would need to be made, as follows:

- The interest paid in each time period would be equal to $50 ($100/2).
- The interest would be discounted at a rate of 4% (8%/2) for 10 periods. (There would be 10 interest payments made over the 5 years.)
- Similarly the $1,000 face value would be discounted at a rate of 4% for 10 periods.

Other key points to understand about bond valuation are listed next.

- When the market interest falls, the lower coupon rates mean interest paid on old bonds exceeds interest paid on new bonds. This results in **reinvestment rate risk** from the perspective of the bondholder. The reinvestment rate on coupon bonds rises and falls with market interest rates, which leads to reinvestment rate risk.
- Bond price moves inversely with market interest rate. If the market interest rate rises, the bond price declines. Conversely, if the market interest rate falls, the bond price rises.
- The magnitude of interest rate changes influences bond prices—the greater the moves in interest rates, the greater the swings in bond prices.
- As the maturity date approaches, the price of a bond will approach par value. This movement of bond prices toward the principal (par or face) value is called **convergence**.

Stocks

A **stock** is an equity investment instrument; it signifies an ownership position (equity) in a corporation. Stockholders (or shareholders) who buy stock (shares) in a corporation have a claim on the corporation's assets and profits based on the proportional shares of stock owned. Their claims, however, are subordinate to all debt holders. In addition, common stockholders' claims are subordinate to preferred stockholders' claims. The differences between common and preferred stocks are discussed later in this section under "Common Stock" and "Preferred Stock."

The level of equity ownership takes into consideration the number of shares outstanding. The term **outstanding share** refers to the number of shares of a corporation's stock held by shareholders.

Ownership is calculated by dividing the number of shares an investor owns by the total number of shares outstanding. For example, if a company has 10,000 shares of stock outstanding and an investor owns 200 of them, that investor owns 2% of the company.

Market Value of a Stock

A stock's **market value** (the last reported sale price for outstanding shares) determines the firm's **market capitalization**. Market capitalization (or **cap**) is determined by multiplying the current common stock market price per share by the number of outstanding common stock shares. A public corporation with 30 million shares outstanding that trade at $30 each has a market capitalization of $900 million.

Market capitalization is one of many methods used to categorize types of stocks. Figure 2B-10 shows stock classifications based on market capitalization. Corporations usually are classified as large cap, medium cap (mid cap), small cap, or micro cap, depending on their market capitalization.

Figure 2B-10 Categories of Stocks Based on Capitalization

Large cap	$15 billion and over
Mid cap	Between $2 billion and $15 billion
Small cap	Between $300 million and $2 billion
Micro cap	Below $300 million

A large-cap stock is the stock of a company with a market capitalization that is large relative to other companies. Large-cap stocks frequently offer regular dividends, and the underlying company's size generally lessens the risk of company failure.

A mid-cap stock is a stock with a market capitalization that is between that of large- and small-cap stocks. Similar to large-cap stocks, mid-cap stocks also have a large volume of shares to trade, but the companies are smaller and less mature than large-cap stocks. Typically, these companies offer a greater potential for growth than larger companies, but the risk is also greater.

A small-cap stock is a stock with a market capitalization that is relatively small compared to the average company. Small-cap stocks have the potential for dramatic growth, but they also have the potential for greater volatility.

Investment returns for the different types of stocks often move in a different cycles. Micro-cap stocks are considered to be the riskiest group of all.

Other common stock classifications are listed next.

- *Blue-chip stocks.* Stocks of the largest and most consistently profitable publicly traded corporations
- *Growth stocks.* Stocks of corporations that have strong growth potential, with sales, earnings, and market share growing faster than the overall economy
- *Cyclical stocks.* Stocks of corporations whose earnings are highly dependent on economic conditions (e.g., economic upturns and slowdowns)
- *Defensive stocks.* Conservative stocks that are relatively stable and impervious to most economic conditions
- *Value stocks.* Stocks that appear inexpensive when compared to earnings and other performance measures
- *Income stocks.* Stocks of typically solid performers with good track records that usually generate a steady dividend income stream
- *Speculative stocks.* Stocks that are risky investments in corporations that have yet to prove their true worth

Two additional stock classifications are common stock and preferred stock. Common stock and preferred stock have several distinguishing differences (as well as some similarities). Their distinct features offer corporations and investors a variety of risks and rewards.

The common and preferred stock classifications are the focus of the remaining content on stocks.

Common Stock

Common stock provides equity ownership in a corporation. That is, the owner of a common stock has an interest in the assets of the corporation and a share in the earnings. The interest, as noted earlier, is subordinate to all debt holders and to holders of preferred stock. Common stock equity sometimes is referred to as residual equity. Collectively, however, common stock holders own the corporation. Common stock has no maturity date, but shareholders may liquidate their investments by selling stock shares in the secondary market.

With common stock, there is no guarantee that an investor will make money. The equity position in a common stock means that the owner shares in the corporation's fortunes and misfortunes.

Common stock **market value per share** is the current trading price of the stock. If the stock increases in value, shareholders benefit from capital appreciation of their investment and potentially receive a dividend. A dividend (or payout) represents a share in profits.

Voting Rights

Ownership of common stock gives shareholders the right to vote on important company matters, such as these:

- Election of members of the corporate board of directors
- Policies and changes in corporate bylaws
- Approval of stock option plans
- Mergers and acquisitions
- Appointment of auditors

Shareholders typically get one vote for each share of stock owned. Companies administer voting rights in one of two methods: traditional or cumulative.

Traditional Voting

Traditional voting (also known as majority voting, majority-rule voting, or statutory voting) is a corporate voting system in which shareholders voting for the board of directors are limited to one vote per share for any single nominee. The total number of votes for each stockholder equals the number of shares owned times the number of positions open. For example, in an election in which five director candidates are running for open board positions, a shareholder owning 500 shares could cast 500 votes for each candidate, for a total of 2,500 votes.

This traditional majority method of voting precludes minority interests from electing any of their own (minority) candidates.

Cumulative Voting

A **cumulative voting** system allows shareholders to cast different numbers of votes for different candidates. Continuing with the five director position example, the shareholder owning 500 shares could distribute the votes equally to the five candidates, distribute the votes among some combination of the candidates, or cast all 2,500 votes for a single candidate.

Cumulative voting attempts to give minority shareholders more voice in corporate governance by increasing their chances to elect a certain number of directors.

Some corporations issue different classes of stocks with different voting rights. In situations in which a class of shareholders is allowed extra voting rights, a small group of individuals could control the direction of the corporation while owning less than a majority of shares.

Shareholders typically cast votes by mail using a proxy statement. In addition, they may cast votes in person at the corporation's annual meeting. Some corporations allow votes to be cast by telephone or over the Internet.

A **proxy statement** is a legal document that is mailed out to all shareholders shortly before the annual meeting. The proxy statement lists the business concerns to be addressed at the annual meeting and includes a ballot for voting on company initiatives and electing the board members. Submitting a proxy ballot authorizes someone else at the meeting (usually the management team) to vote on the investor's behalf. If the management team receives proxies for over 50% of the shares voted, the team can select the entire board of directors. However, if investors do not return their proxy statements, their votes are not counted. With fewer shares being voted at the meeting, the subsequent number needed to constitute a majority is lowered. In effect, then, unreturned proxies become votes in favor of whatever the board of directors wants.

Preemptive Rights

Most common stocks have preemptive rights. By definition, **preemptive rights** allow current shareholders to maintain their proportional ownership in the corporation should the company issue additional stock. Shareholders with preemptive rights have the right (but not the obligation) to purchase new shares before anyone else so that they can maintain their current level of equity ownership.

Liquidating Value

In the event of default or liquidation, common stock shareholders have the last claim on assets of the corporation. Specifically, they have residual rights to a corporation's assets only after the claims of bondholders, other debt holders, and preferred stockholders are paid in full. But common stock shareholders also have limited liability and are not responsible for the corporation's debts. Their losses are limited to the par or stated value of the stock.

Common Stock Valuation

The return rates for a common stock can vary. As noted previously, in some years, no dividend may be paid. In other years, dividends paid may be more or less than the previous year, depending on the company's dividend policy, profitability, and availability of funds.

Valuation for a common stock requires careful projection of future growth and future dividends. Such projections are largely determined by annual dividends, dividend growth, and discount rates.

There are three potential valuation scenarios. Over time, dividends may remain fixed (zero growth), grow at a constant rate, or grow at an unusual (variable) rate. Investors use valuation models to compare their results to existing prices to determine whether a stock is over-, under-, or properly valued.

Use of the Dividend Discount Model

The **dividend discount model (DDM)** is a method to value common stock where the intrinsic value of the common stock is based on the discounted value (the PV) of all expected future dividends.

Dividend discount models are a type of discounted cash flow (DCF) analysis. There are several different DCF models and, in turn, different DDMs, that an organization can use. There is no one best method. The method used should take into consideration:

- *Measure of cash flow.* The dividends and free cash flows to equity
- *Expected holding period.* Whether the expected period is finite (limited) or infinite
- *Pattern of expected dividends.* Zero growth (no growth), growth, stable (constant) growth, or supernormal growth

The most common models used for valuing common stock are these:

- Basic dividend discount model
- Zero dividend growth model
- Constant dividend growth model
- Variable dividend growth model

Each is described with an example.

Basic Dividend Discount Model

The basic dividend discount model is represented by this formula:

$$V_s = \sum_{t=1}^{\infty} \frac{D_t}{(1+k_s)}$$

where:

V_s = intrinsic value of a share of common stock
D_t = expected dividends per share on the common stock in period t
k_s = investor's required rate of return on the common stock (cost of equity)

This basic dividend discount model assumes that an investor buys a common stock and plans to hold it indefinitely. For this reason, it is sometimes referred to as an infinite period valuation model.

Zero Dividend Growth Model

The next formula can be used for zero growth valuation.

$$V_0 = \frac{D_1}{(1+k_s)^1} + \frac{D_2}{(1+k_s)^2} + \frac{D_3}{(1+k_s)^3} + \ldots + \frac{D_\infty}{(1+k_s)^\infty}$$

where:

V_0 = common stock price to be estimated
$D_1 = D_2 = \ldots = D_n = D_\infty$ a constant annual dividend per share on the common stock
k_s = investor's required rate of return on the common stock (cost of equity)

The required rate of return depends on the risk associated with the common stock. Investors expect a high rate of return if an investment is risky. In other words, a higher payoff must be offered to entice investors to invest their money.

The formula may be further simplified:

$$V_0 = \frac{D}{k_s}$$

For example: A company pays an annual cash dividend of $5 per share at the end of each year. Analysts expect no change in the policy. With a required rate of return of 12%, here is how to determine the value of the common stock:

$$V_0 = \frac{D}{k_s} = \frac{\$5}{0.12} = \$41.67$$

The zero growth model is a special case of the constant dividend growth model (**Gordon's model**).

Constant Dividend Growth Model

The constant growth dividend discount model is a valuation approach that assumes dividends per share grow at a constant rate each period that is not expected to change. The model represents a single-stage growth pattern. Substituting $D_0(1+g)^t$ for D_t in the basic model results in the next formula.

$$V_s = \sum_{t=1}^{\infty} \frac{D_0(1+g)^t}{(1+k_s)^t}$$

where:

    D_0 = dividends per share on the common stock in the current period
    g = constant dividend growth rate
    k_s = investor's required rate of return on the common stock (cost of equity)
    t = time period

If k_s is greater than g, the formula can be further simplified to what is commonly known as the Gordon constant growth model (or Gordon's model):

$$V_0 = \frac{D_1}{k_s - g}$$

where:

    V_0 = estimated value of common stock
    D_1 = expected dividends per share on the common stock in year 1
    k_s = required rate of return on the common stock
    g = constant (annual) dividend growth rate

For example: A company just paid a $3 dividend per share last year. Analysts expect dividends to grow at a constant rate of 6% per year. If investors expect to receive a 12% return, what is the intrinsic value of the ABC stock?

In this example:

$D_1 = \$3.00\ (1.06) = \$3.18$
$k_s = 0.12$
$g = 0.06$

$$V_0 = \frac{D_1}{k_s - g} = \frac{\$3.18}{0.12 - 0.06} = \frac{\$3.18}{0.06} = \$53.00$$

Key points about the relationship between the required rate of return (k_s) and the growth rate (g) are summarized in Figure 2B-11.

Figure 2B-11 Gordon Model Key Points

If...		Then:
The difference between k_s and g *widens*	✦	The stock value falls.
The difference between k_s and g *narrows*	✦	The stock value rises.
The difference between k_s and g *shows small changes*	✦	Large changes in the stock's value can result.

Variable Dividend Growth Model

This method estimates the stock price when dividends grow at a different rate for two or more periods of time. When a common stock has varying growth rates of dividends:

- Future dividends must be projected separately.
- Projected dividends must be discounted back to the present using PV interest tables.
- The PV of the terminal at the end of the growth period must be calculated.
- All PVs are added together.

For example: Company J paid an annual cash dividend of $5 per share last year. Analysts expect dividends will grow at an annual rate of 20% for the next three years and then level to a normal growth rate of 5%. With a required rate of return of 12%, here is how to determine the price of the common stock today.

$$P_3 = \frac{D_3(1+g)}{k_s - g}$$

$$= \frac{\$8.64(1.05)}{0.12 - 0.05} = \frac{\$9.07}{0.07} = \$129.57$$

where:

$D_1, D_2, D_3 =$ dividends in years 1, 2, 3, respectively
$P_3 =$ common stock price in year 3
$k_s =$ required rate of return on the common stock
$g =$ constant (annual) dividend growth rate

Year	Income		PVIF* at 12%		PV of Income
1	$D_1 = \$5(1.20) = \$6.00$	×	0.8929	=	$5.36
2	$D_2 = \$6.00(1.20) = 7.20$	×	0.7972	=	5.74
3	$D_3 = \$7.20(1.20) = 8.64$	×	0.7118	=	6.15
	$P_3 = 129.57$	×	0.7118	=	92.23
				Total PV	$109.48

* PVIF = PV interest factor.

In this example, the price of the common stock at the end of year 3 is $129.57. When the discounted values are summed, the estimated stock price is $109.48.

Use of Relative (or Comparable) Valuation Models

Relative valuation is another valuation approach that defines the term *comparable* and chooses a standardized measure of value to compare companies. Value typically is some form of multiple earnings, book value of equity, or sales. Assets may be cheap based on intrinsic value but expensive based on relative valuation and how the market currently prices the assets.

Essentially the same variables considered in DCF valuation models (e.g., required rate of return, expected growth rate, etc.) are used in relative valuation estimates. The major difference between the two valuation approaches is that the assumptions underlying DCF valuation are explicit (clearly defined or formulated) and those applying to relative valuation models are implicit (the assumptions provide conditions that they satisfy).

Choosing comparable firms is fundamental to relative valuation. A comparable firm is one having similar business and industry characteristics to the individual firm being valued.

In relative valuation, an analyst:

- Attempts to control/minimize differences across firms (such as size).
- Computes the multiple for each comparable firm and then averages them.
- Computes the multiple for the individual firm to be valued.
- Compares the multiple for the individual firm to the average.
- Evaluates any differences between the two multiples based on characteristics of the individual firm (such as growth or risk).

For example, looking at these price/earnings (P/E) ratios, where the comparable firms' P/E equals 18 and the individual firm's P/E equals 10, an analyst might consider the individual firm's stock as cheap (or undervalued) because the multiple is less than average. Conversely, if the multiple were higher than average, the stock would be considered expensive (or overvalued).

Three common relative valuation models are price/earnings (P/E) ratios, price-to-book (P/B) ratios, and price-to-sales (P/S) ratios.

Price/Earnings Ratios

The **price/earnings (P/E) ratio** is the most common multiple used to estimate the value of common stock. Earnings power, as measured by earnings per share (EPS), is the primary determinant of investment value. There are two versions of the P/E ratio; the difference between the two is how earnings are calculated in the denominator.

The **trailing P/E** ratio uses earnings over the most recent 12 months. This P/E ratio is common in the popular financial press.

$$\text{Trailing P/E} = \frac{\text{Market Price per Share}}{\text{EPS over Previous 12 Months}}$$

The **leading P/E** ratio uses next year's expected earnings (either expected earnings for the next fiscal year or the next four quarters).

$$\text{Leading P/E} = \frac{\text{Market Price per Share}}{\text{Forecasted EPS over Next 12 Months}}$$

Leading P/E ratios rely on the DDM to develop a constant multiplier model for a stable firm and then explain factors in the DDM that affect a stock's P/E ratio.

For example: A company reports $10 million in earnings in the previous fiscal year. An analyst forecasts a $1.00 EPS over the next 12 months. The company has 15 million shares outstanding at a market price of $15 per share. Given this information, here is how to determine the trailing and leading P/E ratios:

$$\text{Previous year EPS} = \frac{\$10,000,000}{\$15,000,000} = \$0.67$$

$$\text{Trailing P/E} = \frac{\$15.00}{\$0.67} = 22.39$$

$$\text{Leading P/E} = \frac{\$15.00}{\$1.00} = 15.0$$

Advantages of using P/E ratios include:

- They are commonly used in the investment community.
- Research shows a significant relationship between P/E differences and long-run average stock returns.

Some of the disadvantages of using P/E ratios are:

- If earnings are negative, the resulting P/E ratio is useless.
- Volatility in earnings can make the interpretation of P/E ratios difficult.
- Management discretion (that is within allowable accounting practices) can distort earnings.

Price-to-Book Ratios

A **price-to-book (P/B) ratio** (or **price-to-book value ratio**) shows how much the market is willing to pay for equity. Book value is a cumulative amount that typically is a positive value, even if a company reports a loss and has a negative EPS. The P/B ratio is represented as:

$$\text{P/B Ratio} = \frac{\text{Market Value of Equity}}{\text{Book Value of Equity}} = \frac{\text{Market Price per Share}}{\text{Book Value per Share}}$$

where:

$$\text{Book Value of Equity} = \text{Common Shareholders' Equity}$$
$$= (\text{Total Assets} - \text{Total Liabilities}) - \text{Preferred Stock}$$

For example: The next equation uses information shown in the table to calculate the P/B ratio for a company.

Book Value of Equity in Year 1 (millions)	Sales Year 1 (millions)	Shares Outstanding Year 1 (millions)	Price 15 May, Year 1
$14,015	$9,450	3,400	$9.50

$$\frac{\text{Book Value per}}{\text{Share}} = \frac{\text{Total Stockholders' Equity} - \text{Preferred Equity}}{\text{Number of Common Shares Outstanding}}$$

$$= \frac{\$14,015}{3,400} = \$4.12$$

$$\text{P/B Ratio} = \frac{\text{Market Price per Share}}{\text{Book Value per Share}} = \frac{\$9.50}{\$4.12} = \$2.31$$

Advantages of using P/B ratios are listed next.

- Even when EPS is negative, book value is a cumulative amount and is usually a positive value.
- A book value measure is more stable than EPS, so it may be more useful than a P/E ratio when EPS is high, low, or volatile.
- Book value provides an appropriate measure of net asset value for firms holding largely liquid assets (e.g., finance, investment, insurance, and banking).
- P/B ratios can be used to value a company that is expected to go out of business.

- Research shows that P/B ratios help explain differences in long-run average returns.

  Disadvantages of using P/B ratios are listed next.

- P/B ratios ignore the value of nonphysical assets (e.g., customer goodwill or human capital).
- P/B ratios can be misleading when there are substantial differences in the size of the assets in the firms being compared.
- The true investment made by shareholders can be obscured by different accounting conventions.
- Technological change and inflation can result in substantial differences between the book and market value of assets.

Price-to-Sales Ratios

A **price-to-sales (P/S) ratio** shows how much the market is willing to pay for a dollar of sales. The P/S ratio is an increasing function of net profit margin, the dividend payout ratio, and growth rate; it is a decreasing function of risk.

The P/S ratio is represented as:

$$\text{P/S Ratio} = \frac{\text{Market Value of Equity}}{\text{Total Sales}} = \frac{\text{Market Price per Share}}{\text{Sales per Share}}$$

For example: The next equation uses information shown in the table to calculate the P/S ratio for a company.

Book Value of Equity in Year 1 (millions)	Sales Year 1 (millions)	Shares Outstanding Year 1 (millions)	Price 15 May, Year 1
$14,015	$9,450	3,400	$9.50

$$\text{Sales per Share} = \frac{\text{Sales}}{\text{Number of Shares Outstanding}}$$

$$= \frac{\$9,450}{3,400} = \$2.78$$

$$\text{P/S Ratio} = \frac{\text{Market Price per Share}}{\text{Sales per Share}} = \frac{\$9.50}{\$2.78} = 3.42$$

Advantages of P/S ratios are listed next.

- The ratio provides meaningful measure even for distressed firms.
- Sales figures tend to be more reliable than EPS and book value because they are not as easy to manipulate or distort as EPS and book value.

- P/S multiples tend to be more stable because they are not as volatile as P/E multiples.
- P/S ratios are useful for valuing a range of stocks from mature or cyclical industries to start-up companies with no record of earnings.
- Research shows significant relationships between differences in P/S ratios and differences in long-term average stock returns.

Disadvantages of P/S ratios are listed next.

- High sales are not necessarily indicative of operating profits measured by earnings and cash flow.
- P/S ratios do not capture differences in cost structures across companies.
- Although P/S ratios are less subject to distortion than EPS and book value, revenue recognition practices can distort sales forecasts.

Preferred Stock

Similar to common stock, **preferred stock** also provides partial ownership in a corporation. However, there are some important differences. To a degree, preferred stock is more similar to bonds than to common stock. For that reason, preferred stock often is described as a hybrid form of security having characteristics of both debt and equity.

Equity Characteristics

A preferred stock generally offers a fixed dividend; the dividend amount does not fluctuate based on earnings. The term *preferred* also implies that shareholders have a right to receive their specified dividend before common stockholders are paid any dividends.

A fixed dividend reduces investor risk, but it also limits financial rewards. Preferred stock has less volatility when markets fall. But shareholders cannot count on large price gains in rising markets. In fact, the dividend is not guaranteed. The board of directors (which votes on dividend issues) does not have to pay the fixed dividend if it so chooses.

Voting Rights

Preferred stockholders usually do not have the voting rights that common stockholders have. Special voting privileges may be granted if the corporation is unable to pay the fixed dividend or if defaults on a loan agreement or bond indenture.

Liquidating Value

In the event of default or bankruptcy, preferred stockholders have a greater claim on the company's assets than common stockholders. Because preferred stock takes precedence over common stock, preferred stockholders have a greater chance of getting some of their investment back if the corporation fails than do common stock shareholders. Should asset liquidation take place, preferred stockholders are paid only after short- and long-term debt holder claims are satisfied.

Unique Features

A corporation cannot deduct the dividends paid to shareholders on its tax return. This is a principal drawback to using preferred stock in corporate financing.

Other important characteristics of preferred stock are described next.

Cumulative Dividends

Unlike a common stock dividend, which a company is not required to pay, a preferred stock dividend is an obligation regardless of the corporation's earnings. When issuing preferred stock, a corporation often commits to offer a fixed annual dividend. However, the payment is discretionary if the company does not have sufficient earnings to pay. In some situations, unpaid dividends for preferred stock may accumulate.

Many preferred stocks have a cumulative dividends feature that requires that all unpaid cumulative dividends on the preferred stock to be paid from future earnings before common stock dividends are paid. It should be noted that if the corporation has no intention of paying out common stock dividends, there is no requirement to pay the cumulative preferred stock dividends in arrears.

Participating Feature

A participating feature allows preferred stockholders to participate in increasing dividends when common stockholders' dividends reach a certain amount. The exact amount of participation varies and is determined by some predetermined formula that relates additional preferred stockholder payouts to increases in common stockholder payouts.

Participating preferred stock gives preferred stockholders a prior claim on income and the opportunity for additional return. Unfortunately for investors, the participating feature is not as common as the cumulative feature; most preferred stock returns are limited to the fixed dividend rate.

Call Provision

Preferred stock issues have a stated call price (or redemption price). A call price is specified at issuance; it is set above the original issue price and may decrease over time.

A call provision grants the preferred stock issuer the right to buy back (or call) all or part of an issue at the call price rather than attempting to retire the issue by more expensive methods, such as purchasing the stock in the open market or offering a preferred stockholder a price over market value or another security in its place.

Convertible Feature

Preferred stock issues sometimes have a convertible feature (or conversion feature). Convertible preferred stock can be converted into a specified amount of common stock at the option of the holder. Corporations set a fixed ratio for the number of shares of common stock that can be exchanged for the convertible preferred stock. Once converted, the preferred stock issue is retired.

When preferred stock issues have both call provisions and conversion features, a corporation can force conversion by calling the stock if the current market value price of preferred stock is significantly higher than the call price (due to the conversion feature).

As noted, common stocks do not have a maturity date. Unless preferred stock has a mandatory redemption, preferred stock has no maturity date. The call provision and the convertible feature give a corporation flexibility in retiring preferred stock issues (which do not have mandatory redemption) rather than potentially having them outstanding in perpetuity.

Preferred Stock Valuation

If a company pays a fixed dividend at the end of each year, the valuation is determined as shown:

$$V_p = \frac{D}{(1+k)^1} + \frac{D}{(1+k)^2} + \frac{D}{(1+k)^3} + \ldots + \frac{D}{(1+k)^\infty}$$

where:

V_p = market value of the preferred stock
D = constant annual dividends per share on the preferred stock
k = discount rate
∞ = infinity

This equation can be further simplified:

$$V_p = \frac{D}{k}$$

Once the information about the dividend and discount rate is available, the value of the preferred stock is a straightforward calculation.

For example: A company issues preferred stock. Par value of the preferred stock is $100, and each share pays an annual cash dividend of $7 per share. The discount rate for similar preferred stock in the market is 8%. Here is how to determine the value of the preferred stock issued by the parent company.

$$V_p = \frac{D}{k}$$

$$= \frac{\$7}{0.08} = \$87.50$$

Although the annual dividend rate is constant, changes in the discount rate will affect the stock price over time.

- If the market discount rate goes down, the value of the preferred stock will increase.
- If the market discount rate goes up, the value of the preferred stock will decrease.

Derivatives

A **derivative** is a financial instrument whose characteristics and value are derived from the underlying price or value of some other, more basic financial instrument. The underlying asset (also known as an **underlying** or **underlier**) could be a bond, an equity investment, a commodity, or currency.

A derivative involves a contract between two parties. Payment is exchanged between the two parties. The amount of the payment can be either:

- A predetermined amount triggered by a specific event (e.g., the price of the underlying asset exceeding some minimum value); or
- An amount resulting from the change in value of a specified quantity of the underlier. The specified quantity of the underlier is referred to as the **notional amount** (or face amount) of the contract.

Accounting Standards Codification (ASC) Topic 815, *Derivatives and Hedging* (formerly FASB Statement No. 133 and relevant amendments), deals with accounting rules for derivatives. In defining a derivative, ASC Topic 815 notes these points:

- It includes one or more underlying assets.
- It has one or more notional amounts or payment provisions or both.
- It requires no initial net investment, or it has a smaller investment than other types of contracts that would be expected to have a similar response to changes in market factors.
- The net settlement (contract payment) must be a cash payment, delivery of an asset that can be easily converted to cash, or another derivative.

Inevitably, new derivatives will be developed. In specifying these characteristics (rather than defining a derivative in terms of financial instruments considered to be derivatives), FASB's intent was to ensure that ASC Topic 815 can be applied to new derivatives—as long as their characteristics are similar to those outlined in this topic and relevant authoritative literature.

Corporations do not use derivatives to raise money but buy or sell them to protect against adverse changes in market factors. For example, a corporation might use a derivative to manage the risk associated with an underlying investment and protect against fluctuations in its value.

Conceptually, there are two basic types of derivatives: options and forward contracts. Subsequent content concentrates on these derivative instruments. Other derivative instruments (e.g., futures and swaps) are some combination or variation of options and forwards. Their characteristics are briefly discussed next.

Derivatives are complex instruments, which can be risky. The information on derivatives contained in this text is intended to provide an overview.

Much of this content summarizes information from:

- *Accounting for Derivatives and Hedging* by Mark A. Trombley (McGraw-Hill Higher Education, 2002)
- AFP Learning System: *Treasury*

Many other resources are available on the subject of derivatives. For additional guidance on buying and selling derivatives, consulting such resources is strongly advised.

Options

An **option** (or option contract) is a contract between two parties wherein the purchaser of the contract has the right (but not the obligation) to buy or sell a given amount of an underlying asset.

Key Characteristics and Terminology

Some of the notable characteristics and terminology associated with option contracts are listed next.

- The party with the option to buy or sell is the owner of the option (also known as the buyer or holder of the option). The other party is the writer or seller of the option.
- The underlying asset may be tangible (such as shares of stock, a commodity, or currency) or intangible (such as an index value or an interest rate).
- A **call option** is a type of option contract giving the owner the right (but not the obligation) to buy the underlying asset (also called the underlier) from the writer at a fixed price during the specified time period.
- A **put option** is a type of option contract giving the owner the right (but not the obligation) to sell to the writer the underlying asset at a fixed price during the specified time period.
- **Strike price** (or **exercise price**) refers to the fixed price of the contract.
- **Exercise date** (also known as **maturity date** or **expiration date**) is the last day on which the buyer can exercise (buy or sell) the underlying asset.
- The **premium** is the initial purchase price of the option; it is usually stated on a per-unit basis. The writer (seller) of an option contract receives an upfront premium from the buyer (owner) of the contract. This premium obligates the writer to fulfill the contract (sell or buy the underlying asset) if the buyer chooses to exercise the option.
- A **European option** is a contract allowing the owner to exercise the option only on the maturity date.
- An **American option** is a contract allowing the owner to exercise the option at any time during the exercise period.

Payoff Structure

Different payoffs are possible with options.

- An option is referred to as **at-the-money** if the underlying asset price equals the strike price.
- An option that is generally referred to as **in-the-money** requires a payment to the owner if the contract is exercised immediately.
- The option is **out-of-the-money** if there is no incentive for the holder to exercise the option.
- A call option is referred to as out-of-the-money if the strike price exceeds the price of the underlying asset; it is referred to as in-the-money if the price of the underlying asset exceeds the strike price.
- A put option is referred to as in-the-money if the strike price exceeds the price of the underlying asset; it is referred to as out-of-the-money if the price of the underlying asset exceeds the strike price.

Simplified examples of call and put option payoffs are presented next.

Call option example. A 30-day option contract is made between a buyer and a seller for a commodity; the strike price is $50 per unit. The premium is $2 per unit. Two scenarios are possible at maturity:

1. If the market price is equal to or less than the strike price of $50, the owner (buyer) would not exercise the option because buying the commodity at the current market value price would be cheaper than exercising the option. The buyer loses $2 for the option premium.
2. If the market price is greater than the strike price plus the option premium ($50 + $2 = $52), the owner (buyer) would exercise the option and make a profit.

Put option example. A 60-day option contract is made between a buyer and a seller for a commodity; the strike price is $30 per unit. The premium is $1 per unit. Two scenarios are possible at maturity:

1. If the market price is equal to or greater than the strike price of $30, the owner would not exercise the option. The owner can make more money by selling the commodity at the current market value price than by exercising the option. The loss is $1 for the option premium.
2. If the market price is less than the strike price minus the option premium ($30 − $1 = $29), the owner makes a profit by exercising the option.

At the time an option contract is set, neither party is required to own the underlying asset. In an option involving shares of stock, for example, the writer of the option does not have to currently own the shares of stock. The writer can offer the buyer the option to buy the stock without actually owning it. However, if the owner exercises the call option, the writer must deliver the stock. If the writer does not already own the stock, the writer must buy the shares specified by the contract on the open market and deliver them to the option owner. If current market value exceeds the strike price, the option writer receives only the strike price per share as payment. The difference between the strike price and the market value must be taken as a loss.

Options have an asymmetric payoff profile. Call option owners have the opportunity for unlimited gain with limited possible losses. If the option is not exercised, it expires. No units are exchanged, and the owner's loss is limited to the premium—the price paid to acquire the option. Call option writers may experience unlimited potential losses (unless the contract is covered, which means that the writer already owns the underlier). Put option owners face limited gain and limited losses, and put option writers face only limited losses (but also limited gain).

Options typically are used for leverage or protection. Using an option for leverage provides the owner with equity in the underlying asset for the premium payment (which is a fraction of the actual market value). Because options provide the right to acquire the underlying asset at a fixed price for a limited time, they offer protection by guarding against price fluctuations up to the maturity date. This limits risk to forfeiture of the option premium (unless the underlier is not already owned).

A payoff diagram for the call option example on the preceding page is shown in Figure 2B-12.

Figure 2B-12 Call Option Payoffs

As shown in this figure:

- The market value (market price) differs from the minimum value (minimum price).
- Market value exceeds minimum value in the shaded area between the curved and straight lines.

Investors are willing to pay a premium above minimum price as long as the option price continues to increase. However, as the curved market value line collapses toward the minimum value line, investors are reluctant to pay a premium for the option because any further increase in the option price will produce a minimal increase in the option value.

Price and Value of Options

To a degree, the price or value of an option depends on the expected future value of the underlying asset (as shown in the simple examples).

These factors influence the theoretical value of an option:

- Current price of the underlying asset
- Time until expiration of the option
- Volatility in price of the underlying asset
- Strike price of the option
- The interest rate on risk-free income securities (usually Treasury bills) expiring at the same time as the option contract
- PV of any expected dividends or interest for common stocks or interest-bearing securities

In practice, mathematical formulas are required to calculate theoretical option values. Furthermore, balance sheet accounting requires that a derivative must be shown at fair value on the balance sheet as either an asset or a liability (depending on the specific contract). Accountants must be able to determine the fair value of derivatives.

Financial Accounting Standards Board (FASB) ASC Topic 820, *Fair Value Measurements and Disclosures* (as formerly addressed in FASB Statement No. 157), provides a methodology for determining the fair value of financial instruments (including derivatives) by using a hierarchy of inputs (Level 1, Level 2, Level 3) and requires using valuation techniques consistent with conventional approaches (market, income, and/or cost). This hierarchy and these valuation techniques are further elaborated on and discussed in Part 1 of the CMAexcel Learning System. Several pricing models are used in practice to value option-related derivatives while meeting the requirements of ASC Topic 820. They include the Black-Scholes model, the binomial lattice model, and Monte Carlo simulation.

The Black-Scholes model is best suited for valuing plain-vanilla options (non-complex option derivatives and those with the most standard components—an expiration date and straightforward strike price). Both the binomial lattice model and Monte Carlo simulation are better suited for valuing more complex options. The binomial lattice model involves the construction of a binomial "tree," which has steps that consider the different paths the option's underlying asset can take during the term of the option. At each step, the model can take into account different values in various parameters, such as a change in the exercise price over the life of the option. In comparison, the Black-Scholes model can take into account only a constant exercise price over the life of the option. Therefore, the binomial lattice model provides a more accurate estimate of a complex option than does the Black-Scholes model. Similarly, the Monte Carlo simulation involves running a large number of simulations using random quantities for uncertain variables and looking at the distribution of results to determine the expected value of the option price. Since the Monte Carlo simulation can address variability, it too is a better model than Black-Scholes to use when valuing option-related derivatives.

Forward Contracts

A forward contract is a customized agreement between two parties to buy or sell a specific amount of an asset at a future date for a set price. Forwards are fundamentally different from options because both parties are obligated to perform according to the terms of the contract.

Key Characteristics and Terminology

Some of the notable characteristics and terminology associated with forwards are listed next.

- In a forward contract, one party purchases the contract; the other party is usually referred to as the counterparty.
- The underlying asset may be tangible (such as a commodity or currency) or intangible (such as a stock index or a debt instrument).
- The party who agrees to buy the underlying asset on a specified future date assumes a **long position** (or is said to be long a forward contract).
- The party who agrees to sell that underlying asset on the specified date assumes a **short position** (or is said to be short a forward contract).
- The delivery price (or contract price) is the purchase/sale price specified in the contract.
- The delivery date (or maturity date) refers to the specified future date of the contract; delivery of the contract takes place at maturity.
- The amount of the underlying asset and the delivery date are set at the time the contract is negotiated; no initial payment (premium) is made.

The counterparty in a forward contract is often a bank or a dealer or trader in foreign exchange (FX) markets (as the most common application of forwards is with FX payments). In many cases, these entities serve as "market makers" and facilitate private contracts between two parties.

Forward contracts are not traded on organized exchanges. This is a key distinction from futures contracts, which are traded on standardized exchanges.

Payoff Structure

In the absence of a premium payment, the initial value of the contract to both parties is zero. The contract has no value when it is written. The forward price determines the value of the contract. A long position gains value when the underlying asset price rises and loses value when the asset price falls. Conversely, the short position gains value when the underlying asset price falls and loses value when the asset price rises.

Forwards have symmetrical payoffs; gains and losses for favorable and unfavorable positions are equal. As the value of the underlying asset changes, the value of the long and short positions in a forward contract becomes proportionally positive or negative, depending on the position held.

Forward contract example. A simple scenario illustrating use of a forward contract might be a U.S. importer with a 60-day invoice due in euros. Purchasing a forward contract for euros deliverable in 60 days locks in the exchange rate regardless of the fluctuation that occurs in the currency exchange rate during the 60-day period.

Futures Contracts

A **futures contract** (or futures) is a forward-based contract conceptually similar to a forward contract but different in execution. The basic difference is that unlike forwards (which are often privately negotiated by an intermediary), futures are standardized contracts traded on organized exchanges.

For example, in the United States, futures are traded on these exchanges:

- New York Mercantile Exchange (e.g., for metals, petroleum, and fiber)
- Chicago Board of Trade (e.g., for livestock, wood, and meat)
- International Money Market wing of the Chicago exchange (e.g., for foreign currency futures)

The exchanges dictate notional amounts and maturity dates. They also require daily settlements during the contract based on changes in the underlying asset. Gains and losses are marked against a margin account.

Futures usually are closed out before maturity. They rarely are settled by actual delivery. Final settlement generally is accomplished through a cash payment. The payoff profile from a long position and a short position in a futures contract looks exactly the same as the payoff profiles from a forward contract.

Swaps

A **swap** is a private agreement between two parties (called "counterparties") to exchange (or swap) future cash payments. Similar to a forward contract, a swap agreement usually is facilitated by an intermediary. Swaps are characterized by a series of forward contracts and the exchange of payments on specified payment dates.

The most common type of swap is an interest rate swap—where two parties (usually assisted by an intermediary) exchange future interest payments on a notional amount. The principal amount is notional because it never changes hands and is used only to calculate the payment amounts.

The simplest type of interest swap, called a "plain vanilla interest rate swap," involves trading fixed interest rate payments for floating-rate payments:

- Party A agrees to pay Party B a series of future payments that are equal to a *predetermined fixed interest rate* multiplied by the notional principal.
- Party B agrees to pay Party A a series of future payments that are equal to a *floating interest rate* multiplied by the same notional principal.

At the initiation of the swap in a single currency, Party A and Party B typically do not swap the notional principal. When payments are due, net interest is paid by the counterparty that owes it. That is, the appropriate counterparty pays the difference between the fixed-rate and variable-rate payments. At the conclusion of the swap, there is no transfer of funds because the parties did not initially swap the notional principal.

The main motivation for using interest rate swaps is to reduce exposure to adverse changes in interest rates. The parties convert a fixed-rate obligation (or investment) into a floating-rate obligation (or vice versa) that might be desirable to match the fixed or floating character of their assets and liabilities.

For example: Assume the two parties, A and B, both want to borrow $10 million for five years. Party A has a better credit rating than Party B. Each party has been offered these terms:

	Fixed Rate	Floating Rate
Party A	10.00%	6-month LIBOR* + 0.50%
Party B	11.00%	6-month LIBOR + 1.00%

* London Interbank Offered Rate

Also assume:

- Party A wants to borrow at a floating rate.
- Party B wants to borrow at a fixed rate.
- Party A has a better credit rating than Party B and pays lower interest rates than in fixed and floating markets.
- Party B pays more than Party A in both markets but relatively less in the floating-rate market at a floating rate of the London Interbank Offered Rate (LIBOR) plus 1 percentage point.

Because Party A has a comparative borrowing advantage in the fixed-rate market and Party B has a comparative borrowing advantage in the floating-rate market, the two parties enter into an interest rate swap agreement that produces a net advantage, which typically is split between the two parties.

A potential risk in using swaps is that either counterparty may default on the agreed-on interest payment stream and thus potentially leave the other party liable for the original payment stream. The use of a third-party intermediary can help to mitigate such risks.

There are other forms of interest swaps as well as many other types of swaps. Some of the more common ones are currency rate swaps, where an obligation in one currency is converted to another currency, and commodity swaps, where a floating price for a commodity is exchanged for a fixed price.

Other Long-Term Financial Instruments

In addition to the investment instruments described thus far, corporations can use other instruments as sources for long-term financing. Figure 2B-13 summarizes key features about leases, convertible securities, and warrants.

Figure 2B-13 Other Long-Term Financial Instruments

Instrument	Description	Key Characteristics

Lease	Legal contract through which the owner (the lessor) of an asset grants another party (the lessee) the right to use the asset for a certain period of time in return for a specified payment	• Binds the lessee to make payments specified in the lease contract.
		
		• Can take various forms:
		  • Operating leases: short-term, cancelable leases where the lessor bears the risk of ownership.
		  • Financial lease (also known as full payout or capital lease): usually noncancelable and fully paid out (amortized) over its term and where the lessee bears the risks (i.e., the lessee bears the responsibility for maintenance, insurance, and taxes).

Convertible security	A fixed income security or a preferred stock that includes an option to exchange that security for a stated number of shares of another security	• Typically used to convert the security into a specified number of shares of an equity security. • Allows a corporation to raise funds at a cost of capital lower than a straight bond or common stock issue; when convertibles are exchanged, debt is removed from the balance sheet.
Warrant	Long-term call option to purchase common stock directly from the corporation	• Gives bondholders or preferred stockholders the right to purchase shares of common stock at a given price. • Derives value from the investor's expectation that the stock price will increase beyond the strike price.

Cost of Capital

The cost of capital is a composite of the costs of various sources of funds comprising a firm's capital structure. It represents the minimum rate of return that must be earned on new investments so that shareholders' interests won't be diluted.

Cost of Capital, Defined

A corporation's management team is charged with ensuring efficiency and profitability from assets as well as minimizing the cost of the funds that the firm incurs from investments. In fulfilling this fiduciary responsibility, management makes various financing decisions that affect the firm's capital structure.

Corporations derive capital essentially from two sources: lenders and shareholders. The total capital of a firm represents a combination of debt capital and equity capital. These capital components are described next.

- **Debt capital** is that portion of total capital derived from the issuance of interest-bearing instruments such as notes, bonds, or loans.
- **Equity capital** is that portion of total capital derived from permanent investments by shareholders, as either paid-in capital or retained earnings. A firm may issue new shares of common or preferred stock, or it may choose to retain earnings instead of distributing them as dividends.

Every activity a firm does to generate capital—either explicit or implicit—has a cost associated with it. The overall **cost of capital** represents a proportional average of the various components a firm uses for financing.

The cost of capital should be considered in capital structure decisions. Corporations can benefit from using the cost of capital to benchmark investment decisions and to manage working capital (e.g., receivables, inventories, and payables) more efficiently. The cost of capital also can be valuable to use in measuring and evaluating performance. For example, the actual and expected return on capital or net assets may be compared with the cost of capital associated with each.

Calculating the Cost of Capital

The cost of capital is found by determining costs for the individual types of capital and then multiplying each component cost by its proportion in the firm's total capital structure. Here is the general formula for the cost of capital:

$$k_a = p_1 k_1 + p_2 k_2 + \ldots + p_n k_n$$

where:

k_a = cost of capital (expressed as a percentage)
p = proportion that element comprises of the total capital structure
k = cost of an element in the capital structure
$1, 2, n$ = different types of financing (each with its own cost and proportion in the capital structure)

Cost of Capital Example

Consider a corporation that uses the types of financing shown in Figure 2B-14.

Figure 2B-14 Cost of Capital Example

Type (n)	After-Tax Cost (k)	% of Capital Structure (p)
Debt	4%	30%
Preferred stock	8%	20%
Common equity	18%	50%

$$k_a = p_1 k_1 + p_2 k_2 + \ldots + p_n k_n$$
$$= 0.30(4\%) + 0.20(8\%) + 0.50(18\%) = 1.2 + 1.6 + 9 = 11.8\%$$

In calculating the cost of capital, using the current or prospective cost of the various capital components is generally more appropriate than relying on historical costs. A primary use of the cost of capital is investing new capital in such projects as new products, equipment, or facilities. Therefore, relevant costs are the marginal costs associated with incremental funds the firm plans to raise, not historical costs of capital that the firm had already raised.

Primary considerations in determining the costs of capital are how to determine:

- The cost (k) of each individual capital component.
- The respective weights (p) in the total capital structure of the firm.

Cost of Individual Capital Components

Determining the cost of each component in a firm's capital structure is the first step in calculating the cost of capital. Corporations typically use three methods of financing: debt, preferred stock, and common equity (either retained earnings or the issuance of additional common stock).

Cost of Debt

The cost of debt represents the required rate of return that providers of debt capital (e.g., loans and bonds) require. The basic formula for the after-tax cost of debt is:

$$\text{After-Tax Cost of Debt} = k_d(1-t)$$

where:
k_d = before-tax cost of debt
t = firm's marginal tax rate

Considerations in determining the after-tax cost of debt are:

- What interest rate (k_d) should be used?
- How should different types of debt be handled?
- What effect do income taxes have on the interest rate?

This formula does not reflect any flotation costs because most debt is privately placed.

The before-tax cost of debt is greater than the after-tax cost of debt because a firm can deduct interest payments when determining taxable income. The higher the tax rate, the lower the after-tax cost of debt.

For example: Consider the next example where Blane Company's debt consists of 6% interest-bearing bonds, which are selling at par. The anticipated tax rate is 35%. The cost of debt would be:

$$\text{After-Tax Cost of Debt} = k_d(1-t)$$
$$= 6\%(1-0.35)$$
$$= 3.9\%$$

The current replacement cost (market value) of debt is used in calculating the cost of capital. But with one or more types of debt involved, a weighted average of yields to maturity should be used to calculate the cost of debt.

The weighted average cost of debt is calculated as shown in Figure 2B-15.

Figure 2B-15 Weighted Average Cost of Debt Using Yields to Maturity

1 Debt	2 Market Value (millions)	3 % of Total	4 Yield to Maturity*	5 = (3 × 4) Weighted Cost
Issue A	$45	10.0%	11.2%	1.12%
Issue B	125	27.8	12.4%	3.45
Issue C	280	62.2	13.1%	8.15
Total:	$450	100.0%		12.72%

*Yield to maturity on a bond is the rate of discount that equates the present value of all interest and principal payments with the current price of the bond.

> Weighted average cost of debt before taxes: 12.72%
> Adjustment for income taxes (1 – 0.45 = 0.55) × 0.55
> Weighted average cost of debt after income taxes: 6.996%

Cost of Preferred Stock

The cost associated with preferred stock is a function of the dividend paid (if any) to shareholders and flotation costs. The cost of preferred stock needs to reflect flotation costs, as they can be substantial. Flotation costs include direct costs (such as underwriting fee, filing fees, legal fees, and taxes) and indirect costs (such as management time working on the new issue). Flotation costs are deducted from the selling price of the preferred stock to determine net proceeds.

The general formula for the cost of preferred stock is:

$$k_p = \frac{D_p}{P_p - F}$$

where:

k_p = component cost of preferred stock
D_p = preferred stock dividend
P_p = the current price per share (current or prospective cost)
F = flotation costs as a dollar amount

For example: Blane Company's preferred stock pays an $8 dividend per share and sells for $100 per share. If the firm issued new shares of preferred, it would incur underwriting and other fees (flotation costs) of $2 per share. Here is how the cost of preferred stock would be calculated for the company:

$$k_p = \frac{D_p}{P_p - F} = \frac{\$8}{\$100 - \$2} = \frac{\$8}{\$98} = 8.16\%$$

In this example, the cost of the preferred stock is shown based on an annual dividend payment. If the dividend payment was quarterly, the same formula could be used and the quarterly rate multiplied by 4 to get the nominal annual rate.

Flotation costs sometimes may be given as a percentage of the issue. In the last example, the flotation costs were 2%. Thus, the denominator of the cost of preferred stock would become $P_p (1 - F\%)$, where F is a percentage, not a dollar amount.

Because preferred stock dividends are not tax deductible, they represent an outflow of after-tax funds. A preferred stock (par of $100) with an 11% dividend costs the firm $11 in after-tax earnings. If the firm has a 35% tax rate, it must earn $1.54 before taxes for each dividend dollar paid.

When a corporation has more than one issue of preferred stock outstanding, the weighted average rate on all preferred stock should be used.

Cost of Common Equity

The **cost of common equity** (or **cost of equity**) is the most difficult capital component to calculate. As noted previously, equity consists primarily of common stock issues, paid-in capital, and retained earnings. The cost of equity is the expected, required, or actual rate of return on the firm's common stock, which, if earned, will leave the market value of the stock unchanged. The rate is difficult to estimate because common stock has no fixed contractual payments.

There are various methods, ranging from simple to complex, for estimating the cost of equity. Three of these methods are:

1. Historical rate of return
2. Dividend growth model
3. Capital asset pricing model (CAPM)

Each method has distinct advantages and limitations. Firms may use more than one method to determine a reasonable estimate. The choice of the appropriate method is often a function of the information available for a given situation.

As noted earlier, companies raise equity in one of two ways:

1. Internally, by retaining earnings
2. Externally, by selling new shares of common stock

Mature companies tend to generate most equity internally. Flotation costs make the cost of raising new equity in the market more expensive. Additionally, if the stock is underpriced, losses result from selling stock shares below the correct value. Stated another way, firms generally use lower-cost retained earnings (internal equity) before issuing a new common stock (external equity) because of flotation costs and potential losses from under-pricing.

Estimating the Cost of Internal Equity Using Historical Rate of Return

As the name implies, the historical rate of return method of determining the cost of equity capital involves the historical rate stockholders have earned. It considers the rate of return earned by an investor who bought the stock in the past, held it to the present, and sold it at current market prices.

For example: Consider a situation in which an issue of a common stock share purchased for $100 five years ago sells today for $110. Dividends of $8 were paid annually. Using the historical method, the average rate of return for the investor was 10% a year ($8 dividend plus $2 average annual gain / $100). The 10% is then used as the estimate of the current rate of return on the stock and the firm's cost of equity capital.

Using the historical method implies that:

- The firm's performance will not change substantially in the future.
- No significant changes in interest rates will occur.
- Investor attitude toward risk will not change.

Although this historical method is relatively easy to calculate, the limitation is that the future rarely remains the same as the past.

Estimating the Cost of Internal Equity (Retained Earnings) Using the Dividend Growth Model

The dividend growth model reflects a market value approach. The underlying logic of this model is that the market price of a stock equals the cash flow of expected future incomes, both dividends and market price appreciation, discounted to their present value. This means that when the present value of the future incomes equals the market price, the discount rate equals the cost of equity capital. An underlying assumption is that incomes will grow at a constant compound rate.

The formula for calculating dividend growth is:

$$k_s = \frac{D_1}{P_0} + g$$

where:

k_s = cost of internal equity capital
D_1 = dividend per share at time 1
P_0 = market price per share at the time 0
g = expected dividend growth rate

For example: If Blane Company's stock is currently selling at $50 per share, the dividend at the end of the first year is expected to be $3.50 per share, and future dividends are expected to grow at 5% per year, the cost of equity capital would be:

$$k_s = \frac{\$3.50}{\$50} + 5\% = 12.00\%$$

Similar to other methods for calculating the cost of equity capital, the dividend growth rate involves an estimate. In this case, the estimate is for the value of g. The model is useful only if market expectations are for dividends to grow at that rate. Investors must believe that the past trends of earnings per share will continue. If this is the case, the trend (expressed as a percentage) can be used.

Estimating the Cost of Internal Equity (Retained Earnings) Using the Capital Asset Pricing Model

The CAPM is useful in measuring the cost of equity capital for a firm.

The CAPM implies that the rate of return on any security equals the riskless rate of interest plus a premium for risk. The riskless rate is usually based on the current or anticipated rate on long-term U.S. Treasury bonds or short-term U.S. Treasury bills. The premium for risk is derived from the security's beta.

The formula for applying the CAPM to estimate the cost of equity capital is:

$$k_e = R_f + \beta(k_m - R_f)$$

where:

k_e = cost of internal equity capital
R_f = risk-free rate (e.g., the rate on T-bonds or a 30-day T-bill)
β = stock's beta estimate (obtained from a brokerage firm or investment advisory service, or calculated by the firm)
k_m = estimate of the return on the market as a whole or on an average stock value

The term $(k_m - R_f)$ is called the "market risk premium," which is somewhere in the area of 5% to 7%, depending on the date of the estimate and the data sources used by the analysts. Firms often add 6% to the T-bond rate to obtain the rate of return for the market as a whole.

For example: If the T-bond rate is 8%, a firm's stock beta is 0.9, and the expected rate of return for the market is 14%, Blane Company's cost of equity capital using the CAPM would be:

$$k_e = 8\% + 0.9(14\% - 8\%)$$
$$= 8\% + 5.40\%$$
$$= 13.40\%$$

Using the CAPM involves estimates for each term in the equation. Challenges arise in deciding:

- Whether to use long-term or short-term T-bond rates for R_f.
- Estimating the future beta investors expect.
- Estimating the expected rate of return for the market as a whole.

Estimating the Cost of New Equity (Issuing Additional Common Stock) Using the Dividend Growth Model

Determining the cost of new common stock (k_e) must consider flotation costs and possible under pricing losses. The constant growth dividend discount model (DDM) formula used to calculate the cost of existing equity (k_s) can be adjusted to account for both factors. The formula for calculating the cost of new equity is:

$$k_e = \frac{D_1}{P_0 - (F+U)} + g$$

where:

k_e = cost of external equity capital
D_1 = dividend per share at time 1
g = expected dividend growth rate
P_0 = market price per share at time 0
U = under-pricing losses

For example: Suppose Blane Company can issue stock for $50 per share, before $5 from flotation costs and under-pricing losses. The dividend at the end of the first year is expected to be $3.50 per share, and future dividends are expected to grow at 5% per year. The estimated cost of new equity capital would be:

$$k_e = \frac{D_1}{P_0 - (F+U)} + g$$

$$= \frac{\$3.50}{\$50 - \$5} + 0.05 = 12.78\%$$

Comparing the cost of new equity (12.78%) to the cost of internal equity (12%), the difference is the flotation costs and under-pricing losses. These factors make the cost of new equity more costly by almost 1 percentage point.

Estimating the cost of capital, especially when the cost of equity is involved, is not exact. Decision making about inputs and the different models themselves can result in substantial differences in estimates.

Weighted Average Cost of Capital

Once the different capital components have been determined, the final goal is to calculate the relative importance of each source in the total capital structure of the firm. In other words, the individual components must be weighted to show the extent to which each one contributes to the total value of the firm's capital structure.

The **weighted average cost of capital (WACC)** is the firm's overall cost of capital and represents the risks associated with typical or average projects. Many companies use this WACC formula:

$$\text{WACC} = \sum_{i=1}^{n} w_i k_i$$

where:

n = total number of capital components

w_i = percentage of total permanent capital represented by each capital component

k_i = after-tax cost of each capital component

Because WACC includes all sources of permanent financing in a firm's capital structure, the sum of the weighted components must equal 1.0.

Three weighting schemes commonly are used to calculate WACC: book value weights, market value weights, and target value weights.

1. **Book value weights** measure the proportion of each type of capital based on accounting (book) values shown on the firm's balance sheet.
2. **Market value weights** represent current proportions of each type of capital in the firm's capital structure at current market prices.
3. **Target value weights** represent the weights based on the firm's optimal (target) capital structure.

Book values remain stable because they do not depend on changing market values for debt and equity. They represent historical costs. However, using book values can skew WACC because book values may differ substantially from the market.

Many believe that market value weights are the most accurate way to compute WACC because market weights consider the effects of changing market conditions and the current prices of each security. Some debate exists, however, between the merits of using weights based on the actual market or the target market capital structure. Because target weights represent the best estimate of how the firm will raise money in the future, they make sense if the firm is migrating toward the target structure.

For example: Management considers the mix as optimal and wants to maintain this target structure in raising future capital. If Blane Company raises new capital in target proportions, here is how to determine the firm's WACC.

Capital Component	Weight	After-Tax Cost	WACC
Long-term debt	0.40	3.90%	1.560%
Preferred stock	0.10	8.16%	0.816%
Common (internal) equity	0.50	11.80%	5.900%
			8.276%

Using the average cost of the historical rate of return (10.0%), dividend growth model (12.0%), and the CAPM (13.4%), the cost of common (internal) equity (retained earnings) is (10.0% + 12.0% +13.4%) / 3 = 11.8%. If management thought that one method of estimating the cost of retained earnings was better than another, it could use that cost instead of determining an average based on several methods.

Thus, Blane Company's WACC before using external equity would be 8.276% and is calculated as shown:

$$WACC = (0.40)\,(3.9\%) + (0.10)\,(8.16\%) + (0.50)\,(11.8\%)$$
$$WACC = 1.56\% + 0.816\% + 5.9\% = 8.276\%$$

Marginal Cost of Capital

Companies do not have unlimited sources of funds for investments; they do not have the ability to satisfy all of their potential investment desires.

Market investors evaluate the financial merits of different companies, compare them, and determine reasonable limits for individual companies, beyond which investors will not make funds readily available. Should a firm attempt to extend financing beyond its market-determined limit, those funds are available only at high costs. (Recall that raising external capital has flotation costs, making the cost of new equity higher than the costs of retained earnings.)

The **marginal cost of capital (MCC)** is the last dollar of new capital that the firm raises. The **weighted marginal cost of capital (WMCC)** is the incremental cost of financing beyond the previous MCC level. The **marginal cost of capital schedule** sets a series of ranges and specifies the incremental costs a firm will incur when financing exceeds the maximum limit in each range.

MCC Schedules

There are five steps to develop an MCC schedule:

1. Determine the appropriate weights of the new financing.
2. Calculate the component cost of capital associated with each amount of capital raised.
3. Calculate the range of total new financing at which the cost of the new components increases.
4. Calculate the MCC for each range of total new financing.
5. Plot an MCC schedule.

Setting MCC Schedule Break Points

Establishing the range of total new financing at which the cost of the new components increases requires setting break points. A **break point (BP)** is defined as the total financing a firm can raise before the cost of capital increases.

The formula for calculating an MCC break point is:

$$BP_{RE} = \frac{TF_i}{w_i}$$

where:

   BP_{RE} = break point for capital component i

   TF_i = total amount of funds available from capital component i

   w_i = percentage of total permanent capital represented by capital component i

Using this formula, a BP can be determined by dividing the total amount of funds available for a particular capital component at a stated cost by its capital structure weight.

An MCC schedule may include several BPs.

For example: Blane Company's expects to have $50 million in earnings available during the next year to pay out cash dividends to common shareholders or to reinvest. The firm expects to have a 40% dividend payout ratio. Thus, the company will have $30 million [($50) (1 – 0.40)] in new retained earnings. Given the company's capital structure of 40% debt, 10% preferred, and 50% equity, what is the BP for retained earnings?

$$BP_{RE} = \frac{TF_i}{w_i}$$

$$= \frac{\$30 \text{ million}}{0.50} = \$60 \text{ million}$$

Thus, Blane Company can raise $60 million before having to issue external equity as the equity component of its financing mix. This $60 million will consist of $24 million in debt (0.40 × $60 million), $6 million in preferred stock (0.10 × $60 million), and $30 million in internal equity (Retained Earnings – 0.50 × $60 million)). If the company has a capital budget greater than $60 million, it will need to use more expensive common stock as the equity component. Thus, the company's marginal cost of capital will increase due to the higher cost of common stock compared with retained earnings.

Calculating the MCC

Blane Company wants to calculate its MCC after the retained earnings BP. Based on the DDM, the firm's cost of retained equity is 12% but its cost of new equity is 13% when considering flotation costs and under pricing. Thus, the difference of 1 percentage point represents an estimate of the flotation and under pricing costs. Management decides to add 1 percentage point to the cost of common (internal) equity previously calculated. Thus, the estimated cost of new common stock is 12.8% (i.e., 11.8% + 1.0%).

For example: Here is how to calculate Blane Company's MCC after the retained earnings BP of $60 million.

Capital Component	Weight	After-Tax Cost	WACC
Long-term debt	0.40	3.90%	1.560%
Preferred stock	0.10	8.16%	0.816%
Common (internal) equity	0.50	12.80%	6.400%
			8.776%

Thus, the MCC after $60 million increases to 8.776%. The MCC schedule is plotted in Figure 2B-16.

Figure 2B-16 MCC Schedule for Blane Company

The MCC recognizes the responses of investors to increased financing requirements. The market imposes limits on different levels. Excessive levels lead to successively higher costs of capital.

Income Taxes Impact on Capital Structure and Capital Investment Decisions

Taxes can affect a firm's capital structure in these ways:

- Firms with large taxable income (unshielded from taxes) possibly can reduce taxes through more debt financing—which increases the total cash flows distributed to debt and equity holders.
- Firms with volatile operating earnings pose a higher business risk and lower the probability that they will be able to use tax deductions from borrowing during lower-income years. These firms may not want to borrow as much as other firms that have lower business risk.

Use of Cost of Capital in Investment Decisions

Corporations must decide where to invest income to gain the highest possible rate of return within the firm's risk profile. Firms can use the cost of capital as a discount rate of return to evaluate the present value of project cash flows or as a hurdle (threshold) rate to evaluate the internal rate of return.

Cost of capital provides a benchmark for assessing whether the risk and returns on a firm's securities are high or low. These ratings are important for two reasons:

1. High risk means a high cost of capital; low risk is indicative of a low cost of capital.
2. A high cost of capital (discount rate) typically means a low valuation of the firm's securities; a low cost of capital means a high valuation for securities.

The sale of securities provides a corporation with necessary funds for investments. If the value of securities is low, the cost of financing increases. Conversely, financing costs decrease when the value of securities is high.

Ultimately, the solvency of a firm depends on its total risk. Management must consider the impact of various investments on the total risk of the firm.

Knowledge Check:
Long-Term Financial Management

The next questions are intended to help you check your understanding and recall of the material presented in this topic. They do not represent the type of questions that appear on the CMA exam.

Directions: Answer each question in the space provided. Correct answers and section references appear after the knowledge check questions.

1. Which statement accurately describes bond yields?

    ☐ **a.** Higher-quality bonds typically pay lower yields than lower-grade bonds.

    ☐ **b.** Short-term bonds typically pay higher yields than long-term bonds.

    ☐ **c.** Fixed interest rate bonds earn more than zero coupon bonds.

    ☐ **d.** Secured bonds typically pay higher yields than unsecured bonds.

2. Which type of bond is **most** attractive to buy on the secondary market when interest rates are low?

    ☐ **a.** Aaa- or AAA-rated bond

    ☐ **b.** Zero coupon bond

    ☐ **c.** Floating rate bond

    ☐ **d.** U.S. Treasury bond

    For questions 3 through 8, match the financial instruments with the appropriate description.

    a. An agreement between two parties to buy or sell a specific amount of an asset at a future date for a set price

    b. A private agreement between two parties to exchange future cash payments

    c. Long-term call option to purchase common stock directly from the corporation

    d. An instrument providing a limited ownership interest in a corporation and a fixed dividend

    e. A contract allowing the purchaser the right to buy or sell the underlying asset at a stated price on or before a specific date

    f. An instrument providing equity interest in the assets of the corporation and a share in the earnings

3. _____ Common stock

4. _____ Preferred stock

5. _____ Option

6. _____ Forward contract

7. _____ Warrant

8. _____ Swap

9. The price of a bond

☐ **a.** increases as market interest rates increase.

☐ **b.** decreases as market interest rates decrease.

☐ **c.** is independent of market interest rates.

☐ **d.** moves inversely to market interest rate changes.

10. Using the constant dividend growth model (Gordon's model), the value of a common stock with a current dividend of $4, a dividend growth rate of 5%, and a required rate of return of 16% would be

☐ **a.** $25 per share.

☐ **b.** $36.36 per share.

☐ **c.** $38.18 per share.

☐ **d.** $80 per share.

11. The value of a 6%, $50 par, preferred stock with a required rate of return of 8% would be

☐ **a.** $37.50 per share.

☐ **b.** $42.86 per share.

☐ **c.** $50 per share.

☐ **d.** $53 per share.

12. What is the approximate cost of capital for a firm given the following information?

Type	After-Tax Cost	% of Capital Structure
Debt	8%	34%
Preferred stock	9%	26%
Common equity	10%	40%

☐ **a.** 8%

☐ **b.** 9%

☐ **c.** 10%

☐ **d.** 27%

13. Which factor makes determining the cost of debt challenging?

☐ **a.** Interest costs can be calculated in a variety of ways.

☐ **b.** Retained earnings are subject to dividend payments.

   ☐ **c.** Common stock has no fixed contractual payments.

   ☐ **d.** The firm's future performance levels are difficult to estimate.

14. An underlying premise in applying the capital asset pricing model to estimate a firm's cost of equity capital is

   ☐ **a.** investor attitudes toward risk will not change.

   ☐ **b.** incomes are expected to grow at a constant compound rate.

   ☐ **c.** individual capital components must be weighted based on their contributions to the firm's capital structure.

   ☐ **d.** the return rate equals the riskless rate of return plus a premium for risk.

Match the following terms to their description.

15. _____ Cost of capital	**a.** The after-tax interest rate a company pays on all of its capital debt (e.g., loans and bonds)
16. _____ Cost of debt	**b.** Its expected return is normally higher than debt but lower than retained earnings
17. _____ Cost of preferred stock	**c.** The weighted average of the various components a firm uses for financing its investments
18. _____ Cost of common equity	**d.** The expected, required, or actual rate of return on the firm's stock that, if earned, will leave the market value of the stock unchanged

19. What is the after-tax cost of a 6% bond selling at 101 when the effective tax rate is 40%?

   ☐ **a.** 3.6%

   ☐ **b.** 3.56%

   ☐ **c.** 5.94%

   ☐ **d.** 6%

20. What is the after-tax cost of a 5% preferred stock with a 2% flotation cost when the effective tax rate is 40%?

   ☐ **a.** 5%

   ☐ **b.** 3%

   ☐ **c.** 5.1%

   ☐ **d.** 3.06%

21. What is the after-tax cost of a common stock selling at $40 per share when the current dividend is $3 per share and the dividend growth rate is 4%? Assume the effective tax rate is 40%.

☐ **a.** 11.5%

☐ **b.** 7.5%

☐ **c.** 7.8%

☐ **d.** 11.8%

22. What is the after-tax cost of a common stock selling at $40 per share that has a beta coefficient of 1.8? Assume an effective tax rate of 40%, a 90-day Treasury bill rate of 2%, and a required market rate of return of 8%.

☐ **a.** 12.8%

☐ **b.** 7.68%

☐ **c.** 16.4%

☐ **d.** 9.84%

Knowledge Check Answers: Long-Term Financial Management

1. Which statement accurately describes bond yields? [**See** *Bond Yields.*]

    ☑ **a.** Higher-quality bonds typically pay lower yields than lower-grade bonds.

    ☐ **b.** Short-term bonds typically pay higher yields than long-term bonds.

    ☐ **c.** Fixed interest rate bonds earn more than zero coupon bonds.

    ☐ **d.** Secured bonds typically pay higher yields than unsecured bonds.

2. Which type of bond is **most** attractive to buy on the secondary market when interest rates are low? [**See** *Bond Interest.*]

    ☐ **a.** Aaa- or AAA-rated bond

    ☐ **b.** Zero coupon bond

    ☑ **c.** Floating rate bond

    ☐ **d.** U.S. treasury bond

    For questions 3 through 8, match the financial instruments with the appropriate description.

    a. An agreement between two parties to buy or sell a specific amount of an asset at a future date for a set price

    b. A private agreement between two parties to exchange future cash payments

    c. Long-term call option to purchase common stock directly from the corporation

    d. An instrument providing a limited ownership interest in a corporation and a fixed dividend

    e. A contract allowing the purchaser the right to buy or sell the underlying asset at a stated price on or before a specific date

    f. An instrument providing equity interest in the assets of the corporation and a share in the earnings

3. __f__ Common stock

4. __d__ Preferred stock

5. __e__ Option

6. __a__ Forward contract

7. __c__ Warrant

8. __b__ Swap

9. The price of a bond [**See *Bond Valuation.***]

☐ **a.**   increases as market interest rates increase.

☐ **b.**   decreases as market interest rates decrease.

☐ **c.**   is independent of market interest rates.

☑ **d.**   moves inversely to market interest rate changes.

10. Using the constant dividend growth model (Gordon's model), the value of a common stock with a current dividend of $4, a dividend growth rate of 5%, and a required rate of return of 16% would be [**See *Constant Dividend Growth Model.***]

☐ **a.** $25 per share.

☐ **b.** $36.36 per share.

☑ **c.** $38.18 per share.

☐ **d.** $80 per share.

11. The value of a 6%, $50 par, preferred stock with a required rate of return of 8% would be [**See *Preferred Stock Valuation.***]

☑ **a** $37.50 per share.

☐ **b.** $42.86 per share.

☐ **c.** $50 per share.

☐ **d.** $53 per share.

12. What is the approximate cost of capital for a firm given the following information? [**See *Calculating the Cost of Capital.***]

Type	After-Tax Cost	% of Capital Structure
Debt	8%	34%
Preferred stock	9%	26%
Common equity	10%	40%

☐ **a.**   8%

☑ **b.**   9%

☐ **c.**   10%

☐ **d.**   27%

13. Which factor makes determining the cost of debt challenging? [**See *Cost of Debt.***]

☑ **a.**   Interest costs can be calculated in a variety of ways.

☐ **b.**   Retained earnings are subject to dividend payments.

☐ **c.**   Common stock has no fixed contractual payments.

☐ **d.**   The firm's future performance levels are difficult to estimate.

14. An underlying premise in applying the capital asset pricing model to estimate a firm's cost of equity capital is [**See *Cost of Common Equity*.**]

   ☐ **a.** Investor attitudes toward risk will not change.

   ☐ **b.** Incomes are expected to grow at a constant compound rate.

   ☐ **c.** Individual capital components must be weighted based on their contributions to the firm's capital structure.

   ☑ **d.** The return rate equals the riskless rate of return plus a premium for risk.

Match the following terms to their description.

15. __c__ Cost of capital	**a.** The after-tax interest rate a company pays on all of its capital debt (e.g., loans and bonds)
16. __a__ Cost of debt	**b.** Its expected return is normally higher than debt but lower than retained earnings
17. __b__ Cost of preferred stock	**c.** The weighted average of the various components a firm uses for financing its investments
18. __d__ Cost of common equity	**d.** The expected, required, or actual rate of return on the firm's stock that, if earned, will leave the market value of the stock unchanged

19. What is the after-tax cost of a 6% bond selling at 101 when the effective tax rate is 40%? [**See *Cost of Debt*.**]

   ☐ **a.** 3.6%

   ☑ **b.** 3.56%

   ☐ **c.** 5.94%

   ☐ **d.** 6%

20. What is the after-tax cost of a 5% preferred stock with a 2% flotation cost when the effective tax rate is 40%? [**See *Cost of Preferred Stock*.**]

   ☐ **a.** 5%

   ☐ **b.** 3%

   ☑ **c.** 5.1% **Cost of Preferred Stock = $5 / (100 − 2) = 5.1%**

   ☐ **d.** 3.06%

21. What is the after-tax cost of a common stock selling at $40 per share when the current dividend is $3 per share and the dividend growth rate is 4%? Assume the effective tax rate is 40%. [**See *Estimating the Cost of New Equity (Issuing Additional Common Stock) Using the Dividend Growth Model*.**]

    ☑ **a.**   11.5% = ($3/$40) + 4%

    ☐ **b.**   7.5%

    ☐ **c.**   7.8%

    ☐ **d.**   11.8%

22. What is the after-tax cost of a common stock selling at $40 per share that has a beta coefficient of 1.8? Assume an effective tax rate of 40%, a 90-day Treasury bill rate of 2%, and a required market rate of return of 8%. [**See *Estimating the Cost of Internal Equity (Retained Earnings) Using the Capital Asset Pricing Model*.**]

    ☑ **a.**   12.8%

    ☐ **b.**   7.68%

    ☐ **c.**   16.4%

    ☐ **d.**   9.84%

Raising Capital

In Topic 2: Long-Term Financial Management of this section, securities, such as common stock and preferred stock and debt (containing nonconvertible features), as well as methods for their valuation, were discussed as a means for providing capital to, or financing, a corporation. This topic addresses other means through which a corporation may raise capital, including approaches that involve intermediate-term (one to ten years) sources and other long-term (over ten years) sources, namely convertible securities.

The final part of this topic covers other matters relevant to the raising of capital for corporations, such as the capital markets within which the raising of capital occurs; the role of investment bankers, underwriters, and credit rating agencies; insider trading; and a corporation's dividend policies and stock repurchase transactions.

READ the Learning Outcome Statements (LOS) for this topic as found in Appendix B and then study the concepts and calculations presented here to be sure you understand the content you could be tested on in the CMA exam.

Intermediate-Term Sources

Intermediate-term sources for raising capital include the following:

- Term loans
- Equipment financing loans
- Operating leases
- Capital (financial) leases

Each of these sources is discussed separately below.

Term Loans

Term loans are debt obligations having one- to ten-year maturities. The primary issuers of term loans are commercial banks, savings and loan associations, insurance companies, pension funds, the U.S. Small Business Administration (SBA), Small Business Investment Companies (SBICs), Industrial Development Authorities

(IDAs), and equipment suppliers. Term loans are used most often to finance small facility and equipment additions. Large additions usually are financed through stock or bond issues or retained earnings. Term loans are used to finance moderate increases in current assets under these circumstances:

- The cost of stock or bond issuance is prohibitive.
- The loan will be paid off from intermediate-term earnings.
- The increase in working current assets is intermediate term rather than permanent.

Most term loans are secured. In addition, lenders will attach other conditions to term loans. Among them are compensating balances on commercial bank loans, various security provisions, protective covenants, and default provisions. Security provisions include these five:

1. Assignment of payments due
2. Assignment of portions of inventory or receivables
3. Assignment of cash surrender values of key executive life insurance policies
4. Liens on the borrower's inventory, receivables, property, plant, and equipment
5. Pledges of marketable security investments held by the borrower

Protective covenants may be positive or negative.

Default provisions allow the lender to demand immediate repayment of the term loan when certain conditions occur. Among the conditions are:

- Failure of the borrower to pay interest, principal, or both as specified in the loan agreement
- Discovery by the lender of financial statement misrepresentations made by the borrower
- Failure of the borrower to observe any of the covenants specified in the loan agreement

Since term loans are negotiated privately between the borrower and the lender, they are less costly than public offerings of stock or the issuance of bonds. The interest on term loans is usually a bit higher than the prime bank lending rate. Generally the rates are 0.25 to 2.5 percentage points above the prime rate.

Term loans normally require that the principal be amortized (paid off) over the life of the loan. In other words, a term loan is basically an installment loan. The installments may be monthly, quarterly, semiannual, or annual.

For example: Suppose a company borrows $100,000 at 9% per annum payable in eight equal installments, the first occurring at the end of the first year. Given that the present value (PV) of the annuity of eight payments at 9% equals $100,000, the annual payment (R) is computed as:

$$R = \$100,000 \: / \: 5.535 = \$18,067$$

The 5.535 is the PV of annuity factor for $i = 9\%$ and $n = 8$ periods and can be found in the Present Value of Annuity Table in Appendix A.

Each payment of $18,067 would consist of principal repayment and interest as shown in Figure 2B-17.

Figure 2B-17 Amortization Table

End of Year	Annual Annuity Amount	Interest	Principal Repayment	Remaining Balance
0	$0	$0	$0	$100,000
1	18,067	9,000	9,067	90,933
2	18,067	8.183	9,884	81,049
3	18,067	7,294	10,773	70,276
4	18,067	6,324	11,743	58,533
5	18,067	5,267	12,800	45,733
6	18,067	4,116	13,951	31,782
7	18,067	2,860	15,207	16,575
8	18,067	1,492	16,575	$0
Total	$144,536	$44,536	$100,000	

Equipment Financing Loans

Equipment financing loans often use the equipment purchased as collateral for the intermediate-term loan. Such loans are secured either through a conditional sales contract or a chattel mortgage. In a conditional sales contract (sometimes referred to as a purchase money mortgage), the seller holds the title to the equipment until the buyer makes all of the payments stipulated in the loan agreement. Such contracts are used almost exclusively by equipment sellers.

A chattel mortgage is a lien on personal (as opposed to real) property. Real property (real estate) consists of land and buildings. Equipment is personal property. Chattel mortgages occur most commonly when a commercial bank makes a direct equipment financing loan to a borrower.

Mathematically, equipment loans are handled as a term loan, as shown in the previous example.

Leases

Leasing is a way of obtaining the use of an asset for a specified period of time without actually having an ownership interest in the asset. The lessor (property owner) allows the user (lessee) to use the asset for the specified period. In return, the lessee agrees to make periodic lease payments to the lessor. Leases may be operating, capital (financing), or leveraged. The advantages and disadvantage of leases and the calculation of the net advantage to leasing also are covered.

Operating Leases

An operating lease, sometimes called a "service or maintenance lease," provides the lessee with the use of the leased asset on a period-by-period basis. The period of an operating lease usually is considerably shorter than the asset's economic life. An example of an operating lease is a rental of an asset. For example, a company might rent a truck for three months (the duration of its business season). Determination of the rental (lease) payments is discussed under capital leases. An operating lease is technically a short-term financing method. The focus here, then, is on capital leases.

Capital Leases

A **capital (financing) lease** is essentially a "disguised" installment purchase. Capital leases are noncancellable and involve the transfer of the rights and obligations of ownership from the lessor to the lessee. Title to the asset, however, remains with the lessor. The lessor sets the lease payments on a capital lease so as to amortize the cost of the asset over the lease term and to provide it with a sufficient return on its investment.

The determination of the lease payment involves three steps:

1. Compute the lessor's amount to be amortized.
2. Compute the annual after-tax lease income the lessor must earn to receive the desired return on its investment.
3. Convert the lease income required to the lease payment.

For example: Suppose a lessor desires to lease out a piece of equipment costing $100,000 for five years with five annual lease payment each made at the beginning of the year. The lessor will depreciate the asset using straight line (with no salvage value) over five years for both book and tax. However, the asset can be sold by the lessor at the end of its life for $10,000. Assuming the lessor requires an 11% return on its investment and faces a 40% effective tax rate, what would be the required lease payment?

The required lease payment would be calculated as shown.

Step 1. Compute the lessor's amount to be amortized.

The amount to be amortized would be the initial cost of the equipment ($100,000) less the PV of the tax savings on the depreciation and the PV of the after-tax residual.

- The annual depreciation would be $20,000 (100,000 / 5).
- The tax savings per year would be $8,000 (the tax rate of 40% × $20,000).
- The PV of the tax shield would be $29,568 [$8,000 × 3.696 (PV of annuity for $i = 11\%$ and $n = 5$ periods)].
- The PV of the after-tax residual would be $3,558 = [$10,000 (1 − 0.4) × 0.593 (PV of a lump sum for $i = 11\%$ and $n = 5$ periods)] = $6,000(0.593).
- Therefore, the amount to be amortized = $100,000 − $29,568 − $3,558 = $66,874.

Step 2. Compute the annual after-tax income the lessor must earn to receive the desired 11% return on the $66,874.

The PV of the annual after-tax income required (R) at the 11% required rate must be equal to $66,874. Since lease payment are made at the beginning of each year, the Rs form an annuity starting at time = 0 and ending at time = 4.

Therefore,

$$R + 3.102R = \$66,874$$
$$4.102R = \$66,874$$
$$R = \$16,303$$

The 3.102 is the PV of annuity factor for $i = 11\%$ and $n = 4$ periods.

Step 3. Convert the lease income required to the lease payment.

The lease payment would equal the required income divided by 1 minus the effective tax rate. Therefore, lease payment = $\$16,303 / (1 - 0.4) = \$16,303 / 0.6 = \$27,172$.

Leasing Advantages

Leasing offers five advantages.

1. The primary advantage of leasing is flexible financing, because leasing agreements generally have fewer restrictive covenants than loan agreements.
2. Another advantage is in cash flow management. The lessee may be able to make lower payments on a lease as opposed to a term loan because of income tax benefits and/or a lowered interest rate.
3. Some leases provide 100% financing, whereas loans usually require a down payment.
4. A lessee avoids the risk of the asset becoming obsolete.
5. Leasing may be expedient as it often avoids some or all of the time-consuming capital budgeting process.

Leasing Disadvantages

There are two disadvantages of leasing.

1. *Cost.* A company with good credit opportunities may find purchasing to be more cost efficient than leasing.
2. *Loss of flexibility.* It is not unusual for a lessor to deny the lessee the right to make changes to a leased asset, and there is often a penalty for the early cancellation of a lease.

Net Advantage of Leasing

Lease evaluation by the lessee is essentially a lease versus borrow and buy decision analysis. It involves the calculation of the **net advantage of leasing (NAL)**. The NAL compares the PV cost of leasing an asset with the PV cost of borrowing to own the asset. If the cost of borrowing to own is greater than the cost of leasing, the NAL is positive and the asset should be leased.

The NAL is calculated as shown:

1. Installed cost of asset
2. Less: PV of the after-tax lease payment at the cost of borrowing
3. Less: PV of the depreciation tax shield at the cost of borrowing

4. Plus: PV of the after-tax operating costs incurred if owned and not leased at the cost of borrowing
5. Less: PV of the after-tax salvage value at the organization's target rate of return
6. Equals: NAL

The NAL model assumes that the lease is treated as an operating lease for tax purposes by the lessee. The assumption is critical. Both the cost of borrowing and the target rate of return used in the model are after tax.

The installed cost of the asset includes the purchase price less discounts plus freight, installation, and tryout costs. The installed cost is the depreciation base.

NAL Example

For example: A firm leases an asset for six years. The asset has an installed cost of $50,000, and the annual lease payment (due at the beginning of each year) are $10,000. Assume that the asset will be depreciated using the Modified Accelerated Cost Recovery System (MACRS) with a 5-year life. Assume also that the firm faces a 40% tax rate, its after-tax cost of debt is 6%, its after-tax target rate of return is 15%, and the asset's salvage value (pretax) is $20,000.

The NAL for this lease shown in Figure 2B-18 is –$1,296, indicating a net disadvantage to leasing. Therefore, the firm should borrow and purchase the asset.

Other Long-Term Sources

Other long-term sources for raising capital, such as convertible debt and convertible preferred stock, are discussed below.

Convertible Debt

Convertible debt is normally a debenture (unsecured bond) that is convertible to the debt issuer's common stock at the debt holder's option. A convertible bond is, in essence, a deferred equity offering. The issuer of the convertible bonds is expecting that these securities will be converted to common stock, which would make it unnecessary to repay the bond principal at a later date.

Convertible bonds are exchangeable for common stock at a stated conversion price. For example, suppose the ABC Corporation issues convertible bonds with a conversion price of $25. That means that each $1,000 bond is convertible to 40 (1,000 / 25) shares of common stock. The conversion ratio is 40.

Normally, the conversion price is set at 15% to 30% above the common stock price at the time of the bond issuance (roughly $19 to $22 in the example). When the common stock price exceeds the conversion price of $25, it would be profitable for bondholders to convert. In order to insure (force) conversion, convertible bond usually are callable at a set price.

Figure 2B-18 NAL Calculation

End of Year	Installed Asset Cost	Lease Payment After-Tax	Depreciation	Depreciation Tax Shield	Additional After-Tax Operating Costs If Owned	NAL Cash Flows Except Salvage	PV Lump-Sum Factor @ 6%	PV	After-Tax Salvage .6 (20,000)	PV Lump-Sum Factor @ 15%	PV of Salvage	NAL
(1)	(2)	(3)	(4)	(5)	(6)	(7) = (2) − (3) − (5) + (6)	(8)	(9) = (7) × (8)	(10)	(10)	(12)	(13) = (9) − (12)
0	$50,000	$6,000				$44,000	1.000	$44,000				$44,000
1		6,000	$10,000	$4,000	$450	−9,550	.943	−9,006				−9,006
2		6,000	16,000	6,400	450	−11,950	.890	−10,636				−10,636
3		6,000	9,600	3,840	450	−9,390	.840	−7,888				−7,888
4		6,000	5,760	2,304	450	−7,854	.792	−6,220				−6,220
5		6,000	5,760	2,304	450	−7,854	.747	−5,867				−5,867
												−5,679
6			2,880	1,152	450	−702	.705	−495	$12,000	.432	$5,184	−1,296

(1) End of Year

(2) Installed Asset Cost

(3) The after-tax lease payment equals the total lease payment ($10,000) times 1 minus the marginal tax rate (40%). The benefit of the tax deductibility of lease payment is assumed to be received at approximately the same time the lease payment are made, reflecting the quarterly payment of taxes.

(4) MACRS depreciation is computed using the 5-year MACRS rates times the asset cost. The MACRS rates are 20%, 32%, 19.2%, 11.52%, 11.52%, and 5.76%, respectively, over the six years.

(5) The depreciation tax shield is equal to the depreciation in column (4) times the marginal tax rate (40%).

(6) Column (6) is equal to $750 pretax cost times 1 minus the marginal tax rate (40%).

(7) Column (7) is the total of the cash flows needed to compute the NAL that are discounted at the after-tax cost of debt. It is equal to the asset cost (2), less the after-tax lease payments (3), less the depreciation tax shield (5), plus the additional after-tax operating costs incurred if the asset is owned (6).

(8) The after-tax cost of debt is 6% [10% pretax cost times 1 minus the marginal tax rate (40%)].

(9) The PV is equal to the cash flows in column (7) times the present value interest factor (PVIF) factors in column (8).

(10) The after-tax salvage value is equal to the pretax salvage ($20,000) times 1 minus the marginal tax rate (40%).

(12) The PV of the salvage is equal to the after-tax salvage times the PVIF for 15% and 6 years, where the 15% represents the weighted average cost of capital.

(13) The NAL is equal to the sum of the PV cast flows from column (9) minus the PV of the after-tax salvage from column (12).

Source: From R. Charles Moyer, James R. McGuigan, and William J. Kretlow. *Contemporary Financial Management (with Thomson ONE - Business School Edition and InfoTrac®)*, 10E. © 2006 South-Western, a part of Cengage Learning, Inc. Reproduced by permission. www.cengage.com/permissions

Because convertible bonds possess both debt and equity characteristics, their market value is a function of both the common stock value (conversion value) and their value as straight debt. The buyer of the convertible will pay a premium for the equity portion. The equity portion of a convertible bond is the difference between the market price of the convertible and what its value would be as a straight bond. For example, suppose a convertible bond sells for $1,012 per $1,000 bond and its value as a straight bond is $718. The equity portion of the convertible issue would be $294 ($1,012 − $718) per bond.

Convertible Preferred Stock

A convertible preferred stock behaves like a convertible bond. Convertible preferred stocks are not commonly issued. It is important to note, however, that prior to any conversion, convertible bonds are considered to be a part of a corporation's liabilities, not equity.

Other Capital-Raising Matters

Other matters related to rasing capital focus on: the capital markets within which the raising of capital occurs; the role of investment bankers, underwriters, and credit rating agencies in the capital-raising process; insider trading; and a company's dividend policies and stock repurchase transactions.

Capital Markets

The discussion of capital markets that follows encompasses the key factors and contributions in regard to the issuance and trading of debt and equity securities in the capital-raising process.

Primary and Secondary Markets

The migration of a company from private to public ownership often occurs when a private company finds that it needs access to additional funds. The *primary market* and the *secondary market* are terms referring to where securities are created and where they are traded among investors. The initial offering of securities to investors occurs in the primary market. Subsequent trading is facilitated through the secondary market. These markets are further discussed below.

Role of Investment Banks and Underwriters

Investment banks are financial institutions that assist companies and governments in issuing securities, for the purpose of raising capital. The services of an investment bank include providing advice, selling securities, and underwriting. An underwriter bears some or all of the risks of selling and holding the securities in exchange for a premium.

Underwriters may form an underwriting syndicate, which is a group of financial institutions that join together to sell new securities and, possibly, offer to buy the unsold shares. Sometimes, especially with securities that have a higher risk such as unseasoned offerings, an underwriter signs a best efforts agreement that requires him or her to use all efforts to sell as much of an issue as possible to the public, but the underwriter does not take responsibility for unsold shares. An underwriter may issue a tombstone ad to announce (but not offer for sale) a new security issue. The ad gets its name from the bold black border surrounding the information.

As the need for expansion funds grows and exceeds money that can be raised through such sources as personal investments, trade credit, lines of credit, loans and venture capital, management goes to investment bankers who agree to underwrite a stock offering. By definition, the **primary market** is the market in which investors have the first opportunity to buy a newly issued security.

Underwriters help the firm prepare a prospectus. A stock prospectus is a formal written offer to sell securities to the public. It is filed with the SEC and made available to all investors. The prospectus includes details such as how the security is valued, the issue price per unit, usage, size, and goal of the issuing company.

The primary market is basically synonymous with an initial public offering (IPO). Through the underwriting process, investment banks buy all the public shares at a set price. The corporation receives money that can be used for financing operations. Investment banks earn money from the spread between the offering price of an IPO issue to public and the price of the IPO issue paid to the issuer. An investment bank may join an underwriting syndicate consisting of the originating house (the investment banker dealing with the issuer) and other investment banking firms selected by the issuer. The originating house is referred to as the syndicate manager or underwriting manager.

The investment bank or syndicate (group of investment banks) normally sets up a best efforts agreement with the IPO issuer. In a best efforts agreement, the investment bank or syndicate agrees to use all reasonable efforts to sell as much of the issue to the public. The investment bank or syndicate can purchase either an entire issue from the issuer or merely the amount of the issue required by the issuer's demand. The investment bankers often use tombstone ads to sell and issue. A tombstone ad is an advertisement placed in a financial journal or in the financial pages of a regular newspaper. Tombstone ads are often framed to look, at first glance, like graveyard tombstones.

Investment bank or syndicate placements may be private (to one or more private investor) or public (to the public in general).

After the IPO, the stock shares are traded in the secondary market, but the corporation does not receive any additional income. The stock price then is determined by how much investors are willing to pay for the stock at the time of purchase.

After a firm goes public, it may continue to issue new stocks in the primary market. The only difference is that the stocks are no longer IPOs but seasoned (subsequent or secondary) offerings.

By definition, the **secondary market** is a market in which an investor purchases an asset from another investor rather than an issuing corporation. This is the defining characteristic of the secondary market—investors trade among themselves. They buy and sell previously issued securities from other investors without the involvement of the issuing companies.

The secondary market is generally synonymous with the stock market and includes the New York Stock Exchange (NYSE), NASDAQ, and all major exchanges around the world.

Role of Credit Rating Agencies

Standard & Poor's, Moody's, and Fitch are the three largest bond credit rating agencies. The purpose of the agencies is to assign a rating to each debt security based on creditworthiness of the company or government issuing the security. This rating then is used to determine the market rate of interest on the debt security. When the market interest rate of a debt security is higher than its stated rate, the security will sell at a discount. When the market interest rate equals a debt security's stated rate, it will sell at par (face) value. When the market interest rate is lower than the stated rate, the security will sell at a premium.

Market Efficiency

The U.S. security markets are relatively efficient. The markets quickly reflect information relevant to the value of a security. The idea of market efficiency is called the "efficient market hypothesis (theory)." The hypothesis has three forms:

1. Strong form
2. Semistrong form
3. Weak form

The strong form of the theory states that all information (public or private) is incorporated in a security price. Therefore, it is not possible for insiders to earn abnormal profits. The semistrong form states that all publicly available information (no private information) is incorporated in a security price. Therefore, abnormal returns from insider trading are possible. The weak form of the theory says that security prices reflect all recent price movements only. Therefore, technical analysis will not provide a basis for abnormal returns.

Securities Registration

The Securities and Exchange Commission (SEC) is charged with the regulation of the sale of securities across U.S. state borders. The Securities Act of 1933 regulates the sale of new securities (initial offerings including initial public offerings [IPOs], i.e., the primary market). The Securities Exchange Act of 1934 regulates the secondary security markets and financial reporting by SEC registrants.

The Securities Act of 1933 requires that investors receive significant information concerning securities being offered for public sale and prohibits deceit and fraud in the sale of securities. In order to accomplish these objectives, companies desiring to issue securities to the public file registration statements that include:

- A description of the company's properties and business
- A description of the security to be offered for sale

- Information about the management of the company
- Financial statements certified by independent accountants

Some of the more common forms used for registering securities include Form S-1, S-2, and S-3. Form S-1 is used for IPOs and for companies that do not qualify for streamlined registrations. Form S-2 is available for companies that have not defaulted on any obligation or dividend on preferred stock and that have been filing timely SEC reports for at least three years. Requirements for the use of Form S-3 are similar to those of Form S-2 except the company needs to have filed timely reports for only at least one year, and it must have a public float or market value of its common stock of at least $75 million.

Whichever form is used, each includes all information about the offering in Part 1 of the offering prospectus and all of the other company-specific information needed in the prospectus. When using Forms S-2 and S-3, the company-specific information can be incorporated by reference to previously issued SEC reports available through the SEC's online database system, called EDGAR (www.sec.gov/edgar.shtml).

Insider Trading

Insider trading involves the directors and management of a corporation buying or selling the corporation's securities to gain an advantage over investors who are not privy to the information.

The Insider Trading Act of 1984 specifies civil penalties for illegal insider trading of up to three times the profit gained or three times the loss avoided from the illegal trading. The Insider Trading and Securities Fraud Enforcement Act of 1988 stipulates that brokers, dealers, and investment advisors must enact and enforce policies to prevent insider trading and to prevent the firm, its employees, or any associated persons from misusing material nonpublic information.

Dividend Policy

The discussion of dividend policy covers the types of dividends a corporation may issue, the impact of stock splits, various types of dividend policies a corporation may employ, and the dividend payout process.

Types of Dividends

With common stock, there is no guarantee that an investor will make money. The equity position in a common stock means that the owner shares in the corporation's fortunes and misfortunes.

Common stock **market value per share** is the current trading price of the stock. If the stock increases in value, shareholders benefit from capital appreciation of their investment and potentially receive a dividend.

A dividend (or payout) represents a share in profits. Corporations are not required to pay dividends unless declared by the board of directors. Payments vary based on earnings and how much the board decides to pay out. Corporations usually pay cash dividends quarterly, but they may also pay dividends in kind or in the form of stock.

- A **cash dividend** is paid in the form of cash, usually a check. Cash dividends typically are taxable.
- **Dividends in kind** involve a dividend paid in assets other than cash. In the past, Wrigley Chewing Gum paid dividends in gum.
- **Stock dividends** are paid as additional shares of stock (rather than cash). They allow a corporation to conserve cash for investment purposes while still rewarding investors. When a corporation issues a stock dividend, there typically are no tax consequences until shareholders sell their shares.
- **Liquidating dividends** are dividends that exceed the corporation's retained earnings. They are not taxable.

Stock Splits

Stock splits involve the issuance of new stock shares to replace the existing shares. A two-for-one stock split, for example, involves replacing each existing share with two new shares. The two-for-one split doubles authorized, issued, treasury, and outstanding shares and cuts the par or stated value of the stock in half.

Corporations typically split stocks to lower the price of a stock, make the price more appealing, and stimulate trading. The rationale is that when the price of the stock is high, individual investors may be reluctant to buy shares either because the shares cost so much or because of concern that the stock price has peaked in value.

Stocks can be split in various increments: two for one, three for one, three for two, and so on. In a two-for-one split, a stockholder with 100 shares would turn in the 100 shares and receive 200 new shares. If the stock is trading at $100 a share, the price drops to about $50 a share. If the stock price drops to exactly $50, the total market value remains the same (200 shares at $50 a share versus the original 100 shares at $100; both equal $10,000). Although the total market value initially remains the same, stockholders may profit if the price eventually goes up.

A stock also may undergo a **reverse split**. In a reverse split, the number of shares decreases, and the price increases accordingly. For example, in a one-for-two reverse split, 100 shares of stock trading at $1 a share become 50 shares worth $2 a share. A reverse split often is used to keep a stock at the stock market's minimum listing price or to increase the stock's general attractiveness to investors who shy away from low-priced stocks. Stock splits and reverse splits do not result in any taxable gain or loss.

In general, dividends are considered an incentive to own common stock. Corporations offering regular dividends generally have progressed beyond the growth phase, tend not to derive much benefit from reinvesting profits, and, therefore, choose to share those profits as dividends. Thus, the stage of a company's life cycle tends to affect its dividend policy.

If corporate earnings decline, a company may decide to reduce or omit its cash dividend, which may signal a decline in the company's future prospects and result in a lower stock price.

Dividend Policies

The issue that corporations face in selecting a dividend policy is how much the corporation should return to the shareholders versus how much it should reinvest in the business. The policy is determined by the board of directors, which generally meets quarterly to declare and approve a quarterly dividend or to approve the decision not to pay a dividend. The determinants of dividend policy are:

- *Shareholder preferences*. Dividend versus corporation growth.
- *Liquidity*. Short-run cash position.
- *Solvency*. The corporation cannot declare a dividend if insolvent
- *Borrowing capacity*. If low, the corporation may wish to reinvest earnings rather than issue dividends.
- *Earnings stability*. Stable earnings correlate with regular, stable dividends.
- *Growth opportunities*. If high, the corporation may wish to reinvest earnings rather than issue dividends.
- *Inflation*. If high, the corporation may need the earnings to reinvest.
- *Capital impairment restrictions*. Legal capital or appropriations (reservations) of retained earnings.
- *Restrictive covenants*. From term loans, bond indentures, or leasing agreements.
- *Taxes*. Dividends are ordinary income to the recipient whereas stock appreciations are treated as capital gains.

There are four basic dividend policies:

1. Passive residual
2. Stable dollar
3. Constant dividend payout ratio
4. Small regular plus extras

A company following the **passive residual** policy reinvests earnings as long as there are opportunities whose returns exceed the company's required rate of return. Any residual is returned to the shareholders.

A corporation using a **stable dollar** policy pays a regular constant dividend as long as the corporation has the ability to do so. There is evidence that most corporations and shareholders prefer the predictability of stable dividends. Changes in dividends are equated with changes in profitability and, consequently, changes in stock prices.

In contrast, a company using a **constant dividend payout ratio** will have dividends that vary from year to year. This method calculates dividend payments as a constant or fixed percentage of each year's earnings per share.

Historically, dividend payouts in the United States have been between 40% and 60% of earnings. However, because most corporations are reluctant to reduce dividends, dividend payout ratios tend to increase when earnings drop and decrease when earnings rise.

At the option of the investor, some companies provide a dividend reinvestment plan in which the investor does not receive the dividend as cash. Instead, the dividend is used to purchase new shares of the company stock, which allows the investor to have immediate reinvestment of earnings and lowered transaction costs and the company to maintain value and thereby increase stock price.

Many corporations pay a regular small quarterly dividend plus year-end extras in high-earnings years. Large companies, such as U.S. Steel and DuPont, often have followed this policy.

Dividend Payout Process

Four dates are relevant to the dividend payout process:

1. Declaration date
2. Payment date
3. Record date
4. Ex-dividend date

A dividend declaration would state that Company X declares a dividend today payable on a set date to shareholders of record on a date between the declaration and payment dates. On the declaration date, the corporation reduces its retained earnings and sets up the dividend payable.

The ex-dividend date is a date set by the stock exchange handling the stock. The date usually is four business days prior to the record date, which allows the exchange time to record ownership changes. For example, suppose the record date is March 3 and the ex-dividend date is February 27, investors who purchase the stock prior to February 27 are eligible for the March 3 dividend while investors purchasing the stock after February 27 are not entitled to the dividend. Investors would expect the stock price to decline by the dividend per share between February 27 and March 3 when it is selling ex-dividend. Research indicates that stock prices decline by slightly less than the dividend per share.

Stock Repurchases

Corporations often repurchase their own stock shares. Repurchased shares may be retired and returned to authorized shares or held in the corporation's treasury as treasury stock.

Shares normally are retired when a corporation is attempting to go private by eliminating nonmanagement shareholders and taking the corporation's stock off the exchange on which it had been trading.

Corporations hold repurchased shares (treasury stock) for use in the future. Potential uses of the shares include:

- Stock ownership plans, such as employee stock ownership plans
- Employee retirement plans
- Mergers and acquisitions
- Stock options and warrants

A corporation may also purchase its own shares in order to control the share price, especially when management believes the market price is unreasonably low.

Knowledge Check: Raising Capital

The next questions are intended to help you check your understanding and recall of the material presented in this topic. They do not represent the type of questions that appear on the CMA exam.

Directions: Answer each question in the space provided. Correct answers and section references appear after the knowledge check questions.

1. How much are the annual payments on a 6-year, 8%, $1,000,000 term loan? The present value of annuity factor 6 years at 8% is 4.623. The PV of a lump-sum factor for 6 years at 8% is .630.

   ☐ **a.** $216,310

   ☐ **b.** $246,667

   ☐ **c.** $80,000 for each of the first 5 years and $1,080,000 at the end of year 6

   ☐ **d.** Not determinable given the data

2. What is the first-year interest portion of the annual payment on a $200,000, 5-year, 7% term loan? The first-year principal payment on the term loan is $34,778.

   ☐ **a.** $14,002

   ☐ **b.** $20,777

   ☐ **c.** $12,545

   ☐ **d.** $22,232

3. A lessor calculates an annual after-tax income from a lease to be $18,500. Assuming the lessor faces a 35% effective annual tax rate, the lease payment required by the lessor would be how much?

   ☐ **a.** $12,025

   ☐ **b.** $28,462

   ☐ **c.** $52,857

   ☐ **d.** Not determinable given the data

4. In determining the net advantage of leasing (NAL), the expected after-tax salvage of the asset leased is discounted at what rate?

   ☐ **a.** The lessee's target rate of return

   ☐ **b.** The lessee's borrowing rate

   ☐ **c.** The lessee's after-tax borrowing rate

   ☐ **d.** The lessee's after-tax target rate of return

5. The straight debt value of a convertible bond at issue is normally

    ☐ **a.**   greater than the market value of the bond at issue.

    ☐ **b.**   less than the market value of the bond at issue.

    ☐ **c.**   the same as the market value of the bond at issue.

    ☐ **d.**   equal to its value as an equity instrument.

6. Primary security markets handle

    ☐ **a.**   only debt security issues.

    ☐ **b.**   only blue-chip stock issues.

    ☐ **c.**   debt or equity IPOs.

    ☐ **d.**   only equity securities.

7. Which of the following is **true** regarding the efficient market theory?

    ☐ **a.**   The semistrong form has been supported by research.

    ☐ **b.**   None of its forms has been supported by research.

    ☐ **c.**   The weak form has been supported by research.

    ☐ **d.**   The strong form has been supported by research.

8. The four dates related to the dividend process are the:

    I.   payment date.

    II. ex-dividend date.

    III. declaration date.

    IV. record date.

    The proper chronological order of these dates is:

    ☐ **a.**   III, IV, II, I

    ☐ **b.**   II, III, IV, I

    ☐ **c.**   II, III, I, IV

    ☐ **d.**   III, II, IV, I

9. Which of the following is **not** a basic dividend policy?

    ☐ **a.**   Passive residual

    ☐ **b.**   Small regular plus extras

    ☐ **c.**   Variable dividend payout ratio

    ☐ **d.**   Stable dollar

Knowledge Check Answers: Raising Capital

1. How much are the annual payments on a 6-year, 8%, $1,000,000 term loan? The present value of annuity factor 6 years at 8% is 4.623. The PV of a lump-factor for 6 years at 8% is 0.630. [**See *Term Loans*.**]

    ☑ **a.** $216,310

    ☐ **b.** $246,667

    ☐ **c.** $80,000 for each of the first 5 years and $1,080,000 at the end of year 6

    ☐ **d.** Not determinable given the data

2. What is the first-year interest portion of the annual payment on a $200,000, 5-year, 7% term loan? The first-year principal payment on the term loan is $34,778. [**See *Term Loans*.**]

    ☑ **a.** $14,002

    ☐ **b.** $20,777

    ☐ **c.** $12,545

    ☐ **d.** $22,232

3. A lessor calculates an annual after-tax income from a lease to be $18,500. Assuming the lessor faces a 35% effective annual tax rate, the lease payment required by the lessor would be how much? [**See *Capital Leases*.**]

    ☐ **a.** $12,025

    ☑ **b.** $28,462

    ☐ **c.** $52,857

    ☐ **d.** Not determinable given the data

4. In determining the net advantage of leasing (NAL), the expected after-tax salvage of the asset leased is discounted at what rate? [**See *Net Advantage of Leasing*.**]

    ☐ **a.** The lessee's target rate of return

    ☐ **b.** The lessee's borrowing rate

    ☐ **c.** The lessee's after-tax borrowing rate

    ☑ **d.** The lessee's after-tax target rate of return

5. The straight debt value of a convertible bond at issue is normally [**See *Convertible Debt*.**]

    ☐ **a.** greater than the market value of the bond at issue.

    ☑ **b.** less than the market value of the bond at issue.

    ☐ **c.** the same as the market value of the bond at issue.

    ☐ **d.** equal to its value as an equity instrument.

6. Primary security markets handle [**See *Role of Investment Banks and Underwriters.***]

   ☐ **a.** only debt security issues.

   ☐ **b.** only blue-chip stock issues.

   ☑ **c.** debt or equity IPOs.

   ☐ **d.** only equity securities.

7. Which of the following is **true** regarding the efficient market theory? [**See *Market Efficiency.***]

   ☑ **a.** The semistrong form has been supported by research.

   ☐ **b.** None of its forms has been supported by research.

   ☐ **c.** The weak form has been supported by research.

   ☐ **d.** The strong form has been supported by research.

8. The four dates related to the dividend process are the:

   I.   payment date.

   II.   ex-dividend date.

   III. declaration date.

   IV.   record date.

   The proper chronological order of these dates is: [**See *Dividend Payout Process.***]

   ☐ **a.** III, IV, II, I

   ☐ **b.** II, III, IV, I

   ☐ **c.** II, III, I, IV

   ☑ **d.** III, II, IV, I

9. Which of the following is **not** a basic dividend policy? [**See *Dividend Policy.***]

   ☐ **a.** Passive residual

   ☐ **b.** Small regular plus extras

   ☑ **c.** Variable dividend payout ratio

   ☐ **d.** Stable dollar

Working Capital Management

THE BASIC COMPONENTS OF AN ORGANIZATION's working capital are cash, marketable securities, accounts receivable, and inventory. This topic looks at working capital and the management of each of these components.

 READ the Learning Outcome Statements (LOS) for this topic as found in Appendix B and then study the concepts and calculations presented here to be sure you understand the content you could be tested on in the CMA exam.

Working Capital Terminology

The term *working capital* (or current capital) generally refers to the funds a company holds in current (short-term) asset accounts. *Net working capital* refers specifically to the difference between a firm's current assets and its current liabilities. Net working capital provides a measure of immediate liquidity and indicates how much cash a firm has available to sustain and build its business. Depending on a firm's level of current liabilities, the number may be positive or negative.

Working capital management refers to decisions made about a firm's short-term assets and liabilities. Working capital management policies are generally categorized as aggressive, conservative, or moderate.

An **aggressive working capital management** policy focuses on high profitability potential, despite the cost of high risk and low liquidity. Aggressive asset management results in capital being minimized in current assets versus long-term investments. Aggressive financing policies include higher levels of lower-cost short-term debt and less long-term capital investments. Although this lowers capital costs, it increases the risk of short-term liquidity problems. With an aggressive policy, current assets will be less than current liabilities.

A **conservative working capital management** policy focuses on low-risk, low-return working capital investment and financing. A conservative policy places a greater proportion of capital in liquid assets but at the sacrifice of some profitability.

Conservative policy uses higher-cost capital but postpones the principal repayment of debt or avoids it entirely by using equity. With a conservative policy, current assets will be much greater than current liabilities.

A **moderate** (or **matching**) **working capital management** policy uses risk and return and financing strategies that match the maturity of the assets with the maturity of the financing. The hedging approach to financing involves matching maturities of debt with specific financing needs. A moderate policy seeks a balance between current assets and current liabilities.

Effective working capital management is important for all businesses. Firms need to review the complete operations of their working capital management programs to ensure efficiencies in:

- *Cash management.* Managing cash inflows and outflows
- *Marketable securities management.* Managing short-term investments and borrowing portfolios
- *Accounts receivable management.* Managing cash receivables and disbursements
- *Inventory management.* Maintaining stock of items at desired levels (e.g., raw materials, work in progress, or finished products)

Working capital management consists of cash and securities management, receivables management, inventory management, and short-term credit management. Its goal is to minimize both the operating cycle and the cash cycle.

The operating cycle is the number of days of inventory on hand plus the receivables collection period. The cash cycle is the operating cycle less the accounts payable (A/P) payment cycle. Both cycles are minimized by decreasing the number of days' inventory on hand and the receivables collection period while maximizing the A/P payment cycle. Subsequent content examines each of these working capital components in more detail.

Cash Management

Cash management describes the collective activities by which a corporation administers and invests its cash. The primary goal of cash management is to use cash as efficiently as possible and in a manner that is consistent with the firm's strategic objectives and risk management profile.

Finance and treasury departments are integrally involved in cash management. Working together, they must ensure that the necessary cash resources are available in a timely manner to sustain business operations, starting with the purchase of raw materials and other resources and continuing through to payment for those materials and resources, the sale of goods and services, and the collection of sales receipts.

Factors Influencing Cash Levels

Liquidity requirements and a firm's profitability and risk policies are the primary determinants of its cash levels.

Liquidity Requirements

Liquidity refers to the ability to convert assets into cash quickly without incurring loss. A firm's cash inflows (incoming cash) and cash outflows (cash expenditures) are rarely synchronized—which means that they are not for the same amount and do not occur at the same time. A business needs to monitor net working capital to cover the imbalances of cash inflows and outflows and ensure sufficient liquidity. Ultimately, an efficient cash management system can increase a firm's overall liquidity. In turn, increased liquidity can lead to increased profitability and reduced risk of insolvency.

Profitability and Risk Policies

Profitability typically varies inversely with liquidity. A firm must determine the optimal levels of investment in current assets as well as the appropriate mix of short- and long-term financing necessary to support liquidity requirements. Such investments must take into account the interrelationship and trade-offs between profitability and risk. For example, offering more liberal credit terms to vendors may increase receivables. Thus, the firm may have to sell short-term securities, reduce cash balances, and/or increase short-term funding from banks to generate cash flows. Trying to reduce idle cash in bank accounts may result in increased transaction costs. Clearly, the optimum mix of debt or equity financing can vary greatly from one company or industry to another.

The effective management of liquidity, profitability, risk, and cash requires a cash management system that must address the day-to-day management of:

- *Collections.* How to bring funds into the firm from customers or other sources
- *Concentration.* How to concentrate funds where they can be used most effectively by moving cash from deposit banks (field banks) and other banks in the firm's collection system to a primary concentration bank
- *Disbursements.* How to move funds from the concentration bank to the firm's disbursement bank(s) for payments to employees, vendors, investors, and other payees
- *Banking relations.* How to manage relationships with banks and other financial service providers
- *Cash forecasting.* How to forecast future cash flows and predict potential shortages or surpluses
- *Information management.* How to develop and maintain appropriate information systems for collecting and analyzing financial data
- *Investing and borrowing.* How to invest excess cash balances and meet short-term borrowing requirements
- *Compensation.* How to cover wages and other financial benefits earned from labor

Once again, the magnitude of these operations will vary according to the size and nature of the business enterprise. A large international corporation would, of course, have a much more complex cash management system than a small domestic company that occupies one facility.

Motives for Holding Cash

Corporations need sufficient financial resources (e.g., cash balances in banks and securities as well as backup lines of credit and other short-term borrowing arrangements) to maintain adequate liquidity. The reasons businesses need to manage liquidity typically are summarized as being driven by transactions, precautionary, or speculative motives.

- The **transactions motive** for holding cash addresses the unsynchronized nature of cash flows. A firm must have sufficient cash reserves or near-cash reserves to meet financial payments arising from ordinary business operations (e.g., small purchases, employee compensation, taxes, and dividends).
- The **precautionary motive** for holding cash is to provide a buffer for unexpected cash needs. The unpredictable nature of cash inflows and outflows means that a firm must maintain sufficient levels of cash or near-cash balances to cover expenses.
- The **speculative motive** involves the use of surplus liquid reserves to take advantage of short-term investments or other temporary situations that may arise. For example, the price of a raw material suddenly may decline and offer a substantial savings if purchased with reserve funds.

Ensuring proper levels of liquidity necessitates continuous measuring, monitoring, and forecasting activities. Excess liquidity and insufficient liquidity both have disadvantages:

- Excess liquidity can translate into a loss of potential earnings because funds are not used profitably.
- Insufficient liquidity can result in a variety of negative costs, such as delayed payments, additional interest from unexpected borrowing, or brokerage and administrative costs if securities must be sold. In the worst-case scenario, excessive liquidity deficits can lead to insolvency and bankruptcy.

Management of Cash Flows

Forecasting data and financial controls contained in a cash budget provides a starting point for cash management. But efficient cash management also involves day-to-day activities pertaining to collection, disbursement, and temporary investments. These types of cash flows must be managed:

- **Cash inflows.** Funds collected from customers; funds obtained from banks, lenders, and other financial sources; and funds received from investors and other sources
- **Concentration flows.** Internal transfers among a firm's business units and between various bank accounts the firm owns to create liquid reserves
- **Cash outflows.** Funds distributed from the firm's liquid reserves to employees, vendors, shareholders, and other payees of the company

The timing of these cash flows is important to maintain adequate liquidity, optimize cash resources, and manage risk. The challenge in cash flow timing is to be able to meet current and future financial obligations in a timely manner while minimizing nonearning (idle) cash balances, borrowing any necessary funds at an acceptable cost, and controlling the firm's exposure to financial risks.

A firm generally benefits from shortening the timing of cash inflows and lengthening the timing of cash outflows. Speeding up accounts receivable (A/R) allows a business access to funds sooner; slowing down A/P provides a longer time frame for the firm to use the money it has on hand. Naturally, both must be managed carefully so as not to jeopardize vendor and customer relations and the firm's credit standing with suppliers and lenders.

Businesses can use various techniques to speed up collections and control disbursements.

Methods to Speed Up Cash Collections

A **collection system** is the set of banking arrangements and processing procedures used to process customer payments and gather incoming cash.

A firm's collection system affects the timing of cash inflows. Firms generally attempt to speed up cash collections by reducing collection float. **Collection float** is the time interval between when the maker mails a check and when the funds are available for the receiving firm to use.

Collection float has three components:

1. **Mail float.** The time between when a check is mailed and when it is received by the payee or a processing site
2. **Processing float.** The time between when the payee or processing site receives a check and when it is deposited at a financial institution
3. **Availability float.** The time interval between when the check is deposited and when the firm's account is credited with the collected funds

Figure 2B-19 presents a simple representation of collection float.

Figure 2B-19 Components of Collection Float

Payor mails check	Firm receives check	Firm deposits check	Funds available
Mail float	Processing float	Availability float	

In attempting to reduce collection float, important considerations include the optimal number and location of collection points, whether to use a lockbox system or an electronic payment system, and how to manage the concentration banking system.

Collection Points

Depending on the nature of the business, firms collect payments from customers over the counter, through the mail, and electronically (via home banking, telecommunications, personal computers, and the Internet). Over-the-counter receipts may be cash, checks, or credit cards. Mail receipts are normally checks or credit cards. Electronic receipts are usually credit cards. In general, the more collection points available, the shorter the collection float, especially if collection points are closer to customers or near Federal Reserve banks (for faster check-clearing purposes). However, there may be higher operating costs associated with additional collection points.

Lockbox System

A **lockbox system** is an arrangement between a firm and a banking institution in which all deposits are received directly by the bank and immediately deposited into the firm's account.

The arrangement sets up the bank's post office box number for all remittances rather than the firm's address. The lockbox process is transparent to customers because the remittance envelopes and statements show the firm's name, not the bank's name. Some firms have multiple collection locations in the form of a lockbox network.

In setting up a lockbox system, a firm usually requests that the bank photocopy all checks received, attach a photocopy of the check to the remittance, and include the envelope (which often notes an address change) or anything else sent with the payment.

A lockbox system ensures that deposits are handled on the day they are received, which dramatically reduces processing float. Depending on the lockbox location(s), mail float and availability float also can be shortened. Once the day's receipts are deposited, the bank forwards a validated deposit slip and, if requested, the check photocopies and remittance documents to the company.

The main drawback of a lockbox system is the cost associated with the additional banking services. Lockboxes have fixed and variable costs.

Fixed lockbox costs may include recurring (e.g., annual or monthly) fees for renting the post office box, preparing deposits, transmitting remittance data, balance reporting, and other account maintenance activities. Typically all fixed costs are bundled into a single lockbox maintenance charge.

Examples of variable lockbox costs include per-item deposit and processing charges, charges for transmitting remittance data, and photocopying and microfilming charges.

To decide whether to use a lockbox system, a firm needs to compare the added costs of the system with the potential income that can be gained from having accelerated funds availability, as shown:

Net Benefit from Lockbox = Reduction in Float Opportunity Cost
+ Reduction in Internal Processing Costs
− Lockbox Processing Costs

Float opportunity cost is a function of:

- Dollar amount of the collected items.
- Total collection time for the items.
- A firm's current investment or borrowing rate.

The lockbox system is profitable if the income is greater than the costs.

For example: A company is considering a lockbox proposal. The company has $96 million in annual sales ($8 million per month). The annual volume of checks is 12,000, and the batch of checks is of average size is $8,000. Internal check processing cost (assuming no lockbox) is $0.20 per item. The annual opportunity cost for the company is 8%.

A lockbox processor proposes to charge $8,500 per year plus a $0.45 processing cost per item.

Figure 2B-20 Lockbox Example

		Without a Lockbox	
Batch	**Dollar Amount**	**Collection Float Days**	**Total Dollars**
1	$1,400,000	× 1 =	$5,600,000
2	4,400,000	× 2 =	8,800,000
3	2,200,000	× 6 =	13,200,000
Total Deposits	$8,000,000	Total Float Cost	$27,600,000
		Divided by 30 calendar days	$920,000
		Annual cost of float ($920,000 × 0.08)	$73,600

		With a Lockbox	
Batch	**Dollar Amount**	**Collection Float Days**	**Total Dollars**
1	$1,400,000	× 3 =	$4,200,000
2	4,400,000	× 1 =	4,400,000
3	2,200,000	× 4 =	8,800,000
Total Deposits	$8,000,000	Total Float Cost	$17,400,000
		Divided by 30 calendar days	$580,000
		Annual cost of float ($580,000 × 0.08)	$46,400
		Annual cost of float without a lockbox	$73,600
		Annual cost of float with a lockbox	($46,400)
		Lockbox float savings	$27,200
		Fixed lockbox costs	($8,500)
		Variable lockbox costs (12,000 × $0.45)	($5,400)
		Savings of internal processing costs (12,000 × $0.20)	$2,400
		Net dollar benefit of a lockbox	$15,700

Based on the cost-benefit analysis that examined the trade-off between the savings from float reduction and the cost of the lockbox, the economic benefit to the company is $15,700.

An **electronic payment system** facilitates a payment or a transfer in an electronic format. Because electronic systems bypass mail and manual processing, they can guarantee funds availability on the payment date. In the United States, two of the primary electronic payment methods are the automated clearing house system and Fedwire.

The **automated clearing house (ACH)** system provides an electronic alternative to checks. Payment information is processed and settled electronically. In the United States, the Federal Reserve is the main operator of ACH. Increased reliability, efficiency, and cost-effectiveness are the primary benefits. ACH also offers the capability to transfer more information about a payment than is possible on a check.

Fedwire is the Federal Reserve's funds transfer system. It provides a real-time method of immediately transferring funds between two financial institutions via their respective Federal Reserve bank accounts. Although reliable and secure, the system is relatively expensive to use.

A **concentration banking system** systematically transfers deposits received from field banks and/or lockbox banks to the firm's disbursement bank to create a centralized inventory of liquid reserves held as cash or for short-term credit or investment transactions.

Some banks require a **compensating balance**, which is a non-interest-bearing deposit maintained in the company's deposit accounts at the bank for account service charges, lines of credit, or investments. The balance requirement can be specified as a percentage of the total commitment, the unused amount of the commitment, or the outstanding borrowings.

In general, cash concentration reduces idle balances in field banks, improves control over a firm's cash inflows and outflows, and facilitates more effective investments. Naturally, there are administrative and control costs associated with a cash concentration system. Cost should be weighed against the expected value of the benefits provided.

Methods to Slow Down Payments

A **disbursement system** is the set of banking arrangements, payment mechanisms, and processing procedures used to disburse funds to employees, vendors, suppliers, tax agencies, and other payees (e.g., shareholders and/or bondholders).

A firm's disbursement system affects the timing of cash outflows and disbursement float. **Disbursement float** is the time interval between when the maker mails a check and when funds are deducted from the maker's account.

Disbursement float has three components. The first two are mail float and processing float, the same two components that are part of collection float. The third component, which is different in disbursement float, is called **clearing float**—the time interval between when the check is deposited by the payee and when the firm's account is debited.

A simple representation of disbursement float is shown in Figure 2B-21.

Typical costs associated with disbursement systems are time-value costs, excess balances, transaction costs, payee relations, and information and control costs.

Figure 2B-21 Components of Disbursement Float

Banks and other institutions offer companies a variety of services to help control disbursement system costs. In particular, a zero balance account system is one way a firm can improve management of the disbursement process.

A **zero balance account (ZBA)** is a disbursement account against which a firm can write checks even though the balance is maintained at zero. A transfer from a master account located in the same bank covers any checks debited against the ZBA.

Firms often have several subsidiary ZBAs (e.g., separate ZBAs for payroll, dividends, and other payables) under one master disbursing account. Furthermore, some ZBAs may be used for collections as well as disbursements. Funding is automatic. Credits and debits are posted daily; the bank transfers just enough funds between the master account and the ZBA to keep the balance of the ZBA at zero.

The benefits of a ZBA system include control over account balances and the elimination of idle excess balances in subsidiary accounts. Firms can invest the master account balance in securities more accurately. ZBAs also can facilitate decentralization of payables for firms with multiple locations by providing local check-writing authorization while maintaining funding control at headquarters. However, those individuals in a company with final cash management authority must forecast the timing of check clearing accurately and ensure that the master account has sufficient reserves to cover the associated ZBAs.

Although the overall goal of a disbursement system is to make payments in a timely, accurate, and cost-effective manner, firms sometimes deliberately attempt to slow down the clearance of payments. Centralized payables and the use of payable through drafts are two methods of slowing down payments.

- Having **centralized payables** means payments are made through a single account (usually headquarters or a centralized processing center). Centralizing the payment function provides greater assurance that checks and funds will be disbursed when desired than with a decentralized payables system, where the likelihood of excess balances is greater (as well as increased transfer, reconciliation, and administrative costs). Concentrations of excess cash can be used for loan repayments or investments. In some cases, the improved access to cash position information possible with a centralized account can allow a firm to earn a greater investment return by being able to hold the money longer. However, a centralized payables system requires careful monitoring to ensure that delayed payments do not result in the loss of cash discounts or damage relations with payees.

- A **payable through draft (PTD)** is a payment instrument that is drawn against the maker, not the maker's bank. Unlike an ordinary check, a PTD is not payable on demand when presented at a bank. Therefore, the responsibility for paying the draft lies with the firm making the check. When the maker's bank receives the check, the bank must present it to the issuer for final acceptance. At that time, the firm deposits the funds to cover the draft. Using a PTD delays the time the firm has to have funds available and allows it to maintain smaller bank balances. The potential downside of a PTD is that banks typically impose higher service charges and suppliers may prefer checks.

Electronic Commerce

From a cash management perspective, **electronic commerce** (or **e-commerce**) refers to the application of information and network technology to facilitate business relationships among trading partners. Many formats and communication protocols are included under the umbrella of e-commerce, including the Internet, internal intranet networks, Web-based commerce, and electronic data interchange (EDI) and the EDI subsets of electronic funds transfer (EFT) and financial EDI (FEDI).

Although many transactions among North American companies are still paper based, e-commerce provides an alternative. The primary benefits of e-commerce include:

- Increased productivity because it basically eliminates manual processing
- Reduced cycle time
- Lower error rates
- Improved cash flow forecasting
- Improved communication capabilities

Hardware and software requirements and their associated costs, security issues, and the education and training of internal personnel and trading partners are the basic considerations in implementing e-commerce. Properly implemented and supported, e-commerce can facilitate stronger ties between a company and its vendors and customers.

Complex or simple, a cash management system should fulfill these objectives:

- Speed cash inflows.
- Slow cash outflows.
- Minimize idle cash.
- Minimize administrative costs connected with cash flows.
- Maintain good relations with customers and suppliers.
- Minimize the costs of providing backup liquidity.
- Maximize the value of financial information provided to management.

Marketable Securities Management

Corporations need cash to meet their ongoing financial obligations. Although some amount of cash reserves is prudent, holding an excessive level involves several costs. Holding too much cash idle in bank accounts not only incurs maintenance costs but also results in a loss of potential interest income. That is why companies hold a short-term investment portfolio of interest-earning marketable securities.

Marketable securities are investments that mature in a year or less. They generally are classified as short-term investments (although balance sheet accounting differentiates securities with original maturities of three months or less as cash equivalents and those maturing in a year or less as short-term investments).

Why Companies Hold Marketable Securities

Specifically, companies invest in marketable securities for three main reasons:

1. *Reserve liquidity.* To provide a source of near cash (or instant cash) and cover any working capital imbalances resulting from insufficient cash inflows or unforeseen cash needs
2. *Controllable outflows.* To earn interest on funds that are being held for predictable downstream cash outflows (such as interest payments, taxes, dividends, or insurance policies)
3. *Income generation.* To earn interest on surplus cash for which the company has no immediate use

Variables in Marketable Securities Selection

Before investing in a marketable security, careful consideration should be given to the choice. Safety, marketability, yield, maturity, and taxability are characteristics that firms typically evaluate.

Safety

Safety (preservation of principal) is considered the guiding principle or most basic test in selecting a security. Although a certain degree of risk is inherent in any investment, a firm must assess the specific risk associated with a security and weigh that risk against the potential for financial returns (or losses). Firms tend to look for short-term instruments that offer both safety and some level of income generation.

Marketability

The marketability of a security refers to the owner's ability to sell the security in large volumes relatively quickly without a substantial price concession. High marketability is a function of the availability of a large secondary market. A security with less active secondary markets is considered to be less liquid.

Yield

A security's yield (return) is related to its interest rate. Some securities offer variable interest, others pay a fixed rate, and some (e.g., U.S. Treasury bills) pay no interest but are sold at a discount and redeemed at face value. For variable-rate securities, the longer the time to maturity, the greater the potential price variation due to interest rate movements. Yield has an inverse relationship with liquidity; the more liquid a security, the lower its yield. In turn, yield has a positive relationship to risk. In general, the higher the risk, the higher the expected return. Yields on safe, short-term securities tend to be quite low.

Maturity

The term *maturity* refers to the life of the security and represents the date on which the obligation it represents is settled. Maturity dates vary. Short-term securities often are chosen based on a maturity date on which the firm has forecasted a need for cash. Some securities may be designated for quick liquidity while others may be earmarked for less immediate use.

Taxability

A company should evaluate the tax implications of the security. A firm's effective tax rate will determine the advantage of tax-exempt alternatives and the after-tax rate from taxable investments. The interest earned on all securities except municipal notes and bonds is taxable.

Types of Marketable Securities

There are two major markets for debt and equity instruments: the capital market and the money market. Stocks and long-term bonds are bought and sold in the capital market. The money market is where short-term debt securities that mature in one year or less trade.

Unlike the capital market, which has specific exchanges (e.g., the New York Stock Exchange), the money market is a group of markets. Major issuers of money market securities are the U.S. government, foreign government securities dealers, commercial paper (CP) dealers, bankers' acceptance (BA) dealers, and other money market brokers specializing in short-term instruments.

Figure 2B-22 provides an overview of various types of money market securities.

Figure 2B-22 Types of Marketable Securities

Instrument	Description
U.S. Treasury securities	Direct obligations of the U.S. Treasury; backed by the full faith and credit of the U.S. government.
	Interest rates provide a reference point and market indicator for other securities.
	Considered "safe" investments because they are free of default risk, are actively traded on a large secondary market, and are highly marketable.
	Common types include:
	Treasury bills (or T-bills): do not bear interest; sold at a discount and mature to face value in one year or less.
	Treasury notes (or T-notes): bear interest semiannually; mature within one to ten years.
	Treasury bonds (or T-bonds): similar to T-notes but have maturities longer than ten years; generally not purchased for a short-term portfolio except when the bond is close to maturity.

Federal agency securities (agency securities)	Interest-bearing securities usually offered and redeemed at face value.
	Generally not backed by the full faith and credit of the U.S. government but still considered relatively safe investments and free of default risk.
	Typically smaller issues than Treasury securities; not quite as marketable but still highly liquid.
	Limited tax exposure; many are exempt from state/local income taxes but not state franchise taxes.
Repurchase agreements (repos)	Purchase of a security from another party, usually a bank or security dealer who agrees to buy it back at a specified date for a fixed price.
	Commonly involve U.S. Treasury securities as the underlying security to be repurchased at a rate slightly less than the U.S. Treasury securities offer.
	Varying maturity, starting with overnight repurchase agreements.
	Generally considered a relatively safe investment (because of the government underlier).
	Often transferred to a third party to ensure that securities are available for sale if the issuer defaults.
Bankers' acceptances (BAs)	Essentially time drafts that result from commercial trade financing; frequently involve international transactions.
	Involve a letter of credit "accepted" by a bank; typically implies the BA is backed by that bank.
	Varying maturities and denominations.
	Liquidity is provided by an active secondary market of dealers.
Commercial paper	Unsecured short-term loan issued by a corporation.
	Negotiable instrument but typically held to maturity because of a weak secondary market; typically higher yield than similar securities because of its low marketability.
	Maturity ranges from 1 to 270 days.
	May be interest bearing or discounted; usually are discounted.
	Generally rated by credit rating agencies (e.g., Moody's or Standard & Poor's) to help investors assess risk.
Auction rate preferred stock	Equity usually purchased by other corporations that invest in short-term debt instruments.
	Dividend rate is reset regularly (usually every seven weeks) to keep the price from fluctuating.
	Investors usually have the opportunity to sell the stock if they do not want the adjusted rate (unless the auction process fails).
	Desirable because of the 70% dividend exclusion allowance on the dividend income.
Negotiable certificates of deposit (CDs)	Interest-bearing deposits issued by banks or saving and loan institutions that can be traded in money markets; generally sold at face value in denominations of $1 million.
	Most mature between one and three months; some can be for several years.
	Offer fixed and variable interest rates.
	Not guaranteed by the Federal Deposit Insurance Corporation if in excess of $100,000; therefore, issuing bank should be investigated carefully.
	Highly marketable if issued by a large, established bank.
	Common types include:
	Eurodollar (or euro) certificates of deposit (CDs)—dollar-denominated CDs issued by foreign branches of U.S. banks and foreign banks, primarily in London.
	Yankee CDs—CDs issued by U.S. branches of foreign banks.
	Thrift CDs—CDs issued by savings and loan associations, savings banks, and credit unions.
Eurodollar deposits	Typically nonnegotiable dollar-denominated time deposits held by banks outside the United States (although not necessarily in Europe); not subject to U.S. banking regulations.
	May be purchased through most large U.S. banks.
	Maturities range from overnight to several years; most are six months or less.
Short-term municipals	State and local government issues.
	Two common types:
	CP instrument with float interest rate reset weekly.
	Longer-term note with a one- to two-year maturity.
	Short-term municipal has great price stability and better marketability.

Accounts Receivable Management

The term **accounts receivable (A/R)** refers to the money customers owe a company resulting from its decision to sell products and services on a credit basis. An item is classified as an account receivable after it is sold and an invoice is sent. An account receivable is treated as an asset (normally short-term) on the company's balance sheet.

Why Companies Carry Accounts Receivable

Credit is often described as a sales tool. In deciding to extend credit and carry A/R, companies consider these factors:

- General economic conditions
- Target market (e.g., terms necessary to attract new customers and needs of current customers)
- Industry practices (e.g., credit terms competitors offer)
- Potential profit from interest income for credit terms

As with other current assets, A/R have profitability and risk trade-offs. Extending credit may stimulate sales and profits. But a company incurs costs for carrying receivables and runs the risk of potential bad-debt losses. Companies must have efficient and effective policies and procedures in place for managing A/R.

The general factors that influence the management of a company's receivables are:

- Defined credit policies and terms of sale
- Provisions for the evaluation of customer creditworthiness and the determination of customer credit lines
- Prompt A/R billing and collection
- Accurate and up-to-date A/R records
- Provisions for follow-up on overdue accounts and initiation of collection procedures (if necessary)

Managing credit and A/R activities at a company involves the sales, accounting, and finance functions. The decision as to whether to grant credit to a customer considers five things called the five C's of credit granting. Listed in the normal order of priority, they are:

- Character (the customer's reputation)
- Conditions (the customer's financial condition and the state of the economy)
- Cash flow (the customer's cash position)
- Credit (the customer's credit rating and status)
- Collateral (against the receivable)

Credit Terms

Credit terms stipulate the form and timing of payment extended to a customer for the receipt of goods and services as well as the discount terms (if any). The **credit**

period is the net due date (e.g., 20 days, 30 days). **Discount terms** are stated in terms of the credit period and the cash discount given for early payment. The **cash discount** is the percentage of reduction allowed for early payment. For example, terms of 5/10 net 30 mean that the total amount is due in 30 days of the invoice date, but the buyer can take a 5% discount by paying within 10 days.

Common terms of credit that companies offer are described in Figure 2B-23.

Figure 2B-23 Types of Credit Extension

Form	Description
Open account (open book credit)	Seller's invoice represents the formal obligation between buyer and seller and records the sale as an account receivable.
	Customer receives an invoice for each transaction or a monthly statement showing invoices for the period.
	Full payment is due according to specified credit terms and any discounts; fees generally are charged for late payments.
	Includes periodic review of creditworthiness.
	Most common type of credit.
Installment credit	Requires the customer to make equal monthly payments consisting of principal plus interest.
	May involve a written contract specifying terms of the obligation, credit terms, interest rate, and so on.
	Often used for large-value consumer purchases (e.g., automobiles).
Revolving credit	Provides ongoing credit without requiring approval of individual transactions as long as an account is in good standing (e.g., credit outstanding is below an established limit, and payments are current).
	Assesses an interest charge based on the average amount outstanding for the period if the account is past due.
Letter of credit (L/C)	Involves a letter of credit instrument where a bank guarantees the seller (not the buyer) payment for an agreed-on purchase.
	Buyer typically pays a fee for opening an L/C.
	Commonly used for import/export transactions.

Extending the Credit Period

Extending the credit period and changing the discount terms can affect both the profitability and the risk associated with A/R. Specific formulas are available to calculate the effect of changes in credit periods and cash discounts. A firm extends a credit period with the expectation of increased profitability from increased sales.

For example: A firm changes credit terms from net 30 to net 60; the credit period is increased from one month to two months. The more liberal credit terms encourage additional sales. But the extended collection period results in additional carrying costs for the firm as customers slow down their payments.

In extending a credit period, the firm must compare the profitability of additional sales with the opportunity costs of the additional receivables. If the increased sales profits exceed the required return on investment for the additional receivables, the change in the credit period is worthwhile.

Changing the Discount Terms

A firm offers a cash discount or varies an existing one in an attempt to speed up payment of receivables.

For example: A firm's current collection period averages 60 days with no cash discount given. The firm decides to offer the discount terms of 2/10, net 45. After one month, 70% of the firm's customers (in dollar volume) take advantage of the cash discount.

In changing the discount terms, the firm must determine if the increased speed in collections offsets the cost of offering the discount. If the opportunity costs of accelerated collections are greater than the cost of the discount, the discount is worthwhile; if the savings do not offset the cash discount, the discount is not a good idea.

Default Risk

A receivable is only as good as the probability of it being paid. The term *bad debts* generally refers to the slowness in the collection of receivables and the portion of receivables in default. Default occurs when a customer fails to meet the terms of an obligation. **Default risk** is the risk that a company (or an individual) will not be able to pay interest or principal on debt obligations.

To minimize default risk, firms need to set and maintain credit standards for credit extension, billing, and collection. Credit information on an applicant may be gathered from internal and external sources.

Typical sources of internal credit information are listed next.

- A credit application completed by an applicant
- An agreement form completed by an applicant
- A firm's records on past dealings with the applicant (e.g., payment history)

External sources of credit information are listed next.

- *Financial statements.* Review of audited (or unaudited) financial statements and related ratios that can be compared to industry averages
- *Trade references.* Contact with other companies regarding their actual payment experiences with the applicant
- *Banks and other lenders.* For standardized credit information about the applicant's financial condition and available credit
- *Agencies.* Local and national agency reports on the credit history of most companies

Factors Contributing to Optimal Credit/Collection Policies

Credit and collection policies involve an assessment of the creditworthiness of the buyer, the credit terms extended, and the level of collection procedures required. At the very least, the gains derived from credit and collection policies should be equal to the costs associated with them.

To maximize the profitability of credit and collection polices, a firm needs to vary these policies. The optimal solution is reached based on the best possible combination of credit standards, credit terms, and collection expenditures. Typically, the next relationships have been found to exist:

- In the absence of credit standards, sales revenues and contribution margins are maximized but are often offset by large bad-debt losses, collection costs, and high costs from carrying very large receivables.
- With tighter credit standards, sales revenues and contribution margins decline but so do the average collection period, bad-debt losses, and receivable carrying costs.
- The optimal credit policy would be the one that considers the costs and benefits of credit granting and attempts to maximize net benefits.

Inventory Management

Understanding inventory management requires an understanding of these basic inventory control terms:

- **Stock** refers to all the goods a company stores and represents a supply that is kept for future use.
- **Inventory** is a list of all the items held in stock.
- An **item** is a single type of product kept in stock or one entry in the inventory.
- A **unit** is the standard size or quantity of a stock item.

Given these definitions, the concepts of inventory control and inventory management can be explained.

Inventory control (or **stock control**) refers to the collective activities and procedures that ensure that the right amount of each item is held in stock. Inventory control requires that the organization be able to answer three questions. They are:

1. What do we have?
2. How much do we have?
3. Where is it?

Inventory management refers to the process of determining and maintaining the required level of inventory that will ensure that customer orders are properly filled on time. Inventory management requires that the organization answer three additional questions. They are:

1. What to order (or make)?
2. When to order (or make)?
3. How much to order (or make)?

Why Companies Carry Inventory

Inventories are carried to compensate for the variability between the supply of an item and the demand for it. Inventory control involves balancing conflicting costs—balancing the cost of holding sufficient stock to provide a specified level of customer service with the cost of purchasing the inventory. The point at which those costs intersect provides answers to many inventory control issues, such as what to keep in stock, when orders should be placed, how much should be ordered, and so on.

To some degree, every company holds inventory. But holding inventory is costly because of storage and handling costs, the danger of inventory obsolescence, and the costs associated with tied-up capital. When capital is tied up, businesses must forgo other profitable opportunities for investments. These disadvantages and costs for holding inventory lead to the question: Why do companies carry inventory?

At a simplistic level, inventory provides a buffer between supply and demand. But there are many other reasons for holding inventory, including:

- Coverage for mismatches between supply and demand rates
- Efficient servicing of customer demands that are larger than expected or at unexpected times
- Coverage for delayed or insufficient supplier deliveries
- Economies in purchasing (such as price discounts on large orders or savings on purchases when prices are low and expected to rise)
- Economies in production
- Maintenance of consistent levels of operation
- Coverage for emergencies

In general, the level of inventory should be increased only if the benefits outweigh the costs of maintaining the additional inventory.

Economic Order Quantity

Economic order quantity (EOQ) represents the optimum order size—the quantity of a regularly ordered item to be purchased at a point in time that results in minimum total cost (i.e., the sum of ordering costs and carrying costs).

Ordering Costs

Ordering costs include the marginal costs of placing a purchase or production order. They are the marginal cost of computer time to prepare orders and the cost of the supplies used to generate an order. Fixed costs of ordering, such as salaries, are irrelevant.

The more frequently orders are placed, the more costs incurred by the ordering process. The general relationship between ordering cost (per order) and order quantity (number of units per order) is shown in the first frame of Figure 2B-24. The rationale is thus built for ordering larger quantities at one time to minimize ordering costs.

Carrying Costs

Carrying costs (also called storage costs or holding costs) are the marginal costs of carrying the inventory. They include marginal storage and handling costs, obsolescence and deterioration costs, insurance, taxes, and the cost of the funds invested in inventories. Carrying costs rise as the order size grows and decline when items are ordered in smaller amounts.

Figure 2B-24 EOQ and the Relationship Between Carrying Cost, Ordering Cost, and Order Quantity

The second frame of Figure 2B-24 depicts this simple relation between carrying cost (per order) and order quantity (number of units per order).

EOQ can be determined when ordering and carrying costs are related to demand. The last frame in Figure 2B-24 illustrates EOQ.

The EOQ formula is:

$$EOQ = \sqrt{\frac{2FD}{C}}$$

where:

    F = marginal cost per order

    D = total inventory units demanded

    C = carrying (carrying or holding) cost per inventory unit

If the carrying costs decrease, the EOQ increases. If total inventory units demanded or marginal cost per order decrease, EOQ also decreases.

EOQ is based on these assumptions:

- Lead time is constant and known.
- Demand occurs at a relatively stable and known rate.
- Operating and storage costs are known.
- Replenishment is instantaneous; there are no stock-outs.
- The demand for the item in question is independent.

EOQ principles also can be applied to the quantities of an item to be manufactured.

For example: Assume that a manufacturer of financial calculators uses 10,000 units of an item annually. Its order cost is $75 per order and the storage cost is $1.50 per unit per year. The EOQ would be:

$$\text{EOQ} = \sqrt{\frac{2(10,000)(\$75)}{\$1.50}} = \sqrt{1,000,000} = 1,000 \, \text{units}$$

If the company uses 10,000 units per year and its EOQ is 1,000, the company would reorder 10 times a year (10,000 / 1,000).

Although widely used, EOQ analysis has these weaknesses:

- Assumptions sometimes are unrealistic and inaccurate; situations where all relevant factors (demand, lead time, and costs) are known with complete certainty are rare.
- Calculations are based on estimated costs and forecast demands.
- In manufacturing environments, where setup costs are high, large quantities lead to excess capacity and inventory.
- Too much capacity leaves too much capital tied up in inventory.

Impact of Lead Time and Safety Stock

In practice, replenishment is not instantaneous, and when stock-outs occur, they typically have myriad associated costs. Stock-outs can result in reduced profits from lost sales, loss of goodwill, loss of future sales, and loss of reputation. In manufacturing, disruptions in production can be considerable and costly, ranging from rescheduling issues to employee layoffs and premium prices for emergency orders and special deliveries from suppliers.

Such shortage issues can be minimized or avoided by shortening lead time and having some level of safety stock.

Lead Time

Lead time is the time between placing an order and getting the units in stock and ready for use. Lead time may vary for several reasons. Effective inventory management attempts to keep lead time short by reducing the time for:

- Order preparation (the time to gather order information and prepare the order).
- Order delivery to a supplier (the time to get the order to a supplier via electronic transmissions, telecommunications, or mail).
- Order processing and fulfillment by the supplier.
- Order delivery from the supplier.
- Process delivery (getting the items into stock).

Safety Stock

Safety stock (or **buffer stock**) generally refers to a quantity of stock planned and held in inventory to protect against fluctuations in supply and demand or as protection against production forecast errors and or short-term changes in backlog.

Where EOQ analysis is based on the theoretical assumption that demand and lead time are known with certainty, safety stock uses a model involving probability.

Safety stock analysis attempts to address the uncertainty found in inventory systems, particularly the real-world uncertainty in demand and lead time.

Determining the level of safety stock to maintain involves balancing the probability and cost of a stock-out with the cost of carrying sufficient safety stock to avoid this possibility. Specific calculations (which are beyond the scope of this text) are used. These general concepts apply:

- The greater the uncertainty in forecasted demand, the more safety stock a firm may wish to consider.
- The greater the uncertainty in lead time to replenish a stock-out, the more safety stock a firm may want to maintain.

Safety stock analysis considers all costs associated with stock-outs. But the final factor is the cost of carrying additional inventory and loss of interest income from tying up working capital. If not for these costs and loss of interest-earning investments, a firm theoretically could carry sufficient safety stock to prevent stock-outs from ever occurring.

Reorder Points

When to order an item is a function of the lead time for the item, its usage rate, and the safety stock of the item maintained. The item has to be ordered so that the usage of the item over the lead time does not cut into the safety stock of the item. The reorder point (ROP) specifies the level of inventory on hand that would trigger an order. The formula for an ROP is:

$$ROP = UL + \text{Safety Stock}$$

where:
U = usage rate (demand per unit of time [D/t])
L = lead time

For example: Suppose an item has a demand of 10,000 units over 50 weeks, a safety stock of 400 units, and a lead time of three weeks. The ROP would be:

$$ROP = UL + \text{Safety Stock} = (10,000/50)\,(3) + 400 = (200)\,(3) + 400$$
$$= 600 + 400 = 1,000$$

An order would be triggered when the inventory on hand reaches 1,000 items.

Just-in-Time Systems and Kanban

Basic principles of just-in-time (JIT) systems and Kanban are covered in Part 1 of the *Wiley CMAexcel Learning System*. These concepts are also appropriate to mention in the context of inventory control.

The underlying objective of JIT systems is to minimize all waste in manufacturing operations by meeting production targets with the minimum amount of materials, equipment, operators, and so on. This is accomplished by completing all operations just at the time they are needed. Kanban is the simple manual method of control used in conjunction with JIT to ensure that all materials actually do arrive just as they are needed.

Some similarities exist between EOQ and JIT/Kanban systems. For example, both monitor stock levels and place orders for replenishment with fixed quantities. However, a major difference is that with JIT and Kanban, activity reduces stock to its reorder level, and replenishments occur only after each withdrawal. The choice of EOQ versus JIT depends on a variety of factors specific to the organization.

JIT and Kanban systems have been described as deceptively simple. Careful evaluation and planning are required for effective implementation. But when JIT and Kanban are well conceived and properly adopted as a means of inventory control, they can reduce stocks of raw materials and work in progress dramatically. In turn, such reductions translate to additional cost savings by:

- Reducing the manufacturing and warehousing space needed
- Lowering property and overhead expenses
- Reducing the investments for stock

In the end, JIT and Kanban can lead to more efficient use of working capital.

Inventory Management Metrics

There are two measures of effective inventory management: inventory turnover and number of days on hand. The inventory turnover is calculated as shown:

$$\text{Inventory Turnover} = \frac{\text{Cost of Goods Sold}}{\text{Average Inventory}}$$

The average inventory often is calculated by adding the beginning and ending balances for the period and dividing by 2.

The days on hand is calculated as shown:

$$\text{Days on Hand} = \frac{365}{\text{Inventory Turnover}}$$

For example: Suppose a company has a beginning inventory of $24,000 and an ending inventory of $36,000 and cost of goods sold of $240,000. Its inventory turnover would be:

Inventory Turnover = $240,000 / [($24,000 + $36,000) / 2]

= $240,000 / ($60,000 / 2)

= $240,000 / $30,000 = 8 times per year

Its days on hand would be:

Days on Hand = 365 / 8 = 45.6 days

Types of Short-Term Credit

Businesses usually meet short-term borrowing needs in one of two ways:

1. By raising funds externally through financial intermediaries (e.g., through banks and financial institutions or by investing in money markets)
2. By issuing CP

The vast majority of businesses rely on financial intermediaries to perform the lending function.

Several types of short-term credit arrangements are possible, including the use of:

- Accrued expenses
- Trade credit
- Unsecured short-term bank loans (lines of credit and revolving credit)
- Secured short-term loans (collateralized A/R and collateralized inventory)
- Commercial paper
- Bankers' acceptances

A brief description of each is presented next.

Accrued Expenses

Accrued expenses represent the amount a firm owes but has not yet paid for wages, taxes, interest, and dividends. The most common accrued expenses are wages and taxes.

Accrued expenses are considered a spontaneous source of interest-free financing. Businesses can use current funds to fulfill immediate cash needs up to the point the accrued expenses become due for payment. In that respect, accrued expenses must be used with discretion.

Trade Credit

Trade credit is a source of short-term financing created when a supplier grants credit terms to customers on purchases. Trade credit often is the largest source of short-term credit for small firms.

Trade credit represents an indirect loan with these terms:

- A seller supplies goods according to predefined credit terms.
- The credit appears as A/R on the seller's books and A/P on the customer's books.
- The credit represents cash the customer may keep until the specified final payment date.

An open account (where a seller gives the buyer a specified time period to pay for goods or services) is the most common type of trade credit.

Unsecured Short-Term Bank Loans

An **unsecured short-term bank loan** is a form of bank credit that is not backed by a pledge of specific collateral or assets. Such loans are made based on the financial soundness and creditworthiness of the borrower.

Unsecured short-term bank loans are negotiated between the bank and the business. A loan agreement stipulates the terms of the loan (e.g., interest to be paid, payment terms, maturity date, etc.). The borrower signs a **promissory note** as a formal obligation to repay the loan according to the specified terms.

Unsecured short-term bank loans generally are considered self-liquidating, meaning that the assets the company purchases with the loan or the current assets held by the company will generate sufficient cash flows to pay off the loan. For example, unsecured short-term bank loans are popular instruments to finance seasonal buildups in A/R or inventory.

Lines of credit and revolving credit are two types of unsecured loans that provide quick and ready sources of short-term financing for businesses.

Lines of Credit

A **line of credit** (or credit line) is an agreement allowing a firm to borrow up to a specified limit during a particular time period. The borrower has access to the credit amount (which is generally substantial) but pays interest only on actual borrowing. Borrowing against a line of credit is done through a specific short-term note. A sequence of short-term notes can be issued against the same line of credit. Maturities of the short-term notes vary; generally notes range from overnight to 90 days (although some may be longer).

Technically, lines of credit are set up for a set period (usually a year), but most are renewed on an ongoing basis at maturity. Many lines of credit are kept in force for years.

Revolving Credit

Revolving credit (also known as a revolver or a revolving credit agreement) allows a business to borrow, repay, and reborrow up to a specified amount. Credit terms of a revolver are similar to those of a line of credit. Although revolvers often are used for short-term borrowing, many times the term is longer (ranging from two to five years).

Secured Short-Term Loans

A **secured short-term loan** (or **asset-based borrowing**) is a form of credit based on the pledging of an asset for collateral. A/R and inventory are the most common assets used in this form of secured lending; equipment, real estate, or other tangible property is sometimes used as collateral.

In a **collateralized accounts receivable** type of arrangement, the lender spends time evaluating the borrower's business; the volume of customer purchases, the timeliness of customer payments, delinquency rates, and the number of bad-debt write-offs are all considered. Based on this evaluation, an advance rate is determined, stated as a percentage of the A/R outstanding. The percentage is then applied to the amount of pledged A/R and determines the maximum amount that can be borrowed. When a loan is in force, the borrower's customers typically make payments directly to the lender, who applies them to the outstanding loan balance.

Collateralized inventory is similar to A/R financing. The amount of credit is limited by the advance rate and determined as a percentage of inventory. The advance rate also considers the risk that the borrower may not be able to sell the inventory (due to changes in market conditions, fluctuating commodity prices, or inventory obsolescence or spoilage). In general, lenders are more willing to collateralize raw materials and finished goods than work in progress. On occasion, some lenders may calculate different advance rates for different types of inventories. Generally, the advance rate is much less for inventory than for A/R.

Commercial Paper

Commercial paper (CP) is an unsecured promissory note issued by a corporation. CP is sold at a discount from par value and is backed by a promise of the corporation to buy back the paper at maturity by paying par value.

The major credit rating agencies usually rate the CP of a specific issuer. CP typically is sold in denominations of $100,000. For public issues, maturities range from overnight to 270 days. Some private issues may have maturities longer than 270 days.

CP interest rates vary. The rate is market based and is a function of the issuing company's credit rating, the size of the issue, and general market short-term interest rates.

Most CP is sold through dealers (either investment banking institutions or commercial banks). Some companies may sell their CP issues directly to investors.

In general, the use of CP for short-term financing:

- Provides a broad distribution for borrowing, which results in more funds at lower rates than other methods provide.
- Allows the borrower to avoid the expense of maintaining a compensating balance with a commercial bank.
- Promotes the name of the borrower because of the broad market the borrower's name becomes more widely known.

Bankers' Acceptances

A **bankers' acceptance (BA)** is a negotiable short-term instrument used primarily to finance the import and export of goods. Some issues may be used for the domestic shipment and storage of readily marketable staples.

A BA is a time draft drawn by a borrower and accepted by the bank on which it is drawn. Accepting the draft implies that the bank assumes obligation for the payment of the draft at maturity.

BAs are readily marketable and often are discounted in the money market. The borrower receives discounted proceeds as an advance and is obligated to pay the full draft amount to the accepting bank at maturity. The accepting bank pays the investor who purchased the BA.

Short-Term Credit Management

Different short-term credit options have different costs for the borrower. This section looks specifically at three types of short-term financing costs:

1. Costs incurred by not taking cash discounts extended with trade credit
2. The effective annual interest rate associated with unsecured short-term bank loans
3. Factoring costs associated with collateralized secured short-term bank loans

Cash Discounts Extended with Trade Credit

Trade credit represents cash a firm can invest up until the specified payment date (e.g., 30, 60, or 90 days). The longer the payment period, the longer the firm can use the funds.

The amount of short-term financing cost the firm saves depends on the days of credit. For example, if a firm were to use credit worth $100,000 for 30 days rather than borrowing that amount from another source at a cost of 2%, the firm would save $2,000 ($100,000 × 0.02).

Firms grant trade credit to help facilitate a sale. Discounts are offered as incentives for customers to pay early and reduce the cost of carrying receivables. The customer must weigh the discount against the option of using the trade credit and decide whether it is beneficial to take the discount and pay early. Generally, a firm saves money by taking the discount rather than extending the credit up to the original payment date.

The formula for determining the cost of foregoing a cash discount (and, therefore, delaying payment beyond the discount period) is as follows:

$$\text{EID} = \frac{\text{DR}}{1 - \text{DR}} \times \frac{365}{\text{N} - \text{DP}}$$

where:
EID = effective rate of interest for forgoing the cash discount
DR = discount rate
N = net payment period
DP = discount period

For example: Credit terms are 2/10 net 30. The effective interest rate of foregoing the cash discount is:

$$\text{EID} = \frac{0.02}{1 - 0.02} \times \frac{365}{30 - 10}$$

$$= 37.24\%$$

If the firm can borrow funds elsewhere for less than 37.24%, it should do so and take the discount for early payment of the trade credit. However, if borrowing exceeds 37.24% (or funds are not available elsewhere), the firm might want to delay payment until the net due date.

Effective Annual Interest Rate

Banks charge interest for unsecured short-term bank loans. They generally assess a commitment fee, and they also may charge a compensating balance.

Interest Rate

The interest rate charged consists of a spread added to a base rate such as prime, the British Bankers' Association (BBA) London Interbank Offered Rate (LIBOR), or the Fed rate for T-bills. In determining the interest rate, banks evaluate the customer's ability to repay the loan. The rate charged reflects the bank's assessment of the loan risk. The rate usually is variable and will be adjusted according to the changes in the base rate.

Commitment Fee

In addition to interest, banks often charge a commitment fee for holding lines of credit or revolvers available for the borrower. The commitment fee is some percentage of the line or the unused portion of the line.

Compensating Balance

Some banks also may require a compensating balance. The compensating balance designates the percentage of the loan the bank may require the borrower to hold on deposit without earning interest or offsetting other service charges. A compensating balance may be specified as a percentage of the total commitment, the unused portion of the commitment, or the outstanding borrowings.

A commitment fee and a compensating balance effectively reduce the amount of funds the borrower can use. In doing so, they also increase the effective annual interest rate charged for the loan. In other words, the effective annual interest rate is higher than the initial interest rate quoted by the bank.

The formula for effective annual rate of interest is

$$\text{EI} = \left(\frac{\text{PR} + \text{CF}}{1 - \text{CB}} \right) \left(\frac{365}{\text{M}} \right)$$

where:

EI = effective rate of interest

PR = principal interest charge (%)

CF = commitment fee (%)

CB = compensating balance (%)

M = loan length in days

For example: A firm negotiates a one-year loan for $1 million with an interest rate of 12%. The commitment fee is 0.25 % of the total amount, and the compensating balance is 10% of the line.

$$EI = \left(\frac{0.12 + 0.0025}{1 - 0.10} \right)\left(\frac{365}{365} \right) = \left(\frac{0.1225}{0.9} \right) = 13.6\%$$

The quoted rate is 12%, but the effective annual interest rate the firm actually will pay is 13.6%.

Factoring Costs

Factoring is the sale or transfer of A/R in a secured short-term loan to a third party (factor). A factor is a company specializing in the financing and management of receivables.

Factoring receivables is governed by a contract between the factor and the client. A factor makes credit checks on accounts and charges a percentage commission on the receivables, depending on the amount and the quality of the receivables and the overall financial soundness of the client. The factor also charges interest, which usually is variable.

A factor can liquidate collateralized assets in the event the client cannot repay the loan. To protect itself against default risk, the factor typically applies a **haircut** to the current value of the receivables. This means that the loan amount will be for substantially less than the face value of the receivables. Applying a haircut provides a buffer for the factor. Should the factor have to sell the assets at distressed prices, the factor still has a chance of covering the default loan amount.

For example: The face value of A/R is $200,000. The haircut is 15%, and the total charges (interest charges and commission) are $30,000.

The proceeds of the loan to the borrowing firm would be $140,000.

$170,000	Face value of A/R × the haircut [$200,000 × (1 − 15%)]
− 30,000	Total charges
$140,000	Loan proceeds

In some cases, factoring arrangements are transparent to the customer, who continues to make payments to the firm, which, in turn, endorses the payments to the factor. In other cases, the customer is notified of the transfer and has to make payments directly to the factor. Most arrangements are without recourse, which means that the selling company would not be liable for any receivables not collected by the factor.

Factoring arrangements also can be set up for inventories. But because inventories are the least liquid current assets, the haircut is higher and a trust receipt is required. A **trust receipt** allows the borrower to sell goods out of stock and remit proceeds to the factor.

Maturity Matching or Hedging Approaches to Financing

Maturity matching is a working capital management approach that hedges risk by matching the maturities of the company's assets and liabilities. Thus, the company attempts to finance short-term projects with short-term financing and long-term projects with long-term assets.

Hedging is a method of reducing exposures to adverse fluctuations in prices, interest rates, or foreign exchange rates. Companies hedge an investment by taking an offsetting position in a second investment instrument.

The reason for investing capital in foreign operations generally is motivated by the desire to capture a return in excess of that required. Additional contributing factors include the desire to:

- *Capitalize on gaps in international markets.* Where domestic markets may offer only normal rates of return, international investments across different markets may present distinct opportunities to earn excess returns.
- *Lower operating costs.* Lower labor costs and other cost efficiencies are possible through expansion into foreign markets.
- *Secure necessary raw materials.* Companies lack sufficient raw materials and invest abroad to acquire them. Consider how mining companies and oil companies go offshore to secure necessary resources for operations.

Investments in international markets, production facilities, and raw materials all can help a firm secure a rate of return higher than through domestic activities alone.

There are some key risks associated with international opportunities, including taxation, political risks, and exchange rate risk exposures.

Taxation

Taxation becomes complex due to different tax laws and different treatments of foreign investments. The U.S. government taxes firms with international operations differently than domestic companies. Individual countries tax the income of foreign companies doing business in their country.

Political Risks

The potential for political instability in many countries, ranging from mild interference in operations to expropriation, warrants careful consideration.

Exchange Rate Risk Exposures

A fundamental risk results from changes in currency exchange rates. Three specific types of exchange-rate risks are translation, transactions, and economic.

1. **Translation exposure** is related to the accounting treatment of changes in exchange rates. There can be accounting gains or losses when assets and liabilities are translated from foreign operations into the parent company's currency.
2. **Transactions exposure** is the gain or loss that occurs when settling a specific foreign transaction, such as the purchase or sale of a foreign product or the settlement of open-credit terms.
3. **Economic exposure** is the change in value of a company resulting from unanticipated changes in exchange rates. Economic exposure is a function of expected future cash flows.

Maturity matching and hedging are two methods a firm can use to manage exchange risk exposure. Although beyond the scope of this text, there exist many maturity-matching strategies and hedging activities that firms can use to offset the risk of loss from a change in foreign currency rates.

Knowledge Check: Working Capital Management

The next questions are intended to help you check your understanding and recall of the material presented in this topic. They do not represent the type of questions that appear on the CMA exam.

Directions: Answer each question in the space provided. Correct answers and section references appear after the knowledge check questions.

1. The transactions motive for holding cash is **best** described as

   ☐ **a.** using surplus liquid reserves to take advantage of short-term investments or other temporary situations.

   ☐ **b.** synchronizing cash inflows and outflows so that excess cash balances can be invested in short-term instruments.

   ☐ **c.** providing a buffer for unexpected cash needs that result from the unpredictable nature of cash inflows and outflows.

   ☐ **d.** maintaining sufficient cash or near-cash reserves to meet financial payments arising from ordinary business operations.

2. Which of the following techniques will **not** speed up collections?

   ☐ **a.** Lockbox system

   ☐ **b.** ACH and Fedwire processing

   ☐ **c.** Payable through draft

   ☐ **d.** Cash concentration banking system

For questions 3 through 7, match each type of marketable security with its characteristic.

3. ＿＿ Federal agency securities	**a.** Interest-bearing deposits issued by banks or saving and loan institutions that can be traded in money markets
4. ＿＿ Commercial paper	
5. ＿＿ Bankers' acceptances	**b.** Time drafts that result from commercial trade financing
6. ＿＿ Negotiable certificates of deposit	
7. ＿＿ Auction rate preferred stock	**c.** Relatively safe investment and free of default risk
	d. Equity usually purchased by other corporations that invest in short-term debt instruments
	e. Unsecured short-term loan issued by a corporation

8. A primary benefit that a firm expects to gain from lengthening a credit period is

 ☐ **a.** increased profitability resulting from increased sales.

 ☐ **b.** increased revenue from interest charges on past due accounts.

 ☐ **c.** fewer collections procedures necessary for past due accounts.

 ☐ **d.** improved inventory control resulting from relatively stable demand.

9. Which of the following statements accurately characterizes economic order quantity (EOQ) and safety stock principles?

 ☐ **a.** Both models advocate reducing stock to a predetermined reorder level.

 ☐ **b.** EOQ analysis assumes demand and lead time are known with certainty; safety stock uses a model involving probability.

 ☐ **c.** EOQ analysis and safety stock both assume that demand varies but lead time is known with certainty.

 ☐ **d.** Both models are based on the premise that there is no true measure of certainty in inventory control.

For questions 10 through 15, match each short-term credit arrangement with its characteristic.

10. ____ Accrued expenses	**a.** Negotiated arrangements exemplified by lines of credit and revolvers
11. ____ Trade credit	**b.** Negotiable short-term instrument used primarily to finance the import and export of goods
12. ____ Unsecured short-term bank loans	
13. ____ Secured short-term loans	**c.** Lending based on an advance rate; typically stated as a percentage of accounts receivable or inventory
14. ____ Commercial paper	**d.** An indirect loan between a supplier and customers for purchases
15. ____ Bankers' acceptance	**e.** Spontaneous interest-free financing used to fulfill cash needs up to the point at which they become due for payment
	f. An unsecured promissory note issued by a corporation and sold at a discount from par value

16. What is the effective annual interest rate on a $5 million loan with an interest rate of 8%, a commitment fee of 0.25%, and a compensating balance of 10%?

 ☐ **a.** 8%

 ☐ **b.** 8.64%

 ☐ **c.** 9.17%

 ☐ **d.** 11.11%

Knowledge Check Answers: Working Capital Management

1. The transactions motive for holding cash is **best** described as [**See Motives for Holding Cash.**]

    ☐ **a.** using surplus liquid reserves to take advantage of short-term investments or other temporary situations.

    ☐ **b.** synchronizing cash inflows and outflows so that excess cash balances can be invested in short-term instruments.

    ☐ **c.** providing a buffer for unexpected cash needs that result from the unpredictable nature of cash inflows and outflows.

    ☑ **d.** maintaining sufficient cash or near-cash reserves to meet financial payments arising from ordinary business operations.

2. Which of the following techniques will **not** speed up collections? [**See Methods to Speed Up Cash Collections.**]

    ☐ **a.** Lockbox system

    ☐ **b.** ACH and Fedwire processing

    ☑ **c.** Payable through draft

    ☐ **d.** Cash concentration banking system

For questions 3 through 7, match each type of marketable security with its characteristic.

3. __c__ Federal agency securities	**a.** Interest-bearing deposits issued by banks or saving and loan institutions that can be traded in money markets
4. __e__ Commercial paper	
5. __b__ Bankers' acceptances	
6. __a__ Negotiable certificates of deposit	**b.** Time drafts that result from commercial trade financing
7. __d__ Auction rate preferred stock	**c.** Relatively safe investment and free of default risk
	d. Equity usually purchased by other corporations that invest in short-term debt instruments
	e. Unsecured short-term loan issued by a corporation

8. A primary benefit that a firm expects to gain from lengthening a credit period is [**See Credit Terms.**]

    ☑ **a.** increased profitability resulting from increased sales.

    ☐ **b.** increased revenue from interest charges on past due accounts.

☐ **c.** fewer collections procedures necessary for past due accounts.

☐ **d.** improved inventory control resulting from relatively stable demand.

9. Which of the following statements accurately characterizes economic order quantity (EOQ) and safety stock principles? [**See *Economic Order Quantity*.**]

☐ **a.** Both models advocate reducing stock to a predetermined reorder level.

☑ **b.** EOQ analysis assumes demand and lead time are known with certainty; safety stock uses a model involving probability.

☐ **c.** EOQ analysis and safety stock both assume demand varies but lead time is known with certainty.

☐ **d.** Both models are based on the premise that there is no true measure of certainty in inventory control.

For questions 10 through 15, match each short-term credit arrangement with its characteristic.

10. __e__ Accrued expenses	**a.** Negotiated arrangements exemplified by lines of credit and revolvers
11. __d__ Trade credit	
12. __a__ Unsecured short-term bank loans	**b.** Negotiable short-term instrument used primarily to finance the import and export of goods
13. __c__ Secured short-term loans	**c.** Lending based on an advance rate; typically stated as a percentage of accounts receivable or inventory
14. __f__ Commercial paper	
15. __b__ Bankers' acceptances	**d.** An indirect loan between a supplier and customers for purchases
	e. Spontaneous interest-free financing used to fulfill cash needs up to the point at which they become due for payment
	f. An unsecured promissory note issued by a corporation and sold at a discount from par value

16. What is the effective annual interest rate on a $5 million loan with an interest rate of 8%, a commitment fee of 0.25%, and a compensating balance of 10%? [**See *Effective Annual Interest Rate*.**]

☐ **a.** 8%

☐ **b.** 8.64%

☑ **c.** 9.17%

☐ **d.** 11.11%

Corporate Restructuring

CORPORATE RESTRUCTURING INVOLVES CHANGES in corporate ownership, asset structure, and/or capital structure. This topic looks at the means by which corporate restructuring can take place (e.g., by mergers, acquisitions, leveraged buyouts, various types of divestitures, and tracking stocks). It also covers various takeover defense tactics, the evaluation of factors for restructuring (e.g., benefits or synergies), valuing a business for merger or acquisition, business failure issues such as bankruptcy, and forced reorganizations.

 READ the Learning Outcome Statements (LOS) for this topic as found in Appendix B and then study the concepts and calculations presented here to be sure you understand the content you could be tested on in the CMA exam.

Mergers and Acquisitions

Businesses often grow by acquiring, or combining with, other businesses. Often the acquisition is facilitated through a merger. A **merger** (acquisition) is a type of business combination in which an acquiring company absorbs a second company, and the second company ceases to exist as a separate legal entity subsequent to the merger. In effect, the second company is merged into the acquiring company, which remains in business as the legal entity of the then-combined companies of two or more companies. For example, Company A purchases Company B and Company C. Company A continues with Company B subsumed. Another way of looking at it in equation form is as follows: $A + B = A$. A merger can be financed through a combination of cash, debt/borrowings, and/or stock (equity securities). Mergers may be horizontal (combining of two or more companies in the same industry), vertical (company combining with its suppliers or customers), or conglomerate (combining of companies not in the same industry and not having a buyer–seller relationships). Approval of the shareholders of each company to the merger transaction is required.

A **consolidation** is a type of business combination, similar to a merger, that creates an entirely new company (that remains in business and retains legal existence) from the merged companies. Again, the acquired companies are merged into the newly formed company and cease to exist as separate legal entities subsequent to the consolidation. For example, Company A and Company B merge to form Company C, or $A + B = C$.

An **acquisition** is the purchase of all of another company's assets or the purchase of a controlling interest in the acquiree's (target company's) outstanding voting stock (e.g., common stock). An acquisition transaction in which the target company's assets are purchased requires a vote of the target company's shareholders. In a stock acquisition, a formal vote of the target company stockholders is not required, and the acquisition can be executed even when the target company's management and board of directors are hostile to the proposed acquisition. In such a case, the acquirer company can make a tender offer for a controlling interest of the target company's outstanding voting stock directly to the target company's shareholders. A tender offer is a public, open offer or invitation (e.g., takeover bid), usually announced in a newspaper advertisement, by an acquirer company to the stockholders of a target company, for those stockholders to "tender" their stock for sale at a specified price during a specified time.

Takeover Defense Tactics

Takeovers of a company may be friendly or hostile. In a hostile takeover, the target company often tries to prevent the takeover. To do so, the target company will use a host of different defense tactics in their attempt to ward off the takeover. Those defense tactics, often called "shark repellants," include those listed below:

- **Staggering terms for the board of directors** instead of all of them coming up for election at the same time.
- **Golden parachutes** for key executives providing exorbitant pay and benefits if discharged through a merger.
- **Corporate charter rules** requiring a supermajority (such as 80%) of the shareholders to approve a takeover.
- **Poison pills**, or securities that have value only when an unfriendly bidder obtains control of a certain percentage of the target's shares. An example would be a bond having a poison put. A poison put allows the bondholders to force the target to redeem the bonds, making the potential takeover less attractive.
- **Fair price provisions** (or shareholders' rights plans) involve warrants issued to shareholders that permit the purchase of the target company's stock at a fraction of the market price in the event of a takeover attempt.
- A **white knight defense**, which involves the target finding a friendlier buyer with which to merge.
- A **"Pacman" defense**, in which the target company attempts to buy out the so-called hostile buyer.
- **Litigation**, where the target company challenges one or more aspects of a tender offer, in an attempt to delay the takeover.
- **Greenmail**, which is a targeted repurchase of the target company's stock (by the target company) after the potential acquirer has purchased a large number of shares of the target company's stock. Essentially, the potential acquirer is offered the opportunity to sell its acquirer shares back to the target company at an amount substantially in excess of the stock's market value.

- **Delisting the public company stock and going private or pursuing an LBO**. In an LBO transaction, the management and/or other employees of the target company purchase the company using large amounts of debt, thus preventing the acquirer company from gaining control over the target company.
- **"Lobster traps"** in which the target company issues a charter preventing individuals with more than 10% of convertible securities from converting them to voting stock. This catches the "large lobsters" and lets the small ones escape.
- **Selling off the crown jewels**, is a tactic in which the target company sells off or disposes of certain assets that make it a desirable target.
- Other tactics include flip-in and flip-over rights, creating an employee stock ownership plan (ESOP), and a reverse tender offer.

Divestitures

A **divestment** is the opposite of an investment. A divestment (or divestiture) involves the sale of an operating unit or the reduction or elimination of a company's assets. There are a variety of reasons why a company might look to divest an operating unit or reduce or eliminate certain assets; these reasons include raising capital for its core business operations, refocusing on the company's operations, or due governmental antitrust litigation. Some typical divestiture methods used by companies include spin-offs, equity carve-outs, and split-ups.

Spin-Offs

In a **spin-off transaction**, an independent company is created through the sale or distribution of new shares of an existing business or division of a parent company. These shares are distributed on a pro rata basis to existing shareholders of the parent company. In essence, a spin-off is a type of dividend to existing shareholders. A business wishing to streamline its operations may sell unproductive or unrelated subsidiary businesses as spin-offs. For example, a company might spin off one of its mature businesses that is experiencing little growth so that it can focus on high-growth related businesses. The company or business spun off is expected to be worth more as an independent company than as part of the larger business. Recent examples of this include Expedia's spin-off of TripAdvisor in 2011, and Sears Holding Corporation's spin-off of Sears Canada in 2012. The AT&T breakup in 1984 is considered to be one of the most successful spin-offs in history. During the breakup, AT&T gave each of its shareholders one share of stock in each of its seven regional telephone companies for every ten shares of AT&T they owned.

Equity Carve-Outs

An **equity carve-out** (also known as a split-off initial public offering [IPO] or a partial spin-off) is a type of corporate reorganization in which a company (parent) creates a new subsidiary and subsequently facilitates an IPO of the new subsidiary without fully spinning it off. The parent company usually offers only a minority share (typically up to 20%) of the newly created subsidiary company to outsiders, thereby retaining management control. Equity carve-outs increase the access to capital markets, enabling the carved-out subsidiary strong growth opportunities and a degree of autonomy (such as its own board of directors) while retaining access to resources at the parent company. Often an equity carve-out ultimately results in the parent company fully spinning off the subsidiary company.

Split-Ups

A split-up occurs when a single company splits into two or more separately run companies. Shares of the original company are exchanged for shares in each of the new companies. The exchange ratios are determined by the parent's board of directors and approved by its shareholders prior to the split-up. After the split-up, the original company ceases to exist.

Split-ups are executed either for strategic reasons or because of a government mandate resulting from monopolistic concerns. Strategic split-ups are an attempt to break the original company into separate companies whose overall shareholder value exceeds the shareholder value of the original company.

Evaluating Factors for Restructuring

The overall objective of corporations that enter into restructuring transactions is to maximize shareholder wealth. Mergers and acquisition transactions enable an acquirer company to cease a number of benefits through operating or financial synergies with an acquiree (target) company that the acquirer company may not have been able realize prior to the merger or acquisition. Some examples include the acquirer company's ability to:

- Obtain another company's assets, skills, or technology
- Achieve economies of scale.
- Obtain resources, such as through the combination of sales forces, facilities, and outlets.
- Obtain additional distribution channels and global expansion of the products and services.
- Obtain customers.
- Grow faster than internally possible.
- Diversify product and services offerings.
- Utilize net operating loss carryforwards.

Similarly, companies consider divesting existing business units or assets for a host of reasons. Motives include:

- Divesting businesses that are not part of the company's core operations so that it can focus on what it does best.

- To obtain necessary funds.
- To realize greater market value than the company may be able to realize as a whole.
- To create stability in the company's stock price, which may be experiencing fluctuations as a result of volatility of one or more of the company's business units.
- Getting rid of underperforming or failing businesses that may be depressing earning and/or draining cash flows.
- Pressure from regulatory agencies and/or stockholders.

Valuing a Business for Merger or Acquisition

Three major techniques or methods are used to value a target company for merger or acquisition:

1. Discounted cash flow method (DCF)
2. Adjusted book value method
3. Comparative price/earnings (P/E) ratio method

Conceptually, the DCF method is the soundest of the three methods. It compares the present value (PV) of the cash flow benefits to be derived from the merger with the PV of the merger costs. The discount rate used in computing the PV of the cash benefits typically would be the acquiring company's after-tax required rate of return. The merger cash flow benefits are the target company's expected future free cash flows. The PV of the merger costs is often just the original purchase price.

For example: Suppose the after-tax free cash flow from a merger is estimated to be $2,000,000 per year and is expected to last for 15 years. Assuming the acquiring company's required rate of return is 14%, the PV of the postmerger cash flow benefits would be $2,000,000 × 6.142 = $12,284,000. The number 6.142 represents the PV of an annuity at 14% for 15 years. The price offered by the acquirer company typically would be less than or equal to the $12,284,000 calculated.

The **adjusted book value** method for valuing a business in a merger or acquisition transaction involves determining the market value of the target company's assets and subtracting the value of its liabilities. Because identifying market valuations for the target company's assets and liabilities can be both difficult and costly, this method is not commonly used.

The **comparative P/E ratio method** establishes the exchange of the acquiring company's stock for the target company's stock so as to obtain a desired postmerger P/E ratio.

For example: Suppose the ABC Corp. is considering acquiring XYZ Co. in a stock-for-stock exchange. Financial data for the two companies is shown in Figure 2B-25.

If no synergistic benefits are expected, what is the maximum exchange ratio ABC should agree to if it wants no dilution in earnings per share (EPS)? For this to occur, the combined EPS would have to be at least $5.00 per share. To maintain a $5.00 EPS, the combined number of common shares outstanding would have to be 8 million ($40 million in combined net income divided by the required $5.00 EPS).

Figure 2B-25 Financial Data for ABC Corp. and XYZ Co.

	ABC	XYZ	Combined
Sales (millions)	$600	$75	$675
Net income (millions)	$30	$10	$40
Common shares outstanding (millions)	6	4	?
Earnings per share	$5.00	$2.50	?
Common stock price per share	$50	$20	$50

Therefore, ABC would trade 2 million of its shares for the 4 million XYZ shares, resulting in a 1-for-2 (0.5-for-1) exchange ratio.

Business Failures

An organization is **technically insolvent** when it is unable to meet current obligations even though the value of its assets exceeds its liabilities. It is **legally insolvent** when its liabilities exceed the value of its assets. It is **bankrupt** when it files a bankruptcy petition in accordance with the U.S. 2005 Bankruptcy Reform Act as amended in 2008. A bankruptcy may be a corporate reorganization filed under Chapter 11 of the Act or a formal bankruptcy (liquidation) under Chapter 7 of the Act.

Chapter 11 Reorganization

Chapter 11 provides a debtor company the opportunity to restructure its business. A variety of actions may be used, such as restructuring of existing loans, acquisition of new financing with priority of company earnings, rejection of specific contracts, and the cancellation of certain contracts. A trustee, often the debtor as debtor in possession, acts as trustee of the business during the reorganization. During the period of reorganization, the automatic stay provision requires all creditors to cease collection attempts. The court must approve the reorganization plan, and may convert the case to a Chapter 7 liquidation if it is in the best interests of the creditors.

Chapter 7 Bankruptcy

Chapter 7 involves a corporate liquidation. In liquidation, a referee normally is appointed to handle the administrative aspects of the bankruptcy procedure. The referee arranges a meeting of the creditors. The creditors select a trustee who liquidates the business and pays the creditors according to the priority of claims set forth in Chapter 7.

The priority of claims states that first secured claims are satisfied by the proceeds from the sale of the secured assets. The amount paid each secured claim holder is the lesser of the amount of the claim and the amount received from the sale. If the amount of the claim is less than the amount of the sale, the secured creditor receives the amount of the claim and the difference becomes available to satisfy the unsecured creditors. If the amount of the claim exceeds the amount of the sale, the secured creditor receives the amount of the sale and the difference becomes an amount considered an unsecured creditor claim.

The order of priority for unsecured creditors is described next.

1. First-priority creditors are paid in a specific order:
   a. Expenses for the administration of the bankruptcy
   b. Business expenses incurred after the petition has been filed but before the trustee has been appointed
   c. Unpaid wages for services performed during the three months prior to the bankruptcy filing and not to exceed $2,000 per employee
   d. Unpaid contributions to employee benefit plans not to exceed $2,000 per employee
   e. Customer layaway deposits not to exceed $900 per customer
   f. Taxes owed to federal, state, and local governments
2. General and unsecured creditors are paid next.
3. If any monies remain, preferred shareholders receive their liquidation values.
4. Common shareholders receive any monies remaining on a pro rata basis.

Other Forms of Corporate Restructuring

There are other forms of restructuring that can help a company to meet its primary goal of maximizing shareholder wealth, weathering tough economic times, or simply ensuring its long-term viability. In addition to mergers and acquisitions and key divestiture techniques (previously discussed), as well as Chapter 7 bankruptcy liquidations and Chapter 11 bankruptcy reorganizations (also previously discussed), companies may decide to pursue other changes in ownership, asset structure, or capital structure in order facilitate the necessary restructuring.

For example, a company may choose to go private. This can be accomplished by repurchasing outstanding common stock shares and retiring them. In doing so, the stock is delisted and is no longer traded. These types of transactions are often executed through a leveraged buyout (LBO). An LBO (as previously introduced in the context of takeover defense tactics) is a type of acquisition by which the management (or other employees) of a company buy the company using little equity and significant amounts of debt with the company's assets serving as collateral for the debt. A company can benefit from an LBO because of the savings it realizes from a reduction in administrative costs associated with it having been a public company. Additionally, managers/employees, who then become owners in the company, have greater incentives and greater operational flexibility.

Alternatively, a private company can pursue restructuring through an initial public offering (IPO) of its stock and becoming a public company.

A company may also restructure its ownership by setting up an employee stock ownership plan (ESOP) whereby the company transfers its ownership to its employees. ESOPs are commonly used to provide a market for the shares of departing owners of successful closely-held companies, to motivate and reward employees, or to take advantage of incentives to borrow money for acquiring new assets in pretax dollars. ESOPs also provide major tax benefits, including (but not limited to) tax deductibility of contributions of stock and cash contributions to the ESOP. ESOPs were also discussed previously as a tactic company can use in defending itself from a potential takeover.

Letter stock, also known as **tracking stock** or targeted stock, is yet another restructuring technique a company can pursue. Tracking stock are specialized equity offerings issued by a company (parent) that are based on the operations of a specific division or strategic business unit (SBU) of a diversified organization. They are issued for the purpose of tracking the performance of the SBU. All revenues, expenses, income, and cash flows of the SBU being tracked are separated from the parent company and attached to the SBU's tracking stock. The tracking stock is, therefore, separately traded at a price related to the operations of the SBU being tracked. Tracking stock often is used to separate a high-growth SBU from a larger parent that has been experiencing losses. The parent and its shareholders, however, still control the tracked SBU.

The most popular tracking stock is the QQQ (formerly known as the quadruple-Qs or the QQQQ), an exchange-traded fund whose return mirrors the returns of the NASDAQ 100 index. Another tracking stock is Standard & Poor's Depository Receipts (SPDR S&P 500). SPDR S&P 500 returns mirror the returns of the S&P 500 index.

Companies can also restructure through changes in their asset or capital structure. This might be facilitated through a liquidation of assets of an underperforming operating unit where the assets of that operating unit are sold piecemeal. An asset restructuring can also be executed through a sale-leaseback transaction. In a sale-leaseback transaction, a company sells certain property or assets and then leases them back from the buyer. Doing so allows the company to free up capital and raise money while retaining possession and use of the property or asset. As it relates to restructuring through changes in its capital structure, a company (as an alternative to bankruptcy) may work with its creditors through a debt restructuring. Debt restructuring is a process that allows a company to reduce and renegotiate its delinquent debts in order to improve or restore liquidity so that it can continue its operations.

Knowledge Check:
Corporate Restructuring

The next questions are intended to help you check your understanding and recall of the material presented in this topic. They do not represent the type of questions that appear on the CMA exam.

Directions: Answer each question in the space provided. Correct answers and section references appear after the knowledge check questions.

1. A merger may be any of the following **except**

   ☐ **a.** horizontal.

   ☐ **b.** vertical.

   ☐ **c.** cross-functional.

   ☐ **d.** conglomerate.

2. Potential defenses against hostile takeovers include

   ☐ **a.** poison pills.

   ☐ **b.** white knights.

   ☐ **c.** Pacman.

   ☐ **d.** all of the above.

3. Which of the following is **not** a type of divestiture?

   ☐ **a.** A spin-off

   ☐ **b.** An equity carve-out

   ☐ **c.** An equity carve-up

   ☐ **d.** A split-up

4. Techniques used to value and evaluate potential mergers and acquisitions include:

   ☐ **a.** adjusted book value.

   ☐ **b.** discounted cash flow.

   ☐ **c.** comparative P/E ratios.

   ☐ **d.** all of the above.

5. Which of the following is **not** a priority unsecured creditor in a bankruptcy proceeding?

   ☐ **a.** An unsubordinated debenture

   ☐ **b.** Federal, state, and local taxes owed

   ☐ **c.** Customer deposits subject to limits

   ☐ **d.** Unpaid wages subject to limits

Knowledge Check Answers: Corporate Restructuring

1. A merger may be any of the following **except** [See *Mergers and Acquisitions.*]
   - ☐ **a.** horizontal.
   - ☐ **b.** vertical.
   - ☑ **c.** cross-functional.
   - ☐ **d.** conglomerate.

2. Potential defenses against hostile takeovers include [**See *Takeover Defense Tactics.***]
   - ☐ **a.** poison pills.
   - ☐ **b.** white knights.
   - ☐ **c.** Pacman.
   - ☑ **d.** all of the above.

3. Which of the following is **not** a type of divestiture? [**See *Divestitures.***]
   - ☐ **a.** A spin-off
   - ☐ **b.** An equity carve-out
   - ☑ **c.** An equity carve-up
   - ☐ **d.** A split-up

4. Techniques used to value and evaluate potential mergers and acquisitions include: [**See *Valuing a Business for Merger or Acquisition.***]
   - ☐ **a.** adjusted book value.
   - ☐ **b.** discounted cash flow.
   - ☐ **c.** comparative P/E ratios.
   - ☑ **d.** all of the above.

5. Which of the following is **not** a priority unsecured creditor in a bankruptcy proceeding? [**See *Chapter 7 Bankruptcy.***]
   - ☑ **a.** An unsubordinated debenture
   - ☐ **b.** Federal, state, and local taxes owed
   - ☐ **c.** Customer deposits subject to limits
   - ☐ **d.** Unpaid wages subject to limits

International Finance

AS GOODS ARE TRADED BETWEEN COUNTRIES, they must be paid for. The cost of imported goods to a country depends on the value of its currency in relation to the value of the currency of the exporting country.

In addition to using currency to pay for goods and services, investors purchase and sell currencies as a form of hedge investment. For example, if an investor feels that the American dollar will soon be declining against the Japanese yen, she will trade dollars for yen in order to profit from the change in rates. If she is correct, later she will be able to purchase more dollars than she sold with the same amount of yen.

This topic looks at fixed, flexible, and floating exchange rates; means of managing transaction exposure; financing and paying for international trade; transfer pricing; and diversification of international assets.

 READ the Learning Outcome Statements (LOS) for this topic as found in Appendix B and then study the concepts and calculations presented here to be sure you understand the content you could be tested on in the CMA exam.

Foreign Currency Exchange

As any international traveler knows, one currency can be exchanged for another. A U.S. citizen who travels to England, exchanges U.S. dollars (USD) for British pounds (GBP); the same traveler, when crossing the channel to France, may exchange USD or GBP for euros. In effect, the traveler is buying one currency with another currency at a price determined by the rate of exchange.

One difficulty in following currency rates is that many exchange rates are subject to change in the currency marketplace. In other words, like other commodities, currencies can depreciate or appreciate in value in the global marketplace. When tangible objects, such as real estate or works of art, appreciate in value, they simply have a higher price tag. Intangible goods, such as stocks and bonds, also carry higher prices when they appreciate and lower prices when they depreciate in value. The same is true of currencies, although in a less straightforward manner.

When a currency appreciates in value, it has more buying power in relation to another specific currency; when it depreciates in value, it has less buying power in relation to other specific currencies. As a result of appreciation, a currency will buy more units of another currency; therefore, the holder of the currency can buy more goods than before. Travelers experience this when their home currency appreciates against the currency of the country they are visiting, allowing them to purchase better hotel accommodations, eat at better restaurants, and purchase more goods to bring home. If their home currency depreciates against that of the other country, the opposite happens, and they may have to scale back or even cancel their visit.

Shortly after World War II, the rate of exchange between USD and British pounds was about $4 to £1. When visiting the United States, Winston Churchill could "buy" $4 with approximately £1, whereas President Truman, when visiting London, would have needed about $4 to purchase £1. As the years passed, the pound gradually depreciated against the USD (or the USD appreciated in relation to the pound) until at one point in the 1990s, the two currencies were very nearly equal in value. The dollar then began depreciating against the pound (the pound appreciated against the dollar) until the pound rose in dollar value to nearly $2 per £1. That was pleasant for British travelers to the United States and not so good for U.S. travelers to Great Britain.

Fluctuations in exchange rates continue constantly—unless the exchange is fixed, as described later in this topic. These constant changes can be viewed on the Internet at Web sites such as www.xe.com.

Another difficulty is that the same exchange rate looks different depending on which country's viewpoint is taken. That is, one can quote the USD–GBP exchange rate as the number of pounds required to buy one dollar or the number of dollars required to buy one pound.

Exchange rate quotes are said to be either direct or indirect, depending on which currency is quoted in terms of the other.

For example: Assume that John is a U.S. citizen planning to tour Britain. He lands at Heathrow Airport in London, and the tour director says he will need 500 GBP for his various expenses. A direct quote tells John how many dollars are required to buy 1 GBP. An indirect quote is the inverse amount—the number of pounds John can receive in exchange for 1 USD.

Figure 2B-26 illustrates the relationship between direct and indirect quotes.

Figure 2B-26 Relationship Between Direct and Indirect Quotes

Type of Quote	Currency Relationship (U.S. Perspective)	Example
Indirect quote	Foreign currency/domestic currency	USD 1 = 0.531536 GBP
Direct quote	Domestic currency/foreign currency	1 GBP = 1.88134 USD

This may not be intuitively satisfying. If a shopper goes into the grocery store with $3 in her pocket intending to buy potatoes, the listed price will tell her how many dollars are required to buy a pound of potatoes. The grocery store provides direct quotes on potatoes.

Although understanding exchange rates is easiest in relation to transactions by John, the U.S. traveler, the impact of exchange rates goes far beyond the purchases of international tourists. International trade is facilitated by the currencies of the trading nations. Purchases of oranges from Mexico will be made in Mexican pesos; purchases of American merchandise will be made in USD. For a consumer in a foreign country to purchase U.S. merchandise, he or she must have USD (or its country must, to facilitate national trading). Thus, there is a market for exchange of foreign currencies.

Fixed, Flexible, and Floating Currency Exchange Rates

Exchange rates have evolved from fixed rates in the first half of the twentieth century to flexible or floating rates.

Fixed Currency Exchange Rates

In a **fixed exchange rate system**, each country is required to maintain its currency at or near a certain value in relation to other currencies or to another measure, such as the value of gold. In 1944, the United Nations Monetary and Financial Conference (commonly known as the Bretton Woods Conference) was convened to regulate the international monetary and financial situation at the end of World War II. Among other actions, the conference established a system in which world currencies were pegged to the value of the USD, with the dollar set at a certain value in relation to gold, and the USD was designated the medium of foreign exchange. (The initial value of the dollar, $35 per ounce of gold, was maintained until the 1960s.)

In a fixed system, governments can take various actions to offset the changes that normally would result from fluctuations in the supply and demand for the currency. One straightforward method is to intervene in the currency market, using a nation's currency reserves to buy or sell dollars in the marketplace, thus increasing or decreasing the supply and thereby decreasing or increasing its price in terms of other currencies.

Assume, for example, that under the old fixed rate system, the Swiss franc's value is fixed at 2 francs to 1 dollar. And assume that demand for the franc increases in the world exchange markets to 1.90 francs to 1 dollar. (Remember, as the franc strengthens, or the dollar weakens, traders will be able to buy more dollars with fewer francs.) To restore the dollar's value against the franc, the U.S. Treasury could dip into its reserves of Swiss francs and use them to buy USD in the marketplace, thus reducing the available supply of dollars and increasing the supply of francs, until the exchange rate settles at 2 francs to 1 dollar.

Instead of intervening in exchange markets to buy or sell currency, the U.S. government might react to a depreciating dollar by other means. For example, if the dollar's decline were a reaction to a trade imbalance, the government might enact trade policies to decrease a trade deficit or increase a surplus. This would bring dollars back into the country and increase the demand for dollars to purchase U.S. goods abroad, thus raising the dollar's value in exchange for other currencies.

Nations also can place controls on currency exchange to make a currency easier or more difficult to acquire, or they can make domestic macroeconomic adjustments that decrease or increase the supply of the country's currency in the markets. For instance, if domestic price inflation were reducing the value of the dollar, the Fed might raise interest rates. This would reduce the domestic demand for money by making it more costly to borrow funds, and it also would make dollars more valuable in currency markets by increasing the interest paid on dollar-based bonds. Thus, the supply of dollars would be reduced and the demand increased, raising the currency's value from both the supply and demand sides.

Flexible or Floating Exchange Rates

A **flexible** or **floating exchange rate** is a system wherein the exchange rates for currencies are determined by market supply and demand just as are the prices of other financial assets, such as stocks and bonds. Thus, the value of the currency floats according to market action. Figure 2B-27 summarizes the features and claimed benefits of fixed and floating exchange rates.

Figure 2B-27 Benefits of Fixed and Floating Exchange Rates

Exchange Rate Type	Essential Features	Claimed Benefits
Fixed	Exchange rates do not vary.	• **Promote monetary discipline** Fixed rate systems (such as the gold standard described earlier) include restrictions on each country's monetary and fiscal policies, thus preventing governments from pursuing policies designed to expand or contract the country's money supply arbitrarily. • **Prevent speculation** Because rates are fixed, there is no incentive to buy or sell currencies in hopes of benefiting from future rate changes. • **Reduce uncertainty** Because rates are fixed, prices remain stable and predictable, removing uncertainty about the value of future payments received for exports.
Floating	Exchange rates alter with supply and demand.	• **Allow monetary autonomy** When rates are allowed to float with supply and demand, government monetary policy is not restricted by the demands of exchange rate agreements, such as a requirement to buy or sell currency to maintain a set rate. • **Allow trade balance adjustment** Floating rates allow a country to adjust automatically to changes in international trade, whereas fixed rate structures make such adaptation difficult—and usually too late.

With floating exchange rates, the short-run rates are a function of the interest rate differentials between countries. In the medium range, exchange rates are a function of trade imbalances. In the long run, exchange rates move toward purchasing power parity between the countries.

In a **managed floating exchange rate system**, the currency rate normally fluctuates according to supply and demand but is also supported by currency interventions by central banks in order to stabilize or alter rates. Monetary intervention by central banks is based on recognition that changing economic conditions may require changes in exchange rates to avoid persistent payment deficits and surpluses. A managed floating exchange rate system allows for more volatility in exchange rates than did the fixed rates under the Bretton Woods agreement.

Changes in foreign currency exchange rates can be disruptive to an economy and discourage the flow of trading. Speculators in foreign currency exchange add to the problem by purchasing and selling currencies as commodities. As a result, the usual intervention in the managed float system is for a central bank to manage or stabilize the exchange rate in a way similar to the monetary controls used by the Federal Reserve Board in the United States—purchasing or selling the currency in order to control supply and demand.

In 1987, the G-7 nations (the group of seven nations consisting of the United States, Japan, Germany, the United Kingdom, France, Italy, and Canada) agreed to stabilize the USD, which had been declining rapidly in the previous two years due to large U.S. trade deficits. The G-7 nations purchased large amounts of dollars to prop up the dollar's value. In 1994, the USD again eroded in value relative to the Japanese yen and the German mark. This was due again to a sizable U.S. trade deficit and foreign selling of U.S. investments and trading of USD for other foreign currencies, which severely increased the market supply of USD. To counteract this decline, the central banks of the United States and 16 allies purchased large amounts of USD to lower supply and restabilize the dollar.

Floating exchange rate systems have both advantages and disadvantages. Trade growth has not been found to diminish under the floating exchange rate system. Proponents believe that managed float has enabled nations and the world to prevent severe economic turmoil. Floating exchange rates facilitate international adjustments to negative or dangerous economic developments, and proponents believe that such events would put unbearable pressures on a fixed rate system.

Opponents of managed floating exchange rate systems believe that managed float results in excessively volatile exchange rates. Volatility has occurred even when the underlying economic and financial conditions of a particular nation have been stable. Opponents believe that managed float has not resolved balance of payments imbalances as flexible rates were presumed to do.

Opponents of managed systems feel that managed float lacks clear rules and guidelines to make the system viable in the long run. Nations inevitably will be tempted to intervene, not merely to smooth out short-term or speculative fluctuations but to prop up their currency if it is chronically weak and to manipulate the value of the currency to achieve domestic stabilization goals. Some fear that the future will bring more managing and less floating.

Currency Fluctuations

Currencies float in relation to each other. If one currency goes down in value, other currencies will be relatively higher in value. The exchange rate is determined as a trading relationship between two currencies. Six factors affect exchange rates:

1. Differences in inflation rates
2. Differences in interest rates
3. Current-account deficits
4. Level of public debt
5. Ratio of exports to imports, also known as the terms of trade
6. Political and economic stability

Determinants of exchange rates are changes in consumer tastes, income changes, changes in relative price (to be discussed shortly), speculation by investors in foreign currencies (which increase demand—buying—or supply—selling), and interest rates. If interest rates are high in one country relative to another, they will attract foreign investments into that country. As a result, the demand on the currency of that country will increase the currency's exchange rate.

Changes in a foreign currency will affect the cost of importing that country's goods. If the foreign currency is down relative to the currency of the importing country, its currency and products will be cheaper for the importing country. If the foreign currency is up relative to the importing country's currency, currency and products will be more expensive and its products will be more expensive for imports.

Companies that denominate transactions in foreign currencies are responsible for managing exchange rate risks. Currency futures, currency options, and currency swaps are tools used to manage those risks. **Currency futures**, also called "FX futures" and "foreign exchange futures," are contracts to exchange a number of foreign currency units for another at a specific date for a specific price (exchange rate.) **Currency options** provide the option, but not the requirement, to make the same type of exchange as a currency future. The benefit of the currency option is that the option does not need to be exercised unless it is beneficial. In a **currency swap**, two parties agree to exchange the principal and interest aspects of a loan in one currency for equivalent aspects of another loan in a different currency. Currency swaps closely resemble interest rate swaps, except that they may involve the exchange of principal.

The difference in the cost of imports is called the "relative price." For example, suppose that Italy is exporting product A to the United States for €50 and the United States is exporting product B to Italy for $50. The exchange rate determines what the relative cost will be to consumers in the United States importing Italian goods and to consumers in Italy importing American goods.

If the exchange rate ($/€) is 1.25:

- The relative price of product A for U.S. consumers is 1.25($/€) × €50 = $62.50.
- The relative price of product B for Italian consumers is € (1/1.25) = .8 (€/$) × $50 = €40.

If, two months later, the price of product A is still €50 in Italy but has fallen to $60 (from $62.50) in the United States, we can conclude that the dollar has risen in value (appreciated) relative to the euro. Correspondingly, the euro has fallen relative to the dollar, and product B, still at $50 in the United States, will now cost a European buyer €41.67. We can calculate the exchange rate based upon the real versus relative price as shown:

$$\$60 / €50 = 1.2 \ (\$/€)$$
$$€41.67 / \$50 = .8334 \ (€/\$)$$

Another way to show the fluctuation in exchange rates is on a graph. Figure 2B-28 demonstrates an increase in the value of the euro relative to the USD.

Figure 2B-28 Equilibrium for USD and Euro Exchange Rate

Figure 2B-28 shows an increasing demand for the euro from demand line D to demand line D_1. This occurs in the case of a balance of payments deficit resulting from increased exports, increased income for Europeans, and increased demand on the euro. Notice that, for the quantity supplied of euros, it would cost more in USD to purchase euros as the demand increases.

Risk and Rate of Return for Foreign Investment

One of the risks of holding any financial asset is that it may prove to be unfavorable and decline in value. International investment that spans a number of countries is seen as a way of diversifying that risk.

Consider the example of investors in Country A and Country B, both of which grow coffee. In international trade, residents of each country purchase 50% ownership in the farm cooperatives of the other. When climate and economic conditions are good in Country A and Country B experiences drought, each investor earns the same on their portfolio. If, for example, Country A harvests 75 tons of coffee and Country B harvests only 25 tons, each country earns a return of 50 tons. In this instance, the investor in Country B benefits from diversification. In another year, in which Country B produces 100 tons of coffee and Country A produces 50 tons, each will recognize a return of 75 tons. In this case, Country A benefits from diversification.

Similar diversification will aid investors in the case of adverse interest rate changes in one country; diversification of portfolio assets in other countries will minimize the impact of the adverse change.

When considering an international investment, a company naturally wants to consider the potential rate of return of its new foreign investments. But it also should consider the impact on the risk of its overall portfolio.

An investment in a developing country, for example, may promise a higher rate of return than domestic operations. But higher rates of return tend to be correlated with higher risk. In this case, risk means variability.

For example: Assume that Luxury Luggage, Inc., a domestic U.S. company, starts an operation overseas that returns 45% one year followed by a return of −5% the next. That may be a mean rate of return of 20% ([45% + −5%] / 2 = 40% / 2 = 20%), but if Luxury Luggage has a conservative outlook on risk, it is likely to prefer an investment with more predictable returns, such as 20% followed by 18% followed by 19%. That is only a 19% return, but the risk profile is more consistent with a conservative outlook. Investors in the company will not be subjected to those nerve-wracking quarters when returns drop precipitously, causing the risk averse to sell their investments. Lenders, too, tend to be more amenable to providing funds for investments with stable rates of return, because fluctuating returns means lean quarters that may jeopardize the ability to cover loan obligations.

Investing overseas, however, is a form of diversification. And diversification actually tends to reduce risk as the investor—Luxury Luggage, in this case—multiplies the number of investments in its portfolio. For risk reduction to work, though, diversification requires more than mere multiplication of investments. If all the investments have the same characteristics, they will not alter the risk profile of the portfolio.

If, for example, Luxury Luggage maintains assembly plants in ten locations, each of which earns a 20% return in year 1, an 18% return in year 2, and a 22% return in year 3, it has done nothing to alter the risk–return relationship of maintaining only one of those operations.

Diversification evens out variability—reduces risk, in other words—if the earnings in one location tend to be up when earnings elsewhere are down. This is a simple way of saying that a company considering an overseas investment must look at the expected rate of return plus the variability of the return (standard deviation, in statistical terms) but must do so in light of the correlation of those good and not-so-good years.

For example: Assume that Luxury Luggage is considering two new locations for assembly plants. Its financial department concludes that the two locations offer the potential returns and risk shown in Figure 2B-29.

Figure 2B-29 Rate of Return and Risk in Countries A and B

Country	Mean Return Rate	Standard Deviation
A	18%	8%
B	22%	13%

Assume that Luxury Luggage currently is making a 16% return from its U.S. operation, with a standard deviation of 10%. If it ships half of its business to the new location, the resulting rate of return is easy to calculate because it is a simple average. For the combined operations in the United States and Country A, the mean rate of return will be 17% (16% + 18% / 2 = 17%). And for Country B, the mean return will be 19% (16% + 22% / 2).

If rate of return were the only consideration, Country B would be the easy choice for the new location. But Country B, with its standard deviation of 13%, involves greater risk. And the company cannot determine how much risk is involved by simply averaging the standard deviations. Instead, it will have its financial experts put their computer programs to work to determine the correlation coefficients and come up with standard deviations for the two potential combinations of domestic and overseas operations.

It is quite possible that Country B, although riskier when considered alone, may counterbalance Luxury Luggage's weak domestic quarters with its own stronger quarters, so that the two operations together have a lower standard deviation than either one separately.

There always will be political risk in international investments. In the event of political upheaval, adverse changes may result for the foreign investor, including nationalization of assets and seizing of the assets from that investor. The political risk of investing in another country is tied to the possibility of financial upheaval in the country, which ultimately can be tied to politics. The Asian crisis in 1997 was exacerbated by the withdrawal of loans by nervous foreign investors. Those investors lost their money by refusing to roll over loans, but other investors who may have been willing to roll over loans or continue to invest lost their capital anyway as economies collapsed.

Other risks associated with international projects include currency fluctuations and inflation risks.

Multinational Budgeting and Financing

Comparative advantage is the ability of a firm or individual to produce goods and/or services at a lower opportunity cost than other firms or individuals. Each country can benefit by focusing on production of goods or services that provide an advantage when compared with other goods or services that could be produced within that country. Assuming the free flow of capital across borders, multinationals also can consider investing in goods or services according to the absolute advantage offered, no matter where production might take place.

Like domestic capital budgeting, investing in capital projects across borders focuses on analysis of long-term cash flows. This is true whether the project involves setting up new operations similar to one's domestic businesses (e.g., opening a new chain of stores) or acquiring existing businesses. However, the next issues, among others, arise in addition to those involved in budgeting for domestic capital investment.

Returns and Risks

Expected returns may have to be adjusted in light of political and economic risks. Doing business in foreign countries may involve more risk than doing business domestically, or the opposite may be true, depending on the countries involved. Investors will shy away from putting money into unstable, unpredictable situations unless expected returns justify the added risk. Methods of providing more attractive returns include offering a higher rate of return, budgeting for higher cash flows, and shortening the time horizon for returns.

Overall Cash Flows versus Local Cash Flows

The parent company's cash flows must be considered separately from the foreign operation's cash flows. From the foreign operation's point of view, cash flows are self-contained.

For example: If a division in Vietnam generates an acceptable return, the manager on site will be satisfied. Management at the headquarters in the United States, however, has to balance cash flows in Vietnam against all other cash flows in the firm's other divisions in the Philippines and the Dominican Republic, as well as in the United States. If the cash flows in Vietnam are earned by diverting business from operations elsewhere, headquarters may have to change its overall strategy.

Currency Considerations

Because of currency exchange rate fluctuations, future investment returns may be reduced in value when translated from the local currency back into dollars. Those returns also may be enhanced in value by currency fluctuations. To analyze the impact of currency fluctuations, budgets can be projected with several different assumptions about future exchange rates to judge the impact each might have on the returns from the investment. (The method of doing this is called "sensitivity analysis," which is covered in Part 1, Section E: Internal Controls.) Risk also can be hedged by various currency investment strategies.

Effects of Inflation

Different long-term rates of inflation in the foreign and domestic countries can affect an overseas capital project in several ways. Inflation will affect the local market by its impact on the price of resources and the price of the product or service produced. It also may affect demand for the product, depending on price elasticity. Currency exchange rates also respond to inflation; high inflation rates correlate with depreciating currency, and low inflation correlates with a strengthened currency. Finally, potential sources of borrowed funds will be more or less attractive depending on the rate of inflation. Inflation generally favors the borrower and penalizes the lender; inflated currency makes the initial amount, as well as fixed payments, easier to repay. These various effects of inflation—on prices, currency exchange rates, and financing—must be considered together; some may be favorable and some harmful.

Taxation

Tax rates can vary considerably among countries, and they must be taken into account when determining where to make capital investments. If a multinational company has divisions that buy and sell among themselves, it can benefit from differential tax rates in the various countries by the way it sets transfer prices. Divisions in high-tax countries generally should record the lowest profits on such transfers, while divisions in low-tax jurisdictions should record the highest profits.

Different Accounting Standards

Accounting standards may be different between countries of the parent company and the across-border division or subsidiary. This creates added cost and complexity when analyzing returns according to the two systems.

Financing and Paying for International Trade

Forms of Payment in International Trade

If Company A in Europe ships products to Company B in the United States, how and when does money change hands? A number of instruments are used.

The import-export business involves a degree of payment risk when money changes hands across borders. Like any seller, an exporter of goods risks nonpayment, and like any buyer, an importer risks paying for items that never appear or show up damaged or defective. Importers and exporters handle these risks through a number of different methods of payment.

- A **letter of credit** is a letter sent by a lender to an exporter on behalf of an importer stating that the bank will accept a draft (bill of exchange) with appropriate accompanying documentation and will back the obligation of the importer. A confirmed letter of credit also includes the guarantee of a bank in the exporter's country.

- A **sight draft** is a bill for imports that is payable immediately. This is similar to a cash on demand (COD) order, where the importer pays for the goods when they arrive with proper documentation. A sight draft is also called a "demand draft."
- A **time draft** is a bill that must be paid at a specified time in the future or upon completion of specified requirements by the exporter.
- A **consignment** is when the exporter sends goods to the importer to be sold. The importer sends money to the exporter as the goods are sold.
- An **open account** occurs when the exporter mails documents to the importer (buyer) before there is any obligation on the part of the importer. Essentially, the importer has no obligation. This arrangement can be risky for the exporter, as it runs the risk of default by the buyer. An open account is most likely between two countries that have conducted business successfully in the past.
- Importers sometimes **prepay** for goods or services. This subjects the importer to the maximum amount of payment risk and therefore is suitable only for transactions between counterparties with sound reasons to trust one another, such as units of the same multinational company.

Methods of Financing Foreign Trade

Import-export transactions also can be financed in several different ways.

Bankers' Acceptance

Bankers' acceptances (BAs) are forms of time drafts drawn to finance the export, import, domestic shipment, or storage of goods. A BA is accepted when a bank writes on the draft its agreement to pay it at maturity. A bank will accept the draft from either the drawer of the BA or the holder of the instrument.

BAs are traded at discounts from face value in the secondary market. For example, if Company A ships from Country A to Company B in Country B, Company B will arrange with the bank to pay the costs of the imported goods at a specified time in the future. The BA will be sent to the exporter, who can sell the BA in the market at a discount rate in order to finance export expenses. The holder of the BA at the time of its maturity presents it to the guaranteeing bank for payment at face value.

Denominating Transactions in a Foreign Currency

A company may transact business (buying inventory or selling products) in the local currency (USD) or in a foreign currency. If the company decides to transact in the foreign currency, also called "denominating the transaction in the foreign currency," there is the risk that the foreign currency will appreciate or depreciate relative to the local currency, creating a gain or loss. For example, suppose a U.S. company denominated the sale of merchandise for €1,000 when the euro had a spot exchange rate of $1.40 with terms of net 30 (due in full in 30 days). If the euro has appreciated in value to $1.45 by the date of receipt, the company receives the €1,000, which are now worth $1,450 instead of the original $1,400, creating a gain of $50. Alternatively, if a company was the buyer in this transaction, a $50 loss would be created because $1,450 would be required to satisfy the €1,000 payment. Many companies choose to transfer the risk of changing currency rates with currency swaps, currency options, currency futures, or other techniques, such as countertrading, forfaiting, or cross-border factoring.

Countertrade

The term **countertrade** means exchanging goods or services with other goods or services (in whole or in part) rather than with money. Countertrade covers a wide range of commercial mechanisms for reciprocal trade. It involves the exchange of goods or services to finance purchases rather than using cash. Barter is probably the oldest and best-known example. Other methods of countertrade have evolved to meet the requirements of a more sophisticated world economy. In its various forms, countertrade represents 10% to 15% of world trade.

Countertrade facilitates trade flows and investments into countries that have difficulty externalizing hard currency or that impose certain **counterpurchases** (or offset obligations) on sellers of products, projects, and technologies. It focuses on ways to create financing and investment solutions to mitigate sovereign/political and commercial risk.

On the downside, countertrade exposes participants to several risks, such as pricing risk, the risk of handling unfamiliar goods, and the risk of receiving goods in poor condition. Pricing risk results from the fluctuation of exchange rates. Over a long term countertrade contract, the value of the goods received may vary considerably in world currencies. Perhaps the most common problem experienced by countertraders is having to handle goods with which they are not familiar, leading to expense and liability involved in handling or reselling the goods. Countertraders also risk receiving goods in poor condition or of substandard quality—a risk shared by those who purchase goods and services.

Forfaiting

Forfaiting refers to the purchase of receivables for goods or services from an exporter in order for the seller to obtain immediate cash without affecting the exporter's existing credit line. Forfaiting is typically without recourse, meaning that the purchaser of the receivables obligation does not have the ability to go back to the exporter in the event of nonpayment.

A typical forfaiting transaction includes these characteristics:

- A credit period of at least 180 days
- The ability to settle the receivable in most major currencies
- A letter of credit or a guarantee is made by a bank
- A promissory note, a bill of exchange, a deferred-payment letter of credit, and/or a letter of guarantee

Cross-Border Factoring

A **factor** is a financial institution that buys a firm's accounts receivable and collects on the accounts. Cross-border factoring occurs when there is a network of factors across borders. The exporter's factor may contact factors in other countries to handle collection of accounts receivables, including those from imports.

Foreign Currency Loans

Companies may borrow foreign currencies when financing transactions or operations in another country. The methods of handling foreign currency transactions are varied and complicated, but one aspect of such borrowing is important to know: the impact of exchange rate changes on the cost of borrowing.

The effective interest rate on a currency loan (the actual cost of borrowing) combines the nominal interest with the effects of changing exchange rates. If the borrowed currency depreciates during the term of the loan, the interest rate effectively decreases, because the amount owed will be less in terms of the weaker currency. The opposite happens when the foreign currency appreciates, making the loan effectively more costly.

Assume, for example, that Accountemps International (AI), a U.S. company with operations in Germany, wants to borrow euros when the USD is trading at par with the euro—1 USD purchases 1 euro. And assume that the 90-day interest rate available on loans from Deutschebank is 5% and the company borrows €1,000,000 for repayment in 90 days. On day 1 of the loan's term, the €1,000,000 is equal to $1,000,000.

Assuming interest is due in 90 days, at the time of repayment, the nominal rate of 5% will require an interest payment of €12,328.70 and a principal and interest repayment of €1,012,328.70.

Interest on Euro Loan

$1,000,000 \times (0.05 \times 90 / 365) = €12,328.70$

Debt Repayment in Euros

$$
\begin{aligned}
\text{Principal} &= 1,000,000 \\
\text{Interest} &= 12,328.70 \\
\text{Total Repayment} &= 1,012,328.70
\end{aligned}
$$

If the euro has appreciated against the USD to, for example, 0.95 euro/1 USD (fewer euros are required to purchase 1 USD), then AI's repayment of 1,012,328.70 will require USD 1,065,609.10.

Principal and Interest Repayment at €0.95 / $1

€1,012,328.70 / .95 [Euro / USD exchange rate] = $1,065,609.10

The effective interest rate combines the interest expense with the extra $65,609.10 required to repay the principal.

Effective Interest Rate on Euro Loan

65,609.10 / 1,000,000 = 6.56%

The net loss on this transaction, for accounting purposes, is $53,280.40 [$1,012,328.70 – $1,065,609.10].

If the euro had depreciated in value, the effective interest rate would have been less than the nominal 5% rate.

Assume the exchange rate at the time of repayment was €1.05/$1 (more euros are required to purchase USD than at the beginning):

Principal and Interest Repayment at €1.05 Euro / $1

1,012,328.70 Euro / 1.05 [Euro / USD Exchange Rate] = USD 964,122.57

Effective Interest Rate on Euro Loan

$964,122.57 − $1,000,000 = −$35,877.43
−35,877.50 / 1,000,000 = −3.59%

The net gain on this transaction, for accounting purposes, is $48,206.20 [$1,012,328.70 − $964,122.57].

Because of the positive change in the exchange rate, AI "paid" a negative rate of interest. In other words, the firm actually made more on the currency exchange than it paid in nominal interest. (This is the sort of result that encourages speculation in foreign currencies.)

Transfer Pricing

Transfer pricing is the pricing of a product when selling from one part of a company to another. When the buyer and seller divisions are in different countries, the objective of transfer pricing is to minimize the company's effective worldwide income tax obligations. To accomplish this task, a company sets a high transfer price (perhaps based on the market price) on goods shipped to a division in a country with relatively higher taxes and sets a low transfer price (perhaps based on direct costs) on goods shipped to a division in a country with relatively lower taxes.

For example: If the income tax rate in the United States is 30% and the income tax rate in a foreign country is 40%, the company will use a high transfer price when selling from the United States to the foreign country in order to tax the gross profit at the 30% rate. The higher cost to the foreign division will yield a lower gross profit and, therefore, decrease the taxable income at the 40% rate, as shown:

	North Division U.S. Division (30% Tax Rate)	South Division Foreign Division (40% Tax Rate)	Total Both Divisions
Sales			
10,000 units × $15 per unit	$ 150,000	–	–$ 150,000
20,000 units × $18 per unit	–	$ 360,000	$ 360,000
Total sales	$ 150,000	$ 360,000	$ 510,000
Expenses			
Variable:			
10,000 units × $7 per unit	$ 70,000	–	$ 70,000
20,000 units × $10 per unit	–	$ 200,000	200,000
Fixed:	50,000	65,000	115,000
Total expenses	$ 120,000	$ 265,000	$ 385,000
Operating income	$ 30,000	$ 95,000	$ 125,000
Operating expenses	10,000	40,000	50,000
Taxable income	$ 20,000	$ 55,000	$ 75,000
Income tax	$ 6,000	$ 22,000	$ 28,000

Transfer price of an additional 1,000 units from U.S. to Foreign at market ($15):

	U.S. Division	Foreign Division	Totals Both Divisions
Increase in sales	$ 15,000	$ 18,000	$ 33,000
Increase in costs	7,000	15,000	22,000
Net increase in taxable income	$ 8,000	$ 3,000	$ 11,000
Increase in income taxes	$ 2,400	$ 1,200	$ 3,600

Transfer price of an additional 1,00 units from U.S. to Foreign at variable cost ($7):

	U.S. Division	Foreign Division	Totals Both Divisions
Increase in sales	$ 7,000	$ 18,000	$ 25,000
Increase in costs	7,000	7,000	14,000
Net increase in taxable income	$ –	$ 11,000	$ 11,000
Increase in income taxes	$ –	$ 4,400	$ 4,400

Transfer pricing has become an important component in global tax minimization. Creative transfer pricing approaches, applied in the context of acquisitions, divestitures, plant relocations, research and development activities, and global restructuring transactions, assist in the management and minimization of global tax rates.

Legal and Social Issues in Global Business

There are many legal challenges in international business, including disparities between international law and the laws of individual nations; continuing debate about free trade versus protectionism, particularly in regard to developing countries; and differing customs between countries.

Disparities Between International and Domestic Law

Different countries have different laws for how to conduct business. Some businesses may choose to do business in nations in which they can conduct certain activities not allowed in their own countries. For example, some firms have moved their businesses to Caribbean island nations that do not charge taxes, simply to avoid U.S. taxes.

The U.S. Foreign Corrupt Practices Act forbids an American company doing business overseas to pay bribes to a foreign government official for obtaining contracts or business. This can pose an ethical dilemma because it places the American company at a disadvantage in a country where bribes are the standard mode of doing business.

Free Trade versus Protectionism

Although the governments of most nations generally believe that free trade and open markets are avenues toward greater world wealth, the controversy over free trade versus protectionism continues within and between nations.

Many people in developed countries fear loss of jobs as businesses move their production operations overseas to countries that have lower wage levels and fewer costly environmental and worker protection laws. Those in developing countries disagree with protectionist acts, such as agricultural subsidies. Some resent that they have been required, as developing nations, to be completely open to free trade while tariffs and subsidies still exist in developed nations, such as the United States and the European nations.

Among leaders of international organizations as well as heads of nations, there is disagreement about the pace of opening markets and privatizing businesses in emerging markets. Some leaders want to push developing nations to rapidly privatize businesses (private ownership as opposed to government ownership of the business) and to open markets to free trade. However, other economists believe that opening a market too soon or privatizing businesses in a country too quickly results in a lack of stability. They believe that businesses in a developing country need time to develop stable business practices before tariffs are removed.

Differing Customs

Businesses managing international offices also must deal with the customs, practices, and attitudes in the workplace that can differ greatly between countries, in areas such as vacation time, work schedule, benefits, employee supervision, and social position.

Threat of Expropriation

One significant risk of operating a business in a foreign country is the threat of expropriation. Certain countries may expropriate private company assets and, usually, expel the U.S. workers and managers. **Expropriation** is forceful confiscation and redistribution of private property outside of common laws, such as those of eminent domain. An international company should consider the potential risk of expropriation before operating in a foreign country.

Diversification of International Assets

Diversification means reducing risk by investing in a variety of assets. A diversified portfolio is one in which values do not move up and down in perfect synchrony. Thus, the diversified portfolio is less risky than the weighted average risk of total assets. More risk-averse companies seek to diversify to a greater extent in order to limit unexpected foreign currency gains and losses.

Knowledge Check: International Finance

The next questions are intended to help you check your understanding and recall of the material presented in this topic. They do not represent the type of questions that appear on the CMA exam.

Directions: Answer each question in the space provided. Correct answers and section references appear after the knowledge check questions.

1. Last year, import of a European product that cost €100 cost $125. This year, the same import, which has not changed price in euros, costs $140. Which of the following is true?

   ☐ **a.** The exchange rate of USD for euros has increased from 0.80 to .71.

   ☐ **b.** The exchange rate of USD for euros has decreased from 1.25 to 1.40.

   ☐ **c.** The exchange rate of USD for euros has decreased from 0.71 to 0.80.

   ☐ **d.** The exchange rate of USD for euros has increased from 1.25 to 1.40.

2. All of the following are risks specific to foreign investment **except**

   ☐ **a.** political risk.

   ☐ **b.** foreign currency fluctuation risk.

   ☐ **c.** interest rate risk.

   ☐ **d.** potential nationalization of businesses by the foreign country.

3. An American firm that sells products from all over the world wishes to import a collection of Chinese art. The Chinese art dealer needs cash in order to finance the shipment, but the American art dealer does not wish to pay for the imported art before it arrives. What can the American importer use to meet both her needs and those of the exporter?

   ☐ **a.** Consignment agreement

   ☐ **b.** Bankers' acceptance

   ☐ **c.** Sight draft

   ☐ **d.** Letter of credit

4. An American company has three foreign subsidiaries: X, Y, and Z. The corporate income tax is 45% in X's country, 35% in Y's country, and 40% in Z's country. How can the American company use transfer pricing to improve its combined after-tax earnings?

   ☐ **a.** By increasing the price that X charges Y

   ☐ **b.** By decreasing the price that Y charges Z

   ☐ **c.** By reducing the price that X charges Y

   ☐ **d.** No combination of increases or reductions in transfer prices

Knowledge Check Answers: International Finance

1. Last year, import of a European product that cost €100 cost $125. This year, the same import, which has not changed price in euros, costs $140. Which of the following is true? [**See *Currency Fluctuations.***]

   ☐ **a.** The exchange rate of USD for euros has increased from 0.80 to .71.

   ☐ **b.** The exchange rate of USD for euros has decreased from 1.25 to 1.40.

   ☐ **c.** The exchange rate of USD for euros has decreased from 0.71 to 0.80.

   ☑ **d.** The exchange rate of USD for euros has increased from 1.25 to 1.40.

2. All of the following are risks specific to foreign investment **except** [**See *Risk and Rate of Return for Foreign Investment.***]

   ☐ **a.** political risk.

   ☐ **b.** foreign currency fluctuation risk.

   ☑ **c.** interest rate risk.

   ☐ **d.** potential nationalization of businesses by the foreign country.

   Interest rate risks are not unique to foreign investments. In fact, diversification in different countries can minimize interest rate risk.

3. An American firm that sells products from all over the world wishes to import a collection of Chinese art. The Chinese art dealer needs cash in order to finance the shipment, but the American art dealer does not wish to pay for the imported art before it arrives. What can the American importer use to meet both her needs and those of the exporter? [**See *Financing and Paying for International Trade.***]

   ☐ **a.** Consignment agreement

   ☑ **b.** Bankers' acceptance

   ☐ **c.** Sight draft

   ☐ **d.** Letter of credit

4. An American company has three foreign subsidiaries: X, Y, and Z. The corporate income tax is 45% in X's country, 35% in Y's country, and 40% in Z's country. How can the American company use transfer pricing to improve its combined after-tax earnings? [**See *Methods of Financing Foreign Trade.***]

   ☐ **a.** By increasing the price that X charges Y

   ☐ **b.** By decreasing the price that Y charges Z

   ☑ **c.** By reducing the price that X charges Y

   ☐ **d.** No combination of increases or reductions in transfer prices

Practice Questions: Corporate Finance

Directions: This sampling of questions is designed to emulate actual exam questions. Read each question and write your response on another sheet of paper. See the "Answers to Section Practice Questions" section at the end of this book to assess your response. Validate or improve the answer you wrote. For a more robust selection of practice questions, access the **Online Test Bank** at www .wileycma.com.

Question 2B1-AT05

Topic: Risk and Return

Using the capital asset pricing model (CAPM), the required rate of return for a firm with a beta of 1.25 when the market return is 14% and the risk-free rate is 6% is

- ☐ **a.** 7.5%.
- ☐ **b.** 14.0%.
- ☐ **c.** 16.0%.
- ☐ **d.** 17.5%.

Question 2B1-AT06

Topic: Risk and Return

The expected rate of return for the stock of Cornhusker Enterprises is 20%, with a standard deviation of 15%. The expected rate of return for the stock of Mustang Associates is 10%, with a standard deviation of 9%. The stock that would be considered riskier is

- ☐ **a.** Mustang, because the coefficient of variation is higher.
- ☐ **b.** Cornhusker, because the standard deviation is higher.
- ☐ **c.** Cornhusker, because the coefficient of variation is lower.
- ☐ **d.** Mustang, because the return is lower.

Question 2B2-LS04

Topic: Long-Term Financial Management

Which of the following statements about correlation and return variability **best** describes a portfolio with a limited number of stocks representing different industries?

- ☐ **a.** Low correlation and low portfolio return variability
- ☐ **b.** Low correlation and high portfolio return variability
- ☐ **c.** High correlation and high portfolio return variability
- ☐ **d.** High correlation and low portfolio return variability

Question 2B2-LS05

Topic: Long-Term Financial Management

If a firm's goal is to minimize portfolio risk, the **best** strategy would be to include

- ☐ **a.** investments with low betas and highly correlated returns.
- ☐ **b.** investments with high betas and low correlated returns.
- ☐ **c.** diversified investments with high betas.
- ☐ **d.** diversified investments with low betas.

Question 2B2-CQ06

Topic: Long-Term Financial Management

Cox Company has sold 1,000 shares of $100 par, 8% preferred stock at an issue price of $92 per share. Stock issue costs were $5 per share. Cox pays taxes at the rate of 40%. What is Cox's cost of preferred stock capital?

- ☐ **a.** 8.00%
- ☐ **b.** 8.25%
- ☐ **c.** 8.70%
- ☐ **d.** 9.20%

Question 2B2-CQ07

Topic: Long-Term Financial Management

Bull & Bear Investment Banking is working with the management of Clark Inc. in order to take the company public in an initial public offering. Selected financial information for Clark is as shown next.

Long-term debt (8% interest rate)	$10,000,000
Common equity: Par value ($1 per share)	3,000,000
Additional paid-in capital	24,000,000
Retained earnings	6,000,000
Total assets	55,000,000
Net income	3,750,000
Dividend (annual)	1,500,000

If public companies in Clark's industry are trading at 12 times earnings, what is the estimated value per share of Clark?

- ☐ **a.** $9.00
- ☐ **b.** $12.00
- ☐ **c.** $15.00
- ☐ **d.** $24.00

Question 2B2-LS13

Topic: Long-Term Financial Management

A long-term call option to buy common stock directly from a corporation is a

- ☐ **a.** forward contract.
- ☐ **b.** warrant.
- ☐ **c.** convertible security.
- ☐ **d.** futures contract.

Question 2B2-LS15

Topic: Long-Term Financial Management

An analyst observes a 15-year, 7% option-free bond with semiannual coupons. The required yield on this bond was 7%, but suddenly it drops to 6.5%. The price of this bond

- ☐ **a.** will increase.
- ☐ **b.** will decrease.
- ☐ **c.** will stay the same.
- ☐ **d.** cannot be determined without additional information.

Question 2B2-LS23

Topic: Long-Term Financial Management

What is the after-tax cost of debt for a 6% interest-bearing bond at an anticipated tax rate of 38%?

- ☐ **a.** 3.80%
- ☐ **b.** 3.72%
- ☐ **c.** 4.40%
- ☐ **d.** 6.00%

Question 2B2-CQ09

Topic: Long-Term Financial Management

The Hatch Sausage Company is projecting an annual growth rate for the foreseeable future of 9%. The most recent dividend paid was $3.00 per share. New common stock can be issued at $36 per share. Using the constant growth model, what is the approximate cost of capital for retained earnings?

- ☐ **a.** 9.08%
- ☐ **b.** 17.33%
- ☐ **c.** 18.08%
- ☐ **d.** 19.88%

Question 2B2-CQ10

Topic: Long-Term Financial Management

Angela Company's capital structure consists entirely of long-term debt and common equity. The cost of capital for each component is shown next.

Long-term debt	8%
Common equity	15%

Angela pays taxes at a rate of 40%. If Angela's weighted average cost of capital is 10.41%, what proportion of the company's capital structure is in the form of long-term debt?

- ☐ **a.** 34%
- ☐ **b.** 45%
- ☐ **c.** 55%
- ☐ **d.** 66%

Question 2B2-CQ15

Topic: Long-Term Financial Management

Thomas Company's capital structure consists of 30% long-term debt, 25% preferred stock, and 45% common equity. The cost of capital for each component is shown next.

Long-term debt	8% before tax
Preferred stock	11%
Common equity	15%

If Thomas pays taxes at the rate of 40%, what is the company's after-tax weighted average cost of capital?

- ☐ **a.** 7.14%
- ☐ **b.** 9.84%
- ☐ **c.** 10.94%
- ☐ **d.** 11.90%

Question 2B3-AT13

Topic: Raising Capital

Arch Inc. has 200,000 shares of common stock outstanding. Net income for the recently ended fiscal year was $500,000, and the stock has a price/earnings ratio of 8. The board of directors has just declared a three-for-two stock split. For an investor who owns 100 shares of stock before the split, the approximate value (rounded to the nearest dollar) of the investment in Arch stock immediately after the split is

- ☐ **a.** $2,000.
- ☐ **b.** $1,333.
- ☐ **c.** $3,000.
- ☐ **d.** $4,000.

Question 2B4-CQ08

Topic: Working Capital Management

Shown next are selected data from Fortune Company's most recent financial statements.

Marketable securities	$10,000
Accounts receivable	60,000
Inventory	25,000
Supplies	5,000
Accounts payable	40,000
Short-term debt payable	10,000
Accruals	5,000

What is Fortune's net working capital?

- ☐ **a.** $35,000
- ☐ **b.** $45,000
- ☐ **c.** $50,000
- ☐ **d.** $80,000

Question 2B4-CQ10

Topic: Working Capital Management

The Rolling Stone Corporation, an entertainment ticketing service, is considering the next means of speeding cash flow for the corporation:

Lockbox system. A lockbox system would cost $25 per month for each of its 170 banks and would result in interest savings of $5,240 per month.

Drafts. Drafts would be used to pay for ticket refunds based on 4,000 refunds per month at a cost of $2.00 per draft, which would result in interest savings of $6,500 per month.

Bank float. Bank float would be used for the $1,000,000 in checks written each month. The bank would charge a 2% fee for this service, but the corporation will earn $22,000 in interest on the float.

Electronic transfer. Items over $25,000 would be transferred electronically; it is estimated that 700 items of this type would be made each month at a cost of $18 each, which would result in increased interest earnings of $14,000 per month.

Which of these methods of speeding cash flow should Rolling Stone Corporation adopt?

- ☐ **a.** Lockbox and electronic transfer only
- ☐ **b.** Bank float and electronic transfer only
- ☐ **c.** Lockbox, drafts, and electronic transfer only
- ☐ **d.** Lockbox, bank float, and electronic transfer only

Question 2B6-AT14

Topic: International Finance

A U.S.-based infant clothing company, Tiny Tot, is interested in importing fabric from China. Which of the following should Tiny Tot arrange first for the Chinese company to ship the merchandise?

- ☐ **a.** Bill of lading
- ☐ **b.** Time draft
- ☐ **c.** Letter of credit
- ☐ **d.** Sight draft

Question 2B6-AT18

Topic: International Finance

An appreciation of the U.S. dollar against the Japanese yen would

- ☐ **a.** make U.S. goods more expensive to Japanese consumers.
- ☐ **b.** increase the translated earnings of U.S. subsidiaries domiciled in Japan.
- ☐ **c.** increase the cost of buying supplies for U.S. firms.
- ☐ **d.** make travel in Japan more expensive for U.S. citizens.

Question 2B6-AT19

Topic: International Finance

Technocrat Inc., located in Belgium, currently manufactures products at its domestic plant and exports them to the United States, since production is less expensive at home. The company is considering the possibility of setting up a plant in the United States. All of the following factors would encourage the company to consider direct foreign investment in the U.S. **except** the

- ☐ **a.** expectation of more stringent trade restrictions by the United States.
- ☐ **b.** depreciation of the U.S. dollar against Belgium's currency.
- ☐ **c.** changing demand for the company's exports to the United States due to exchange rate fluctuations.
- ☐ **d.** widening of the gap in production costs between locations in the United States and Belgium.

To further assess your understanding of the concepts and calculations covered in Part 2, Section B: Corporate Finance, practice with the **Online Test Bank** for this section. **REMINDER:** See the "Answers to Section Practice Questions" section at the end of this book.

Decision Analysis

Decision making is a key activity in every organization. In any business, a wide variety of decisions have to be made on a daily basis. Decisions may range from small to large-scale in scope and can be individual decisions or group decisions. Furthermore, a given decision can have short- and/or long-term consequences in regard to the resources involved in reaching the decision as well as the financial impact.

Management accountants often are called on to provide critical data used in the decision-making process. This section reviews fundamental information that management accountants need to know about the decision-making process, the importance of relevant cost and revenue data, the use of cost/volume/profit, and marginal analyses.

Management decision making also involves the setting of prices for goods and services. The current competitive, global environment demands careful setting and managing of output prices. Management accountants assist price setters by providing cost information for short-run and long-run pricing, market-based pricing, cost-based pricing, target pricing, target costing, and target rate of return pricing. Management accountants also help price setters apply the laws of supply and demand to pricing decisions.

Risk management is a required component of decision making and pricing. The objective of risk management is to reduce risk to an acceptable level. The management accountant often is involved in the assessment and management of risk. In particular, management accountants help identify threats to the organization and their probabilities, controls against the threats and their effectiveness, and the losses incurred by not preventing or detecting threats prior to their occurrence.

Learning Outcome Statements Overview: Decision Analysis

Section C.1. Cost/Volume/Profit Analysis

A. Demonstrate an understanding of how cost/volume/profit (CVP) analysis (break-even analysis) is used to examine the behavior of total revenues, total costs, and operating income as changes occur in output levels, selling prices, variable costs per unit, or fixed costs.
   a. Break-even analysis is used to determine how many units must be sold in order to have net operating income equal zero, given a firm's cost structure. Total costs are broken out between variable and fixed costs and compared against revenues in order to determine the level of sales needed. The factors that go into determining a break-even point are sales price per unit, variable costs per unit, and total fixed costs.
      i. Sales price—As selling price per unit increase, the break-even point (in units) decreases.
      ii. Variable costs per unit—As variable costs per unit increase, the break-even point (in units) increases.
      iii. Total fixed costs—As fixed costs increase, the break-even point (in units) increases.

B. Calculate operating income at different operating levels.
   a. Operating income—Total revenues from operations less total costs from operations (excluding income taxes).

   Operating Income = Total Oprating Revenues – Total Operating Costs

C. Differentiate between costs that are fixed and costs that are variable with respect to levels of output.
   a. Fixed costs—Costs that are not affected by changes in the level of output. Rent is an example of a fixed cost.
   b. Variable costs—Costs that increase and decrease proportionately to changes in output level. Direct material is an example of a variable cost.

D. Explain why the classification of fixed vs. variable costs is affected by the time frame being considered.
   a. The classification of costs as fixed or variable can be affected by the time horizon being considered. In other words, some variable costs may be reclassified as fixed. Given an extended period of time, a fixed cost, although it is

not variable, may change. Salaries may be fixed in a short time period, but layoffs may occur if levels of output decrease dramatically.

E. Calculate contribution margin per unit and total contribution margin.

    a. Contribution margin per unit is computed by subtracting the *variable* costs per unit from the unit selling price.

$$\text{Contribution Margin} = \text{Unit Selling Price} - \text{Variable Cost per Unit}$$

F. Calculate the break-even point in units and dollar sales to achieve targeted operating income or targeted net income.

    a. In order to calculate the break-even point, you will need to compute contribution margin percentage (CMP):

$$\text{Contribution Margin Percentage} = \frac{\text{Unit Contribution Margin (UCM)}}{\text{Selling Price per Unit}}$$

    b. The formula for computing a desired operating income is:

$$\frac{\text{Target Income}}{\text{(Units)}} = \frac{\text{Fixed Costs} + \text{Target Income}}{\text{UCM}}$$

    Note: In computing break-even, target income is set to zero.

    c. The formula is slightly different in order to compute break-even in dollar sales:

$$\text{Break-even Point in Dollars} = \frac{\text{Fixed Costs}}{\text{(UCM/Selling Price per Unit)}}$$

G. Demonstrate an understanding of how changes in unit sales mix affect operating income in multiple-product situations.

    a. Since companies usually have more than one product with varying levels of profitability, break-even analysis becomes more complicated. If sales vary among total units sold on multiple products, the break-even point will vary. Profits tend to be greater if higher-margin items comprise a larger proportion of the product or service mix.

H. Calculate multiple-product break-even points given percentage share of sales, and explain why there is no unique break-even point in multiple-product situations.

    a. To determine the break-even point for a company with multiple products, you must compute the weighted average contribution margin per unit as follows:

$$\text{Weighted Average UCM} = \frac{\begin{array}{c}\text{(Product A UCM Number of Units Sold)} + \\ \text{(Product B UCM} \times \text{Number of Units Sold)}\end{array}}{\begin{array}{c}\text{Product A Number of Units Sold} + \\ \text{Product B Number of Units Sold}\end{array}}$$

b. Once that is figured, you can use the next break-even point formula to get the total units that need to be sold:

$$\text{Break-Even Point} = \frac{\text{Fixed Costs}}{\text{Weighted Average UCM}}$$

I. Define, calculate and interpret margin of safety and margin of safety ratio.
   a. Margin of safety—Defines how far an organization is past the break-even point at its current sales volume level. For example, if the unit break-even point is 100 units and the company sells 150 units, it would have a margin of safety of 50 units.

$$\text{Margin of Safety} = \text{Planned Sales} - \text{Break-Even Sales}$$

   b. Margin of safety ratio—Measures the percentage above the break-even point in units. In the example, the margin of safety ratio is 50% (50/100).

$$\text{Margin of Safety Ratio} = \frac{\text{Margin of Safety}}{\text{Planned Sales}}$$

J. Explain how sensitivity analysis can be used in CVP analysis when there is uncertainty about sales.
   a. When there is uncertainty in unit selling price, variable costs, or fixed costs, a company can use sensitivity analysis to determine what effect certain changes to those variables will have on overall break-even point. For example, what if fixed costs increased by 10%? Or what if we were able to sell this unit for only $75 per unit instead of $80? You can alter the formulas mentioned above to compute the revised break-even to see how sensitive it would be to changes in variables.

K. Analyze and recommend a course of action using CVP analysis.
   a. Using the data above, you should be able to recommend a course of action to management to increase overall profitability. Some recommendations could include:
      i. Focus on Product A instead of Product B.
      ii. Convert variable costs of production (labor) to fixed costs of production (automated machines).
      iii. Find ways to reduce variable costs.

L. Demonstrate an understanding of the impact of income taxes on CVP analysis.

$$\text{Price Elasticity of Demand (E)} = [\text{Change in Quantity/Average of Quantities}] \times [\text{Change in Price/Average of Prices}]$$

   a. Income taxes are computed on net operating income and need to be taken into account in order to compute a target net income. In the equations above, target income needs to be adjusted for the tax effects of operating income. For example, if the target net income is $90,000 and the tax rate is 40%, a company would have to achieve an operating income of $150,000: (90,000 / (1 – tax rate)). The $150,000 number can then be used in the formula above, or you can substitute $90,000 with (90,000 / (1.00 – .6)).

Section C.2. Marginal Analysis

A. Identify and define relevant costs (incremental, marginal, or differential costs), sunk costs, avoidable costs, explicit and implicit costs, and relevant revenues.

    a. Relevant costs and relevant revenues (also called "incremental, marginal, or differential costs")—Those that differ among options and are future oriented. Costs and revenues that already have been incurred (historical costs) or committed are sunk and are irrelevant in decision making.

    b. Sunk costs—Costs that have already been incurred and cannot be recovered.

    c. Avoidable costs—Costs that will not be incurred if a particular activity is not performed.

    d. Explicit costs—Represent clear costs that are easily identified and accounted for (i.e., direct materials, sales commissions, etc.).

    e. Implicit costs—Costs represented by lost opportunity of the next best use of a company's resources. Implicit costs can account for the time it takes to make a product that can't be spent on another aspect of the business.

B. Explain why sunk costs are not relevant in the decision-making process.

    a. Sunk costs are costs that have already been incurred and cannot be recovered. Since they cannot be recovered regardless of the decision you are trying to make, they shouldn't be factored into the decision-making process.

C. Demonstrate an understanding of and calculate opportunity costs.

    a. Implicit costs are not as easily identified in the decision-making process but need to be considered to make an informed decision. If a company is deciding on whether to make or buy a product, it needs to take into account the lost revenue from other items that it is not able to sell if it focuses on making another product (opportunity cost). For example, assume a company is deciding whether to make Product B or buy Product B from an outside party. If it decides to make Product B, it will have to reduce the amount of Product A that it makes and sells. If Product A that has a contribution margin of $5 and the company needs will have to reduce production by 10,000 units, then the opportunity cost to be used in the decision is $50,000. Product B would have to generate more income to cover the cost of not producing Product A.

D. Calculate relevant costs given a numerical scenario.

    a. The CMA exam will test your proficiencies to certain scenarios of whether to make versus buy, introduce a new product, processes a product further, accepting special orders, or adding segments to the existing business. In all of those scenarios, you will need to determine which costs are relevant to the decision. Relevant costs are those that differ among options and are future oriented. Costs and revenues that already have been incurred (historical costs) or committed are sunk and are irrelevant in decision making. For example, a relevant cost is how much it would cost to expand operations to produce a product. The money already spent on research and development to test the feasibility of the product is not relevant as it can never be recovered.

E. Define and calculate marginal cost and marginal revenue.
   a. Marginal cost—The cost of the next unit produced.
   b. Marginal revenue—The revenue derived from the sale of the next unit.

F. Identify and calculate total cost, average fixed cost, average variable cost, and average total cost.
   a. Total cost—The total of variable costs plus all fixed costs.
   b. Average fixed cost—Total fixed costs divided by production volume. The average fixed cost should decrease as production volume increases within the relevant range.
   c. Average variable cost—Total variable costs divided by production volume. The average variable cost should remain unchanged as production volume increases within the relevant range.
   d. Average total cost—Total costs (variable plus fixed) divided by production volume. The average total cost should follow a linear curve, as mentioned above.

G. Demonstrate proficiency in the use of marginal analysis for decisions such as (a) introducing a new product or changing output levels of existing products, (b) accepting or rejecting special orders, (c) making or buying a product or service, (d) selling a product or performing additional processes and selling a more value-added product, and (e) adding or dropping a segment.

   In making decisions for any of these areas, you need to consider only relevant revenues and costs associated with future actions. Any prior revenues and costs associated are not factored into the decision. A comparison needs to be built to determine total future profitability of decision 1 versus total future profitability of decision 2. [For more information, see Topic 2: Marginal Analysis (in book).]

H. Calculate the effect on operating income of a decision to accept or reject a special order when there is idle capacity and the order has no long-run implications.
   a. Making a determination about whether to accept or decline a special order request involves an assessment of profitability (based on relevant costs and revenues and opportunity costs) as well as consideration of capacity utilization. When there is excess capacity, the decision to accept or reject a special order can be determined based on the additional revenue minus the additional costs (which are typically only variable costs). Fixed costs are considered irrelevant for this situation as they would be incurred regardless of whether the special order is accepted.

I. Identify and describe qualitative factors in make-or-buy decisions, such as product quality and dependability of suppliers.
   a. After analyzing all relevant costs in a decision to make versus buy, you must understand other qualitative factors that don't have a cost associated with them, such as:

      i. Unique knowledge of external suppliers.

      ii. Unusually skilled labor.

      iii. Access to rare materials.

      iv. Quality control issues.

J. Calculate the effect on operating income of a make-or-buy decision.

    a. Making a determination about whether to make or buy involves an assessment of profitability based on relevant costs and revenues and opportunity costs. Additional explicit costs are determined for both decisions as well as implicit factors, such uses of the idle facility if it is outsourced, the reduction in workforce, and others.

K. Calculate the effects on operating income of a decision to sell or process further and of a decision to drop or add a segment.

    a. Just like the other decisions already described, making a determination about whether to make or buy involves an assessment of profitability based on relevant costs and revenues and opportunity costs. Once-manufactured products can be sold or processed further into a new product or a product with additional value added. If the additional revenue exceeds the additional costs to process, the decision should be made to process further.

L. Identify the effects of changes in capacity on production decisions.

    a. Changes in capacity are relevant costs that need to be considered in any of the marginal analysis scenarios. Reducing capacity by adding a product line has an opportunity cost that needs to be taken into account when computing marginal operating income.

M. Demonstrate an understanding of the impact of income taxes on marginal analysis.

    a. Income taxes are a relevant cost that needs to be considered in any marginal analysis scenarios.

N. Recommend a course of action using marginal analysis.

    a. Making a determination about any of marginal analysis scenarios involves an assessment of profitability based on relevant costs and revenues and opportunity costs. Qualitative considerations aside, if the relevant revenues exceed the relevant costs, then the decision should be made to accept the project. See Topic 2: Marginal Analysis for more detailed analysis.

Section C.3. Pricing

A. Identify different pricing methodologies, including market comparables and cost-based and value-based approaches.

    a. Market comparable pricing uses as a price the price of another item having similar characteristics. It is commonly used in real estate appraisal. Cost-based pricing is commonly used when the product can be readily differentiated from products of the competition. Value-based (value-optimized pricing) or market-based pricing sets prices based on customer expectations and demand as well as customers' perceived value of the product.

B. Differentiate between a cost-based approach and a market-based approach to setting prices.

 a. Cost-based approach—Looks at the costs to develop a product or service and sets a price to recoup those costs and make a desired profit.

 b. Market-based approach—Price is based on a relationship between supply and demand and what a consumer is willing to pay for the good.

C. Calculate selling price using a cost-based approach.

 a. Under cost-based pricing, a firm:

  i. Determines the costs to produce and sell a product at a certain volume level.

  ii. Identifies a reasonable return (markup).

  iii. Adds the markup to the cost.

  iv. Adjusts the markup as necessary in response to market forces.

Selling Price = Unit Cost + (Markup % on Unit Cost × Unit Cost)

D. Demonstrate an understanding of how the pricing of a product or service is affected by the demand for and supply of the product or service as well as the market structure within which it operates.

 a. Two market methods help determine prices:

  i. Demand-based concept—If the demand for the product is high, the price will be set high. If demand is low and/or there are numerous substitutes for the product, the price will be set low.

  ii. Competition-based concept—It sets the price according to the price offered by competitors of identical and substitutable products.

E. Demonstrate an understanding of the impact of cartels on pricing.

 a. A cartel is a formal agreement among competitors to fix prices, marketing, and/or production. Cartels are designed to increase profits and decrease competition by creating barriers to entry and forcing supply and demand to ensure a certain price is paid for the good or service.

F. Demonstrate an understanding of the short-run equilibrium price for the firm in (1) pure competition; (2) monopolistic competition; (3) oligopoly; and (4) monopoly using the concepts of marginal revenue and marginal cost.

 a. Pure competition—For a product being sold in a purely competitive market, marginal revenue is equal to average revenue, which is equal to market price. In other words, in pure competition, a firm must sell at the market price since it is competing with a large number of competitors with a standardized product. In the short run, profit is maximized at the output level when marginal revenue (MR) equals marginal cost (MC): MR = MC.

 b. Monopolistic competition—Products may be differentiated but are not identical and, therefore, are not substitutable. Firms behave like monopolies in the short run and typically ignore the impact of other firms in an attempt to increase marginal net revenues (relevant costs and revenues). In the short run, profit is maximized at the output level when marginal revenue equals marginal cost: MR = MC.

      c. Oligopoly—An industry with only a few large firms. The firms usually depend on each other for pricing decisions.

      d. Monopoly—One company owns the entire market for a particular good. Firms typically sell fewer products at higher prices, resulting in higher net marginal revenue. In order to maximize profits, the monopolist firm usually sets price and output where marginal revenue equals marginal cost: $MR = MC$.

G. Identify techniques used to set prices based on understanding customers' perceptions of value, competitors' technologies, products and costs.

      a. There are various techniques to set prices if the company is not operating in pure competition and therefore must sell at whatever the market will pay. These techniques take into account supply and demand but also consider the total cost of production, desired profit levels, and perceived value. Some of these methods are described further below.

H. Define and demonstrate an understanding of target pricing and target costing, and identify the main steps in developing target prices and target costs.

      a. Target pricing—A method whereby the selling price of a product is calculated to produce a certain rate of return according to a specific volume of production. The target price represents the maximum allowable price that can be charged for the product or service. It is an estimate of the amount that potential customers would be willing to pay based on their value perceptions—their needs and expectations for products and services, quality, timeliness, and price.

      b. Target costing—A comprehensive cost management process that determines a target cost for a product or service and then develops a prototype that can be made profitably for the identified amount. The main steps in developing target costs are:

          1. Establish target price based on market needs, competition, perceived value, and so on.

          2. Establish the desired target profit margin based on risk and return.

          3. Determined allowable cost to meet profit margin based on price and output.

          4. Implement plan to achieve allowable costs using tools described below.

I. Define value engineering.

      a. Value engineering—A principal technique in closing the gap between current cost and allowable cost. It is the systematic analysis of a product or service design, materials, specifications, and production processes in the context of customer requirements.

J. Calculate the target operating income per unit and target cost per unit.

      a. Target operating income per unit—The operating income a company strives for on each unit of product or service sold at the target volume. Target operating income typically is set by management as a percentage of total sales.

         For example, if a company desires to have a target operating income of 15% of sales and it expects to sell 12,000 units at $75 per unit ($900,000), the target operating income would be $135,000. The target operating income per unit would be $11.25 ($135,000/12,000).

  b. Target cost per unit—The estimated long-run product or service cost per unit at the target volume. Target cost per unit is calculated by subtracting target price per unit from target operating income per unit.

  From the example above, target cost would be $63.75 ($75.00 – 11.25).

K. Define and distinguish between a value-added cost and a non-value-added cost.

  a. Value-added costs—Costs that convert resources into products or services consistent with customer requirements. They are costs that customers perceive as adding value or utility to a product or service. Value-added costs might be costs associated with design, assembly, tools, and machinery.

  b. Non-value-added costs—Costs that are not critical to customer preferences and often are not known by the customer, such as rework costs, special delivery charges, and cost of obsolete inventory.

L. Define the pricing technique of cost plus target rate of return.

  a. Cost plus target rate of return pricing technique—Attempts to price a product in order to generate a target rate of return on investment.

M. Calculate the price elasticity of demand using the midpoint formula.

  a. Price elasticity of demand—Measures the sensitivity of the quantity demanded of a product to a change in price. The formula is:

$$\text{Price Elasticity of Demand } (E_d) = \frac{\text{\% Change in Quantity Demanded of Product X}}{\text{\% Change in Price of Product X}}$$

N. Define and explain elastic demand and inelastic demand.

  a. Elastic demand—A product has an elastic demand if a small change in price results in a large change in the quantity demanded.

  b. Inelastic demand—A product is said to have an inelastic demand if a large change in price results in a small change in quantity demanded.

O. Estimate total revenue, given changes in prices and demand as well as elasticity.

  a. When a firm faces an elastic demand curve, it can increase its revenue by lowering prices and thereby increasing the (elastic) demand. When a firm faces an inelastic demand curve, however, it can increase revenues by raising prices—because the higher price will not decrease the (inflexible) demand.

P. Discuss how pricing decisions can differ in the short-run and in the long-run.

  a. In the short run, there are certain costs that would be incurred whether a product is sold or not. Therefore, those costs should not be considered in the pricing of a product. In the long run, changes can be made to production capacity, labor, overhead, and so on that have an effect on the overall cost of the product.

Q. Define product life cycle and explain why pricing decisions might differ over the life of a product.

  a. Product life cycle—Begins with research and development and works all the way through the decline stage of a product. Sometimes life cycle costing is used to estimate the total life costs of a product in order to price a product to recover those costs plus a desired return.

R. Evaluate and recommend pricing strategies under specific market conditions.

    a. Refer to the types of markets a firm operates in above. The type of market it competes in is going to dictate its pricing strategy. The competitive landscape will also dictate the elasticity of the product and what effect changes in price will have on the product.

Cost/Volume/Profit Analysis

Cost/volume/profit (CVP) analysis is a method for analyzing the interrelationships among total cost, volume, and profits in an organization. CVP analysis examines the interactions among the:

- Selling prices of products and services;
- Sales volume (the level of activity);
- Per-unit variable costs;
- Total fixed costs; and
- Mix of products and services sold.

Managers can apply CVP analysis data in a wide variety of decision-making situations, such as:

- Raising or lowering prices for existing products and services;
- Introducing a new product or service;
- Setting prices for new products and services;
- Expanding product and service markets;
- Deciding whether to replace an existing piece of equipment; and
- Deciding whether to make or buy a product or service.

 READ the Learning Outcome Statements (LOS) for this topic as found in Appendix B and then study the concepts and calculations presented here to be sure you understand the content you could be tested on in the CMA exam.

CVP Terminology and Assumptions

Cost/volume/profit analysis uses certain terms in specific ways:

Cost generally refers to a resource expended to achieve a specific objective.

A **cost driver** is any factor that affects costs. A change in a cost driver will result in a change in the total cost of a related cost object. Examples of cost drivers are the number of units manufactured or the number of packages shipped. In CVP analysis, the cost driver used is normally units produced and sold.

A **cost object** is anything for which cost data is accumulated. Products, product lines, customers, jobs, and organizational business units are examples.

A **fixed cost** is a cost that remains constant, in total, regardless of changes in the level of activity within a relevant range. Fixed costs have to be changed by management action. Fixed costs either are committed, facility-related costs, such as rent and depreciation resulting from prior management decisions, or discretionary (managed or budgeted) fixed costs, such as advertising, indirect labor or selling, and administrative salaries set by management during the annual budgeting process.

A **variable cost** is a cost that varies, in total, in direct proportion to changes in the level of activity within a relevant range. Variable costs include: direct materials; direct labor; variable overhead, such as utilities and supplies; variable selling costs, such as shipping and sales commissions; and variable administrative costs, such as royalties paid for the use of a patent.

The **relevant range** is the range of activity within which the variable and fixed cost functions remain valid.

Revenues are inflows of assets received in exchange for products or services. Revenues are the sum of the price multiplied by the number of units sold for each product.

A **revenue driver** is a factor that affects revenue, such as advertising and promotion costs, the selling prices of units, or the number of units sold.

Total costs (or total expenses) are made up of total variable costs and total fixed costs. Total variable costs are the sum of unit variable cost multiplied by the number of units sold for each product. Total costs are represented as:

Total Costs = Total Variable Costs + Total Fixed Costs

Operating income is total revenues from operations less total costs from operations (excluding income taxes). Operating income generally is represented as:

Operating Income = Total Operating Revenues − Total Operating Costs

Companies generally exclude financing costs from operating income for analytical purposes, because such costs are not related to operations (i.e., nonoperating).

Net operating income is the after-tax operating income for a period. Net operating income is represented as:

Net Operating Income = Operating Income − Operating Income Taxes

Operating income taxes are calculated by taking the relevant tax rate and multiplying it by operating income. Therefore, net operating income is also calculated as:

Net Operating Income = (1 − Relevant Tax Rate) (Operating Income)

Activity level (also known as output level, measure of output, or output) refers to the number of units produced or sold during a period. Activity level nomenclature can vary across industries. For example, instead of units, airlines use passenger miles, hospitals may use patient days or beds occupied, hotels use rooms occupied, and colleges and universities use student credit hours.

Four assumptions underlie CVP analysis. They are:

1. *Linearity.* Revenue and cost functions are linear over the relevant range.
2. *Certainty.* The parameters (prices, unit variable costs, and fixed costs) are known or can be reasonably estimated.
3. *A single product or a defined product mix.* A defined product mix allows the analyst to look at a hypothetical weighted average product.
4. *Production is equal to sales.* This is the critical limiting assumption since according to conventional generally accepted accounting principles (GAAP), full absorption costing operating income is a function of the difference between production and sales. The use of variable costing and a contribution margin approach to operating income determination relieves the need for this assumption.

Fixed and Variable Cost Behavior

Cost behavior generally refers to how a cost will react to changes in business activity levels. As the business output changes, a given cost may rise, fall, or remain constant.

A key assumption in CVP analysis is that costs can be classified as either fixed or variable with respect to activity level—the amount of goods produced or services provided by a company. Figure 2C-1 summarizes how fixed and variable costs behave in total and on a per-unit basis within the relevant range. Note in the figure how fixed and variable costs behave differently if they are viewed as total costs or on a per-unit basis.

Figure 2C-1 Fixed and Variable Cost Behavior Within Relevant Range

Type of Cost	Behavior in Total	Behavior per Unit
Fixed	Not affected by changes in activity level. They have to be changed by management decision.	Increase and decrease inversely to changes in activity level (e.g., fixed cost per unit increases as activity level falls and decreases as activity level rises).
Variable	Increase and decrease proportionately to changes in activity level.	Remain constant.

Examples of costs that are fixed irrespective of the environment in which they are incurred (e.g., manufacturing, retail, or service) include insurance premiums, rental charges, property taxes, salaries, and advertising.

In manufacturing environments, variable costs include direct materials, direct labor, variable overhead, sales commissions, shipping costs, and royalties. For a merchandising business, variable costs include costs of goods sold, sales commissions, and some billing costs. In a service environment such as a hospital, variable costs include the cost of prescription drugs, hospital supplies, and patient meals.

Fixed and Variable Classifications Over Time

The classifications of costs as fixed and variable can be affected by the time horizon being considered. In other words, some variable costs may be reclassified as fixed. Given an extended period of time, a fixed cost, although it is not variable, may change.

Generally, these principles apply to fixed and variable cost classifications over time:

- The shorter the time period, the higher the percentage of total costs that can be viewed as fixed.
- The longer the time horizon, the more costs that can be viewed as variable.
- Overall, whether a cost is fixed or variable is often a function of:
  - Relevant range
  - Time frame
  - The given decision situation

The example in Figure 2C-2 further illustrates fixed and variable cost behavior.

Figure 2C-2 Fixed and Variable Cost Behavior

	Total Cost at 10,000 Units	Cost per Unit	Total Cost at 25,000 Units	Cost per Unit	Total Cost at 50,000 Units	Cost per Unit
Direct materials	$16,000	$1.60	$40,000	$1.60	$80,000	$1.60
Direct labor	25,000	2.50	62,500	2.50	125,000	2.50
Distribution	13,000	1.30	32,500	1.30	65,000	1.30
Depreciation	50,000	5.00	50,000	2.00	80,000	1.60
Rent	25,000	2.50	25,000	1.00	40,000	0.80

The per-unit costs for materials and labor are fixed over the relevant range of capacity. Total costs for depreciation and rent are fixed whether the company produces one or 25,000 units. However, when sales increase beyond the plant's capacity of 25,000 units, the company would need to add on to its production line. Per-unit costs would increase as additional equipment and space would be required.

Total Revenues and Total Costs

The CVP model assumes that total revenues and total costs are linear within a relevant range of activity level. Stated another way, within a limited range of output, total costs are expected to increase at an approximately linear rate. Figure 2C-3 shows a simple representation of this linear relationship.

Figure 2C-3 CVP Graph of Total Revenues, Total Costs, and Output Levels

Break-Even Analysis

CVP analysis is sometimes referred to as break-even analysis. Technically, break-even analysis is only one part of CVP analysis.

A **break-even point**, also called the **operating break-even point**, is the output level at which total revenues and total costs are equal. At break-even, operating income is zero. Above the break-even point, there is an operating income; below break-even, there is an operating loss.

Determining the break-even point is a key part of CVP analysis and assessing how various what-if decision alternatives will affect operating income. The break-even point may be determined using three different methods: an equation method, a contribution margin method, and a graph method. Each of these methods is described for Company K, given this scenario:

A Company K sales representative travels to a client's location to promote a new product. The unit selling price for the product is $200. The fixed costs for the product are $4,000. The unit variable costs for the product are $100, and the current quantity of the product sold is 75.

Equation Method

A common equation method for computing the break-even point is:

$$\text{Revenues} - \text{Variable Costs} - \text{Fixed Costs} = \text{Operating Income}$$

or

$$(\text{USP} \times Q) - (\text{UVC} \times Q) - \text{FC} = \text{OI}$$

where:
USP = unit selling price
Q = quantity sold to break even
UVC = unit variable costs
FC = fixed costs
OI = operating income

At the break-even point, operating income is zero. Setting operating income to zero and substituting the numbers in the equation, the break-even point for the example (expressed in units) is calculated as shown:

$$(\text{USP} \times Q) - (\text{UVC} \times Q) - \text{FC} = \text{OI}$$

$$(\$200 \times Q) - (\$100 \times Q) - \$4{,}000 = \$0$$

$$\$100 \times Q = \$4{,}000$$

$$Q = \frac{\$4{,}000}{\$100} = 40 \text{ Units}$$

In this example, selling fewer than 40 units will be a loss; selling 40 units will be break-even; selling more than 40 will make a profit.

Contribution Margin Method

The contribution margin method is an algebraic adaptation of the equation method. **Contribution margin** represents the amount remaining from sales revenue after variable expenses are deducted. It is found by taking revenues and subtracting all costs of the output that vary with respect to the number of output units. The contribution margin method is based on this equation:

$$\text{Contribution Margin Method for Break-Even} = (USP \times Q) - (UVC \times Q) - FC$$

$$(USP \times Q) - (UVC \times Q) - FC = OI$$

$$(USP - UVC) \times Q = FC + OI$$

$$UCM \times Q = FC + OI$$

$$Q = \frac{FC + OI}{UCM}$$

where:

USP = unit selling price

Q = quantity sold to break even

UVC = unit variable costs

FC = fixed costs

OI = operating income

UCM = unit contribution margin ($USP - UVC$)

Setting operating income to zero and inserting the numbers in the contribution margin method, the break-even point (expressed in units) for the example is calculated as follows:

$$\text{Break-Even Number of Units} = \frac{\text{Fixed Costs (FC)}}{\text{Unit Contribution Margin (UCM)}}$$

$$= \frac{\$4,000}{\$100} = 40 \text{ Units}$$

A contribution income statement highlights the contribution margin by grouping line items by cost behavior patterns. A contribution margin income statement confirms the contribution margin break-even calculations.

Figure 2C-4 Contribution Income Statement for Company K

Sale revenues ($200 × 40)	$8,000
Variable costs ($100 × 40)	4,000
Contribution margin	4,000
Fixed costs	4,000
Operating income	$0

Contribution Margin Percentage/Contribution Margin Ratio

The contribution margin may be expressed as a percentage instead of a dollar amount per unit. Contribution margin percentage (also called "contribution margin ratio," or CMR) may be calculated in two ways. Contribution margin percentage often is represented as the contribution margin per unit divided by selling price:

$$\text{Contribution Margin Percentage} = \frac{\text{Unit Contribution Margin (UCM)}}{\text{Selling Price per Unit}}$$

$$= \frac{\$100}{\$200} = 0.50 \text{ or } 50\%$$

Contribution margin percentage also can be calculated as contribution margin divided by total revenues. If 40 packages are sold:

$$\text{Contribution Margin Percentage} = \frac{\text{Contribution Margin}}{\text{Total Revenues}}$$

$$= \frac{\$4,000}{\$8,000} = 0.50 \text{ or } 50\%$$

The contribution margin percentage or CMR provides the contribution margin per dollar of revenues. In this example, it indicates that 50% of each dollar (equal to $0.50) is contribution margin.

Variable Cost Percentage

Variable cost percentage is the complement of the contribution margin percentage. In other words:

$$\text{Contribution Margin Percentage} + \text{Variable Cost Percentage} = 1$$

In the example given, contribution margin percentage = 50%, so variable cost percentage = 50%. Given variable costs are $100 per unit and variable cost percentage is 50%, selling price is:

$$\$100/0.50 = \$200$$

Graph Method

A CVP graph (or break-even chart) shows the interrelationships among cost, volume, and profit graphically.

- The activity level (unit volume) is shown on the horizontal (X) axis.
- Dollars are shown on the vertical (Y) axis.
- Total costs and total revenues are both plotted as lines with their point of intersection being the break-even point.

Figure 2C-5 shows a CVP graph of break-even analysis.

Figure 2C-5 CVP Graph of Break-Even Analysis

Margin of Safety

The **margin of safety (MOS)** defines how far an organization is past the break-even point at its current sales volume level. The MOS can be calculated and expressed in sales units, in sales dollars, or as a percentage. The data for the break-even analysis just covered stated that Company K is operating at a sales level of 75 units or $15,000 (75 units times a price of $200) in sales dollars. The MOS in units, therefore, is 35 units (75 less the break-even of 40). The MOS in sales dollars is $7,000 ($15,000 less the break-even of $8,000). The MOS ratio or percentage is 46.7% of the current level of operations (35 units past break-even divided by the 75 units being sold) or 87.5% of the break-even level of operations (35 units past break-even divided by the 40-unit break-even.

Margin of safety computations (as required for the CMA examination) can, therefore, be stated as follows:

Margin of Safety (dollars) = Planned Sales−Break-Even Sales

$$\text{Margin of Safety Ratio (or Percentage)} = \frac{\text{Margin of Safety}}{\text{Planned Sales}}$$

Using Break-Even Analysis to Calculate Target Profit

Break-even analysis also can be used to determine how many units must be sold to earn a target profit level—either a targeted operating income or a targeted net income. Building on the previous scenario and setting a target operating income of $8,000 for Company K, here is how the calculations in units and dollar sales would look in the equation, the contribution margin, and the graph methods.

Equation Method

The equation used in this case is:

$$\text{Revenues} - \text{Variable Costs} - \text{Fixed Costs} = \text{Target Operating Income}$$

or

$$(\text{USP} \times \text{QT}) - (\text{UVC} \times \text{QT}) - \text{FC} = \text{TOI}$$

where:

USP = unit selling price
QT = quantity sold to earn the target operating income
UVC = unit variable costs
FC = fixed costs
TOI = target operating income

Setting the target operating income to $8,000 for Company K, the number of units that must be sold is calculated as:

$$(\text{USP} \times \text{QT}) - (\text{UVC} \times \text{QT}) - \text{FC} = \text{TOI}$$
$$(\$200 \times \text{QT}) - (\$100 \times \text{QT}) - \$4,000 = \$8,000$$
$$\$100 \times \text{QT} = \$4,000 + \$8,000$$
$$\$100\text{QT} = \$12,000$$
$$\text{QT} = \frac{\$12,000}{\$100} = 120 \text{ Units}$$

Contribution Margin Method

With the contribution margin method, setting operating income for Company K to $8,000, the numerator would consist of fixed costs plus the target operating income:

$$QT = \frac{FC + TOI}{UCM}$$

$$= \frac{\$4,000 + \$8,000}{\$100}$$

$$= \frac{\$12,000}{\$100} = 120 \text{ Units}$$

The contribution income statement is shown in Figure 2C-6.

Figure 2C-6 Contribution Income Statement

Sale revenues ($200 × 120)	$24,000
Variable costs ($100 × 120)	12,000
Contribution margin	12,000
Fixed costs	4,000
Operating income	$8,000

Calculating the break-even point in terms of revenues is also possible. Recall the previous calculation of contribution margin percentage or CMR:

$$\text{Contribution Margin Percentage} = \frac{\text{Contribution Margin}}{\text{Total Revenues}}$$

$$= \frac{\$4,000}{\$8,000} = 0.50 \text{ or } 50\%$$

In this example, 50% of each dollar (or $0.50) is contribution margin. To break even, the contribution margin must equal the fixed costs of $4,000. To earn $4,000 of contribution margin, revenues must equal $8,000.

$$\text{Break-Even Revenues} = \frac{\text{Fixed Costs}}{\text{Contribution Margin \%}}$$

$$= \frac{\$4,000}{0.50} = \$8,000$$

Graph Method

Figure 2C-7 shows a profit-volume graph and how changes in output affect operating income. The level of fixed costs at zero output is $4,000. Each unit beyond the break-even point contributes to operating income.

Figure 2C-7 Profit-Volume Graph

At the 60-unit level, for example, operating income would be:

$$(\$200 \times 60) - (\$100 \times 60) - \$4,000 = \$2,000$$

Analysis of Multiple Products

Sales mix (or **revenue mix**) refers to the relative proportions of products or services sold. Most companies have multiple products and/or services. Generally, the different offerings are not equally profitable. Businesses typically strive for the sales mix that yields the highest profits. Profits tend to be greater if a larger proportion of the product or service mix comprises higher-margin items.

Consider the next budget projections shown in Figure 2C-8 for ABAB Products, a company with two products (A and B).

Figure 2C-8 Budget Projections

	Product A	Product B	Total
Number of units sold	100	50	150
Revenues per unit ($200 and $125)	$20,000	$6,250	$26,250
Variable costs per unit ($125 and $75)	12,500	3,750	16,250
Contribution margin per unit ($75 and $50)	7,500	2,500	10,000
Fixed costs ($4,000)			4,000
Operating income			$6,000

Because of the multiple products, there is no unique number of units for a break-even point. The number depends on the sales mix. The next equation can be used when the sales mix (two units of product A for each unit of product B sold) is constant:

$$\text{Revenues} - \text{Variable Costs} - \text{Fixed Costs} = \text{Operating Income}$$

Using the ABAB Products numbers, the number of units of each product that must be sold is calculated as shown:

Revenue $-$ Variable Costs $-$ Fixed Costs $=$ Operating Income
$[\$200 \, (2S) + \$125S] - [\$125 \, (2S) + \$75S] - \$4{,}000 = 0$
$\$525S - \$325S = \$4{,}000$
$\$200S = \$4{,}000$
$S = 20$
$2S = 40$

where:
   $2S$ = number of units of product A to break even
   S = number of units of product B to break even

When the sales mix is 40 units of product A and 20 units of product B, the break-even point is 60. Alternate sales mixes would result in different break-even points.

Weighted Average Contribution Method

The weighted average contribution method is another way to apply CVP analysis to a company producing multiple products. To determine the break-even point, the weighted average contribution margin per unit is computed for each of the products at the budgeted sales mix. Returning to the previous sales mix of Product A and Product B:

Weighted Average UCM

$$= \frac{(\text{Product A UCM} \times \text{Number of Units Sold}) + (\text{Product B UCM} \times \text{Number of Units Sold})}{\text{Product A Number of Units Sold} + \text{Product B Number of Units Sold}}$$

where:
UCM = unit contribution margin

$$= \frac{(\$75 \text{ per unit} \times 100 \text{ units}) + (\$50 \text{ per unit} \times 50 \text{ units})}{100 \text{ units} + 50 \text{ units}}$$

$$= \frac{\$7{,}500 + \$2{,}500}{150} = \frac{\$10{,}000}{150} = \$66.67 \text{ per unit}$$

The break-even point then is calculated as shown.

$$\text{Break-Even Point} = \frac{\text{Fixed Costs}}{\text{Weighted Average UCM}}$$

$$= \frac{\$4,000}{\$66.67 \text{ per unit}} = 60 \text{ units}$$

The ratio of Product A to Product B sales is 100:50 (or, 2:1), wso the break-even point is:

$$60/3 = 20 \times 2 = 40 \text{ units of Product A}$$
$$60/3 = 20 \text{ units of Product B}$$

At this mix, the contribution margin is \$4,000 (Product A \$75 per unit × 40 units + Product B \$50 per unit × 20 units), which is exactly equal to the company's fixed costs of \$4,000. Because the contribution margin equals fixed costs at 60 units, the company is just breaking even.

The break-even point in revenues for multiple products can also be calculated using the weighted-average contribution margin percentage.

$$\text{Weighted Average Contribution Margin \%} = \frac{\text{Total Contribution Margin}}{\text{Total Revenues}}$$

$$= \frac{\$10,000}{\$26,250} = 0.3809523 \text{ or } 38.05923\%$$

$$\text{Total Revenues Required to Break Even} = \frac{\text{Fixed Costs}}{\text{Weighted Average Contribution Margin \%}}$$

$$= \frac{\$4,000}{0.3809523} = \$10,500$$

Figure 2C-9 shows the breakdown of total revenues, total variable costs, and total contribution margin at the break-even point.

Figure 2C-9 Budget Projections at Break-Even

	Product A	**Product B**	**Total**
Number of units sold	40	20	60
Revenues ($200 and $125)	$8,000	$2,500	$10,500
Variable costs ($125 and $75)	5,000	1,500	6,500
Contribution margin ($75 and $50)	$3,000	$1,000	4,000
Fixed costs ($4,000)			4,000
Operating income			$0

Using data from Figure 2C-9, the $10,500 of total revenues is broken down between Product A and B in this way: 76.2% for A ($8,000/$10,500) and 23.8% for B ($2,500/$10,500). The break-even revenues of $10,500 should be split in the same ratio. This results in:

- Break-even revenues for Product A of $8,000 (76.2% × $10,500)
- Break-even revenues for Product B of $2,500 (23.8% × $10,500)

At a selling price of $200 for Product A and $125 for Product B:

- Break-even for Product A = 40 units ($8,000/$200)
- Break-even for Product B = 20 units ($2,500/$125)

The effects of changes in the sales mix on the operating income depend on how the original proportions of higher- and lower-margin items have changed. These general principles usually apply:

- A shift from high-CM items to low-CM items may cause operating income to fall even though total sales may increase.
- A shift from low-CM items to high-CM items may cause operating income to rise even though total sales may decrease.

Businesses often attempt to maximize revenues through their sales mixes. Many factors can influence decisions as to which products to produce in what quantity and what products to emphasize. Sometimes the best decision may not always be to produce the items having the highest CM per unit. For example, a product may have a high CM, but the company may not be able to sell sufficient units to break-even. In most cases (especially when a plant is operating at full capacity), management should focus on each product's CM and select those having the highest CM per unit of the constraining resource.

A **constraining resource** is a resource that restricts or limits the production or sale of products or services. In manufacturing, examples of constraining resources include contribution per machine hour, contribution per direct labor, or the availability of direct materials, purchased parts and components, or skilled labor. In a retail environment, display space footage can be a constraining resource. Financial and sales factors also can be constraining resources in either environment.

A challenge arises when trying to maximize total operating income for a variety of products when each has multiple constraining resources. A company may need to stock minimum quantities of products even if these products are not very profitable. A hardware store, for example, may have to carry less profitable items to ensure that it has a wide range of products that customers need.

Income Taxes and CVP Analysis

As noted earlier, net operating income often is represented by operating income minus income taxes. To determine net income, the only change in the equation method for CVP analysis is to modify the target operating income to allow for taxes.

For example: Figure 2C-10 shows the role of taxes for Company K, using a tax rate of 40% and the company's contribution income statement, where the target operating income is $8,000.

Figure 2C-10 Contribution Income Statement for Company K

Sale revenues ($200 × 40)	$8,000
Variable costs ($100 × 40)	4,000
Contribution margin	4,000
Fixed costs	4,000
Operating income	$0

$$\text{Target Net Operating Income} = \text{Operating Income} - (\text{Operating Income} \times \text{Tax Rate})$$
$$= \text{Operating Income} \times (1 - \text{Tax Rate})$$
$$\text{Operating Income} = \frac{\text{Target Net Income}}{1 - \text{Tax Rate}}$$

Returning to the equation method and taking income taxes into account:

$$\text{Revenues} - \text{Variable Costs} - \text{Fixed Costs} = \frac{\text{Target Net Operating Income}}{1 - \text{Tax Rate}}$$

For Company K, the equation is now:

$$\$200Q - \$100Q - \$4,000 = \frac{\$8,000}{1 - 0.40}$$

$$\$200Q - \$100Q - \$4,000 = \$13,333$$

$$\$100Q = \$17,333$$

$$Q = 173.33 \text{ units}$$

The contribution income statement in Figure 2C-11, which includes the effect of income taxes, is proof of the equation.

Figure 2C-11 Income Taxes and Target Operating Income

Revenues ($200 × 173.33)	$34,666
Variable costs ($100 × 173.33)	17,333
Contribution margin	17,333
Fixed costs	4,000
Operating income	13,333
Income taxes ($13,333 × 0.40)	5,333
Net operating income	$8,000

Sensitivity Analysis and CVP

Sensitivity analysis in CVP analysis involves asking what-if questions regarding changes in the volume (Q) and in the parameters (prices, unit variable costs, and fixed costs). Recall that the original break-even example, Company K, involved a firm producing and selling a product with a unit selling price of $200. The fixed costs for the product are $4,000. The unit variable costs for the product are $100, and the current quantity of the product sold is 75. The break-even point for the product was determined to be 40 units, or $8,000 in sales.

Sensitivity analysis could ask: What would the break-even point in units be if the price (USP) increased by 10% while unit variable costs (UVC) increased by 12% and fixed costs (FC) increased to $4,104? The new break-even point in units (Q) would be 38 units and can be calculated as shown:

$$Q = FC/(USP - UVC)$$

where:
Q = quantity sold to break even
FC = fixed costs
USP = unit selling price
UVC = unit variable cost

$Q = 4,104/[200(1.1) - 100(1.12)] = 4,104/(220 - 112) = 4,104/108$
  = 38 Units (a drop of 2 units or 5% from the original break-even point of 40 units)

Another example of sensitivity analysis would be: What happens to operating income (OI) when volume (Q) increases past the break-even point of 38 units just computed?

The OI would increase by the USP less the UVC [unit contribution margin (UCM)] multiplied by the number of units past the break-even point. Thus, the OI would increase by \$108 (\$220 − \$112) for every additional unit sold past the break-even point.

Many other what-if questions regarding changes in volume and/or changes in parameters can be posed and solved using sensitivity analysis.

Knowledge Check:
Cost/Volume/Profit Analysis

The next questions are intended to help you check your understanding and recall of the material presented in this topic. They do not represent the type of questions that appear on the CMA exam.

Directions: Answer each question in the space provided. Correct answers and section references appear after the knowledge check questions.

1. In the CVP model, total revenues and total costs

    ☐ **a.** remain constant within a limited range of output.

    ☐ **b.** increase and decrease inversely to changes in activity level.

    ☐ **c.** increase and decrease proportionately to changes in activity level.

    ☐ **d.** increase at a linear rate within a relevant range of activity.

2. All of the following statements accurately describe a break-even point **except**

    ☐ **a.** operating income is zero.

    ☐ **b.** total revenues and total costs are equal.

    ☐ **c.** above break-even signifies profits; below break-even signifies loss.

    ☐ **d.** below break-even signifies profits; above break-even signifies loss.

Match the following terms with their description.

3.	_____ Relevant range	**a.**	How a cost will react to changes in business activity levels
4.	_____ Activity level	**b.**	The activity range over which the variable and fixed cost functions remain valid
5.	_____ Cost behavior		
6.	_____ Contribution margin	**c.**	Relative proportions of products or services sold
7.	_____ Sales mix	**d.**	Number of units produced and sold
		e.	Amount remaining from sales revenue after variable expenses are deducted

8. Given fixed costs of $8,000, variable costs of $100, and a unit contribution margin of $200, how many units must be sold to reach a target operating income of $34,000?

   ☐ **a.** 130

   ☐ **b.** 140

   ☐ **c.** 210

   ☐ **d.** 260

Questions 9 and 10 refer to these data:

Sale revenues (20,000 units)	$1,200,000
Less variable costs	900,000
Contribution margin	300,000
Less fixed costs	240,000
Operating income	$60,000

9. Calculate the company's contribution margin ratio and variable cost ratio.

10. Compute the company's break-even point in both unit and sales dollars.

**Knowledge Check Answers:
Cost/Volume/Profit Analysis**

1. In the CVP model, total revenues and total costs [**See *CVP Terminology and Assumptions*.**]

    ☐ **a.**   remain constant within a limited range of output.

    ☐ **b.**   increase and decrease inversely to changes in activity level.

    ☐ **c.**   increase and decrease proportionately to changes in activity level.

    ☑ **d.**   increase at a linear rate within a relevant range of activity.

2. All of the following statements accurately describe a break-even point **except** [**See *Break-Even Analysis*.**]

    ☐ **a.**   operating income is zero.

    ☐ **b.**   total revenues and total costs are equal.

    ☐ **c.**   above break-even signifies profits; below break-even signifies loss.

    ☑ **d.**   below break-even signifies profits; above break-even signifies loss.

Match the following terms with their description.

3. __b__ Relevant range	**a.**	How a cost will react to changes in business activity levels
4. __d__ Activity level	**b.**	The activity range over which the variable and fixed cost functions remain valid
5. __a__ Cost behavior		
6. __e__ Contribution margin	**c.**	Relative proportions of products or services sold
7. __c__ Sales mix	**d.**	Number of units produced and sold
	e.	Amount remaining from sales revenue after variable expenses are deducted

8. Given fixed costs of $8,000, variable costs of $100, and a unit contribution margin of $200, how many units must be sold to reach a target operating income of $34,000? [**See *Equation Method*.**]

   ☐ **a.** 130

   ☐ **b.** 140

   ☑ **c.** 210

   ☐ **d.** 260

To calculate the number of units needed to achieve a target profit, use this formula:

QT = (FC + TOI)/UCM

QT = ($8,000 + $34,000) / $200 = 210 units

Questions 9 and 10 refer to these data:

Sale revenues (20,000 units)	$1,200,000
Less variable costs	900,000
Contribution margin	300,000
Less fixed costs	240,000
Operating income	$60,000

9. Calculate the company's contribution margin ratio and variable cost ratio. [**See *Contribution Margin Percentage/Contribution Margin Ratio*.**]

   Contribution Margin Ratio = Contribution Margin / Sales

   Contribution Margin Ratio = $300,000 / $1,200,000 = 25%

   Variable Cost Ratio = Variable Costs / Sales

   Variable Cost Ratio = $900,000 / $1,200,000 = 75%

10. Compute the company's break-even point in both unit and sales dollars. [**See *Break-Even Analysis*.**]

    Break-Even Point in Units = Fixed Costs / Unit Contribution Margin

    Fixed Costs = $240,000

    Unit Contribution Margin = Total Contribution Margin / Number of Units

    Unit Contribution Margin = $300,000 / 20,000 Units = $15

    Break-Even Point in Units = $240,000 / $15 = 16,000 Units

    Break-Even Point in Dollars = Fixed Costs / Contribution Margin Ratio

    Fixed Costs = $240,000

    Contribution Margin Ratio = Contribution Margin / Sales

    Contribution Margin Ratio = $300,000 / $1,200,000 = 0.25

    Break-Even Point in Dollars = $240,000 / 0.25 = $960,000

Marginal Analysis

DECISION MAKING INVOLVES A CHOICE between at least two alternatives. In some situations, there are several alternatives to consider. But other decisions may require choosing between only two alternatives, one of which may be the status quo. Regardless of the number or types of options, the costs and benefits of the various alternatives need to be evaluated during the decision process.

Marginal analysis (also known as incremental or differential analysis) is a method of analyzing short-term decisions. It emphasizes incremental cost increases or decreases rather than total costs and benefits associated with an action (or set of alternative actions). The short term is defined as the lesser of the time frame over which capacity is fixed, or one year. It is generally applied to these types of decisions:

- Special orders and pricing
- Make or buy
- Sell or process further
- Add or drop a segment
- Maximize contribution per unit of the limiting factor

The key factor in applying marginal analysis is deciding which information is relevant to the decision. Relevant costs and relevant revenues are those that differ among options and are future oriented. Costs and revenues that already have been incurred or committed are sunk and are irrelevant in decision making. Stated another way, any costs, including allocated costs, that do not differ between alternatives should be ignored in marginal decision analyses. Historical costs are irrelevant.

This topic takes a closer look at the application of marginal analysis in organizational decision making.

 READ the Learning Outcome Statements (LOS) for this topic as found in Appendix B and then study the concepts and calculations presented here to be sure you understand the content you could be tested on in the CMA exam.

Special Orders and Pricing

A special order pricing decision involves a situation in which a firm has a one-time opportunity to accept or reject a special order for a specified quantity of its product or service. Making a determination about whether to accept or decline a special order request involves an assessment of profitability (based on relevant costs and revenues and opportunity costs) as well as consideration of capacity utilization. If the relevant revenue exceeds the relevant costs (including opportunity costs), the special order will be profitable.

If there is excess capacity—more than enough to cover the order—the firm needs to identify variable costs associated with the special order (unit variable costs multiplied by the number of units) and any additional fixed costs (avoidable fixed costs) that might by caused by accepting the order. Such costs are relevant costs and determine the minimum acceptable (break-even) price. If the price offered for the special order times the number of units involved is greater than the unit variable costs plus the avoidable fixed costs, the order is profitable and should be accepted.

If the firm is operating at or near capacity, the minimum acceptable price is the normal sale price. When there is no excess capacity, a special order should be taken only if the price offered exceeds the normal price. In the case of full capacity, a firm also must consider whether accepting the order could result in the loss of other more profitable sales. The opportunity costs resulting from lost sales that have a higher contribution margin should be evaluated.

Special-Order Cost Analysis

Consider this scenario:

> The unit selling price for a product is $4.
> The average variable cost per unit is $2.75.
> The average fixed cost per unit is $1.
> The total cost per unit is $3.75.
> Normal production is 500,000 units.
> Fixed costs are $500,000.
> A special order for 50,000 units is offered at a selling price of $3.50 per unit.

Excess Capacity

In the case of excess capacity, the correct analysis for the decision is to compare the relevant costs to the special order price. Relevant costs include the cost to produce a unit ($2.75) and the special order price offered per unit ($3.50). The fixed cost per unit ($1) remains the same whether the order is accepted or not; it is not relevant. There is a $0.75 ($3.50 − $2.75) contribution to income for each unit sold, or a total contribution of $37,500 (50,000 units × $0.75). The order is profitable and should be accepted.

A common error in evaluating a special order decision is to focus on the total cost per unit. If the total cost per unit is used as the comparison figure, the order probably would be rejected because the unit cost ($3.75) exceeds the special order price ($3.50).

At or Near Full Capacity

Assuming that the firm is operating at or near full capacity, the proper decision analysis should consider the opportunity cost arising from any lost sales. For example, if the special order would result in the loss of other sales that have a higher contribution margin ($1), the opportunity cost of lost sales is $50,000 (50,000 × $1). The net contribution loss for the order is $12,500 ($50,000 − $37,500). Accepting the special order would reduce total profits by $12,500, so the order should be rejected.

In relevant-cost analysis scenarios, fixed costs are irrelevant unless they are avoidable. For example, a special order might require additional indirect labor, such as inspectors or material handlers to fulfill it; this would increase manufacturing costs and make the added (avoidable) fixed costs relevant for the decision.

As the term *special order* implies, special orders are unexpected and infrequent. They are short term and are accepted in those infrequent situations when they can increase total contribution. Accepting special order pricing on a regular (long-term) basis can erode profits.

Make versus Buy

Make versus buy, as used here, refers to short-term outsourcing. *Outsourcing* describes a company's decision to purchase a product or service from an outside supplier rather than producing it in-house. The definition of *short term* implies that the organization has the capacity to produce the product in question. Reaching a decision about whether to make or buy involves a comparison of the relevant costs to make the item internally with the cost to purchase externally. In some situations, opportunity costs and qualitative factors also need to be considered.

Relevant costs represent the short-term costs to make the item in-house. They are the incremental or differential costs, which include the variable costs to manufacture the product as well as any avoidable fixed costs related to manufacturing the product and any forgone contributions caused by manufacturing the product. Relevant costs are those that can be avoided or eliminated by buying externally.

Irrelevant costs are those unavoidable costs that will not change regardless of whether the firm makes or buys the item. They are the sunk costs or future costs that will remain in place even if the item is bought externally. Typically, these are fixed overhead costs and any depreciation costs.

If the relevant costs are less than the purchase price, the decision should be to keep production inside. If the outside purchase price is less than these avoidable costs, the logical decision is to outsource.

Make versus Buy Cost Analysis

Consider this scenario: AAPartCo manufactures 5,000 units of a part each year. The cost of manufacturing one unit of the part at this volume is shown in Figure 2C-12:

Figure 2C-12 AAPartCo Manufacturing Cost

Direct materials	$2.50
Direct labor	3.50
Variable overhead	1.50
Fixed overhead	1.00
Total cost per unit	$8.50

The company can buy unlimited quantities of the part from an outside supplier at a unit cost of $7.75. Because the relevant costs are $7.50 ($8.50 − $1 for fixed overhead that will remain), the part should not be outsourced. At the 5,000-unit level, this translates to an additional $1,250 (5,000 × $0.25) in favor of continuing to make the item internally.

Consideration of Avoidable Fixed Costs and Other Opportunity Costs

Avoidable fixed costs and other opportunity costs should be considered in a make-or-buy decision. A common make-or-buy opportunity cost is whether some part of the fixed overhead could be avoided by outsourcing. For example, perhaps an inspector could be eliminated. Another common opportunity cost is whether some part of the space being used during internal production could be used for another purpose, such as the manufacture of some alternative product or renting it to another organization.

If the space now being used to produce an item internally has no alternative use and would remain idle, the opportunity cost is zero. But if the space could be used for some other purpose, that opportunity cost should be considered when evaluating an outsourcing offer.

Returning to the AAPartCo example, if the company could eliminate 50% of the fixed costs per unit and also recoup $6,000 a year by leasing the space to another company, the economic benefits from outsourcing change the decision. In this situation, the $6,000 is an avoidable fixed cost and the opportunity cost per unit from renting out the space is $1.20 ($6,000 / 5,000 units). The relevant cost to make is now $9.20 ($7.50 original relevant cost from before plus $0.50 of fixed cost that could be avoided if the firm outsources [i.e., opportunity cost #1] plus $1.20 of lost rent [i.e., opportunity cost #2]). The relevant cost to buy is $7.75. Comparing the two, the potential savings from outsourcing is now $1.45 per unit, or $7,250 in total ($1.45 × 5,000 units) in favor of buying externally.

Consideration of Qualitative Factors

The make-or-buy marginal analysis of relevant costs has a key role in the decision to outsource. But there is more to successful outsourcing than the potential profit margins. In addition to the profit alternatives in make-or-buy decisions, firms also need to evaluate the qualitative factors of dealing with an external supplier. Examples of such qualitative factors include the need to tap an external supplier's unique knowledge, unusually skilled labor, or access to rare materials.

The desire to control quality traditionally has been the driving factor in the decision to make rather than buy. Increasingly, buying and selling organizations are forming quasi-partnerships and alliances and collaborating on improving products and services. Buying companies now often temper the make-or-buy decision with the potential for mutually advantageous supplier relationships. If the buying organization can be assured that established quality and service levels will be consistent with its needs and that the supplier's practices will be improved continuously, lower prices can result. The flip side is that erratic order-giving to suppliers (making parts during slack times and buying them during prosperous times) can backfire and potentially create problems in securing parts when sales demand is high but there are shortages of material and workers.

The final decision to outsource to an external supplier should not ignore the supplier's reputation for dependability and quality in:

- Ensuring on-time delivery and a smooth flow of parts and materials.
- Maintaining acceptable quality control.
- The strategic aspects of retaining control over core competencies are also important. Any outsourcing of an internal capability essential to maintaining competitive position requires careful consideration.

Sell or Process Further

Sell or process further concerns the decision to sell a product or service before an intermediate processing step or to add further processing and then sell the product or service for a higher price. Common examples of sell or process further include decisions to:

- Add features to a product to enhance functionality.
- Improve the flexibility or quality of a service.
- Repair defective products so they can be sold in the usual manner (rather than selling them for a discount in a defective state).

Sell-or-process-further decisions require analysis of relevant costs. In many situations, such decisions also involve consideration of joint products or services. A key point in this type of sell-or-process-further decision is that all costs that have already been incurred, such as joint costs, are irrelevant.

Joint products or joint services involve situations in which two or more products or services are produced from a single common input. For example, gasoline, diesel fuel, and heating oil are three joint products that are prepared (refined) from crude oil. The split-off point is the point in the production process at which the joint products can be recognized as separate products. **Joint costs** describe the costs incurred up to the split-off point.

The reason joint costs are irrelevant is that they are common costs that must be incurred to get the product or service to the split-off point. Because joint costs are not directly attributable to any of the intermediate products or services or the end products or services, they are irrelevant in deciding what to do from the split-off point forward.

For sell-or-process-further decisions, continuing to process a product or service is profitable as long as the incremental revenue received (the revenue attributable to the added processing) exceeds the incremental processing costs incurred. This rule also applies to processing beyond the split-off point in the case of joint products and services. Figure 2C-13 summarizes the steps in a sell-or-process-further decision.

Figure 2C-13 Sell-or-Process-Further Decision-Making Steps

Step 1	Determine the selling price for a product or service, or determine the selling price of each product or service in a joint production process at the split-off point.
Step 2	Determine the selling price of each product or service if it were processed further.
Step 3	Calculate the incremental revenue from processing further; subtract the Step 1 amount from the Step 2 amount.
Step 4	Calculate the incremental costs.
Step 5	Compare the incremental revenue to the incremental costs by subtracting the cost of processing further (or the separable costs of processing each product or service beyond the split-off point; Step 4) from the incremental revenue (Step 3). A positive net value supports processing further, and a negative result indicates selling before processing further (or at the split-off point).

Sell-or-Process-Further Cost Analyses

Example 1

Consider this scenario involving a simple comparison of incremental costs and incremental revenue:

The unit production cost for a product is $4,200.

The unit selling price for a product is $5,000.

The incremental processing cost per unit is $1,500.

The new unit selling price is $5,800.

Given this information, the product should be sold as is and not processed further. The incremental revenue is $800 ($5,800 − $5,000). The incremental cost to process further ($1,500) exceeds the incremental revenue and would result in a $700 loss from further processing ($800 − $1,500 = −$700).

Example 2

Consider this scenario involving joint products:

> A company processes raw material A into joint products B and C.
>
> Each 100 units of raw material A yield 60 units of product B and 40 units of product C.
>
> Raw material A costs $5 per unit.
>
> Processing 100 units of raw material A into joint products B and C costs $100.
>
> Product C can be sold immediately for $5 per unit, or it can be processed further and sold for $15 per unit. Additional processing costs are $4 per unit.

Given this information, there is a net benefit of $6 per unit to process product C further:

> The incremental revenue for processing further is $10 ($15 − $5, which is the selling price for product C after further processing minus the selling price for product C at the split-off point).
>
> The incremental cost for processing further is $4.
>
> The net benefit of $6 is the incremental revenue minus the incremental cost ($10 − $4).
>
> The raw material A cost ($5) and the $100 to process raw material A into products B and C are joint costs incurred up to the split-off point; they are irrelevant costs.

Add or Drop a Segment

A short-run decision to keep or drop an existing product or a service or whether to add a new one is largely determined through relevant cost analysis and the impact the decision will have on net operating income. Avoidable and other opportunity costs must be determined. Only those costs that are avoidable are relevant to consider in the decision analysis.

For example, given a product line made up of five different products, deciding to drop one of those products from the sales mix solely on the basis of its recent net operating loss is generally unwise. Instead, there should be an analysis to distinguish between traceable fixed costs and common fixed costs for the product. The traceable fixed costs are potentially avoidable costs if the product is dropped. The common fixed costs are unavoidable costs and will remain whether the product is dropped or kept. Common fixed costs are irrelevant.

Once avoidable fixed costs are identified, their associated contribution margin can be determined and the decision to add, drop, or keep a segment can be made with greater assurance:

If the avoidable fixed costs saved are less than the contribution margin amount that will be lost, the decision should be to keep the segment.

If the avoidable fixed costs saved are greater than the contribution margin amount lost, the decision should be to eliminate the segment because overall net operating income should improve.

If there are other opportunity costs, such as the forgone contribution from an alternative product or the ability to rent out the space released by not producing the product, these costs need to be added to the avoidable fixed costs in the add or drop decision process.

Add-or-Drop-a-Segment Cost Analysis

Example 1

Consider the income statement in Figure 2C-14 for a product segment reporting losses.

Figure 2C-14 Income Statement

Sales		$500,000
Variable expenses		200,000
Contribution margin		300,000
Fixed expenses:		
General factory overhead*	$60,000	
Salary of product manager	90,000	
Depreciation of equipment†	50,000	
Product advertising	100,000	
Rent for factory space‡	70,000	
General administrative expenses*	30,000	400,000
Net loss		$(100,000)

*Represents allocated common costs that would be redistributed to other product lines if the product is dropped.

† For equipment that has no resale value and does not wear out through use.

‡ For space owned by the company.

Based on evaluation of this income statement, as shown in Figure 2C-15, the company should keep the product.

Allocated common costs (*) are unavoidable and would still be incurred.

The equipment depreciation (†) is an unavoidable expense.

Figure 2C-15 Cost Analysis

Lost contribution margin	($300,000)
Savings from avoided fixed costs:	
Salary of product manager	90,000
Product advertising	100,000
Net loss from dropping the line	($110,000)

The factory space (‡) rental cannot be eliminated.

The fixed costs that can be saved by dropping the product are less than the contribution margin, so the company is better off in the short run keeping the product line.

Example 2

Consider the income statement in Figure 2C-16 showing segment margin for a product.

Figure 2C-16 Income Statement

	Segment A	Company	Company without Segment A
Sales	$500,000	$4,000,000	$3,500,000
Variable expenses	200,000	2,000,000	1,800,000
Contribution margin	300,000	2,000,000	1,700,000
Fixed expenses:			
General factory overhead*	$60,000	$600,000	600,000
Salary of product manager	90,000	400,000	310,000
Depreciation of equipment†	50,000	300,000	300,000
Product advertising	100,000	300,000	200,000
Rent for factory space‡	70,000	200,000	200,000
General administrative expenses*	30,000	100,000	100,000
Net loss	$(100,000)	$100,000	$(10,000)

*Represents allocated common costs that would be redistributed to other product lines if the product is dropped.

† For equipment that has no resale value and does not wear out through use.

‡ For space owned by the company.

As the schedule of operating data shows, in this case, the company should keep Segment A. Overall net income is greater with the segment. Avoidable fixed costs saved from discontinuing Segment A are not as much as the contribution margin amount that will be lost.

Maximize Contribution per Unit of the Limiting Factor

When the firm's ability to meet customer demand is constrained by one factor that determines capacity, the firm's goal becomes maximizing contribution margin per unit of capacity (the limiting factor).

For example: Barlow Company manufactures three products: A, B, and C. The selling price, variable costs, and contribution margin for one unit of each product are shown in Figure 2C-17.

Figure 2C-17 Barlow Company Products

	Product		
	A	B	C
Selling price	$180	$270	$240
Less variable expenses:			
Direct materials	24	72	32
Other variable expenses	102	90	148
Total variable expenses	126	162	180
Contribution margin	$54	$108	$60
Contribution margin ratio	30%	40%	25%

The same raw material is used in all three products. Barlow Company has only 5,000 pounds of raw material on hand and will not be able to obtain any more for several weeks due to a strike at its supplier's plant. Management is trying to decide which product(s) to concentrate on next week in filling its backlog of orders. The material costs $8 per pound. The next process can be used to determine which products the company should work on next week.

First, the company needs to determine each product's contribution per pound of material, and identify the product that maximizes contribution per pound, as shown in Figure 2C-18.

Figure 2C-18 Barlow Products Contribution Margin per Pound of Material

	A	B	C
(1) Contribution margin per unit	$54	$108	$60
(2) Direct material cost per unit	$24	$72	$32
(3) Direct material cost per pound	$8	$8	$8
(4) Pounds of material required per unit (2) ÷ (3)	3	9	4
(5) Contribution margin per pound (1) ÷ (4)	$18	$12	$15

The company should concentrate its available material on product A, as shown in Figure 2C-19.

Figure 2C-19 Total Contribution Margin

	A	B	C
Contribution margin per pound (from Figure 2C-18)	$18	$12	$15
Pounds of material available	× 5,000	× 5,000	× 5,000
Total contribution margin	$90,000	$60,000	$75,000

Although product A has the lowest contribution margin per unit and the second lowest contribution margin ratio, it is preferred over the other two products because it has the greatest amount of contribution margin per pound of material, and material is the company's constrained resource.

Income Taxes and Marginal Analysis

The decision-making process requires identifying the various types of relevant costs. A relevant cost may be variable or fixed. Typically, most variable costs are relevant because they are different for each alternative and have not been committed; the majority of fixed costs are irrelevant because they usually are the same for all options. The only relevant fixed costs are those that are avoidable.

One erroneous assumption is classifying depreciation expenses as relevant costs. The depreciation of facilities or equipment is a portion of a committed cost. The purchase cost is allocated over the life of the asset. For this reason, depreciation expenses are sunk costs and usually irrelevant in decision analysis.

The exception to classifying depreciation expenses as irrelevant costs is when tax effects are considered. When income taxes are taken into consideration, depreciation has a positive effect because it reduces taxable income and subsequent tax expense. In this context, depreciation reduces the company's tax liability.

Economic versus Accounting Concepts of Marginal Revenue and Marginal Costs

The economic concept of costs includes both explicit costs—such as direct labor; direct material; overhead; and selling, general, and administrative costs—as well as implicit costs not included in accounting records or in the determination of accounting income. The implicit costs, however, *are* included in the determination of economic income. Implicit costs include the opportunity cost of capital provided to the firm by its owners. Accounting costs include only explicit costs; implicit costs are excluded.

Cost analysis performed by management accountants can be similar to analysis done by economists but may have subtle differences. For example, the economic definition of marginal cost is the cost of the next unit produced. In performing marginal analysis, management accountants use unit variable costs (UVCs) as a surrogate for marginal costs. Likewise, the economic definition of marginal revenue is the revenue derived from the sale of the next unit. Management accountants use unit selling price (USP) as a surrogate for marginal revenue.

Total costs (TC), as noted earlier, are calculated by adding together all variable costs (VC) plus all fixed costs (FC). Using Q as production volume, average variable costs would then equal variable cost divided by production volume, or (AVC) = VC/Q, and average fixed costs would equal fixed costs divided by production volume, or (AFC) = FC/Q. Therefore, average total costs would be calculated by adding together average variable costs plus average fixed costs, or (ATC) = AVC + AFC.

Knowledge Check: Marginal Analysis

These questions are intended to help you check your understanding and recall of the material presented in this topic. They do not represent the type of questions that appear on the CMA exam.

Directions: Answer each question in the space provided. Correct answers and section references appear after the knowledge check questions.

1. For a firm that has excess capacity, a special order pricing decision should

   ☐ **a.** consider the opportunity costs from potential lost sales.

   ☐ **b.** compare relevant costs to the special order price.

   ☐ **c.** compare the total cost per unit and the special order price.

   ☐ **d.** evaluate any joint costs incurred up to the split-off point.

2. A make-or-buy cost analysis involves all of these factors **except**

   ☐ **a.** comparison of relevant internal costs with the cost to purchase externally.

   ☐ **b.** consideration of opportunity costs.

   ☐ **c.** evaluation of an external supplier.

   ☐ **d.** comparison of incremental revenue with incremental costs.

3. What is the profit or loss of a decision to sell or process a product further given the following information?

   • The unit production cost for the product is $10,000.

   • The unit selling price for the product is $6,000.

   • The incremental processing cost per unit is $1,000.

   • The new unit selling price is $6,650.

   ☐ **a.** −$350

   ☐ **b.** −$650

   ☐ **c.** +$350

   ☐ **d.** +$650

4. When making an add/drop product decision, common corporate costs should be

   ☐ **a.** considered to be avoidable.

   ☐ **b.** ignored.

   ☐ **c.** allocated based on sales.

   ☐ **d.** allocated based on relative contribution margins.

5. Given the information shown for the four products produced by Huron Machining, which product should Huron produce first? There is unlimited demand for each product.

   Product A: Price = $100; Unit Contribution = $40; Contribution per Machine Hour = $10

   Product B: Price = $80; Unit Contribution = $50; Contribution per Machine Hour = $8

   Product C: Price = $75; Unit Contribution = $35; and Contribution per Machine Hour = $12

   Product D: Price = $110; Unit Contribution = $55; Contribution per Machine Hour = $11

   ☐ **a.** Product A

   ☐ **b.** Product B

   ☐ **c.** Product C

   ☐ **d.** Product D

Knowledge Check Answers: Marginal Analysis

1. For a firm that has excess capacity, a special order pricing decision should. **[See *Special Orders and Pricing.*]**

   ☐ **a.** consider the opportunity costs from potential lost sales.

   ☑ **b.** compare relevant costs to the special order price.

   ☐ **c.** compare the total cost per unit and the special order price.

   ☐ **d.** evaluate any joint costs incurred up to the split-off point.

2. A make-or-buy cost analysis involves all of the following factors except **[See *Make versus Buy Cost Analysis.*]**

   ☐ **a.** comparison of relevant internal costs with the cost to purchase externally.

   ☐ **b.** consideration of opportunity costs.

   ☐ **c.** evaluation of an external supplier.

   ☑ **d.** comparison of incremental revenue with incremental costs.

3. What is the profit or loss of a decision to sell or process a product further given the following information? **[See *Sell-or-Process-Further Cost Analyses.*]**

   The unit production cost for the product is $10,000.

   The unit selling price for the product is $6,000.

   The incremental processing cost per unit is $1,000.

   The new unit selling price is $6,650.

   ☑ **a.** −$350

   ☐ **b.** −$650

   ☐ **c.** +$350

   ☐ **d.** +$650

   New Unit Selling Price − Unit Selling Price Before Further Processing − Cost of Further Processing = Profit/(Loss) of Product That Is Processed Further

   $6,650 − $6,000 − $1,000 = − $350

4. When making an add/drop product decision, common corporate costs should be **[See *Add or Drop a Segment.*]**

   ☐ **a.** considered to be avoidable.

   ☑ **b.** ignored.

   ☐ **c.** allocated based on sales.

   ☐ **d.** allocated based on relative contribution margins.

5. Given the information shown for the four products produced by Huron Machining, which product should Huron produce first? There is unlimited demand for each product. [See *Maximize Contribution per Unit of the Limiting Factor.*]

Product A: Price = $100; Unit Contribution = $40; Contribution per Machine Hour = $10

Product B: Price = $80; Unit Contribution = $50; Contribution per Machine Hour = $8

Product C: Price = $75; Unit Contribution = $35; and Contribution per Machine Hour = $12

Product D: Price = $110; Unit Contribution = $55; Contribution per Machine Hour = $11

- ☐ **a.** Product A
- ☐ **b.** Product B
- ☑ **c.** Product C
- ☐ **d.** Product D

Huron should select the product with the highest contribution margin per machine hour.

Pricing

T O SURVIVE IN TODAY'S COMPETITIVE ENVIRONMENT, a company must manage both costs and prices carefully. Long-term financial success depends on whether prices charged for products and services exceed costs and provide sufficient reserves to fund growth, finance reinvestment, and deliver a satisfactory return to investors. Management accountants have a key role in collecting, analyzing, measuring, and reporting information crucial to cost and pricing decisions.

READ the Learning Outcome Statements (LOS) for this topic as found in Appendix B and then study the concepts and calculations presented here to be sure you understand the content you could be tested on in the CMA exam.

Setting Prices

Pricing decisions generally refers to the collective decisions a company makes about what to charge for its products and services. There is no universally accepted method of setting prices. Yet pricing decisions can be critical in the success or failure of a business. Prices set too high tend to discourage sales; prices set too low may not cover costs.

Relevant product and service costs are an important part of pricing decisions. Earlier sections introduced the concepts of cost-behavior patterns, cost traceability, cost drivers, and cost relevance. Such contemporary cost system elements:

- Use activities and operations as intermediate cost objects to trace costs to final cost objects.
- Assign costs to final cost objects based on cost drivers.
- Provide multiple views of costs (e.g., by resources consumed, activities consumed, and drivers consumed).
- Facilitate cost management of a product or a service by making the various causal relationships visible to managers.

A well-designed cost management system increases the likelihood of good pricing decisions and helps an organization to meet its strategic objectives. Other factors, such as supply and demand and the time horizon for a product or service, also influence decisions.

This topic begins by considering how prices are set. Traditional pricing based on supply and demand are covered first, including the impact of the time horizon. Then market-based pricing (both demand-based pricing and competition-based pricing) is explained. Cost-based pricing methods are discussed next, then target costing is explained and illustrated. The remainder of the topic includes discussions about supply and demand, market equilibrium, price elasticity of demand, and governmental intervention in market operations.

Supply and Demand Considerations

Traditional pricing practices in situations in which there are few competitors and demand exceeds supply are to mark up product or service costs to yield a sufficient profit. As long as demand remains strong and the competition is limited, any increases in costs can be offset with price increases.

The primary pitfall of pricing based on supply and demand in this manner is that it provides little incentive for cost management. Many companies—in various industries—have priced their products and services out of the market by perpetually increasing prices to cover costs. Furthermore, unless there are strong barriers to market entry (such as technological superiority or large capital investment requirements), such pricing creates the opportunity for competitors to enter the marketplace. As competition increases and supply exceeds demand, surviving by marking up costs to yield good profits becomes problematic.

Demand-based pricing uses customer demand and customers' perceived value of the product as the primary pricing basis. Demand-based pricing includes price skimming, penetration pricing, yield management, price points, psychological pricing, bundle pricing, value-based pricing, and premium pricing.

Time Horizons

Pricing decisions are often categorized as short run or long run.

Short-run pricing decisions have implications for a year or less. Many are for a time period of six months or less. Short-run decisions apply to one-time and short-run special product purchase orders or responses to competitive market conditions that require more immediate product line and output volume adjustments.

Long-run pricing decisions have a time horizon greater than one year. Long-run decisions generally focus on a product or service in a major market.

The time horizon—short run or long run—ultimately dictates which product or service costs are relevant to pricing. Some pricing decisions may have both short- and long-run implications.

Short-Run Costing and Pricing

Consider this scenario illustrating costing and pricing for a one-time special order. Company K has decided to bid on a one-time opportunity with a quick turnaround.

Excess manufacturing capacity is available, so the order will have no effect on existing sales. Current variable and fixed costs per unit are shown in Figure 2C-20 for a normal production run of 100,000 units.

Figure 2C-20 Fixed and Variable Costs for Company K

	Variable Cost per Unit	Fixed Cost per Unit	Variable and Fixed Costs per Unit
Manufacturing			
Direct materials	$10	—	$10
Packaging	5	—	5
Direct labor	6	—	6
Manufacturing overhead	8	$10	18
Total manufacturing costs	29	10	39
Advertising and commissions	4	12	16
Distribution	7	5	12
Total costs	$40	$27	$67

The variable manufacturing overhead ($8) represents utility costs. At the normal production run of 100,000 units, details of the total fixed manufacturing overhead costs and the fixed manufacturing overhead costs per unit are shown in Figure 2C-21.

Figure 2C-21 Fixed Manufacturing Overhead Unit Costs

	Total Fixed Manufacturing Overhead Costs	Fixed Manufacturing Overhead Cost per Unit
Depreciation	$300,000	$3
Materials procurement	100,000	1
Salaries	200,000	2
Engineering	400,000	4
Total fixed manufacturing overhead costs	$1,000,000	$10

The one-time special order is for 10,000 units. If the company decides to bid on the order, the current fixed manufacturing costs ($1,000,000) will continue to be incurred. The only additional expenditures the company would incur are for materials procurement ($10,000) and engineering setups ($25,000).

The firm requesting the bid has indicated that any offer in excess of $35 per unit would be noncompetitive. The company must determine what short-term price to bid for this special offer.

Relevant costs must be analyzed. Only the additional materials procurement and engineering manufacturing costs are relevant. Advertising and distribution costs are irrelevant to the pricing decision. Existing fixed manufacturing costs are also irrelevant because they will remain whether Company K accepts the special order or not. Relevant costs are summarized in Figure 2C-22.

Figure 2C-22 Relevant Cost Data

Direct materials (10,000 units × $10)		$100,000
Packaging (10,000 units × $5)		50,000
Direct labor (10,000 units × $6)		60,000
Variable manufacturing overhead (10,000 units × $8)		80,000
Fixed manufacturing overhead		
Materials procurement	$10,000	
Engineering	25,000	
Total fixed manufacturing overhead costs		35,000
Total relevant costs		$325,000

Based on this relevant cost data, per-unit relevant costs are $32.50 ($325,000 / 10,000 units). This is below the $35 price deemed as competitive. Any bid above the cost per unit ($32.50) and below $35 will contribute to the company's operating income. For example, a short-term price of $34 would result in a profit of $15,000 [10,000 × ($34.00 − $32.50)].

As noted in the discussion of special order pricing in Section C, Topic 2: Marginal Analysis, making a price decision based on the total cost per unit would be misleading and probably would result in not bidding on the business. In this example, if the total cost per unit is used as the comparison figure, the order would be rejected because the company's unit cost ($67) exceeds the bid ceiling price ($35). Even if only the variable cost per unit was used in the analysis, the order would have been rejected ($40 compared to the bid ceiling of $35).

Long-Run Costing and Pricing

Accurate cost information is essential in the decisions a company makes about what to charge for a product or service and how to best compete in the marketplace. Analysis methods make assumptions regarding costs and prices. To the extent that these constraints are stable, the analyses have a greater probability of accuracy.

Given an extended time horizon, stable and predictable costs are much preferred for pricing decisions. Stable long-run costs lead to greater price stability and reduce the need for continuous monitoring of suppliers' prices and other relevant cost data. Stable long-run costs also improve other planning decisions and foster stronger, longer-term buyer and seller relationships. Forecasting becomes easier and customer relations become stronger.

In the previous example, the company must cover all costs (including fixed overhead) in the long run. With excess capacity, no additional fixed overhead costs are incurred as production increases, and, therefore, the more units produced, the lower the total unit cost.

Market-Based Pricing

Companies often must compete in markets in which products and services have little differentiation. Market-based pricing generally prevails in such product or service parity situations, whereby the market prices of identical and substitutable products determine the market price.

Two market methods help determine prices. The first is the demand-based concept. If the demand for the product is high, the price will be set high. If demand is low and/or there are numerous substitutes for the product, the price will be set low. The second market method to help determine selling price is the competition-based concept, which sets the price according to the price offered by competitors of identical and substitutable products.

In market-based pricing circumstances:

- Market forces strongly influence the price set for a product or service.
- Customers are reluctant to pay more than the prevailing market price.
- Companies typically charge the prevailing market rate.
- Companies consider what customers expect, want, and value.
- Companies determine the intensity of competitive rivalries.
- Companies anticipate how customers and competitors will react to its pricing.

Because the selling price cannot be changed easily, a company using this strategy should determine a cost/benefit analysis using the market price. If costs to produce and sell will not result in an acceptable level of profit, the company typically makes the decision not to remain in the market for that product.

In market-based pricing, companies make decisions about product and service features as well as pricing decisions based on anticipated customer and competitor reactions. The general goal is to avoid setting prices that could lead to costly market destabilizing or competitive price warfare. As such, the market-based approach is a logical pricing approach in highly competitive and commodity-type markets such as airlines, oil, gas, minerals, and many farm products.

Cost-Based Pricing

The **cost-based pricing** (or **cost-plus pricing**) approach looks at the costs to develop a product or service and sets a price to recoup those costs and make a desired profit. Cost-based pricing is appropriate when some level of product or service differentiation exists and a company can exercise modest discretion in setting prices. Where market-based pricing is fairly restricted by market conditions, cost-based pricing considers market reactions as one factor in setting prices.

Under cost-based pricing, a firm:

- Determines the costs to produce and sell a product at a certain volume level.
- Identifies a reasonable return (markup).
- Adds the markup to the cost.
- Adjusts the markup as necessary in response to market forces.

With cost-based pricing, the markup typically is expressed as a percentage of cost. A predetermined markup is applied to the cost base to determine a target selling price.

Selling Price = Unit Cost + (Markup % on Unit Cost × Unit Cost)

For example, consider a product with these total costs:

Direct materials	$50
Direct labor	40
Variable factory overhead	20
Total product costs	$110

Total fixed overhead costs are $100,000 ($100 per unit at the 1,000 unit level).

Selling and administrative (S&A) expenses are $ 500,000 ($500 per unit at the 1,000 unit level).

The challenges of cost-based pricing are determining what costs to use and what the final markup should be. There are three cost-plus methods to determine the selling price of a product:

1. Variable cost
2. Product cost
3. Total cost

In this example, variable costs are $50 + $40 + $20 = $110. The product costs are $210, and the total costs are $710 per unit ($110 + $500 S&A Expenses per Unit + $100 Fixed Overhead per Unit).

The formula for the selling price in these methods requires computing the markup and adding it to the costs. The markup is different under all three methods. For the variable cost markup, the computation is:

$$\text{Markup Percentage} = \frac{\text{Desired Profit} + \text{Total Fixed Costs} + \text{Expenses}}{\text{Total Variable Costs}}$$

At a level of 1,000 units in the example, with a desired profit of $200,000, the markup is computed to be [$200,000 + $100,000 + $500,000] /$110,000 = 727% at the 1,000 unit level. The selling price will be:

$$\text{Selling Price} = \text{Markup per Unit} + \text{Costs per Unit}$$

So in this case, selling price = [(727% ×$110) + $110] = $910.
The product cost markup is computed as:

$$\text{Product Cost Markup Percentage} = \frac{\text{Desired Profit} + \text{Expenses}}{\text{Total Product Costs}}$$

The total cost markup is computed as:

$$\text{Total Cost Markup Percentage} = \frac{\text{Desired Profit}}{\text{Total Costs}}$$

Under all three cases, the selling price will remain $910.

In the end, the desired markup is evaluated and may be modified based on the prices competitors charge for similar products and the anticipated reactions of customers to alternative prices.

Target Pricing

The traditional pricing approaches discussed thus far are all based on the idea that:

Price = Unit Cost + Unit Profit

This equation presumes that a product or service has been developed, costs have been or can be identified, and the item is ready to be marketed once a price is set.

Target costing offers a fundamentally different way to look at the relationship of price and costs. The underlying concept of target costing is:

Cost = Competitive Price − Unit Profit

The cost for the product or service is computed by starting with the anticipated selling price and deducting the desired profit.

Keep in mind that both unit cost and unit profit are functions of volume. Increased volumes lower unit costs and raise unit profits while decreased volumes raise unit costs and lower unit profits.

Target Costing Process

Just as there is no universal definition for target costing, no definitive list of steps exists for target costing. Target costing practices in any company tend to evolve based on specific business circumstances. However, Statement on Management

Accounting (SMA) *Implementing Target Costing*, notes that the steps shown in Figure 2C-23 are common to most target costing applications.

Figure 2C-23 Target Costing Steps

Establish a target price in the context of market needs and competition.

Establish the target profit margin.

Determine the allowable cost that must be achieved.

Calculate the probable cost of current products and processes.

Establish the target cost—the amount by which costs must be reduced.

Establish the cross-functional team to be involved in the implementation process from the earliest design stages.

Use tools such as concurrent engineering, value engineering, and quality function deployment in the design process.

Implement cost reductions (e.g., through life-cycle costing) once production is under way.

Target Costing

Various definitions of target costing exist. SMA *Implementing Target Costing* lists these characteristics as common to most definitions:

- A competitive market environment
- A situation in which market prices drive cost (and investment) decisions
- Implementation of cost planning, cost management, and cost reduction early in product or service design and development
- Cross-functional team involvement, including management accounting

Essentially, **target costing** is a comprehensive cost management process that determines a target cost for a product or service and then develops a prototype for that product or service that can be made profitably for the identified amount. It is a proactive methodology whereby product and service costs are managed early on during the design and development processes rather than in the later stages of product development and production.

The fundamental objective of target costing is to enable businesses to manage operations profitably in a competitive market. As such, the foundation for target costing is the determination of market- and price-based costs. The cross-functional participation of research and design, engineering, production, marketing, and accounting is necessary to ensure that the proposed product or service, when sold, generates the desired profit margin. Stated another way, the cross-functional team is given the responsibility to design and develop the product or service so that it can be made for the target cost.

Target Cost

In defining **target cost**, SMA *Implementing Target Costing* indicates that the term means different things to different companies. For some, target cost is the same as allowable cost (see next heading). Other definitions describe target cost as the difference between the allowable cost and the current cost—the amount by which costs must be reduced to achieve the allowable costs.

Allowable Cost

Allowable cost is the difference between the target price (set by market forces) and the target profit (set by management). In effect, the allowable cost represents the maximum unit cost, given an expected volume that a firm can commit to a product to achieve the company's profit objective. Target operating income per unit and target cost per unit are required in order to calculate allowable cost. Remember that both targets are functions of target volume.

- Target operating income per unit is the operating income a company strives for on each unit of product or service sold at the target volume.
- Target cost per unit is the estimated long-run product or service cost per unit at the target volume.

Target cost per unit is determined by subtracting target operating income per unit from the target price. When a unit is produced for the target cost and sold at the target price, a company will be able to achieve its target operating income.

Consider the next scenario illustrating target operating income per unit and target cost per unit. Due to increasing market competition, a firm needs to reduce its per-unit selling price from $100 to $75. At this lower price, the firm expects to increase annual sales from 10,000 units to 12,000. Management wants to earn a 15% target operating income on sales revenues. Total current cost per unit at 12,000 units would be $80. Figure 2C-24 shows target revenues and cost.

Figure 2C-24 Target Revenues and Cost

Total Target Sales Revenues	=	12,000 Units × $75 = $900,000
Total Target Operating Income	=	15% × $900,000 = $135,000
Target Operating Income per Unit	=	$135,000 / 12,000 = $11.25
Target Cost per Unit	=	Target Price − Target Operating Income per Unit
	=	$75.00 − $11.25 = $63.75

In target pricing, the market price of a product is taken as a given. The target cost per unit usually is lower than the full product or service cost per unit. This is the case in the example just presented, where the target cost per unit is $63.75 and the current (full) cost per unit is $80. But in order to make money, a company must recover all of its costs. Thus, all costs—both fixed and variable—are relevant in target cost calculations. Under these circumstances, businesses constantly are challenged in target costing to improve a product or service and the associated production processes throughout the entire life cycle of the item.

Target Price

In target costing, the **target price** represents the maximum allowable price that can be charged for the product or service. It is an estimate of the amount that potential customers would be willing to pay based on their value perceptions—their needs and expectations for products and services, quality, timeliness, and price. A target price also reflects the firm's understanding of the market competition—its capabilities and probable responses. In the final outcome, a target price should result in an acceptable price to customers as well as an acceptable price to the organization.

Designing a Proposed New Product or Service under Target Costing

Figure 2C-25 summarizes basic techniques (as identified in SMA *Implementing Target Costing*) that firms use to design a proposed new product or service and establish its target price and target margin.

Figure 2C-25 Target Costing Process Techniques

Technique	Description
Market assessment tools	Any of several methods to assess the market and customers' wants and needs in regard to a proposed product or service including surveys, focus groups, interviews, and customer comment cards with current, prospective, or former customers.
Reverse engineering (teardown analysis)	The acquisition and disassembly of competitors' products to investigate their design, material(s), likely manufacturing processes, attributes, quality, and costs.
Industry and competitive analysis	Analysis techniques used to develop an understanding of competitors and how to best position a firm and its products and services to a competitive advantage. This may include any variety of strategies (such as Michael E. Porter's strategies) for conducting comprehensive industry and competitive analysis.
Financial planning and analysis	Detailed financial planning and statement analysis to examine the relationships between process, volume, and revenue. This approach also looks at cost and investments in the aggregate and for specific segment lines and individual products (or services); it allows a comparison to the proposed product or service.
Internal cost analysis	Determination of product and service costs and related investments for current offerings in order to estimate the costs of the proposed new product or service under existing and proposed product/service and process characteristics. This technique often involves activity-based management (ABM) and activity-based costing (ABC) to identify costs associated with specific cost-incurring activities.
Cost tables	Maintenance and use of detailed databases of cost information based on various manufacturing variables; facilitate cost projections for the proposed new product or service, assuming the use of different designs, materials, manufacturing processes, and end user functions. This technique helps managers determine in advance the effect of alternative choices.

Industry and competitive analysis used in combination with market assessment and reverse engineering data help to facilitate setting of the target price. Financial planning and analysis facilitates the determination of the target profit margin. Internal cost analysis and cost tables facilitate the comparison of allowable and current costs and the determination of the target cost.

Once the target cost is identified, the challenge of achieving it ensues. The emphasis on cross-functional teams promotes a high degree of interdependence among all functions in the organization. Companies will try to adapt different approaches to arrive at a product/service and process design that achieves the target cost. Most firms use some elements of concurrent engineering, value engineering, quality function deployment, and life-cycle costing.

Concurrent Engineering

Concurrent engineering is a process in which an organization designs a product or service using input and evaluations from all business units and functions early in the process, anticipating problems and balancing the needs of all parties. The emphasis is on maintaining customer requirements and upstream prevention rather than downstream correction.

Value Engineering

Value engineering is a principal technique in closing the gap between current cost and allowable cost. It is the systematic analysis of a product or service design, materials, specifications, and production processes in the context of customer requirements.

A differentiation is made between value-added costs and non-value-added costs. **Value-added costs** are those costs that convert resources into products or services consistent with customer requirements. They are costs that customers perceive as adding value or utility to a product or service. Conversely, non-value-added costs are not critical to customer preferences. In a manufacturing environment, examples of value-added costs might be costs associated with design, assembly, tools, and machinery. Examples of non-value-added costs could be special delivery charges, rework costs, or the cost of obsolete inventory.

In practice, the distinction between value-added and non-value-added costs can be somewhat difficult to assess. Some costs may fall in both categories, given specific circumstances. In manufacturing, testing costs or ordering costs often are difficult to differentiate between value-added and non-value-added.

The objective in value engineering is to balance overall costs and benefits and increase the ultimate value of the product. The process is best achieved using cross-functional teams, as trade-offs among design, development, production, and cost are involved. Management accountants often are called on to assess the potential savings resulting from the elimination of non-value-added activities and associated costs.

For the most part, the terms *value engineering* and *value analysis* are used interchangeably. Some firms use *analysis* for the design and development stages and *engineering* for the postdevelopment stage.

Quality Function Deployment

Quality function deployment (QFD) is a structured method in which customer requirements for a product or service are translated into appropriate technical requirements at each stage of development and production. The QFD process is often referred to as "listening to the voice of the customer."

Product Life-Cycle Costing and Life-Cycle Costing

Target costing assumes that the price of a product or service is stable or decreasing over time because of market conditions—due to competition on price, quality, and functionality. Companies must respond to these competitive pressures through a product's or service's life cycle.

Products and services pass through stages of existence. The product-life-cycle concept assumes that products:

- Have a limited life.
- Pass through phases, each of which has different opportunities and threats to sales.
- Require different marketing strategies in different life-cycle phases.

There are four phases in the life of a product or service:

1. *Market introduction.* High costs, slow sales volume, low competition, a need to create demand, and little profit.
2. *Growth.* Decreased costs due to economies of scale, increased sales volume, increased competition, increased profitability but sometimes with lowered sales prices.
3. *Maturity.* Costs are lowered, sales are at their peak, competition is high, prices tend to drop, and differentiation is needed to maintain market share.
4. *Saturation and decline.* Sales volume decreases, profits decrease, and sales prices decrease.

Target costing is designed to reduce the overall costs of a product or service over its entire life cycle. In applying target costing principles, firms must periodically redesign products and services to reduce price and improve value simultaneously.

Life-cycle costing tracks and accumulates all actual costs associated with a product or service throughout its life cycle. Capturing all costs provides important information for a variety of planning decisions to minimize overall costs.

Cost-Plus Target Rate of Return Pricing

Earlier discussions of cost-based pricing described the general formula of setting a price as adding a markup percentage to the cost base. A cost-plus target rate of return is one method of determining the markup based on the target rate of return on investment.

The **target rate of return on investment** is the target operating income a firm must earn divided by its invested capital. Companies often specify a target rate of return on investment.

Consider the next scenario illustrating cost-plus target rate of return pricing:

Full costs per unit for a product are $1,000.

The number of units expected to be sold is 10,000.

The pretax target rate of return is 20%.

Invested capital (long-term or fixed assets plus current assets) is $10,000,000.

Total target operating income is 20% × $10,000,000, or $2,000,000.

Target operating income per unit is $2,000,000 / 10,000 units, or $200.

Based on this information, the desired target operating income per unit is $200. Given the full product costs per unit of $1,000, the markup percentage that this translates to is:

$$\$200/\$1,000 = 20\%$$

The 20% markup represents operating income per unit as a percentage of full product cost per unit.

Peak Load Pricing Considerations

Thus far, all the pricing methods discussed have been based on costs in some manner. In some circumstances, non-cost factors must be considered in setting a price. Peak load pricing is such a situation.

Peak load pricing is the practice of charging more or less for a product or service based on demand and physical capacity limits. With peak load pricing, prices differ among market segments even though there is no significant difference in the outlay costs.

Prices may go up or down with peak load pricing:

- When demand approaches capacity limits, prices go up.
- When slack or excess capacity is available, prices go down.

Peak load pricing is found in a variety of industries, such as airlines, hotels, car rental, electric utilities, and telecommunications.

Laws of Supply and Demand

Pricing decisions must consider the relationship of supply and demand. Demand is inversely related to price, and supply is directly related to price. As prices increase, all other things being equal, demand will decrease. As prices decrease, all other things being equal, demand will increase. As prices increase, all other things being equal, supply will increase. As prices decrease, all other things being equal, supply will decrease.

A market is not merely the corner store with predetermined prices; it is any situation in which buyers and sellers come together (physically or electronically) to exchange goods and services. Buyers create a demand for products or services that sellers create and supply. The demand is the amount of a product or service consumers are willing and able to buy. The supply is the amount producers of goods or services are willing and able to make available for sale.

We examine the relationship between supply and demand in the context of the soybean market.

Demand

A demand schedule is a table of potential demand, with each price matched to its corresponding demand. Figure 2C-26 is a demand schedule for soybeans that Farmer J has constructed.

Figure 2C-26 Demand Schedule for Soybeans

Price of Soybeans per Bushel	Quantity Demanded (per Week)
$6	20
$5	30
$4	40
$3	60

To be meaningful, a demand schedule must indicate a time period. The quantity of soybeans demanded in Figure 2C-26 is for a period of one week. If Farmer J prices soybeans at $6 per bushel, he will be able to sell 20 bushels in the week (making $120). If he prices his soybeans at $4 per bushel, he will be able to sell twice as much, or 40 bushels per week (making $160).

Farmer J must determine which route he will take: produce fewer soybeans and sell less at a higher price, or produce more soybeans and sell more at a lower price.

The demand curve in Figure 2C-27 corresponds to the demand schedule in Figure 2C-26, with the curve showing the quantity demanded at each given price. The demand curve slopes downward, indicating that quantity demanded increases as the price falls and decreases as the price rises.

Figure 2C-27 Demand Curve for Soybeans

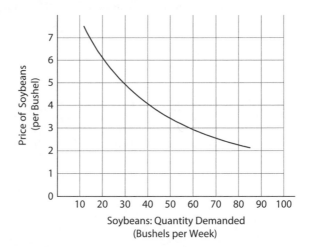

Change in Quantity Demanded

A change in quantity demanded is a movement along the demand curve. If the price of soybeans increases, the quantity demanded will decrease.

Several factors can cause a change in the quantity demanded:

- Part of the law of diminishing marginal utility states that consumers will buy more only if the price is lowered.
- There is an **income effect**; that is, consumer incomes are relatively higher if the price is lowered and consumers are, therefore, able to purchase more.
- The **substitution effect** is the tendency for consumers to purchase more of a product when its price falls, thus in effect substituting that product for others they were buying before (assuming the same amount of income to spend). For instance, if the price of restaurant meals declines, people may eat out more often and at home less often. As the price of one item falls, the price of competitive items, in effect, rises, making consumers less likely to keep buying them. The substitution effect applies more generally. For instance, when the cost of labor rises, employers will tend to use less of it, and if the same work can be automated, employers will tend to substitute machine processes for human labor.

Change in Demand

A change in demand itself is a shift of the entire demand curve. For example, if buyers learn in a news article about the health benefits of soybeans, the demand for soybeans may increase.

This increased demand is shown in Figures 2C-28 and 2C-29.

Figure 2C-28 Increased Demand Schedule for Soybeans

Price of Soybeans per Bushel	Quantity Demanded (per Week)
$6	30
$5	40
$4	50
$3	80

Figure 2C-29 Shift of Demand Curve for Soybeans

Demand is affected by a number of factors:

- **Personal taste.** Different consumers like different goods, and those tastes change over time. Personal taste has an effect on demand based on the number of consumers in the market. As the population increases, decreases, or shifts, buyers enter or leave the market, increasing or decreasing demand.
- **Income.** As income rises, consumers purchase more of most types of goods and services. Such goods are normal goods. The demand for inferior goods decreases as incomes rise. Steak is a normal good while hamburger is an inferior good. The concept of normal versus inferior relates to consumer incomes, not to quality or the perception of quality.
- **Price of related goods.** Substitutes can affect demand for a product or service, as can complements (items that normally are purchased together; e.g., golf clubs and golf bags). If the price of one product drops (golf clubs), there will be an increase in demand for the complementary product (golf bags).
- **Expectations of buyers.** Buyers may anticipate a weak or strong economy and reduce or increase spending, or they may expect price increases and buy products before the increases occur.

Supply

Now that Farmer J has studied the demand for soybeans, he must determine how much he is willing to supply at given prices.

After calculating his production costs and other factors, Farmer J creates his supply schedule (a table of potential supply and corresponding prices), as shown in Figure 2C-30.

Figure 2C-30 Supply Schedule for Soybeans

Price of Soybeans per Bushel	Quantity Supplied (per Week)
$6	100
$5	90
$4	80
$3	65

Farmer J uses the numbers from his supply schedule to graph the supply curve (a graph of potential supply and corresponding prices), shown in Figure 2C-31. Note that the supply curve slopes upward, indicating that supply will increase as the price rises and decrease as the price falls.

Figure 2C-31 Supply Curve for Soybeans

A change in quantity supplied is movement from one point to another on the supply curve. If the price of soybeans drops from $4 to $3, Farmer J will be willing to supply only 65 bushels per week instead of the 80 he is willing to supply at $4 per bushel.

A change in supply itself is represented by a shift of the entire supply curve. Figure 2C-32 shows a change in supply.

Figure 2C-32 Shift in Supply Curve for Soybeans

Changes in supply are caused by:

- **Resource prices**. Resource prices affect the cost of production and, therefore, the quantity a business is willing to supply at a given price.
- **Technology**. Technological advances or increased use of technology can lower production costs, thereby enabling an increase in supply at a given price.
- **Taxes and subsidies**. Changes in taxes can affect costs and thus affect the quantity a producer is willing to supply at various prices. Government subsidies lower costs and increase supply.
- **Prices of similar goods**. The price of similar, substitute, or complementary goods can affect the amount producers are willing to supply.
- **Expectations.** Expectations about the future of a product can affect the industry's willingness to supply the product. For example, after September 11, 2001, manufacturers of American flags added workers to be able to increase production and supply of flags to meet an increased demand.
- **Number of sellers.** As more sellers enter the market, supply is increased, and the supply curve shifts to the right. As sellers leave the market, supply decreases, and the supply curve shifts to the left.

Ultimately, it is the interaction of aggregate supply and aggregate demand that determines prices. Excess supply (a surplus) decreases prices in the face of unchanged demand. Supply shortage, against unchanged demand, results in price increases. Increasing demand for limited resources, such as oil or diamonds, results in increasing prices.

Market Equilibrium

Equilibrium is the price at which quantity supplied equals quantity demanded. Market equilibrium differs depending on the level of competition in the market. In a market with monopolistic competition, where there are products that may be differentiated but are not identical and, therefore, not substitutable, firms behave like monopolies in the short run. Pricing in the short run typically ignores the impact of other firms, increasing marginal net revenues. However, in the long run, firms in monopolistic competition become more like purely competitive firms. In a monopoly, firms typically sell fewer products at higher prices, resulting in higher net marginal revenue, unless they are legally required to do otherwise. In an oligopoly, marginal net revenues are higher than in pure competition, unless and until laws prohibit the lack of competition.

Note that when we discuss equilibrium in the next examples, we are dealing with multiple buyers and sellers (pure competition). The quantities in these examples are now in thousands of bushels, because many more buyers and sellers are included in the determination of market supply and demand.

Equilibrium price and equilibrium quantity are the price and quantity demanded (or supplied) at equilibrium. Market clearing price is another term for equilibrium price. Equilibrium tends to be a rationing function of prices: a price where selling and buying decisions are synchronized, or coordinated. Figure 2C-33 shows equilibrium for soybeans.

Figure 2C-33 Market Equilibrium

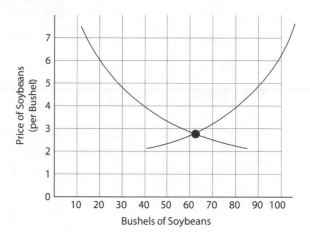

The equilibrium point is the point on the graph of market equilibrium at which the supply curve and the demand curve intersect. The equilibrium price in this example is $2.75 per bushel for soybeans; the equilibrium quantity is 62,000 bushels per week.

Disequilibrium is lack of equilibrium—any price at which quantity supplied and quantity demanded are not equal. A price above equilibrium results in excess supply; a price below equilibrium results in a shortage of supply or excess demand. Disequilibrium can be temporary, such as that which occurs during the growth of one industry and the decline of another (e.g., the move from the VHS video format to DVD).

There is a direct relationship between a shift in the demand curve and the equilibrium price and equilibrium quantity. When demand increases, the equilibrium price increases.

There is an inverse relationship between a shift in the supply curve and the equilibrium price and equilibrium quantity. When supply increases, the equilibrium price decreases.

These rules are based on the assumption that all other things, such as income and economic conditions, are equal.

Figure 2C-34 shows the relationships among supply, demand, and equilibrium.

Figure 2C-34 Effects on Equilibrium of Changes in Supply and Demand

<table>
<tr><td></td><td></td><td colspan="2" align="center">**Demand**</td></tr>
<tr><td></td><td></td><td>**Increase**</td><td>**Decrease**</td></tr>
<tr><td rowspan="4">**Supply**</td><td rowspan="2">**Increase**</td><td>Effect on equilibrium **price** cannot be predicted.</td><td>Equilibrium **price** decreases.</td></tr>
<tr><td>Equilibrium **quantity** will increase.</td><td>Effect on equilibrium **quantity** cannot be predicted.</td></tr>
<tr><td rowspan="2">**Decrease**</td><td>Equilibrium **price** increases.</td><td>Effect on equilibrium **price** cannot be predicted.</td></tr>
<tr><td>Effect on equilibrium **quantity** cannot be predicted.</td><td>Equilibrium **quantity** will decrease.</td></tr>
</table>

Price Elasticity of Demand

The law of demand states that consumers respond to price changes by buying more or less of a product. However, consumer responsiveness to a price change can vary considerably from product to product and between different price ranges for the same product.

Price elasticity of demand is the degree to which consumers will respond to a price change. Similar to the elasticity of a rubber band, the question for the supplier is: How far can I stretch this without breaking it? For products that have elastic or relatively elastic demand curves (two degrees of the same measure), consumers will be very responsive to a change in price. For example, when the price of travel increases, statistics show that travel decreases at a faster rate. If a product is inelastic or relatively inelastic (two measures, again, along the same scale), such as basic foods, consumers are not as responsive to price changes.

A perfectly inelastic demand indicates that a change in price will result in no corresponding change in demand. A perfectly elastic demand indicates that a small decrease in price will result in consumers demanding as much of the product as they can get or a small increase in price will result in demand falling to zero. Perfectly elastic demand happens only in a purely competitive market.

Figure 2C-35 shows perfectly inelastic and perfectly elastic demand curves on a graph.

Figure 2C-35 Perfectly Inelastic and Perfectly Elastic Demand

The formula for price elasticity of demand (a midpoint average) is:

$$\text{Price Elasticity of Demand } (E_d) = \frac{[\text{Change in Quantity/(Average of Quantities)}]}{[\text{Change in Price/(Average of Prices)}]}$$

This formula calculates elasticity of demand as a percentage of price. This is important because a change in price of $1 is different for a car than it is for one bushel of soybeans. Elasticity of demand normally varies over a range of prices. In addition, the percentage of change is calculated based on an average of the starting price and the new price. Although some economists favor using the initial value as the basis of the calculations rather than the average of the initial and ending values, the CMA exam only tests the approach that uses the averages. This approach is called the "midpoint formula" approach.

As an example of the calculation using the midpoint formula approach, consider a change in quantity demanded between prices on the demand curve for soybeans. Assume that at $5 per bushel, the demand is 30,000 bushels, and at $4 per bushel, the demand increases to 40,000 bushels. Note when substituting the values into the formula that the percentage change is calculated by using the midpoints formula—that is, the dollar change is divided by the average of the beginning and ending values to determine the percentage change [(30,000 + 40,000 / 2 and ($5 + $4) / 2). The next computations are made to arrive at the elasticity of demand for soybeans.

$$\% \text{ Change in Quantity Demanded} = \frac{\text{Change in Quantity Demanded}}{\text{Average Quantity Demanded}} = \frac{10,000}{(30,000 + 40,000)/2} = 0.2857$$

$$\% \text{ Change in Price} = \frac{\text{Price Change}}{\text{Average Price}} = \frac{\$1}{(\$5 + \$4)/2} = 0.22$$

$$\text{Elasticity of Demand } (E_d) \text{ for Soybeans} = \frac{\% \text{ Change in Quantity Demanded of Product X}}{\% \text{ Change in Price of Product X}} = \frac{0.2857}{0.22} = 1.30$$

When using the averages of the beginning and ending values, one gets the same answer regardless of whether the values change upward or downward; for example, ($5 + $4) / 2 is the same as ($4 + $5) / 2. When interpreting the price elasticity of demand, the negative sign usually is ignored.

Conclusions can be reached about price elasticity of demand based on a product's elasticity value:

- A price elasticity of demand value greater than 1 is considered elastic or relatively elastic. A percentage change in price results in a larger percentage change in quantity demanded.
- A price elasticity of demand value less than 1 is considered inelastic or relatively inelastic. A percentage change in price results in a smaller percentage change in quantity demanded.
- **Unit elastic demand** is the term used to describe the price range at which a percentage change in price results in an equal percentage change in quantity demanded.

Although it is common to refer simply to price elasticity of demand, one also may see references to price elasticity coefficient or price elasticity coefficient of value. All these terms have the same meaning.

A business uses information about elasticity of demand to determine the selling price that will maximize revenues. Farmer J can create a table of soybean demand based on demand schedules, adding consideration for the elasticity coefficient of price changes of soybeans, as shown in Figure 2C-36. As the unit price drops from $10, at first revenues climb; additional demand is sufficient to offset the decreasing per-unit price. At a price of either $5 or $6 per unit—the unit elastic price—a $1 change in price has no effect on total revenue, which is 150 at either price. As unit price drops to $4 and below, however, the elasticity coefficient becomes negative; revenue actually drops even though demand keeps rising.

Figure 2C-36 Price Elasticity of Demand, Elasticity Coefficient, and Total Revenue

Quantity Demanded (per Week)	Unit Price	Elasticity Coefficient	Total Revenue (Quantity × Price)	Total Revenue Test
5	$10		$50	
		6.33		Elastic
10	9		90	
		3.40		Elastic
15	8		120	
		2.14		Elastic
20	7		140	
		1.44		Elastic
25	6		150	
		1		Unit elastic
30	5		150	
		.692		Inelastic
35	4		140	
		.467		Inelastic
40	3		120	
		.294		Inelastic
45	2		90	
		.158		Inelastic
50	1		50	

Figure 2C-37 shows the elasticity of demand of Product X on the demand curve.

Figure 2C-37 Elasticity of Demand of Product X

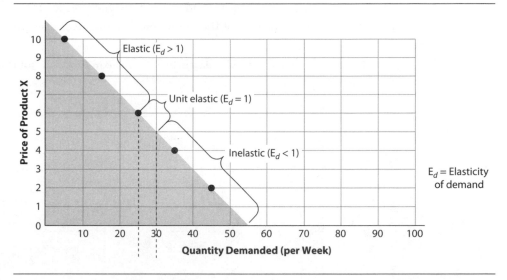

Figure 2C-38 graphs elasticity of demand and total revenues based on the numbers in Figure 2C-36. Note that total revenues are maximized between prices of $5 and $6, where total revenues equal $150. Prices above $6 and below $5 will reduce total revenues.

Figure 2C-38 Total Revenue Curve of Product X

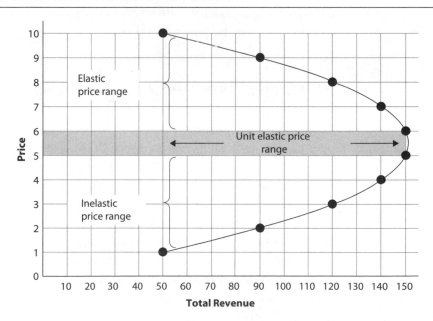

Note that elasticity of demand differs between ranges of prices, with the price more elastic at lower quantities and less elastic at lower prices and higher quantities. In the graph on the right in Figure 2C-39 (a less detailed version of Figure 2C-38), you can see that revenue increases when prices increase, as price goes up in the inelastic portion of the graph, but revenue decreases in the elastic portion.

Figure 2C-39 Impact of Price Elasticity of Demand in Terms of Quantity and Total Revenue

In competitive markets, firms should seek to price their products with regard to elasticity of demand in order to set a price that increases revenues. When a firm faces an elastic demand curve, it can increase its revenue by lowering prices and thereby increasing the (elastic) demand. When a firm faces an inelastic demand curve, however, it can increase revenues by raising prices—because the higher price will not decrease the (inflexible) demand.

Government Intervention in Market Operations

Discussion of the relationship between supply and demand thus far has assumed a pure market, with all things being equal. However, a large focus of many national governments is to ensure stability in markets and employment, and the government sometimes intervenes in the natural market process.

Governments repeatedly apply supply and demand analysis and measures of elasticity of demand in determining economic and trade policies. There are many reasons for governments to control the economy. Government intervention in market operations involves policies that attempt to hold the price at a disequilibrium value that could not be maintained in the absence of intervention. In addition, governments may introduce legislation to deal specifically with pricing and maintaining market competitiveness.

Impact of Cartels on Pricing

A cartel is a formal agreement among competitors to fix prices, marketing, and/or production. Cartels usually occur where there are a small number of sellers (an oligopoly) and usually are in industries with homogenous products. Generally, cartels are designed to increase profits and to decrease competition. Cartels can be categorized as private or public. A public cartel involves a government or governmental agency and generally is protected from legal actions concerning cartel activities. Private cartels, however, are subject to antitrust laws in most nations and generally are prohibited because of the impact of decreased competition and increased pricing.

Knowledge Check: Pricing

The next questions are intended to help you check your understanding and recall of the material presented in this topic. They do not represent the type of questions that appear on the CMA exam.

Directions: Answer each question in the space provided. Correct answers and section references appear after the knowledge check questions.

1. What characteristics differentiate the traditional pricing approach from target pricing?

    ☐ **a.** Traditional pricing is based on the premise that price equals cost plus the profit margin; target costing implies that cost equals the competitive price minus the profit margin.

    ☐ **b.** Traditional pricing is based on the premise that cost equals the competitive price minus the profit margin; target costing implies that price equals cost plus the profit margin.

    ☐ **c.** Traditional pricing marks up prices as a percentage of costs; target costing marks up prices in response to competitors.

    ☐ **d.** Traditional pricing marks up prices in response to competitors; target costing marks up prices as a percentage of costs.

Match each pricing approach with the appropriate characteristic.

2. _____ Market-based price 3. _____ Cost-based price 4. _____ Target price	**a.** Generally used when some level of product or service differentiation exists and a company can exercise modest discretion in setting prices **b.** Generally used in a competitive environment to enable businesses to manage operations profitably **c.** Generally used in product or service parity situations and when a company has little latitude in setting prices

5. Which practice would be **most** useful in a firm's attempt to close the gap between current and allowable costs during the design process?

    ☐ **a.** Reverse engineering

    ☐ **b.** Product life-cycle costing

    ☐ **c.** Value engineering

    ☐ **d.** Quality function deployment

6. What is a primary benefit of involving cross-functional teams in the target costing process?

☐ **a.** Improved analysis of how to gain and sustain competitive advantage

☐ **b.** More accurate input and maintenance of cost table databases

☐ **c.** More realistic market assessment of customer wants and needs

☐ **d.** Better assurance that the proposed product or service generates the desired profit margin

7. Which of the following statements about supply and demand is (are) true?

I. There is a direct relationship between shifts in the demand curve and the equilibrium price and equilibrium quantity.

II. An increase in supply with an increase in demand will result in an increase in equilibrium price and quantity.

III. A perfectly elastic demand would be shown in a graph as a vertical line, while a perfectly inelastic demand is shown as a horizontal line.

IV. A price elasticity of demand value greater than 1 is considered elastic or relatively elastic.

☐ **a.** I

☐ **b.** I and II

☐ **c.** I and IV

☐ **d.** I, II, III, and IV

8. Which of the following statements about supply and demand are true?

I. When demand increases, the price of complementary products will increase.

II. The substitution effect states that when the price of a product decreases, consumers will buy a substitute product.

III. The law of diminishing marginal utility states that consumers will buy more of a product only if the price decreases.

IV. An increase in the quantity supplied without a change in demand will result in a decrease in price.

☐ **a.** I and II

☐ **b.** I, II, and III

☐ **c.** I, III, and IV

☐ **d.** I, II, III, and IV

Knowledge Check Answers: Pricing

1. What characteristics differentiate the traditional pricing approach from target pricing? [**See *Target Pricing*.**]

   ☑ **a.** Traditional pricing is based on the premise that price equals cost plus the profit margin; target costing implies that cost equals the competitive price minus the profit margin.

   ☐ **b.** Traditional pricing is based on the premise that cost equals the competitive price minus the profit margin; target costing implies that price equals cost plus the profit margin.

   ☐ **c.** Traditional pricing marks up prices as a percentage of costs; target costing marks up prices in response to competitors.

   ☐ **d.** Traditional pricing marks up prices in response to competitors; target costing marks up prices as a percentage of costs.

Match each pricing approach with the appropriate characteristic.

2.	__c__	Market-based price	**a.**	Generally used when some level of product or service differentiation exists and a company can exercise modest discretion in setting prices
3.	__a__	Cost-based price		
4.	__b__	Target price	**b.**	Generally used in a competitive environment to enable businesses to manage operations profitably
			c.	Generally used in product or service parity situations and when a company has little latitude in setting prices

5. Which practice would be **most** useful in a firm's attempt to close the gap between current and allowable costs during the design process? [**See *Allowable Cost*.**]

   ☐ **a.** Reverse engineering

   ☐ **b.** Product life-cycle costing

   ☑ **c.** Value engineering

   ☐ **d.** Quality function deployment

6. What is a primary benefit of involving cross-functional teams in the target costing process? [**See Designing a Proposed New Product or Service under Target Costing.**]

   ☐ **a.** Improved analysis of how to gain and sustain competitive advantage

   ☐ **b.** More accurate input and maintenance of cost table databases

   ☐ **c.** More realistic market assessment of customer wants and needs

   ☑ **d.** Better assurance that the proposed product or service generates the desired profit margin

7. Which of the following statements about supply and demand is (are) true? [**See Laws of Supply and Demand.**]

   I. There is a direct relationship between shifts in the demand curve and the equilibrium price and equilibrium quantity.

   II. An increase in supply with an increase in demand will result in an increase in equilibrium price and quantity.

   III. A perfectly elastic demand would be shown in a graph as a vertical line, while a perfectly inelastic demand is shown as a horizontal line.

   IV. A price elasticity of demand value greater than 1 is considered elastic or relatively elastic.

   ☐ **a.** I

   ☐ **b.** I and II

   ☑ **c.** I and IV

   ☐ **d.** I, II, III, and IV

8. Which of the following statements about supply and demand are true? [**See Laws of Supply and Demand.**]

   I. When demand increases, the price of complementary products will increase.

   II. The substitution effect states that when the price of a product decreases, consumers will buy a substitute product.

   III. The law of diminishing marginal utility states that consumers will buy more of a product only if the price decreases.

   IV. An increase in the quantity supplied without a change in demand will result in a decrease in price.

   ☐ **a.** I and II

   ☐ **b.** I, II, and III

   ☑ **c.** I, III, and IV

   ☐ **d.** I, II, III, and IV

Directions: This sampling of questions is designed to emulate actual exam questions. Read each question and write your response on another sheet of paper. See the "Answers to Section Practice Questions" section at the end of this book to assess your response. Validate or improve the answer you wrote. For a more robust selection of practice questions, access the **Online Test Bank** at www.wileycma.com.

Question 2C1-CQ01

Topic: Cost/Volume/Profit Analysis

Following are the operating results of the two segments of Parklin Corporation.

	Segment A	Segment B	Total
Sales	$10,000	$15,000	$25,000
Variable costs of goods sold	4,000	8,500	12,500
Fixed costs of goods sold	1,500	2,500	4,000
Gross margin	4,500	4,000	8,500
Variable selling and administrative	2,000	3,000	5,000
Fixed selling and administrative	1,500	1,500	3,000
Operating income (loss)	$1,000	$(500)	$500

Variable costs of goods sold are directly related to the operating segments. Fixed costs of goods sold are allocated to each segment based on the number of employees. Fixed selling and administrative expenses are allocated equally. If Segment B is eliminated, $1,500 of fixed costs of goods sold would be eliminated. Assuming Segment B is closed, the effect on operating income would be

- ☐ **a.** an increase of $500.
- ☐ **b.** an increase of $2,000.
- ☐ **c.** a decrease of $2,000.
- ☐ **d.** a decrease of $2,500.

Question 2C1-CQ02

Topic: Cost/Volume/Profit Analysis

Edwards Products has just developed a new product with a variable manufacturing cost of $30 per unit. The marketing director has identified three marketing approaches for this new product.

Approach X	Set a selling price of $36 and have the firm's sales staff sell the product at a 10% commission with no advertising program. Estimated annual sales would be 10,000 units.
Approach Y	Set a selling price of $38, have the firm's sales staff sell the product at a 10% commission, and back them up with a $30,000 advertising program. Estimated annual sales would be 12,000 units.
Approach Z	Rely on wholesalers to handle the product. Edwards would sell the new product to the wholesalers at $32 per unit and incur no selling expenses. Estimated annual sales would be 14,000 units.

Rank the three alternatives in order of net contribution, from highest to lowest.

- ☐ **a.** X, Y, Z
- ☐ **b.** Y, Z, X
- ☐ **c.** Z, X, Y
- ☐ **d.** Z, Y, X

Question 2C1-CQ04

Topic: Cost/Volume/Profit Analysis

Elgers Company produces valves for the plumbing industry. Elgers' per unit sales price and variable costs are as shown.

Sales price	$12
Variable costs	8

Elgers' practical plant capacity is 40,000 units. Its total fixed costs aggregate $48,000 and it has a 40% effective tax rate.

The maximum net profit that Elger can earn is

- ☐ **a.** $48,000.
- ☐ **b.** $67,200.
- ☐ **c.** $96,000.
- ☐ **d.** $112,000.

Question 2C1-CQ09

Topic: Cost/Volume/Profit Analysis

Cervine Corporation makes two types of motors for use in various products. Operating data and unit cost information for its products are presented next.

	Product A	Product B
Annual unit capacity	10,000	20,000
Annual unit demand	10,000	20,000

Selling price	$100	$80
Variable manufacturing cost	53	45
Fixed manufacturing cost	10	10
Variable selling and administrative	10	11
Fixed selling and administrative	5	4
Fixed other administrative	2	0
Unit operating profit	$ 20	$10
Machine hours per unit	2.0	1.5

Cervine has 40,000 productive machine hours available. The relevant contribution margins, per machine hour for each product, to be utilized in making a decision on product priorities for the coming year, are

	Product A	Product B
a.	$17.00	$14.00
b.	$18.50	$16.00
c.	$20.00	$10.00
d.	$37.00	$24.00

Question 2C1-CQ10

Topic: Cost/Volume/Profit Analysis

Allred Company sells its single product for $30 per unit. The contribution margin ratio is 45%, and fixed costs are $10,000 per month. Allred has an effective income tax rate of 40%. If Allred sells 1,000 units in the current month, Allred's variable expenses would be

- ☐ **a.** $9,900.
- ☐ **b.** $12,000.
- ☐ **c.** $13,500.
- ☐ **d.** $16,500.

Question 2C1-CQ11

Topic: Cost/Volume/Profit Analysis

Phillips & Company produces educational software. Its unit cost structure, based on an anticipated production volume of 150,000 units, is:

Sales price	$160
Variable costs	60
Fixed costs	55

The marketing department has estimated sales for the coming year at 175,000 units, which is within the relevant range of Phillip's cost structure. Phillip's break-even volume (in units) and anticipated operating income for the coming year would amount to

- ☐ **a.** 82,500 units and $7,875,000 of operating income.
- ☐ **b.** 82,500 units and $9,250,000 of operating income.
- ☐ **c.** 96,250 units and $3,543,750 of operating income.
- ☐ **d.** 96,250 units and $7,875,000 of operating income.

Question 2C1-CQ15

Topic: Cost/Volume/Profit Analysis

For the year just ended, Silverstone Company's sales revenue was $450,000. Silverstone's fixed costs were $120,000, and its variable costs amounted to $270,000. For the current year, sales are forecasted at $500,000. If the fixed costs do not change, Silverstone's operating profits this year will be

- ☐ **a.** $60,000.
- ☐ **b.** $80,000.
- ☐ **c.** $110,000.
- ☐ **d.** $200,000.

Question 2C2-CQ01

Topic: Marginal Analysis

Williams makes $35,000 a year as an accounting clerk. He decides to quit his job to enter a one-year MBA program full-time. Assume Williams doesn't work in the summer or hold any part-time jobs. His tuition, books, living expenses, and fees total $25,000 a year. Given this information, the annual total economic cost of Williams's MBA studies is

- ☐ **a.** $10,000.
- ☐ **b.** $35,000.
- ☐ **c.** $25,000.
- ☐ **d.** $60,000.

Question 2C2-CQ03

Topic: Marginal Analysis

Daily costs for Kelso Manufacturing include $1,000 of fixed costs and total variable costs, as shown:

Unit Output	10	11	12	13	14	15
Cost	$125	$250	$400	$525	$700	$825

The average total cost at an output level of 11 units is

☐ **a.** $113.64.

☐ **b.** $125.00.

☐ **c.** $215.91.

☐ **d.** $250.00.

Question 2C2-CQ04

Topic: Marginal Analysis

Harper Products' cost information for the normal range of output in a month is shown next.

Output in Units	Total Cost
20,000	$3,000,000
22,500	3,325,000
25,000	3,650,000

What is Harper's short-run marginal cost?

☐ **a.** $26

☐ **b.** $130

☐ **c.** $146

☐ **d.** $150

Question 2C2-CQ11

Topic: Marginal Analysis

Refrigerator Company manufactures ice makers for installation in refrigerators. The costs per unit, for 20,000 units of ice makers, are:

Direct materials	$ 7
Direct labor	12
Variable overhead	5
Fixed overhead	10
Total costs	$34

Cool Compartments Inc. has offered to sell 20,000 icemakers to Refrigerator Company for $28 per unit. If Refrigerator accepts Cool Compartments' offer, the plant would be idled and fixed overhead amounting to $6 per unit could be eliminated. The total relevant costs associated with the manufacture of ice makers amount to

☐ **a.** $480,000.

☐ **b.** $560,000.

☐ **c.** $600,000.

☐ **d.** $680,000.

Question 2C2-CQ14

Topic: Marginal Analysis

Capital Company has decided to discontinue a product produced on a machine purchased four years ago at a cost of $70,000. The machine has a current book value of $30,000. Due to technologically improved machinery now available in the marketplace, the existing machine has no current salvage value. The company is reviewing the various aspects involved in the production of a new product. The engineering staff advised that the existing machine can be used to produce the new product. Other costs involved in the production of the new product will be materials of $20,000 and labor priced at $5,000.

Ignoring income taxes, the costs relevant to the decision to produce or not to produce the new product would be

- ☐ **a.** $25,000.
- ☐ **b.** $30,000.
- ☐ **c.** $55,000.
- ☐ **d.** $95,000.

Question 2C2-CQ15

Topic: Marginal Analysis

Current business segment operations for Whitman, a mass retailer, are presented next.

	Merchandise	Automotive	Restaurant	Total
Sales	$500,000	$400,000	$100,000	$1,000,000
Variable costs	300,000	200,000	70,000	570,000
Fixed costs	100,000	100,000	50,000	250,000
Operating income (loss)	$100,000	$100,000	$(20,000)	$ 180,000

Management is contemplating the discontinuance of the Restaurant segment since "it is losing money." If this segment is discontinued, $30,000 of its fixed costs will be eliminated. In addition, Merchandise and Automotive sales will decrease 5% from their current levels. What will Whitman's total contribution margin be if the Restaurant segment is discontinued?

- ☐ **a.** $160,000
- ☐ **b.** $220,000
- ☐ **c.** $367,650
- ☐ **d.** $380,000

Question 2C2-CQ16

Topic: Marginal Analysis

Aril Industries is a multiproduct company that currently manufactures 30,000 units of Part 730 each month for use in production. The facilities being used to produce Part 730 have fixed monthly overhead costs of $150,000 and a theoretical capacity to produce 60,000 units per month. If Aril were to buy Part 730 from an outside supplier, the facilities would be idle and 40% of fixed costs would continue to be incurred. There are no alternative uses for the facilities. The variable production costs of Part 730 are $11 per unit. Fixed overhead is allocated based on planned production levels.

If Aril Industries continues to use 30,000 units of Part 730 each month, it would realize a net benefit by purchasing Part 730 from an outside supplier only if the supplier's unit price is less than

☐ **a.** $12.00.

☐ **b.** $12.50.

☐ **c.** $13.00.

☐ **d.** $14.00.

Question 2C3-CQ01

Topic: Pricing

A market research analyst determined the next market data for a commodity.

Price	Quantity Supplied	Quantity Demanded
$ 25	250	750
50	500	500
75	750	250
100	1,000	0

Based on this information, which one of the following statements is **correct**?

☐ **a.** At a price of $30, there will be excess demand.

☐ **b.** A market clearing price cannot be determined.

☐ **c.** At a price of $80, there will be insufficient supply.

☐ **d.** A market price of $50 cannot exist for very long.

Question 2C3-CQ03

Topic: Pricing

An economic research firm performed extensive studies on the market for large-screen televisions (LSTs). Portions of the results are shown next.

Household Income	LST Sales (units)
$50,000	20,000
60,000	28,000
72,000	39,200

Price of LSTs	LST Sales (units)
$1,000	100,000
900	115,000
810	132,250

The income elasticity of demand for LSTs is

☐ **a.** 0.4.

☐ **b.** 1.5.

☐ **c.** 1.8.

☐ **d.** 2.5.

Question 2C3-CQ04

Topic: Pricing

Jones Enterprises manufactures three products, A, B, and C. During the month of May, Jones's production, costs, and sales data were as shown.

	Products			
	A	B	C	Totals
Units of production	30,000	20,000	70,000	120,000
Joint production costs to split-off point				$480,000
Further processing costs	$-	$60,000	$140,000	
Unit sales price				
At split-off	3.75	5.50	10.25	
After further processing	-	8.00	12.50	

Based on this information, which one of the following alternatives should be recommended to Jones's management?

☐ **a.** Sell both Product B and Product C at the split-off point.

☐ **b.** Process Product B further but sell Product C at the split-off point.

☐ **c.** Process Product C further but sell Product B at the split-off point.

☐ **d.** Process both Products B and C further.

Question 2C3-CQ05

Topic: Pricing

Synergy Inc. produces a component that is popular in many refrigeration systems. Data on three of the five different models of this component are shown next.

	Model		
	A	**B**	**C**
Volume needed (units)	5,000	6,000	3,000
Manufacturing costs			
Variable direct costs	$10	$24	$20
Variable overhead	5	10	15
Fixed overhead	11	20	17
Total manufacturing costs	$26	$54	$52
Cost if purchased	$21	$42	$39

Synergy applies variable overhead on the basis of machine hours at the rate of $2.50 per hour. Models A and B are manufactured in the Freezer Department, which has a capacity of 28,000 machine processing hours. Which one of the following options should be recommended to Synergy's management?

- ☐ **a.** Purchase all three products in the quantities required.
- ☐ **b.** Manufacture all three products in the quantities required.
- ☐ **c.** The Freezer Department's manufacturing plan should include 5,000 units of Model A and 4,500 units of Model B.
- ☐ **d.** The Freezer Department's manufacturing plan should include 2,000 units of Model A and 6,000 units of Model B.

Question 2C3-CQ06

Topic: Pricing

Leader Industries is planning to introduce a new product, DMA. It is expected that 10,000 units of DMA will be sold. The full product cost per unit is $300. Invested capital for this product amounts to $20 million. Leader's target rate of return on investment is 20%. The markup percentage for this product, based on operating income as a percentage of full product cost, will be

- ☐ **a.** 42.9%.
- ☐ **b.** 57.1%.
- ☐ **c.** 133.3%.
- ☐ **d.** 233.7%.

Question 2C3-CQ08

Topic: Pricing

Almelo Manpower Inc. provides contracted bookkeeping services. Almelo has annual fixed costs of $100,000 and variable costs of $6 per hour. This year the company budgeted 50,000 hours of bookkeeping services. Almelo prices its services at full cost and uses a cost-plus pricing approach. The company developed a billing price of $9 per hour. The company's markup level would be

☐ **a.** 12.5%.

☐ **b.** 33.3%.

☐ **c.** 50.0%.

☐ **d.** 66.6%.

Question 2C3-CQ09

Topic: Pricing

Fennel Products is using cost-based pricing to determine the selling price for its new product based on the next information.

Annual volume	25,000 units
Fixed costs	$700,000 per year
Variable costs	$200 per unit
Plant investment	$3,000,000
Working capital	$1,000,000
Effective tax rate	40%

The target price that Fennell needs to set for the new product to achieve a 15% after-tax return on investment (ROI) would be

☐ **a.** $228.

☐ **b.** $238.

☐ **c.** $258.

☐ **d.** $268.

 To further assess your understanding of the concepts and calculations covered in Part 2, Section C: Decision Analysis, practice with the **Online Test Bank** for this section. **REMINDER:** See the "Answers to Section Practice Questions" section at the end of this book.

Risk Management

Risk is the level of uncertainty about future events. Organization managers need to identify, assess, and respond to risks in order for the organization to achieve its goals and objectives and its vision. Risks must be managed to an acceptable level to adequately protect organizational assets and to mitigate losses. Even though risks are difficult to determine and quantify, management should make a best effort to identify, assess, and respond to them. This section focuses on the enterprise risk management (ERM) model. ERM provides a comprehensive approach to risk identification, assessment, and response.

Learning Outcome Statements Overview: Risk Management

Section D.1. Enterprise Risk

A. Identify and explain the different types of risk, including business risk, hazard risks, financial risks, operational risks, and strategic risks.
   a. Hazard risks—Relate to natural disasters, such as storms, floods, hurricanes, blizzards, earthquakes, and volcanoes.
   b. Financial risks—Caused by debt/equity decisions related to financing the business. They include liquidity (short-term bill paying) and solvency (long-term bill paying) risks usually controlled through adequate financial and capital reserves.
   c. Operational risks—Relate to the relationship of fixed and variable costs in the organization's cost structure as well as internal process failures, system failures, personnel, legal, and compliance.
   d. Strategic risks—Include regulatory risk, economic risk, and political risk.
B. Demonstrate an understanding of operational risk.
   a. Operational risk from inadequate or failed internal processes can include product damages and claims and inadequate internal controls.
   b. Operational risk from people can include human resource deficiencies and occupational safety and health accidents.
   c. Operational risk from systems can include business continuity inadequacies and other information technology failures.
C. Define legal risk, compliance risk, and political risk.
   a. Operational risk includes legal and compliance risks that relate to the organization's compliance with laws, relevant regulations, and contractual obligations.
D. Demonstrate an understanding of how volatility and time impact risk.
   a. Risks are a function of volatility (variability) and time. Increased volatility, such as variability in expected returns, translates into increased risk. The longer the time frame, the more the uncertainty and, consequently, the higher the risk. Shorter time frames imply lower risk.
E. Define the concept of capital adequacy (i.e., solvency, liquidity, reserves, sufficient capital, etc.).

    a. Capital adequacy measures how well a financial institution protects its depositors and protects the financial systems around the world. The measure of capital adequacy is called the "capital adequacy ratio" (CAR). For a company, capital adequacy relates to how well it manages solvency, liquidity, and reserves.

F. Explain the use of probabilities in determining exposure to risk, and calculate expected loss, given a set of probabilities.

    a. Assessing risk generally involves the use of probabilities in order to assess the overall exposure to loss. The weighted average of the probability and extent of loss is used to determined total expected loss.

        For example, if there is a 40% chance that a company will suffer a $1,000,000 loss and a 60% chance that the company will suffer a $300,000 loss, the expected loss can be estimated as $580,000 [(.4 × $1,000,000) + (.6 × $300,000)].

G. Define the concepts of unexpected loss and maximum possible loss (extreme or catastrophic loss).

    a. In the example above, it is apparent that the actual loss cannot be $580,000, the amount of the expected loss. If there are two scenarios and one will result in a $1,000,000 loss and the other will result in a $300,000, those are the only two actual losses that can occur. The unexpected loss is the amount of loss that exceeds the expected loss. The maximum possible loss is the $1,000,000.

H. Identify strategies for risk response (or treatment), including actions to avoid, retain, reduce (mitigate), transfer (share), and exploit (accept) risks.

    a. Risks can be mitigated in these ways:

        i. Risk transfer (share)—Risk can be transferred by purchasing insurance policies against the risk itself. For example, a company can purchase property and casualty insurance and bond employees to minimize losses should a threat be carried out.

        ii. Risk avoidance—Ceasing an activity that brings risk to the firm. For example, a firm can shut down (or never open) the zip line operation in an amusement park.

        iii. Exploiting risks—Involves accepting one lower risk to mitigate another higher one. An example is where a company expands into a lower-risk industry, such as health care, while lessening its commitment in a higher-risk industry, such as automotive parts.

I. Define risk transfer (e.g., purchasing insurance, issuing debt).

    a. Risk transfer (share)—Risk can be transferred by purchasing insurance policies against the risk itself. For example, a company can purchase property and casualty insurance and bond employees to minimize losses should a threat be carried out.

J. Demonstrate an understanding of the concept of residual risk, and distinguish it from inherent risk.

    a. Residual risks—Those that remain after any actions management might take with regard to inherent risks.

    b. Inherent risk—The risk of an activity in the absence of any risk mitigating strategies.

K. Identify and explain the benefits of risk management.

    a. Not adequately addressing risk can have substantial negative effects on a business and could potentially put the company out of business. Given the potential ramifications of mismanaging risk, companies should implement a risk management process program that will enable them to avoid risks, reduce the negative effects of risks, prepare to accept some risks, and/or transfer risks to another party (typically by purchasing insurance).

L. Identify and describe the key steps in the risk management process.

    1. Determine the company's tolerance for risk.

    2. Evaluate the company's risk exposure.

    3. Implement an appropriate risk management strategy.

    4. Monitor risk exposure and the strategy.

M. Explain how attitude toward risk might affect the management of risk.

    a. Risk assessment is a function of management's attitude toward risk as well as the estimate of potential risk. For example, the more risk averse a management team is, the more it will be willing to spend on mitigating the risk. Likewise, the greater the potential risk is perceived to be, the more time and money management will be willing to spend to minimize or mitigate the risk.

N. Demonstrate a general understanding of the use of liability/hazard insurance to mitigate risk (detailed knowledge not required).

    a. Purchasing an insurance policy is a strategy to transfer the risk of potential loss to a third party in exchange for a periodic payment.

O. Identify methods of managing operational risk.

    a. Operational risk can be mitigated by having in place adequate internal controls, defined business processes, a trained workforce, and plans for disaster recovery. A company also can shift the organization's cost structure from fixed to variable to mitigate operational risk.

P. Identify and explain financial risk management methods.

    a. Financial risks may be lessened by adjusting the organization's capital structure to minimize the cost of capital. The cost of capital is a function of the mixture of debt, preferred stock, retained earnings, and common stock issued in the organization's capital structure. The proper mix will reduce to an acceptable level bankruptcy risk and agency costs.

Q. Identify and explain qualitative risk assessment tools including risk identification, risk ranking, and risk maps.

    a. Risk identification—Seeks to identify as many threats as possible without evaluating them. Much like a risk brainstorming session.

    b. Risk ranking—After risks have been identified, they are ranked according to their probability of occurrence and the magnitude of loss.

    c. Risk mapping—A tool to see visually the probability of occurrence and the magnitude of loss when evaluating risk.

R. Identify and explain quantitative risk assessment tools including cash flow at risk, earnings at risk, earnings distributions, and earnings per share (EPS) distributions.

    a. Cash flow at risk—A value at risk (VaR) analysis tool using the cash flow figure as the maximum loss within a given time period

    b. Earnings at risk—A VaR analysis tool using the accrual basis earnings as the maximum loss within a given time period

    c. Earnings distributions—Potential returns are plotted on the x axis and the probabilities on the y axis.

S. Identify and explain value at risk (VaR) (calculations not required).

    a. Value at risk (VaR)—The maximum loss within a given period of time and given a specified probability level (level of confidence). VaR is prospective. It quantifies market risk while it is being taken. VaR is depicted graphically using a bell curve.

T. Define enterprise risk management (ERM), and identify and describe key objectives, components and benefits of an ERM program.

    a. Enterprise risk management (ERM)—A comprehensive analysis of all risks facing the organization, including financial, operational, and compliance risk.

    b. Key objectives:

        i. To create, protect, and enhance shareholder value by managing the uncertainties facing an organization. Instead of managing risk in many individual silos, ERM takes an integrated and holistic perspective on risks facing an organization.

    c. The COSO ERM framework includes eight interrelated components that may assist a company in managing risk within its risk appetite and provide reasonable assurance regarding the achievement of entity objectives.

U. Identify event identification techniques and provide examples of event identification within the context of an ERM approach.

    a. Event inventories—Detailed listings of potential events that might occur or are common.

    b. Internal analysis—Analysis drawing on the experiences within the company and the staff within the company to identify risks

    c. Escalation or threshold triggers—Triggers that alert management to areas of concern by comparing current transactions or events with a predefined criteria

    d. Facilitated workshops and interviews—Identify events by drawing on accumulated knowledge and experience of management, staff, and others.

    e. Process flow analysis—Considers the inputs, tasks, responsibilities, and outputs that combine to form a process.

    f. Leading event indicators—Identify the existence of conditions that could give rise to an event by monitoring data related to those events.

    g. Loss event data methodologies—Compilation of historical data detailing specific events that may have triggered losses in the past.

V. Explain the role of corporate governance, risk analytics, and portfolio management in an ERM program.

    a. ERM involves corporate governance, risk analysis, and portfolio management. The organization must be managed properly, management must assess risks, and it must develop a wealth-maximizing portfolio of investments. The investments (assets) include current assets (cash, trading securities, receivables, inventories, and prepayments) and noncurrent assets (property, plant, and equipment, long-term investments, natural resources, and intangibles).

W. Evaluate scenarios and recommend risk mitigation strategies.

    a. The information outlined above details many risk mitigation strategies in order to manage risk within an organization.

X. Prepare a cost-benefit analysis and demonstrate an understanding of its uses in risk assessment and decision making.

    a. The COSO Framework provides some guidance on preparing a cost-benefit analysis. A risk analysis and response cost-benefit analysis involves steps similar to any cost-benefit analysis. The costs of the risks or potential losses are weighed against the cost of preventing the event from occurring. Mitigating factors, and the costs associated with them, are weighed against the benefits of those programs.

Y. Demonstrate an understanding of the COSO ERM conceptual framework.

    a. The COSO ERM framework expands the 1992 *COSO Internal Control— Integrated Framework*. It expands the model from five interrelated components to eight. The eight interrelated components assist a company in managing risk within its risk appetite and assist in providing reasonable assurance regarding the achievement of entity objectives. The components are:

       i. Internal environment

       ii. Objective setting

       iii. Event identification

       iv. Risk assessment

       v. Risk response

       vi. Control activities

       vii. Information and communication

       viii. Monitoring

Enterprise Risk

RISK IS BASED ON HAVING a certain level of uncertainty about future events. Organizations need to identify, assess, manage, and respond to the risks that they have in order to achieve the mission of the company, protect company assets, and avoid unexpected losses. Although risks often are difficult to determine and quantify, management should make a best effort to identify potential risks and their probabilities of occurrence.

Several organizations provide guidance to assist with the design and implementation of an effective enterprise-wide risk management approach. The latter part of this topic focuses on the most widely used and accepted enterprise-risk management framework, the *COSO Enterprise Risk Management Integrated Framework*, which is a comprehensive approach to assessing an organization's risk in many different areas.

 READ the Learning Outcome Statements (LOS) for this topic as found in Appendix B and then study the concepts and calculations presented here to be sure you understand the content you could be tested on in the CMA exam.

Risk and Expected Loss

In a business context, *risk* is defined as the level of exposure to a chance of loss. For example, if a company determines that a particular risk could result in a loss of up to $50,000, the company would be willing to spend up to $50,000 to mitigate the risk. The amount of the loss calculated by the company represents the maximum possible loss (extreme or catastrophic loss). This loss often is referred to as the value at risk (VaR). VaR includes cash flow at risk, earnings at risk, and earnings per share (EPS) distributions (mean and variance). Normal risk models cannot deal with totally unexpected losses such as an atomic attack.

Value at Risk

In managing risk, organizations should not rely solely on historical data. Those managing risk should know about risks at the time those risks are being taken.

As noted, historical performance over long periods of time average rates of return to accommodate fluctuations of unusually high or low returns. But as the name implies, *historical* provides a retrospective indication of risk. When reviewing a portfolio, historical volatility illustrates how risky the portfolio had been over the some previous period of time. It provides no indication about the current market risk of the portfolio. VaR gives organizations the ability to assess current risk.

VaR is the maximum loss within a given period of time and given a specified probability level (level of confidence). Unlike retrospective risk metrics that measure historical volatility, VaR is prospective. It quantifies market risk while it is being taken.

Figure 2D-1 overviews key VaR concepts.

Figure 2D-1 Value at Risk Characteristics

Application	VaR can be applied to any portfolio that can reasonably be marked to market performance on a regular basis. VaR is not applicable to real estate or other illiquid assets.
Time frame/horizon	VaR evaluates a portfolio's performance over a specific period of time, such as a trading day, week, or a month.
Base currency	VaR measures risk in a currency. Any currency can be used.
VaR measurement	A resulting VaR measure summarizes a portfolio's market risk with a single number.

VaR can be calculated using any of these methods: historical method, variance-covariance method, or Monte Carlo simulation.

Historical Method

The historical method reorganizes actual historical returns for a time period by putting them in order from worst to best. The historical method assumes that history will repeat itself, from a risk perspective. A histogram plot correlates frequency of returns with losses. The resulting level of confidence provides a percentage that a worst-case scenario for a daily loss will not exceed. (For example, if we invest $1,000, we are 95% confident that our worst daily loss will not exceed $40 ($1,000 × 4%).)

Variance-Covariance Method

The variance-covariance method assumes that stock returns are normally distributed. Expected (or average) return and a standard deviation are estimated and a normal distribution curve is plotted. Reviewing the normal curve, one can see exactly where the worst percentages lie on the curve. The percentages looked at are a function of desired confidence and the standard deviation.

Monte Carlo Simulation

A Monte Carlo simulation refers to any method that randomly generates trials. This method involves developing a model for future returns and running multiple hypothetical trials through the model.

The CMA candidate is expected to be able to identify and explain VaR, but calculations are not required on the exam.

Types of Risk

Risks can be any of these types:

- Hazards
- Financial
- Operational
- Strategic
- Capital adequacy

Hazard risks relate to natural disasters such as storms, floods, hurricanes, blizzards, earthquakes, and volcanoes.

Financial risks are caused by debt/equity decisions related to financing the business. They include liquidity (short-term bill paying) and solvency (long-term bill paying) risks usually controlled through adequate financial and capital reserves.

Operational risk relates to the composition and mix of fixed and variable costs in an organization's cost structure. An organization is deemed to be exposed to more risk when a greater percentage of the cost structure is comprised of fixed costs. Operational risk also relates to the following risks:

- Internal process failures
- System failures
- Personnel
- Legal and compliance

Legal and compliance risks relate the organization's compliance with laws, relevant regulations, and contractual obligations.

Capital adequacy measures how well a financial institution protects its depositors and protects the financial systems around the world. The measure of capital adequacy is called the capital adequacy ratio (CAR):

$$CAR = \frac{\text{Tier 1 Capital} + \text{Tier 2 Capital}}{\text{Risk} - \text{Weighted Assets}}$$

Tier 1 capital is the capital of a financial institution that can absorb losses without being required to cease trading. Tier 2 capital is capital that can absorb losses in the event of a winding up, so it provides a lesser degree of protection to depositors than does tier 1 capital. Winding up is a process that entails selling all the assets of a business entity, paying off creditors, distributing any remaining assets to the principals, and then dissolving the business. The computation of risk-weighted assets requires an evaluation of each of the financial institution's assets in terms of riskiness and using weights to compute those risk-weighted assets. The CAR is an important factor in determining the riskiness of a financial institution in relation to solvency, liquidity, reserves, and sufficient capital.

Risks are a function of volatility (variability) and time. Increased volatility, such as variability in expected returns, translates into increased risk. The longer the time frame, the more the uncertainty and, consequently, the higher the risk. Shorter time frames imply lower risk.

The remainder of this topic covers risk assessment, risk identification, risk response, risk management, and the enterprise risk management (ERM) model.

Risk Assessment

Risk assessment is a forward-looking survey of the business environment to identify anything that could prevent the accomplishment of organizational objectives. Risk assessment involves the identification of internal and external means that could potentially defeat the organization's internal control structure, compromise assets, or diminish the organization's financial viability. It is a creative process covering both risk identification and risk response. It involves identifying as many potential threats as possible and evaluating them to determine the proper response (i.e., which require action and the priority for that action). The risk response process also should estimate the probability of each threat occurring.

Assessing risks appears to be a quantitative and scientific process, but if risks are assessed and prioritized improperly, unexpected losses can occur. There exist a number of qualitative considerations in assessing risk, such as ranking the risks in order of importance and visualizing the risks with the use of a risk map. A risk map enables an analysis of risks not only on an individual level but also in relation to one another. Additionally, as risk assessments are refreshed over time, a risk map can allow analysis over time. Additionally, the maximum possible loss should be computed and used subjectively in the assessment of risk.

Risk assessment is a function of management's attitude toward risk as well as the estimate of potential risk. For example, the more risk averse a management team is, the more it will be willing to spend on mitigating the risk. Likewise, the greater the potential risk is perceived to be, the more time and money management will be willing to spend to minimize or mitigate the risk.

Ideally, risk assessment activities are performed on a continuous basis by all employees within the organization. However, the process must be driven by those responsible for organization governance: the board of directors and the audit committee. Their commitment and involvement and attitude toward risk must be communicated down through the entire organization. As risks are identified, they are assigned to the appropriate level of management for consideration. The resulting risk assessment culture becomes an integral part of the organization's control environment. In most instances, and typically for strategic risks, the risk assessment process is conducted at regular intervals, usually once a year.

Assessing risk generally involves the use of probabilities. For example, if there is a 40% chance that a company will suffer a $1,000,000 loss and a 60% chance that the company will suffer a $300,000 loss, the expected loss can be estimated as $580,000 [(.4 × $1,000,000) + (.6 × $300,000)]. Determining the estimated amounts and their probabilities involves experience, information, and judgment.

Risk Identification

Risk identification seeks to identify as many threats as possible without evaluating them. Risk identification will naturally drive the process to include as many individuals from the organization as possible, especially those with specific detailed information about the particular risk area being considered. For example, a strategic risk assessment would involve senior management, senior finance people, and the strategic planning area. An operational risk assessment would include those from the operating units because they have the insight into how the business processes actually work and, specifically, what threats would interrupt the accomplishment of operational objectives.

A risk framework can be helpful to facilitate the risk identification process. The framework provides guidance to the risk assessment participants and helps them organize the identified threats. The framework can organize risks by categories and by structural element (e.g., strategy, people, process, technology, data) or by business process (e.g., revenue cycle, disbursement cycle, cash management and treasury, financial reporting, operations).

The risk framework should consider both internal and external factors. Risk assessment participants should be tasked and encouraged to identify threats from both factors. Examples of internal and external risk factors are listed next.

Internal Risk Factors

- Communication methods
- Risk assessment activities
- Appropriateness of internal control activities
- Labor relations
- Training and capability of the employees
- Degree of supervision of employees
- Operational risks
- Financial risks
- Strategic risks

External Risk Factors

- Regulatory changes
- Industry competition
- Relationships with key suppliers
- Relationships with customers
- Recruiting and hiring activities
- International risk
- Hazard risks

Tools, diagnostics, and processes that may be used to support risk identification include:

- Checklists
- Flowcharts
- Scenario analysis
- Value chain analysis
- Business process analysis
- Systems engineering
- Process mapping
- Computed cash flow at risk
- Projected earnings at risk
- Projected earnings distributions
- Projected EPS distributions

Additionally, it is appropriate to consider a hindsight evaluation of risk assessment activities by examining experienced risks that were not identified in prior risk assessments or if they were identified but not properly evaluated or evaluated as lower-risk items. In any case, actions should be made to refine the risk assessment process to identify these risks properly in the future.

Risk Response

The goal of **risk response** is to provide an objective and independent evaluation of the risks facing the organization. Each identified risk item is evaluated, generally by a two-factor scale (risk map) of impact and likelihood:

1. *Impact.* The effect the risk occurrence would have on the organization's objective *if it were to actually occur.* For example, what loss would occur if a particular risk factor occurred and was not detected and corrected?
2. *Likelihood.* The probability or chance that the risk actually will occur.

By graphing or mapping the evaluation of risk items on this two-factor scale, with the origin of the graph being low impact and low likelihood, higher-priority items (i.e., those items with a high impact and high likelihood ratings) will graph in the upper right quadrant.

Risks should be evaluated on the inherent or residual (control) risk level.

- *Inherent risk* is the risk that exists before any controls are implemented to mitigate such risk. It is the probability of a threat occurring.
- *Residual or control risk* is the risk that still exists after all control activities are executed. It is the probability that the control system fails to prevent or detect the occurred threat before it causes damage to the organization.

Initially all inherent risks are considered high-impact, high-likelihood risks because there is no consideration of controls. Controls must be considered in prioritizing risks. Evaluating residual (control) risk involves evaluating control activities that may or may not be effective. For example, a risk could be overlooked because the evaluator is relying on internal controls that do not actually function. For this reason, residual risk evaluation attempts to identify key controls needed to achieve the lower impact and lower likelihood scores and then to verify that those controls are indeed in place and functioning.

Preventive control activities are used to reduce the likelihood of a risk occurrence while detective and corrective controls are used to reduce the impact of a risk occurrence. Preventive controls offer the most cost benefits; corrective controls offer the least cost benefits. Again, the idea is to prevent threats from occurring or, if they cannot be prevented, then to detect and correct them before damage occurs.

Risk response involves reducing risks to an acceptable level. Risks can be mitigated in these ways:

- Risk transfer (e.g., purchasing property and casualty insurance and bonding employees to minimize losses should a threat be carried out)
- Risk avoidance (e.g., avoiding risky activities)
- Exploiting risks (e.g., accepting one lower risk to mitigate another higher one)

An example of exploiting risks would be for a company to expand into a lower-risk industry, such as health care while lessening its commitment in a higher-risk industry, such as automotive parts.

Operational risks may be lessened by shifting the organization's costs from fixed to variable. For example, a company can outsource parts or activities rather than producing or performing them internally.

Financial risks may be lessened by adjusting the organization's capital structure to minimize the cost of capital. The cost of capital is a function of the mixture of debt, preferred stock, retained earnings, and common stock issued in the organization's capital structure. The proper mix will reduce bankruptcy risk and agency costs to an acceptable level.

Risk Management

Given the potential ramifications of mismanaging risk, companies should implement a risk management process program that will enable them to avoid risks, reduce the negative effects of risks, prepare to accept some risks, and/or transfer risks to another party (typically by purchasing insurance). Although the formality and specifics of the process will vary across different organizations, the general steps of a risk management process are summarized in Figure 2D-2.

Figure 2D-2 Steps in the Risk Management Process

Step 1	**Determine the company's tolerance for risk.**
	This step identifies the organizational attitude toward risk. Will the company accept significant financial risks? Does the company want to take on only selective risk exposures? Must the firm eliminate all risks?
Step 2	**Evaluate the risk exposure.**
	During this step, the specific nature of the exposure must be identified (e.g., is the risk related to potential changes in interest rates or foreign exchange rates? If no, what is the primary risk factor?). Then the exposure must be quantified so that a decision can be made as to whether the level of risk is acceptable to the organization.
Step 3	**Implement an appropriate risk management strategy.**
	A risk management strategy identifies what actions (if any) must be taken to manage the risk exposure. A wide variety of strategies is possible.
Step 4	**Monitor the risk exposure and the strategy.**
	Periodic monitoring assesses the status quo or any unexpected changes in the risk exposure (as a result of market volatility, etc.). This step also considers whether the risk management strategy selected is effective. Strategy adjustments may be necessary.

In addition to setting forth specific objectives and strategies with respect to risk management, organizations typically identify the roles and responsibilities of key individuals and establish a hierarchy for decision making. Consideration also is given to how performance results will be measured and reported.

Enterprise Risk Management

ERM is the comprehensive analysis and management of all risks facing the organization, including financial, operational, and compliance risk. Many organizations have implemented an ERM process as part of their corporate governance policies due to increased regulatory pressures or to take greater advantage of business opportunities that may be accompanied by greater levels of risk. A variety of software vendors offer ERM packages with the analytics needed to accomplish an effective ERM.

IMA's Statements on Management Accounting, *Enterprise Risk Management: Frameworks, Elements, and Integration*, states that the goal of ERM is:

> To create, protect, and enhance shareholder value by managing the uncertainties that could either negatively or positively influence achievement of the organization's objectives. Stronger internal controls, more effective corporate governance, and implementation of ERM can lead to improved stability, reaction time, and increased shareholder value. Instead of managing risk in many individual silos, ERM takes an integrated and holistic perspective on risks facing an organization.

Basic components found in most ERM frameworks are listed next.

- Set strategy and objectives.
- Identify risks.
- Assess risks.
- Treat risks.
- Control risks.
- Communicate and monitor.

An effective ERM implementation requires an organizational context that includes these characteristics:

- Tone at the top
- Risk management philosophy and risk appetite
- Integrity and ethical values
- Scope and infrastructure for ERM

In September 2004, the Committee of Sponsoring Organizations of the Treadway Commission (COSO) introduced the *Enterprise Risk Management—Integrated Framework (ERM Framework)*, which expands on the COSO's 1992 *Internal Control—Integrated Framework* model (updated in 2013 and now referred to as the *2013 Internal Control—Integrated Framework*). It is important to note that the 2004 *ERM Framework* is still the applicable framework for referencing ERM, even in light of the 2013 COSO *Internal Control—Integrated Framework* update. The two frameworks are intended to be complementary, and neither supersedes the other. As such, the *ERM Framework* notes that internal control is a part of ERM. The *ERM Framework* includes eight elements; some of the original five elements from the 1992 (and 2013 updated) internal control framework were expanded, and some new elements (e.g., the elements of objective setting, event identification, and risk response, as noted below) were added. The *ERM Framework* takes a more holistic view and broader focus than the 1992 (and 2013 updated) model. With this model, the scope becomes much wider, and higher risks can be mitigated by implementing better strategic control.

The *ERM Framework* includes this definition:

> Enterprise risk management is a process, effected by an entity's board of directors, management and other personnel, applied in strategy setting and across the enterprise, designed to identify potential events that may affect the entity, and manage risk to be within its risk appetite, to provide reasonable assurance regarding the achievement of entity objectives.

This definition recognizes that ERM is an ongoing, fluid process involving the entire organization. Just as the COSO model of control is intended to be a unifying theory of internal control, the COSO *ERM Framework* is intended to be a unifying and comprehensive analysis of risk. The framework includes eight interrelated components:

1. *Internal environment.* The internal environment refers to the organization's risk management philosophy and risk appetite, integrity and ethical values, and the environment in which it operates.

2. *Objective setting.* The new model ensures that management has an established process for setting objectives so it can better identify events that may either aid in the organization's success or threaten to impede it. The objectives should be in line with the overall mission of the organization and consistent with its appetite for risk.

3. *Event identification.* The new model focuses on the process for identifying internal and external events that are relevant to achievement of an entity's objectives. The organization needs established criteria for distinguishing between risks and opportunities and methods for responding to the former and capitalizing on the latter.

4. *Risk assessment.* The model includes a component for assessing risk—determining its probability and degree of importance. Risks are classified as either inherent or residual. Inherent risks are those that the organization will face unless management takes action to avoid or mitigate them. They are the first to be assessed. Residual risks are those that remain after any actions management might take with regard to inherent risks.

5. *Risk response.* Risks are analyzed, considering likelihood and impact, as a basis for determining how they should be managed. Responses to inherent risks are developed first. After completing that task, management develops a residual risk profile that identifies the risks that will remain even after inherent risks have been dealt with. Management then must seek ways to manage acceptable risks and transfer unacceptable risks (perhaps with insurance from outside companies).

6. *Control activities.* Policies and procedures are established and implemented to help ensure that the risk responses are effectively carried out. The COSO model lists six control activities:

   a. The assignment of authority and responsibility (job descriptions)
   b. A system of transaction authorizations
   c. Adequate documentation and records
   d. Security of assets
   e. Independent verifications
   f. Adequate separation of duties

7. *Information and communication.* The COSO model recognizes that relevant information must be identified, captured, and communicated in a form and time frame that enables people to do their jobs successfully. This model assumes that the data communicated are secure and accurate.

8. *Monitoring.* All aspects of internal controls are monitored, and modifications made as necessary. Monitoring is accomplished through ongoing management activities, separate evaluations, or both. Internal auditors, the audit committee, and the disclosure committee as well as management all may be involved in monitoring controls.

The eight components of the COSO *ERM Framework* stretch across the strategic, operational, reporting, and compliance functions of an organization and also are relevant across all of the various reporting units of an organization.

According to the COSO model, ERM encompasses:

- *Aligning risk appetite and strategy.* Management considers the entity's risk appetite in evaluating strategic alternatives, setting related objectives, and developing mechanisms to manage related risks.
- *Enhancing risk response decisions.* ERM provides the rigor to identify and select among alternative risk responses: risk avoidance, reduction, sharing, and acceptance.
- *Reducing operational surprises and losses.* Entities gain enhanced capability to identify potential events and establish responses, reducing surprises and associated costs or losses.
- *Identifying and managing multiple and cross-enterprise risks.* Every enterprise faces a myriad of risks affecting different parts of the organization. ERM facilitates effective response to the interrelated impacts and integrated responses to multiple risks.
- *Seizing opportunities.* By considering a full range of potential events, management is positioned to identify and proactively realize opportunities.
- *Improving deployment of capital.* Obtaining robust risk information allows management to effectively assess overall capital needs and enhance capital allocation.

Source: *Enterprise Risk Management Integrated Framework, Executive Summary,* Copyright © 2004, Committee of Sponsoring Organizations of the Treadway Commission

These capabilities inherent in ERM help management achieve the entity's performance and profitability targets and prevent loss of resources. As noted in the COSO framework, ERM helps ensure effective reporting and compliance with laws and regulations and helps avoid damage to the entity's reputation and associated consequences. In sum, ERM helps an entity get to where it wants to go and avoid pitfalls and surprises along the way. As with any new program, each company should perform a cost–benefit analysis of the ERM before implementation.

ERM involves corporate governance, risk analysis, and portfolio management. The organization must be managed properly, management must assess risks, and it must develop a wealth-maximizing portfolio of investments. The investments (assets) include current assets (cash, trading securities, receivables, inventories, and prepayments) and noncurrent assets (property, plant, and equipment, long-term investments, natural resources, and intangibles).

The COSO ERM Framework provides guidance for management and is available from COSO at www.coso.org. Other sources for ERM information include IMA's Statements on Management Accounting, specifically:

- *Enterprise Risk Management: Frameworks, Elements, and Integration* (2011)
- *Enterprise Risk Management: Tools and Techniques for Effective Implementation* (2007)

Knowledge Check: Enterprise Risk

The next questions are intended to help you check your understanding and recall of the material presented in this topic. They do not represent the type of questions that appear on the CMA exam.

Directions: Answer each question in the space provided. Correct answers and section references appear after the knowledge check questions.

1. Controls should be implemented to reduce risk to

   ☐ **a.** zero.

   ☐ **b.** the level at which management believes the risk benefit is less than its cost.

   ☐ **c.** the level of materiality specified by the external auditors.

   ☐ **d.** the level of materiality specified by the audit committee.

2. The enterprise risk management model looks at

   ☐ **a.** financial risk.

   ☐ **b.** operating risk.

   ☐ **c.** compliance risk.

   ☐ **d.** all of the above.

3. Enterprise risk management is

   ☐ **a.** unrelated to internal controls.

   ☐ **b.** an element of the COSO *Integrated Framework*.

   ☐ **c.** a unified and comprehensive risk analysis model.

   ☐ **d.** all of the above.

4. Risks include all of the following **except**:

   ☐ **a.** hazard risks.

   ☐ **b.** financial risks.

   ☐ **c.** personal risks.

   ☐ **d.** operational risks.

5. Risks

   ☐ **a.** decrease with time.

   ☐ **b.** are independent of time.

   ☐ **c.** cannot be controlled.

   ☐ **d.** are a function of variability.

6. The evaluation phase of risk response looks at

☐ **a.** the likelihood of threats.

☐ **b.** the impact of threats.

☐ **c.** neither a nor b.

☐ **d.** both a and b.

7. The risk identification framework considers

☐ **a.** only external threats.

☐ **b.** both external and internal threats.

☐ **c.** only internal threats.

☐ **d.** risk priorities.

Knowledge Check Answers: Enterprise Risk

1. Controls should be implemented to reduce risk to [See *Risk Response.*]
   - ☐ **a.** zero.
   - ☑ **b.** the level at which management believes the risk benefit is less than its cost.
   - ☐ **c.** the level of materiality specified by the external auditors.
   - ☐ **d.** the level of materiality specified by the audit committee.

2. The enterprise risk management model looks at [See *Enterprise Risk Management.*]
   - ☐ **a.** financial risk.
   - ☐ **b.** operating risk.
   - ☐ **c.** compliance risk.
   - ☑ **d.** all of the above.

3. Enterprise risk management is [See *Enterprise Risk Management.*]
   - ☐ **a.** unrelated to internal controls.
   - ☐ **b.** an element of the COSO *Integrated Framework*.
   - ☑ **c.** a unified and comprehensive risk analysis model.
   - ☐ **d.** all of the above.

4. Risks include all of the following **except:** [See *Types of Risk.*]
   - ☐ **a.** hazard risks.
   - ☐ **b.** financial risks.
   - ☑ **c.** personal risks.
   - ☐ **d.** operational risks.

5. Risks [See *Risk Assessment.*]
   - ☐ **a.** decrease with time.
   - ☐ **b.** are independent of time.
   - ☐ **c.** cannot be controlled.
   - ☑ **d.** are a function of variability.

6. The evaluation phase of risk response looks at [See *Risk Response.*]
   - ☐ **a.** the likelihood of threats.
   - ☐ **b.** the impact of threats.
   - ☐ **c.** neither a nor b.
   - ☑ **d.** both a and b.

7. The risk identification framework considers [**See *Risk Identification.***]

    ☐ **a.** only external threats.

    ☑ **b.** both external and internal threats.

    ☐ **c.** only internal threats.

    ☐ **d.** risk priorities.

Directions: This sampling of questions is designed to emulate actual exam questions. Read each question and write your response on another sheet of paper. See the "Answers to Section Practice Questions" section at the end of this book to assess your response. Validate or improve the answer you wrote. For a more robust selection of practice questions, access the **Online Test Bank** at www.wileycma.com.

Question 2D1-AT16

Topic: Enterprise Risk

Which of the following is **not** an example of a form of political risk associated with foreign direct investment?

- ☐ **a.** Uncontrolled inflation
- ☐ **b.** Nationalization of factories
- ☐ **c.** Change in government regime
- ☐ **d.** Civil war

Question 2D1-AT17

Topic: Enterprise Risk

All of the following are valid reasons for expansion of international business by U.S. multinational corporations, **except** to

- ☐ **a.** secure new sources for raw materials.
- ☐ **b.** find additional areas where their products can be marketed successfully.
- ☐ **c.** protect their domestic market from competition from foreign manufacturers.
- ☐ **d.** minimize their costs of production.

Question 2D1-AT18

Topic: Enterprise Risk

Risk assessment is a process

- ☐ **a.** designed to identify potential events that may affect the entity.
- ☐ **b.** that establishes policies and procedures to accomplish internal control objectives.
- ☐ **c.** that identifies risk but does not include management's response to risk.
- ☐ **d.** that assesses the quality of internal controls throughout the year.

Question 2D1-AT19

Topic: Enterprise Risk

Within a financial risk management context, the term *value at risk* (VaR) is defined as the

☐ **a.** maximum value a company can lose.

☐ **b.** worst possible outcome given the distribution of outcomes.

☐ **c.** most likely negative outcome.

☐ **d.** maximum loss within a certain time period at a given level of confidence.

 To further assess your understanding of the concepts and calculations covered in Part 2, Section D: Risk Management, practice with the **Online Test Bank** for this section. **REMINDER:** See the "Answers to Section Practice Questions" section at the end of this book.

Investment Decisions

Capital is a limited organizational resource, whether it is in the form of debt or equity. Banks have limits as to the volume of credit they can extend. Even the most stable of firms can only borrow up to a certain level or issue a limited amount of shares of common stock to raise capital.

Given the fact that organizations have limited capital resources, every firm must evaluate investment projects carefully. Management accountants often have a key role in deciding whether an investment is sound and worth undertaking. Content in this section begins with an overview of the capital budgeting process and then reviews the fundamental principles that can facilitate intelligent choices between two or more investment alternatives.

Learning Outcome Statements Overview: Investment Decisions

Section E.1. Capital Budgeting Process

A. Define capital budgeting, and identify the steps or stages undertaken in developing and implementing a capital budget for a project.

   a. Capital budgeting—The process of making long-term investment decisions. It is a decision-making process that enables a firm to evaluate the viability of a long-term project and whether it is worth undertaking.

   b. The stages in the capital budgeting process are:

      i. Identification—Identify which type of capital budget expenditures are necessary and consistent with organization goals.

      ii. Search—Investigate investments and search for alternatives.

      iii. Evaluation—Project revenues, costs, risks, and the like.

      iv. Selection—Choose projects with greatest predicted return. (Risk should also be considered.)

      v. Financing—Secure project financing.

      vi. Implementation and control—Implement the project.

B. Identify and calculate the relevant cash flows of a capital investment project on both a pretax and an after-tax basis.

   a. Key points in evaluating capital investment cash flows are:

     • Income statement items that do not affect cash, such as depreciation expense, amortization expense, gains, and losses, are ignored in cash flow analysis problems. Additionally, expenses and revenues are adjusted to remove deferrals and accruals, such as unearned revenues, prepaid expenses, accrued revenues, and accrued expenses.

     • All items affecting cash flows must be examined regardless of whether they are revenues or expenses for the accounting period.

     • Sunk costs are ignored because they are historical costs that are not relevant to the investment decision.

     • Opportunity costs must be included and typically are treated as a cash outlay at the onset of the project.

     • Investments in net working capital are treated as cash outflows at the time they occur and as cash inflows when they are released.

     • The anticipated effects of inflation must be taken into account.

- Depreciation expenses are relevant in capital budgeting only to the extent that they affect the firm's tax obligation. Depreciation provides the firm with non-cash expenses that are tax deductible.

C. Demonstrate an understanding of how income taxes affect cash flows.

    a. In order to accurately project the profitability of a project, a company must identify all the related revenues and expenses, including the income tax effect of those cash flows. Taxes can have a large impact on overall profitability. Capital investments typically are depreciated on an accelerated basis, which provides tax deductions early on in the project timeline.

D. Distinguish between cash flows and accounting profits, and discuss the relevance to capital budgeting of incremental cash flow, sunk cost, and opportunity cost.

    a. Accounting profits typically do not align with the cash flows of a company because of the accrual basis of accounting, treatment of capital expenditures, and other non-cash operating revenues and expenses. For example, the purchase of a piece of equipment would be a cash outflow in year 1 but would show up in the accounting profit only through the process of depreciation over the estimated useful life of the asset.

    b. Incremental cash flow—The additional operating cash flow received or expended from taking on a new project.

    c. Sunk costs—Ignored in capital budgeting because they are historical costs that are not relevant to the investment decision.

    d. Opportunity costs—Included in capital budgeting as a cash outlay at the onset of the project since they provide comparisons against the next best alternative.

E. Explain the importance of changes in net working capital in capital budgeting.

    a. Changes in net working capital (i.e., current assets less current liabilities) must be considered in the initial cash flow of the project as funds are needed to initiate the project. Those cash outflows are not included in accounting profits but are certainly a resource that needs to be funded. If changes in net working capital were ignored, the investment return would be skewed.

F. Discuss how the effects of inflation are reflected in capital budgeting analysis.

    a. Inflation can have a large impact on the real rate of return on a project. If inflation is high, the value of the dollar decreases over time. If inflation is not taken into account, a company may be analyzing cash inflows in year 10 assuming they are equivalent to cash inflows in year 1 in real terms.

G. Define hurdle rate.

    a. Hurdle rate (also called the minimum rate of return)—Determines how rapidly the value of the dollar decreases out in time. Management determines the rate for evaluating capital budgeting projects, and it should include the effects of expected inflation and risk.

H. Identify and discuss qualitative considerations involved in the capital budgeting decision.

    a. Whatever classification scheme a company uses, organizational strategies and objectives will influence the evaluation criteria and decision procedures in making a capital investment. It is important to consider qualitative factors in evaluating capital budgeting projects, such as the impact on employee morale, the support of the company's mission statement, and the company's reputation.

I. Describe the role of the post-audit in the capital budgeting process.

    a. Just as any budgeting process, an audit should be conducted after the capital investment project to compare actual results versus expected results. This data can be used for future decisions and for evaluation purposes.

Section E.2. Discounted Cash Flow Analysis

A. Demonstrate an understanding of the two main discounted cash flow (DCF) methods, net present value (NPV) and internal rate of return (IRR).

    a. Net present value (NPV)—Uses a specified discount rate to bring all subsequent net cash flows after the initial investment to their present values at the time of the initial investment.

    b. Internal rate of return (IRR)—Estimates the discount rate at which the present value of all the subsequent net cash inflows after the initial investment equals the initial cash outlay(s) of the investment.

B. Calculate NPV and IRR.

    a. There are six steps in determining the NPV for a capital project:

        1. Determine the net cash flows for each year.

        2. Identify the required rate of return (RRR).

        3. Determine the discount each year (using the appropriate present value [PV] table) for the RRR in Step 2.

        4. Determine the PV for the net cash flows; multiply the amount for Step 1 by the amount of Step 3.

        5. Total the amounts in Step 4 for all years of the investment.

        6. Subtract the initial investment amount (year 0 cash flow).

Example NPV Computation, 4-Year Project with Uneven Cash Flows, Hurdle Rate 10%

Year	Cash Inflows (Step 1)		Discount Factor at 10% (Steps 2 & 3)		Present Value (Step 4)
1	$60,000	×	0.909	=	$54,540
2	40,000	×	0.826	=	33,040
3	30,000	×	0.751	=	22,530
4	20,000	×	0.683	=	13,660
				(Step 5)	$123,770
				(Step 6)	(90,000)
			Net Present Value		$33,770

b. There are six steps in determining IRR for a capital project with uniform net cash flows:

1. Determine the total initial investment for the project (total cash outflows and commitments).
2. Identify the predetermined criterion cutoff rate of return (the required rate).
3. Determine net cash inflows for each year.
4. Divide the initial investment (Step 1) by the annual cash flow (Step 3) to obtain the IRR factor, which is basically the present value annuity factor for an annuity (PVIFA).
5. Refer to the PV annuity table in Appendix A to locate a discount rate at the specified number of years that matches the IRR factor (or the one closest to it).
6. Compare the IRR rate (Step 5) to the chosen criterion cutoff rate (Step 2). In the NPV example above, the NPV was positive, meaning the rate of return was greater than the hurdle rate, or RRR. In order to determine the IRR on the project in that example you can increase the discount rate (10%) until the NPV gets near zero.

C. Demonstrate an understanding of the decision criteria used in NPV and IRR analyses to determine acceptable projects.

a. An NPV of zero means the investment earns the same rate of return as the RRR. A positive NPV indicates it earns a higher rate than the required rate and should be accepted. A negative NPV indicates it earns a lower rate than the required rate and should be rejected.

b. IRR is compared to the RRR. If the IRR is higher than the RRR, it is an acceptable project as it would result in a positive NPV.

D. Compare NPV and IRR focusing on the relative advantages and disadvantages of each method, particularly with respect to independent versus mutually exclusive projects and the multiple IRR problem.

a. Both NPV and IRR methods weigh heavily on an accurate hurdle rate. If the hurdle rate is inaccurate, then the decision may not be accurate.

b. The advantages of both methods are that they each consider the time value of money, the initial cash investment, and all cash flows after the initial investment.

c. A major difference is that the end result of NPV is a dollar figure whereas the final computation for IRR is a percentage. Thus, NPV has an advantage, because NPV values of individual projects can be added together to estimate the effect of accepting some possible combination of projects.

d. Another major advantage of NPV or IRR is that NPV can be determined easily using different desired rates of return for different periods.

e. If projects are mutually exclusive, the NPV and IRR methods might produce conflicting rankings since NPV can be added together to produce an overall NPV, but IRR rates cannot be added together. That being said, two projects together might produce a positive NPV but each individually might be less than the RRR. This fact needs to be considered when the costs of the projects, the timing and amount of cash flows, and the timelines are different.

E. Explain why NPV and IRR methods can produce conflicting rankings for capital projects if not applied properly.

    a. In comparing two projects with different initial cash outflows, one may produce a high IRR and a low NPV. The other project may produce a lower IRR but a higher NPV. Depending on the method, each project would be selected differently.

F. Identify assumptions of NPV and IRR.

    a. NPV assumes that cash flows are reinvested at the desired rate of return (cost of capital).

    b. IRR assumes that cash flows are reinvested at the internal rate of return instead of the required rate.

G. Evaluate and recommend project investments on the basis of DCF analysis.

    a. The information outlined above provides general guidelines and analysis of whether to accept or reject a project. See Topic 2: Discounted Cash Flow Analysis for additional computations and recommendations of DCF analysis.

Section E.3. Payback and Discounted Payback

A. Demonstrate an understanding of the payback and discounted payback methods.

    a. Similar to the net present value (NPV) and internal rate of return (IRR) techniques, the payback period (PP) does not distinguish between types of cash inflows. As a simple measure of cash inflows, the PP also can be used to evaluate capital investments having uniform net cash flows or uneven cash flows. The payback period of a capital investment assuming uniform cash flows is:

$$\text{Payback Period} = \frac{\text{Total Initial Investment}}{\text{Expected Annual Net Cash Flow}}$$

    b. The payback period of a capital investment, assuming uneven cash flows, is:

$$\text{Payback Period} = \frac{\substack{\text{Years Until Full Recovery +} \\ \text{Unrecovered Cost at the Beginning of the Last Year}}}{\text{Cash Flow During the Last Year}}$$

    c. The discounted payback is similar to the payback method except that it uses present value, or discounted value, of net cash flows. The formulas above can be applied the same with the exception that the annual cash flows must be discounted back to present value before using them in the formula. As a result, you likely won't have a uniform cash flow example using discounted payback.

B. Identify the advantages and disadvantages of the payback and discounted payback methods.
- a. Advantages of the payback method:
  - Uses a simple calculation
  - Produces results that are easy to understand
  - Provides a rough measure of liquidity and risk
- b. Disadvantages of the payback method:
  - Ignores the time value of money
  - Ignores cash flows after the payback period (what if they are negative?)
  - Provides no measure of profitability
  - Promotes the acceptance of short-term projects if the target payback period is too short
- c. The advantage of the discounted payback method is that it addresses the major disadvantage of the payback method in that it does not ignore the time value of money.

C. Calculate payback periods and discounted payback periods.
- a. Using the formulas above, you can calculate the payback periods of any project. [Also refer to Topic 3: Payback and Discounted Payback (in book) for more detailed analysis.]

Section E.4. Risk Analysis in Capital Investment

A. Identify alternative approaches to dealing with risk in capital budgeting.
- a. Sensitivity analysis—A what-if technique evaluating how net present value (NPV), internal rate of return (IRR), and other indicators of the profitability of a project change if the discount rate, labor or materials costs, sales, or some other factor varies from one case to another.
- b. Simulations—Allow testing of a capital investment project before it is accepted. Because the actual future values for cash flows and discount rates for investment projects are not known, hypothetical cash flows and discount rates are assumed and can be studied using a simulation model.
- c. Scenario analysis—Approach to evaluating risk that uses single-point estimates where each possibility is assigned a best-guess estimate. Scenarios (such as best, worst, or most likely case) for each input variable are chosen, and the results are reported.
- d. Monte Carlo analysis—Based on the use of computational algorithms that rely on random sampling in order to compute results. The Monte Carlo method uses computerized simulations are a class of computational algorithms that rely on repeated random sampling to compute their results.

B. Distinguish among sensitivity analysis, scenario analysis, and Monte Carlo simulation as risk analysis techniques.
- a. See item A above for descriptions of sensitivity analysis, scenario analysis, and Monte Carlo simulations.

C. Explain why a rate specifically adjusted for risk should be used when project cash flows are more or less risky than is normal for a firm.

    a. A firm needs to use a risk-adjusted rate when evaluating projects that are outside of the norm for the firm. For example, a company with a required rate of return of 12% should not use only that rate in its computations because projects need to be evaluated on the basis of risk as well. A more risky project might require a 14% hurdle rate in order to compensate the company for the extra risk and uncertainty it is taking on.

D. Explain how the value of a capital investment is increased if consideration is given to the possibility of adding on, speeding up, slowing up, or discontinuing early.

    a. Companies can use another analysis tool called real options valuation (ROV) to value a project. ROV assumes that management can actively modify the project throughout its life by responding to each outcome (in other words, options are exercised) and the possibility of a large negative outcome is reduced or eliminated. The ROV value of a project typically is higher than its net present value. The more real options that are available, the less risk involved and the higher the value of the project.

E. Demonstrate an understanding of real options, and identify examples of the different types of real options (calculations not required).

    a. As discussed above, real options reduce the uncertainty, and therefore risk, of a project. They add more flexibility to mitigate risks throughout the life of a project. Some real options include:

- Abandon—Cease the project by getting rid of assets or diverting the assets to other uses.
- Expand—Start a project out small and increase the investment as the project rolls on.
- Postpone—Delay the project until more information is collected and analyzed.
- Adapt—Option based on the ability of a firm to vary output or production methods in response to demand.

Capital Budgeting Process

S IMPLY STATED, CAPITAL BUDGETING is the process of making long-term invest-ment decisions. It is a decision-making process that enables a firm to evaluate the viability of a long-term project and whether it is worth undertaking.

 READ the Learning Outcome Statements (LOS) for this topic as found in Appendix B and then study the concepts and calculations presented here to be sure you understand the content you could be tested on in the CMA exam.

Capital Budgeting

In the course of business operations, firms make two types of investments: current and capital.

Current investments (or **current expenditures**) are short term in nature because they are investments that can be written off in the same year that the expenses occur. Wages, salaries, many administrative expenses, and expenditures for raw materials in manufacturing are all examples of current investments.

An **operating budget** (or **current budget**) is a plan for the operating expenses and revenues associated with activities for the current time period.

Capital investments (or **capital expenditures**) are long term in nature because they are an investment that requires a current cash outlay today with the expectation of future benefits. The value of the initial cash outlay is gradually reduced (amortized) over a period of years according to Internal Revenue Service (IRS) regulations. Examples of capital investments include expenditures for new or replacement equipment, buildings, and land as well as investments made in research and design (R&D) and the development of new products and services. (Although R&D costs are long-term investments for budgeting purposes, annual R&D costs also are expensed in the current period per the requirements of generally accepted accounting principles [GAAP].)

A **capital budget** is a plan of proposed outlays for acquiring long-term assets and includes the means for financing the acquisition.

A firm's stability and future success often depends on its capital investments. Thus, firms need a sound capital budgeting process to analyze and control long-term capital investments. Firms often have great difficulty recovering money tied up in bad capital investments.

Capital Budgeting Applications

Capital budget proposals can come from a variety of sources. For the process of decision analysis, capital expenditures often are grouped in one of these categories:

- *Expansion projects.* New assets (machines, buildings, etc.) bought with the purpose of expanding business operations
- *Replacement projects.* Replacement of existing machines and equipment
- *Mandatory (compliance) projects.* Required by law to maintain safety in the workplace, safety of consumers, or to protect the environment
- *Other projects.* Allocations for R&D for new products and/or the expansion of existing products as well as various other long-term investments for buildings, land, patents, and the like

Alternate capital expenditure classifications exist, such as:

- Operating efficiency and/or revenue generation
- Competitive effectiveness
- Regulatory, safety, health, and environmental requirements

Whatever classification scheme a company uses, organizational strategies and objectives will influence the evaluation criteria and decision procedures in making a capital investment. It is important to consider qualitative factors in evaluating capital budgeting projects, such as the impact on employee morale, the support of the company's mission statement, and the company reputation.

Project and Time Dimensions in Capital Budgeting

Two important aspects of capital budgeting are the project dimension and the time dimension.

Project Dimension

Where operational budgeting decisions focus on income determination, planning, and control of activities for the current time period, capital budgeting decisions look at projects that span multiple accounting periods. A capital budgeting project related to the development of a new product, for example, might span several years from R&D through product fulfillment and customer service.

Life-cycle costing must be used to accumulate capital budgeting costs and revenues on a project-by-project basis and track income over the entire project. For the new product development example just given, costs must be accumulated for all business functions in the value chain over many accounting periods.

Time Dimension

Typically, a capital budgeting decision depresses reported income for the current period but has the potential to generate high cash inflows in the future. Therefore, capital budgeting decisions cannot be based solely on the current accounting period's income statement.

Certainly income for any given period is important. For publicly traded companies, income reported in a given period can affect the firm's stock price and can affect bonuses. But excessive focus on short-term accounting can result in investment decisions that forgo long-term profitability.

The concept of the time value of money is basic to capital budgeting. The time value of money implies that:

- A dollar (or any other monetary unit) is worth more today than a dollar received tomorrow because that dollar can be invested today to earn a return.
- A dollar tomorrow is worth less than a dollar today because of the interest forgone.

A $10,000 investment made today with the potential for a 15% annual rate of return would be worth $11,500 at the end of the year. But according to the time value of money, had the investment not been made, the opportunity cost is the $1,500 forgone.

Stages of Capital Budgeting

A capital budgeting project consists of a logical progression of activities. The specific names for the stages or steps vary across firms. In general, firms address all of the stages or steps shown in Figure 2E-1.

Figure 2E-1 Stages of Capital Budgeting

Stage 1	**Identification**
	Identify which types of capital budget expenditures are necessary and consistent with organizational goals, objectives, and strategies.
Stage 2	**Search**
	Thoroughly investigate the initial capital investment proposals and explore alternative investments.
Stage 3	**Evaluation**
	Project revenues, financial and nonfinancial benefits, costs, and cash flows for each alternative and compare them for the project's entire life cycle. Management must assess how the project will affect the organization's resources and whether the firm can absorb the costs.

(Continued)

Figure 2E-1 (Continued)

Stage 4	**Selection**
	Choose projects chosen for implementation, which typically means selecting those in which the predicted financial benefits exceed costs by the greatest margin. Consideration also should be given to the nonfinancial (qualitative) outcomes.
Stage 5	**Financing**
	Secure project financing either internally (reinvesting cash) or externally by selling debt and equity in the capital market.
Stage 6	**Implementation and control**
	Implement the capital project and then to initiate the monitoring and evaluation tools necessary to keep the project within the capital budget. Planning factors used at the time the project was selected need to be compared with actual results. Adjustments may need to be made to obtain optimal results throughout the project life cycle.

Incremental Cash Flows

Competent managers and knowledgeable investors always give special attention to the firm's cash position, which is also described as the firm's operating cash flow—hence the saying "Cash is king."

Estimating future cash flows is one of the most important tasks in capital budgeting. A firm must be able to evaluate the difference between its cash flows with and without an investment project and where all relevant costs and benefits have an effect during the project.

Key points in evaluating capital investment cash flows are:

- Income statement items that do not affect cash, such as depreciation expense, amortization expense, gains, and losses, are ignored in cash flow analysis problems. Additionally, expenses and revenues are adjusted to remove deferrals and accruals, such as unearned revenues, prepaid expenses, accrued revenues, and accrued expenses.
- All items affecting cash flows must be examined regardless of whether they are revenues or expenses for the accounting period.
- Sunk costs are ignored because they are historical costs that are not relevant to the investment decision.
- Opportunity costs must be included and typically are treated as a cash outlay at the onset of the project.
- Investments in net working capital are treated as cash outflows at the time they occur and as cash inflows when they are released.
- The anticipated effects of inflation must be taken into account.
- Depreciation expenses are relevant in capital budgeting only to the extent that they affect the firm's tax obligation. Depreciation provides the firm with non-cash expenses that are tax deductible.

Capital investment projects generally begin the same way, with a cash outflow as a payment or commitment of funds. However, during the life of the investment, different cash flow outcomes are possible. The return on the initial cash outflow may decrease cash expenditures or generate additional cash inflows. In some circumstances, both outcomes may occur. Furthermore, based on information provided by the project's monitoring and control activities, funds for additional capital investments may be needed.

Relevant incremental cash flows during a capital investment project are categorized based on the timing of when they occur during the capital investment project: at the start of the project, during the course of the project, or at the end. Figure 2E-2 summarizes characteristics of these capital project cash flow categories.

Figure 2E-2 Cash Inflows and Outflows During a Capital Budgeting Project

Category	Description	Cash Flow Activities
Initiation	Initial cash investment	Outflows to fund the investment and initiate the project
		Commitments for net working capital (i.e., current assets and current liabilities that are non-cash)
		Inflows or outflows if there is an asset being replaced
Operation	Interim incremental net cash flows	Outflows for operating expenditures
		Outflows for additional capital investments (if necessary)
		Commitments for additional net working capital (i.e., current assets and current liabilities that are non-cash) for operations
		Inflows generated by the investment (e.g., revenues and cash savings) and cash released from net working capital no longer needed for operations
Disposal	Incremental net cash flow for the final year	Inflows or outflows related to the investment's disposal
		Cash inflows from the release of net working capital (i.e., current assets and current liabilities that are non-cash) no longer committed to the investment

Cash inflows increase the cash available to the business; cash outflows or cash commitments decrease the cash available to the business. Committing funds to working capital makes those funds unavailable for other uses. Net working capital is the excess of current assets over current liabilities and is considered the amount of additional funds available to meet operational requirements.

Understanding the next concepts is important before examining each of these relevant cash flow categories further.

- **Direct effect** is the immediate effect that a cash inflow, outflow, or commitment has on cash flows.
- **Tax effect** (or indirect effect) is the change in a firm's tax payments caused by the taxability of revenues and the deductibility of expenses.
- **Net effect** (or total effect) is the total of the direct effect and the tax effect.

Initiation Cash Flows

Cash flows during project initiation generally are determined as shown in Figure 2E-3. The cost of the asset is subject to various adjustments, depending on the net effect of all transactions.

Figure 2E-3 Incremental Cash Flows at Initiation

–	Direct effect for the cost of the new asset
–	Additional capitalized expenditures (e.g., for shipping, installation, and modification)
– or +	Increase or decrease in net working capital (i.e., current assets and current liabilities that are non-cash)
+	Net proceeds from the sale of the old asset (if the investment is a replacement project)
– or +	Tax effect due to the sale of the old asset (if the investment is a replacement project)
=	Initiation cash flow

Operation Cash Flows

Following the initial cash outflows necessary to begin a project, a firm hopes to benefit from cash flows generated during subsequent periods. Future cash flows generally can be determined as shown in Figure 2E-4.

Figure 2E-4 Incremental Cash Flows During Operations (per Period)

	Net increase or decrease in operating revenue
– or +	Any net increase or decrease in operating expenses (excluding depreciation)
– or +	Net increase or decrease in tax depreciation charges
=	Net change in income before taxes
– or +	Net increase or decrease in taxes
=	Net effect after taxes
+ or –	Net increase or decrease in tax depreciation charges
=	Incremental cash flow for the operating period

Note that the net increase or decrease in tax depreciation charges is first subtracted or added to determine the net change in income before taxes. The net increase or decrease in tax depreciation is later added back in or subtracted out to determine the incremental cash flow for the period. That is because tax depreciation is a non-cash expenditure that lowers taxable income. It needs to be considered initially to determine the incremental effect that the project has on the firm's acceptance of the project. After the incremental effect is determined, it is added or subtracted once again to avoid understating the project's effect on cash flow.

Disposal Cash Flows

Incremental cash flow at disposal (in the final period, at project termination) is shown in Figure 2E-5, where recognition is given to a few activities associated specifically with project termination:

- The salvage value of any sold or disposed assets
- The net tax effect (the taxes or tax savings) related to the asset disposal
- Any change in net working capital (e.g., the reinstatement of net working capital to cash flow at project termination)

Figure 2E-5 Incremental Cash Flows at Disposal

+	Salvage value of any sold or disposed assets
− or +	Net tax effect (taxes or savings) due to the sale or disposal of assets
+ or −	Recaptured increase or decrease in net working capital level
=	Incremental cash flow at disposal

Incremental Cash Flow Example

Consider this example of incremental cash flow determination involving the purchase of a new machine in a manufacturing operation:

- The cost for the new machine is $80,000.
- Shipping and installation charges for the machine are $20,000.
- The salvage value for the machine after a useful life of four years is $33,000.
- No additional working capital is required.
- The machine will be installed in an area that has no alternative use so there are no opportunity costs.
- The firm's tax rate is 40%.

Incremental cash flows at the initiation of the project can be summarized as in Figure 2E-6.

Figure 2E-6 Incremental Cash Flows at Initiation

Direct effect for the cost of the new asset	($80,000)
Additional capitalized expenditures (shipping or installation)	(20,000)
Initiation cash flow	($100,000)

Projections for net operating revenue (before depreciation and taxes) after the project begins are shown in Figure 2E-7.

Figure 2E-7 Projections for Net Operating Revenue

	Year-End			
	1	2	3	4
Net cash flows	$40,000	$42,000	$50,000	$38,000

Incremental (future) cash flows during operations and at disposal are shown in Figure 2E-8.

Figure 2E-8 Incremental Cash Flows from Operations and Disposal

Operation cash flows (years 1 to 4)	Year-End			
	1	2	3	4
Net change in operating revenue, excluding depreciation	$40,000	$42,000	$50,000	$38,000
Net increase in tax depreciation charges*	(33,330)	(44,450)	(14,810)	(7,410)
Net change in income before taxes	$6,670	($2,450)	$35,190	$30,590
Net increase or decrease in taxes at 40% tax rate	(2,668)	980	(14,076)	(12,236)
Net effect after taxes	$4,002	$(1,470)	$21,114	$18,354
Net increase in tax depreciation charges	33,330	44,450	14,810	7,410
Incremental cash flow for years 1 to 4	$37,332	$42,980	$35,924	$25,764

Disposal cash flows (year 4)				
Salvage value of any sold or disposed assets[†]				$33,000
Net tax effect (taxes due) on the sale or disposal of assets				(13,200)
Disposal cash flow				$19,800

*According to the Modified Accelerated Cost Recovery System (MACRS) depreciation schedule for a three-year asset with a depreciable basis of $100,000, the depreciation rates are year 1 = 33.33%, year 2 = 44.45%, year 3 = 14.81%, and year 4 = 7.41%.

[†]Assumes salvage value is recapture of depreciation and taxed at the ordinary income rate of 40%.

The expected incremental cash flows determined above are summarized in Figure 2E-9. Note that in capital budgeting, the year when the initial cash outflows begin is referred to as year 0.

Figure 2E-9 Expected Incremental Cash Flows

	Year-End				
	0	1	2	3	4
Net cash flows	($100,000)	$37,332	$42,980	35,924	$45,564*

* Year 4 includes operational cash flows of $25,764 and disposal cash flows of $19,800.

This incremental cash flow data provides the relevant information necessary to judge the financial attractiveness of the project. Management would need to assess how the project will affect the organization's resources, and comparisons should be made to other alternatives.

A firm then would need to examine the expected cash inflows and outflows of the capital investment project further using various methods. These methods are explained in detail in the next two topics of this section:

- Discounted cash flow (DCF) analysis
- Payback method

The DCF methods adjust cash flows by incorporating the time value of money. For this reason, they are used widely in assessing long-run investment decisions. An important element of DCF is the determination of the hurdle rate to be used. The hurdle rate, also called the minimum rate of return, determines how rapidly the value of the dollar decreases out in time. The rate is determined by management for evaluating capital budgeting projects and should inherently include the effects of expected inflation and risk.

Income Tax Considerations

Cash flows resulting from capital investments have various tax effects. Under some circumstances, taxes can significantly reduce net cash flows from a project and influence their desirability.

Most tax rules set forth for preparing financial statements under GAAP apply to cash flows from capital investment projects. But there are also special tax rules related to capital investments. In particular, tax rules pertaining to depreciation differ in these ways:

- Depreciation amount allowable
- Depreciation time period
- Depreciation pattern

The tax treatment of a depreciable asset can be complex. Whenever a firm invests in an income-producing asset, the productive life of that asset is estimated. The value of any capital asset decreases as its useful life is expended. For accounting purposes, the asset is depreciated over this period.

However, depreciation may not reflect the true value of a capital asset during its useful life because obsolescence may occur at any time. For example, a superior machine is developed that renders an existing one obsolete even though it is not worn out. Furthermore, the depreciation method a firm chooses may be more of a function of the effect on taxes rather than the ability to make a project's book value reflect its true resale value.

In practice, a variety of factors can complicate depreciation. Thorough investigation of the current and applicable tax code and/or consultation with a tax specialist is advisable.

Depreciation Amount Allowable

While it is important for CMA candidates to understand how depreciation is calculated, candidates are not expected to calculate depreciation amounts on the CMA exam. Depreciation amounts related to capital budgeting decisions will be provided in exam problems. The "Depreciation Pattern" section later in this topic provides an overview of several depreciation methods, so that candidates gain an understanding of the effect that the various methods may have on evaluating a potential investment.

Computing the depreciation amount allowable for an asset requires a determination of the asset's depreciable basis. In tax accounting, **depreciable basis** is the amount that can be written off for tax purposes over a period of years.

Typically, the amount allowable is the original cost of the asset. This includes other capitalized expenditures that are necessary to prepare the asset for use (such as shipping and installation charges). Capitalized expenditures are treated as depreciable cash outlays and not as expenses of the period in which they are incurred.

In some situations, the amount allowable can be greater or less than the original investment costs. Tax credits, for example, can reduce the amount allowable below the original cost, and some tax laws permit companies to claim depreciation amounts for specific assets in excess of the investment made.

Depreciation Time Period

There are three main techniques for determining the depreciation time period for capital investments:

1. The taxpayer estimates the useful life.
2. Tax authorities estimate the useful life.
3. Tax law specifies the allowable life through a series of tax tables, such as the Modified Accelerated Cost Recovery System (MACRS), pronounced "makers."

Generally, the shorter the allowable life of the asset, the fewer periods over which the depreciation of the asset can be claimed. This shorter allowable life results in a higher depreciable amount per year, higher tax deductions, and greater tax savings.

Depreciation Pattern

Tax authorities allow different depreciation patterns (based on the time periods). A variety of depreciation methods are possible. An overview of a few of the more common methods follows.

Straight-Line Depreciation

Straight-line (SL) depreciation allocates expenses equally over the depreciable life of the asset. An equal depreciation amount is taken each year.

The general formula for straight-line depreciation is:

$$\text{Straight-Line Depreciation} = \frac{\text{Cost} - \text{Salvage Value}}{\text{Estimated Useful Life}}$$

For example: An asset costs $10,000 with an estimated useful life of 5 years and a salvage value of $2,000. Using the straight-line depreciation method results in equal depreciation expenses each year over the equipment's 5-year life of:

$$\text{Straight-Line Depreciation} = \frac{\$10,000 - \$2,000}{5} = \$1,600 \text{ per Year}$$

Accelerated Depreciation

Accelerated depreciation refers to any method that writes off a capital investment faster than under straight-line depreciation. More of the depreciable amount is written off in the early years of the investment than with the straight-line method. Sum-of-the-years' digits, declining-balance depreciation, and double-declining-balance depreciation are all examples of accelerated depreciation methods.

Sum-of-the-years' digits (SYD) is one method to reduce the book value of a capital investment rapidly in the early years and at a lower rate in the later years of the asset's life. The SYD method takes into consideration the estimated salvage value in the same manner as the SL method.

For example: Use the same $10,000 asset with a 5-year life and a $2,000 estimated salvage value to determine the amount of depreciation during the first year using the SYD method. Because this asset has an estimated useful life of 5 years, the sum of the numbers is 15 (as $1 + 2 + 3 + 4 + 5 = 15$).

The asset is depreciated in this manner:

- 33.33% (5/15) in the first year.
- 26.67% (4/15) in the second year.
- 20.00% (3/15) in the third year.
- 13.33% (2/15) in the four year.
- 6.67% (1/15) in the fifth year.

Thus, the depreciation for the first year is $2,667 ($8,000 × 0.3333) using the SYD method versus $1,600 using the SL method. During the fifth year, the SYD depreciation is $536 ($8,000 × 0.067) versus $1,600 using the SL method. Compared with depreciation using the SL method, depreciation using the SYD method is higher during the early years but lower in the latter years of an asset's life.

Declining-balance (DB) depreciation decreases the asset's value by reducing its book value by a constant percentage each year. Unlike the SL and SYD methods, the DB method does not explicitly use the salvage value in its calculations. However, depreciation expense will be halted when the cost less salvage value has been depreciated. The general formula for the DB method to determine the depreciation charge in any period is:

$$(1/n) \text{ NBV}$$

where:

n = depreciable life of the asset

NBV = asset's net book value at the start of the year

(cost – accumulated depreciation)

For example: For a $10,000 asset with a 5-year life, the depreciation in the first year would be $2,000. The 1/5 determines the fixed percentage, or 20%, that is applied against the declining net book value each year. The net book value for the second year would be $8,000 (the acquisition cost minus accumulated depreciation). Thus, the depreciation charge for year 2 would be:

$$(0.20)\ \$8,000 = \$1,600$$

The fixed percentage selected is generally the one that reduces book value to salvage value at the end of the asset's estimated life. The asset should never be reduced below the estimated salvage value.

Variations of the DB method use an accelerator or multiplier factor (m) to increase the amount of annual depreciation in the early years of an asset's life, as shown:

 Depreciation Using the DB Method with a Multiplier = $m\ (1/n)$ NBV

where:

m = multiplier

n = depreciable life of the asset

NBV = asset's net book value at the start of the year

(cost less accumulated depreciation)

For example: The double-declining balance (DDB) method doubles the rate in the previous scenario, where $m = 2$, as shown here:

$$2\ (0.20)\ \$10,000 = \$4,000$$

The fixed percentage is now 2 (0.20), or 40%. This fixed percentage applied against the declining net book value in year 2 results in:

$$2\ (0.20)\ \$6,000 = \$2,400$$

In the third year, the charge would be:

$$2\ (0.20)\ \$3,600 = \$1,440$$

In years 1 through 3, the company has a cumulative depreciation expense of $7,840 ($4,000 + $2,400 + $1,440). Because the total depreciation expense is $8,000

($10,000 – $2,000), the depreciation in year 4 is limited to $160 ($8,000 – $7,840) instead of $864 [2 (0.20) $2,160].

There would be no depreciation expense in year 5 because the asset has been fully depreciated to its estimated salvage value.

MACRS tables categorize all business assets into classes (e.g., computers and peripheral equipment, office machinery, office furniture, nonresidential real estate, etc.) and then specify the time period over which the assets can be written off in each class (e.g., three-year property, five-year property, seven-year property, etc.). Depending on the class of an asset, different conventions can be used to adjust the first-year depreciation depending on the placed-in-service date.

The IRS provides special tables to determine the percentage of the item's tax basis that can be depreciated each year. The asset's tax basis does not change over the years, only the percentage used as a multiplier changes.

For example: Assume that the $10,000 asset previously discussed is classified as five-year asset life category. The depreciation rates as a percentage shown in Figure 2E-10 apply to the original basis ($10,000), not the depreciable basis ($10,000 – $2,000).

Figure 2E-10 Five-Year Asset Life Category

Year	% (rounded)
1	20.00
2	32.00
3	19.20
4	11.52
5	11.52
6	5.76

This table is based on the DDB method, which switches to straight-line depreciation. Year 1 is the year in which the asset is placed in service. This table uses the midyear convention, which assumes that the asset is placed in service at midyear. Thus, the company can expense only half of the normal amount of depreciation during year 1.

For the $10,000 asset with an estimated salvage value of $2,000, the depreciation expense for year 1 is 0.20 ($10,000) = $2,000.

Although a full discussion of how income taxes specifically can affect cash inflows and outflows for capital investments is beyond the scope of this text, the next general points can be made about depreciation and tax considerations in profitable companies:

- Depreciation deductions are not cash payments; they are non-cash costs that reduce taxable income and taxes.
- A depreciation expense has an effect on the amount of income taxes a firm must pay for a given period.
- Because depreciation reduces taxable income and reduces the tax outflow, depreciation effectively results in a cash inflow.

- The decrease in the tax liability due to the depreciation charge is referred to as a **depreciation tax shield**.
- This tax shield is equal to the depreciation amount multiplied by the tax rate.

Companies tend to favor accelerated depreciation patterns because they result in larger depreciation deductions and cash savings in years when the cash savings have a higher present value. Compared to the SL method, however, accelerated methods result in lower earnings per share (EPS) during the early years but higher EPS during the later years, holding other factors constant.

Knowledge Check: Capital Budgeting Process

The next questions are intended to help you check your understanding and recall of the material presented in this topic. They do not represent the type of questions that appear on the CMA exam.

Directions: Answer each question in the space provided. Correct answers and section references appear after the knowledge check questions.

1. Capital budgeting is **best** described as

   ☐ **a.** decision making related to current expenditures.

   ☐ **b.** the process of making long-term investment decisions.

   ☐ **c.** the process of planning for short-term investments.

   ☐ **d.** decision making to support operating efficiency.

2. Which of the following items is **not** an example of a capital expenditure?

   ☐ **a.** Heating, ventilation, and air-conditioning system upgrade for Environmental Protection Agency compliance

   ☐ **b.** Purchase of a new assembly machine that will cut labor and maintenance costs

   ☐ **c.** Purchase of a new computer server for the research and development group

   ☐ **d.** Project bonuses paid to salaried employees

3. As it relates to relevant cash flow categories, *direct effect* refers to the

   ☐ **a.** immediate effect that a cash inflow, outflow, or commitment has on cash flows.

   ☐ **b.** change in a firm's tax obligations.

   ☐ **c.** net increase or decrease in tax depreciation charges.

   ☐ **d.** total of the direct effect and the tax effect.

Knowledge Check Answers: Capital Process

1. Capital budgeting is **best** described as [**See** *Capital Budgeting.*]

   ☐ **a.** decision making related to current expenditures.

   ☑ **b.** the process of making long-term investment decisions.

   ☐ **c.** the process of planning for short-term investments.

   ☐ **d.** decision making to support operating efficiency.

2. Which of the following items is **not** an example of a capital expenditure? [**See** *Capital Budgeting.*]

   ☐ **a.** Heating, ventilation, and air-conditioning system upgrade for Environmental Protection Agency compliance

   ☐ **b.** Purchase of a new assembly machine that will cut labor and maintenance costs

   ☐ **c.** Purchase of a new computer server for the research and development group

   ☑ **d.** Project bonuses paid to salaried employees

3. As it relates to relevant cash flow categories, *direct effect* refers to the [**See** *Initiation Cash Flows.*]

   ☑ **a.** immediate effect that a cash inflow, outflow, or commitment has on cash flows.

   ☐ **b.** change in a firm's tax obligations.

   ☐ **c.** net increase or decrease in tax depreciation charges.

   ☐ **d.** total of the direct effect and the tax effect.

Discounted Cash Flow Analysis

VARIOUS TECHNIQUES ARE AVAILABLE to evaluate capital investment projects. This topic discusses one of the more complicated techniques: **discounted cash flow (DCF)** analysis. DCF analysis adjusts cash flows over time for the time value of money. DCF methods are used to evaluate a capital investment by comparing the equivalent present values of all future net cash flows against the initial investment.

Two popular DCF methods are covered:

1. Net present value (NPV) uses a specified discount rate to bring all subsequent net cash flows after the initial investment to their present values at the time of the initial investment. NPV emphasizes the dollar amount at the time of the investment. The NPV method is the preferred method for evaluating capital budgeting projects. It is consistent with the objective of maximizing shareholder wealth. Shareholder wealth is the NPV of the firm's future cash flows at its weighted average cost of capital.

2. Internal rate of return (IRR) estimates the discount rate at which the present value of all the subsequent net cash inflows after the initial investment equal the initial cash outlay(s) of the investment. IRR uses the discount rate as a point of comparison. There are two limitations to using the IRR method:

   a. First, it assumes that the firm reinvests cash inflows earned from a capital budgeting project at the IRR, which may not always be correct.
   b. If any of the cash flows other than the initial investment are negative, the project will have multiple IRRs.

 READ the Learning Outcome Statements (LOS) for this topic as found in Appendix B and then study the concepts and calculations presented here to be sure you understand the content you could be tested on in the CMA exam.

Required Rate of Return

Although each discounted cash flow (DCF) method takes a different approach, net present value (NPV) and internal rate of return (IRR) both use these criteria to evaluate a capital investment:

- Total initial cash flow for the investment
- Expected future cash inflows and outflows from the investment
- Firm's required rate of return for the investment

The capital budgeting process, discussed in Topic 1 of this section, covered total cash flow and incremental cash flows. The next step in the capital budgeting process is to determine if the anticipated cash flows meet the required rate of return and the weighted average cost of capital (WACC) requirements established by the company.

The **required rate of return** represents the minimum future receipts the firm will accept in choosing an investment. Stated another way, it is the return that a firm could expect to receive elsewhere for a capital investment of comparable risk. The required rate of return also is referred to as the desired rate of return, the hurdle rate, the threshold, or the (opportunity) cost of capital.

From a practical standpoint, determining the desired rate of return for all potential investments is challenging as well as time consuming. Identifying and evaluating the gamut of potential investment opportunities available at a given point in time is problematic and costly for a firm. Firms tend to use two methods to expedite the process: a minimum rate of return or the cost of capital (WACC). WACC is the conceptually correct discount rate.

Minimum Rate of Return

Firms typically have a minimum rate of return figure that they use to evaluate investments. This rate usually is based on the firm's strategic objectives, industry averages, and common investment opportunities. When a firm uses a minimum rate of return as an investment benchmark, capital investment projects must meet this rate.

Cost of Capital

The WACC is a weighted average of the various components a firm uses for financing. WACC is found by determining the cost of each individual capital component (e.g., issues of preferred or common stock; borrowing through various forms of debt, such as loans and bonds; or retained earnings) and then multiplying the cost of each by its proportion in the firm's total capital structure.

Recall the general formula for the cost of capital:

$$k_a = w_1 k_1 + w_2 k_2 \ldots + w_n k_n$$

where:

k_a = cost of capital (expressed as a percentage)
w = weight that component comprises of the total capital structure
k = cost of a component in the capital structure
1, 2, and n = different types of financing (each with its own cost and proportion in the capital structure)

Section B: Corporate Finance covers the specific formulas for determining the cost of each component in a firm's capital structure. It also examines how the WACC is used to calculate the relative importance of each source in the total capital structure of the firm (once the individual capital components have been determined).

Recall the formula for the WACC:

$$\text{Weighted Average Cost of Capital} = w_d k_{dt} + w_e k_e$$

where:

w_d = percentage of debt
k_{dt} = after-tax cost of debt
w_e = percentage of equity
k_e = cost of equity

Firms often use WACC to evaluate the cost of capital investments that have risk profiles consistent with the firm's overall risk profile (i.e., projects of average riskiness for the firm).

Thus, in making capital investment decisions, the cost of capital can be applied as the discount rate to evaluate the present value (PV) of project cash flows. It may also provide the basis for the required rate of return and the point of comparison for a capital investment project's internal rate of return.

Net Present Value

Net present value (NPV) is the PV of a project's future cash flows less the initial investment in the project. It discounts all expected future cash inflows and outflows to the present.

In order to calculate NPV, the PV first must be determined.

Present Value Calculation

Present value (PV) is the equivalent dollar value today of future net cash inflows. It is determined by applying an appropriate discount (based on the required rate of return) to the future cash inflow. Discount rate factors can be derived in two ways: by using an algebraic formula or by applying a discount rate factor from a table. The discount rate factor tables simply list the discount rates that are calculated by using the algebraic formula. Some CMA candidates may prefer to use a financial calculator to complete these problems; the financial calculator will calculate the discount factor based on the data that is input by the user. The next formulas can be used to calculate PV amounts using the algebraic approach or the discount rate factor tables.

$$\text{Present Value (PV)} = \frac{\text{Amount of Cash Flow}}{(1+r)^n}$$

where:

r = discount rate

n = number of periods

or

$$\text{Present Value (PV)} = \text{Amount of Cash Flow} \times \text{Discount Rate Factor}$$

Using the algebraic formula, the PV of $20,000, to be received in one year, with a 10% required rate of return would be calculated as shown:

$$\text{Present Value (PV)} = \frac{\text{Amount of Cash Flow}}{(1+r)^n}$$

$$\text{PV} = \$20,000 / (1 + 0.10)^1$$

$$\text{PV} = \$20,000 / 1.1$$

$$\text{PV} = \$18,182$$

The PV of $20,000, to be received in one year, with a 10% required rate of return also can be determined by using the PV of $1 factor table listed in Figure 2E-11. Refer to the figure to locate the appropriate discount rate.

Figure 2E-11 Partial Present Value of $1 Interest Factor Table

(*n*) Periods	10%	11%	12%
1	0.909	0.901	0.893
2	0.826	0.812	0.797
3	0.751	0.731	0.712
4	0.683	0.659	0.636
5	0.621	0.593	0.567
6	0.564	0.535	0.507
7	0.513	0.482	0.452
8	0.467	0.434	0.404
9	0.424	0.391	0.361
10	0.386	0.352	0.322

The discount rate (0.909) taken from the PV interest factor table is the discount factor for 10% in one period.

Present Value (PV) = Amount of Cash Flow × Discount Rate

$$PV = \$20,000 \times 0.909$$

$$PV = \$18,180$$

Note that the PV is $2 different from the amount calculated using the algebraic formula. This is simply due to rounding of the PV interest factor in the table.

Proof of this calculation can be found by determining the cash investment one year from now as shown:

Present value of cash now	=	$18,180
Interest for one year ($18,180 × 10%)	=	1,818
Total cash in one year from now	=	$19,998

In other words, $18,180 is the PV equivalent of a $20,000 cash inflow that will be received one year from now.

Net Present Value Calculation

NPV is the amount in dollars today that an investment earns after yielding the desired rate of return for each period during the life of the investment.

The six steps in determining the NPV for a capital project are listed next.

1. Determine net cash flows for each year.
2. Identify the required rate of return.
3. Determine the discount for each year (using the appropriate PV table) for the required rate of return in Step 2.
4. Determine the PVs for the net cash flows; multiply the amount for Step 1 by the amount for Step 3.
5. Total the amounts in Step 4 for all years of the investment.
6. Subtract the initial investment amount.

NPV can be used to evaluate investments with both uniform net cash flows and with uneven cash flows. Step-by-step examples of both types of calculations are shown next.

Uniform Net Cash Flows Example

Uniform cash flow also is described as an **annuity investment**. An annuity provides a series of equal cash flows over a specified number of periods and requires the use of the PV interest factor annuity table to determine the discount factor. The discount factor varies based on the number of years and the desired rate of return.

For example: Consider this scenario:

- The desired rate of return for an investment over three years is 10%.
- Net cash flows for each year of the investment are $125,000.

Refer to Figure 2E-12 to locate the appropriate discount rate.

Figure 2E-12 Partial Present Value Interest Factor Annuity Table

(*n*) Periods	10%	11%	12%	13%
1	0.909	0.901	0.893	0.885
2	1.736	1.713	1.690	1.668
3	2.487	2.444	2.402	2.361
4	3.170	3.102	3.037	2.974
5	3.791	3.696	3.605	3.517
6	4.355	4.231	4.111	3.998
7	4.868	4.712	4.564	4.423
8	5.335	5.146	4.968	4.799
9	5.759	5.537	5.328	5.132
10	6.145	5.889	5.650	5.426

The discount rate of 2.487 is found using the PV interest factor annuity table for three years at 10%. The PV of the net cash inflows can then be calculated as shown:

$$\text{PV of Net Cash Inflows} = \$125,000 \times 2.487 = \$310,875$$

If an initial cash investment of $300,000 is required, then the PV of the investment is determined by subtracting the initial investment from the PV of the net cash inflow as shown:

$$\text{NPV} = \$310,875 - \$300,000 = \$10,875$$

The NPV calculation in this example indicates that the initial investment of $300,000 will earn $10,875 in current dollars in addition to a 10% return for each of the three years during the life of the investment.

Uneven Cash Flows Example

A project with uneven cash flow projections over its life starts with the net cash inflows generated each year and then discounts them using the PV interest factor table. The discount factor will vary for each year of the investment.

For example: Consider this scenario:

- The total initial investment is $90,000.
- The required rate of return over four years is 10%.
- Annual net cash inflows over the life of the investment are $60,000, $40,000, $30,000, and $20,000.

Refer to the Present Value of $1 Table in Appendix A and locate the appropriate values for the four periods.

Figure 2E-13 shows how the cash flows are discounted using the PV interest factor table excerpt to determine the PV for each year.

Figure 2E-13 Using Net Present Value to Evaluate a Project

Year	Cash Inflows		Discount Factor at 10%		Present Value
1	$60,000	×	0.909	=	$54,540
2	40,000	×	0.826	=	33,040
3	30,000	×	0.751	=	22,530
4	20,000	×	0.683	=	13,660
Total present value of net cash inflows					$123,770
Less initial investment					(90,000)
NPV					$33,770

The NPV calculation indicates that the initial investment of $90,000 will earn $33,770 in current dollars over the life of the project.

Notice how Figure 2E-13 provides a useful worksheet for evaluating the effect of each of the various factors. A 10% decrease in cash inflows or an increase in the discount factor to 11% could be done and would result in a different PV amount. The worksheet also could be useful for doing a comparison of DCFs for a selection of projects. This type of analysis is often part of the risk analysis that is done when evaluating projects.

Net Present Value Interpretation

NPV values may be interpreted in this way:

- An NPV of zero means that the investment earns the same rate of return as the required rate of return.
- A positive NPV indicates that the investment earns a higher rate of return than the required rate; future cash flows are greater than the initial investment cost.
- A negative NPV means that future cash flows will earn a return less than the required rate.

Projects with a positive NPV are acceptable because they add value to the firm. Projects with a negative NPV indicate that the firm would earn less than required in a PV sense. However, a positive NPV does not mean that the project is the best possible investment alternative for a firm. A positive NPV simply means that the investment will earn a higher rate of return than the firm's required rate. Alternate investment opportunities may offer even better returns.

Internal Rate of Return

The **internal rate of return (IRR)** estimates the discount rate that makes the PV of net cash inflows equal to the initial investment. Stated another way, IRR is a discount rate that will make the NPV of an investment zero (if the rate is used as the required rate of return to compute NPV).

Internal Rate of Return Interpretation

The IRR method evaluates a capital investment by comparing the estimated IRR to a predetermined criterion. This criterion is based on whatever rate the firm uses to evaluate investments, such as its minimum rate of return, the rate from another desirable alternate investment, or an industry average. The criterion rate serves as a cutoff point. Projects below this cutoff rate are rejected unless they are mandatory projects.

Internal Rate of Return Calculation

The IRR method has two fundamental steps:

1. Determine the rate of return that makes the PV of net cash inflows equal the investment's initial amount.
2. Compare the estimated rate of return with the firm's required rate of return (the criterion cutoff) to assess the investment's desirability.

Similar to NPV, IRR may be used to evaluate investments with uniform net cash flows and with uneven cash flows. Examples of both types of calculations follow.

Uniform Net Cash Flows Example

The steps in determining IRR for a capital project with uniform net cash flows are:

1. Determine the total initial investment for the project (total cash outflows and commitments).
2. Identify the predetermined criterion cutoff rate of return (the required rate).
3. Determine net cash inflows for each year.
4. Divide the initial investment (Step 1) by the annual cash flow (Step 3) to obtain the IRR factor, which is basically the present value annuity factor for an annuity (PVIFA).
5. Refer to the PV annuity table in Appendix A to locate a discount rate at the specified number of years that matches the IRR factor (or the one closest to it).
6. Compare the IRR rate (Step 5) to the chosen criterion cutoff rate (Step 2).

If the calculated IRR exceeds the criterion cutoff rate, which serves as the desired rate of return, the project is a desirable investment.

For example: Consider this scenario:

- The total initial investment is $35,000.
- The predetermined criterion rate is 10%.
- Net cash inflows for each of the next three years are $15,000.

The IRR factor can then be calculated as shown:

$$\text{IRR factor} = \$35,000 \ / \ \$15,000 = 2.33$$

Refer to the Present Value of an Annuity Table in Appendix A to locate the IRR value.

In this example, IRR equals 13% (using the annuity table for three periods and interpolating to the nearest table value, 2.361).

Because the criterion cutoff rate (serving as the required rate of return) is 10% and the IRR value for the project is very close to 13%, the project is a desirable investment. If the desired rate of return had been 14%, the project should be rejected.

Uneven Cash Flows Example

For a project with uneven cash flow projections, the IRR calculation becomes trial and error and interpolation. Cash flows must be discounted at various rates until a rate is found that makes the PV equal to the initial investment.

In practice, computer spreadsheet programs and financial calculators make determining the IRRs of changing cash flows fairly easy. The next numerical example helps to illustrate the concepts behind the procedures.

For example: Consider this scenario:

- The total initial investment is $10,675.
- The criterion cutoff rate is 10%.
- The predicted annual net cash inflows over the life of the investment are $6,000, $4,000, and $3,000.

Refer to Figure 2E-14 and locate the appropriate values for the three periods.

Figure 2E-14 Partial Present Value Interest Factor Table

(*n*) Periods	10%	11%	12%
1	0.909	0.901	0.893
2	0.826	0.812	0.797
3	0.751	0.731	0.712
4	0.683	0.659	0.636
5	0.621	0.593	0.567
6	0.564	0.535	0.507
7	0.513	0.482	0.452
8	0.467	0.434	0.404
9	0.424	0.391	0.361
10	0.386	0.352	0.322

Figure 2E-15 shows how the cash flows are discounted using the PV interest factor table to determine the PV for each year.

Figure 2E-15 Total Present Value of Net Cash Inflows at 10%

Year	Cash Inflows		Discount Factor at 10%		Present Value
1	$6,000	×	0.909	=	$5,454
2	4,000	×	0.826	=	3,304
3	3,000	×	0.751	=	2,253
Total present value of net cash inflows					$11,011
Total initial investment (cash outflow)					(10,675)
Net present value					$ 336

The NPV for the three years is $336. A positive NPV means that the project is expected to yield a return higher than the one applied (in this case, 10%). Therefore, the next step is to use a higher rate. Figure 2E-16 computes the NPV at a discount rate of 12%. (Refer to the Present Value of $1 Table in Appendix A and locate the appropriate values for the three periods at 12%.)

Figure 2E-16 Total Present Value of Net Cash Inflows at 12%

Year	Cash Inflows		Discount Factor at 12%		Present Value
1	$6,000	×	0.893	=	$ 5,358
2	4,000	×	0.797	=	3,188
3	3,000	×	0.712	=	2,136
Total present value of net cash inflows					$10,682
Total initial investment (cash outflow)					(10,675)
Net present value					$ 7

At a 12% discount rate, the NPV is $7, which implies that the project is expected to yield slightly above 12%. Because the criterion cutoff rate is 10%, the project is acceptable. When NPV is negative, the rate of return is below the computed rate. As an example, Figure 2E-17 computes the NPV at a 14% discount rate. Therefore, the IRR of the project is between 12% and 14%, but much closer to 12%.

Figure 2E-17 Total Present Value of Net Cash Inflows at 14%

Year	Cash Inflows		Discount Factor at 14%		Present Value
1	$6,000	×	0.877	=	$ 5,262
2	4,000	×	0.769	=	3,076
3	3,000	×	0.7675	=	2,025
Total present value of net cash inflows					$10,363
Total initial investment (cash outflow)					(10,675)
Net present value					$ (312)

At a 12% discount rate, the PV for the net cash flows for the three years is $10,682, which is close to the total initial investment of $10,675. Because the criterion cutoff rate is 10%, the project should be accepted.

Comparison of NPV and IRR

The same basic assumptions of risk or uncertainty underlie both the NPV and IRR methods and are based on estimates, some of which are difficult to predict. The more accurate the estimates, the more accurate will be the NPV or IRR. The advantages of DCF methods are that both NPV and IRR consider:

- The time value of money.
- The initial cash investment.
- All cash flows after the initial investment.

A major difference is that the end result of NPV is a dollar figure whereas the final computation for IRR is a percentage. Thus, NPV has an advantage, because NPV values of individual projects can be added together to estimate the effect of accepting some possible combination of projects. Because IRR yields a percentage, multiple projects cannot be added or averaged to evaluate any combination of capital investment projects. In that case, choosing the combination of projects with the highest IRRs is preferable.

Another advantage of the NPV method is its usefulness in evaluating a project in which the required rate of return varies over the life of the project. The total PV of the cash inflows can be determined and compared with the total initial investment to evaluate the attractiveness of a project. Again, using the IRR method, it is not possible to infer if the project is unattractive. Different required returns for each year means that there is no single rate of return or a single IRR value that can be referenced. Different required returns for each year can result in a difference in ranking available capital budgeting projects.

NPV is also more reliable than IRR when there are several alternating periods of net cash inflows and net cash outflows, because it can lead to maximizing shareholder wealth.

Both methods have some reliability cautions:

- NPV is only as reliable as the discount rate that is selected. An unrealistic discount rate can result in an erroneous decision to accept or reject a project.
- A capital investment project should not be accepted solely on the basis of a high IRR value. A high IRR result must be looked at further to assess whether an opportunity to invest cash flows at such a high IRR is realistic.
- NPV and IRR have different reinvestment rate assumptions. NPV implicitly assumes that the firm can reinvest all cash inflows at the required rate of return. By contrast, IRR implicitly assumes that the firm can reinvest all cash inflows at the IRR. The reinvestment rate underlying NPV generally is considered to be the more appropriate assumption.

However, among the various methods available for analyzing capital investments, the DCF methods are theoretically the most reliable. The NPV and IRR methods typically yield similar results as long as there are no differences in:

- Project size (the amount of the initial investment);
- Net cash flow pattern;
- Life of the project; or
- Cost of capital over the life of the project.

If any of the cash flows in the analysis, other than the initial investment, are negative, the IRR will yield multiple answers, which will all be correct and absurd. In such situations, only NPV should be used.

Knowledge Check:
Discounted Cash Flow Analysis

The next questions are intended to help you check your understanding and recall of the material presented in this topic. They do not represent the type of questions that appear on the CMA exam.

Directions: Answer each question in the space provided. Correct answers and section references appear after the knowledge check questions.

Match each term with its application.

1. _____ Present value	**a.** Proportional average of the various capital components a firm uses for financing
2. _____ Net present value	**b.** Estimates the discount rate that makes the present value of net cash inflows equal to the initial investment
3. _____ Internal rate of return	**c.** The amount in dollars today that an investment earns after yielding the desired rate of return for each period during the life of the investment
4. _____ Required rate of return	**d.** Minimum future receipts an investor will accept in choosing an investment
5. _____ Weighted average cost of capital	**e.** The equivalent dollar value today of future net cash inflows

6. What is the importance of the criterion rate in internal rate of return calculations?

☐ **a.** Projects below this rate are rejected.

☐ **b.** Projects above this rate are rejected.

☐ **c.** The rate is used to find the discount rate in a present value annuity table.

☐ **d.** The rate is used to find the discount rate in a present value interest factor table.

Knowledge Check Answers:
Discounted Cash Flow Analysis

Match each term with its application.

1. __e__ Present value	a. Proportional average of the various capital components a firm uses for financing
2. __c__ Net present value	b. Estimates the discount rate that makes the present value of net cash inflows equal to the initial investment
3. __b__ Internal rate of return	c. The amount in dollars today that an investment earns after yielding the desired rate of return for each period during the life of the investment
4. __d__ Required rate of return	d. Minimum future receipts an investor will accept in choosing an investment
5. __a__ Weighted average cost of capital	e. The equivalent dollar value today of future net cash inflows

6. What is the importance of the criterion rate in internal rate of return calculations? **[See *Internal Rate of Return Calculation*.]**

   ☑ **a.** Projects below this rate are rejected.

   ☐ **b.** Projects above this rate are rejected.

   ☐ **c.** The rate is used to find the discount rate in a present value annuity table.

   ☐ **d.** The rate is used to find the discount rate in a present value interest factor table.

Payback and Discounted Payback

THE PAYBACK METHOD IN CAPITAL BUDGETING DETERMINES THE number of years needed to recoup the net initial investment in a capital budgeting project. In other words, the payback represents the break-even point for the investment. The payback method also can incorporate discounted cash flows to evaluate an investment. This method is referred to as the discounted payback method.

READ the Learning Outcome Statements (LOS) for this topic as found in Appendix B and then study the concepts and calculations presented here to be sure you understand the content you could be tested on in the CMA exam.

Uses of the Payback Method

Similar to the net present value (NPV) and internal rate of return (IRR) techniques, the payback period (PP) does not distinguish between types of cash inflows (whether the cash inflow is the result of operations, the disposal of a piece of equipment, the restoration of working capital, etc.). As a simple measure of cash inflows, the PP also can be used to evaluate capital investments having uniform net cash flows or uneven cash flows.

Uniform Net Cash Flows Example

The next calculation determines the payback period of a capital investment assuming uniform cash flows are expected:

$$\text{Payback Period} = \frac{\text{Total Initial Investment}}{\text{Expected Annual Net Cash Flow}}$$

For example: Consider this scenario:

- The total initial investment is $600,000.
- The expected annual net cash flow is $175,000.

In this case, the calculation would be:

$$\text{Payback Period} = \frac{\$600,000}{\$175,000} = 3.43 \text{ Years}$$

Uneven Cash Flows Example

In situations in which the annual cash inflows are uneven, determining payback becomes a cumulative calculation. The net cash inflows are accumulated until the initial investment is recovered. Straight-line interpolation is used if the payback amount falls within a year.

The formula for the payback period is:

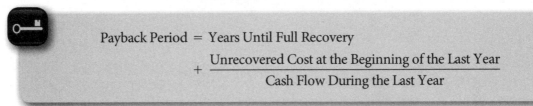

$$\text{Payback Period} = \text{Years Until Full Recovery}$$
$$+ \frac{\text{Unrecovered Cost at the Beginning of the Last Year}}{\text{Cash Flow During the Last Year}}$$

For example: Consider this scenario:

- The total initial investment is $30,000.
- The predicted annual net cash inflows over the life of the investment are $10,000, $12,000, $16,000, and $14,000.

Figure 2E-18 shows the figures.

Figure 2E-18 Payback and Uneven Cash Flows

Year	Net Cash Flow	Cumulative Net Cash Flow
0	− $30,000	− $30,000
1	10,000	− 20,000
2	12,000	− 8,000
3	16,000	8,000
4	14,000	22,000

After two years, the project requires another $8,000 to pay for itself. In year 3, the project is expected to generate $16,000 in net cash inflows. This means that for this investment, payback will occur sometime between year 2 and year 3. The project needs $8,000 more after year 2 to recover its initial investment. Therefore, dividing the unrecovered cost at the beginning of the last year by the cash flow during the last year ($8,000 / $16,000) results in 0.5 years yielding a total payback period for the project of 2.5 years.

$$\text{Payback Period} = 2 + \frac{\$8,000}{\$16,000} = 2.5 \text{ Years}$$

Payback Method Interpretation

When using the payback method, firms typically choose a target payback period (or maximum cutoff period) for a project. The target payback period represents what the firm considers to be the maximum acceptable length of time for a project. Projects with a payback shorter than the target payback period are accepted; those with a payback longer than the target payback period are rejected. In the previous example, if the firm had set the maximum acceptable target payback for the $30,000 investment as 3 years, the investment should be accepted because the actual payback is achieved in 2.5 years.

Typically, the higher the risk of a project, the shorter the target payback period should be because it is desirable to recover riskier investments more quickly. When comparing two or more investment projects, those with shorter payback periods are generally preferable.

Advantages and Disadvantages of the Payback Method

The payback method has distinct advantages and disadvantages as listed in Figure 2E-19.

Figure 2E-19 Advantages and Disadvantages of the Payback Method

Advantages	Disadvantages
Uses a simple calculation	Ignores the time value of money; adds cash flows without regard to timing
Produces results that are easy to understand	Ignores cash flows occurring after the payback period
Provides a rough measure of liquidity and risk	Provides no measure of profitability
	Promotes the acceptance of short-term projects if the target payback period is too short

In some situations, the quick measures of liquidity and risk are beneficial to indicate the risk of losing a capital investment in a high-risk situation. In a rough sense, projects with shorter payback periods are less risky. Projects with shorter paybacks also tend to provide an organization with greater flexibility because the investment funds become available sooner for other projects.

Because of its basic limitations, the payback method can provide only a partial picture of whether an investment is worthwhile. Therefore, it is best used in conjunction with other capital budgeting techniques.

Discounted Payback

The **discounted payback method** addresses one of the shortfalls of the payback period calculation, namely, ignoring the time value of money. Discounted payback uses the PVs of net cash inflows rather than the undiscounted dollar amounts of net cash inflows to determine a payback period.

Similar to the NPV method, the PVs of net cash inflows are estimated using the firm's desired rate of return. The time period necessary for the cumulative NPVs of net cash flows to equal the initial project investment is the present value payback period.

Figure 2E-20 Discounted Payback and Even Net Cash Flow

Year	Net Cash Inflows		Discount Factor at 10%		Present Value of Net Cash Flows	Cumulative Present Value of Net Cash Flows
0	− $16,000		0		− $16,000	− $16,000
1	6,000	×	0.909	=	5,454	− 10,546
2	6,000	×	0.826	=	4,956	− 5,590
3	6,000	×	0.751	=	4,506	− 1,084
4	6,000	×	0.683	=	4,098	3,014

The project will recover its initial investment between year 3 and year 4. The amount needed in year 4 to reach PV payback is $1,084. The discounted payback period is then determined as:

$$\text{Discounted Payback} = 3 + \frac{\$1,084}{\$4,098} = 3.27 \text{ Years}$$

This is in contrast to the simple payback method:

$$\text{Payback Period} = \frac{\$16,000}{\$6,000} = 2.67 \text{ Years}$$

The payback method gives a different answer from the discounted payback calculation because it does not discount cash flows.

Knowledge Check:
Payback and Discounted Payback

The next questions are intended to help you check your understanding and recall of the material presented in this topic. They do not represent the type of questions that appear on the CMA exam.

Directions: Answer each question in the space provided. Correct answers and section references appear after the knowledge check questions.

1. Which of the following statements about using the payback method in capital budgeting is **false**?

    The payback method:

    ☐ **a.** represents the break-even point for an investment.

    ☐ **b.** provides a rough measure of project liquidity.

    ☐ **c.** takes into account the time value of money.

    ☐ **d.** provides a rough measure of project risk.

2. What is the payback period for a capital budgeting project in which the total initial capital investment is $900,000 and the expected annual net cash flow is $150,000?

    ☐ **a.** 3 years

    ☐ **b.** 5 years

    ☐ **c.** 6 years

    ☐ **d.** 7 years

3. Which of the following statements accurately compares the discounted payback and payback methods?

    ☐ **a.** Both methods provide simple measures of project profitability.

    ☐ **b.** Discounted payback uses the present values of net cash inflows; payback does not.

    ☐ **c.** Discounted payback ignores cash flows after the payback period expiration; payback does not.

    ☐ **d.** Both methods distinguish between types of cash inflows.

Knowledge Check Answers: Payback and Discounted Payback

1. Which of the following statements about using the payback method in capital budgeting is **false**?

   The payback method: [See *Advantages and Disadvantages of the Payback Method.*]

   ☐ **a.** represents the break-even point for an investment.

   ☐ **b.** provides a rough measure of project liquidity.

   ☑ **c.** takes into account the time value of money.

   ☐ **d.** provides a rough measure of project risk.

2. What is the payback period for a capital budgeting project in which the total initial capital investment is $900,000 and the expected annual net cash flow is $150,000? [See *Payback Method Interpretation.*]

   ☐ **a.** 3 years

   ☐ **b.** 5 years

   ☑ **c.** 6 years

   ☐ **d.** 7 years

3. Which of the following statements accurately compares the discounted payback and payback methods? [See *Discounted Payback.*]

   ☐ **a.** Both methods provide simple measures of project profitability.

   ☑ **b.** Discounted payback uses the present values of net cash inflows; payback does not.

   ☐ **c.** Discounted payback ignores cash flows after the payback period expiration; payback does not.

   ☐ **d.** Both methods distinguish between types of cash inflows.

Risk Analysis in Capital Investment

BY DEFINITION, RISK IMPLIES UNCERTAINTY AND INSTABILITY. In several areas of Section B: Corporate Finance, risk was discussed extensively as it relates to long-term financial management. In capital budgeting, risk has different implications.

Fundamentally, there are no risk-free capital investments. Consider just a few reasons why that is true:

- Future cash inflows can vary unexpectedly throughout the life of a project.
- The rate of return used in calculations may not be accurate for the life of the project.
- The cost of financing may increase during the life of a project.
- New mandatory regulatory factors can require additional investments at any given point in time.
- The life of the related product or service could be significantly shorter or longer than anticipated.
- Inflationary or recessionary economic conditions may impact the value of cash flows.
- Domestic or global political events may impact project cash flows or the viability of the project as a whole.

Because of all these types of risk associated with capital budgeting, selecting capital investment projects is always a challenge. This topic looks at some of the ways to minimize the uncertainty using various techniques, such as sensitivity analysis, certainty equivalents, the capital asset pricing model, simulations, and specifically adjusted rates.

 READ the Learning Outcome Statements (LOS) for this topic as found in Appendix B and then study the concepts and calculations presented here to be sure you understand the content you could be tested on in the CMA exam.

Sensitivity Analysis

Sensitivity analysis, as it pertains to capital investments, is a what-if technique evaluating how net present value (NPV), internal rate of return (IRR), and other indicators of the profitability of a project change if the discount rate, labor or materials costs, sales, or some other factor varies from one case to another. The purpose is to assess how sensitive the NPV, the IRR, or another specified profitability measure is to a change.

Sensitivity analysis can be used to answer questions such as these:

- What happens to NPV if cash flow increases or decreases by 10% for each year of the project?
- Will NPV remain positive throughout a project if there is no cash inflow in the second year of a three-year project?
- What will happen to NPV if the discount rate increases from 8% to 10% or decreases from 8% to 7%?
- What would happen to the NPV if a major redesign of the product, requiring additional capital investments, is necessary in year 3 in order to address competitive new products?
- What would be the impact on NPV if the project is extended for three years, with decreasing cash flows and increased maintenance costs in the extended years?

To further understand how sensitivity analysis can be used to answer such what-ifs, consider the next scenario.

- Annual net cash inflows over the life of investment A are $2,000 in Y1 and $3,000 in Y2.
- Annual net cash inflows over the life of investment B are $3,600 in Y1 and $1,400 in Y2.
- The total initial investment for each project is $3,200.

Given this information, what happens to each project if the discount rate changes from 10% to 12%? Refer to Figure 2E-21.

Figure 2E-21 Changes in Discount Rate

		Project A at 10%		
Year	Cash Inflows		Discount Factor at 10%		PV
1	$2,000.00	×	0.909	=	$1,818.00
2	3,000.00	×	0.826	=	2,478.00
Total PV of net cash flows					4,296.00
Less initial investment					(3,200.00)
NPV					$1,096.00

Project A at 12%

Year	Cash Inflows		Discount Factor at 10%		PV
1	$2,000.00	×	0.893	=	$1,786.00
2	3,000.00	×	0.797	=	2,391.00
Total PV of net cash flows					4,177.00
Less initial investment					(3,200.00)
NPV					$977.00

Project B at 10%

Year	Cash Inflows		Discount Factor at 10%		PV
1	$3,600.00	×	0.909	=	$3,272.40
2	1,400.00	×	0.826	=	1,156.40
Total PV of net cash flows					4,428.80
Less initial investment					(3,200.00)
NPV					$1,228.80

Project B at 12%

Year	Cash Inflows		Discount Factor at 10%		PV
1	$3,600.00	×	0.893	=	$3,214.80
2	1,400.00	×	0.797	=	1,115.80
Total PV of net cash flows					4,330.60
Less initial investment					(3,200.00)
NPV					$1,130.60

Comparison of Projects A and B

Project	NPV at 10%	NPV at 12%	Dollar Change	NPV % Change
A	$1,096.00	$977.00	($119.00)	–10.86%
B	$1,228.80	$1,130.60	($98.20)	–7.99%

The NPV of each project declines when the discount rate increases from 10% to 12%. The percentage change in the NPV for project A is –10.9%, whereas the change for project B is –8.0%. Thus, project A is more sensitive to changes in the discount rate than project B and poses a higher risk if the discount rate changes. Other changes, such as increasing cash inflows, receiving cash inflows earlier, decreasing cash outflows, and paying cash outflows later, will mathematically increase NPV for a project.

Conversely, the opposites—decreasing cash inflows, receiving cash inflows later, increasing cash outflows, and paying cash outflows earlier—effectively decrease NPV.

Consider how the quality of the sensitivity analysis becomes a value-adding feature of the project. If company managers see that a project has been planned carefully so as to accommodate variances in discount rates, cash flows, and the like, they will be encouraged to support the project knowing that it has been designed or scaled to accommodate these and other potential challenges. Likewise, investors will have more confidence in a company that has a demonstrated capability of project planning and budgeting. This confidence will result in a higher sustained price for the company's stock even when the inevitable project challenges occur.

Another type of sensitivity analysis is real options valuation (ROV). ROV is in direct contrast to discounted cash flow (DCF) analysis such as NPV and IRR, although the computations often involve these techniques in providing inputs of the model. When using DCF analysis, the most likely outcomes are modeled and management flexibility is ignored, implicitly assuming that management is passive with regard to the capital project once it is committed. The uncertainty in DCF techniques is accounted for by adjusting the discount rate. By contrast, ROV assumes that management can actively modify the project throughout its life by responding to each outcome (in other words, options are exercised), and the possibility of a large negative outcome is reduced or eliminated. The ROV value of a project typically is higher than in NPV. The model itself parallels financial options in that there is a strike price, options (such as option to contract, option to abandon, and option to expand), and option terms, which are more fully explained throughout Section B.

Simulations

Simulations allow testing of a capital investment project before it is accepted. Because the actual future values for cash flows and discount rates for investment projects are not known, hypothetical cash flows and discount rates are assumed and can be studied using a simulation model.

In capital budgeting, simulations can be used to approximate:

- Expected NPV, IRR, and profitability index (PI).
- Dispersion about an expected value.

When attempting to evaluate more than one risky investment, the NPV or IRR for each project can be simulated several times and average NPVs, IRRs, and standard deviations can be computed and ranked. Repeating the process many times also allows values to be plotted on a frequency distribution graph to show the distribution of the NPVs and IRRs. The distribution curves enable one to make a reasonable assessment of the risk level of a project.

Many simulation software programs are available. These programs are useful because they can create many more scenarios than can be done by hand. Some of these programs also can draw graphs of the results. One of the best-known computer simulation models in capital budgeting is the Monte Carlo simulation tool, which uses repeated random sampling and computational algorithms to calculate a range of most likely outcomes for the project.

Scenario Analysis

The scenario approach to evaluating risk uses single-point estimates where each possibility is assigned a best-guess estimate. Scenarios (such as best, worst, or most likely case) for each input variable are chosen, and the results are reported. For example, a comparison of a spreadsheet cost construction model is prepared using traditional what-if scenarios. By contrast, Monte Carlo simulations sample probability distribution for each variable to produce hundreds or thousands of possible outcomes, and the results are analyzed to get probabilities of different outcomes occurring.

Monte Carlo Analysis

Monte Carlo analysis is based on the use of computational algorithms that rely on random sampling in order to compute results. The Monte Carlo method uses computerized simulations which are a class of computational algorithms that rely on repeated random sampling to compute their results. Monte Carlo methods often are used in simulating physical and mathematical systems. These methods are most suited to calculation by a computer when it is not feasible to compute an exact result with a deterministic algorithm, such as to model phenomena with significant uncertainty in inputs (as in the calculation of risk in business).

Certainty Equivalents

The **certainty equivalent (CE)** approach to selecting projects attempts to separate the timing of cash flows from their risk. The expected cash flow is converted into an amount that has a higher probability of actually materializing. In other words, a CE factor is used to convert a projected cash flow into a certain cash flow. These cash flows are then discounted at a risk-free rate (such as the rate for a U.S. Treasury bill). In practice, only a small percentage of firms report using the CE approach.

In other words, if a firm has an expected cash flow of $15,000 in year 5 of an investment and the forecaster thinks that an 80% yield (or $12,000) of that expected cash flow is realistic, that amount is then discounted at the risk-free rate.

Six steps are used to determine CEs:

1. Project the expected cash flows of the investment.
2. Identify the CE factors, or the percentages of the expected cash flows that are certain.
3. Multiply the expected cash flows by the CE factors to determine the certain cash flows.
4. Calculate the PV of the project by discounting the certain cash flows at a specified risk-free discount rate.
5. Calculate the NPV of the project by subtracting the initial investment from the PV of the certain cash flows.

6. Evaluate the NPV of the project; a zero or positive value is acceptable, and a negative value should be rejected.

To better understand how CEs are applied, consider the next scenario:

- Annual net cash inflows over the life of a five-year investment are $10,000, $8,000, $7,000, $6,000, and $5,000.
- CE factors are estimated over the life of the investment at 90%, 85%, 70%, 60%, and 45%.
- The total initial investment for the project is $18,000.
- The risk-free rate of return is 3%.

Given this information and applying the CE approach, an evaluation of what the project looks like is shown in Figure 2E-22.

Figure 2E-22 Project Evaluation and Certainty Equivalent Factors

Year	Expected Cash Inflows		Certainty Equivalent Factor		Certain Cash Flow
1	10,000.00	×	0.900	=	$9,000.00
2	8,000.00	×	0.850	=	6,800.00
3	7,000.00	×	0.700	=	4,900.00
4	6,000.00	×	0.600	=	3,600.00
5	5,000.00	×	0.450	=	2,250.00

Year	Certain Cash Inflows		Discount Factor at 3%		Present Value of Certain Cash Flow
1	$9,000.00	×	0.971	=	$8,739.00
2	6,800.00	×	0.943	=	6,412.40
3	4,900.00	×	0.915	=	4,483.50
4	3,600.00	×	0.888	=	3,196.80
5	2,250.00	×	0.863	=	1,941.75
Total PV of net cash inflows					$24,773.45
Less initial investment					(18,000.00)
NPV					$6,773.45

The positive NPV value indicates that the project is acceptable.

Capital Asset Pricing Model

The capital asset pricing model (CAPM) was discussed in Section B: Corporate Finance, as it relates to finding the required rate of return on a stock or portfolio. The CAPM also has application in capital budgeting. The formula for the CAPM in capital budgeting is:

$$E(R)_a = R_f + \beta\,[E(R_m) - R_f]$$

where:

$E(R_a)$ = required rate of return on an asset (project) being evaluated

R_f = risk-free rate

β_a = beta of an asset (project)

$E(R_m)$ = return on a market portfolio

The premise behind using the CAPM in capital budgeting is treating a project in the same manner as a share of stock. The rationale is that the return from a project is linked to the return on the firm's total assets or to the return in an industry, just as a stock or market portfolio. With this assumption, the beta of the company is used as the beta for the project. In the event a project is not a typical investment for a company, an average industry beta can be substituted. Comparing betas among similar companies in similar industries is called the pure play approach.

Once the project's required rate of return is identified, NPV can be calculated. Expected cash flows are discounted using the required rate of return, and the total NPV of cash flows is subtracted from the total initial project investment. A zero or positive NPV means that the project can be accepted as it will preserve the required rate of return.

If multiple projects are being evaluated, the one with the higher beta is considered more risky.

Use of Specifically Adjusted Rates

Under most circumstances, risky capital projects are less desirable than safe investments. Firms typically demand a higher rate of return for riskier projects, or they use conservative estimates for cash flows.

Many firms use their company cost of capital as the yardstick to discount cash flows on all new investments. In situations where new projects are more or less risky than is normal for the firm, using the company rate can create problems.

The firm's cost of capital is an appropriate discount rate when capital projects have the same average risk as the firm's existing business. However, care and discretion must be used in determining what exactly constitutes similar risk.

Using the firm's cost of capital rate arbitrarily for all new projects can lead to accepting or rejecting a project regardless of its risk only because it offers a higher rate of return than the company's cost of capital. The problem is twofold:

1. Good low-risk projects may be rejected.
2. Poor high-risk projects may be accepted.

When in doubt, analysts should assess the relative risks of projects on an individual basis and use a new rate specifically adjusted for the project risk. By doing this, every project has its own opportunity cost of capital.

Qualitative Considerations in Capital Investments

There are a variety of quantitative methods available for evaluating capital budgeting projects. Most of the techniques discussed have distinct strengths and weaknesses. As a result, managers should, and often do, use multiple criteria for evaluating investment projects. Collectively, multiple methods mitigate the potential for estimation errors and/or incorrect decisions that are not in the best interests of the firm or shareholders.

In addition to quantitative methods, a firm also should recognize these important qualitative factors that can influence investment decisions:

- Management may not have the necessary information to make capital budgeting decisions (e.g., type of information or frequency).
- Loan provisions may limit borrowing.
- The firm may have self-imposed capital rationing limits.
- Decision makers may be risk averse.
- Conflict may exist between decisions to take on a project and performance evaluation of managers (e.g., a manager might be concerned about how a project will affect a bonus plan based on reported annual accrual accounting numbers).
- A firm may not have sufficient or qualified personnel to implement capital projects successfully.
- Management may assess whether the investment can increase customer loyalty and retention.

Capital investments often are strategic in nature and are based partly on qualitative factors that are important to consider but difficult to estimate.

Knowledge Check:
Risk Analysis in Capital Investment

The next questions are intended to help you check your understanding and recall of the material presented in this topic. They do not represent the type of questions that appear on the CMA exam.

Directions: Answer each question in the space provided. Correct answers and section references appear after the knowledge check questions.

For questions 1 through 4, match the different approaches to dealing with risk with the appropriate description.

1. _____ Sensitivity analysis	**a.** The use of a hypothetical situation (similar to the real one) to help make a decision
2. _____ Certainty equivalent approach	
	b. A measure of the extent to which one factor varies when another factor changes
3. _____ Capital asset pricing model	
	c. The conversion of projected cash flows into an amount that has a higher probability of actually materializing
4. _____ Simulations	
	d. The use of a firm's beta or an industry beta in an assessment of project risk

5. Which method is **best** suited to comparing the net present values for two capital investment projects when the cash flows vary?

☐ **a.** Sensitivity analysis

☐ **b.** Certainty equivalent approach

☐ **c.** Capital asset pricing model

☐ **d.** Computer simulation

Knowledge Check Answers: Risk Analysis in Capital Investment

For questions 1 through 4, match the different approaches to dealing with risk with the appropriate description.

1. __b__ Sensitivity analysis	a. The use of a hypothetical situation (similar to the real one) to help make a decision
2. __c__ Certainty equivalent approach	b. A measure of the extent to which one factor varies when another factor changes
3. __d__ Capital asset pricing model	c. The conversion of projected cash flows into an amount that has a higher probability of actually materializing
4. __a__ Simulations	d. The use of a firm's beta or an industry beta in an assessment of project risk

5. Which method is **best** suited to comparing the net present values for two capital investment projects when the cash flows vary? [**See Sensitivity Analysis.**]

☑ **a.** Sensitivity analysis

☐ **b.** Certainty equivalent approach

☐ **c.** Capital asset pricing model

☐ **d.** Computer simulation

Directions: This sampling of questions is designed to emulate actual exam questions. Read each question and write your response on another sheet of paper. See the "Answers to Section Practice Questions" section at the end of this book to assess your response. Validate or improve the answer you wrote. For a more robust selection of practice questions, access the **Online Test Bank** at www.wiley.cma.com.

Question 2E1-AT06

Topic: Capital Budgeting Process

In order to increase production capacity, Gunning Industries is considering replacing an existing production machine with a new technologically improved machine effective January 1. This information is being considered:

- The new machine would be purchased for $160,000 in cash. Shipping, installation, and testing would cost an additional $30,000.
- The new machine is expected to increase annual sales by 20,000 units at a sales price of $40 per unit. Incremental operating costs are comprised of $30 per unit in variable costs and total fixed costs of $40,000 per year.
- The investment in the new machine will require an immediate increase in working capital of $35,000.
- Gunning uses straight-line depreciation for financial reporting and tax reporting purposes. The new machine has an estimated useful life of five years and zero salvage value.
- Gunning is subject to a 40% corporate income tax rate.

Gunning uses the net present value method to analyze investments and will employ these factors and rates:

Period	Present Value of $1 at 10%	Present Value of an Ordinary Annuity of $1 at 10%
1	0.909	0.909
2	0.826	1.736
3	0.751	2.487
4	0.683	3.170
5	0.621	3.791

Gunning Industries' initial net cash outflow in a capital budgeting decision would be

- ☐ **a.** $160,000.
- ☐ **b.** $190,000.
- ☐ **c.** $225,000.
- ☐ **d.** $195,000.

Question 2E1-AT07

Topic: Capital Budgeting Process

In order to increase production capacity, Gunning Industries is considering replacing an existing production machine with a new technologically improved machine effective January 1. Gunning Industries is considering this information:

- The new machine would be purchased for $160,000 in cash. Shipping, installation, and testing would cost an additional $30,000.
- The new machine is expected to increase annual sales by 20,000 units at a sales price of $40 per unit. Incremental operating costs are comprised of $30 per unit in variable costs and total fixed costs of $40,000 per year.
- The investment in the new machine will require an immediate increase in working capital of $35,000.
- Gunning uses straight-line depreciation for financial reporting and tax reporting purposes. The new machine has an estimated useful life of five years and zero salvage value.
- Gunning is subject to a 40% corporate income tax rate.

Gunning uses the net present value method to analyze investments and will employ these factors and rates:

Period	Present Value of $1 at 10%	Present Value of an Ordinary Annuity of $1 at 10%
1	0.909	0.909
2	0.826	1.736
3	0.751	2.487
4	0.683	3.170
5	0.621	3.791

Gunning Industries' discounted annual depreciation tax shield for the first year of operation would be:

- ☐ **a.** $13,817.
- ☐ **b.** $15,200.
- ☐ **c.** $20,725.
- ☐ **d.** $22,800.

Question 2E1-AT08

Topic: Capital Budgeting Process

Which one of the following is **most** relevant to a manufacturing equipment replacement decision?

- ☐ **a.** Gain or loss on the disposal of the old equipment
- ☐ **b.** Original cost less depreciation of the old equipment

□ **c.** A lump-sum write-off amount from the disposal of the old equipment

□ **d.** Disposal price of the old equipment

Question 2E2-CQ01

Topic: Discounted Cash Flow Analysis

Calvin Inc. is considering the purchase of a new state-of-art machine to replace its hand-operated machine. Calvin's effective tax rate is 40%, and its cost of capital is 12%. Data regarding the existing and new machines are presented next.

	Existing Machine	New Machine
Original cost	$50,000	$90,000
Installation costs	0	4,000
Freight and insurance	0	6,000
Expected end salvage value	0	0
Depreciation method	straight line	straight line
Expected useful life	10 years	5 years

The existing machine has been in service for seven years and could be sold currently for $25,000. Calvin expects to realize a before-tax annual reduction in labor costs of $30,000 if the new machine is purchased and placed in service.

If the new machine is purchased, the cash flows for the fifth year would amount to

□ **a.** $18,000.

□ **b.** $24,000.

□ **c.** $26,000.

□ **d.** $30,000.

Question 2E2-CQ11

Topic: Discounted Cash Flow Analysis

For each of the next six years, Atlantic Motors anticipates net income of $10,000, straight-line tax depreciation of $20,000, a 40% tax rate, a discount rate of 10%, and cash sales of $100,000. The depreciable assets are all being acquired at the beginning of year 1 and will have a salvage value of zero at the end of six years.

The present value (PV) of the total depreciation tax savings would be:

□ **a.** $8,000.

□ **b.** $27,072.

□ **c.** $34,840.

□ **d.** $87,100.

Question 2E2-CQ14

Topic: Discounted Cash Flow Analysis

Fuller Industries is considering a $1 million investment in stamping equipment to produce a new product. The equipment is expected to last nine years, produce revenue of $700,000 per year, and have related cash expenses of $450,000 per year. At the end of the ninth year, the equipment is expected to have a salvage value of $100,000 and cost $50,000 to remove. The Internal Revenue Service categorizes this as 5-year Modified Accelerated Cost Recovery System (MACRS) property subject to the next depreciation rates.

Year	Rate
1	20.00%
2	32.00%
3	19.20%
4	11.52%
5	11.52%
6	5.76%

Fuller's effective income tax rate is 40% and Fuller expects, on an overall company basis, to continue to be profitable and have significant taxable income. If Fuller uses the net present value method to analyze investments, what is the expected net tax impact on cash flow in year 2 before discounting?

- ☐ **a.** Positive $28,000 impact
- ☐ **b.** $0 impact
- ☐ **c.** Negative $100,000 impact
- ☐ **d.** Negative $128,000 impact

Question 2E2-CQ16

Topic: Discounted Cash Flow Analysis

AGC Company is considering an equipment upgrade. AGC uses discounted cash flow (DCF) analysis in evaluating capital investments and has an effective tax rate of 40%. Selected data developed by AGC are shown next.

	Existing Equipment	New Equipment
Original cost	$50,000	$95,000
Accumulated depreciation	45,000	–
Current market value	3,000	95,000
Accounts receivable	6,000	8,000
Accounts payable	2,100	2,500

Based on this information, what is the initial investment for a DCF analysis of this proposed upgrade?

- ☐ **a.** $92,400
- ☐ **b.** $92,800
- ☐ **c.** $95,800
- ☐ **d.** $96,200

Question 2E3-CQ01

Topic: Payback and Discounted Payback

Hobart Corporation evaluates capital projects using a variety of performance screens, including a hurdle rate of 16%, payback period of 3 years or less, and an accounting rate of return of 20% or more. Management is completing review of a project on the basis of these projections:

Capital investment	$200,000
Annual cash flows	$74,000
Straight-line depreciation	5 years
Terminal value	$20,000

The projected internal rate of return is 20%. Which one of the following alternatives reflects the appropriate conclusions for the indicated evaluative measures?

	Internal Rate of Return	Payback
a.	Accept	Reject
b.	Reject	Reject
c.	Accept	Accept
d.	Reject	Accept

Question 2E3-CQ02

Topic: Payback and Discounted Payback

Quint Company uses the payback method as part of its analysis of capital investments. One of its projects requires a $140,000 investment and has these projected before-tax cash flows:

Year 1	$60,000
Year 2	60,000
Year 3	60,000
Year 4	80,000
Year 5	80,000

Quint has an effective 40% tax rate. Based on these data, the after-tax payback period is

☐ **a.** 1.5.

☐ **b.** 2.3.

☐ **c.** 3.4.

☐ **d.** 3.7.

Question 2E3-CQ03

Topic: Payback and Discounted Payback

Foster Manufacturing is analyzing a capital investment project that is forecasted to produce the following cash flows and net income.

Year	After-Tax Cash Flow	Net Income
0	($20,000)	$ 0
1	6,000	2,000
2	6,000	2,000
3	8,000	2,000
4	8,000	2,000

The payback period of this project will be

☐ **a.** 2.5 years.

☐ **b.** 2.6 years.

☐ **c.** 3.0 years.

☐ **d.** 3.3 years.

Question 2E3-LS02

Topic: Payback and Discounted Payback

Which of the following statements is not true of using the payback method in capital budgeting? The payback method

☐ **a.** provides a rough measure of project risk.

☐ **b.** takes into account the time value of money.

☐ **c.** does not distinguish between types of cash inflows.

☐ **d.** represents the break-even point for an investment.

Question 2E4-CQ01

Topic: Risk Analysis in Capital Investment

Long Inc. is analyzing a $1 million investment in new equipment to produce a product with a $5 per unit margin. The equipment will last 5 years, be depreciated on a straight-line basis for tax purposes, and have no value at the end of its life. A study of unit sales produced these data:

Annual Unit Sales	Probability
80,000	0.10
85,000	0.20
90,000	0.30
95,000	0.20
100,000	0.10
110,000	0.10

If Long utilizes a 12% hurdle rate and is subject to a 40% effective income tax rate, the expected net present value of the project would be

- ☐ **a.** $261,750.
- ☐ **b.** $283,380.
- ☐ **c.** $297,800.
- ☐ **d.** $427,580.

Question 2E4-CQ02

Topic: Risk Analysis in Capital Investment

Parker Industries is analyzing a $200,000 equipment investment to produce a new product for the next 5 years. A study of expected annual after-tax cash flows from the project produced these data:

Annual After-Tax Cash Flow	Probability
$45,000	0.10
50,000	0.20
55,000	0.30
60,000	0.20
65,000	0.10
70,000	0.10

If Parker utilizes a 14% hurdle rate, the probability of achieving a positive net present value is

- ☐ **a.** 20%.
- ☐ **b.** 30%.
- ☐ **c.** 40%.
- ☐ **d.** 60%.

Question 2E4-LS03

Topic: Risk Analysis in Capital Investment

What is a primary caution when using a company's cost of capital as the discount rate to evaluate a capital project?

- ☐ **a.** Evaluation typically rejects high-risk projects.
- ☐ **b.** The cost of capital may need to be risk adjusted.
- ☐ **c.** Low-risk projects are favored.
- ☐ **d.** Opportunity costs can be distorted.

Question 2E4-LS04

Topic: Risk Analysis in Capital Investment

Which type of real option would a firm be **most** likely to choose if there is a high probability that competitors can enter a market and capture profitable future cash flows?

- ☐ **a.** Adapt
- ☐ **b.** Abandon
- ☐ **c.** Postpone
- ☐ **d.** Expand

To further assess your understanding of the concepts and calculations covered in Part 2, Section E: Investment Decisions, practice with the **Online Test Bank** for this section. **REMINDER:** See the "Answers to Section Practice Questions" section at the end of this book.

Professional Ethics

This section covers ethics for both management accountants and financial managers as well as organizations. Management accountants and financial managers confront unique ethical challenges arising from their particular organizational responsibilities. To help accountants in these roles assess the specific ethical demands of their situations, the Institute of Management Accountants has developed the *IMA Statement of Ethical Professional Practice*. This statement, which is available from IMA's Web site in Statement on Management Accounting and is reproduced here, is the basis for this section.

The Institute of Management Accountants' Statement on Management Accounting (SMA) *Values and Ethics: From Inception to Practice* addresses the needs and rewards for organizations that take a proactive stance in creating and maintaining an ethical culture. The SMA states: "All accounting professionals [should be] aware of their responsibility to act as change agents within their organizations, supporting the maintenance of effective controls and ensuring that their organizations have considered, adopted, and fully implemented a company-wide ethics and compliance program, including a code of ethics and a confidential hot/helpline." This SMA, which appears on IMA's Web site, is the basis of this section of the CMA exam.

There are five primary categories for management to focus on in order to effectively maintain the desired ethical atmosphere:

1. Defining values
2. Leadership by example
3. Ethics and internal controls
4. Practical application
5. Measuring and improving ethical compliance

In addition, no company operates in a vacuum. Therefore, it is essential to understand the difference between acts that are legal and those that are ethical.

Note to students: The Ethics section of the CMA exam addresses the subject from the perspective of individual behavior and in particular how individuals use the *IMA Statement of Ethical Professional Practice*. It also addresses the subject from the perspective of the organization. Students should be aware of and focused on the different perspectives being covered. Be sure to carefully review the Learning Outcome Statements related to ethics.

IMA Statement of Ethical Professional Practice

Members of IMA shall behave ethically. A commitment to ethical professional practice includes overarching principles that express our values, and standards that guide our conduct.

Principles

IMA's overarching ethical principles include: Honesty, Fairness, Objectivity, and Responsibility. Members shall act in accordance with these principles and shall encourage others within their organizations to adhere to them.

Standards

A member's failure to comply with the following standards may result in disciplinary action.

I. Competence

Each member has a responsibility to:

- Maintain an appropriate level of professional expertise by continually developing knowledge and skills.
- Perform professional duties in accordance with relevant laws, regulations, and technical standards.
- Provide decision support information and recommendations that are accurate, clear, concise, and timely.
- Recognize and communicate professional limitations or other constraints that would preclude responsible judgment or successful performance of an activity.

II. Confidentiality

Each member has a responsibility to:

- Keep information confidential except when disclosure is authorized or legally required.
- Inform all relevant parties regarding appropriate use of confidential information. Monitor subordinates' activities to ensure compliance.
- Refrain from using confidential information for unethical or illegal advantage.

III. Integrity

Each member has a responsibility to:

- Mitigate actual conflicts of interest, and regularly communicate with business associates to avoid apparent conflicts of interest. Advise all parties of any potential conflicts.

- Refrain from engaging in any conduct that would prejudice carrying out duties ethically.
- Abstain from engaging in or supporting any activity that might discredit the profession.

IV. Credibility

Each member has a responsibility to:

- Communicate information fairly and objectively.
- Disclose all relevant information that could reasonably be expected to influence an intended user's understanding of the reports, analyses, or recommendations.
- Disclose delays or deficiencies in information, timeliness, processing, or internal controls in conformance with organization policy and/or applicable law.

Resolution of Ethical Conflict

In applying the Standards of Ethical Professional Practice, you may encounter problems identifying unethical behavior or resolving an ethical conflict. When faced with ethical issues, you should follow your organization's established policies on the resolution of such conflict. If these policies do not resolve the ethical conflict, you should consider the following courses of action:

- Discuss the issue with your immediate supervisor except when it appears that the supervisor is involved. In that case, present the issue to the next level.
- If you cannot achieve a satisfactory resolution, submit the issue to the next management level. If your immediate superior is the chief executive officer or equivalent, the acceptable reviewing authority may be a group such as the audit committee, executive committee, board of directors, board of trustees, or owners. Contact with levels above the immediate superior should be initiated only with your superior's knowledge, assuming he or she is not involved. Communication of such problems to authorities or individuals not employed or engaged by the organization is not considered appropriate, unless you believe there is a clear violation of the law.
- Clarify relevant ethical issues by initiating a confidential discussion with an IMA Ethics Counselor or other impartial advisor to obtain a better understanding of possible courses of action.
- Consult your own attorney as to legal obligations and rights concerning the ethical conflict.

Learning Outcome Statements Overview: Professional Ethics

Section F.1. Ethical Considerations for Management Accounting and Financial Management Professionals

Ethics may be tested in conjunction with any topic area.

- Provisions of **IMA's Statement of Ethical Professional Practice**
- Evaluation and resolution of ethical issues

Using the standards outlined in **IMA's Statement of Ethical Professional Practice**, the candidate should be able to:

A. Identify and describe the four overarching ethical principles.
   a. Honesty—Requires conscientious application to the task at hand and truthfulness in all analyses and communications.
   b. Fairness—Requires empathetic and just consideration of the needs of others involved in a particular situation and full disclosure of all necessary contextual information.
   c. Objectivity—Requires impartial and dispassionate evaluation of conflicting points of view before arriving at a conclusion.
   d. Responsibility—Requires actions to be performed with faithfulness and loyalty.
B. Evaluate a given business situation for its ethical implications.
   a. The following information contains standards that may be violated in a given business situation, and the chapter materials include a detailed scenario to identify ethical implications and to resolve the conflict. [See Topic 1: Ethical Considerations for Management Accounting and Financial Management Professionals (in book) for more details.]
C. Identify and describe relevant standards that may have been violated in a given business situation and explain why the specific standards are applicable.
   a. Four standards may be violated in a given business situation: competence, confidentiality, integrity, and credibility.
      i. Competence has to do with maintaining appropriate skills and expertise.

ii. Confidentiality has to do with the disclosure of confidential information.

iii. Integrity has to do with mitigating conflicts of interest and abstaining from anything that would discredit the profession.

iv. Credibility has to do with communicating information fairly and objectively and disclosing all relevant information.

D. Recommend a course of action for management accountants or financial managers to take when confronted with an ethical dilemma in the business environment.

a. The *IMA Statement of Ethical Professional Practice* advises:

In applying the Standards of Ethical Professional Practice, you may encounter problems identifying unethical behavior or in resolving an ethical conflict. When faced with ethical issues, you should follow your organization's established policies on the resolution of such conflict. If these policies do not resolve the ethical conflict, you should consider the following courses of action.

1. Discuss problems with immediate supervisor.
2. If immediate supervisor is the CEO or equivalent, the acceptable reviewing authority may be audit committee, executive committee, board of directors or owners.
3. Clarify relevant ethical issues by initiating a confidential discussion with an IMA Ethics Counselor.
4. Consult your own attorney as to your legal obligations and rights.

E. Evaluate and propose resolutions for ethical issues such as fraudulent reporting, manipulation of analyses, results, and budgets.

a. The recommended course of action in any ethical conflict is described above and in greater detail in Topic 1: Ethical Considerations for Management Accounting and Financial Management Professionals in the book.

F. Using the fraud triangle model, the candidate should be able to identify the three components of the triangle.

a. The three components of the fraud triangle are motive (pressure), opportunity, and rationalization. Motive describes the compelling need for funds which drives the fraud. The common motives are lifestyle (cars, houses, etc.) needs, addictive behaviors such as drinking, drugging, and gambling, and short-term cash needs. Opportunity describes the situation, normally a lapse in internal controls, which allows the fraud to occur. Rationalization describes the mind-set of the fraudster. It helps the fraud perpetrator rationalize that what he/she has done is not a crime.

G. Use the model to explain how management accounting and financial management professional can identify and manage the risk of fraud.

a. The management accountant needs to understand the fraud triangle to be aware of employee behavioral issues and changes and managements' tendency to rationalize behavior to help identify potential frauds and the possible perpetrators. In addition, the management accountant needs to be aware of any internal control weaknesses that would create opportunities for fraud.

Section F.2. Ethical Considerations for the Organization

A. Identify the purpose of the U.S. Foreign Corrupt Practices Act.
   a. The FCPA was passed in 1977 as a result of Securities and Exchange Commission (SEC) investigations in the mid-1970s that revealed that hundreds of companies admitted making questionable or illegal payments to foreign government officials to secure favorable action.
B. Identify the practices that the U.S Foreign Corrupt Practices Act prohibits, and explain how to apply this Act to typical business situations.
   a. The FCPA forbids an American company doing business in another country to pay bribes to a foreign government to obtain contracts or secure business.
C. Apply relevant provisions of IMA's Statement on Management Accounting, *Values and Ethics: From Inception to Practice*, to a business situation.
   a. The *Values and Ethics* statement published by the IMA contains many important provisions to assist an organization in developing, adopting, and maintaining an ethical framework. According to the SMA:

> For those in the management accounting profession, the Institute of Management Accountants created The Statement of Ethical Professional Practice. Other major global accounting bodies also maintain codes of ethical conduct. The intent of this Statement on Management Accounting (SMA) . . . is to make all accounting professionals aware of their responsibility to act as change agents within their organizations, supporting the maintenance of effective internal controls and ensuring that their organizations have considered, adopted, and fully implemented a company-wide ethics and compliance program, including a code of ethics and a confidential hot/helpline.
>
> [For additional details on the SMA, see Topic 2: Ethical Considerations for the Organization (in book), or review the SMA itself.]

D. Discuss corporate responsibility for ethical conduct.
   a. Despite the fact that a company may employ many thousands of employees, the organization still has a responsibility to ensure, to the best of its ability, that all of those employees are behaving in an ethical manner. To achieve control, the organization defines the principles of behavior it desires by identifying and documenting the organizational values, creating codes of ethics and conduct, and implementing internal controls.
E. Explain why it is important for an organization to have a code of conduct.

a. In the absence of a defined code of conduct or ethics, employees either will follow their own beliefs and values or look for guidance from leadership to determine the expected course of action. Therefore, it is essential that management hold itself to a higher standard of conduct than expected from those who are supervised.

F. Demonstrate an understanding of the ways ethical values benefit an organization.

a. Research also has shown that strong ethical cultures can impact the bottom line. Improvements like higher levels of productivity, improved interpersonal dynamics, and lower risks of fraud all result in better financial performance for the organization.

G. Demonstrate an understanding of the differences between ethical and legal behavior.

a. The FCPA addresses the problem of questionable or illegal bribes to foreign officials. In many instances, the payments that were being made were not only legal, they were a common business practice in those countries. Many people felt that the FCPA made it difficult for U.S. companies to compete overseas since the practice was so common. Other important legal and ethical issues for international business involve cultural differences and disparities between international law and the laws of individual countries. One country's ethical outrage may be another's ordinary practice, which may create an ethical dilemma for international businesses.

H. Demonstrate an understanding of role of "leadership by example" or "tone at the top" in determining an organization's ethical environment.

a. IMA's SMA, *Values and Ethics: From Inception to Practice*, states the following about the role of leadership in an organization's ethical environment:

> Ethical behavior is not something that applies to someone else— every single individual is responsible for behaving ethically. Nowhere is this more important than the demonstration of ethical behavior that managers and supervisors exhibit in the way they execute their day-to-day work. . . . Leaders—especially those in the most senior positions—are expected to set the "tone at the top," demonstrating through their actions a commitment to the organization's ethical framework and other controls. Senior managers must avoid creating the perception that they are above the rules.

I. Explain the importance of human capital to an organization in creating a climate where "doing the right thing" is expected (i.e., hiring the right people, providing them with training, and practicing consistent values-based leadership).

a. It is not enough for management to hold itself to a higher level of conduct. If an organization wants to create a climate where doing the right thing is the norm, it is important to hire the right people, provide them with adequate training, and then practice consistent values-based leadership. The process begins with hiring the right employees. Once the right employees have been hired, training is the next priority.

J. Explain how an organization's culture impacts its behavioral values.

    a. If employees have been properly trained with ethical values in place, the culture of the company will develop in accordance with its code of ethics. An organization's culture is made up of the accumulated behavioral actions of all of its employees over time. A culture that is in alignment with the organization's core values and code of ethics will tend to strengthen and reproduce the desired ongoing behaviors. This is illustrated by a culture where everyone from a top executive to an entry-level employee understands, shares, and lives the same set of values. The synergy of everyone acting in alignment with values will result in increased productivity, lower risks of fraud, and improved financial results.

K. Explain the importance of an organization's core values in explaining its ethical behavior.

    a. To present a unified presence to customers, shareholders, vendors, the community, and all other stakeholders, it is essential for the organization to define its core values as they relate to the business in which it is involved. In this manner, all employees are provided with the unifying guidance they require to make ethical choices aligned with corporate values.

L. Discuss the importance of employee training to maintaining an ethical organizational culture.

    a. Employee training is a key part of maintaining an ethical organizational culture. In addition to having each employee read and understand the code of ethics, training should explain the concepts that lie behind the code. The training also should translate the high-level corporate-wide ethics statement into expected behavior for specific positions. This makes the code of ethics easier to understand, more memorable, and more likely to be lived.

M. Describe the following methods to monitor ethical compliance: human performance feedback loop and survey tools.

    a. Human performance feedback loop—To improve compliance, performance review systems must be aligned with organizational values and ethics statements. Employee job descriptions, required competencies, and performance objectives should include ethical expectations. Employee reviews, conducted annually (or more frequently), should evaluate the individual's compliance with ethical expectations along with operational goals. For example, an evaluation might rate not only accuracy and timeliness of an employee's reports; it also could rate his performance in treating all others with dignity and respect. Ideally, the feedback used to make this evaluation would include 360-degree input, including both internal and external responses.

    b. Survey tools—Another useful way to measure ethical performance is the use of surveys. Using the organization's code of ethics as a source, surveys could have employees rate how well the organization is doing. For example, employees can be asked the degree to which they agree with statements such as: "This organization respects the dignity of all individuals." The results of surveys will indicate the degree of compliance and provide a method to stimulate an ongoing dialogue with employees.

N. Explain the importance of a whistleblowing framework (e.g., ethics helpline) to maintaining an ethical organizational culture.

   a. A whistleblowing framework provides employees who identify ethically questionable behavior by others with a confidential way to seek advice and report ethical violations. Research has shown that employee hotlines are valuable reporting mechanisms for discovering fraud within an organization. If the hotline is truly anonymous and also can be used by employees to access advice on ethical situations, employees raise issues can more freely without fear of retaliation.

O. Identify the requirements of SOX Section 406—Code of Ethics for Senior Financial Officers

   a. Sarbanes-Oxley Section 406, Code of Ethics for Senior Financial Officers:
      • Requires companies to adopt a code of ethics for senior financial officers.
      • Includes instructions for the timely reporting of "any change in or waiver of the code of ethics" for officers.

P. Discuss the issues organizations face in applying their values and ethical standards internationally.

   a. One country's ethical outrage may be another's ordinary practice, which may create an ethical dilemma for international businesses. On one side, a company may alienate potential trading partners or host countries by an ethnocentric, and apparently arrogant, insistence on the universal rightness of its own practices. On the other side, there is a temptation to follow local custom and practice. Organizations often find it difficult to determine if they should stick to the ethical practices of their home country or follow the ethical practices of the country they are operating in.

Q. Demonstrate an understanding of the relationship between ethics and internal controls.

   a. Internal controls are designed to provide reasonable assurance as to the achievements of the following:
      • Effectiveness of operations.
      • Efficiency of operations.
      • Safeguarding of assets.
      • Reliability of financial reporting.
      • Compliance with laws and regulations.

The 1992 COSO (Committee of Sponsoring Organizations) Integrated Internal Control framework has five elements:

   1. Control environment
   2. Risk assessment
   3. Control activities
   4. Information and communication
   5. Monitoring

Ethics are in the control environment element. The control environment sets the control and ethical tone for the organization. It includes ethical values as well as the management philosophy and style and employee competence. Ethics deal with values relating to human conduct. They look at what is right and what is wrong as well as what is good and what is bad. A code of ethics is a set of moral precepts or rules of conduct to be followed by the organization's personnel.

Ethical Considerations for Management Accounting and Financial Management Professionals

ETHICAL CHALLENGES CAN DERAIL THE career of a management accountant or financial management professional. Therefore, these individuals have an obligation to the public, their profession, the organizations they serve, and themselves to maintain the highest standards of ethical conduct.

This topic addresses the elements and application of the *IMA Statement of Ethical Professional Practice*. By knowing and applying the *IMA Statement of Ethical Professional Practice,* not only will professionals be able to meet their obligations, they also will be perceived as trustworthy sources of information and partners in the organization.

READ the Learning Outcome Statements (LOS) for this topic as found in Appendix B and then study the concepts and calculations presented here to be sure you understand the content you could be tested on in the CMA exam.

Introduction

What should an accountant do if instructed by an immediate superior to record the physical inventory at original cost even though obsolescence has clearly reduced its value? The *IMA Statement of Ethical Professional Practice* is intended to provide guidance to an accountant in this example as well as many other situations that will challenge how accountants do their work.

Ethics is the intellectual discipline that attempts to distinguish right from wrong in human conduct. It is also a practical endeavor that proposes standards of perfect behavior as points of comparison when individuals must choose among various courses of action. Applying perfect standards in an imperfect world is rarely easy or straightforward.

In the situation just described, for example, two opposing ethical principles apply. On one hand, the accountant has a duty under an employment contract to carry out the instructions of a supervisor. On the other hand, it would be unethical for the accountant to record the inventory at cost rather than at its depreciated value. The accountant cannot satisfy both principles at once and must choose between them. Ethics, then, consists of making morally defensible choices within the sometimes ethically ambiguous, perhaps even threatening, conditions of real life.

Two good questions to ask when faced with an ethical dilemma are: "Have I gathered all the information and insight I need to take responsible and objective action?" and "Would I be pleased to have my closest friends learn of my actions?"

IMA Statement of Ethical Professional Practice

Much of this section is excerpted directly from the *IMA Statement of Ethical Professional Practice*. It is recommended that candidates study this statement thoroughly and commit the principles, standards, and resolution of ethical conflict to memory.

Ethical Behavior for Practitioners of Management Accounting and Financial Management

Practitioners of management accounting and financial management have an obligation to the public, their profession, the organizations they serve, and themselves to maintain the highest standards of ethical conduct. In recognition of this obligation, the Institute of Management Accountants has promulgated standards of ethical professional practice. Adherence to these standards, both domestically and internationally, is integral to achieving the objectives of management accounting. Practitioners of management accounting and financial management shall not commit acts contrary to these standards nor shall they condone the commission of such acts by others within their organizations.

IMA Statement of Ethical Professional Practice

Practitioners of management accounting and financial management shall behave ethically. A commitment to ethical professional practice includes overarching principles that express our values and standards that guide our conduct.

Principles

IMA's overarching ethical principles include:

1. Honesty
2. Fairness

3. Objectivity
4. Responsibility

Practitioners shall act in accordance with these principles and shall encourage others within their organizations to adhere to them.

Honesty

The first principle, honesty, requires conscientious application to the task at hand and truthfulness in all analyses and communications. Honesty is one of the key attributes people look for in an accountant or financial professional: "If you can't trust your accountant, who can you trust?" Examples of honesty include: disclosing all necessary and relevant information to outside auditors; refusing to record information that is anything less than accurate; and providing factual information to others so that they can make decisions based on truthful information.

Fairness

Fairness requires empathetic, and just consideration of the needs of others involved in a particular situation and full disclosure of all necessary contextual information. The organization deserves adequate and full disclosure in context so that appropriate actions can be taken within a reasonable time frame. To be fair, that context should be fully spelled out. Examples of fairness include: providing information and feedback objectively; identifying and fixing mistakes; and selecting vendors without bias, prejudice, or favoritism.

Objectivity

Objectivity requires impartial and dispassionate evaluation of conflicting points of view before arriving at a conclusion. For many years, organizations have depended on the objectivity of internal and external financial professionals to support them in making critical business decisions. "Let's ask our accountants" is often the course of action when businesspeople want to determine a reasoned, thorough, dispassionate, legally defensible course of action. Examples of objectivity are stating relevant financial and legal guidelines, maintaining standards for documenting information, and making recommendations on existing data despite pressures to favor one course over another.

Responsibility

Responsibility requires actions to be performed with faithfulness and loyalty. Responsibility to the client and the profession is one of the most important underpinnings for the ethical behavior of financial professionals. This includes not just loyalty to the short-term interests of the client but also to the long-term impact of financial decisions. Examples of responsibility include conveying information at the appropriate time, ensuring information on reports and statements is accurate, and gathering enough information to make an informed decision.

Standards

The *IMA Statement of Ethical Professional Practice* identifies and explains four standards that help define a member's ethical responsibility:

1. Competence
2. Confidentiality
3. Integrity
4. Credibility

A member's failure to comply with these standards may result in disciplinary action.

Competence

Each member has a responsibility to:

1. Maintain an appropriate level of professional expertise by continually developing knowledge and skills.
2. Perform professional duties in accordance with relevant laws, regulations, and technical standards.
3. Provide decision support information and recommendations that are accurate, clear, concise, and timely.
4. Recognize and communicate professional limitations or other constraints that would preclude responsible judgment or successful performance of an activity.

The rules in accounting are as diverse as they are dynamic. Keeping up to date with changes in regulations and the adoption of new laws and standards in the industry is essential. Failing to do so may unknowingly lead to unethical behavior.

Confidentiality

Each member has a responsibility to:

1. Keep information confidential except when disclosure is authorized or legally required.
2. Inform all relevant parties regarding the appropriate use of confidential information. Monitor subordinates' activities to ensure compliance.
3. Refrain from using confidential information for unethical or illegal advantage.

While the confidentiality standard is fairly straightforward, today's technological advances actually may hinder management accountants from following it as diligently as they must. Not only should paper and electronic documents be properly secured, but all conversations, especially those on cell phones, should be conducted only in a private setting and never in public locations, such as airports and cafés.

Integrity

Each member has a responsibility to:

1. Mitigate actual conflicts of interest. Regularly communicate with business associates to avoid apparent conflicts of interest. Advise all parties of any potential conflicts.
2. Refrain from engaging in any conduct that would prejudice carrying out duties ethically.
3. Abstain from engaging in or supporting any activity that might discredit the profession.

Integrity includes the responsibility to communicate both the good and the bad, whether it is news, analysis, judgment, or professional opinion.

Credibility

Each member has a responsibility to:

1. Communicate information fairly and objectively.
2. Disclose all relevant information that could reasonably be expected to influence an intended user's understanding of the reports, analyses, or recommendations.
3. Disclose delays or deficiencies in information, timeliness, processing, or internal controls in conformance with organization policy and/or applicable law.

Credibility ties in closely with the competence standard. In order to be credible, an individual must be competent. Underlying credibility is the management accountant's duty to plan ahead and assess potential risks, gather enough information to be fully informed about all relevant facts, and communicate unfavorable news promptly.

Resolution of Ethical Conflict

Resolving an ethical conflict can be a difficult and often stressful task. Unfortunately, there is no magic formula that will result in the right decision. Each situation is different, and the circumstances are often complex. The *IMA Statement of Ethical Professional Practice* advises:

> In applying the Standards of Ethical Professional Practice, you may encounter problems identifying unethical behavior or in resolving an ethical conflict. When faced with ethical issues, you should follow your organization's established policies on the resolution of such conflict. If these policies do not resolve the ethical conflict, you should consider the following courses of action.
>
> 1. Discuss such problems with the immediate supervisor except when it appears that the supervisor is involved. In that case, present the issue to the next managerial level.

2. If the immediate supervisor is the chief executive officer or equivalent, the acceptable reviewing authority may be a group such as the audit committee, executive committee, board of directors, board of trustees, or owners. Contact with levels above the immediate superior should be initiated only with the superior's knowledge, assuming he or she is not involved. Communication of such problems to authorities or individuals not employed or engaged by the organization is not considered appropriate, unless the member believes there is a clear violation of the law.
3. Clarify relevant ethical issues by initiating a confidential discussion with an IMA Ethics Counselor or other impartial advisor to obtain a better understanding of possible courses of action.
4. Consult your own attorney as to legal obligations and rights concerning the ethical conflict.

Addressing any ethical conflict requires careful consideration and an examination of all the facts before proceeding. This may require:

- Checking data and source material
- Confirming rumors
- Asking more detailed questions
- Probing other people for more information
- Disregarding preconceived ideas

Any of these steps must be done with regard to ethical responsibilities for confidentiality in accordance with the Standards of Ethical Professional Practice.

The next question to consider when faced with an ethical conflict is "What are the alternatives?" Defining the alternatives will provide a framework within which to examine the merits and drawbacks of each option. Attempting to clearly define the choices may reveal a new option.

Consider any rules, laws, or regulations that may apply. What do the rules say? How do they apply to each of the alternatives? Depending on the situation, many different rules and regulations may need to be examined, including the company's code of conduct; local, state and federal laws; generally accepted accounting principles and Financial Accounting Standards Board (FASB) standards, and the IMA's Standards of Ethical Professional Practice.

The company's policies provide a starting point. The IMA Ethics Helpline (1-800-245-1383) is available for members and can offer an outside perspective. It may be necessary to consult with the company's legal or compliance department and, if necessary, a personal attorney, regarding interpretation of laws and regulations as well as the management accountant's legal obligations and rights. When interpreting the rules, it is always best to err on the conservative side.

When someone feels pressured in a particular direction, the human factor of an ethical conflict comes into play. Individuals may feel pressured by professional obligations and personal values, which, in some cases, may conflict. A person's morals, background, experiences, social and economic circumstances, and the ethical culture of the organization all may contribute to an ethical conflict. Professional obligations related to customer expectations, investor goals, departmental quotas, delivery schedules, and many internal and external factors also may compel an individual to choose one option over another. Personal and professional factors differ, so each individual is likely to respond differently to pressure. One strategy is to try to pinpoint the reasons the decision is difficult to make, considering each side.

Finally, the consequences of each alternative need to be considered carefully, including who else will be affected and how they will be affected.

The Fraud Triangle

Often some aspect of fraud underlies ethical situations that a management or financial accounting professional faces. Fraud is simply an act of deceit or trickery or breach of confidence perpetrated for profit or to gain some unfair or dishonest advantage. There are various types of fraud. Fraud against a company, or occupational fraud, can be committed either internally, by employees, managers, officers, or owners of a company, or externally, by customers, vendors, or other parties. Other schemes defraud individuals rather than organizations. Because fraud is so prevalent in the business world today (e.g., Enron and WorldCom debacles), it is important for management and financial accounting professionals to fully understand how and why fraudulent acts occur. This knowledge can provide the management and financial accounting professional with the ability to recognize the potential for fraud and take proactive steps to mitigate its occurrence.

A widely recognized model for explaining the factors that cause someone to commit occupational fraud is the fraud triangle. The fraud triangle consists of three components: pressure, opportunity, and rationalization.

The underlying presumption of this model is that these three factors must be present at the same time in order for an ordinary person to perpetrate a fraud. Pressure, such as a financial need, is the "motive" for committing the fraud. Examples of pressure that commonly lead to fraud include the need to meet earnings expectations to sustain investor confidence, the need to meet productivity targets at work, or simply the inability to pay one's bills. Opportunity, or perceived opportunity, defines the method by which the crime can be committed. The individual fraudster must see some way he or she can use (abuse) his or her position of trust to solve the financial problem with a low perceived risk of getting caught. For instance, an individual committing a fraud (i.e., stealing monies) sees an internal control weakness and, believing no one will notice if funds are taken, begins the fraud with a small amount of money. If no one notices, the amount taken usually grows. Finally, rationalization involves the individual fraudster justifying the crime to him- or herself in a way that makes it an acceptable or justifiable act. Common rationalizations an individual may use include: "I was underpaid; my employer cheated me" or "I was entitled to the money" or "I was only borrowing the money."

It is critical that management or financial accounting professionals understand the fraud triangle and its components and be cognizant of employee behavioral issues and changes that might heighten the likelihood of potential fraud. Additionally, management or financial accounting professionals need to be aware of any internal control weaknesses that might create opportunities for fraud.

Conducting an organizational fraud risk assessment can assist with managing the risk of fraud. Such an assessment involves identifying and evaluating fraud risk factors (e.g., the establishment of unrealistic earnings expectations); identifying possible fraud risk, schemes, and scenarios (e.g., intentional overstatement of sales to meet unrealistic earnings expectations); prioritizing identified fraud risks and assessing their likelihood; evaluating internal controls to mitigate fraudulent activity; and documenting and continually monitoring and updating the fraud risk assessment.

Practice Ethical Scenario

The board of directors of Arivan Corporation recently learned that some members of the senior management team had circumvented the company's internal controls for personal gain. The board appointed a special task force of external auditors and outside legal counsel to investigate the situation.

After extensive review, the task force concluded that for a period of several years, the expenses of the company's chief executive officer, president, and vice president for public relations were charged to an account called the Limited Expenditure Account (LEA). The account was established five years before and was not subject to the company's normal approval and authorization process. Approximately $2,000,000 of requests for reimbursement were routinely processed and charged to LEA. Accounting personnel were advised by the controller to process such requests based on the individual approval of the three executives, even when the requests were not adequately documented.

The vice president for public relations and his department were in charge of political fundraising activities. The task force determined, however, that only a small portion of the $1,000,000 raised in the previous year actually was used for political purposes. In addition, departmental resources were used for personal projects of the three identified executives. The task force also uncovered an additional $4,000,000 of expenditures that were poorly documented so that even the amounts for proper business purposes could not be identified.

The task force noted that these payment practices, as well as LEA, were never disclosed in the internal audit department's audit reports even though company disbursements were tested annually. References to these practices and LEA were included on two occasions in recent years' work papers. The director of internal audit, who reports to the controller, advised that he reviewed these findings with the controller who, in turn, advised that he mentioned these findings to the president. The president recommended that they not be included in the internal audit reports. The task force also noted that the company did not have a formal, published ethics policy.

1. Discuss whether the controller has acted unethically. Reference the relevant standards of ethical practice in your answer.
2. If you were one of the accounting personnel directed to process these transactions, what steps would you take to resolve the ethical conflict?

Think about how you would apply the IMA Statement of Ethical Professional Practice *to answer these questions. Write your ideas on a separate sheet of paper, then read the solutions provided to assess your answers.*

Solution: Question 1

Referring to the *IMA Statement of Ethical Professional Practice,* the controller has acted unethically. Even though the company does not have an ethics policy, members must act in accordance with the principles of honesty, fairness, objectivity, and responsibility. The controller also should encourage others in the organization to adhere to these same principles. Furthermore, the controller has violated specific standards of ethical conduct by advising accounting personnel to process payments with individual authorizations, even when the transactions were not adequately documented, and by advising the director of the internal audit department to not include any references to these improprieties in the audit reports. The specific standards violated are discussed next.

Competence

Perform professional duties in accordance with relevant laws, regulations, and technical standards.

Integrity

- Mitigate actual conflicts of interest. Regularly communicate with business associates to avoid apparent conflicts of interest. Advise all parties of any potential conflicts.
- Refrain from engaging in any activity that would prejudice their ability to carry out their duties ethically.
- Refrain from engaging in or supporting any activity that would discredit the profession.

Credibility

Communicate information fairly and objectively.

Confidentiality

Not an issue in this situation.

Solution: Question 2

Given that the company does not have a formal ethics policy, Arivan most likely does not have an established policy for resolving ethical conflicts. However, if a policy does exist, a management accountant should follow the company's procedures. In the absence of an established ethics policy, or if the procedures fail to resolve the ethical conflict, the management accountant should consider these actions:

- Because the accountant's superior appears to be the cause of this ethical dilemma, the accountant should present the issue to the next highest-level manager in the organization and then proceed to successively higher levels (e.g., audit committee, board of directors, etc.), until the matter is satisfactorily resolved.
- The accountant should not communicate the situation to individuals or authorities outside of Arivan unless there is a clear violation of the law.
- The accountant should clarify the ethical issues with an impartial advisor to obtain a better understanding of possible courses of action.
- The accountant should consult his or her own attorney about personal legal obligations and rights concerning this situation.

Resolving an ethical conflict can be a challenging and often stressful task. In this scenario, there are many levels of authority to transcend before reaching someone who is not involved.

Knowledge Check: Professional Ethics

The next questions are intended to help you check your understanding and recall of the material presented in this topic. They do not represent the type of questions that appear on the CMA exam.

Directions: Answer each question in the space provided. Correct answers and section references appear after the knowledge check questions.

1. The *IMA Statement of Ethical Professional Practice* includes four overarching ethical principles. Name the four principles.

   a. _____

   b. _____

   c. _____

   d. _____

2. The *IMA Statement of Ethical Professional Practice* includes four standards. Name the four standards.

   a. _____

   b. _____

   c. _____

   d. _____

   For questions 3 through 7, match the following rules to the IMA standards of ethical responsibility. More than one standard may apply.

   a. Competence

   b. Integrity

   c. Confidentiality

   d. Credibility

3. _____ Refuse any gift that might influence your actions in your capacity as an accountant.

4. _____ Prepare complete and clear reports.

5. _____ Disclose fully all relevant information that could influence a user's understanding of a report.

6. _____ Communicate unfavorable as well as favorable information.

7. _____ Perform your duties in accordance with applicable laws, regulations, and standards.

8. If an accountant's immediate supervisor instructs the accountant to withhold essential but unpleasant information in a management report, the accountant should:

☐ **a.** do as the supervisor asks and tell no one.

☐ **b.** refuse to do as the supervisor asks and alert an investigative reporter to the problem.

☐ **c.** take the matter to the supervisor's immediate supervisor.

☐ **d.** take the matter directly to the corporate ombudsman.

Knowledge Check Answers: Professional Ethics

1. The *IMA Statement of Ethical Professional Practice* includes four overarching ethical principles. Name the four principles. [**See IMA Statement of Ethical Professional Practice—Principles.**]

    a. **Honesty**

    b. **Fairness**

    c. **Objectivity**

    d. **Responsibility**

2. The *IMA Statement of Ethical Professional Practice* includes four standards. Name the four standards. [**See IMA Statement of Ethical Professional Practice—Standards.**]

    a. **Competence**

    b. **Confidentiality**

    c. **Integrity**

    d. **Credibility**

    For questions 3 through 7, match the following rules to the IMA standards of ethical responsibility. More than one standard may apply.

    a. Competence

    b. Integrity

    c. Confidentiality

    d. Credibility

3. <u>**b**</u> Refuse any gift that might influence your actions in your capacity as an accountant.

4. <u>**a and d**</u> Prepare complete and clear reports.

5. <u>**d**</u> Disclose fully all relevant information that could influence a user's understanding of a report.

6. <u>**b and d**</u> Communicate unfavorable as well as favorable information.

7. <u>**a**</u> Perform your duties in accordance with applicable laws, regulations, and standards.

8. If an accountant's immediate supervisor instructs the accountant to withhold essential but unpleasant information in a management report, the accountant should: [**See Resolution of Ethical Conflict.**]

    ☐ a. do as the supervisor asks and tell no one.

    ☐ b. refuse to do as the supervisor asks and alert an investigative reporter to the problem.

    ☑ c. take the matter to the supervisor's immediate supervisor.

    ☐ d. take the matter directly to the corporate ombudsman.

Ethical Considerations for the Organization

ETHICS IS ABOUT THE INTEGRITY OF THE DECISION MAKING PROCESS that is used to resolve any number of issues," according to Institute of Management Accountants' Statement on Management Accounting (SMA) titled *Values and Ethics: From Inception to Practice.*

At its lowest denominator, ethics is about behavior; more specifically for the organization, the term *ethics* refers to the ability to predict and control employees' behavior to ensure that the company's values and business purpose are being met consistently.

READ the Learning Outcome Statements (LOS) for this topic as found in Appendix B and then study the concepts presented here to be sure you understand the content you could be tested on in the CMA exam.

Corporate Responsibility for Ethical Conduct

Too often in recent years, top executives accused of unethical behavior have stated under oath that they are innocent of any wrongdoing. Despite the fact that companies may employ many thousands of employees, the organization still has a responsibility to ensure, to the best of its ability, that all of those employees are behaving in an ethical manner. To achieve control, the organization defines the principles of behavior it desires by identifying and documenting the organizational values, creating codes of ethics and conduct, and implementing internal controls. All of these documents work together to provide guidance in decision making and selecting daily behavioral choices. This guidance, according to the SMA titled *Values and Ethics: From Inception to Practice*, is a "critical element in the creation of a framework for ethical management." Ultimately these documents create and maintain an ethical culture that actively supports the types of behavior the organization desires.

The size of the organization will determine how extensive each of these documents will be. In general, the larger the company, the more well-defined expected conduct will need to be. In smaller companies that are run by the founder, leading by example often can be as effective at creating an ethical culture as extensive documentation. However, as these smaller companies grow and the founder becomes less and less accessible, there is a danger that the culture will be diluted. Therefore, it is important for even small companies to document their values and behavioral expectations of employees.

Fortunately, making such an effort offers the organization many benefits. It can take years for an organization to build up a reputation for quality or reliability. Yet the behavior of a few or even a single employee can destroy an organization's reputation very quickly. Therefore, companies that take corporate ethical responsibility seriously usually experience improvement in share value, client retention, and attraction of new clients, investors, and employees. In addition, they experience a lowered risk of compliance violations.

Research also has shown that strong ethical cultures can impact the bottom line. Improvements like higher levels of productivity, improved interpersonal dynamics, and lower risks of fraud all result in better financial performance for the organization. According to the IMA's *Values and Ethics: From Inception to Practice:*

> Organizations that succeed in a broad-based deployment of a code of ethics will create a base for enhanced risk assessment, greater transparency for those responsible for organizational governance, and an increased probability that commitments made in words are truly being fulfilled in practice. As a result, CEOs [chief executive officers] and CFOs [chief financial officers] who are required to sign commitments of compliance will do so with a greater degree of knowledge and certainty that their words and the actions of the organization are aligned.

Because working within the letter of the law does not guarantee that individuals are behaving ethically, ethical behavior goes beyond the idea of following legally acceptable procedures. Individuals and organizations behave ethically when their actions are aligned with a set of core values. The challenge for most organizations is that each employee comes into the company with his or her own predefined set of values. To present a unified presence to customers, shareholders, vendors, the community, and all other stakeholders, it is essential for the organization to define its core values as they relate to the business in which it is involved. In this manner, all employees are provided with the unifying guidance they require to make ethical choices aligned with corporate values.

Ethics Starts at the Top

Ideally everyone in an organization, from the board of directors to the CEO to the front-line worker, will answer the next questions in a similar manner:

- What values does this organization believe in?
- What principles drive this organization's decision making?
- By what ethical standards does this organization live?
- What principles/beliefs do managers and leaders demonstrate?

These questions are the basis for articulating a cohesive code of conduct. Once the company's values are defined, they are applied to different areas of the organization to provide daily guidance on what individuals are expected to do and what they are expected not to do. These principles then provide a framework for ethical management and leadership.

Because they are broadly written, these short statements may be interpreted differently by individuals. Therefore, the next step is for senior management to expand each principle into a more specific behavioral profile. The expanded statement includes examples of what type of behavior exemplifies this principle as well as what type of behavior is inconsistent with it. The goal is to create a concrete foundation that can be used to guide operational decisions on a daily basis.

For these principles to become a part of the organizational culture, it is imperative that senior management fully understand the implications that will arise during operational implementation. If the principles cannot be implemented consistently, or if they inadvertently create an environment that is untenable, the end result will be confusion and conflict.

In the absence of a defined code of conduct or ethics, employees either will follow their own beliefs and values or look for guidance from leadership to determine the expected course of action. Therefore, it is essential that management hold itself to a higher standard of conduct than expected from those who are supervised. To be effective, managers will set a good example, follow documented values, keep all promises and commitments, and establish an atmosphere conducive to helping others to adhere to the existing ethics standards.

Applying Ethics in a Corporate Setting

As important as a code of ethics is, ultimately it is only a document. What gives the code life and produces the inherent benefits are the people who live that code. A company's employees are truly its most important asset when creating an ethical culture.

It is not enough for management to hold itself to a higher level of conduct. If an organization wants to create a climate where doing the right thing is the norm, it is important to hire the right people, provide them with adequate training, and then practice consistent values-based leadership.

The process begins with hiring employees. During the interview process, potential candidates should be screened for personal values and expected workplace behaviors as well as skills and aptitudes. Although values are amorphous and difficult to measure, they can be inferred by asking about personal values, using open-ended interview questions about how they would respond to specific circumstances, or inquiring whether certain actions would be considered ethical. Because of the importance of bringing in only the right people and the potential cost of hiring and then firing those who behave unethically, the SMA states that "management accountants should ensure that part of the HR [human resources] budget is allocated for conducting thorough behavioral analysis and that in-depth assessment is mandatory in the case of sensitive positions."

Once the right employees have been hired, training is the next priority. Orientation should contain information specific to the organization's values and any existing codes of conduct or ethics. To reaffirm these beliefs regularly, ongoing training should be provided to all staff. Training programs should be comprehensive, relate to real-world situations faced by employees, and provide a consistent message.

Employee training is a key part of maintaining an ethical organizational culture. In addition to having each employee read and understand the code of ethics, training should explain the concepts that lie behind the code. The training also should translate the high-level corporate-wide ethics statement into expected behavior for specific positions. This makes the code of ethics easier to understand, more memorable, and more likely to be lived.

The SMA specifies that ongoing training should include these expectations:

- General employee behavior and personal conduct
- How ethics are built into work management methods
- How ethics affects specific jobs, processes, activities, and relationships
- How the organization monitors compliance with code
- What routes are open to employees who have compliance issues
- What action is taken when a complaint or issue is identified
- The actions and penalties once noncompliance is proven

Consistent, values-based leadership not only models the desired behaviors for staff, it also translates high-level ethical statements into operational examples appropriate to be applied to day-to-day responsibilities. For example, the statement "We believe that all people have the right to be treated with dignity and respect" conveys a principle. To apply this principle, the management accountant would discuss with his or her staff how it applies when they are performing tasks like requesting documentation, collecting receivables, and educating nonfinancial staff members about financial issues. General ethics training is valuable in creating overall awareness, but most employees are more interested in learning about behavioral issues specific to their position and responsibilities.

An organization's culture is made up of the accumulated behavioral actions of all of its employees over time. A culture that is in alignment with the organization's core values and code of ethics will tend to strengthen and reproduce the desired ongoing behaviors. This is illustrated by a culture where everyone from a top executive to an entry-level employee understands, shares, and lives the same set of values. The synergy of everyone acting in alignment with values will result in increased productivity, lower risks of fraud, and improved financial results.

Measuring and Improving Ethical Compliance

As stated in the SMA *Values and Ethics: From Inception to Practice*, "One of the greatest problems in achieving ethical compliance is the ability of any organization to actually be aware of what is happening on a day-to-day basis and making ethical compliance a core element of its mainstream governance and accountability framework."

Legal and regulatory mandates may serve as a deterrent to unethical behavior. However, management is responsible for instituting internal controls and operational transparency. Because "You cannot manage what you cannot measure," the certification by an organization's CEOs and CFOs that internal controls are adequate (as required under the Sarbanes-Oxley Act [SOX]) constitutes a large part of an organization's ethical compliance framework.

Internal controls provide a framework for identifying and controlling the risks that exist within an organization. They also can be used to assess the amount of risk to which an organization is exposed. Internal controls and an ethical culture are, necessarily, closely related. Internal controls that are in alignment with company values serve to strengthen the culture. At the same time, a vibrant ethical culture provides a strong foundation that compels employees to follow internal controls. Therefore, an effective internal control system becomes an integral part of the organizational culture.

Various tools are available to measure and improve compliance with ethical values; they include the human performance feedback loop, survey tools, and a whistleblowing framework.

Human Performance Feedback Loop

To improve compliance, performance review systems must be aligned with organizational values and ethics statements. Employee job descriptions, required competencies, and performance objectives should include ethical expectations.

Employee reviews, conducted annually (or more frequently), should evaluate the individual's compliance with ethical expectations along with operational goals. For example, an evaluation might rate not only accuracy and timeliness of an employee's reports; it also could rate his performance in treating all others with dignity and respect. Ideally, the feedback used to make this evaluation would include 360-degree input, including both internal and external responses.

The human performance feedback loop also should measure the number of employees completing ethics training and their score on any required testing.

Survey Tools

Another useful way to measure ethical performance is the use of surveys. Using the organization's code of ethics as a source, surveys could have employees rate how well the organization is doing.

For example, employees may be asked the degree to which they agree with statements such as: "This organization respects the dignity of all individuals." The results of surveys will indicate the degree of compliance and provide a method to stimulate an ongoing dialogue with employees.

Whistleblowing Framework

A whistleblowing framework provides employees who identify ethically questionable behavior by others with a confidential way to seek advice and report ethical violations.

Research has shown that employee hotlines are a valuable reporting mechanism for discovering fraud within an organization. If the hotline is truly anonymous and also can be used by employees to access advice on ethical situations, employees raise issues can more freely without fear of retaliation.

A further benefit of implementing a whistleblowing framework is the ability to collect, analyze, and summarize existing and potential ethical problems. This information is essential for identifying opportunities to improve training and internal controls. As stated in the SMA *Values and Ethics: From Inception to Practice,* "Management accountants need to ensure that such processes are in place, that they operate on a fully confidential basis, and that they are capable of generating statistical or event-based reporting through which insight into ethical practice can be created."

Governmental and International Implications for Organizational Ethics

As mentioned earlier, ethical behavior results from actions that are aligned with a core set of values. Governments attempt to legislate broad sets of values by creating laws and regulations that individuals and organizations are required to follow. Although working within the letter of the law does not guarantee that individuals are behaving ethically, understanding and applying applicable laws are a key part of organizational ethics.

The U.S. Foreign Corrupt Practices Act (FCPA) is a good example of this. The FCPA was passed in 1977 as a result of Securities and Exchange Commission (SEC) investigations in the mid-1970s that revealed that hundreds of companies admitted making questionable or illegal payments to foreign government officials to secure favorable action. The FCPA forbids an American company doing business in another country to pay bribes to a foreign government to obtain contracts or secure business.

The cultural values of the United States clearly were the impetus for the creation of the FCPA. However, not all governments in all parts of the world agree with these values. The challenge for the global organization becomes how to get work done in countries where the expectation of a "commission" (in effect, a payment to local government officials) is commonplace.

Ethically, a key question is: When do commissions become bribes? On an organizational level, senior management must ensure that the code of ethics is being applied consistently across all of the business cultures in which it operates. Specifically, managers should investigate how the code of ethics may conflict with existing practices in other countries. It is essential for employees to see that the code of ethics is applied consistently across the entire organization. Doing this may mean bypassing potential business opportunities when they require the organization to act in a manner that is inconsistent with stated ethical values.

Other important legal and ethical issues for international business involve cultural differences and disparities between international law and the laws of individual countries.

One country's ethical outrage may be another's ordinary practice, which may create an ethical dilemma for international businesses. On one side, a company may alienate potential trading partners or host countries by an ethnocentric, and apparently arrogant, insistence on the universal rightness of its own practices. On the other side, there is a temptation to follow local custom and practice.

How should a multinational corporation determine the working conditions and practices it will use when it establishes a subsidiary in another country? Should it accede to local custom even if such employment practices would be anathema in its home country? Or should it risk appearing ethnocentric—and being uncompetitive—by adhering to home-country standards in its subsidiary and, perhaps, openly criticizing the host country's practice?

One response companies have adopted to protest such ethical disparities has been the embargo. Rather than working in a country with problems such as poor treatment of workers or entrenched discrimination, companies may choose to have no business relations with the country. Nations, for their part, may enforce such a position on all domestic corporations. The United States, for example, for many years enforced an embargo on trade with or investment in South Africa, because of that country's discriminatory practice of apartheid. Yet many who opposed apartheid argued against the embargo, asserting that engagement with South Africa would provide a more effective venue for opposing apartheid and its effects from within an established relationship. Further, they argued that such embargoes simply hurt the people they are meant to help. In fact, some companies have set up foreign operations that challenge the hiring and workplace practices of the host country, but doing so requires overcoming significant obstacles and, sometimes, actual danger. There are no easy answers to ethical dilemmas that challenge international business, but such dilemmas cannot be ignored.

Different countries may have different laws for how to conduct business. Some businesses may choose to do business in nations in which they can conduct certain activities not allowed in their own countries. For example, to avoid U.S. taxes, some firms have moved their businesses to Caribbean island nations that do not charge taxes.

Global corporations based in the United States also have to comply with SOX. Section 406 of SOX requires companies to adopt (or explain why they have not adopted) a code of ethics for senior financial officers. The code applies to the firm's principal financial officer and comptroller or principal accounting officer as well as to the principal executive officer.

Section 406 also includes instructions for the timely reporting of "any change in or waiver of the code of ethics" for these officers. The SEC has defined the term *waiver* as company approval for an officer to make a material departure from the code of ethics. An implicit waiver involves the organization's failure to take action within a reasonable period of time after it becomes aware of a material departure from the code of ethics.

SOX Section 406 also defines a code of ethics as:

such standards as are reasonably necessary to promote—

1. honest and ethical conduct, including the ethical handling of actual or apparent conflicts of interest between personal and professional relationships;
2. full, fair, accurate, timely, and understandable disclosure in the periodic reports, required to be filed by the issuer; and
3. compliance with applicable governmental rules and regulations.

The SEC recognizes that a code of ethics needs to be applicable to the specific situation and culture of each company. Therefore, the SEC does not offer any specific wording or provisions that should be included in a code of ethics. However, the SEC did add that a code of ethics also should promote prompt reporting of violations of the code of ethics as well as accountability for adhering to the code.

The next scenario illustrates how these concepts and principles apply to an organization's operations.

Practice Ethical Scenario

Magneto Industries (MI) recently appointed George Parker as CEO following the retirement of the previous CEO. After spending a few weeks reviewing operations and financial results, George is concerned about how MI is doing business. MI reported record earnings over the last several years, with 15% growth per year— unprecedented in the industry.

When George interviewed Bob Gartner, the chief operating officer, Bob shared with George that the equipment used in production is in bad shape. Despite the fact that the equipment is only five years old, it has begun to break down at unexpected times due to lack of preventive maintenance.

Sam Donato, the head of maintenance, explained that the maintenance budget has been reduced by 10% to 15% every year for the last three years. Despite his pleas to the previous CEO to increase the budget and memos explaining the consequences of not properly maintaining the production equipment, he has had to limit his activities to repairs only. Further, he has had to literally glue some of the equipment back together to keep it running. What should have been a temporary fix became permanent when his purchase requests for replacement parts were returned to him unapproved.

One day while George was walking through the plant, he was astonished to see Tom Haskins, the production supervisor, take chewing gum out of his mouth and place it in a piece of machinery. When George asked what he was doing, Tom explained that there was a piece on the machinery that regularly vibrated loose. Tom had noticed that Sam's staff were getting irritated with having to repeatedly come out and glue it in place, so he had started to fix it himself to save time.

While in the plant, George also spoke to a few production employees. The general message that these people communicated was that they were just earning a paycheck while looking for a better job. MI was known for doing as little as possible to maintain its equipment and its workforce.

When he reviews the current-year financials, George is not surprised to see that revenue and production have slipped substantially on a year-to-date basis as compared to the previous year.

1. What values does this organization believe in, and how do they explain what George has witnessed?
2. How has leadership by example impacted the attitude and actions of Tom Haskins?
3. What steps should George take to create a more ethical and values-based culture at MI?
4. What are some of the potential benefits that MI may realize by making these changes?

Solution

1. MI's most important priority is growing the bottom line, no matter what they need to do to accomplish this task. This value resulted in utilizing short-term strategies with long-term consequences. For example, expensive and valuable equipment has been allowed to deteriorate, and employee turnover in the production area is very high.
2. Tom Haskins's attitude and actions are direct results of watching the organization prioritize short-term growth over long-term growth. He has watched the maintenance department glue equipment back together regularly and decided that his contribution to cutting costs is to patch the equipment together himself in the most expedient manner.
3. As CEO, George needs to set the tone at the top and let everyone know that past practices are no longer acceptable. If they don't already exist, George should identify and document MI's values and code of ethics.

   This should be followed by staff training, which should cover not only the values and code of conduct but also include examples of behaviors that are expected and those that are not acceptable. Examples should be specific to the position being trained. Annual reviews should be modified to include measures of the behavior covered in the training.

   All leaders in the organization, such as Bob Gartner and Sam Donato, should be held to a higher level of conduct than those below to set the tone at the top.

   Further, budgets should be set that are sufficient for staff to follow these values. For example, the maintenance budget should be looked at closely to determine what is needed to repair the existing equipment properly and to institute a preventive maintenance plan.

   On an organizational level, MI should implement a whistleblowing framework that employees can use to report unethical behavior. In addition, employees should be educated and encouraged to use this system as a confidential method for gaining advice in ethically challenging situations.

   To measure results, George could do a baseline survey of employees to identify current adherence to values. By repeating the same survey at a later date,

George will be able to measure whether the implemented practices resulted in the expected behavioral changes.

4. In the short run, MI will most likely experience a downturn in growth since unsustainable practices were used to create it. In the long run, MI will experience:

- Sustainable growth as a result of increased production from well-maintained equipment.
- Improved organizational culture.
- Improved reputation for quality and reliability.
- Improved interpersonal dynamics.
- Lower risk of fraud.

Knowledge Check:
Ethical Considerations for the Organization

The next questions are intended to help you check your understanding and recall of the material presented in this topic. They do not represent the type of questions that appear on the CMA exam.

Directions: Answer each question in the space provided. Correct answers and section references appear following these questions.

1. Corporate management is responsible for creating an ethical culture by doing all of the following **except**

   ☐ **a.** identifying and documenting organizational values.

   ☐ **b.** defining principles of behavior.

   ☐ **c.** implementing a whistleblowing mechanism.

   ☐ **d.** creating a code of ethics or conduct.

2. The **most** important reason for creating an ethical culture is:

   ☐ **a.** decreasing risk in the organization.

   ☐ **b.** creating alignment between what an organization believes in and what its employees do.

   ☐ **c.** ensuring compliance with SOX.

   ☐ **d.** increasing net income.

3. For ethics training to be effective, it should contain all of the following elements **except**

   ☐ **a.** Be part of orientation as well as ongoing training.

   ☐ **b.** Relate to real-world situations faced by employees.

   ☐ **c.** Provide a consistent message.

   ☐ **d.** Include a test to evaluate learning.

4. What are three tools available to measure and improve compliance?

   a. _____

   b. _____

   c. _____

5. Which of the following is an example of a metric that an annual review may include to measure compliance with corporate ethical expectations?

   ☐ **a.** Ability to complete work accurately

   ☐ **b.** Has signed off on having received and read the corporate code of ethics

   ☐ **c.** Ability to reach a decision when faced with a problem

   ☐ **d.** Ability to model behavior consistent with the corporate values statement

6. The U.S. Foreign Corrupt Practices Act

   ☐ **a.** forbids an American company doing business overseas to pay bribes.

   ☐ **b.** requires foreign companies doing business in the United States to comply with SOX.

   ☐ **c.** requires foreign companies that want to sell stock in U.S. exchanges to register with the Securities and Exchange Commission.

   ☐ **d.** forbids companies that do business in the United States from paying bribes.

7. Section 406 of the Sarbanes-Oxley Act requires

   ☐ **a.** senior financial officers to have and follow a code of ethics.

   ☐ **b.** organizations to use specific wording in their code of ethics.

   ☐ **c.** senior financial officers to sign off on the annual tax return.

   ☐ **d.** changes to the code of ethics to be reported on a Form 8-K.

Knowledge Check Answers:
Ethical Considerations for the Organization

1. Corporate management is responsible for creating an ethical culture by doing all of the following **except** [See *Ethics Starts at the Top.*]

    ☐ **a.** identifying and documenting organizational values.

    ☐ **b.** defining principles of behavior.

    ☒ **c.** implementing a whistleblowing mechanism.

    ☐ **d.** creating a code of ethics or conduct.

    A whistleblower framework does not create an ethical culture.

2. The **most** important reason for creating an ethical culture is [See *Applying Ethics in a Corporate Setting.*]

    ☐ **a.** decreasing risk in the organization.

    ☒ **b.** creating alignment between what an organization believes in and what its employees do.

    ☐ **c.** ensuring compliance with SOX.

    ☐ **d.** increasing net income.

    The other three answers are likely outcomes but not the defining reason.

3. For ethics training to be effective, it should contain all of the following elements **except** [See *Applying Ethics in a Corporate Setting.*]

    ☐ **a.** Be part of orientation as well as ongoing training.

    ☐ **b.** Relate to real-world situations faced by employees.

    ☐ **c.** Provide a consistent message.

    ☒ **d.** Include a test to evaluate learning.

4. What are three tools available to measure and improve compliance? [See *Measuring and Improving Ethical Compliance.*]

    a. Human performance feedback loop

    b. Survey tools

    c. Whistleblowing framework

5. Which of the following is an example of a metric that an annual review may include to measure compliance with corporate ethical expectations? [See *Measuring and Improving Ethical Compliance.*]

    ☐ **a.** Ability to complete work accurately

    ☐ **b.** Has signed off on having received and read the corporate code of ethics

     ☐ **c.**   Ability to reach a decision when faced with a problem

     ☑ **d.**   Ability to model behavior consistent with the corporate values statement

6. The U.S. Foreign Corrupt Practices Act [**See *Governmental and International Implications for Organizational Ethics.*]**

     ☑ **a.**   forbids an American company doing business overseas to pay bribes.

     ☐ **b.**   requires foreign companies doing business in the United States to comply with SOX.

     ☐ **c.**   requires foreign companies that want to sell stock in U.S. exchanges to register with the Securities and Exchange Commission.

     ☐ **d.**   forbids companies that do business in the United States from paying bribes.

7. Section 406 of the Sarbanes-Oxley Act requires [**See *Governmental and International Implications for Organizational Ethics.*]**

     ☑ **a.**   senior financial officers to have and follow a code of ethics.

     ☐ **b.**   organizations to use specific wording in their code of ethics.

     ☐ **c.**   senior financial officers to sign off on the annual tax return.

     ☐ **d.**   changes to the code of ethics to be reported on a Form 8-K.

Practice Questions: Professional Ethics

Directions: This sampling of questions is designed to emulate actual exam questions. Read each question and write your response on another sheet of paper. See the "Answers to Section Practice Questions" section at the end of this book to assess your response. Validate or improve the answer you wrote. For a more robust selection of practice questions, access the **Online Test Bank** at www.wileycma.com.

Question 2F1-AT01

Topic: Ethical Considerations for Management Accounting and Financial Management

As management accountants progress in the profession, they often have the responsibility to supervise the work of less experienced workers. Which of the following is an ethical responsibility of the supervisor?

- ☐ **a.** Hire new workers who will fit in socially with existing staff.
- ☐ **b.** Maximize the profit or minimize the cost of the department.
- ☐ **c.** Ensure that workers handle confidential information appropriately.
- ☐ **d.** Encourage the workers to develop relations with customers.

Question 2F1-AT02

Topic: Ethical Considerations for Management Accounting and Financial Management

Sam Smith has been offered a pair of tickets to the pro football team if Smith purchases a computerized inventory control system from a specific vendor. Which of the following steps should Smith take?

- ☐ **a.** Refuse any further conversations with the vendor.
- ☐ **b.** Review his company's policies on gifts from vendors.
- ☐ **c.** Sign the contract for the system if the price of the ticket is less than $50.
- ☐ **d.** Consult with the audit committee of the board of directors.

Question 2F1-AT03

Topic: Ethical Considerations for Management Accounting and Financial Management

John Moore was recently hired as assistant controller of a manufacturing company. The company controller, Nancy Kay, has forecasted a 16% increase in annual earnings. However, during the last quarter of the year, John estimates that the company will report only a 12% increase in earnings. When he reports this to Nancy, she tells him that meeting the numbers won't be a problem. She explains that there are several jobs in production that will finish after the end of the fiscal year, and she will record the associated revenue in the accounting system for the current year.

What is the first step that John Moore should take at this time?

- ☐ **a.** Notify the audit committee of the issue.
- ☐ **b.** Contact his lawyer to determine his rights.
- ☐ **c.** Discuss the issue with the chief financial officer of another company, who does not know any employees at John's company.
- ☐ **d.** Follow his organization's established policies regarding the resolution of this type of conflict.

Question 2F2-AT01

Topic: Ethical Considerations for the Organization

The Foreign Corrupt Practices Act is a U.S. law that prohibits U.S. companies from

- ☐ **a.** making "corrupt" payments to foreign officials for the purpose of obtaining or retaining business.
- ☐ **b.** making products in overseas markets that do not comply with the same safety and environmental regulations as for domestically produced products.
- ☐ **c.** exporting to countries that do not comply with U.S. human rights regulations.
- ☐ **d.** selling products for corrupt, unethical, or illegal purposes.

Question 2F2-AT02

Topic: Ethical Considerations for the Organization

Which of the following actions will most likely result in a successful foreign business venture in Islamic countries?

- ☐ **a.** Employ Islamic people.
- ☐ **b.** Behave in a manner that is consistent with Islamic ethics.
- ☐ **c.** Have property in an Islamic nation.
- ☐ **d.** Adhere to Islamic beliefs.

To further assess your understanding of the concepts and calculations covered in Part 2, Section F: Professional Ethics, practice with the **Online Test Bank** for this section. **REMINDER:** See the "Answers to Section Practice Questions" section at the end of this book.

Essay Exam Support Materials

Writing an effective essay exam is a special challenge. It tests your written communication skills in addition to your knowledge of the content. Essay questions also test your understanding of how specific pieces of information relate to one another, and your ability to apply your knowledge to real-life situations. The next information is included to help you learn more about how to respond to the exam part content in written essay form.

Preparing for the Essay Portion of the Exam

The essay portion of the CMA exam can draw from any of the LOS and content from Part 2: Financial Decision Making. It requires understanding the content and being prepared to evaluate the issues presented as well as making recommendations for the resolution of specific situations.

Your study plan should help you learn the content, learn how to respond to the content in multiple-choice questions, and learn to respond to essay questions presented on the content. This is a significant part of the challenge of the CMA exams. One way to meet this challenge is to break it down into smaller challenges—learn the content first, then practice multiple-choice exam-type questions, then learn how to respond to essay questions.

How to Write Essay Answers

The CMA exam essay questions require you to discuss the main points of a specific topic and then examine their implications. When developing your responses, you must support your answers with evidence of your thinking in order to demonstrate your knowledge and comprehension of a topic and your ability to apply that knowledge via thoughtful analysis.

You will be expected to present written answers that:

- Directly respond to the questions asked.
- Are presented in a logical manner.
- Demonstrate an appropriate understanding of the subject matter.

Clues within the questions can be used to help you formulate and organize your responses. Verbs such as *analyze, apply, explore, interpret,* and *examine* can help delineate the requirements of the question. Using the same verbs within your answer will help ensure that you are responding directly and completely to the specific questions being asked.

Candidates are expected to have a working knowledge of using word processing and electronic spreadsheets. They are also expected to have an understanding of basic financial statements, time value of money concepts, and elementary statistics. The essay portion of the exam is computer driven. Answers are entered using a text editor similar to Microsoft Notepad. Some questions may require a spreadsheet similar to, but not exactly the same as, Microsoft Excel.

Writing Skills

The essay section of the CMA exam is a way to assess your ability to analyze, evaluate, and effectively communicate about business situations. Written communication is an important skill required in today's business environment.

The Institute of Certified Management Accountants (ICMA) assesses your writing skills in the essay portion of the CMA exam. The assessment is based on these criteria:

- Use of standard English
- Organization
- Clarity

Use of Standard English

The use of standard English is an integral part of expressing ideas in a business environment. Assessment of the use of clear and concise terminology as is standard to the English language will be administered on the essay portion of the exam.

Organization

When answering essay questions, organizing your answers in a logical manner is important to effective business writing skills. As you read through the question, order your thoughts in a manner that exercises your process of thinking. Make sure that your answer has a clear beginning, outlining what you will be answering, followed by the answer, backed up by CMA content-specific facts, and a summary of what you just described.

Clarity

Being clear in your response is as important as the use of standard English and organization of your response on the CMA exam. Assessors of the essay portion of the CMA exam will look at the answer and critique based on whether the answer is clearly expressed and that the answer is supported by CMA content-specific rationale. When answering, read your answer thoroughly to make sure that your response is clear and that the reader will understand how you are attempting to answer the questions.

Using Standard English, Organization, and Clarity in Your Responses to the Essays

When reading through the essay examples, work through the problems as if you were actually answering the questions on the actual CMA exam. When working through the essays, pay close attention to the key words in the question, organize your response, and start writing the answer to the question. When answering, make sure that you are answering the question in a clear and concise manner and make sure that you use standard English. Once complete, compare your answer to the answer provided in the textbook. Pay close attention to the way the answer is organized, the key words that are used, and way the answer is presented. Compare the textbook answer to your answer to see how you did.

Essay Exam Study Tips

ON THE ACTUAL FOUR-HOUR CMA EXAM, the essay portion of the exam will begin once you complete the multiple-choice section or after three hours, whichever comes first. This means you will have at least one hour to complete the two essay questions presented.

To make the best use of your time to complete the essay portion:

- Prior to taking the exam, take the online tutorial to become familiar with the testing screens. The tutorial is not part of your testing time and may be repeated. However, total tutorial time is limited to 20 minutes.
- Briefly skim through both essay questions and get an idea what each question is asking you to do (i.e., describe, analyze, calculate, etc.).
- You have one hour to complete the full essay exam (more if you have finished the multiple-choice section earlier than the three-hour limit). Determine how much time you will dedicate to each essay question.
- Start with the question you know best. Begin by writing key words, thoughts, facts, figures, and anything else that can be used to answer the question.
- As you answer one question, issues related to the other may occur to you. Write that information next to the appropriate question. This will build your confidence and give you a starting place when you begin to answer the second question.

To answer each question:

- Read the entire question for requirements.
- Be aware of the verb clues that delineate what is being asked. This will help you formulate and organize your answer. Note that you may have more than one task—for example, define abc and interpret its applicability to xyz.
- Write the basic requirements in the answer space so that you are sure to address them.
- Begin your answer with one or two sentences that directly answer the question. If possible, rephrase the question's essential terms in a statement that directly answers the question.
- Use bullet points to show main ideas, and support each point with sufficient detail to show that you understand all the issues relevant to the question.
- Make it as easy as possible for graders to give you points. The goal in grading is to award you points, so show your thinking clearly and effectively. Do not write too little or too much.

- Finish your essay with one or two sentences that summarize your main point(s).
- Proofread your answer for logic, thoroughness, and clarity.
- Keep track of time. Do not spend too much time on one question.
- If you do not have enough time to write a full essay, write an outline of your main points to show what you know in order to get partial credit.

Examples of Essay Question Answers

EACH ESSAY QUESTION ACTUALLY CONSISTS of several related questions based on one scenario. The question as a whole is worth a set number of points and is graded against a scorecard to ensure consistent grading. The scorecard lists appropriate terms, topics, and ideas that address the answer. Presented here are two essay questions drawn from previous exams. The first essay question is followed by an example of an answer that would be awarded maximum points—a "best" answer. How these points are awarded is shown on a scorecard similar to ones used by the Institute of Certified Management Accountants (ICMA).

Following the second essay question are two answers that were awarded fewer points because they do not address all the issues. The "good" answer meets some but not all of the criteria. The "better" answer covers more of the requested information, as shown on the scorecard, and receives more points.

As you will see, the goal of the graders is to give test takers points rather than take them away. If test takers earn more credits than the maximum allowable points, they can be awarded only the maximum allowable number of points.

There are two types of essay questions: questions that ask for a **written response** and questions that ask for a **series of calculations, tables, or charts for a response**.

Note: The questions, answers, and scorecards used in these examples were provided by the ICMA and are used with their permission unless otherwise indicated.

Example Question 1: Amur Company

Amur Company manufactures three lawn care component parts: fuel systems, transmission assemblies, and electrical systems. For the past five years, manufacturing overhead has been applied to products on standard direct labor hours for the units actually produced. The standard cost information is shown next.

Exhibit A shows standard cost information.

Exhibit A Standard Cost Information

	Fuel Systems	Transmission Assemblies	Electrical Systems
Units produced and sold	10,000	20,000	30,000
Standard labor hours	2.0	1.5	1.0
Standard direct material cost per unit	$25.00	$36.00	$30.00
Budgeted and actual manufacturing overhead		$3,920,000	

The current direct labor rate is $10 per hour. New machinery that highly automates the production process was installed two years ago and greatly reduced the direct labor time to produce the three products. The selling price for each of the three products is 125% of the manufacturing cost.

Amur's segment of the lawn care component industry has become very competitive, and the company's profits have been decreasing. Eric West, Amur's controller, has been asked by the president of the company to analyze the overhead allocations and pricing structure. West thinks that future allocations should be based on machine hours and direct labor hours rather than the current allocation method, which is based on direct labor hours only. West has determined the additional product information shown in Exhibit B.

Exhibit B Additional Product Information

	Fuel Systems	Transmission Assemblies	Electrical Systems
Standard machine hours	2.0	4.0	6.0
Manufacturing overhead:			
Direct labor cost		$560,000	
Machine cost		$3,360,000	

Questions

1. By allocating all of the budgeted overhead based on direct labor hours, calculate the unit manufacturing cost and unit sales price for each of the three products manufactured at Amur Company.
2. Prepare an analysis for Amur Company using the appropriate cost driver(s) determined by Eric West for manufacturing overhead. Calculate the unit manufacturing cost and unit sales price for each of the three products.
3. Based on your calculations in Questions 1 and 2, prepare a recommendation for the president at Amur Company to increase the firm's profitability.

Sample "Best" Answer for Amur Business Scenario

Question 1

The allocation of all of Amur Company's budgeted manufacturing overhead based on direct labor hours results in the unit manufacturing costs and unit sales prices for its three products is calculated as follows:

Fuel systems

> Units: 10,000
>
> Standard labor hour/unit: 2.0
>
> **Total standard labor hours: 20,000**
>
> Direct material: $25.00
>
> Direct labor at $10/hour: $20.00
>
> Overhead at $49/DLH[1]: $98.00
>
> **Total cost: $143.00**
>
> **Sales price (125% of cost): $178.75**

Transmission Assemblies

> Units: 20,000
>
> Standard labor hour/unit: 1.5
>
> **Total standard labor hours: 30,000**
>
> Machine hours per unit: 4.0
>
> **Total machine hours: 80,000**
>
> Direct material: $36.00
>
> Direct labor at $10/hour: $15.00
>
> Overhead at $49/DLH[1]: $73.50
>
> **Total cost: $124.50**
>
> **Sales price (125% of cost): $155.63**

Electrical Systems

> Units: 30,000
>
> Standard labor hour/unit: 1.0
>
> **Total standard labor hours: 30,000**
>
> Direct material: $30.00
>
> Direct labor at $10/hour: $10.00
>
> Overhead at $49/DLH[1]: $49.00
>
> **Total cost: $89.00**
>
> **Sales price (125% of cost): $111.25**

Note:

[1] Total manufacturing overhead of $3,920,000 / 80,000 total direct labor hours = $49.00 per direct labor hour.

Question 2

When the cost drivers identified by Eric West are used to allocate manufacturing overhead, the unit manufacturing costs and unit sales prices for the three products manufactured at Amur Company are calculated as follows:

Fuel systems

> Units: 10,000
>
> Standard labor hour/unit: 2.0
>
> **Total standard labor hours: 20,000**
>
> Machine hours per unit: 2.0
>
> **Total machine hours: 20,000**
>
> Direct material: $25.00
>
> Direct labor at $10/hour: $20.00
>
> Overhead DLH at $7/hr[1]: $14.00
>
> Overhead Machine hrs at $12/hr[2]: $24.00
>
> **Total cost: $83.00**
>
> **Sales price (125% of cost): $103.75**

Transmission Assemblies

> Units: 20,000
>
> Standard labor hour/unit: 1.5
>
> **Total standard labor hours: 30,000**
>
> Machine hours per unit: 4.0
>
> **Total machine hours: 80,000**
>
> Direct material: $36.00
>
> Direct labor at $10/hour: $15.00
>
> Overhead DLH at $7/hr[1]: $10.50
>
> Overhead Machine hrs at $12/hr[2]: $48.00
>
> **Total cost: $109.50**
>
> **Sales price (125% of cost): $136.88**

Electrical Systems

> Units: 30,000
>
> Standard labor hour/unit: 1.0
>
> **Total standard labor hours: 30,000**
>
> Machine hours per unit: 6.0
>
> **Total machine hours: 180,000**
>
> Direct material: $30.00
>
> Direct labor at $10/hour: $10.00
>
> Overhead DLH at $7/hr[1]: $7.00

Overhead Machine hrs at $12/hr[2]: $72.00

Total cost: $119.00

Sales price (125% of cost): $148.75

Notes:

[1] Direct labor overhead of $560,000 / 80,000 total direct labor hours = $7.00 per direct labor hour.

[2] Machine overhead of $3,360,000 / 280,000 total machine hours = $12.00 per machine hour.

Question 3

The summary of the revised margins for each of Amur Company's three products, assuming the sales prices developed in Question 1 (allocation of all manufacturing overhead based on direct labor hours) is compared to revised costs developed in question 2 (allocation of manufacturing overhead based on cost drivers), is as follows:

Fuel Systems

Current price: $178.75

Revised cost: $83.00

Gross profit (loss): $95.75

Margin: 54%

Transmission Assemblies

Current price: $155.63

Revised cost: $109.50

Gross profit (loss): $46.13

Margin: 30%

Electrical Systems

Current price: $111.25

Revised cost: $119.00

Gross profit (loss): ($7.75)

Margin: NA

Based on this analysis, fuel systems and transmission assemblies are producing a higher return than Amur Company previously thought. Fuel systems are the most profitable (54% gross margin) followed by transmission assemblies; however, electrical systems are losing money on a full-cost basis.

Recommendations for improving profitability include:

- Focus on fuel systems, through actions such as increasing marketing expenditures and reducing the price to increase sales.
- Improve profitability of electrical systems through changes to the manufacturing process to reduce the machine hours required.
- Decrease marketing of this electrical system, and increase the selling price if possible.

Scoring of "Best" Answer for Amur Business Scenario

The Amur question would be graded against a scorecard similar to the one shown next. Note that:

- The scorecard addresses more issues than is required by the question. This is done to accommodate variations between test takers and to provide the greatest opportunity for a maximum score. The goal of the graders is to give test takers points rather than taking them away. If test takers earn more credits than the maximum allowable points, they will be awarded only the maximum allowable points.
- At times, the process is more important than the numeric answers. Test takers should show all work/calculations to earn the maximum allowable points.
- Explanations add points.
- Formatting is not judged. You will be using simple text editing, such as Microsoft Notepad, so you may not be able to make charts and should use dashes for bullets.

Amur Scorecard

Amur—Total allowable points 17

Question 1: Maximum allowable points = 5
Issues to address

Unit manufacturing cost and price (DLH allocation) =

Total labor hrs = Standard Hr / Unit × Units for each product

Totals all product labor hrs / (80,000)

Overhead of $3,920,000 / 80,000 DLH = Overhead rate

Includes unit direct materials cost in product cost

Direct labor = $10 × Standard DLH per unit

OH/Unit for each product = OH rate × Standard DLH/Unit

DM + DL + OH = Product cost / ($143($89)) / ($124.5)

Sales price = 125% × Product cost

Question 2: Maximum allowable points = 5

Unit manufacturing cost and price (Cost driver allocation) =

Total machine hours = (Standard hour / Unit) × Units for each product

Totals all product machine hours / (280.000)

Machine OH = $3,360, 000 / 280,000)

DL OH = $560,000 / 80,000 hours / ($7 per DHL)

OH / unit for each product = OH rate × standard MH / unit

OH / unit for each product = OH rate × standard DLH / unit

Includes DM and DLH for each product

Totals all costs / ($83) / ($109.50) / ($119)

Sales price = 125% × Product cost

Question 3: Maximum allowable points = 7
Issues to address
Recommendation
Increase emphasis on fuel systems
Margin/profit highest
Increase emphasis on transmission
Margin/profit is high
Increase marketing to generate sales
Decrease price to stimulate sales
Other recommendations to leverage profitability
Decrease emphasis on electrical systems
Margin is lower/losing money
Improve manufacturing process
Raise price if market will bear it
Other recommendations to deal with electrical systems

Example Question 2: Zylon Corporation

Business Scenario

Jeff Frankie is the chief financial officer of Zylon Corporation, a manufacturer and distributor of electronic security devices primarily suited for residential applications. Frankie is currently in the process of preparing the Y2 annual budget and implementing an incentive plan to reward the performance of key personnel. The final operating plans will then be presented to the board of directors for approval.

Frankie is aware that next year may be very difficult due to announced price increases to major customers. Zylon's president has put pressure on management to achieve the current year's earnings per share amounts. Frankie is, therefore, considering introducing zero-based budgeting in order to bring costs into line with revenue expectations.

Duke Edwards, Zylon's manufacturing director, is attempting to convince Frankie to build budgetary slack into the operating budget. Edwards contends that productivity is burdened by an abnormal amount of product design changes and small lot size production orders that incur costly setup times.

Questions

1. Explain at least three advantages and at least three disadvantages of budgetary slack from the point of view of Zylon Corporation's management group as a whole.
2. Describe how zero-based budgeting could be advantageous to Zylon Corporation's overall budget process.

Sample "Better" Answer for Zylon Business Scenario

Question 1

At least three advantages and three disadvantages of budgetary slack from the point of view of Zylon Corporation's management group as a whole include the following:

Advantages

1. It provides flexibility for operating under unknown circumstances, such as an extra margin for discretionary expenses in case budget assumptions on inflation are incorrect, or adverse circumstances arise.
2. Additional slack may be included to offset the costly setups from design changes and/or small lot size orders.
3. The increased pressure to meet Y1 earnings per share targets may result in postponing expenditures into Y2 or aggressively pulling sales into Y1. Budgetary slack in Y2 may compensate for shifting those earnings from Y2 into Y1.

Disadvantages

1. It decreases the ability to highlight weaknesses and take timely corrective actions on problem areas.
2. It decreases the overall effectiveness of corporate planning. Actions such as pricing changes or reduced promotional spending may be taken from a perceived need to improve earnings, when eliminating the budgetary slack could accomplish the same objective without marketplace changes.
3. It limits the objective evaluation of departmental managers and performance of subordinates by using budgetary information.

Question 2

Zero-based budgeting (ZBB) could be advantageous to Zylon Corporation's overall budget process for the following reasons:

- The ZBB process evaluates all proposed operating and administrative expenses as if they were being initiated for the first time. Each expenditure is justified, ranked, and prioritized according to its order of importance to the overall corporation, not just its role in one department.
- The focus is on evaluation of all activities rather than just incremental changes from the prior year. This allows addressing activities that have been ongoing to determine if they are still useful in the current environment. The objectives, operations, and costs of all activities are evaluated, and alternative means of accomplishing the objectives are more likely to be identified.

Scoring of "Better" Answer for Zylon Business Scenario

The Zylon question would be graded against a scorecard similar to the one shown. Note that:

- The scorecard addresses more issues than is required by the question. This is done to accommodate variations between test takers and to provide the greatest opportunity for a maximum score. The goal of the graders is to give test takers points rather than taking them away. If test takers earn more credits than the maximum allowable points, they can be awarded only the maximum allowable points.
- At times, the process is more important than the numeric answers. Test takers should show all work/calculations to earn the maximum allowable points.
- Explanations add points.
- Formatting is not judged. You will be using simple text editing such as Microsoft Notepad, so you may not be able to make charts and should use dashes for bullets.

Zylon Scorecard

Zylon Total allowable points 12

Question 1: Maximum allowable points = 6

Issues to address

Advantages

Provides flexibility under uncertainty

Extra margin for discretionary expenses

If assumptions wrong or adverse circumstances

Offsets unexpected setup costs

    Design changes

    Small lot sizes

Can compensate for earnings timing shifts

    Pressure to meet EPS

    Postponing expenses or accelerating sales

Other

    Explanation

Disadvantages

Decreases ability to ID weakness and take action

    Expenses are overstated in budget

Decreases effectiveness of overall planning process

Unnecessary actions taken such as

    Price changes or promotional spending cuts

    When eliminating slack would have solved problem

Limits objective evaluation of employees

    Measured against inflated budget

Other

    Explanation

Question 2: Maximum allowable points = 6

Issues to address

Advantages

Each expense is justified and ranked

    Each exp is evaluated as it were first time

(Continued)

Unnecessary activities can be eliminated
    All activities are evaluated
    Ongoing activities must be justified
Slack can be reduced
    Expenses must be grounded in realistic assumptions
Alternative means can be identified
    Are forced to evaluate processes
Other
    With explanation

Sample "Good" Answer for Zylon Business Scenario

A good answer would address enough of the identified three issues on the Zylon scorecard to earn a score of 70% or 80% of the maximum allowable points. A good answer for the Zylon scenario is shown next. It addresses the issues but does not go beyond the question to provide explanations and clarification.

Question 1

At least three advantages and three disadvantages of budgetary slack from the point of view of Zylon Corporation's management group as a whole include the following:

Advantages

- It provides operating flexibility.
- Additional slack may be included to offset costs.
- Zylon will need to postpone expenditures.

Disadvantages

- It decreases the ability to highlight weaknesses and take timely corrective actions on problem areas.
- It decreases the overall effectiveness of corporate planning.
- It limits the objective evaluation of departmental managers and performance of subordinates.

Question 2

Zero-based budgeting (ZBB) could be advantageous to Zylon Corporation's overall budget process for these reasons:

- The ZBB process evaluates all proposed operating and administrative expenses as if they were being initiated for the first time.
- The focus is on evaluation of all activities.

Practice Essay Questions and Answers

The next essay questions, and the answers that appear beginning at page 629, were adapted from the *Revised CMA Exam, Questions and Answers: Part 4* (2005 and 2008) books supplied by the Institute of Certified Management Accountants and are used with their permission (unless otherwise indicated).

The focus of the questions will be on the test taker's ability to apply concepts presented in the part being tested to a business scenario.

The answers supplied are meant to serve as samples of answers that address 80% or more of the points listed on the question grading guide. There are generally more points on the grading guide than points that can be awarded (i.e., there may be 110 possible points but only 100 that can be awarded in total), so answers scoring 80% may vary among test takers. Thus, the answers presented here represent one possible answer, not a definitive correct answer.

Part 2 Section A Questions

Question 2A-ES01

The accounting staff of CCB Enterprises has completed the preparation of financial statements for the 2005 calendar year. The statement of income for the current year and the comparative statement of financial position for 2005 and 2004 are reproduced here.

The accounting staff calculates selected financial ratios after the financial statements are prepared. Average balance sheet account balances are used in computing ratios involving income statement accounts. Ending balance sheet account balances are used in computing ratios involving only balance sheet items. The ratios have not been calculated for 2005. Financial ratios that were calculated for 2004 and their respective values are:

- Times interest earned   5.16 times
- Return on total assets   12.5%
- Return on operating assets   20.2%
- Return on common stockholders' equity   29.1%

CCB Enterprises
Statement of Income
Year Ended December 31, 2005
($000 omitted)

Revenue	
Net sales	$800,000
Other	60,000
Total revenue	$860,000
Expenses	
Cost of goods sold	$540,000
Research and development	25,000
Selling and administrative	155,000
Interest	20,000
Total expenses	$740,000
Income before income taxes	120,000
Income taxes (40% tax rate)	48,000
Net income	$72,000

CCB Enterprises Comparative Statement of Financial Position
December 31, 2005 and 2004
($000 omitted)

Assets	2005	2004
Current assets		
Cash and short-term investments	$26,000	$21,000
Receivables, less allowance for doubtful accounts ($1,100 in 2005 and $1,400 in 2004)	48,000	50,000
Inventories, at lower of FIFO cost or market	65,000	62,000
Prepaid items and other current assets	5,000	3,000
Total current assets	$144,000	$136,000
Other assets		
Investments, at cost	$106,000	$106,000
Deposits	10,000	8,000
Total other assets	$116,000	$114,000
Property, plant, and equipment		
Land	$12,000	$12,000
Buildings and equipment, less accumulated depreciation ($126,000 in 2005 and $122,000 in 2004)	268,000	248,000
Total property, plant, and equipment	$280,000	$260,000
Total assets	$540,000	$510,000

Liabilities and Stockholders' Equity

Current liabilities		
Short-term loans	$22,000	$24,000
Accounts payable	72,000	71,000
Salaries, wages, and other	26,000	27,000
Total current liabilities	$120,000	$122,000
Long-term debt	160,000	171,000
Total liabilities	$280,000	$293,000
Stockholders' equity		
Common stock, at par	$44,000	$42,000
Paid-in capital in excess of par	64,000	61,000
Total paid-in capital	$108,000	$103,000
Retained earnings	152,000	114,000
Total stockholders' equity	$260,000	$217,000
Total liabilities and stockholders' equity	$540,000	$510,000

Questions

A. Explain how the use of financial ratios can be advantageous to management.

B. Calculate the following financial ratios for 2005 for CCB Enterprises (round your answer to three decimal places):

1. Times interest earned
2. Return on total assets
3. Return on operating assets
4. Return on common stockholders' equity
5. Total debt ratio
6. Total debt to equity ratio
7. Current ratio
8. Quick (acid-test) ratio

Question 2A-ES02

Renbud Computer Services Co. (RCS) specializes in customized software development for the broadcast and telecommunications industries. The company was started 30 years ago by three people to develop software primarily for a national network to be used in broadcasting national election results. After sustained and manageable growth for many years, the company has grown very fast over the last three years, doubling in size. This growth has placed the company in a challenging financial position for the coming year.

Within 30 days, RCS will need to renew its $300,000 loan, a current liability, with the Third State Bank of San Marcos. Harvey Renbud, president of RCS, is concerned about renewing the loan because of the low amount of cash on hand. The bank has requested RCS's last year's income statement, comparative balance sheets for the last two years, and six ratios relating to operating performance and liquidity.

RCS Financial Statements

Renbud Computer Services Co.
Income Statement
Last Year

Net revenues		$2,500,000
Expenses		
Cost of product services	$1,500,000	
Selling and administration	300,000	
Depreciation and amortization	200,000	
Interest	60,000	
Income taxes	150,000	
Total expenses		$2,210,000
Net income		$ 290,000

Renbud Computer Services Co.
Balance Sheet
Past Two Years

Assets	Last Year	Two Years Ago
Cash	$50,000	$50,000
Accounts receivable, net	350,000	250,000
Operating supplies and other	70,000	60,000
Equipment, net	1,100,000	900,000
Furniture and fixtures, net	120,000	100,000
Other long-term assets	240,000	200,00
Total assets	$1,930,000	$1,560,000
Liabilities and shareholders' equity		
Accounts payable	$150,000	$130,000
Taxes payable	140,000	120,000
Note payable (Third State Bank)	300,000	200,000
Bonds payable (due in 2002)	400,000	400,000
Total liabilities	990,000	850,000
Capital stock (1,000 shares)	100,000	100,000
Retained earnings	840,000	610,000
Total shareholders' equity	710,000	940,000
Total liabilities and shareholders' equity	$1,930,000	$1,560,000

Questions

A. Explain why the Third State Bank of San Marcos would be interested in Renbud's comparative financial statements.

B. Using Computer Services Co.'s comparative financial statements, ratio calculations, and industry ratios, calculate these financial ratios for RCS Co.:
1. Current ratios for the past two years
2. Accounts receivable turnover for last year
3. Total asset turnover for last year
4. Return on shareholders' equity for last year
5. Debt to equity ratio for the last two years
6. Net profit margin percentage (return on sales) for last year

C. Briefly discuss the limitations and difficulties that can be encountered in using ratio analysis.

Question 2A-ES03

In the Statements of Financial Accounting Concepts (SFACs), the Financial Accounting Standards Board (FASB) set forth the fundamentals on which financial accounting and reporting standards are to be based. Specifically, the FASB intends that these concept statements establish objectives and concepts that can be used to develop standards for financial accounting and reporting, and to resolve new and emerging problems. Knowledge of the FASB objectives and concepts should enable those affected by financial accounting standards to better understand the content and limitations of the information provided by financial accounting and reporting. **SFAC No. 8** Chapter 1 discusses the objective of general-purpose financial reporting by a reporting entity, and **SFAC No. 5** recommends the composition of a full set of financial statements.

Question

Identify and describe the major sections of the statement of cash flows.

Question 2A-ES04

Sentech Scientific Inc., a manufacturer of test instruments, is in contract negotiations with the labor union that represents its hourly manufacturing employees. Negotiations have reached an impasse, and it appears that a strike is imminent. The controller has called the general accounting manager into his office to discuss liquidity issues if and when a strike does occur.

The controller asks the accounting manager to recommend measures to assess liquidity if a strike were to occur. Although some of the nonunion employees probably could produce test instruments during a strike, the controller would rather be conservative and assume no shipments during this time frame. Since customers may go to other sources to obtain the products they need during a strike, cash receipts for current outstanding amounts owed by customers may not be paid on a timely basis.

Questions

A. Define *liquidity*, and explain its importance to Sentech.
B. Identify three measures that could be used to assess liquidity, and explain how to calculate these measures.
C. Determine which liquidity measure identified above would **best** fit the controller's requirements, and explain why. Include in your discussion the reasons why the other measures would not be as appropriate.

Question 2A-ES05

Chargrille Inc. is a U.S. firm that manufactures barbecue grills. The majority of the component parts are acquired from a company in Mexico, then shipped to the United States, where the grills are assembled, packaged, and shipped to dealers. Helen Adams, the treasurer, is developing the revision to the cash budget for the second quarter utilizing these forecasted parameters:

Sales Data

	March	April	May	June	July
U.S.—Unit Sales	70,000	80,000	75,000	65,000	65,000
Canada—Unit Sales	50,000	50,000	60,000	45,000	35,000

- Selling price: In U.S. = 50 US dollars (USD); in Canada = 60 Canadian dollars (CAD)
- Variable expenses: U.S. labor = 10 USD per unit

  U.S. materials = 5 USD per unit
  Mexican imported parts = 350 Mexican pesos (MXN) per unit

- Overhead per month = 400,000 USD
- An interest payment on long term-debt of 500,000 USD is due in June.
- An income tax payment of 1,000,000 USD is due in June.
- Collections are assumed to occur in the month following the sale.
- Products are manufactured and the cash is expended one month prior to the sale.
- The cash balance at the end of March is assumed to be 1 million USD.
- Forward exchange rates are assumed to be:

	April	May	June
CAD per USD	1.20	1.19	1.18
MXN per USD	11.3	11.4	11.5

Questions

A. Develop the monthly cash flow budget in U.S. dollars (USD) for April, May, and June, showing the beginning cash balance, cash receipts, cash disbursements, and ending cash balance for each month. (Use the spreadsheet to enter your responses.)

B. Identify and discuss the potential impact of currency fluctuations on receipts and cash disbursements that Chargrille is exposed to based on the calculations you made in Question A.

C. If the spot rate (per 1 USD) on the Canadian dollar is 1.20 and it is 11.00 on the Mexican peso at the time Adams is preparing the budget revision, identify whether the U.S. dollar is expected to appreciate or depreciate during the second quarter relative to the:

 1. Canadian dollar

 2. Mexican peso

D. Identify and discuss two alternatives available to reduce the foreign exchange rate risk to which Chargrille is exposed.

Question 2A-ES06

Giga Industries is a large, publicly held manufacturer of telecommunications equipment. The firm developed the next forecast for the upcoming year.

Balance Sheet (thousands of dollars)		
Current assets		$100,000
Fixed assets	750,000	
Accumulated depreciation	200,000	
Net fixed assets		550,000
TOTAL ASSETS		$650,000
Current liabilities		$50,000
Long-term debt		150,000
Shareholders' equity		
Preferred stock	50,000	
Common—par of $2	100,000	
Common—premium	200,000	
Retained earnings	100,000	
		450,000
TOTAL LIABILITIES and EQUITY		$650,000

Income Statement (thousands of dollars)	
Revenue	$2,000,000
Depreciation expense	50,000
Other expenses	1,775,000
Earnings before interest & taxes	175,000
Interest expense	15,000
Taxes (40% effective rate)	64,000
Net income	96,000
Preferred stock dividends	5,000
Earnings for common stock	$91,000

The product development team has developed a new line of state-of-the-art switching devices and is proposing a major capital investment of $200 million for a new division of the firm that will manufacture and sell the new line. An extensive financial analysis was prepared using estimates for each year of the estimated 10-year product life and presented to the board of directors indicating that the project would result in a positive net present value (NPV) of $60 million and an internal rate of return (IRR) of 25%. A board member commented that the project looked very promising but expressed concern about the impact on earnings. The controller was asked to develop a revised forecast for the coming year, assuming the project was approved.

Questions

A. You are preparing the revised forecast for the controller. For each of the next assumptions, show the balance sheet and/or income statement account that would be affected, the amount of the change, and if the change increases or decreases the account. Assume no flotation costs on all financing.

  1. The $200 million investment in fixed assets will be made on January 1 and will be depreciated on a 10-year straight-line basis for financial statement and income tax purposes.

  2. On January 1, $75 million of 10-year bonds will be issued at par with annual interest of 10% payable December 31 with principal to be repaid at maturity.

  3. On January 1, $25 million of preferred stock will be issued with an annual dividend rate of 14% payable December 31.

  4. On January 1, 4 million new shares of common stock will be issued to net the firm $25 per share. Common stock dividends are expected to be $0.50 payable December 31, as in the original forecast.

  5. During the initial year of operation, the new product is expected to produce cash revenue of $60 million and have cash expenses (other than depreciation) of $30 million.

B. Assume that the tax rate is expected to remain at 40% and that taxes are paid on December 31. Calculate the change in net income resulting from the transactions in question A.

C. Since financial theory indicates that project decisions should be made based on NPV and IRR, why would a large public company be concerned about the effect on earnings in the first year?

Question 2A-ES07

Foyle Inc. has prepared the comparative income statements for the three most recent fiscal years that are shown below. While profitable, Foyle has been losing market share and is concerned about future performance. Also presented are data about Foyle's largest competitor and the industry average.

	Year 1	Year 2	Year 3	Competitor	Industry Average
Revenue	$20,000	$24,000	$30,000	$45,000	$28,000
Cost of goods sold	12,000	12,000	18,000	21,600	14,000
Gross profit	8,000	12,000	12,000	23,400	14,000
Sales and marketing	2,000	2,000	2,000	5,000	3,000
General and administrative	1,500	2,000	3,000	3,150	2,500
Research and development	1,500	2,000	1,000	4,000	1,500
Operating income	$ 3,000	$ 6,000	$ 6,000	$11,250	$ 7,000

Questions

1. Using the three Foyle Inc. statements,
    a. prepare a comparative common-size statement using revenue as the base measure.
    b. prepare a common base-year income statement using year 1 as the base year. Show your calculations.
2. Calculate Foyle's growth rate of both revenue and operating income for year 2 and year 3. Show your calculations.
3. By evaluating Foyle's performance against the performance of Foyle's largest competitor and the industry average, identify and discuss three areas that Foyle should target for further investigation and performance improvement. Support your discussion with data.

Question 2A-ES08

Income statements for Bockman Industries, a retailer, are shown next for the past two years.

	Year 2	Year 1
Revenues	$6,400,000	$6,000,000
Cost of goods sold	3,100,000	2,850,000
Gross margin	3,300,000	3,150,000
Selling expenses	950,000	880,000
Administrative expenses	1,120,000	1,050,000
Loss due to strike	20,000	0
Interest expense	30,000	30,000
Income before taxes	1,180,000	1,190,000
Income tax expense	472,000	476,000
Income from continuing operations	708,000	714,000
Discontinued operations, net	72,000	0
Net income	$ 780,000	$ 714,000
Earnings per share	$2.50	$2.30

Questions

1. Prepare common-size income statements (vertical analysis) for Bockman Industries for the two years presented.
2. Prepare a memo to the controller of Bockman identifying and describing a possible explanation for each of the following.
   a. An increase in sales along with the change in the gross margin percentage
   b. An increase in sales along with the increase in selling expenses
   c. An increase in sales along with the increase in administrative expenses
3. Assume that Bockman has no preferred stock outstanding and that any change in the number of shares of common stock occurred at the beginning of year 2. If the shareholders' equity at the end of year 2 totaled $7,363,200, calculate Bockman's book value per share.

Question 2A-ES09

Knight, Inc. and Day, Ltd. are large firms in the same industry. Each firm has $200 million of assets and produces $50 million of earnings before interest and taxes (EBIT), and both are subject to a 40% income tax rate. Knight finances 30% of its assets with debt at a before-tax cost of 10%. Day finances 60% of its assets with debt at a before-tax cost of 15%.

Questions

1. Develop a summary balance sheet and a summary income statement for each of the two companies based on the information provided. Round dollar amounts to the nearest million.
2. Calculate the return on equity for each company, to the nearest tenth of a percent.
3. Based on the information given, identify which company has the higher level of risk. Explain your answer.
4. Describe and explain four implications (or costs) of financial distress.

Question 2A-ES10

McMullen Industries is planning a major expansion of its facilities in several major markets. The new fixed assets to be acquired are estimated to cost $500 million, and McMullen is discussing financing arrangements with an investment banking firm. The summarized income statement and balance sheet for McMullen are shown next.

McMullen Industries
Income Statement
(millions of dollars)

Sales	$5,500
Cost of goods sold	3,100
Gross profit	2,400
Selling, general, and administrative	1,600
Operating profit	800
Interest expense	100
Pretax income	700
Taxes (40%)	280
Net income	$420
Earnings per share	$7.00

Balance Sheet
(millions of dollars)

Current assets	$ 100
Net fixed assets	3,000
Total assets	3,100
Current liabilities	50
Long-term debt	1,000
Common stock:	
Par value ($2/share)	120
Additional paid-in capital	1,000
Retained earnings	930
Net common equity	2,050
Total liabilities and equity	$3,100

One financing option is the issuance of new shares of common stock. The investment banker estimates that new shares can be issued at a price of $100 per share. McMullen pays an annual dividend of $2 per share every December 31. Another option is to issue $500 million of 20-year mortgage bonds at 6% with principal repayment beginning in year 10. Interest is payable annually on December 31.

Questions

1. Disregarding issue costs and assuming the financing is in place for the full year, develop a pro forma income statement (including earnings per share) and balance sheet by adjusting the income statement and balance sheet above to reflect the acquisition of the new facilities and associated financing for the:
   a. Common stock alternative
   b. Debt alternative
2. Discuss the following financial measures and calculate each for the common stock and debt alternatives:
   a. Financial leverage ratio
   b. Working capital

3. Is the debt issue viable if McMullen has a covenant in one of its prior debt agreements stating that the company must maintain a debt-to-equity ratio below 60%? Show your calculations.
4. Using the DuPont approach to return on equity, calculate: net profit margin, asset turnover, equity multiplier, and return on equity for:
   a. Common stock alternative
   b. Debt alternative
5. Identify and briefly discuss five factors that influence a company's capital structure.

Part 2 Section B Questions

Question 2B-ES01

The Gershenfeld Foundation was established 25 years ago to encourage, promote, and support research in the physical sciences. A wide range of industrial corporations contribute money in support of the foundation's work. The foundation has awarded research grants at a rate commensurate with its contributions and portfolio earnings.

Gershenfeld's contributions have increased significantly the past few months. The results of the foundation's recent fund drive exceeded the expectations of the board of trustees. New research grants are being reviewed and evaluated, but a final decision on which grants to fund and the amount of funding will not be made for at least 60 days. Thus, Gershenfeld has an excess cash position that is expected to continue for two months.

The board of trustees has instructed the foundation's executive director to invest the excess cash during this interim period. The executive director has been instructed to earn the highest possible yield while maintaining marketability and safety of principal. The types of investments that the executive director is considering for the use of $3.5 million of excess cash are (1) certificates of deposit, (2) U.S. Treasury bills, and (3) preferred stock of domestic corporations.

Questions

A. Define each of the next financial instrument characteristics and explain the effect each has on the yield of investments.
   1. Default risk
   2. Marketability
   3. Maturity
B. Evaluate each type of investment being considered by Gershenfeld's executive director in terms of default risk, marketability, and maturity.
C. Discuss the suitability of each type of investment being considered by the executive director for Gershenfeld Foundation's particular situation.

Question 2B-ES02

Atrax Corporation is now a diversified company that was originally founded as a textile and milling company by Adam Traxal. During the 1980s and early 1990s, before any diversification, Atrax's earnings had leveled off to about $2.25 per share. The growth possibilities in this industry were limited so that the demand for expansion funds has been low. There were large internal cash flows during this period, and Atrax regularly paid out 65% of its earnings as cash dividends. By the middle 1990s, this large dividend payout had become a trademark of Atrax's common stock.

The firm began diversifying into high-technology, growth companies in 1994 in an effort to reduce its business risk from its dependence on a single source of sales. Traxal thought such diversification was essential to maintain Atrax's financial health. The diversification program has been successful as far as Traxal is concerned. Atrax is no longer completely dependent on a single source of sales. The earnings have grown moderately to $2.80 per share since 1994 despite the issuance of additional common shares. The price of the Atrax common stock has increased so that the price/earnings (P/E) ratio is slightly higher than it was in 1994. In addition, the 65% cash dividend payout ratio has been maintained during the expansion period.

At first the diversification program was easily financed by the excess funds that were generated internally. Eventually though, the firm began to recognize the need to use external sources—long-term debt and/or additional issues of common stock—to finance its expansion programs. One consequence of the several common stock offerings was to dilute Traxal's control over the firm because he was unable to purchase his pro rata share of the additional offerings due to a shortage of personal funds. The Traxal family holdings amounted to 54% of the firm's stock in 1994, but their ownership has now fallen to around 35%. However, Traxal still is able to maintain effective control over the firm because no other stockholder owns more than 4% of the total stock.

Traxal believes that continued expansion is important for Atrax. Traxal is against any additional issues of common equity because he still cannot generate the personal funds necessary to purchase additional stock to maintain his present equity position. However, further expansion could be greatly hampered if additional issues of common equity are not employed. Traxal has instructed his staff to suggest alternative proposals that would allow him to maintain control of Atrax and still continue the firm's diversification program. Summaries of three proposals are presented next.

Proposal 1

The acquisition program would continue and be financed out of earnings, not paid out as dividends and from long-term debt issues and preferred stock issues. The current 65% cash dividend payout ratio would be maintained, and there would be no additional issues of common stocks. However, there would be an increase in long-term debt and preferred stock issues.

Proposal 2

The acquisition program would continue, and cash dividends would be reduced. The staff estimates that acquisitions could be financed with internally generated funds and a minimum amount of long-term debt. No additional common equity would be required. Atrax probably could distribute cash dividends equal to 10% to 20% of earnings. This proposal would not significantly change Atrax's current debt-to-equity relationship. In an attempt to appease stockholders who face a drop in their cash dividends, a stock dividend would be paid.

Proposal 3

The acquisition program would continue and be financed entirely by internally generated funds by reducing the cash dividend payout rate to zero, if necessary. No additional long-term debt or shares of common stock would be employed.

Questions

A. Adam Traxal finds Proposal 1 interesting but wonders what effect it would have on the rest of the firm and on the market value of Atrax Corporation's common stock. Assuming that the price of a firm's stock is the product of its current earnings per share and its historical price/earnings ratio, indicate the ways in which implementing Proposal 1 would operate to affect the market price of Atrax's common stock.

B. Adam Traxal considers Proposal 3 to be the least attractive because cash dividends might be reduced to zero. Explain what the probable short-term and long-term effects would be on the market price of Atrax's common stock if the acquisition program is dependent on reducing the cash dividend payout ratio to zero.

C. Adam Traxal considers Proposal 2 the most appealing because dividends still would continue to be distributed.

   1. Would Traxal be able to maintain his current equity position of 35% if stock dividends were distributed? Explain your answer.
   2. Explain how, if at all, the market price of Atrax's common stock probably would be affected if this proposal is adopted.
   3. Compare and contrast Proposal 2 with Proposal 3 in terms of the probable effects on the market price of Atrax's common stock.

Question 2B-ES03

Kravel Corporation is a diversified company with several manufacturing plants. Kravel's Dayton plant has been supplying parts to truck manufacturers for over 30 years. The last shipment of truck parts from the Dayton plant will be made December 31, 2006. Kravel's management currently is studying three alternatives relating to its soon-to-be-idle plant and equipment in Dayton.

Alternative 1

Wasson Industries has offered to buy the Dayton plant for $3,000,000 cash on January 1, 2007.

Alternative 2

Harr Enterprises has offered to lease the Dayton facilities for four years beginning on January 1, 2007. Harr's annual lease payments would be $500,000 plus 10% of the gross dollar sales of all items produced in the Dayton plant. Probabilities of Harr's annual gross dollar sales from the Dayton plant are estimated as shown next.

Annual Gross Dollar Sales	Estimated Probability
$2,000,000	0.1
4,000,000	0.4
6,000,000	0.3
8,000,000	0.2

Alternative 3

Kravel is considering the production of souvenir items to be sold in connection with upcoming sporting events. The Dayton plant would be used to produce 70,000 items per month at an annual cash outlay of $2,250,000 during 2007, 2008, and 2009. Linda Yetter, vice president of marketing, has recommended a selling price of $5 per item and believes the items will sell uniformly throughout 2008, 2009, and 2010.

The adjusted basis of the Dayton plant as of the close of business on December 31, 2006, will be $4,200,000. Kravel has used straight-line depreciation for all capital assets at the Dayton plant. If the Dayton plant is not sold, the annual straight-line depreciation charge for the plant and equipment will be $900,000 each year for the next four years. The market value of the plant and equipment on December 31, 2010, is estimated to be $600,000.

Kravel requires an after-tax rate of return of 16% for capital investment decisions and is subject to corporate income tax rates of 40% on operating income and 20% on capital gains.

Questions

A. Calculate the present value (at December 31, 2006) of the expected after-tax cash flows for each of the three alternatives available to Kravel Corporation regarding the Dayton plant. Assume all recurring cash flows take place at the end of the year.

B. Discuss the additional factors, both quantitative and qualitative, Kravel Corporation should consider before a decision is made regarding the disposition or use of the idle plant and equipment at the Dayton plant.

Question 2B-ES04

Langley Industries plans to acquire new assets costing $80 million during the coming year and is in the process of determining how to finance the acquisitions. The business plan for the coming year indicates that retained earnings of $15 million will be available for new investments. As far as external financing is concerned, discussions with investment bankers indicate that market conditions for Langley securities should be as listed next.

- Bonds with a coupon rate of 10% can be sold at par.
- Preferred stock with an annual dividend of 12% can be sold at par.
- Common stock can be sold to yield Langley $58 per share.

The company's current capital structure, which is considered optimal, is shown next.

Long-term debt	$175 million
Preferred stock	50 million
Common equity	275 million

Financial studies performed for Langley indicate that the cost of common equity is 16%. The company has a 40% marginal tax rate. (Ignore floatation costs for all calculations.)

Questions

A. Determine how Langley should finance its $80 million capital expenditure program, considering all sources of funds. Be sure to identify how many new shares of common stock will have to be sold. Show your calculations.

B. Calculate Langley's weighted incremental cost of capital that it could use to assess the viability of investment options.

C. Identify how each of the next events, considered individually, would affect Langley's cost of capital (increase, decrease, no change). No calculations are required.

  1. The corporate tax rate is increased.

  2. Banks indicate that lending rates will be increasing.

  3. Langley's beta value is reduced due to investor perception of risk.

  4. The firm decides to significantly increase the percentage of debt in its capital structure since debt is the lowest-cost source of funds.

Question 2B-ES05

Crenshaw Manufacturing has decided to acquire new equipment for its manufacturing facilities and currently is deciding how to finance the acquisition. The equipment has an initial purchase and installation cost of $2 million, will be utilized for five years, and is expected to have a salvage value of $200,000 at the end of the five-year period. The estimated economic life of the equipment is six years. Maintenance cost is expected to be $75,000 per year. Crenshaw has an effective income tax rate of 40%. Crenshaw is considering two options:

  1. *Purchase the equipment.* Crenshaw would depreciate the property for financial statement purposes on a straight-line basis over five years and for federal income tax purposes as three-year property using the MACRS general depreciation system and the half-year convention producing tax depreciation rates (rounded) of 33%, 45%, 15%, and 7% for years 1 through 4 respectively. In addition to maintenance costs, Crenshaw would have to pay insurance of $25,000 per year and property taxes of $50,000 per year.

2. *Lease the equipment through Morton Financial, a third-party lessor.* Morton provided a quote of $600,000 per year due at the year-end as the lease payment. Morton would be responsible for insurance and property taxes, but Crenshaw would be responsible for maintenance.

Crenshaw's financial analysis department realizes that the financial community views leasing as a form of debt financing and therefore evaluates the lease versus buy decision as 100% debt financing. Crenshaw could issue debt at a before-tax cost of 10% in today's market.

Questions

A. Should Crenshaw purchase or lease the new equipment? Support your recommendation with calculations that show the net financial advantage.

B. If Crenshaw decides to lease the equipment, should the lease be classified as an operating or a capital lease for financial accounting and reporting purposes? Support your answer.

C. Identify three reasons why firms in general may consider leasing as an alternative to ownership.

Question 2B-ES06

Henderson Inc. needs to raise $15 million for its research and development program. Its investment banker suggested raising the funds through the issuance of original issue discount bonds. The bonds would be outstanding for five years, have a semiannual coupon rate of 6%, and a maturity value of $1,000 each. The current market conditions require a yield of 8%, given Henderson's bond rating. Henderson's marginal income tax rate is 40%. Ignore the issue expense of the bonds and round all calculations to the nearest dollar. Assume the bonds are issued on the first day of the fiscal year.

Questions

A. What is the issue price of each bond? Show your calculations.

B. How many bonds will Henderson have to issue? Show your calculations.

C. Determine the net after-tax cash flows per bond to Henderson relating to the bonds at issuance (time = 0) and for each of the five years they are outstanding. Show your calculations.

D. Assume that at the end of three years, interest rates are 6% for bonds rated the same as Henderson's and maturing at the same time. What would a rational investor be willing to pay for one of Henderson's bonds? Show your calculations.

Question 2B-ES07

Han Electronics Inc. is an electronics retailer with a fitness equipment retailer subsidiary. Han is a mature company with declining sales while the subsidiary is growing and profitable. The management of Han is considering several strategic options for the company as a whole. They considered purchasing additional companies to continue to diversify their product mix or split out some or all of the subsidiary into a separate company so that each company could go in a different direction. Ultimately, the concern is that Han is failing. Management wants to maximize shareholder value, turn the company around, and continue as a going concern.

Questions

1. **a.** Define mergers and acquisitions.
   b. Does this scenario describe a merger or an acquisition?
   c. Identify three possible synergies or benefits of mergers and acquisitions.
2. **a.** Identify and describe these two types of divestitures: spin-offs and equity carve-outs.
   b. Identify whether either of these divestiture types is described in the scenario above.
3. **a.** Define bankruptcy and identify the different types of bankruptcy.
   b. What is the priority of creditors in a bankruptcy proceeding?

Question 2B-ES08

OneCo, Inc. produces a single product. Cost per unit, based on the manufacture and sale of 10,000 units per month at full capacity, is shown next.

Direct materials	$4.00
Direct labor	1.30
Variable overhead	2.50
Fixed overhead	3.40
Sales commission	.90
	12.10

The $0.90 sales commission is paid for every unit sold through regular channels. Market demand is such that OneCo is operating at full capacity, and the firm has found it can sell all it can produce at the market price of $16.50.

Currently, OneCo is considering two separate proposals:

a. Gatsby, Inc. has offered to buy 1,000 units at $14.35 each. Sales commission would be $0.35 on this special order.
b. Zelda Productions, Inc. has offered to produce 1,000 units at a delivered cost to OneCo of $14.50 each.

Questions

1. What would be the effect on OneCo's operating income of each of the following actions?
   a. Acceptance of the proposal from Gatsby but rejection of the proposal from Zelda
   b. Acceptance of the proposal from Zelda but rejection of the proposal from Gatsby
   c. Acceptance of both proposals

2. Assume Gatsby has offered a second proposal to purchase 2,000 units at the market price of $16.50 but has requested product modifications that would increase direct materials cost by $.30 per unit and increase direct labor and variable overhead by 15%. The sales commission would be $.35 per unit.
   a. Should OneCo accept this order? Explain your recommendation.
   b. Would your recommendation be different if the company had excess capacity? Explain your answer.
3. Identify and describe at least two factors other than the effect on income that OneCo should consider before making a decision on the proposals.

Part 2 Section C Questions

Question 2C-ES01

Microeconomic theory suggests that the quantity demanded for any good is a function of relative prices, consumer real income, and consumer tastes. If tastes are held constant, changes in the other two independent variables will induce a change in the dependent variable (i.e., the quantity demanded for a particular good). The concept that measures the responsiveness of quantity demanded to changes in the independent variable is called "elasticity of demand."

Questions

A. Define the concept of price elasticity of demand.
B. Explain the significance of the price elasticity of demand concept for a firm's management.

Question 2C-ES02

Candice Company has decided to introduce a new product. The new product can be manufactured by either a capital-intensive method or a labor-intensive method. The manufacturing method will not affect the quality of the product. The estimated manufacturing costs for each of the two methods are shown next.

	Capital Intensive		Labor Intensive	
Raw materials		$5.00		$5.60
Direct labor	.5DLH* @ $12	6.00	.8DLH @ $9	7.20
Variable overhead	.5DLH @ $6	3.00	.8DLH @ $6	4.80
Directly traceable incremental fixed manufacturing costs		$2,440,000		$1,320,000

*DLH = direct labor hour

Candice's market research department has recommended an introductory unit sales price of $30. The incremental selling expenses are estimated to be $500,000 annually plus $2 for each unit sold regardless of the manufacturing method used.

Questions

A. Calculate the estimated break-even point in annual unit sales of the new product if Candice Company uses the
1. capital-intensive manufacturing method.
2. labor-intensive manufacturing method.
B. Determine the annual unit sales volume at which Candice Company would be indifferent between the two manufacturing methods.
C. Candice's management must decide which manufacturing method to employ. One factor it must consider is operating leverage.
1. Explain operating leverage and the relationship between operating leverage and business risk.
2. Explain the circumstances under which Candice should employ each of the two manufacturing methods.
D. Identify the business factors other than operating leverage that Candice must consider before selecting the capital-intensive or labor-intensive manufacturing method.

Question 2C-ES03

The City of Blakston owns and operates a community swimming pool. The pool is open each year for 90 days during the summer months of June, July, and August. A daily admission is charged to patrons of the pool. By law, 10% of all recreational and sporting fees must be remitted to a state tourism promotion fund. The city manager has set a goal that pool admission revenue, after subtracting the state fee and variable costs, must be sufficient to cover the fixed costs. Variable costs are assumed to be 15% of gross revenue. Fixed costs for the three-month period total $33,000. The next budget for the pool has been prepared for the current year.

Adult admissions: 30 per day × 90 days × $5.00	$13,500
Student admissions: 120 per day × 90 days × $2.50	27,000
Total revenue	40,500
State tourism fee	4,050
Net revenue	36,450
Variable costs	6,075
Fixed costs	33,000
Expected deficit	$ (2,625)

The city manager is trying to determine what admission mix is necessary to break even and what actions could be taken to eliminate the expected deficit.

Questions

A. Given the anticipated mix of adult and student admissions, how many total admissions must the pool have in order to break even for the season?

   B. Regardless of the admissions mix, what is the highest number of admissions that would be necessary to break even for the season?

   C. Regardless of the admissions mix, what is the lowest number of admissions that would be necessary to break even for the season?

Question 2C-ES04

Kolobok, Inc., produces premium ice cream in a variety of flavors. Over the past several years, the company has experienced rapid and continuous growth and is planning to increase manufacturing capacity by opening production facilities in new geographic areas. These initiatives have put pressure on management to better understand both their potential markets and associated costs. Kolobok's management identified three aspects of its current operation that could affect the new market expansion decision: (1) a highly competitive ice cream market, (2) the company's current marketing strategy, and (3) the company's current cost structure.

    Since the company began operations in 1990, Kolobok has used the markup approach for establishing prices for six-gallon containers of ice cream. The product prices include the cost of materials and labor, a markup for profit and overhead cost (a standard $20), and a market adjustment. The market adjustment is used to appropriately position a variety of products in the market. The goal is to price the products in the middle of comparable ice creams offered by competitors while maintaining high quality and high differentiation. Sales for 2007 based on Kolobok's markup pricing are presented next by product.

Product	Material and Labor	Markup	Market Adjustment	Unit Price	Boxes Sold	Total Materials and Labor	Total Sales
Vanilla	$29.00	$20.00	$1.00	$50.00	10,200	$295,800	$510,000
Chocolate	28.00	20.00	7.00	55.00	12,500	350,000	687,500
Caramel	26.00	20.00	2.00	48.00	12,900	335,400	619,200
Raspberry	27.00	20.00	2.00	49.00	13,600	367,200	666,400
Total					49,200	$1,348,400	$2,483,100

    For the year 2007, Kolobok's before-tax return on sales was 7%. The company's overhead expenses were $500,000; selling expenses, $250,000; administrative expenses, $180,000; and interest expenses, $30,000. Kolobok's marginal tax rate is 30%.

    Kolobok is considering replacing markup pricing with target costing and has prepared the next table to better compare the methods. Kolobok tries to appeal to the top 30% of the retail sales customers, including restaurants and cafés. In positioning Kolobok's products, three dimensions are considered: price, quality, and product differentiation. Accordingly, there are three main competitors in the market:

Competitor A. Low cost, low quality, high standardization

Competitor B. Average cost, moderate quality, average differentiation

Competitor C. High cost, high quality, high differentiation

Product	Competitor Pricing A	Competitor Pricing B	Competitor Pricing C	Kolobok Target Prices
Vanilla	$49	$55	$55	$53
Chocolate	50	53	56	53
Caramel			51	50
Raspberry		51	52	50

Kolobok also has been reviewing its purchasing, manufacturing, and distribution processes. Assuming that sales volumes will not be affected by the new target prices, the company believes that improvements will yield a $125,000 decrease in labor expense and a 25% reduction in overhead expense.

Questions

A. Describe target costing.

B. Analyze and compare the two alternative pricing methods: markup pricing and target costing.

C. Assuming that the sales volumes will not be affected by the new product pricing based on target costing and that the process improvements will be implemented, calculate Kolobok's before-tax return on sales using the proposed target prices.

D. Recommend which pricing method (markup or target) Kolobok should use in the future and explain why.

Question 2C-ES05

Pearson Foods is the second largest company in the breakfast cereal and fruit juice markets. For the past five years, Pearson's profits have exceeded the industry average, and management has decided to pursue a plan for growth. Two promising opportunities are being evaluated.

1. Enter the high-energy, low-fat cereals market. This project would entail developing new products using new or expanded facilities and would be financed out of earnings and through a series of long-term debt offerings over the next two years. The debt offerings would raise Pearson's debt as a percentage of total capital from 22% to 30% at the end of the two-year period.

2. Acquire Safin Bakery, a long-established and well-known bread and bakery goods company. The acquisition could be completed by the end of the calendar year and would be financed by cash and long-term notes. The debt as a percentage of total capital would rise to 40% by the end of the calendar year. Safin Bakery would be merged into Pearson Foods but operate independently as a separate division for two years. At the end of two years, Pearson would be able to consolidate the administrative, financial, and operating functions.

Both projects meet the investment criteria established by Pearson's management, and the treasurer will be preparing an evaluation of the two projects in terms of financing differences, impact on profitability, and operational and managerial problems.

Questions

A. As part of a risk assessment process, identify the strategic advantages and disadvantages of Pearson Foods' opportunity to use internal expansion by developing new products for the high-energy, low-fat cereals market.

B. As part of a risk assessment process, identify the strategic advantages and disadvantages of Pearson Foods' opportunity to use external expansion by acquiring Safin Bakery.

Question 2C-ES06

David Burns is the manager of the Electrical Division of Madison Inc. The budget for the upcoming year has just been finalized and is summarized next.

Budget Component	Amount
Revenue	$17,050,000
Expenses	
Direct labor (300,000 hours @ $20/hr)	6,000,000
Employee benefits	2,400,000
Tools and equipment	1,800,000
Materials	2,000,000
Material procurement and handling	200,000
Overhead	3,100,000
Pretax profit	$1,550,000

The budget meets the firm's general guideline of a pretax profit equal to 10% of cost. Various components of the budget are described next:

- Direct labor represents the wage costs of employees (craft personnel, job site supervisors, engineers, etc.) who work on specific projects and are directly billable to customer projects. Madison charges this to customers based on the number of hours employees work on the project times the average wage per hour.
- Employee benefits include the cost to Madison of paid time off (vacations, holidays, and sickness), pensions, health and life insurance, and payroll taxes. This is charged to customers as a percentage of direct labor.
- Tools and equipment includes the cost of small tools; larger equipment, such as cranes, backhoes, and generators; and vehicles, including maintenance, fuel, insurance, and so on. This is charged to customers as a percentage of direct labor charged to the job.
- Materials include materials acquired by Madison for use on customer projects, the cost of which is passed directly on to the specific customers.
- Material procurement and handling represents the cost incurred by Madison to purchase, warehouse, and deliver materials (referenced in the preceding bullet point) to job sites. This is charged to customers as a percentage of the material cost.
- Overhead includes the salary and benefit costs of employees not directly chargeable to projects (administrative and corporate staff as well as senior management) and other corporate expenses for facilities and supplies, most of which are relatively fixed. This is charged to customers as a percentage of all other costs incurred on the project.

Questions

A. David Burns received a call from Colby Architects asking for a price quote for a component of electrical work to be done on an office building project. Based on the detailed specifications, Burns estimated that the job would require 10,000 direct labor hours and materials costing $200,000. He decided to develop a cost proposal for other cost elements based on the percentages inherent in the budget, including a pretax profit equal to 10% of cost. Determine the amount of the quote. Show your calculations.

B. Madison measures the performance of its managers, including Burns, based on their ability to achieve budget targets, focusing on pretax profit as a percentage of billable cost for each project completed. Identify three advantages and three disadvantages of a performance measurement and incentive compensation system linked to the budget for a firm such as Madison.

C. Two weeks after submitting his bid, Burns received a call from Colby stating that if Madison could meet the lowest fixed cost bid of $695,000, it would be awarded the contract. Identify the factors that Burns should consider in deciding whether to accept the fixed price of $695,000.

D. If Burns decides to accept the contract for the fixed price of $695,000, identify two reasons that he can use to justify his decision. Explain your answer.

Question 2C-ES07

Charlene Roberts is the controller for PARKCO, a company that owns and operates several parking garages in a large midwestern American city. Recently, the management of PARKCO has been investigating the viability of building a parking garage in an area of the city that has experienced rapid growth. Some years ago, PARKCO acquired the necessary land at a cost of $425,000 and had worthless buildings on the land demolished at a cost of $72,000. Since then, the land has been rented by various construction companies as a temporary storage site for building materials while the construction companies completed projects in the area. PARKCO has averaged revenue of $5,000 per year for this use of the property.

Roberts is currently assembling financial information relating to the proposed garage. In addition to the information already presented, she received from the CFO, John Demming, these projections:

Number of parking spaces in the proposed garage	840
Number of parking spaces rented at the monthly rate	420
Average number of parkers paying the daily rate (for each of the 20 business days per month)	180
Fixed costs to operate the garage per month	$30,000

Roberts estimates that the monthly variable cost of servicing each monthly parker is $12 and that the price of a monthly parking space would be $75. The estimated cost per daily parker is $2, and the daily parking rate is expected to be set at $8. The parking garage would operate 20 business days per month.

Roberts believes, based on PARKCO's past experience with similar garages, that the projected number of monthly and daily parkers was too high. When she questioned Demming, he replied, "This garage is going to be built no matter what your past experiences are. Just use the figures I gave you."

Questions

1. **a.** Define sunk cost and opportunity cost.
   b. How are these two types of cost recorded in the accounting records?
   c. Identify the sunk costs and opportunity costs, if any, in the PARKCO scenario and show the amount of each.
2. Using the data in the scenario, calculate pretax operating income. Show your calculations.
3. Roberts is uncomfortable with the implications of Demming's statement and has turned to the *IMA Statement of Ethical Professional Practice* for guidance. Based on this guidance,
   a. Identify the ethical principles that should guide the work of a management accountant.
   b. Identify the standards, and describe how they would or would not apply in the circumstances described.
   c. Identify the steps Roberts should take to resolve this situation.

Part 2 Section D Questions

Question 2D-ES01

Upton Industries is a successful manufacturing firm. Until now, Upton has operated exclusively in the United States, but now it wants to expand its production and sales into international markets. Paul Jordan, the CEO of Upton Industries, is concerned about the risks associated with this expansion. He has asked you, as the firm's management accountant, to answer a few questions before he makes the final decision whether to expand the firm internationally.

Questions

A. Discuss the types of financial, operational, and compliance risks that Upton Industries might face if it expands into international markets.
B. To mitigate these risks, Paul Jordan wants to buy an enterprise risk management (ERM) software package. However, before he does, he wants you to explain the benefits that the firm might derive from implementing an ERM system as well as any limitations on these benefits. What would you tell him?
C. Jordan wants the implementation of an ERM to be a success, but he is concerned about how this plan will fit with the corporate culture at Upton Industries. Discuss the key organizational characteristics that would increase the chance that an ERM will be successful.

Question 2D-ES02

EZ-Food runs a fleet of lunch trucks that sell sandwiches, sodas, coffee, and snacks throughout the city. So far, EZ-Food has operated strictly on a cash basis, but now the firm is considering whether to offer weekly credit to its regular customers by allowing them to sign for their food Monday through Thursday and then pay their tabs on Friday. The manager of EZ-Food has developed the risk map shown next. Point A represents the manager's assessment of the impact and likelihood of a few credit customers refusing to pay their bills. Point B shows his assessment of the impact and likelihood of a significant number of customers making late payments. Point C indicates his assessment of a computer virus destroying the records of the amounts that customers owe.

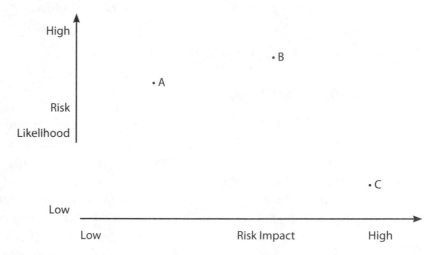

Questions

A. Based on this risk map, which risk should he consider as the highest priority? Explain.
B. Assuming that EZ-Food is unwilling to accept these risks, discuss strategies that the firm could use to avoid, reduce, or transfer each one.
C. The manager of EZ-Food is confused about the difference between inherent risk and residual risk. How would you explain the difference to him?

Question 2D-ES03

Buy-More, Inc. is a chain of retail clothing stores. Recently the firm discovered a serious problem with internal controls over its inventory. Buy-More estimates that there is currently a 5% chance that this problem could result in a $1,000,000 loss. The firm has come up with several possible ways to deal with this problem. Option A: New electronic inventory tags would cost $25,000 and would reduce the chance of the loss to 2%. Option B: Installing $30,000 of surveillance equipment would reduce the chance of the loss to 1%. Option C: If electronic inventory tags and surveillance equipment are both used, the firm estimates there would only be a 0.1% chance of the loss.

Questions

A. Would you consider Option A (electronic inventory tags) and Option B (surveillance equipment) to be controls to prevent inventory theft or controls to detect and correct inventory theft? Explain.

B. What is the expected value of Buy-More's loss if the firm does nothing to fix the problem with the internal controls over its inventory?

C. What is the net benefit (cost) of Option A (electronic inventory tags), Option B (surveillance equipment), and Option C (both electronic inventory tags and surveillance equipment)?

D. Based only on the estimates of benefits and costs, which option should Buy-More implement? Explain.

E. What other factors might be relevant to this decision?

Part 2 Section E Questions

Question 2E-ES01

Miranda Wells joined Sycamore Corporation four months ago as a financial analyst and has been assisting Jake Richter, the controller, in evaluating capital projects. Soon Wells will be making her first presentation to the management committee responsible for selecting capital projects, and she has been working diligently to ensure that her analysis is correct. The management committee will be considering two mutually exclusive projects at this meeting. Both projects require the same initial investment and have the same project lives. Wells has used several capital budgeting methods to evaluate each project and presents the data as a table.

	Project A	Project B
Accounting rate of return	34%	26%
Internal rate of return	16%	19%
Net present value	$2.6 million	$3.5 million
Payback period	4 years	5 years

After completing her analysis, Wells believes Project B is superior to Project A. She intends to recommend Project B to the management committee and Richter agrees.

Questions

A. For each of the four capital budgeting methods used by Miranda Wells to evaluate the two projects at Sycamore Corporation, explain the merits and limitations of each method.

B. Explain why Wells and Richter believe that Project B is superior to Project A.

C. Identify three qualitative considerations that generally should be considered in capital budget evaluations.

Question 2E-ES02

Cambridge Automotive Products (CAP) Inc., a multinational corporation, is a major supplier of a broad range of components to the worldwide automobile and light truck market. CAP is in the process of developing a bid to supply an ignition system module to Korea Auto Corporation (KAC), a South Korean automobile manufacturer, for a new line of automobiles for the next four-year production cycle. The request for proposal issued by KAC specifies a quantity of 200,000 modules in the first year and 250,000 units in years 2 through 4 of the contract. CAP marketing specialists believe that, in order to be competitive, a bid of 100,000 South Korean won (KRW) per unit is appropriate. Other relevant data are shown next.

- Manufacturing specialists estimate that a $12 million (U.S. dollars) investment in equipment (including installation) is required.
- The equipment is expected to last the four-year life of the contract, at which time it would cost $1.4 million to remove the equipment, which would be sold for a scrap value of $900,000.
- Direct labor and material expenses are estimated at $40 per unit.
- The change in indirect cash expenses associated with this contract is expected to be $3 million per year.
- The new product will require additional investment in inventory and accounts receivable balances at the outset, amounting to $1.2 million during the four-year time period. This investment will be recovered at the end of the four-year contract.
- CAP is subject to U.S. income tax at an effective rate of 40%.
- For tax purposes, assume that the initial $12 million cost of the equipment is depreciated evenly over the four-year period.
- The company economist estimates that the exchange rate will average 1,250 KRW per U.S. dollar for the four-year time period.

Questions
A. Calculate the after-tax incremental cash flows in U.S. dollars for these periods:
   1. Period 0
   2. Period 1
   3. Period 4 operating cash flow
B. The assumptions used to develop the cash flows are subject to various degrees of estimation error. For each of three different cash flow variables, identify and discuss one potential risk that could affect the estimates made by CAP.

Question 2E-ES03

Grubstake Mining Ltd. (GML) owns and operates the Dusty Coal Mine, among its other business ventures. The Dusty Coal Mine is a strip mine that has been in operation for a number of years and is expected to operate for another 15 years. Environmental regulations require mine operators to reclaim the land and restore it to its original configuration and vegetation state once mining ceases. GML has been setting aside money for this purpose in an external trust fund managed by a major commercial bank, and currently the balance in the fund is $3 million. Assume that income tax regulations currently allow both the deposits to the trust fund and the earnings on the funds to be exempt from taxation.

GML would like to establish a uniform charge per ton for reclamation costs to be included in contracts with customers for future sales. It is estimated that the reclamation cost in today's dollars is $14 million, and that amount is expected to increase by 4% per year. The trust fund is expected to earn income at a rate of 7% per year on its investments. Annual sales from the mine are expected to be 1,350,000 tons per year over the next 15 years.

Questions

A. Calculate the cost per ton that GML should include in its contracts in order to accumulate a sufficient amount in the trust fund to be able to pay the cost to reclaim the land at the end of the 15-year period.

B. Identify and discuss four uncertainties that GML faces over the 15-year period as far as reclamation is concerned. For each uncertainty, describe what the effect would be on the reclamation cost per ton.

C. Without performing any calculations, discuss the effect on GML if the next changes were to be made in the tax regulations.

  1. Amounts collected for reclamation would be considered taxable income, even if they are deposited in external trust funds.

  2. Currently earnings on the trust funds are taxable.

Question 2E-ES04

Ultra Comp is a large information technology firm with several facilities. The firm's audit committee has determined that management must implement more effective security measures at its facilities. A security improvement team has been formed to formulate a solution. Janet Lynch is the financial analyst assigned to the team. She has determined that a six-year time horizon is appropriate for the analysis and that a 14% cost of capital is applicable. The team is investigating three vendors:

  1. Vendor A is a new entrant to the security industry and is in the process of introducing its security system, which utilizes new technology. The system would require an initial investment of $4 million and have a life of six years. A net cash outflow of $500,000 per year for salaries, operation, maintenance, and all costs related to the system also would be required.

  2. Vendor B is an established firm in the security industry and has a security system that has been on the market for several years. The system requires an initial investment of $1 million and will have a useful life of three years. At the end of the three-year period, Ultra Comp would have to replace the hardware at an estimated cost of $1,250,000, based on current technology. A net cash outflow of $750,000 per year for salaries, operation, maintenance, and all other related costs would also be required.

3. Vendor C is a nationally recognized firm in the security industry and has proposed to Ultra Comp that it provide a total security solution. Vendor C would provide all hardware and personnel to operate and maintain a security system as called for by the specifications of Ultra Comp for all its locations. Ultra Comp would be required to sign a six-year contract at a cost of $1,400,000 per year.

Questions

A. Ultra Comp utilizes the net present value (NPV) method to quantify the financial aspects of corporate decisions. Calculate the NPV of each of the three alternatives.

B. Based on financial considerations, which of the three alternatives should the team recommend? Explain why.

C. Define *sensitivity analysis*, and discuss how Ultra Comp could use this technique in analyzing the three vendor alternatives.

D. Identify and briefly discuss three nonfinancial considerations that the Ultra Comp team should consider prior to making a recommendation to senior management.

Question 2E-ES05

Dominion Industries is evaluating whether to manufacture and market a new model coffeemaker to broaden its product line. A cross-functional team has analyzed the market and cost structure for the new product, and the analysis has produced these data:

Unit selling price	$110
Variable cost per unit	$45
Fixed costs (excluding depreciation)	$600,000
Capital investment	$3,500,000
Working capital investment	$500,000

The team recognizes that the unit sales level is the most difficult variable to forecast and has conducted market research indicating that the sales distribution could be estimated in this way:

Units per year	Probability
20,000	15%
22,000	20%
25,000	30%
26,000	20%
28,000	15%

The product is expected to have a life of 10 years, the working capital is fully recovered, and there is no salvage expected from the capital investment at the end of its life. For purposes of this analysis, use straight-line depreciation and assume a 30% effective income tax rate. Dominion has a cost of capital of 14%.

Questions

A. What is the expected net present value of the investment in this new product? Show your calculations.

B. What is the probability that this investment will produce a positive net present value? Show your calculations.

C. Corporate financial managers recognize that, in general, new capital investment projects involve a variety of risks, depending on the situation.

    1. Identify three techniques or methods that can be used to quantify and assess risk.

    2. For each technique identified, describe the technique and indicate how it is utilized.

Question 2E-ES06

Right-Way Stores is a chain of home improvement stores with 150 locations. Right-Way has identified an attractive site for a new store, and Jim Smith, director of financial planning, has been asked to prepare an analysis and make a recommendation for or against opening this proposed new store.

In preparing his analysis, Smith has determined that the land at the proposed site will cost $500,000 and the new store will cost $3.5 million to build. The building contractor requires full payment at the start of construction, and it will take one year to build the store. Right-Way will finance the purchase of the land and construction of the new building with a 40-year mortgage. The mortgage payment will be $118,000 payable annually at year-end. Fixtures for the store are estimated to cost $100,000 and will be expensed. Inventory to stock the store is estimated to cost $100,000. Concerned about the possibility of rising prices, the company expects to purchase the fixtures and inventory at the start of construction. Advertising for the grand opening will be $50,000, paid to the advertising agency on retainer at the start of construction. The new store will begin operations one year after the start of construction.

Right-Way will depreciate the building over 20 years on a straight-line basis and is subject to a 35% tax rate. Right-Way uses a 12% hurdle rate to evaluate projects. The company expects to earn after-tax operating income from the new store of $1,200,000 per year.

Questions

A. What is Right-Way's total initial cash outflow? Show your calculations.

B. Calculate the annual expected cash flow from the proposed new store. Show your calculations.

C. Right-Way management evaluates new stores over a five-year horizon as management believes there is too much uncertainty after five years of operation. Calculate the net present value (NPV) for the store for the first five years of operation. Show your calculations.

D. Based solely on your answer to C, would you recommend that Right-Way build this store? Explain your answer.

E. How would you use sensitivity analysis to test your confidence in the recommendation? No calculations are required.

Question 2E-ES07

Bell Company is a large diversified manufacturer organized into profit centers. Division managers are awarded a bonus each year if the division exceeds profit goals. Although division managers are generally given control in operating their division, all capital expenditures over $500,000 must be approved by the home office. Bob Charleson was recently appointed division manager of the Central Division.

Twelve months ago, Charleson's predecessor, who has been fired, was able to convince the home office to invest $700,000 in modern manufacturing equipment with an expected life of 5 years. Included within the $700,000 investment was a special packaging machine at a cost of $200,000. This packaging machine has a 5-year useful life and a zero salvage value. Charleson has just learned of a new packaging process that would save the Central Division $60,000 a year in packaging cost over the 5-year life of the equipment. As a result of the introduction of new technology, the current packaging machine could be sold for $75,000. Acquisition and installation of the new packaging process equipment would cost $210,000. Central Division's cost of capital is 10%, and it has an effective income tax rate of 40%. The new equipment has a zero salvage value and is depreciated over 5 years on a straight-line basis.

Questions

1. Calculate the net present value of acquiring the new packaging process. Show your calculations.
2. From a financial standpoint, should Bell Company invest in the new packaging technology? Explain your answer.
3. Identify and explain three nonfinancial or behavioral factors that could cause Charleson to change the investment decision made in the previous question.
4. **a.** Identify and explain one problem with a profit-based compensation system such as Bell's.
   b. Recommend an alternative compensation system that would better align managers' behavior with organizational goals. Explain your answer.

Question 2E-ES08

Grandeur Industries is currently in the process of reviewing capital budget submissions from its various divisions. Grandeur uses the capital asset pricing model (CAPM) for a variety of purposes, including the determination of benchmark investment returns. The company's overall cost of capital is 16%, and its beta value is 1.2. The risk-free rate is 4%, and the expected return on the market is 14%. The next projects from different divisions are under consideration, and there is no capital rationing in effect.

Project	Internal Rate of Return	Project Beta
A	16%	1.4
B	18%	1.6
C	12%	0.7
D	17%	1.1

Questions

1. **a.** Calculate the required return for all four projects. Show your calculations.
   b. Which of the four projects under consideration should Grandeur accept? Support your decision.
2. Define capital rationing.
3. **a.** Define and explain beta.
   b. Describe four factors that would impact the beta value that is chosen for use in evaluating a project.

Question 2E-ES09

Orion Corp. is a logistics and transportation company. The finance director, John Kochar, is in the process of evaluating a number of proposed capital investment projects. The next information relates to the firm's finances.

- Some years ago the firm issued 10,000 bonds, each with a face value of $1,000 and paying an annual coupon rate of 9.2%. These bonds are now trading at $1,040 per bond. A coupon payment on these bonds was made yesterday, and the bonds mature next year.
- The firm has no other debt or preferred stock outstanding.
- The firm has 2,000,000 shares of common stock outstanding. The stock is currently selling for $14.80 per share, and the firm is expected to pay a dividend of $1.48 per share next year. The dividend is expected to grow at a constant rate of 4% per year in the foreseeable future.
- The firm's corporate tax rate is 30%.

Kochar is reviewing the capital investment projects shown next. All projects are in Orion's usual line of business and are being considered independently of each other. The listed information is available. (Note that the net present values of the projects are estimated using the weighted average cost of capital.)

Project	Initial Outlay	IRR	NPV
A	$450,000	17.0%	$18,800
B	$128,000	19.5%	$2,300
C	$262,000	16.2%	$9,800
D	$180,000	10.5%	−$7,000
E	$240,000	16.5%	$22,500
F	$160,000	11.1%	−$900

The firm is also evaluating another proposed capwital investment, Project X, that is in a completely different line of business from Orion's usual operations. The project is expected to be financed from the existing capital structure and does not fall within any capital rationing restrictions. The next forecasted net after-tax cash flows relate to Project X.

Year 0	Year 1	Year 2	Year 3	Year 4
–$200,000	$60,000	$80,000	$80,000	$80,000

Questions

1. Based on the information provided, calculate Orion's weighted average cost of capital. Show your calculations.
2. Referring to Projects A through F:
   a. Identify which projects should be accepted by Orion. Provide a brief defense of the decision criteria that you have used in arriving at your recommendations.
   b. Assume that the firm faces a capital constraint of $700,000. Identify the project or projects the firm should undertake. Provide a brief explanation for your recommendations.
3. Referring to Project X, state whether the firm should use its weighted average cost of capital to evaluate this project. Explain your answer.
4. Based on an analysis of two firms with operations similar to Project X, Kochar has determined that the project's beta is 1.5. The risk-free rate is 5%, and the market risk premium is 10%.
   a. Calculate the net present value of Project X and provide a recommendation on whether the project should be accepted. Show your calculations.
   b. Calculate the project's profitability index and provide an interpretation of this measure. Show your calculations.
5. In the past, the firm has typically used the payback period method for evaluating risky projects and accepted projects with a payback period less than 3 years.
   a. Calculate the payback period for Project X. Based on the firm's payback period threshold, what decision should the firm make regarding the project?
   b. Provide one reason why using the payback period can result in the firm making a suboptimal decision.

Part 2 Section F Questions

Question 2F-ES01

Borealis Industries has three operating divisions: Sandstone Books, Corus Games, and Sterling Extraction Services. Each division maintains its own accounting system and method of revenue recognition.

Sandstone Books

Sandstone Books sells novels to regional distributors, which then sell to independent bookstores and retail chains in their territory. The distributors are allowed to return up to 25% of their purchases to Sandstone, and the distributors have the same return allowance with the bookstores. The returns from distributors have averaged 20%

over the past five years. During the fiscal year just ended, Sandstone's sales to distributors totaled $15,000,000. At year-end, $6,800,000 of sales are still subject to return privileges over the next six months. The balance of the book sales, $8,200,000, had actual returns of 19%. Sales from the previous fiscal year totaling $5,500,000 were collected in the current fiscal year, with 21% of sales returned. Sandstone records revenue in accordance with the method referred to as revenue recognition when the right of return exists as the company's operations meet all the applicable criteria for use of this method.

Corus Games

Corus Games supplies video arcades with new games and updated versions of standard games. The company works through a network of sales agents in various cities. Orders are received from the sales agents along with down payments; Corus then ships the product directly to the customer, f.o.b. shipping point. The customer is billed for the balance due plus the actual shipping costs. During the fiscal year just ended, Corus received orders for $12,000,000 from the sales agents along with $1,200,000 in down payments. Customers were billed $150,000 in freight costs and $9,180,000 for goods shipped. After an order has been shipped, the sales agent receives a 12% commission on the product price. The goods are warranted for 90 days after sales, and warranty returns have been about 3% of sales. Corus recognizes revenue at the point of sale.

Sterling Extraction Services

Sterling specializes in the extraction of precious metals. During the fiscal year just ended, Sterling entered into contracts worth $36,000,000 and shipped metals worth $32,400,000. One quarter of the shipments was made from inventories on hand at the beginning of the year, and the remaining shipments were made from metals that were mined during the year. Sterling uses the completion-of-production method to recognize revenue, because the operations meet the specified criteria (i.e., reasonably assured sales prices, interchangeable units, and insignificant distribution costs).

Questions

The chief executive officer (CEO) of Sterling Extraction Services has asked the controller, "How do you know which orders were filled from inventory? I want you to take another look at the revenue calculation. At the current level, our incentive payments will be much lower than expected. Besides, I promised the board of directors that this year's revenue would exceed last year's by at least 12%; I don't like not keeping my promises."

The controller is very uncomfortable with the implications of the CEO's statement and has turned to the *IMA Statement of Ethical Professional Practice* for guidance. According to this guidance:

A. Identify the principles that should guide the work of a management accountant.
B. Identify and describe the standards that would be violated if the controller of Sterling were to manipulate the revenue calculation.
C. Identify the steps the controller should take to resolve this situation.

Question 2F-ES02

Alex Raminov is a management accountant at Carroll Mining and Manufacturing Company (CMMC), a large processor of ores and minerals. While working late one night to complete the footnotes for the financial statements, Raminov was looking for a file in his supervisor's office and noticed a report regarding procedures for disposing of plant wastes. According to handwritten notes on the face of the report, CMMC had been using a residential landfill in a nearby township to dump toxic coal cleaning fluid wastes over a considerable period of time. The report stated that locating a new dump site was urgent because the current one was nearing capacity.

Raminov realized that it was possible CMMC had been improperly disposing of highly toxic fluids in a landfill that was restricted to residential refuse. In addition to the obvious hazards to residents of the area, there could be legal problems if and when the authorities were notified. The financial consequences of cleanup actions, as well as the loss of CMMC's generally good environmental reputation, could be catastrophic for the company.

Raminov asked his supervisor how this item was to be included in the footnotes and inquired whether an accrual for cleanup costs was anticipated. His supervisor told him to "forget about this matter" and that he had no intention of mentioning one word about waste disposal in this year's financial statements.

Questions

A. Using the categories outlined in *IMA Statement of Ethical Professional Practice*, identify the standards that are specifically relevant to Alex Raminov's ethical conflict and explain why the standards are applicable to the situation.
B. According to the *IMA Statement of Ethical Professional Practice*, what further steps, if any, should Raminov take in resolving his ethical dilemma?
C. If he continues to be rebuffed by his employer, should Raminov notify the appropriate authorities? Should he anonymously release the information to the local newspaper? Explain your answers.

Question 2F-ES03

Amy Kimbell was recently hired as an accounting manager for Hi-Quality Productions Inc., a publicly held company producing components for the automotive industry. One division, Alpha, uses a highly automated process that had been outsourced for a number of years because the capital investment required was high and the technology was constantly changing. Two years ago, the company decided to make the necessary capital investment and bring the operation in house. Since all major capital investments must be approved by the board of directors, the budget committee for the Alpha Division recommended the $4 million investment to the board, projecting a significant cost savings.

In her new job as accounting manager, Kimbell is on the budget committee for the Alpha Division. The board has requested from the committee a postaudit review of the actual cost savings. While working on the review, Kimball noted that several of the projections in the original proposal were very aggressive, including an unusually high salvage value and an excessively long useful life. If more realistic projections had been used, Kimbell doubts that the board would have approved the investment.

When Kimbell expressed her concerns at the next meeting of Alpha's budget committee, she was told that it had been the unanimous decision of the committee to recommend the investment because it was thought to be in the best long-term interest of the company. According to the committee members, the postaudit report would not discuss these issues; the committee members believe that certain adjustments to the review are justified to ensure the success of the Alpha division and the company as a whole.

Questions

A. Using the categories outlined in the *IMA Statement of Ethical Professional Practice*, identify the standards that are specifically relevant to Kimbell's ethical conflict and explain why the identified standards are applicable to the situation.

B. According to the *IMA Statement of Ethical Professional Practice*, what specific actions should Kimbell take to resolve her ethical conflict?

Question 2F-ES04

Pro-Kleen specializes in cleaning carpets and upholstery for residences and businesses. Three years ago, the company upgraded its equipment in order to remain competitive and take advantage of new technology. At that time, Pro-Kleen purchased two truck-mounted steam cleaners; the details are shown next.

Purchase date	March 15, 2005
Cost	$200,000
Estimated life	8 years
Salvage value	$20,000

Pro-Kleen takes one-half year's depreciation in both the year of acquisition and the year of disposal and uses the straight-line method for calculating depreciation expense.

Based on recent information, John Morgan, Pro-Kleen's assistant controller, has changed the estimated useful lives of the equipment to five years. The salvage value of the equipment has been reduced to $10,000 due to unexpected obsolescence. These revisions are effective January 1, 2008. After revising the depreciation amounts for the current year's financial reporting, Morgan was told by the controller, Eileen Ryan, that the revision was significant enough to change the small profit projected for the year into a loss. As a result, Ryan has asked Morgan to reduce by half the total depreciation expense for the current year.

Questions

A. Referring to the specific standards outlined in the *IMA Statement of Ethical Professional Practice*, identify and discuss the specific ethical conflicts that Ryan's instruction presents to Morgan.

B. According to the *IMA Statement of Ethical Professional Practice*, identify the steps that Morgan should take to resolve this situation.

Question 2F-ES05

United Forest Products (UFP) is a $1 billion corporation with many large timber and wood processing plants. The company is decentralized into divisions that operate as profit centers. The majority of the centers are evaluated on cost control and the achievement of budgeted output and profits. If target numbers are met, all division employees participate in a profit-sharing plan, and senior management potentially can receive substantial bonuses.

Charlene White is the controller of the Allegheny Division of UFP. Over the past six months, she discussed the division's performance several times with the president of the Allegheny Division, William Jefferson, and it became apparent that the division would not meet its targeted goals unless drastic changes were made. The Allegheny Division is actually a cost center that has been required to use a non-market-based transfer price, but it is evaluated as a profit center. Jefferson realized this problem and told White that the only way to meet budget was "to maximize output and make some serious changes in our cost control." Several weeks later, White noted a dramatic increase in the profitability of the division.

When analyzing the monthly profit and loss details, White noted only a slight increase in output but a significant decrease in the purchase cost of raw timber. She knew her responsibilities required her to understand fully how this sudden change was taking place and began investigating. At the log yard where timber is received and scaled to determine its price, she noticed that a trucker-timber contractor was quite aggravated when he was given the scale report (board feet and quality). When she asked one of the employees what was bothering the contractor, he said, "Are you kidding? You wouldn't believe how much we've been lowering scale measures the last three months!" Further conversations revealed that Jefferson had apparently told the division's mill workers to significantly reduce both the size scale (in inches of log diameter) and quality measures of logs sold to the mill. The impact has been a significant reduction in the price paid to contractors for timber purchased by the division.

White suspects that Jefferson has instructed employees to deliberately give logging contractors arbitrary and inaccurate evaluations of raw material quantity and quality, an unethical business practice.

Questions

A. Identify and discuss Charlene White's ethical conflict, and determine if she has an obligation to act. Be sure to refer to the relevant standards outlined in the *IMA Statement of Ethical Professional Practice* to support your answer.
B. According to the *IMA Statement of Ethical Professional Practice*, what steps should White take to resolve the perceived ethical dilemma?
C. Explain how the performance evaluation system affected behavior at the Allegheny Division, and recommend improvements to the system.

Question 2F-ES06

GRQ Company is a privately held entity that refines a variety of natural raw materials used as primary inputs for the steel industry. The firm has done well over the last several years, and most members of senior management have received bonuses well in excess of 60% of their base salaries. Also, both the chief financial officer and the chief executive officer have earned bonuses in excess of 100% of their base salaries. GRQ has projected this trend of successful earnings and bonuses to continue.

All-American Steel Company (AAS) has tendered a very generous offer to acquire GRQ. At the same time, several top GRQ executives, who own over 40% of GRQ's stock, have learned that the primary supplier of their major raw material will not renew their contract at the end of the current fiscal year. GRQ has no other vendors available within the United States to competitively provide this raw material in the amount needed to support their continued record of profitable operations.

As part of the due diligence process, an analyst with AAS has asked John Spencer, controller of GRQ, if he knows of any material event that would impact earnings over the next several years. Spencer, who also participates in the bonus program, is aware that GRQ's primary supplier will no longer provide raw materials to the firm beyond the end of the current fiscal year. He spoke with Bob Green, the CFO of GRQ, telling him that while the profit projections for the remainder of the current year will match the earnings of prior years, it is obvious that projected earnings for the next year will be greatly reduced. Green informed Spencer that the executive committee had met and decided that only members of top management were to be made aware of the situation with their key supplier. Accordingly, Spencer should not inform AAS of the situation with the supplier.

Questions

A. Referring to the specific standards outlined in the *IMA Statement of Ethical Professional Practice*, identify and discuss Spencer's ethical obligations.
B. According to the *IMA Statement of Ethical Professional Practice*, identify the steps that Spencer should take to resolve the dilemma.

Question 2F-ES07

CenturySound, Inc. produces cutting-edge high-end audio systems that are sold primarily through major retailers. Any production overruns are sold to discount retailers, under CenturySound's private label SoundDynamX. The discount retail segment appears very profitable because the basic operating budget assigns all fixed expenses to production for the major retailers, the only predictable market.

Several years ago, CenturySound implemented a 100% testing program. On average approximately 3% of production is found to be substandard and unacceptable. Of this 3%, approximately two thirds are reworked and the remaining one third are scrapped. However, in a recent analysis of customer complaints, George Wilson, the cost accountant, and Barry Ross, the quality control engineer, have ascertained that normal rework does not bring the audio systems up to standard. Sampling shows that about 25% of the reworked audio systems will fail after extended operation within one year.

Unfortunately, there is no way to determine which reworked audio systems will fail because testing will not detect this problem. CenturySound's marketing analyst has indicated that this problem will have a significant impact on the company's reputation and customer satisfaction if the problem is not corrected. Consequently, the board of directors would interpret this problem as having serious negative implications on the company's profitability.

Wilson has included the audio system failure and rework problem in his written report that has been prepared for the upcoming quarterly meeting of the board of directors. Due to the potential adverse economic impact, Wilson has followed a long standing practice of highlighting this information.

After reviewing the reports to be presented, the plant manager was upset and said to the controller, "We can't trouble the board with this kind of material. Tell Wilson to tone that down. People cannot expect their systems to last forever."

The controller called Wilson into his office and said, "George, you'll have to bury this one. The probable failure of reworks can be referred to briefly in the oral presentation, but it should not be mentioned or highlighted in the advance material mailed to the board."

Wilson feels strongly that the board will be misinformed on a potentially serious loss of income if he follows the controller's orders. Wilson discussed the problem with Ross, the quality control engineer, who simply remarked, "That's your problem, George."

Questions

A. Identify and discuss the ethical considerations that George Wilson should recognize in deciding how to proceed in this matter. Support your answer by referring to the specific standards outlined in the *IMA Statement of Ethical Professional Practice*.

B. According to the *IMA Statement of Ethical Professional Practice*, what are the steps Wilson should take in order to resolve the situation?

Question 2F-ES08

Ambyt Inc., a manufacturer of high-value integrated control devices, became a publicly owned company through an initial public offering less than two years ago. The company had been a privately held firm for over 15 years and has retained its senior management team. The CEO recommended to the CFO that they hire an assistant to prepare the additional reports required of a public company rather than continuing to rely on the outside accounting firm that has been preparing them since the IPO. Wayne Grant, who has experience preparing SEC filings, was hired six months ago to fill this role and reports to the CFO. On July 3, Grant prepared the quarterly reports for the period ending June 30, with information from the Sales and Accounting Departments. Ambyt treats sales and administrative expenses as period expenses; these expenses average about 14% of sales. Parts of the statements are shown next.

Income Statement for Period Ending June 30

Sales	$14,321,000
Less returns and allowances	128,000
Net sales	14,193,000
Cost of goods sold	9,651,000
Gross profit	4,542,000
Selling & administrative expenses	2,024,000
Income from operations	$ 2,518,000

Partial Balance Sheet as of June 30

Current assets	
Cash	$ 269,419
Accounts receivable	2,278,444
Notes receivable	558,000
Inventories	896,000
Short-term investments	532,000
Prepaid expenses	24,222
Supplies	58,798
Total current assets	$4,616,883
Current liabilities	
Accounts payable	$1,639,000
Notes payable	580,000
Accrued wages	421,000
Taxes payable	187,000
Other liabilities	66,000
Total current liabilities	$2,893,000

On July 4, Grant learned from the shipping supervisor that a large order of control devices scheduled to be shipped on June 28 would not be ready until July 6 due to an unauthorized work stoppage by the production machinists. Later the same day, Grant learned that the manager for the Sales Department had included the sale in the June 30 report because the work stoppage was not authorized by the machinist union and therefore was beyond its control. The revenue reported for this sale was $1,250,000 with an associated cost of goods of $715,000.

With this information, Grant determined that he should change the reports he prepared for the period. He discussed this situation with the CFO. The CFO refused to consider the change, explaining that consistent earnings growth is a primary driver of share price. With Amybt shares trading at a P/E of 22, the share price would likely fall even though there was no real problem with production. The CFO stated that although production delays were not common, they had occasionally occurred throughout his years with Amybt and this was not a "big deal."

Questions

1. According to the *IMA Statement of Ethical Professional Practice*, what further steps, if any, should Wayne Grant take in resolving this situation?
2. Should the large shipment originally scheduled for June 28 be included in Ambyt's June 30 Income Statement? Explain your answer.
3. Assuming Grant revises the reports to exclude the sale from the period,
   a. calculate the revised Income from Operations for the period ending June 30.
   b. describe the changes that would be made to Ambyt's June 30 Balance Sheet.
   c. explain how the revisions will impact Ambyt's Cash Flow Statement.
4. Some of Grant's colleagues have been enthusiastic about his new employer's prospects and have been considering the purchase of a large number of shares. Grant is concerned that the share price will fall because of the revised statements and has suggested that they "wait a while" before making the purchase. Discuss Grant's actions with regard to the *IMA Statement of Ethical Professional Practice* by identifying any standards that are specifically relevant and explaining why they are applicable to this situation.

Question 2F-ES09

Global Manufacturing is a Canadian company that processes a wide range of natural resources. Two years ago the company acquired Zeta Manufacturing, a raw material processing firm located in the United States. Over the last year, profits have fallen in the U.S.-based subsidiary. Laura Hammon, the manager of manufacturing accounting for Zeta Manufacturing, has been asked to identify the problems that have impaired the firm's profits.

She has reviewed the monthly production cost reports and discovered that the per unit costs have been consistently increasing over the last year. Since the subsidiary used an actual cost system, Hammon convinced the president and the production manager that a thorough assessment of each product's cost and the implementation of a standard cost system would help to solve the problem.

Within six months, Hammon installed a fully operational standard cost system for the division. After several months of using the new cost system, Hammon is perplexed by unexplainable efficiency and yield variances, which result in material inventory write-downs at the end of each month. The work-in-process account is charged with the actual input costs of direct materials and direct labor, plus a predetermined rate for normal spoilage. At the end of the month, the work-in-process account is relieved by the standard cost per unit multiplied by the number of good units produced. This leaves a balance in the account that should be consistent with the uncompleted units still in process, but when compared to a physical inventory, there is a significant shortage of product in process, resulting in a write-down of inventory.

When Hammon explained her problems to the production manager, he scoffed and said, "It's your crazy standard cost system that is messed up." The production manager says that Hammon's cost system is poorly designed and does not track product costs accurately. Hammon is convinced there is nothing wrong with the design of the standard cost system. She knows that the inventory write-downs have no effect on the production manager's compensation; however, she has heard that his bonus is partially affected by the actual amount of spoilage. She decides to further examine the provision for normal spoilage as well as the actual spoilage reported.

During the following month, she monitored the records of disposal truck traffic that left the plant at night. It would require only one truck nightly to dispose of the spoilage included in her standard cost. The records reflected an average of three disposal trucks leaving the plant each night. This unexplained traffic of disposal vehicles has caused her to be skeptical about the actual spoilage reported by the production manager.

Questions

1. Does Hammon have an ethical responsibility to determine what may explain the unusual inventory write-downs at Zeta Manufacturing? Support your answer by referring to the specific standards outlined in IMA's *Statement of Ethical Professional Practice*.
2. According to the *IMA Statement of Ethical Professional Practice*, what are the steps that Hammon should take in order to resolve the situation?

Question 2F-ES10

The government of a developing country invited several companies to bid on a project to enhance its telecommunications infrastructure. Robert James is vice president of global sales for SouthComm, a large telecommunications company based in the United States. James obtained all of the details required to bid on the project and was able to submit the bid before the deadline. A few weeks after the deadline had passed, he telephoned the deputy minister of the country to find out the status of the project. During that conversation, the deputy minister invited James to a special meeting to present SouthComm's proposal in detail. James spent several days preparing for the meeting and then traveled to the country. During the meeting, James presented the details of SouthComm's proposal for over an hour to the deputy minister and vice deputy. He then answered questions from the men for about 20 minutes. When there were no more questions, James told the deputy and vice deputy that SouthComm was extremely interested in winning the bid for the project and asked if there was anything else he could do to convince them that SouthComm was the best company to select to do the project.

The deputy and vice deputy then spoke between themselves in their native language for several minutes. Finally, the vice deputy told James that SouthComm's bid would be guaranteed to win if a commission of $1 million were paid to the country's government. James knew that this "commission" request was nothing more than a bribe and explained that such a payment would be against U.S. laws as well as SouthComm's corporate policy. The vice deputy then stood up, said good-bye, and shook James's hand.

Questions

A. Why would SouthComm have a corporate policy against these types of payments?
B. James later shared this experience with Rita Lane, who holds a similar position with a large U.S. multinational company. Lane said that such requests are commonplace in global business and that she would do it as long as that practice is acceptable in the foreign country. Do you agree with Lane's opinion?

Question F-ES11

Morgan Company manufactures engine lubricants. During the manufacturing process, some by-products are produced that have no resale value. The by-products are considered hazardous to the environment and should be disposed of in a very specific manner, following hazardous material protocol. Morgan pays an outside company to come onsite and haul away the hazardous materials. Morgan's sales have been much lower than expected this quarter, and there is a lot of pressure to lower costs.

John Lark has worked in the company's controller's office for ten years and is very familiar with the plant floor processes. While walking the plant floor one day, he sees that one of the workers is putting the by-product in the large trash receptacle instead of placing it in the hazardous material bin. When he inquires about why that is being done, the worker explains he is following a management directive and that disposing of the by-product in the trash would save the company the money that would have to be paid to the hazardous materials company.

Questions

A. Is the management of Morgan Company acting in an ethical manner? What are some of the potential risks that Morgan Company will expose itself to by making decisions like this in order to cut costs?
B. What changes should be made to create a stronger ethical environment? What are some of the potential benefits that Morgan Company could realize by creating a more ethical corporate culture?

Part 2 Section A Answers

Answer to Question 2A-ES01

Answer A:

Among the management accountants' responsibilities are the measurement of economic events and transactions and the communication of information about them to interested parties, including management. Financial ratios are a part of this communication process that includes analysis, interpretation, and evaluation of the financial statements. Ratios display a relationship among various elements of financial data and are used to assist management in interpreting and explaining financial statements. They can be effective tools in evaluating a company's liquidity, debt position, and profitability. Financial ratios are an important part of evaluating a company's past performance and are useful in projecting its financial future.

Answer B:

1. Times interest earned $= \dfrac{\text{Income Before Income Taxes} + \text{Interest Expense}}{\text{Interest Expense}}$

$$= \frac{\$120,000 + \$20,000}{\$20,000}$$

$$= 7 \text{ times}$$

2. Return on total assets $= \dfrac{\text{Net Income} + \text{Interest Expense} - \text{Tax Savings}}{\text{Average Total Assets}}$

$$= \frac{\$72,000 + \$20,000 - (\$20,000 \times 0.4)}{(\$540,000 + \$510,000) / 2}$$

$$= 0.16 = 16\%$$

3. Return on operating assets

$$= \frac{\text{Operating Income}}{\text{Average Operating Assets (Total} - \text{Other)}}$$

$$= \frac{(\text{Income Before Taxes}) - (\text{Other Revenue}) + \text{Interest Expense}}{[('05 \text{ Total Assets} - \text{Other Assets}) + ('04 \text{ Total Assets} - \text{Other Assets})] / 2}$$

$$= \frac{\$120,000 - \$60,000 + \$20,000}{[(\$540,000 - \$116,000) + (\$510,000 - \$114,000)] / 2}$$

$$= 0.195 = 19.5\%$$

4. Return on common stockholders' equity

$$= \frac{\text{Net Income}}{\text{Average Common Stockholders' Equity}}$$

$$= \frac{\$72,000}{(\$260,000 + \$217,000) / 2}$$

$$= 0.302 = 30.2\%$$

5. Total debt ratio $= \dfrac{\text{Total Liabilities}}{\text{Total Assets}}$

$\qquad\qquad\quad = \dfrac{\$280,000}{\$540,000}$

$\qquad\qquad\quad = 0.519 = 51.9\%$

6. Total debt/equity ratio $= \dfrac{\text{Total Liabilities}}{\text{Total Stockholders' Equity}}$

$\qquad\qquad\qquad\qquad = \dfrac{\$280,000}{\$260,000}$

$\qquad\qquad\qquad\qquad = 1.077$

7. Current ratio $= \dfrac{\text{Current Assets}}{\text{Current Liabilities}}$

$\qquad\qquad\quad = \dfrac{\$144,000}{\$120,000}$

$\qquad\qquad\quad = 1.2$

8. Quick (acid-test) ratio $= \dfrac{\text{Cash and Short} - \text{Term Investments} + \text{Net Receivables}}{\text{Current Liabilities}}$

$\qquad\qquad\qquad\qquad = \dfrac{\$26,000 + \$48,000}{\$120,000}$

$\qquad\qquad\qquad\qquad = 0.617$

Answer to Question 2A-ESO2

Answer A:

Third State Bank would be interested in comparative financial statements so that it could analyze trends in data and operating results. Trends are important because they may point to basic changes in the nature of the business.

Ratio analysis would give some indication of the company's short-term solvency and help Third State Bank assess the level of risk involved. The ratios also would be useful in analyzing how RCS is performing compared to industry averages and thus serve as a benchmark for comparison to other companies. Ratios reduce absolute dollar amounts to more meaningful data in order for the bank to compare ratios to prior periods, other companies, and the industry. Ratios can be used to show how well the company is being managed and to highlight areas for further investigation. If the ratios do not appear favorable compared to the company's own past and to other companies in its industry, the bank may consider adjusting the dollar level and/or the interest rate of the note or may even decide not to renew the note.

Answer B:

Calculations of selected financial ratios for Renbud Computer Services Co. are presented next.

1. Current Ratio

$$\text{Current Ratio} = \frac{\text{Current Assets}}{\text{Current Liabilities}} = \frac{\text{Cash} + \text{Net A/R} + \text{Operating Supplies}}{\text{A/P} + \text{Taxes Payable} + \text{Notes Payable}}$$

$$\text{Last Year:} \atop \text{(in '000)} = \frac{\$50 + \$350 + \$70}{\$150 + \$140 + \$300} = \frac{\$470}{\$590} = 0.797 \text{ to } 1$$

$$\text{Two Years Ago:} \atop \text{(in '000)} = \frac{\$50 + \$250 + \$60}{\$130 + \$120 + \$200} = \frac{\$360}{\$450} = 0.8 \text{ to } 1$$

2. Accounts Receivable Turnover

$$\text{A/R Turnover} \atop \text{(in '000)} = \frac{\text{Net Sales}}{\text{Average Receivables}} = \frac{\$2,500}{(\$350 + \$250)/2} = \frac{\$2,500}{\$300} = 8.333 \text{ times}$$

3. Asset Turnover

$$\text{A/R Turnover} \atop \text{(in '000)} = \frac{\text{Net Sales}}{\text{Average Total Assets}} = \frac{\$2,500}{(\$1,930 + \$1,560)/2} = \frac{\$2,500}{\$1,745} = 1.433 \text{ times}$$

4. Return on Shareholders' Equity (SE)

$$\text{Return on SE} \atop \text{(in '000)} = \frac{\text{Net Income} - \text{Preferred Dividends}}{\text{Average Common Equity}} = \frac{\$290 - \$0}{(\$940 + \$710)/2} = \frac{\$290}{\$825}$$

$$= 0.352 = 35.2\%$$

5. Debt to Equity Ratio

$$\frac{\text{D/E Ratio}}{\text{(in '000)}} = \frac{\text{Total Current and Long-Term Debt}}{\text{Total Shareholders' Equity}}$$

$$\frac{\text{Last Year:}}{\text{(in '000)}} = \frac{\$990,000}{\$940,000} = 1.053 \text{ to } 1$$

$$\frac{\text{Two Years ago:}}{\text{(in '000)}} = \frac{\$850,000}{\$710,000} = 1.197 \text{ to } 1$$

6. Net Profit Margin Percentage (Return on Sales)

$$\frac{\text{Net Profit Margin}}{\text{Percentage (in '000)}} = \frac{\text{Net Income}}{\text{Net Sales}} = \frac{\$290}{\$2,500} = 0.116 = 11.6\%$$

Answer C:

The difficulties and limitations of ratio analysis include these:

1. Although ratios are useful as a starting point in financial analysis, they are not an end in themselves. Ratios can be used as indicators of what to pursue in a more detailed analysis.
2. Difficulties can arise in making industry average comparisons.
   - Different companies could use different accounting methods (e.g., FIFO versus LIFO inventory valuation).
   - Even though two companies are in the same industry, they may not be comparable because they are focused on different aspects of the business. For example, two companies may be in the oil industry, but one may be primarily a marketer of oil and the other may be a refinery.
   - Companies may be conglomerates that operate in many different industries.
3. The ratios are only as good as the data on which they are based. If accounting policies are questionable, the resulting ratios would also be questionable.

Answer to Question 2A-ES03

The major sections of the statement of cash flows describe the cash flows from these areas:

- Operating activities, which involve the cash effects of transactions that enter into the determination of net income, such as cash receipts from sales and cash payments to suppliers and employees
- Investing activities, which include making and collecting loans, and obtaining and disposing of investments and long-term assets

- Financing activities, which include borrowing and repaying cash from creditors (long-term debt) and obtaining funds from owners (investments) while providing a return on their investment (dividends)

Answer to Question 2A-ES04

Answer A:

Liquidity is the ability of an asset to be converted into cash without significant price concessions. Liquidity is important to Sentech because current obligations will continue if there is a strike. Understanding the company's ability to meet its obligations even if normal cash receipts are not forthcoming would give management an indication of whether—and for how long—it could weather a strike. Lack of liquidity can limit a company's financial flexibility, making it unable to take advantage of discounts and other profitable opportunities. Liquidity problems also can lead to financial distress or bankruptcy.

Answer B:

Measures of liquidity include:
- Current ratio: Current Assets / Current Liabilities
- Quick ratio (or acid-test ratio): (Cash + Marketable Securities + Accounts Receivable) / Current Liabilities
  - The quick ratio excludes inventory and prepaid expenses from cash resources.
- Cash ratio: (Cash + Marketable Securities) / Current Liabilities
  - Only cash and securities that are easily convertible into cash are used.
- Net working capital: Current Assets – Current Liabilities
- Net working capital ratio: Net Working Capital / Total Assets
- Sales to working capital: Sales / Average Net Working Capital
- Accounts receivable turnover: Net Sales / Average Gross Receivables
  - This ratio also can be calculated in days.
- Inventory turnover: Cost of Goods Sold / Average Inventory
  - This ratio can also be calculated in days.

Answer C:

Based on the parameters set down by the controller, either the quick ratio or the cash ratio would be best. The reason that these ratios are best is because they focus on the most liquid assets, excluding prepaid expenses and inventories. During a strike, inventories would not be a source of cash. The cash ratio excludes receivables as well and would be the most conservative measure. The cash ratio would reflect the fact that the collection of receivables would be slowed during a strike.

Answer to Question 2A-ES05

Answer A:

Unit Sales	Mar	Apr	May	Jun	Jul
U.S.	70,000	80,000	75,000	65,000	65,000
Canada	50,000	50,000	60,000	45,000	35,000
Total Sales	120,000	130,000	135,000	110,000	100,000

Cash Receipts		Apr	May	Jun	
U.S.					
Units		70,000	80,000	75,000	
Price (USD)		50	50	50	
Collections		3,500,000	4,000,000	3,750,000	
Canada					
Units		50,000	50,000	60,000	
Price (CAD)		60	60	60	
USD/CAD		0.833	0.840	0.847	
Collections (USD)		2,500,000	2,521,008	3,050,847	
TOTAL RECEIPTS (USD)		6,000,000	6,521,008	6,800,847	
Disbursements:					
Labor @ 10 USD/unit		1,350,000	1,100,000	1,000,000	
Overheads		400,000	400,000	400,000	
U.S. Materials @ 5 USD/unit		675,000	550,000	500,000	
Mexican Import @ 350 MXN/unit		47,250,000	38,500,000	35,000,000	
USD/MXN		0.0885	0.0877	0.0870	
Mexican Import in USD		4,181,416	3,377,193	3,043,478	57%
Interest				500,000	
Income Taxes				1,000,000	
TOTAL DISBURSEMENTS (USD)		6,606,416	5,427,193	6,443,478	
Beginning Cash Balance		1,000,000	393,584	1,487,399	
Ending Cash Balance		393,584	1,487,399	1,844,769	

Answer B:

Chargrille is exposed to currency fluctuations in both its receipts and disbursements. Approximately 41% of the unit sales and collections relate to Canadian customers. If exchange rates of Canadian dollars to U.S. dollars were 10% higher than the forecasted amounts, collections for the quarter would be approximately $800,000 USD less. On the disbursement side, approximately 57% of the disbursements for the quarter relate to the imported parts from Mexico. If the exchange rates of Mexican pesos to USDs were 10% lower than the forecasted amounts, disbursements for the quarter would be approximately $1 million USD greater. An unfavorable variance of 10% from the budgeted exchange rates would bring the cash balance at the end of the quarter from $1.8 million USD to approximately zero.

Answer C:

If the spot rate (CAD/USD) on the CAD is currently 1.20 and is expected to drop steadily to 1.18 by the end of June, it will take fewer Canadian dollars to buy one U.S. dollar. Therefore, the USD is depreciating relative to the CAD. If the spot rate (MXN/USD) on the Mexican peso is currently 11.0 and is expected to rise steadily to 11.5 by the end of June, it will take more Mexican pesos to buy one U.S. dollar. Therefore, the USD is appreciating relative to the MXN.

Answer D:

Chargrille can buy or sell forward currencies as a means of hedging exchange rate exposure. For example, if Adams forecasts the disbursements in pesos for April, May, and June while she is preparing the budget in March, she could purchase 47 MXN for delivery in 30 days, 38 million MXN for delivery in 60 days, and 35 million MXN for delivery in 90 days at the going forward rates for those periods, thereby locking in the exchange rate and quantifying those disbursements. Of course, during the intervening time periods, the U.S. dollar could appreciate, depreciate, or remain stable relative to the MXN. The cost of the forward market hedge can be thought of as insurance. Another option available would be the currency futures market, which allows firms to purchase or sell futures contracts on an organized exchange. Again, the costs associated with buying and selling futures contracts increase the firm's costs; however, they also can reduce the risk of sharp unexpected fluctuations in exchange rates.

Answer to Question 2A-ES06

Answer A:

1. Using the straight line method, $200 million depreciated over 10 years equals $20 million per year. Depreciation expense increases by $20 million. The purchase will decrease cash and increase gross fixed assets by $200 million. The depreciation expense will increase accumulated depreciation and decrease net fixed assets by $20 million.
2. Long-term debt increases by $75 million. Cash, which is part of current assets, also will increase by $75 million. The annual interest expense is $75 million × 10% = $7.5 million.
3. Preferred stock (part of equity) increases by $25 million. Cash, part of current assets, will increase by $25 million. The preferred dividend will increase by $25 million × 14% = $3.5 million.
4. Common stock, part of equity, will increase by $2 par × 4 million = $8 million. The common stock premium, part of Equity, will increase by $23 × 4 million = $92 million. Cash, part of current assets, will increase by $25 × 4 million = $100 million.
5. Revenues increase by $60 million, operating expenses increase by $30 million, and cash increases by $30 million.

Answer B:

The revised forecast is shown next.

Balance Sheet (thousands of dollars)

	Original	Changes	Revised
Current assets	100,000	16,000	116,000
Fixed assets	750,000	200,000	950,000
Accumulated depreciation	200,000	20,000	220,000
Net fixed assets	550,000	180,000	730,000
TOTAL ASSETS	650,000	196,000	846,000
Current liabilities	50,000	0	50,000
Long-term debt	150,000	75,000	225,000
Shareholders' equity			
Preferred stock	50,000	25,000	75,000
Common—par	100,000	8,000	108,000
Common—premium	200,000	92,000	292,000
Retained Earnings	100,000	(4,000)	96,000
	450,000	121,000	571,000
TOTAL LIABILITIES and EQUITY	650,000	196,000	846,000

Income Statement (Thousands of Dollars)

	Original	Changes	Revised
Revenue	2,000,000	60,000	2,060,000
Depreciation Expense	50,000	20,000	70,000
Other Expenses	1,775,000	30,000	1,805,000
Earnings Before Interest and Taxes	175,000	10,000	185,000
Interest	15,000	7,500	22,500
Taxes (40% effective rate)	64,000	1,000	65,000
Net Income	96,000	1,500	97,500
Preferred Stock Dividends	5,000	3,500	8,500
Earnings for Common Stock	91,000	(2,000)	89,000

Answer C:

Public companies are concerned about the effect on earnings for several reasons, including:

- Analysts and investors closely follow earnings and are especially concerned when they drop or do not grow as much as expected.
- Earnings growth is a factor in many valuation formulas. The firm is concerned about the market value of the common stock.

- The firm is expecting to raise $200 million to finance the expansion. Reduced earnings forecasts could result in the debt issue having a higher interest rate, the preferred stock to require a higher dividend rate, and the common stock to be issued at a lower market price.
- Estimates of sales volume growth of the new line could be provided. Growth is very important to investors in valuing the stock of a firm.
- The effect on earnings in the initial year is not indicative of the future prospects for the new line.
- The firm is experiencing a high level of certain costs (specify the types of costs as promotion, start-up, etc.) early in the product life cycle, which will be reduced in coming years. Of course, management must believe this to be true.

Answer to Question 2A-ES07

Answer 1:

a.

	Year 1	Year 2	Year 3
Revenue	100%	100%	100%
Cost of goods sold	60%	50%	60%
Gross profit	40%	50%	40%
Sales and marketing	10%	8.3%	6.7%
General and admin.	7.5%	8.3%	10%
Research and dev.	7.5%	8.3%	3.3%
Operating income	15 %	25%	20%

b.

	Year 1	Year 2	Year 3
Revenue	100%	120%	150%
Cost of goods sold	100%	100%	150%
Gross profit	100%	150%	150%
Sales and marketing	100%	100%	100%
General and admin.	100%	133%	200%
Research and dev.	100%	133%	66.7%
Operating income	100%	200%	200%

Answer 2:

Revenue

Year 2: ($24,000 − $20,000)/$20,000 = 20%

Year 3: ($30,000 − $24,000)/$24,000 = 25%

Operating income

Year 2: ($6,000 − $3,000)/$3,000 = 100%

Year 3: ($6,000 − $6,000)/$6,000 = 0%

Answer 3:

Foyle's gross profit margin 50% was comparable in year 2 to competitor 52% and industry average 50%, but Foyle has fallen to 40% in year 3. Foyle's operating income percentage 25% was the same in year 2 to competitor and industry average at 25%, but Foyle has fallen to 20% in year 3.

Foyle in year 3 has lower sales and marketing than competitor and industry average (6.7% versus 11.1% and 10.7%), but higher in general and administration (10% versus 7% and 8.9%). Foyle's research and development is substantially below both competitor and industry average (3.3% versus 8.9% and 5.4%).

Answer to Question 2A-ES08

Answer 1:

	Year 2	Year 1
Revenues	100.0%	100.0%
Cost of Goods Sold	48.4	47.5
Gross Margin	51.6	52.5
Selling Expenses	14.8	14.7
Administrative Expenses	17.5	17.5
Loss Due to Strike	3	
Interest Expense	.5	.5
Income before Taxes	18.4	19.8
Income Tax Expense	7.4	7.9
Income from Continuing Operations	11.1	11.9
Discontinued Operations	1.1	—
Net Income	12.2	11.9

Answer 2:

a. Sales increased but the gross margin percentage decreased. This could be caused by:
- a change in the product mix.
- a decrease in the selling price which resulted in selling more units but if the cost per unit did not change or increased, the gross margin percentage would increase.
- an increase in the cost of goods that was not passed along to customers; sales could have increased because the competition raised its prices.

b. Selling expenses remained fairly constant as a percentage of sales. This could be caused by:
- nearly all of the selling expenses being variable costs.
- increased advertising to boost sales.

c. Administrative expenses remained at a constant percentage of sales. Since most of these costs are fixed, when sales rise, the costs as a percentage of sales should decrease. The constant percentage could be caused by:
- moving outside of the relevant range of year 1's activity, causing step-fixed costs to increase.
- poor budgeting procedures or poor cost controls that allow administrative spending in proportion to sales.

Answer 3:

Number of shares outstanding = $780,000 / $2.50 = 312,000

Book value = $7,363,200 / 312,000 = $23.60

Answer to Question 2A-ES09

Answer 1:

Knight, Inc. Summary Balance Sheet

Assets	$200 million	Debt	$60 million
		Equity	140 million
		Total Liabilities and Equity	$200 million

Day, Ltd. Summary Balance Sheet

Assets	$200 million	Debt	$120 million
		Equity	80 million
		Total Liabilities and Equity	$200 million

Knight, Inc. Summary Income Statement

EBIT	$50 million
Interest $60m × 10%	6 million
Earnings before tax	44 million
Tax at 40%	17.6 million
Net Income	$26.4 million

Day, Ltd. Summary Income Statement

EBIT	$50 million
Interest $120m × 15%	18 million
Earnings before tax	32 million
Tax at 40%	12.8 million
Net Income	$19.2 million

Answer 2:

Return on Equity

	NI	Equity	ROE
Knight, Inc.	$26.4 million	$140 million	18.86%
Day, Ltd	$19.2 million	$80 million	24.00%

Answer 3:

Day, Ltd. has higher risk, as measured by debt/equity or debt/total assets ratios. Day has higher fixed interest payments. Knight, Inc. is better able to weather a downturn in industry.

Answer 4:

Costs of financial distress include higher interest rates; inaccessibility to debt or equity finance; might have to forgo attractive projects; drop in value of equity; bankruptcy; increased intrusion by creditors; loss of customers, suppliers, employees.

Answer to Question 2A-ES10

Answer 1:

Pro Forma Income Statements and Balance Sheets (millions of dollars)

Income Statement		Pro Forma	
	Current	**Stock (1)**	**Debt**
Sales	$5,500	$5,500	$5,500
COGS	3,100	3,100	3,100
GP	2,400	2,400	2,400
SG&A	1,600	1,600	1,600
Operating Income	800	800	800
Interest Expense	100	100	130
Pretax Income	700	700	670
Income Taxes (40%)	280	280	268
Net Income	$420	$420	$402
Earnings per Share	$7.00	$6.46	$6.70

[1]$500 million @6% = $30 million. Interest Expense for debt is $100 + $30 = $130 million

EPS — Stock: Net Income/Revised # of shares = $420/65 where 65 = 60 (current) + 5 (issued).

Balance Sheet		Pro Forma	
	Current	**Stock (1)**	**Debt**
Current Assets	100	90	82
Net Fixed Assets	3,000	3,500	3,500
Total Assets	**3,100**	**3,590**	**3,582**
Current Liabilities	50	50	50
Long-Term Debt	1,000	1,000	1,000
Common Stock:			
Par Value ($2/share)	120	130	120
Additional Paid-in Capital	1,000	1,490	1,000
Retained Earnings	930	920	912
Net Common Equity	2,050	2,540	2,032
Total Liabilities and Equity	**3,100**	**3,590**	**3,582**

[1]To raise $500 million, McMullen must issue 5,000,000 shares at $100 per share. Two dollars per share is recorded in the "Par Value" account and the remaining $98/share is recorded as "Additional Paid-in Capital".

For stock at year end div of $10 million (5,000,000 shares @ $2) paid out of cash so Current Assets are $100 − $10 = $90, $10 million comes out of R/E $930−$10 = $920.

For debt interest after tax requires a payment of $18 million ($500 * 6.00% * (1 − 40%)) so Current Assets are $100 − $18 = $82 and retained earnings are $18 lower.

Answer 2:

a. Financial leverage ratio measures relation between total assets and the common equity capital. The greater the proportion of assets financed by common equity capital, the lower the financial leverage ratio. A higher financial leverage ratio enhances return on equity. The risk inherent in a change in profitability is greater when the financial ratio leverage is higher.

			Pro Forma		
	Common Stock			**Debt**	
Total assets	3,590	141.34%	Debt	3,582	176.28%
Net Common Equity	2,540			2,032	
	Stock			**Debt**	
Alternate 1 Debt/	1,050		Debt/	1,550	
Equity	2,540		Equity	2,032	
=	41.34%		=	76.28%	
Alternate 2 Debt/	1,050		Debt/	1,550	
Assets	3,590		Assets	3,582	
=	29.25%		=	43.27%	

b. Working capital is a measure of liquidity. It is the excess of current assets over current liabilities. Working capital provides a safety cushion to creditors. It measures liquid reserve available to meet contingencies

	Current Assets		**Current Liabilities**	**Working Capital**
Common	90	less	50	40
Debt Alt	83	less	50	32

Answer 3:
Debt Covenant Test

LT Debt/Equity	49%	39%	74%
Total Debt to Equity	51%	41%	76%

Debt/equity ratios can be defined in various ways. Whether the ratio is defined as long-term debt to equity or as total debt (short- and long-term) to equity, the result is a ratio greater than 60% if debt is issued. The debt issue is, therefore, not viable.

Answer 4:

	(NP Margin)	×	(Asset turnover)	×	(Equity multiplier)	=	ROE
	Net Profit	×	Net Sales		Total Assets		Net profit
	Net Sales		Total Assets		Shareholder's Equity		Shareholder's Equity
Stock	$420		5,500		3,590		$420
	$5,500		3,590		2,540		2,540
	0.07636364		1.532033		1.413386		0.16535433
Debt	$402		5,500		3,582		$402
	$5,500		3,582		2,032		2,032
	0.07309091		1.5355455		1.762795		0.19783465

Answer 5:

- Companies with relatively stable sales are able to take on more debt, and, therefore, more fixed charges than companies in highly cyclical industries or other business situations presenting above normal risks.
- Firms with assets that are suitable as security for loans (i.e. property and equipment) are in a better situation to use debt financing.
- A firm with relatively low operating risk, as measured by the degree of operating leverage or some other measure, is in a better position to have more debt in its capital structure.
- Firms anticipating relatively high growth rates are better able to take on more debt.
- The higher a firm's effective tax rate, the more valuable the tax deductibility (tax shield) of interest payments.
- Those firms having significant amounts of equity controlled by management may be reluctant to issue additional stock since it would dilute control. Debt would be the option if new funds need to be raised.
- Management's attitude toward risk or level of conservatism can have an influence on how much capital structure risk a firm assumes.
- Rating agency assessments of a company can have a definite impact on financial structure. For example, if a rating agency informed management that its bonds would be downgraded if it issued more debt, then the firm would most likely issue common stock if it needed to raise additional capital.
- Market conditions at a specific time have an influence over whether debt or equity is issued. Issues such as whether a firm's stock price is currently depressed

or if interest rates were perceived as being either very high or very low, have an influence on the method of financing and, therefore, the capital structure.
- Maintaining financial flexibility, especially for a growth firm, is very important. That means that at any point in time a firm should not be borrowed to capacity, allowing it the option of issuing debt in the event of favorable conditions. Firms that are at their debt limit have little financial flexibility.

Part 2 Section B Answers

Answer to Question 2B-ES01

Answer A:

1. Default risk is the probability of a security issuer being unable to meet its contractual obligations of interest and principal payments. A greater default risk increases the yield because the investor is paid a premium for the default risk.
2. Marketability of a security is the ability to buy and sell the security on a secondary market and relates to the owner's ability to convert it into cash. A lower marketability increases the yield because the investor is paid a premium for the lack of marketability.
3. Maturity is the length of time remaining until a security is redeemed by the original issuer. A longer maturity means an investor has a greater exposure to risk. This risk increases the yield.

Answer B:

Type of Investment	Default Risk	Marketability	Maturity
Certificate of deposit (CD)	Default risk is that of the issuing bank failing, a probability that is low in most cases.	A poor secondary market exists for the negotiable CDs of the large money market banks.	Original maturities are short term and generally range from 30 days to one year.
U.S. Treasury bills	Default risk is negligible because the bills are guaranteed by the U.S. government.	Market activity is excellent, and transaction costs involved in the sale in the secondary market are small.	Treasury bills are auctioned weekly by the U.S. Treasury with short-term maturities of three months, six months, and one year.
Preferred stock of domestic corporations	Not applicable.	Marketability is very good for a listed issue. The realized price dimension of marketability is not as good because of the volatility of preferred stock prices.	Preferred stock has no maturity.

Answer C:

Certificates of deposit (CD) are a suitable investment for Gershenfeld in its situation. The most common denomination is $100,000, so its appeal is mostly to large investors such as Gershenfeld. CDs carry an acceptable default risk and can be purchased with the desired maturity of two months. Yields on CDs are greater than those on U.S. Treasury bills.

U.S. Treasury bills also are a suitable investment for Gershenfeld in its situation. They are the most conservative of the three types of investments being considered, having the lowest default risk and greatest marketability. However, the yield on U.S. Treasury bills would be less than the yield on CDs.

Preferred stock of domestic corporations is not a suitable investment for Gershenfeld in this situation. Such a stock purchase is generally considered a long-term investment.

Answer to Question 2B-ES02

Answer A:

An increase in long-term debt and preferred stock issues would increase Atrax's degree of financial leverage and its debt-to-equity ratio. This action has two primary effects from the stockholders' perspective:

1. The variability of earnings per share (EPS) and return on equity (ROE) will be greater, and EPS and ROE will increase at a faster rate and be at a higher level whenever the firm earns more than its cost of capital. The increased EPS will exert an upward influence on the value of Atrax's common stock.
2. The variability of EPS and ROE increases Atrax's financial risk. This increased risk exposure will exert a downward influence on the common stock value and will be reflected in a lowered price/earnings ratio.

The net effect on the price of Atrax's common stock will depend on which influence is stronger. The price of the stock probably will rise because Atrax is continuing to diversify for the purpose of reducing its business risk exposure. Therefore, investors are likely to accept the increased financial risk as long as stockholders believe that Atrax is not overusing debt and preferred stock (i.e., is not going beyond its optimal capital structure).

Answer B:

The short-term effect probably will be a decrease in the market price of Atrax's common stock. Atrax's high payout ratio coupled with its limited earnings growth means Atrax probably has attracted conservative investors dependent on dividend income. These investors probably will sell their stock due to the change in dividend policy. In addition, investors may interpret the elimination of cash dividends as a decrease in earnings.

The long-term effect probably will be an increase in the market price of the stock. The funds diverted from the payment of cash dividends will be used in the capital expansion and diversification program. This should lead to increased earnings in the future while also decreasing Atrax's business risk. Investors interested in capital gains (rather than dividend income) probably would be attracted to Atrax, which also should result in a positive effect on the market price of the stock.

Answer C:

1. Yes, Traxal would be able to maintain his current equity position of 35% if stock dividends were distributed because all stockholders will receive additional shares of stock in proportion to their current ownership interest in Atrax.

2. The probable short-term effect would be a decrease in the market price of Atrax's stock, because current investors will seek to sell their stock as a consequence of the change in dividend policy and the implied connotations of reduced earnings. The stock dividends give no substantive value to stockholders who expect a cash dividend. However, the price of the stock may not fall as much as reducing the payout ratio to zero because some current investors may misinterpret the nature of a stock dividend or may accept the reduced cash dividends in the short-term when coupled with the hope for potential capital gains in the long-term.

   The probable long-term effect would be an increase in the market price of Atrax's stock because growth-oriented investors should be attracted to Atrax for the capital gain potential. In addition, a nominal dividend payout will act as a downward stabilizer on stock price movements. Furthermore, if Atrax's diversification program is successful, the reduced business risk and increased future earnings should exert a positive influence on the stock price.

3. Proposal 2 is more likely to result in a smaller drop in the stock price than Proposal 3 in the short term due to the higher cash dividends and less negative reaction to an implied earnings decline. The long-term effect on stock prices is less certain. Proposal 3 probably would result in higher stock prices due to increased future earnings growth because all internally generated funds could be reinvested.

Answer to Question 2B-ES03

Answer A:

Alternative 1—Wasson Industries	
Adjusted basis of Dayton Plant	$4,200,000
Less: Proceeds from sale of plant to Wasson	3,000,000
Loss on sale of plant	$1,200,000
Multiply by: Applicable income tax rate[1]	40%
Decrease in income taxes	$480,000

[1]When net losses exceed net gains, the loss is treated as ordinary income for income tax purposes; thus, the 40% tax rate is used.

Determine the after-tax cash flow and apply the discount factor.

Proceeds from sale of plan to Wasson	$3,000,000
Add: Decrease in income taxes	480,000
After-tax cash flow	$3,480,000
Multiply by: Discount factor	1.00
Present value of after-tax cash flows	$3,480,000

---

[1]The income taxes should be recognized in the years in which the sales occur. The amount of tax is based on sales revenue less costs excluding the depreciation. The depreciation tax shield is shown separately; refer to footnote 2. The income tax charge is $780,000 [($4,200,000 − 2,250,000) × .40].

Alternative 2—Harr Enterprises

Cash flows from annual lease payments

Annual Gross Dollar Sales	Estimated Probability	Expected Value of Sales
$2,000,000	0.1	$200,000
4,000,000	0.4	1,600,000
6,000,000	0.3	1,800,000
8,000,000	0.2	1,600,000
Expected annual gross sales		$5,200,000
Multiply by: Percentage payable to Kravel		.10
Variable portion of lease payment		$520,000
Add: Fixed portion of lease payment		500,000
Before-tax cash flow from lease		$1,020,000
Less: Income tax (40%)		408,000
After-tax cash flow from lease		$612,000
Multiply by: Discount factor		2.798
Present value of after-tax cash flow from lease		$1,712,376

Depreciation tax shield

Annual depreciation	$ 900,000
Multiply by: Tax rate	.4
Income tax shield from depreciation	$360,000
Multiply by: Discount factor	2.798
Present value of depreciation tax shield	$1,007,280

Sale of Dayton plant (12/31/2010)

Estimated cash value of plant (12/31/2010)	$600,000
Gain or loss computation on sale of plant	
Adjusted basis 12/31/2006	$4,200,000
Less: Depreciation (900,000 × 4)	3,600,000
Adjusted basis 12/31/2006	600,000
Less: Proceeds	600,000
Gain/loss	-0-

After-tax cash flow from sale	$600,000
Multiply by: Discount factor	.552
Present value of sale of Dayton plant	$331,200

Present value of after-tax cash flows

PV of after-tax cash flow from lease	$1,712,376
PV of depreciation tax shield	1,007,280
PV of sale of Dayton plant	331,200
Total present value of after-tax cash flows	$3,050,856

[2]The depreciation charge would be included in the calculation of cost of goods sold. Thus, the recognition of the depreciation charge for income tax purposes in 2007, 2008, and 2009 would be deferred one year. The depreciation tax shield for 2007 and 2008 is $360,000 ($900,000 × .40). The depreciation recognized for income tax purposes in 2010 would be $1,800,000 which consists of the 2009 depreciation charge included in the 2010 cost of goods sold and the 2010 depreciation charge recognized in 2010 when the plant is presumably being used as a warehouse. Thus, the depreciation tax shield in 2010 is $720,000 ($1,800,000 × .40).

	Alternative 3—Souvenir Items			

	2007	2008	2009	2010
Revenue (70,000 × 12 × $5)	$ -0-	$4,200,000	$4,200,000	$4,200,000
Annual cash outlays	2,250,000	2,250,000	2,250,000	-0-
Annual cash flows	$(2,250,000)	$1,950,000	$1,950,000	$4,200,000
Less income taxes[1]	-0-	780,000	780,000	780,000
After-tax cash flows	$(2,250,000)	$1,170,000	$1,170,000	$3,420,000
Depreciation tax shield[2]	-0-	360,000	360,000	720,000
Salvage[3]				600,000
Net after-tax cash flows	$(2,250,000)	$1,530,000	$1,530,000	$4,740,000
Discount factors	.862	.743	.641	.552
Present value of after-tax cash flows	$(1,939,500)	$1,136,790	$980,730	$2,616,480

[3]There is no gain or loss on the sale of the plant; thus, the cash flow is equivalent to the proceeds (see Alternative 2).

Net present value of after-tax cash flows:

2007	–$1,939,500
2008	1,136,790
2009	980,730
2010	2,616,480
Total	$2,794,500

Answer B:

The additional factors Kravel Corporation should consider before making a decision regarding the disposition or use of the idle plant and equipment at the Dayton Plant include those listed next.

- Kravel should consider the risks involved for each of the alternatives. Alternative 1 is the least risky because it would be completed on January 1, 2007, whereas Alternatives 2 and 3 would involve activities through 2010.

- Kravel should consider the accuracy of the cash flow estimates and discount rates used in the cash flow analysis.
- Kravel should consider the fit between the timing of the cash flows for each alternative and the cash needs of the corporation.
- Kravel should consider the likelihood of an opportunity to resume the production of truck parts at the Dayton plant. Alternative 1 eliminates that possibility, and Alternative 2 precludes it until 2011.

Answer to Question 2B-ES04

Answer A:

Financing Plan (Dollars in Millions)

	Current Structure	Percent of Total	Funds Needed	Retained Earnings	External Sources
Debt	$175	35%	$28		$28
Preferred	50	10%	8		8
Common	275	55%	44	$15	29
Totals	$500	100%	$80	$15	$65

Financing sources will be:

New debt	$28 million
New preferred stock	8 million
Retained earnings	15 million
New common stock[1]	29 million
Total	$80 million

[1]$29 million / $58 per share = 500,000 new common shares

Answer B:

Weighted Incremental Cost of Capital

	% of Capital Structure	Cost	Weighted Cost
Debt	35%	6.00%[1]	2.10%
Preferred	10%	12.00%	1.20%
Common	55%	16.00%	8.80%
Cost of capital			12.10%

[1]Pretax 10% x (1 – Tax Rate) = 6.00%

Answer C:

1. If the corporate tax rate is increased, the after-tax cost of debt would be reduced, thereby reducing the cost of capital. In other words, the tax shield of debt becomes more valuable to the firm.
2. When the banks indicate they are raising rates, the rest of the debt market generally raises rates. The higher cost of debt will increase the overall cost of capital.

3. Beta is a measure of risk. According to the capital asset pricing model, the cost of equity is directly related to risk. As risk is reduced, the cost of equity is reduced, and, correspondingly, the overall cost of capital is reduced.

4. In general, a significant increase in the percentage of debt in the capital structure (especially in this case where the current structure is deemed optimal) results in more risk for the firm. This increases its cost of debt and its cost of equity. The increase in the cost of equity most likely will offset the fact that debt has a lower relative. The result here is that the cost of capital should increase.

Answer to Question 2B-ES05

Answer A:

Ownership Alternative	$t=0$	$t=1$	$t=2$	$t=3$	$t=4$	$t=5$
Purchase Price **(a)**	(2,000)					
Insurance **(b)**		(25)	(25)	(25)	(25)	(25)
Property Taxes **(c)**		(50)	(50)	(50)	(50)	(50)
Tax Depreciation **(d)**		660	900	300	140	
Salvage **(e)**						200
Income Tax Savings **(g)**: 40% × **(−b−c+d−e)**		294	390	150	86	(50)
Net Cash Flows **(a+b+c+e+g)**	(2,000)	219	315	75	11	75
Present Value factor @ 6%*	1.000	0.943	0.890	0.840	0.792	0.747
Present value	(2,000)	207	280	63	9	56

NPV = (1,385)

* The discount rate to be used is the after-tax cost of debt (10% × (1 − 0.4))

Lease alternative	$t=0$	$t=1$	$t=2$	$t=3$	$t=4$	$t=5$
Lease payment		(600)	(600)	(600)	(600)	(600)
Tax savings		240	240	240	240	240
Net cash flows		(360)	(360)	(360)	(360)	(360)
PV factor @ 6%*	1.000	0.943	0.890	0.840	0.792	0.747
Present value		(339)	(320)	(302)	(285)	(269)

NPV = (1,516)

*The discount rate to be used is the after-tax cost of debt (10% × (1 − 0.4)).

Conclusion: Ownership is more economic since NPV of ownership ($1,385,000) is less than NPV of leasing ($1,516,000), giving a net advantage to ownership of $131,000 on an NPV basis.

Answer B:

Accounting Standards Topic ASC 840 *Leases* (formerly Statement of Financial Accounting Standards No. 13), establishes standards of financial accounting and reporting for leases by lessees and lessors. The Statement defines a lease as an agreement conveying the right to use property, plant, or equipment (land and/or depreciable assets) usually for a stated period of time.

The criterion for classifying leases is that if at its inception a lease meets one or more of the next four criteria, the lease shall be classified as a capital lease by the lessee. Otherwise, it shall be classified as an operating lease.

a. The lease transfers ownership of the property to the lessee by the end of the lease term.
b. The lease contains a bargain purchase option.
c. The lease term is equal to 75% or more of the estimated economic life of the leased property.
d. The present value at the beginning of the lease term of the minimum lease payments, excluding executory costs such as insurance, maintenance, and taxes to be paid by the lessor, including any profit thereon, equals or exceeds 90% of the excess of the fair value of the leased property to the lessor at the inception of the lease

In the case of the lease that Crenshaw is evaluating, criteria **a** and **b** are not met since no ownership is transferred at the end and there is no bargain purchase option. Criterion **c** is met since the lease term is equal to the 5 year life of the equipment. Criterion **d** is also met. The lease payment of $600,000 less the executory costs of insurance and property taxes results in a minimum lease payment of $525,000. The present value of this at the Crenshaw's incremental borrowing rate of 10% is $1.99 million, greater than 90% of fair value of the leased property.

The result is that Crenshaw must classify the lease as a capital lease.

Answer C:

- A lessor may be better able to take full advantage of tax benefits, such as accelerated depreciation, than the lessee who may not be a positive taxable income situation. In that case, the lessor may pass those benefits on to the lessee in the lease payment.
- A lessor may be in a better position to realize a high residual value for the equipment. That is often the case where the lessor is a manufacturer of the equipment or a dealer in the equipment as opposed to being a financial institution.
- Certain property, such as general use assets (vehicles, construction equipment, general-purpose buildings, etc.), lend themselves to leasing since the property can be sold or released after the initial term.

Although most financial analysts agree that leasing is basically a form of debt financing, firms may be able to utilize the leverage available from leasing to a greater extent than they could utilize bond financing.

Answer to Question 2B-ES06

Answer A: Issue price of each bond

Maturity value $1,000.00
PV of $1,000 due in 5 years, at 8%, compounded semiannually
= $1,000 × 0.676 = $676.00

PV of $30 paid semiannually for 5 years, compounded semiannually
= $30 × 8.111 = $243.33

Issue price of bond = $919.33

Discount on bonds payable = $1,000.00 − $919.33 = $80.67

Answer B: How many bonds to issue

Funds needed of $15,000,000 / $919.22 per bond = 16,316 bonds

Answer C: Net after-tax cash flows per bond

	Year 0	Year 1	Year 2	Year 3	Year 4	Year 5
Issue bond	$919					
Cash interest		($60)	($60)	($60)	($60)	($60)
Bond interest		(14)	(15)	(16)	(17)	(19)
Total interest		(74)	(75)	(76)	(77)	(79)
Tax savings		29.60	30	30.40	30.80	31.60
Repay bond						(1,000)
Net cash flow	919	(30.40)	(30)	(29.60)	(29.20)	(1,028)
# of bonds	16,316	16,316	16,316	16,316	16,316	16,316
Total cash flow	$14,999,788	($496,006)	($489,480)	($482,954)	($476,427)	($16,779,374)

Answer D: Rational Investor Calculation

	Amount	PV factor	Present Value
PV of $1,000 due in 2 years @ 6%	$1,000	0.888	$888.00
(4 periods @ 3%)			
PV of $30 paid semiannually	30	3.717	111.51
(4 periods @ 3%)			
Market value of bond			$999.51

Note: Would round to $1000 with sufficient numbers in the PV factor.

Answer to Question 2B-ES07

Answer 1:

a. A merger is the combination of two or more companies in which only one firm survives as the legal entity. An acquisition is when one company acquires another as part of its overall business strategy.

b. The scenario describes a potential strategic acquisition as management was hoping to work on product mix.

c. Some of the synergies of a business combination are the economies realized where the performance of the combined firm exceeds that of its previously separate parts. There are economies of scale where the benefits of size cause the average unit cost to falls as volume increases. Acquisitions can increase sales, market share, or help a company gain market dominance. There may be other marketing and strategic benefits, or the acquisition might bring technological advance to the product table, or it may fill a gap in the product line which would enhance sales made throughout the firm. It may be possible for duplicate facilities to be eliminated after a merger or departments like marketing, accounting, purchasing, and other operations can be consolidated. The sales force may be reduced to avoid duplication of effort in a particular territory. The companies may be able to concentrate a greater volume of activity into a given facility and into a given number of people to have a more efficient utilization of resources.

Answer 2:

a. A spinoff is a form of divestiture resulting in a subsidiary or division becoming an independent company. Ordinarily, shares in the new company are distributed to the parent company's shareholders on a pro-rata basis. An equity carve-out is a public sale of stock in a subsidiary in which the parent usually retains majority control. Only the spinoff is described in the scenario above.

b. The spinoff would be if Electronics Inc were to decide to split the subsidiary off into its own separate company.

Answer 3:

a. The main types of bankruptcy are Chapter 7—which is liquidation, or the sale of assets of a firm, and Chapter 11 which is rehabilitation of an enterprise through its reorganization.

b. In distributing the proceeds to creditors, the priority in a bankruptcy proceeding is as follows:

1. Administrative expenses associated with liquidating the property, including trustees fee and attorney fees.
2. Creditor claims that arise in the ordinary course of the debtors business from the time the case starts to the time a trustee is appointed.
3. Wages earned by employees within 90 days of the bankruptcy petition, limited to $2,000 per employee.
4. Claims for contributions of employee benefit plans for services rendered within 180 days of the bankruptcy petition (limited to $2,000 per employee).
5. Claims of customers who make cash deposits for goods or services not provided by the debtor (limited to $900 per customer).
6. Taxes owed.
7. Unsecured claims either filed on time or tardily filed if the creditor did not know of the bankruptcy.
8. Unsecured claims filed late by creditors who had knowledge of the bankruptcy.
9. Fines and punitive damages.
10. Interest that accrues to claims after the date of the petition.

Answer to Question 2B-ES08

Answer 1:

The cost to produce the units is irrelevant, because OneCo can sell all that it produces at a market price of $16.50. The net realizable value per unit is $15.60 ($16.50 − .90).

a. The first option would decrease net income by $1,600. The net realizable value per unit sold to Gatsby is $14.00 ($14.35 − .35). In order to supply Gatsby, OneCo would be displacing sales in the regular market having a NRV of $15.60. That reduction of $1.60 per unit × 1,000 units would decrease net income by $1,600.

Alternate solution: Normal profit per unit is $4.40 ($16.50 − $12.10). The profit per unit sold to Gatsby is $2.80 ($14.35 − $11.55). Gatsby cost is $11.55 ($4.00 + $1.30 + $2.50 + $3.40 + .35). The difference of $1.60 per unit ($4.40 − $2.80) × 1,000 units would decrease net income by $1,600.

b. The second option would increase net income by $1,100. The extra units could be sold in the regular market at a NRV of $15.60. The cost is $14.50. Thus, profits would increase by $1.10 per unit, or $1,100 in total.

Alternate solution: Selling Price $16.50 − Cost to purchase from Zelda $14.50 − Sales commission $.90 = profit per unit $1.10. Increase in net income $1.10 @ 1,000 units = $1,100.

c. The third option would decrease income by $500. Regular business is unaffected. As explained above, the 1,000 units bought cost $14.50 each, and the NRV of the new units sold is $14.00. The net difference is .50 per unit.

Alternate solution: Action 1 Decrease in Net Income of $1,600 + Action 2 Increase in Net Income of $1,100 = Net Decrease in Net Income of $500.

Answer 2:

a. Direct Material $4.00 + $.30 = $4.30. Direct Labor $1.30 @ 1.15 = $1.495. Variable Overhead $2.50 @ 1.15 = $2.875. Cost $12.42 ($4.30 + $1.495 + $2.875 + $3.40 + .35). Profit per unit $4.08 ($16.5 + 12.42). Market profit $4.40 ($16.50 − $12.10). Decrease in net income ($4.08 − $4.40) = −.32 @ 2,000 = decrease $640. Do not accept proposal.

b. If there is excess capacity, accept the proposal, revenue would contribute to fixed costs.

Answer 3:

Other factors to consider are: the effect on market price/competition, effect on sales force/commissions, quality of Zelda products, and follow-on Gatsby business. There may be other considerations. Some other considerations are: impact on employees; reaction of customers.

Part 2 Section C Answers

Answer to Question 2C-ES01

Answer A: Price elasticity of demand

1. Price elasticity of demand is the percentage change in the quantity demanded of a commodity relative to (divided by) the percentage change in the price of that same commodity.

Answer B:

1. If the price elasticity coefficient of a commodity is greater than 1, the demand for that commodity is classified as elastic. This indicates that the demand for the

commodity is very sensitive to changes in price. If the price elasticity coefficient of a commodity is less than 1, the demand for that commodity is classified as inelastic. This indicates that the demand for the commodity is not sensitive to a change in price. A commodity with a price elasticity of 1 is classified as having unitary elasticity.

2. There is a relationship between changes in total revenue and the price elasticity of demand that would be useful to a firm's management. If demand is elastic, a change in price will cause total revenue to change in the opposite direction. If demand is inelastic, a change in price will cause total revenue to change in the same direction. When unit elasticity exists, an increase or decrease in price will leave total revenue unchanged.

Answer to Question 2C-ES02

Answer A:

	Capital	Intensive	Labor	Intensive
Selling price		$30.00		$30.00
Variable costs:				
Raw materials	$5.00		$5.60	
Direct labor	6.00		7.20	
Variable overhead	3.00		4.80	
Variable selling	2.00	16.00	2.00	19.60
Contribution margin	$14.00		$10.40	

1.
2.

Answer B:

Candice Company would be indifferent between the two manufacturing methods at the volume (x) where total costs are equal.

$$\$16x + \$2,940,000 = \$19.60x + \$1,820,000$$
$$\$3.60x = \$1,120,000$$
$$x = 311,111 \text{ units}$$

Answer C:

1. Operating leverage is the extent to which a firm's operations employ fixed operating expenses. The greater the proportion of fixed expenses used to produce a product, the greater the degree of operating leverage. Thus, Candice's capital-intensive manufacturing method utilizes a greater degree of operating leverage.

   The greater the degree of operating leverage, the greater the change in operating income (loss) relative to a small fluctuation in sales volume. Thus, there is a higher degree of variability in operating income if operating leverage is high. The greater the operating leverage and the resultant variability in operating income, the greater the degree of business risk.

2. Candice should employ the capital-intensive manufacturing method if annual sales are expected to exceed 311,111 units and the labor-intensive manufacturing method if annual sales are not expected to exceed 311,111 units.

Answer D:

Candice must consider these business factors other than operating leverage before selecting a manufacturing method:

- Variability or uncertainty with respect to demand, both quantity and selling price
- The ability to produce and market the new product quickly
- The ability to discontinue the production and marketing of the new product while incurring the least amount of loss

Answer to Question 2C-ES03

Answer A:

The contribution margin is 75%[1] or $3.75 per adult admission, and $1.875 per student admission. The mix is 20% adult (30/150) and 80% student 120/150. The weighted average contribution margin (WACM) is:

$$WACM = .20 \ (\$3.75) + .80 \ (\$1.875) = \$2.25$$

The break-even point is fixed cost / WACM, or

$$\$33,000 \ / \ \$2.25 = 14,667 \text{ per season.}$$

[1]100% − State Fee of 10% − Variable Cost of 15%

Answer B:

The highest number to break even assumes that all admissions are students:

$$\$33,000 \ / \ \$1.875 = 17,600 \text{ per season}$$

Answer C:

The lowest number to break even assumes that all admissions are at the adult rate:

$$\$33,000 \ / \ \$3.75 = 8,800 \text{ per season}$$

Answer to Question 2C-ES04

Answer A:

Target costing is focused on market pricing or the prices of a firm's most direct competitors. The process for determining product pricing involves five steps:

1. Determine the market price.
2. Determine the desired profit.
3. Calculate the target cost at market price less the desired profit.
4. Use value engineering to identify ways to reduce product cost.

5. Use continuous improvement and operational controls to further reduce costs and increase profits.

Answer B:

The main difference between the two methods of pricing is a different starting point for determining product price. Markup pricing is based on existing costs and a desired return. The price is then determined by adding the product cost and the desired markup. This method provides little incentive to reduce costs as long as sales are profitable.

Using target costing, product prices are determined by reviewing competitive pricing and setting prices according to market strategies and positioning. Target costing moves from the existing market prices to the process of managing the product costs in order to earn a desired return. Target costing motivates process improvements. The process is intended to increase or maintain sales while increasing product profitability by reducing product costs through the elimination of non-value-added activities.

Answer C:

Calculate earnings before taxes:

Sales*	$2,528,100	
Less material and labor	1,223,400	(1,348,400 − 125,000)
Less overhead	375,000	(500,000 × .75)
Contribution	929,700	
Selling expense	250,000	
Admin expense	180,000	
Interest expense	30,000	
Earnings before taxes	$ 469,700	
*Vanilla	$53 × 10,200	540,600
Chocolate	$53 × 12,500	662,500
Caramel	$50 × 12,900	645,000
Raspberry	$50 × 13,600	680,000
		$2,528,100

Answer D:

The preferable pricing method for Kolobok is target costing as it is projected to significantly increase the return on sales from 7% to 18.6% ($469,700 / $2,528,100) while maintaining the existing sales level. Target costing also will motivate management to improve internal processes to reduce costs to further improve profitability, particularly for any product where the proposed target price is lower than the previous price. This method also will force Kolobok to be continually aware of the actions of its competitors and trends in the marketplace in order to make adjustments when needed.

Answer to Question 2C-ES05

Answer A:

The strategic advantages that Pearson Foods could realize by expanding internally through the development of new products for the low-fat, high-energy food market include these:

- The new products complement the existing product line, creating operational efficiencies and brand loyalty.
- The company would incur less debt than if it purchases another company.
- The company could capitalize on the low-fat diet trend.
- The company has management know-how in the industry.

The strategic disadvantages that Pearson Foods could realize by expanding internally through the development of new products for the low-fat, high-energy food market include these:

- New product development requires large outlays for research, new facilities, test marketing, and so on.
- New product development decreases cash availability.
- The increased debt ratio could increase the firm's risk, and thus its stock price is at risk.
- The company would incur the risk of product failure.
- It takes a long time to develop a new product and realize profits.

Answer B:

The strategic advantages that Pearson Foods could realize by expanding externally through the acquisition of Safin Bakery include these:

- The acquisition would result in immediate, quantifiable earnings and cash flows.
- The company would acquire a complete company with a proven track record and established markets.
- Managerial and technical expertise would be in place already.
- Safin's established distribution channels could provide new markets for Pearson's other products.
- The addition of Safin would diversify Pearson's product base.
- The acquisition could create synergies for both companies, accomplishing together what they could not do alone.
- Safin could create new growth possibilities for Pearson's employees.

The strategic disadvantages that Pearson Foods could realize by expanding externally through the acquisition of Safin Bakery include these:

- In order to make the acquisition, the company would have to incur a large amount of debt, which could impair its financial flexibility, debt rating, and stock price.
- Pearson lacks knowledge and experience with Safin's products.

- Safin would have to be integrated with Pearson in two years—including the computer system, the accounting system, and the culture.
- An independent operation could lead to suboptimal decisions.

Answer to Question 2C-ES06

Answer A:

Colby Quote Based on Budget Proportions

Revenue	Budget	Colby Quote
	$17,050,000	
Direct Labor		
Hours	300,000	10,000
Rate per Hour	20	20
Total Amount	**6,000,000**	200,000
Employee Benefits	2,400,000	
Percent of Direct Labor	40%	40%
Total Amount		80,000
Tools and Equipment	1,800,000	
Percent of Direct Labor	30%	30%
Total Amount		60,000
Materials	2,000,000	200,000
Procurement and Handling	200,000	
Percent of Material Cost	10%	10%
Total Amount		20,000
Subtotal	12,400,000	560,000
Overhead	3,100,000	
Percent of Above Costs	25%	25%
Total Amount		140,000
Total Cost	$15,500,000	700,000
Pretax Profit		
Percent of Total Cost	10%	10%
Total Amount		70,000
Amount of Colby Quote		$770,000

Answer B:

Madison's performance measurement system can be expected to produce these benefits:

- Aligning the performance measurement system with the budget results in everyone working toward the same goals and targets.
- Focusing on earning a profit on each job provides incentives to managers to constantly be cost conscious.
- If the firm is profitable, employees will be able to share in the rewards. When the firm is not profitable, it does not have the expense of bonuses.

Drawbacks to such a system include these:

- If the budget is revised during the year, the firm faces the dilemma of changing the performance measures, which often upsets employees.
- Although the overall target of 10% may be reasonable, a firm such as Madison cannot expect every project to earn 10%. Focusing on all projects completed during the year may be more realistic.
- Utilizing company average percentages for various cost elements may not be appropriate for all projects. For example, some projects may utilize a significant amount of equipment (as a percentage of labor) compared to other projects. A more appropriate way to charge for major equipment may be to have a rate per day (or per hour, as appropriate) for such equipment and charge the customer based on the number of days (or hours) utilized.

Answer C:

Factors that David Burns should consider include:

- The overall workload for the firm. If there are other more profitable projects that could be undertaken, possibly this project should be turned down. If there are no other alternative projects, this one could be advantageous even though it does not show a 10% profit.
- Burns should identify the primary out-of-pocket (incremental, or marginal) costs for the project and compare them to the contract amount. If the out-of-pocket costs exceed the contract amount, the job should be rejected. If the out-of-pocket costs are less than the contract amount, Madison would receive some contribution toward fixed costs. Direct labor ($200,000), benefits ($80,000), and materials ($200,000) are the primary incremental costs in this case and amount to $480,000. This leaves $215,000 ($695,000 less $480,000) to cover other costs, most of which are primarily fixed.
- Burns should assess the importance of a relationship with Colby. If Colby is a critical customer, that would influence the decision. Also, if Colby has not been a customer before, it may be important to take the job for strategic reasons and establish a relationship, even if this first job does not meet the target profit.
- Of course, Burns will be considering the impact on his performance of accepting a project with a less-than-10% profit. However, he should place the interests of his employer above his own in making a decision on whether to accept the contract.

Answer D:

Reasons that Burns can use to justify his decision include:

- Strategic value of having Colby as a customer.
- Other more profitable opportunities were not available.
- This project involved a significant amount of material costs that are a pass-through to the customer. Therefore, the practice of adding 25% for company overhead is not totally appropriate in this case.

Answer to Question 2C-ES07

Answer 1:

a. Sunk cost is cost already incurred, and thus is irrelevant to the decision at hand.
b. Opportunity cost is the profit foregone (given up) by choosing one course of action over another. Only sunk costs are recorded as incurred, because they result from transactions. There is no accounting recording of events that could have happened (opportunity costs), so they are not recorded in the accounting system.
c. The costs to buy and clear the land ($425,000 and $72,000) would be considered sunk costs, as they have already been incurred. The annual rent that from the construction companies (averaging $5000) would be considered opportunity costs going forward, because PARKCO would have to give them up.

Answer 2:

$$\text{\# of leases} \times (\text{monthly rate} - \text{monthly cost}) = \text{monthly CM}$$

$$420 \times (\$75 - \$12) = \$26,460 \text{ monthly CM}$$

$$\text{\# of days} \times \text{parkers/day} \times (\text{daily rate} - \text{daily cost}) = \text{daily CM}$$

$$20 \times 180 \times (\$8 - \$2) = \$21,600 \text{ daily CM}$$

$$\$26,460 + 21,600 = \$48,060 \text{ total CM}$$

$$(30,000) \text{ fixed cost}$$

$$\$18,060 \text{ pretax operating income}$$

Answer 3:

a. Honesty, Fairness, Objectivity and Responsibility.
b. Under Competence: Prepare complete and clear reports and recommendations after appropriate analysis of relevant and reliable information.

Under Integrity: Communicate favorable as well as unfavorable information and professional judgment or opinions.

Under Credibility: Disclose fully all information that could reasonably be expected to influence an intended user's understanding of the reports, comments, and recommendations presented.

Part 2 Section D Answers

Answer to Question 2D-ES01

Answer A:

Financial risk depends on the way that Upton finances its international expansion. Financing the expansion through debt reduces the firm's solvency. Debt financing is generally riskier than equity financing because the debt must eventually be paid back. In addition, Upton should consider the effect of its financing choice on the firm's liquidity. If the firm chooses debt financing, the interest on the debt must be paid regularly, which will decrease the cash available to pay other obligations in each period. The best way to mitigate financial risk is to make sure that the firm has adequate capital reserves.

Upton's operational risk comes from the relationship between the firm's fixed and variable costs. If Upton has a high ratio of fixed costs to variable costs, the firm would be riskier because it would have to sell more units just to cover its high fixed costs and break even. By contrast, if the ratio of fixed costs to variable costs is low, Upton would face less operational risk since it would have to sell fewer units to cover its relatively low fixed costs.

Compliance risk is the risk that the firm will fail to follow laws or regulations. This risk would be very high for Upton as it expands into different countries because each country has its own set of rules for contracts, taxes, labor conditions, environmental protection, and the like.

Answer B:

The primary goal of an ERM is to align a firm's risk tolerance with its strategy by helping the firm to identify risks and choose the best ways to deal with them so that it has a better chance of achieve its goals. This process is especially important for firms that face multiple risks and cross-enterprise risks. By using an ERM, the firm should experience fewer operational surprises and losses, should make better use of its capital, and should be in a stronger position to take advantage of opportunities that become available. However, the firm should never spend more on its ERM system than the value of the benefits it expects to receive.

Answer C:

Tone at the top: It is not enough to buy a software package. The board of directors and top managers must demonstrate their commitment to integrating their ERM strategy with their decisions across all areas of the business.

Risk management philosophy and tolerance: Risk-averse, risk-neutral, and risk-seeking firms can all implement successful ERM systems. The key is for decision makers to be clear about the amount of risk that they can tolerate so that they can design an appropriate risk management strategy. Obviously, firms with a low tolerance for risk should plan to invest more energy and resources to their ERM.

Integrity and values: Strong corporate ethics can reduce the risk of agency issues between managers and their supervisors and decrease the chance that managers will try to game the system.

Scope and infrastructure: As firms become more complex and diversified, it becomes increasingly important for them to have ERM systems that integrate their departments and divisions across all aspects of the business.

Answer to Question 2D-ES02

Answer A:

Point B (late payments) should have the highest priority because the manager feels that it is likely to occur and would have a high impact on the firm. Point A (bad debt) is also highly likely, but the manager believes that the impact to the firm is fairly low. Point C (computer virus) would have a serious impact on the firm, but the manager thinks that the likelihood is low.

Answer B:

The risks of bad debt and slow payment could be avoided if the firm simply chooses not to offer credit. These risks can be reduced by running a credit check on customers or at least obtaining employment information about each credit customer, and these risks can be transferred if the firm decides to accept credit cards instead.

The risk of a computer virus destroying records could also be avoided if the firm chooses not to offer credit. The firm can reduce this risk by keeping backup records on paper or an electronic storage medium, or the firm can transfer this risk by outsourcing the record-keeping function to another firm.

Answer C:

Inherent risk is the risk that exists before any steps are taken to reduce it, whereas residual risk is the risk that remains after those steps are taken. For example, if EZ-Food extends credit to its regular customers, there is a certain amount of inherent risk that customers may not pay on time. Choosing to do credit checks on these customers will reduce this risk but will not eliminate it entirely. The risk that remains is called the residual risk.

Answer to Question 2D-ES03

Answer A:

Electronic inventory tags function as preventive controls because their high visibility may discourage thieves. These tags also function as detective/corrective controls because they sound an alarm when merchandise is removed from the store.

Surveillance equipment is designed to identify thieves, so it is primarily for detection and correction of theft. However, if the equipment is installed so that it is visible, it may also serve to prevent theft.

Answer B:

Expected Loss = Risk × Exposure = 0.05 × \$1,000,000 = \underline{\$50,000}

Answer C:

Step 1: Expected Loss = Risk × Exposure
Step 2: Loss Reduction = Expected Loss without That Option − Expected Loss with that Option
Step 3: Net Benefit (Cost) = Loss Reduction − Cost of That Option

Option A (electronic inventory tags):
Expected Loss = 0.02 × \$1,000,000 = \$20,000
Loss Reduction = \$50,000 − \$20,000 = \$30,000
Net Benefit = \$30,000 − \$25,000 = \underline{\$5,000 net benefit}

Option B (surveillance equipment):
Expected Loss = 0.01 × \$1,000,000 = \$10,000
Loss Reduction = \$50,000 − \$10,000 = \$40,000
Net Benefit = \$40,000 − \$30,000 = \underline{\$10,000 net benefit}

Option C (both electronic inventory tags and surveillance equipment):
Expected Loss = 0.001 × \$1,000,000 = \$1,000
Loss Reduction = \$50,000 − \$1,000 = \$49,000
Net Cost = \$49,000 − (\$25,000 + \$30,000) = \underline{(\$6,000) net cost}

Answer D:

Based only on estimated benefits and costs, Buy-More should implement Option B because its net benefit is greater than for Option A or Option C.

Answer E:

- How reliable are these estimates?
- What is the firm's tolerance for risk?
- How critical is the \$1,000,000 loss to Buy-More? If Buy-More is a multibillion-dollar firm, it can base its decision strictly on the estimated costs and benefits.

However, if Buy-More is small, then a $1,000,000 loss could threaten the firm's ability to achieve its goals or even its continued existence.

- If Buy-More has a low tolerance for risk and/or if the potential loss of $1,000,000 would be a severe threat, can the firm buy insurance to reduce the risk of loss even further?

Part 2 Section E Answers

Answer to Question 2E-ES01

Answer A:

Accounting rate of return. The merits of the accounting rate of return (ARR) method are that the method is relatively simple to use and easy to understand. It considers the profitability of the projects under consideration. The limitations of the ARR method include ignoring cash flows and the time value of money.

Internal rate of return. The merits of the internal rate of return (IRR) method are that it considers the time value of money and measures the true economic return of the project and productivity of the capital invested in the project. The limitations of the IRR method are that the answer is stated as a percentage rather than a dollar amount, making it more difficult to understand and explain to management. The IRR method also unrealistically assumes that cash flows are reinvested at the IRR of the project.

Net present value method. The merits of the net present value (NPV) method are that it considers the time value of money and size of the investment. The NPV method measures the true economic return of the project, the productivity of the capital investment, and the change in the organization's shareholders' wealth. The limitations of the NPV method include the assumption that all cash flows are reinvested at the discount (hurdle) rate, and it does not calculate a project's rate of return.

Payback method. The merits of the payback method are that it considers cash flows and provides a measure of the liquidity and risk of the investment. The limitations of the payback method are that it neglects the time value of money and the project's profitability.

Answer B:

Miranda Wells and Jake Richter are basing their judgment on the results of the net present value and internal rate of return calculations. These are both considered better measures because they include cash flows, the time value of money, and the project's profitability. Project B is better than Project A for both of these measures.

Answer C:

At least three qualitative considerations that generally should be considered in capital budget evaluations include:

1. Quicker response to market changes and flexibility in production capacity
2. Strategic fit and long-term competitive improvements from the project, or the negative impact to the company's competitiveness or image if it does not make the investment
3. Risks inherent in the project, business, or country for the investment

Answer to Question 2E-ES02

Answer A:

The analysis shown next yields the next after-tax incremental cash flows:

1. Period 0   ($13,200,000)
2. Period 1   4,200,000

$ Millions

		Year			
Cash Flow Element	**0**	**1**	**2**	**3**	**4**
Revenue		$16.0	$20.0	$20.0	$20.0
Equipment	($12.0)				
Equipment Salvage					$0.9
Equipment Removal					($1.4)
Direct Labor and Materials		($8.0)	($10.0)	($10.0)	($10.0)
Indirect Costs		($3.0)	($3.0)	($3.0)	($3.0)
Net Working Capital	($1.2)				$1.2
Total Cash Flow Before Tax	($13.2)	$5.0	$7.0	$7.0	$7.7
Cash Taxes		($0.8)	($1.6)	($1.6)	($1.4)
Net Cash Flow, After Tax	($13.2)	$4.2	$5.4	$5.4	$6.3
Memo: Calculation of Cash Taxes					
Tax Profit Before Tax and Depreciation		$5.0	$7.0	$7.0	$6.5
Tax Depreciation		($3.0)	($3.0)	($3.0)	($3.0)
Tax Profit Before Tax		$2.0	$4.0	$4.0	$3.5

3. The Period 4 operating cash flow is $5,400,000 calculated as shown next.

Revenue	$20,000,000
Direct labor and material	(10,000,000)
Indirect costs	(3,000,000)
Before tax cash flow	7,000,000
Tax effect[1]	(1,600,000)
After tax cash flow	$ 5,400,000

[1]$7,000,000 − $3,000,000 = $4,000,000 x 40% = ($1,600,000)

Answer B:

Cash flow variables with potential risks that could affect the estimates made by CAP include these:

- Volume estimates generally are subject to a high degree of estimation error due to the variety of external factors that impact the volume realized in the future. Competitive forces, consumer acceptance of the new product, and general economic conditions are just a few of the factors that could influence the ultimate demand realized for the new car by KAC, which would impact the demand for ignition system modules from CAP. Since there are a number of fixed costs, including equipment and indirect costs, deviations in volume could have a significant impact on the cash flows and the financial success of the project.
- Exchange rates are another important variable. Since CAP is a U.S. company with a cost structure consisting of U.S. dollar–denominated expenses, there is exchange risk resulting from a revenue stream in the Korean won. The net cash flows from the project in U.S. dollars will be dependent on the exchange rate in effect when each of the KRW denominated payments is received.
- Direct costs are another potential variance, given that the actual productivity of its workforce, the reliability of its manufacturing systems, and unit materials costs could vary substantially from what CAP projects. In a competitive bidding situation, there may be pressure to bid as low as possible to increase the chances for success. If the firm has used best-case assumptions for its cost structure, negative variances in the assumptions for direct costs could decrease the amount of cash flow generated from the project relative to expectations.
- The estimates for the cost of the equipment removal and the salvage value of the equipment could vary significantly as these costs will occur several years in the future and could negatively impact the expected cash flow.

Answer to Question 2E-ES03

Answer A:

The required cost per ton can be calculated as shown:

Required Fund at the End of Year 15

Amount in today's dollars	$14,000,000
Future value factor (15 years, 4%)	1.801
Required fund	$25,214,000
Value of current fund at the end of year 15	
Current fund value	$ 3,000,000
Future value factor (15 years, 7%)	2.759
Value in 15 years	$ 8,277,000
Estimated additional amount needed in year 15	
Required fund	$ 25,214,000
Value of current fund in 15 years	8,277,000
Additional amount needed	$ 16,937,000

Annual funding required	
Additional amount needed	$ 16,937,000
FV of Annuity factor (15 years, 7%)	÷ 25.129
Annual funding required	$ 674,002
Cost per ton	
Annual funding required	$ 674,002
Annual output (tons)	÷ 1,350,000
Cost per ton	$ 0.50

Answer B:

Major uncertainties and their effect on the charge per ton could include these:

- *Estimate of the cost in today's dollars for the reclamation.* Since the reclamation will not be done for 15 years, there is considerable uncertainty. The technology could change, resulting in higher or lower cost. The law or associated regulations could also change.
- *Rate of escalation of the reclamation cost.* Future cost increase levels are difficult to project.
- *Estimated earnings level of the fund.* The 15-year horizon is a long period of time. Investment returns from the equities and fixed income markets can fluctuate significantly from year to year.
- *Tax regulation changes.* Changes in tax regulations would affect the annual amount deposited to the fund because earnings could become taxable.
- *Changes in mine output.* Total output could be different and/or the yearly amounts may not be uniform as projected.

Answer C:

Changes in tax regulations could affect the analysis in these ways:

1. If amounts collected for reclamation and deposited in external funds were taxable,
   - GML would have to charge its customers more each year.
   - The charge per ton would initially be adjusted by dividing the amount by (1–Tax Rate) and offsetting that by an amount equal to the present value of the tax benefit in 15 years when reclamation occurs and a tax benefit is received.

2. If the earnings on the fund were taxable,
   - The charge per ton would have to increase to offset the tax payments.
   - GML may want to communicate to the trustee that it should be more aggressive (i.e., take more risk) so it earns higher pretax returns.
   - GML may want the trustee to invest in tax exempt instruments. This decision should take into account the yields of tax exempt versus taxable instruments.

Answer to Question 2E-ES04

Answer A:

The table shows the net present value of each of the alternatives.

	Time	Amount	14% PV Factor	Present Value
Vendor A				
Initial investment	0	$4,000,000	1.000	$4,000,000
Annual cash outflow	1 – 6	500,000	3.889	1,944,500
NPV				**$5,944,500**
Vendor B				
Initial investment	0	$1,000,000	1.000	$1,000,000
Replacement	3	1,250,000	0.675	843,750
Annual cash outflow	1 – 6	750,000	3.889	2,916.750
NPV				**$4,760,500**
Vendor C				
Annual cash outflow	1 – 6	$1,400,000	3.889	5,444,600
NPV				**$5,444,600**

Answer B:

Ultra Comp should select Vendor B. It is the optimal choice from a financial point of view as it meets the requirements at the lowest cost. Since the decision has already been made to implement a new security system, the issue is to decide on a system that meets the requirements at the lowest cost.

Answer C:

Sensitivity analysis is a tool to test the impact of changing investment assumptions on the resulting net present values. The method helps determine the "sensitivity" of outcomes to changes in the parameters. It shows how the output of the model depends on the input of the model.

Answer D:

Nonfinancial factors that Ultra Comp should consider prior to making a recommendation include these:

- Vendor A technology may be more effective in the long term even though it is the highest-cost solution. However, there is a risk involved in the fact that this is new technology and may not prove effective.

- Vendor B technology is known to be effective and should be satisfactory for the near term. However, there is uncertainty in the long term.
- Since Vendor C is a nationally recognized leader, it may be in a better position to manage the security of Ultra Comp, especially as new developments arise.
- Ultra Comp should review the management capability and the financial stability of each of the vendors.
- Ultra Comp should contact previous clients of each of the vendors to determine their level of satisfaction with the quality and customer service of each vendor.

Answer to Question 2E-ES05

Answer A:

Sales

(a) Units	(b) Probability	(c) Weighted (a) × (b)
20,000	15%	3,000
22,000	20%	4,400
25,000	30%	7,500
26,000	20%	5,200
28,000	15%	4,200
	Expected value	**24,300**

Unit selling Price = $110

Revenue = $110 × 24,300 =	$2,673,000
Total Variable Cost $45 × 24,300 =	(1,093,500)
Fixed Costs	(600,000)
Depreciation on New Equipment	(350,000)
Earnings Before Taxes	629,500
Taxes @ 30%	(188,850)
Net Income	440,650
Add back Depreciation	350,000
Annual Cash Flow, Years 1–9	$790,650
PV Annuity Factor (14%, 9 years)	4.946
PV of Annual Cash Flows	$3,910,555
Add Working Capital Recovery, Year 10	1,290,650
PV Factor, 14%, Year 10	0.270
PV of Year 10 Flows	$348,476
Initial Period Costs: Capital Investment	(3,500,000)
Working Capital	(500,000)
NPV	$259,031

Answer B:

NPV for Each Possibility

Unit Sales	20,000	22,000	25,000	26,000	28,000
Revenue@ $110	$2,200k	$2,420k	$2,750k	$2,860k	$3,080k
Variable Cost@ $45	900	990	1,125	1,170	1,260
Fixed Cost	600	600	600	600	600
Pretax Cash Flow	$700k	$830k	$1,025k	$1,090k	$1,220k
Times (1 − 0.3)	490	581	717.5	763	854
Depreciation Shield	105	105	105	105	105
After-Tax Cash Flow	595	686	822.5	868	959
PV Annuity Factor	4.9464	4.9464	4.9464	4.9464	4.9464
PV, Annual Cash Flow, 1 − 9	$2,943k	$3,393k	$4,068k	$4,293k	$4,744k
Year 10 Flow	1,095	1,186	1,322	1,368	1,459
PV Factor	0.2697	0.2697	0.2697	0.2697	0.2697
PV Year 10	295	320	357	369	393
Initial Costs	4,000	4,000	4,000	4,000	4,000
NPV	($762k)	($287k)	$425k	$662k	$1,137k
Result	Neg.	Neg.	Pos.	Pos.	Pos.
Probability	15%	20%	30%	20%	15%

Shortcut method:

PV of Inflows = $3,500k + 500k − 500k × 0.270 = $3,865 for Break-Even

Annual Break-Even Flow $4,000,000 / 5.216 = $740,989

600,000 × .7 = 420,000; 350,000 × .3 = 105,000

$740,989 + $420,000 − $105,000 = $1,055,989 Total After-Tax Break-Even CM

$65 Pretax CM × .7 = $45.50 After-Tax CM

$1,055,989 / $45.50 Unit CM = 23,209 Units

35% Probability of Selling < 22,000 Units, 65% Probability of Selling > 22,200 Units

Answer C:

Techniques or methods that can be used to factor risk into a capital budget analysis are:

Sensitivity Analysis

Sensitivity analysis is a technique used to test the sensitivity of net present value (NPV) to a change in one or more input variable. A variable is changed by specified amounts or percentages, and the resulting NPV is calculated to get a picture of how sensitive NPV is to that variable. This method gives the analyst a feel for the riskiness of a project and points to the sensitive variables that he or she may want to investigate further to obtain more accurate estimates or to hedge the risk in certain cases.

Risk-Adjusted Discount Rates

This method recognizes the fact that there is a relationship between risk and return. Projects with higher-than-average levels of risk should earn higher-than-average returns in order to compensate for the risk. This results in using the company's cost of capital to evaluate projects of average risk to the firm and requiring projects with significantly higher risk to earn higher returns. Those projects determined to be less risky than average can be evaluated using discount (hurdle) rates less than the average cost of capital. Since risk cannot be measured precisely, the incremental adjustments above or below the average cost of capital are in many cases judgmental, but at least an attempt to balance risk and return is made.

Certainty Equivalent

The certainty equivalent method is one that also attempts to reflect the risk return relationship. Using this method, the expected cash flows are adjusted to reflect their risk. In this manner, those cash flow elements that are perceived to be riskier (e.g., unit sales levels in a very competitive market) are adjusted to reflect that risk while other cash flows that are perceived to have minimal risk (e.g., property taxes on a building) have correspondingly different adjustments. Since risk is accounted for by adjusting the cash flows, the resulting certainty equivalent cash flows are discounted at the risk-free rate. With this method, as with others, the adjustments are generally made utilizing judgment.

Break-Even Analysis

Break-even analysis is a somewhat simplistic way to attempt to get a handle on the risk of a project. Using this method, the analyst determines which cash flow variable (generally revenue) is most uncertain, then models the project's NPV and determines the value of the variable in question (say, revenue) that produces an NPV of zero. The analyst then determines the likelihood that the break-even revenue level will be met or exceeded. Variables other than revenue also can be analyzed in this way.

Simulation

Monte Carlo simulation, which grew out of work on the mathematics of casino gambling, ties together sensitivities and input variable probability distributions. The first step is to specify the probability distribution of each uncertain cash flow variable. This information is input to a computer program, which then chooses at random a value for each uncertain variable, based on its probability distribution. The value selected for each uncertain variable then is used along with the other input assumptions to determine the net cash flows for each year and the resulting project NPV. This process is repeated hundreds of times, and the resulting NPVs are plotted to make up a probability distribution, which may be plotted to visually show the distribution. The primary advantage of this method is that it shows the range of outcomes along with their associated probabilities rather than merely a point estimate of NPV.

Decision Trees

A decision tree is a tool used to help the analyst choose between several courses of action. The method is especially useful in more complex capital budget situations where there are alternative courses of action. For example, if a firm was analyzing a venture involving first performing research and development and then having to decide on the basis of the outcome of the R&D whether to proceed to build a facility to manufacture a product, a decision tree could be helpful. It provides a structure within which the analyst can lay out options and investigate the possible outcomes of choosing those options. This helps to form a picture of the decision points and their potential outcomes. A probability is assigned to each potential outcome. From each decision point, branches of the tree lead to possible outcomes. Each of these possible outcomes produces an expected value for NPV along with a probability. Those values are weighted to see if the project is worth initiating. An advantage of this method is that it forces decision makers to identify the probable outcomes and determine what they would do if the alternative outcomes occurred.

Answer to Question 2E-ES06

Answer A:

$500,000 + $3,500,000 + $100,000 + $100,000 + $50,000 = $4,250,000 million.

Answer B:

The scenario tells us that the after tax operating income is $1,200,000. We find the depreciation expense by dividing the building cost into the depreciation period: $3,500,000/20 = $175,000 annual depreciation expense.

Assuming that interest on the mortgage is not considered when we discount a cash flow, or it is included in (taken out to arrive at) the $1.2 million, and there is no change in working capital, we can calculate the cash flow in three ways:

1. Simply add the $1,200,000 and the $175,000 to get $1,375,000.
2. Find total net income:
   $1,200,000 After-Tax Operating Income / (1 − .35) = $1,846,150 Taxable Income

The tax on this is $646,154, getting us back to $1,200,000 net income. Add back the $175,000 depreciation to get $1,375,000.

3. Use depreciation tax shield: Start with the $1,846,154 taxable income. Adding the $175,000 depreciation, we get before tax cash flow of $2,021,154. The tax on this is $707,404, but the depreciation tax shield is $61,250, resulting in $1,375,000 cash flow.

Answer C:

The factor for a five-year annuity at 12% from our table is 3.605. So the value of five years of cash flow is $4,956,875. But the store will open, and cash flows will start one year after spending the zero period costs, so this value needs to be discounted one more year, to $4,425,781.

The NPV is $4,425,781 − $4,250,000 = $175,000.

Answer D:

Yes, Right-way should build the store. The positive NPV (even ignoring values past five years) will add to the value of the company. The benefit of the future cash flows is greater than the costs to open to the store.

Answer E:

Sensitivity analysis shows how much small changes in the inputs affect the decision. Especially if we had a computer, we could try other assumptions about the store's forecast after tax operating income, the input with the most uncertainty. The costs of construction also may be underestimated, even the tax rate and the hurdle rate may possibly change over the next five years. How much will these have to change to turn a successful, positive NPV store into an unsuccessful, negative NPV store?

Answer to Question 2E-ES07

Answer 1:

1. The net present value is calculated as follows:

New packaging process equipment	$210,000 × 1.00	$(210,000)
Sale of existing packaging equipment	$ 75,000 × 1.00	75,000
Tax benefit from sale	$ 34,000 × .9090	30,906
Depreciation tax shield—new	$ 42,000 × .4 × 3.791	63,689
Loss of annual tax shield—old	$ 40,000 × .4 × 3.170	(50,720)
Annual after-tax savings 10%@ 5 year	$ 36,000 × 3.791	136,476
Net present value		$ 45,351

Annual depreciation on old equipment $200,000/5 = $40,000

Book value at end of first year $200,000 − $40,000 = $160,000

Loss on sale of old equipment:

Sale price	$75,000	
Book value	160,000	($85,000)

Tax benefit = $85,000 × 40% tax rate $34,000

Annual depreciation on new equipment $210,000/5 = $42,000

Answer 2:

The net present value at 10%, the firm's cost of capital, is positive. A positive NPV indicates that the project earns more than the firm's cost of capital, and thus should be accepted.

Answer 3:

Nonfinancial and behavioral factors that could cause the company to change the investment decision made solely on the basis of financial terms include:

- Charleson's bonus may be negatively affected by the decision to replace the packaging equipment with the new technology, since the sale yields a short-term accounting loss of $85,000. Such a loss may cause the Central Division to miss its profit targets, and Charleson to miss his bonus.
- What kind of a warranty will the new equipment have? Since the technology is new, there may be some risk of it not working reliably.
- There will be a learning curve and therefore increased training costs.

Answer 4:

a. A profit-based compensation system such as Bell Company's may not lead to optimal decisions because it is based on accounting profit, which does not necessarily capture the changes in the company's value. Also it is focused only on the short term.

b. A better alternative would be a system that is based on market value. This would align the company's goal of maximizing shareholder value with the manager's goal of maximizing his or her bonus, and focus on long term results.

Answer to Question 2E-ES08

Answer 1:

a.& b. The Capital Asset pricing Model (CAPM) when used in an investment analysis context postulates that the return on an investment should be at least equal to the risk-free rate plus a risk premium. The risk premium is based on the risk (volatility) of the investment relative to the overall market (as measured by beta) times the incremental return on the market above the risk-free rate. The model can be expressed as follows;

$$\text{Required Return} = r_f + (r_m - r_f) \times \beta$$

Where:

r_f = risk-free rate

r_m = return on the market

β = the beta value for the investment, a measure of risk

For the various projects:
Project A: Required return = 4% + (14% – 4%) x 1.4 = 18%

Since the internal rate of return (IRR) of 16% is less than the required 18%, the project should be **REJECTED.**

Project B: Required return = 4% + (14% − 4%) × 1.6 = 20%

Since the IRR of 18% is less than the required 20%, it should be **REJECTED.**

Project C: Required return = 4% + (14% − 4%) × 0.7 = 11%

Since the IRR of 12%, is greater than the required 11%, it should be **ACCEPTED.**

Project D: Required return = 4% + (14% − 4%) × 1.1 = 15%

Since the IRR of 17%, is greater than the required 15%, it should be **ACCEPTED.**

The capital asset pricing model allows firms (users) to assess the size of risk premium necessary to compensate for bearing risk. It is a way to estimate the required rate of return on a security or investment. Once the required return has been determined it lets the user know if the expected return from the investment is sufficient to warrant acceptance of the investment.

Answer 2:

Capital rationing is where funds are limited to a fixed dollar amount and must be allocated among competing projects.

Answer 3:

a. Beta = Measure of a stock's volatility in relation to market.

Market beta = A stock that moves > market, beta > 1; if < market, < 1.

High beta stocks are riskier but potential for higher returns and vice versa.

b. Factors that have an influence on the beta value for a project include:
- The industry that the division undertaking the project is in and its risk characteristics.
- Experience the division has with similar projects, if any.
- Ability of the division to realize estimated returns on projects in the past.
- Strength of the management team of the division.
- Level of competition expected.
- The geographical location of the project. Certain countries are more risky to operate in than others.
- The degree to which the project involves new technology or unproven operating conditions.

Answer to Question 2E-ES09

Answer 1:

The weighted average cost of capital for the firm can be computed as follows.

	Market Value	Proportion	Cost
Bonds	$10,400,000[1]	0.26	5.0[3]
Common Stock	$29,600,000[2]	0.74	14.0[4]
Totals	$40,000,000	1.00	

[1] $10,000 \times 1040.00 = \$10,400,000$.

[2] $2,000,000 \times \$14.80 = 29,600,000$.

[3] $\text{Price} = \$1040.00 = \dfrac{92 + 1000}{(1 + k_d)}$

So, $k_d = \dfrac{1092}{1040} - 1 + 5\%$

[4] $k_e = D_1 + g = 1.48 = 0.04 = 14\% \ P_0 \ 14.80$

$\text{WACC} = 0.26 \times 0.05(1 - 0.3) + 0.74 \times 0.14 = 11.27\%$

Answer 2:

a. The ranking of projects based on the net present value, which is the preferred criterion, is as follows.

Project	Initial Outlay	IRR	NPV
E	$240,000	16.50%	$22,500
A	$450,000	17.00%	$18,800
C	$262,000	16.20%	$9,800
B	$128,000	19.50%	$2,300
F	$160,000	11.10%	–$900
D	$180,000	10.50%	–$7,000

So, the firm should accept projects E, A, C and B. The reason for using the NPV is that this criterion maximizes the value of the firm while using the IRR can give misleading results.

b. Since there is a capital constraint, the projects need to be ranked based on the profitability index, as follows.

Project	Initial Outlay	IRR	NPV	PI[1]
E	$240,000	16.50%	$22,500	0.094
A	$450,000	17.00%	$18,800	0.042
C	$262,000	16.20%	$9,800	0.037
B	$128,000	19.50%	$2,300	0.018
F	$160,000	11.10%	–$900	–0.006
D	$180,000	10.50%	–$7,000	–0.039

[1] Profitability index = NPV / Initial Outlay.

The firm should accept projects E and A which uses $690,000 and provides the highest NPV per dollar invested.

Answer 3:

The weighted average cost of capital cannot be used to evaluate the project because it is not in the same line of business as the firm's current operations. It is likely that the project would alter the firm's business risk in which case using the weighted average cost of capital would be inappropriate. The firm should use a project-specific hurdle rate that reflects the project's systematic risk.

Answer 4:

a. Based on the CAPM, the project's hurdle rate $= 0.05 + 0.10 \times 1.5 = 20\%$. The project's net present value is:

$$NPV = ((\$60,000 \times .833) + (\$80,000 \times .694 + (\$80,000 \times .579) +$$

$$(\$80,000 \times .482)) - \$200,000 = -\$9620.00$$

Since the NPV is negative the project should be rejected.

b. Profitability index $= NPV / \text{Initial Investment} = -9.620/200,000 = -0.0481$

The profitability index scales the net present value by the initial investment on the project and provides an estimate of the project's *NPV* per dollar invested. In this case the project generates a negative *NPV* of 4.81 cents per dollar invested.

Question 5:

a. The project's payback period $= 2 + 60 / 80 = 2.75$ years.
   Based on the threshold payback period that the firm uses it would accept the project because the firm recovers its initial investment in less than 3 years.
b. The project should be rejected because it has a negative *NPV*. The payback period leads to a suboptimal decision because it ignores the time value of money. The payback period also ignores the cash flows in later years but in this case even with year 4's net cash flows the project's *NPV* remains negative.

Part 2 Section F Answers

Answer to Question 2F-ES01

Answer A:

The overarching principles identified in the *IMA Statement of Ethical Professional Practice* that should guide the work of a management accountant are honesty, fairness, objectivity, and responsibility.

Answer B:

If the controller were to manipulate the revenue in accordance with the implied wishes of the chief executive officer, these standards would be violated:

Competence

- Perform professional duties in accordance with relevant laws, regulations, and technical standards.

Integrity

- Mitigate actual conflicts of interest, regularly communicate with business associates to avoid apparent conflicts of interest. Advise all parties of potential conflicts.
- Refrain from engaging in any conduct that would prejudice carrying out duties ethically.
- Abstain from engaging in or supporting any activity that might discredit the profession.

Credibility

- Communicate information fairly and objectively.
- Disclose all relevant information that could reasonably be expected to influence an intended user's understanding of the reports, analyses, or recommendations.
- Disclose delays or deficiencies in information, timeliness, processing, or internal controls in conformance with organization policy and/or applicable law.

Answer C:

To resolve this situation, the controller should follow Sterling's policy for resolving ethical issues. If there is no policy or the policy does not resolve the situation, the controller should consider:

- Discussing the issue with the immediate supervisor unless the supervisor is involved, in which case the issue should be presented to the next higher level. If the CEO is the controller's immediate supervisor, the acceptable reviewing authority may be the audit committee or the board of directors. Communication with those outside the organization is not appropriate unless there is a clear violation of the law.
- Having a confidential discussion of the issues with an IMA ethics counselor or other impartial advisor and may consult an attorney to discuss legal obligations and rights concerning the ethical conflict.

Answer to Question 2F-ES02

Answer A:

The standards from the *IMA Statement of Ethical Professional Practice* that specifically relate to Alex Raminov and the situation at Carroll Mining and Manufacturing are these:

Competence

- Perform professional duties in accordance with relevant laws, regulations, and technical standards. It appears that CMMC is not in compliance with the relevant laws and regulations regarding the dumping of toxic materials; at a minimum, Raminov has an obligation to report this situation to higher authorities in the company.

Confidentially

- Keep information confidential except when disclosure is authorized or legally required. This standard may or may not relate to the CMMC situation, depending on the requirements of the environmental regulations in effect in the jurisdiction where CMMC is operating. Raminov may be required by law to disclose the information.

Integrity

- Refrain from engaging in any conduct that would prejudice carrying out duties ethically.
- Abstain from engaging in or supporting any activity that might discredit the profession.
- If Raminov does not report the apparent illegal dumping to those in authority at CMMC, his behavior would not be considered ethical under these standards, and his lack of action would discredit the profession.

Credibility

- Communicate information fairly and objectively.
- Disclose all relevant information that could reasonably be expected to influence an intended user's understanding of the reports, analyses, or recommendations.
- Disclose delays or deficiencies in information, timeliness, processing, or internal controls in conformance with organization policy and/or applicable law.
- All of these standards make it clear that Raminov has an obligation to act objectively in this matter and report the situation to those in authority at CMMC. The risks and exposures of illegal dumping should be disclosed in the financial reports that Raminov is preparing.

Answer B:

Initially, Raminov should follow CMMC's policy regarding the resolution of an ethical conflict. If there is no policy or the policy does not resolve the issue, he should consider the courses of action recommended in the *IMA Statement of Ethical Professional Practice.*

Since Raminov's immediate supervisor appears to be involved in the dumping situation, he should submit the issue to the next higher level. If the situation is not satisfactorily resolved, Raminov should approach successive levels of authority (e.g., chief financial officer, audit committee, board of directors). He can also contact an IMA ethics counselor or other impartial advisor to discuss possible courses of action.

Raminov should consult an attorney regarding his legal obligations and rights in this ethical conflict.

Answer C:

It is not considered appropriate for Raminov to inform authorities or individuals not employed or engaged by CMMC unless he believes there is a clear violation of the law. In discussions with his attorney, Raminov should clarify his obligations under the law. If CMMC does not take action after Raminov has informed the appropriate in-house authorities, he may be obligated to inform the regulatory agency involved. He should not under any circumstances anonymously release this information to the local newspaper.

Answer to Question 2F-ES03

Answer A:

The standards from the *IMA Statement of Ethical Professional Practice* that specifically relate to Amy Kimbell and the situation at Hi-Quality Productions are these:

Competence

- Provide decision support information and recommendations that are accurate, clear, concise, and timely.
- Recognize and communicate professional limitations or other constraints that would preclude responsible judgment or successful performance of an activity.
- Amy Kimbell has an ethical conflict because she has been told to keep quiet about errors she has discovered in the original budgeting process. The incorrect data used make the decision support data provided suspect and the decisions made based on that data risky.

Integrity

- Refrain from engaging in any conduct that would prejudice carrying out duties ethically.
- Abstain from engaging in or supporting any activity that might discredit the profession.
- Amy Kimball has an ethical conflict as she has an obligation to disclose the errors in the budgets presented but has been told not to. If she does not correct the situation, she will not be carrying out her duties ethically and therefore will discredit her profession.

Credibility

- Communicate information fairly and objectively.
- Disclose all relevant information could reasonably be expected to influence an intended user's understanding of the reports, analyses, or recommendations.
- It is clear that the budget committee has not been objective in its presentation of information and therefore has distorted the decisions based on that information. Kimbell should correct the information so that future expectations are realistic.

Answer B:

Initially, Kimbell should follow Hi-Quality Productions' policy regarding the resolution of an ethical conflict. If there is no policy or the policy does not resolve the issue, she should consider the courses of action recommended in the *IMA Statement of Ethical Professional Practice*.

Kimbell should present her findings to her immediate supervisor. If her immediate supervisor is involved in the incorrect budgeting situation or if the supervisor takes no action, she should submit the issue to the next higher level. If the situation is not satisfactorily resolved, Kimbell should approach successive levels of authority (e.g., chief financial officer, audit committee, board of directors). She can also contact an IMA ethics counselor or other impartial advisor to discuss possible courses of action. Kimbell should consult an attorney regarding her legal obligations and rights in this ethical conflict.

Answer to Question 2F-ES04

Answer A:

The standards from the *IMA Statement of Ethical Professional Practice* that specifically relate to John Morgan and the situation at Pro-Kleen are these:

Competence

- Perform professional duties in accordance with relevant laws, regulations, and technical standards.

Integrity

- Refrain from engaging in any conduct that would prejudice carrying out duties ethically.
- Abstain from engaging in or supporting any activity that might discredit the profession.

Credibility

- Communicate information fairly and objectively.
- Disclose all relevant information that could reasonably be expected to influence an intended user's understanding of the reports, analyses, or recommendations.

Answer B:

Initially, Morgan should follow Pro-Kleen's policy regarding the resolution of an ethical conflict. If there is no policy or the policy does not resolve the issue, he should consider the courses of action recommended in the *IMA Statement of Ethical Professional Practice.*

Since Morgan's immediate supervisor appears to be involved in the situation, he should submit the issue to the next higher level. If the situation is not satisfactorily resolved, Morgan should approach successive levels of authority (e.g., chief financial officer, audit committee, board of directors). He can also contact an IMA ethics counselor or other impartial advisor to discuss possible courses of action. Morgan should consult an attorney regarding his legal obligations and rights in this ethical conflict.

Answer to Question 2F-ES05

Answer A:

Management accountants should not condone the commission of unethical acts by others within their organizations. It is stated that the low-quality, low-size estimates sought by Jefferson were unethical business practices. Therefore, Charlene White should take action to resolve this situation. Specific standards that relate to this situation include these:

Competence

- Perform professional duties in accordance with relevant laws, regulations, and technical standards.

Integrity

- Mitigate actual conflicts of interest, regularly communicate with business associates to avoid apparent conflicts of interest. Advise all parties of any potential conflicts.
- Refrain from engaging in or supporting any activity that might discredit the profession.

Credibility

- Communicate information fairly and objectively.
- Disclose fully all relevant information that could reasonably be expected to influence an intended user's understanding of the reports, analyses, or recommendations.

Answer B:

Initially, White should follow UFP's policy regarding the resolution of an ethical conflict. If there is no policy or the policy does not resolve the issue, she should consider the courses of action recommended in the *IMA Statement of Ethical Professional Practice.*

Since White's immediate supervisor appears to be involved in the situation, she should submit the issue to the next higher level. If the situation is not satisfactorily resolved, White should approach successive levels of authority (e.g., corporate chief financial officer, audit committee, board of directors). She can also contact an IMA ethics counselor or other impartial advisor to discuss possible courses of action. White should consult an attorney regarding her legal obligations and rights in this ethical conflict.

Answer C:

The performance evaluation system directly affected performance at the Allegheny Division. The employees were paid bonuses on the basis of profitability but had no control over revenue because of the transfer pricing that was negotiated elsewhere. The division should be evaluated as a cost center only. The evaluation criteria should include quality standards that must be met in order to preclude the behavior exhibited.

Answer to Question 2F-ES06

Answer A:

Under *competence*, Spencer has a responsibility to "maintain an appropriate level of professional competence." He must perform his duties in accordance with relevant laws, regulations and technical standards (e.g., FASB No. 5, *Accounting for Contingencies*).

Under *confidentiality*, he must keep information confidential except when disclosure is authorized or legally required and inform his subordinates of the same requirement. He must refrain from using or appearing to use confidential information for unethical or illegal advantage personally.

Under *integrity*, Spencer must "avoid actual or apparent conflicts of interest and advise all appropriate parties of any potential conflict." He must also "refrain from engaging in any activity that would prejudice his ability to carry out his duties ethically." He should also "refrain from engaging in any activity that would discredit the profession."

Finally, under *credibility*, Spencer must "communicate information both fairly and objectively." He should "disclose fully all relevant information that could reasonably be expected to influence an intended user's understanding of the reports and recommendations presented."

Answer B:

According to the *IMA Statement of Ethical Professional Practice* Spencer should first follow the established policies of the organization he is employed by in an effort to resolve the ethical dilemma. If such policies do not exist or are not effective, he should follow the steps as outlined in "Resolution of Ethical Conflict."

First, he should discuss the problems with his immediate superior except when it appears the superior is involved. Since his superior is the chief financial officer, who gave him the instructions to ignore the situation and not consider the financial ramifications of nondisclosure, he should proceed to the next higher level, which is the chief executive officer of GRQ Company. If this step is not successful in solving the dilemma, he should proceed up the chain of command, which in this case would appear to be the board of directors of GRQ.

However, he should note that except where legally prescribed, communication of such internal problems should not be discussed with authorities or individuals not employed or engaged by the organization.

Spencer should clarify relevant ethical issues by confidential discussion with an objective advisor (e.g., IMA ethics counselor) to obtain a better understanding of possible courses of action. He should consult his own attorney as to his legal obligations and rights concerning the ethical conflict.

According to the provisions of the Sarbanes-Oxley Act of 2002 (SOX), employees are to be provided with a means to report such matters to top management of the organization. When deemed appropriate, they may report these matters to the appropriate external parties (e.g., the Securities and Exchange Commission, Justice Department, Environmental Protection Agency, etc.) as the matter dictates. Candidates should be given some credit for being aware of this provision made by SOX.

Answer to Question 2F-ES07

Answer A:

According to the *IMA Statement of Ethical Professional Practice*, Wilson in this situation has a responsibility to demonstrate:

- Competence by preparing complete and clear reports and recommendations after appropriate analyses of relevant and reliable information.
- Confidentiality by refraining from disclosing confidential information acquired in the course of their work except when authorized, unless legally obligated to do so.
- Integrity by communicating unfavorable as well as favorable information and professional judgments or opinions as well as refraining from engaging in or supporting any activity that would discredit the profession.
- Objectivity by communicating information fairly and objectively and disclose fully all relevant information that could reasonably be expected to influence an intended user's understanding of the reports, comments, and recommendations presented.

Answer B:

Wilson should first discuss this matter with his superior, the controller, unless his superior is involved; in that case, he should go to the next managerial level. If a satisfactory solution cannot be reached with his superior, Wilson should move up the chain of command. Unless his superior is involved, Wilson should inform his superior when he goes to higher levels of management. If his superior is the chief executive officer, Wilson should go to an acceptable reviewing authority, such as the audit committee, executive committee, board of directors. Wilson can clarify ethical issues by having a confidential discussion with an objective advisor (e.g., an IMA ethics counselor) to determine a possible course of action. He may also consult with his own attorney. If Wilson is unable to resolve the ethical dilemma, there may be no other course than to resign and submit an informative memorandum to an appropriate representative of the organization.

Answer to Question 2F-ES08

Answer 1:

According to the *IMA Statement of Ethical Professional Practice*, Resolution of Ethical Conflict, Mr. Grant should "submit the issue to the next management level," and he should inform his direct supervisor.

Answer 2:

Revenue for a manufacturing company is usually properly recognized when the product is delivered. The product was not delivered during the period, and the revenue cannot be recognized during the period. The reason for the delay in delivery has no bearing on the timing of the revenue recognition.

Answer 3:

a. The entry for Sales will be decreased by the $1,250,000 sale amount. The entry for Cost of Goods Sold will decrease by $715,000, resulting in a net adjustment of −$535,000 to the Income from Operations entry. The Income from Operations will be $1,982,400. The Selling Expenses and Administration Expenses are period expenses and are not affected by the timing of the sale.

b. Accounts Receivable will decrease by the amount of the sale, to $1,028,444. Inventories will rise by only the cost of goods amount of $715,000, not the full sales amount.

c. The income statement change will be accompanied by changes to the Inventory and Accounts Receivable entries on the balance sheet. The Cash Flow statement entries for Changes in Inventory and Changes in Accounts Receivable will be altered (as will the Net Income entry if using the indirect method to construct the statement). Entries to Income Taxes Payable will also be altered.

Answer 4:

According to the *IMA Statement of Ethical Professional Practice*, Mr. Grant has an ethical responsibility to keep the information confidential and refrain from using the information for unethical or illegal advantage. Although he has not divulged any confidential information, he has used that information to provide an unethical and illegal advantage to his colleagues. He has behaved unethically, and perhaps illegally, if he meets the SEC's definition of an "insider."

Answer to Question 2F-ES09

Answer 1:

Yes, under the standards of "competency" and "objectivity," Hammon must "maintain an appropriate level of professional competence" to analyze the nature of the technical problem. She must also prepare "complete and clear reports" to management, and after appropriate analysis, report to them "relevant and reliable information" about what she believes may explain the inventory unusual inventory write-downs.

The standard of professional competence requires Hammond to determine what may explain the write-down based on available information. It also requires members to "perform their professional duties in accordance with relevant laws, regulations and technical standards" and to "prepare complete and clear reports and recommendations after appropriate analysis of relevant and reliable information has been performed."

Under the standard of integrity, she needs to refrain from either actively or passively subverting the attainment of the organization's legitimate and ethical objectives. Under objectivity, she would have a responsibility to communicate the information she found fairly and objectively.

Answer 2:

According to the *IMA Statement of Ethical Professional Practice*, Hammon should follow the guidelines established by the organization to resolve such ethical dilemmas. If such do not exist, or if they fail to resolve the dilemma, she should follow the chain of command by going to her immediate superior, which in this case would appear to be the division controller. If this is not successful, she should proceed up the chain of command until the dilemma is resolved. This would include the CEO of the division as well as the controller of Canadian parent company.

She should not disclose the nature of such problems unless it is legally prescribed to anyone who is not an employee or one who is engaged by the organization. Hammon should clarify the relevant ethical issues by confidential discussion with an objective advisor (e.g., the IMA Ethics Counseling Service) to obtain a better understanding of possible courses of action. She should consult her own attorney as to her legal obligations and rights concerning the ethical conflict. However, in this case, since a distortion of the financial statements or a similar situation does not appear to exist, this step may not be necessary.

Finally, if the ethical conflict exists after exhausting all level of internal review, she may have no other recourse on significant matters than the resign from the organization and submit an informative memorandum to an appropriate representative of the organization. Depending the nature of the overall nature and extent of the ethical conflict, it may also be appropriate to notify other parties. (Doing so seems necessary in this situation, since external fraudulent financial reporting does not appear to exist.)

Answer to Question 2F-ES10

Answer A:

SouthComm may have a corporate policy against these types of payments because such a policy is in alignment with the Foreign Corrupt Practices Act (FCPA). The FCPA forbids any U.S. company doing business overseas to pay bribes to a foreign government for obtaining contracts or business. Firms or any of their representatives who violate the FCPA are subject to both civil and criminal penalties. The "commission" mentioned in this scenario is not a commission but would be classified as a bribe. So, in addition to being unethical, the bribe in this scenario would also be illegal.

Answer B:

Lane is assuming that as long as a practice such as this is done on a regular basis, that would make it acceptable. However, that is not the case. The FCPA forbids U.S.

companies from paying bribes to obtain business—regardless of the local laws or customs.

Answer to Question 2F-ES11

Answer A:

No, Morgan Company is not acting in an ethical manner. Knowingly disposing of hazardous materials without taking necessary precautions is unethical and also may be illegal. If discovered by individuals outside the company, the long-term effect on the company's reputation as well as the environment would significantly outweigh any short-term cost savings that the company may realize.

Answer B:

Morgan Company should consider these changes:

- Set a strong tone from the top regarding ethical behavior. A strong and consistent message from top management often has a noticeable effect on the corporate culture and employee behavior.
- Create an ethics code of conduct and have regular training sessions for all employees to ensure that they are all aware of the company's ethics policies.
- Establish a process for employees to report possible ethics violations, such as a whistleblower framework. This process also could be in place for employees who wish to seek advice on possible questionable issues.
- Reexamine the company's budget to ensure that it is reasonable and that favorable results can be achieved without resorting to unethical behavior.

Creating a more ethical corporate culture could result in many benefits for Morgan Company, some of which include:

- A more positive organizational culture.
- Lower turnover rate among employees.
- Higher employee productivity.
- Improved business reputation in the community.
- Improvements in business and financial performance.

Answers to Section Practice Questions

Section A: Financial Statement Analysis

Question 2A1-AT01
Topic: Basic Financial Statement Analysis

Gordon has had the following financial results for the last four years:

	Year 1	Year 2	Year 3	Year 4
Sales	$1,250,000	$1,300,000	$1,359,000	$1,400,000
Cost of goods sold	750,000	785,000	825,000	850,000
Gross profit	$500,000	$515,000	$534,000	$550,000
Inflation factor	1.00	1.03	1.07	1.10

Gordon has analyzed these results using vertical common-size analysis to determine trends. The performance of Gordon can **best** be characterized by which one of the following statements?

- ☐ **a.** The common-size gross profit percentage has decreased as a result of an increasing common-size trend in cost of goods sold.

- ☐ **b.** The common-size trend in sales is increasing and is resulting in an increasing trend in the common-size gross profit margin.

- ☐ **c.** The common-size trend in cost of goods sold is decreasing, which is resulting in an increasing trend in the common-size gross profit margin.

- ☐ **d.** The increased trend in the common-size gross profit percentage is the result of both the increasing trend in sales and the decreasing trend in cost of goods sold.

Explanation: The correct answer is: **a.** The common-size gross profit percentage has decreased as a result of an increasing common-size trend in cost of goods sold.

Gross profit percentage is calculated as shown:

Gross Profit Percentage = (gross profit) / (sales)

Gross Profit Percentage in Year 1 = $500,000 / $1,250,000 = 40%

Gross Profit Percentage in Year 2 = $515,000 / $1,300,000 = 39.6%

Gross Profit Percentage in Year 3 = $534,000 / $1,359,000 = 39.3%

Gross Profit Percentage in Year 4 = $550,000 / $1,400,000 = 39.3%

The decrease in gross profit percentage is caused by an increasing common-size (percent of sales) trend in cost of goods sold.

Question 2A1-AT02

Topic: Basic Financial Statement Analysis

In assessing the financial prospects for a firm, financial analysts use various techniques. An example of vertical, common-size analysis is

☐ **a.** an assessment of the relative stability of a firm's level of vertical integration.

☐ **b.** a comparison in financial ratio form between two or more firms in the same industry.

☐ **c.** advertising expense is 2% of sales.

☐ **d.** comparison in financial form between two or more firms in different industries.

Explanation: The correct answer is: **c.** advertising expense is 2% of sales.

Vertical analysis looks at all items in the income statement (sales adjustments, expenses, gains, losses, other revenues, and taxes) and includes a column that shows these items as a percentage of sales. This approach allows the analyst to compare the income statements of companies of different sizes, since the comparison will be done on a percentage basis rather than on an absolute dollar basis.

Question 2A1-AT03

Topic: Basic Financial Statement Analysis

When preparing common-size statements, items on the balance sheet are generally stated as a percentage of _____ and items on the income statement are generally stated as a percentage of _____.

☐ **a.** total assets; net sales

☐ **b.** total shareholders' equity; net income

☐ **c.** total assets; net income

☐ **d.** total shareholders' equity; net sales

Explanation: The correct answer is: **a.** total assets; net sales.

Common-size balance sheets express all assets, liabilities, and equities as a percentage of the balance sheet footing (total assets). Common-size income statements express all sales adjustments, expenses, gains, losses, other revenues, and taxes as a percentage of sales.

Question 2A1-LS01

Topic: Basic Financial Statement Analysis

Which of the following statements is **true** regarding common-size statements?

☐ **a.** Common-size statements can be used to compare companies of different sizes.

☐ **b.** Common-size statements indexed over two years for two companies, with both showing a 10% increase in profits, show that both companies would make equally attractive investments.

☐ **c.** Horizontal common-size statements can be made only for companies with at least ten years of operational data.

☐ **d.** All of the above.

Explanation: The correct answer is: **a.** Common-size statements can be used to compare companies of different sizes.

Common-size statements alone showing a 10% increase in profits for two companies do not indicate that both are equally attractive investments. One of the companies may have shown an increase in profits from $10 to $11, while the other may have shown an increase in profits from $1,000,000 to $1,100,000. Horizontal common-size statements do not require ten years of data.

Question 2A1-LS02

Topic: Basic Financial Statement Analysis

A common-size statement is helpful

☐ **a.** for figuring out how assets are allocated.

☐ **b.** for determining the next investment the company should make.

☐ **c.** for considering whether to buy or sell assets.

☐ **d.** in comparing companies of different sizes.

Explanation: The correct answer is: **d.** in comparing companies of different sizes.

A common-size statement shows each major section of the financial statement valued at 100%, with its elements as percentages of the total, and is helpful when comparing companies of different sizes and when making comparisons from one year to another within the same company.

Question 2A2-CQ01

Topic: Financial Ratios

Broomall Corporation has decided to include certain financial ratios in its year-end annual report to shareholders. Selected information relating to its most recent fiscal year is provided next.

Cash	$10,000
Accounts receivable	20,000
Prepaid expenses	8,000
Inventory	30,000
Available-for-sale securities	
At cost	9,000
Fair value at year-end	12,000
Accounts payable	15,000
Notes payable (due in 90 days)	25,000
Bonds payable (due in 10 years)	35,000
Net credit sales for year	220,000
Cost of goods sold	140,000

Broomall's working capital at year-end is

- ☐ **a.** $40,000.
- ☐ **b.** $37,000.
- ☐ **c.** $28,000.
- ☐ **d.** $10,000.

Explanation: The correct answer is: **a.** $40,000.

The term *working capital* as used by accountants is calculated by subtracting current liabilities from current assets.

Working Capital = Current Assets − Current Liabilities

Current assets include cash, accounts receivable, prepaid expenses, inventories, and available-for-sale securities. (Available-for-sale securities are carried at fair value, not cost.)

Current Assets = $10,000 + $20,000 + $8,000 + $30,000 + $12,000 = $80,000

Current liabilities include accounts payable and notes payable due in 90 days.

Current Liabilities = $15,000 + $25,000 = $40,000

Working Capital = $80,000 − $40,000 = $40,000

Question 2A2-CQ02

Topic: Financial Ratios

Birch Products Inc. has the following current assets:

Cash	$250,000
Marketable securities	100,000
Accounts receivable	800,000
Inventories	1,450,000
Total current assets	$2,600,000

If Birch's current liabilities are $1,300,000, the firm's

- ☐ **a.** current ratio will decrease if a payment of $100,000 cash is used to pay $100,000 of accounts payable.

- ☐ **b.** current ratio will not change if a payment of $100,000 cash is used to pay $100,000 of accounts payable.

- ☐ **c.** quick ratio will decrease if a payment of $100,000 cash is used to purchase inventory.

- ☐ **d.** quick ratio will not change if a payment of $100,000 cash is used to purchase inventory.

Explanation: The correct answer is: **c.** quick ratio will decrease if a payment of $100,000 cash is used to purchase inventory.

The quick ratio is calculated as follows:

Quick Ratio = (Cash + Marketable Securities + Account Receivables) / (Current Liabilities)

Current Assets = (Cash + Marketable Securities + Receivables)

The quick ratio could be expanded as shown:

Quick Ratio = [(Cash + Marketable Securities + Receivables) − Inventories − Prepayments] / (Current Liabilities)

The purchase of inventory for cash will decrease the numerator of the quick ratio formula without affecting the current liabilities in the denominator. This will result in a decrease in the quick ratio.

Question 2A2-CQ08

Topic: Financial Ratios

Lowell Corporation has decided to include certain financial ratios in its year-end annual report to shareholders. Selected information relating to its most recent fiscal year is provided next.

Cash	$10,000
Accounts receivable (end of year)	20,000
Accounts receivable (beginning of year)	24,000
Inventory (end of year)	30,000
Inventory (beginning of year)	26,000
Notes payable (due in 90 days)	25,000
Bonds payable (due in 10 years)	35,000
Net credit sales for year	220,000
Cost of goods sold	140,000

Using a 365-day year, compute Lowell's accounts receivable turnover in days.

☐ **a.** 26.1 days

☐ **b.** 33.2 days

☐ **c.** 36.5 days

☐ **d.** 39.8 days

Explanation: The correct answer is: **c.** 36.5 days.

The accounts receivable turnover in days is calculated as shown:

Accounts Receivable Turnover in Days = (365 days)
/ (Accounts Receivable Turnover per Year)

Accounts Receivable Turnover per Year = (Net Credit Sales for Year)
/ (Average Accounts Receivable
Balance for Year)

Average Accounts Receivable Balance for Year = (Beginning Balance
+ Ending Balance) / 2

Average Accounts Receivable Balance for Year = ($20,000 + $24,000) / 2

Average Accounts Receivable Balance for Year = $44,000 / 2 = $22,000

Turnover per Year = $220,000 / $22,000 = 10 Times

Turnover in Days = 365 Days / 10 Times per Year = 36.5 days

Question 2A2-CQ14

Topic: Financial Ratios

Cornwall Corporation's net accounts receivable were $68,000 and $47,000 at the beginning and end of the year, respectively. Cornwall's condensed income statement is shown next.

Sales	$900,000
Cost of goods sold	527,000
Operating expenses	175,000
Operating income	198,000
Income tax	79,000
Net income	$119,000

Cornwall's average number of days' sales in accounts receivable (using a 365-day year) is

☐ **a.** 8 days.

☐ **b.** 13 days.

☐ **c.** 19 days.

☐ **d.** 23 days.

Explanation: The correct answer is: **d.** 23 days.

The average number of days in accounts receivable is calculated as shown:

Average Number of Days in Accounts Receivable
= (# Days in Year) / (Accounts Receivable Turnover per Year)

Accounts Receivable Turnover per Year
= (Net Credit Sales for Year) / (Average Accounts Receivable Balance for Year)

Average Accounts Receivable Balance for Year = (Beginning Balance
+ Ending Balance) / 2

Average Accounts Receivable Balance for Year = ($68,000 + $47,000) / 2

Average Accounts Receivable Balance for Year = $115,000 / 2 = $57,500

Accounts Receivable Turnover per Year = $900,000 / $57,500
= 15.65 Times per Year

Average Number of Days in Accounts Receivable = 365 days / 15.65 Times
= 23 Days

Question 2A2-CQ21

Topic: Financial Ratios

Marble Savings Bank has received loan applications from three companies in the auto parts manufacturing business and currently has the funds to grant only one of these requests. Specific data, shown next, have been selected from these applications for review and comparison with industry averages.

	Bailey	Nutron	Sonex	Industry
Total sales (millions)	$4.27	$3.91	$4.86	$4.30
Net profit margin	9.55%	9.85%	10.05%	9.65%
Current ratio	1.82	2.02	1.96	1.95
Return on assets	12.0%	12.6%	11.4%	12.4%
Debt/equity ratio	52.5%	44.6%	49.6%	48.3%
Financial leverage	1.30	1.02	1.56	1.33

Based on this information, select the strategy that should be the **most** beneficial to Marble Savings.

☐ **a.** Marble Savings Bank should not grant any loans as none of these companies represents a good credit risk.

☐ **b.** Grant the loan to Bailey as all the company's data approximate the industry average.

☐ **c.** Grant the loan to Nutron as both the debt to equity ratio and degree of financial leverage are below the industry average.

☐ **d.** Grant the loan to Sonex as the company has the highest net profit margin and degree of financial leverage.

Explanation: The correct answer is: **c.** Grant the loan to Nutron as both the debt to equity ratio and degree of financial leverage are below the industry average.

The debt to equity ratio and the degree of financial leverage both measure an organization's risk. The lower the debt to equity ratio, the lower the risk. Similarly, the lower the degree of financial leverage, the lower the risk. In the case of Nutron, both the debt to equity ratio and the degree of financial leverage measures are below industry averages. Therefore, it is the least risky of the three choices.

Question 2A2-CQ29

Topic: Financial Ratios

The following information concerning Arnold Company's common stock was included in the company's financial reports for the last two years.

	Year 2	Year 1
Market price per share on December 31	$60	$50
Par value per share	10	10
Earnings per share	3	3
Dividends per share	1	1
Book value per share on December 31	36	34

Based on the price/earnings information, investors would **most likely** consider Arnold's common stock to

☐ **a.** be overvalued at the end of year 2.

☐ **b.** indicate inferior investment decisions by management in year 2.

☐ **c.** show a positive trend in growth opportunities in year 2 compared to year 1.

☐ **d.** show a decline in growth opportunities in year 2 compared to year 1.

Explanation: The correct answer is: **c.** show a positive trend in growth opportunities in year 2 compared to year 1.

The company's P/E (price/earnings) ratio increased from year 1 to year 2. The P/E ratio is calculated by taking the market price per share and dividing it by the earnings per share.

P/E Ratio = (Market Price per Share) / (Earnings per Share)

P/E Ratio, Year 1 = $50 / $3 = $16.67

P/E Ratio, Year 2 = $60 / $3 = $20

Since the P/E ratio is increasing from year 1 to year 2, it is showing a positive trend in growth opportunities in year 2 compared to year 1.

Question 2A2-CQ30

Topic: Financial Ratios

Devlin Inc. has 250,000 shares of $10 par value common stock outstanding. For the current year, Devlin paid a cash dividend of $3.50 per share and had earnings per share of $4.80. The market price of Devlin's stock is $34 per share. Devlin's price/earnings ratio is

- ☐ **a.** 2.08.
- ☐ **b.** 2.85.
- ☐ **c.** 7.08.
- ☐ **d.** 9.71.

Explanation: The correct answer is: **c.** 7.08.

The P/E ratio is calculated by taking the market price per share and dividing it by the earnings per share.

P/E Ratio = (Market Price per Share) / (Earnings per Share)

P/E Ratio = $34 / $4.80 = 7.08

Question 2A3-CQ01

Topic: Profitability Analysis

For the year just ended, Beechwood Corporation had income from operations of $198,000 and net income of $96,000. Additional financial information is given next.

	January 1	December 31
7% bonds payable	$95,000	$77,000
Common stock ($10 par value)	300,000	300,000
Reserve for bond retirement	12,000	28,000
Retained earnings	155,000	206,000

Beechwood has no other equity issues outstanding. Beechwood's return on shareholders' equity for the year just ended is

- ☐ **a.** 19.2%.
- ☐ **b.** 19.9%.
- ☐ **c.** 32.0%.
- ☐ **d.** 39.5%.

Explanation: The correct answer is: **a.** 19.2%.

Return on shareholders' equity is calculated as shown:

Return on Shareholders' Equity = (Net Income − Preferred Stock Dividends) / (Average Shareholders' Equity)

Shareholders' Equity = Common Stock + Reserve for Bond Retirement + Retained Earnings

Average Shareholders' Equity = (Beginning Balance + Ending Balance) / 2

Average Shareholders' Equity = ($300,000 + $12,000 + $155,000
+ $300,000 + $28,000 + $206,000) / 2

Average Shareholders' Equity = ($1,001,000) / 2 = $500,500

Since there are no preferred stock dividends, return on shareholders' equity = $96,000 / $500,500 = 0.192, or 19.2%.

Question 2A3-AT01

Topic: Profitability Analysis

For a given level of sales and holding all other financial statement items constant, a company's return on equity (ROE) will

- ☐ **a.** decrease as its total assets increase.
- ☐ **b.** increase as its debt ratio decreases.
- ☐ **c.** decrease as its cost of goods sold as a percentage of sales decrease.
- ☐ **d.** increase as its equity increases.

Explanation: The correct answer is: **a.** decrease as its total assets increase.

To analyze ROE, use the DuPont model for return on investment (ROI) and multiply it by the leverage factor. This would appear as:

DuPont Model ROI = Net Income / Sales × Sales / Average Assets

Leverage Factor = Assets / Equity

ROE = DuPont Model ROI × Leverage Factor

ROE = Net Income / Sales × Sales / Average Assets × Assets / Equity

All other things being equal, the return on equity will decrease as total assets increase.

ROE will decrease as the debt ratio decreases.

As cost of goods sold as a percentage of sales decreases, profit will increase along with ROE.

As the level of equity increases, ROE will decrease.

Question 2A3-LS01

Topic: Profitability Analysis

BDU Company has net income of $500,000 and average assets of $2,000,000 for the current year. If its asset turnover is 1.25 times, what is its profit margin?

- ☐ **a.** 0.25
- ☐ **b.** 0.31
- ☐ **c.** 0.36
- ☐ **d.** 0.2

Explanation: The correct answer is: **d.** 0.2

Profit Margin = Net Income / Sales

Calculate sales by rearranging the next formula:

Asset Turnover = Sales / Assets

Sales = (Asset Turnover) (Assets)

Sales = (1.25) ($2,000,000) = $2,500,000

Profit Margin = $500,000 / $2,500,000 = 0.2

Question 2A3-LS05

Topic: Profitability Analysis

Which of the following must be considered in measuring income?

I. Estimates regarding future events.

II. Accounting methods used by the company.

III. The degree of informative disclosure about results of operations.

IV. Different needs of users.

- ☐ **a.** I and II only
- ☐ **b.** II and III only
- ☐ **c.** I, II, III, and IV
- ☐ **d.** I, II, and IV only

Explanation: The correct answer is: **c.** I, II, III, and IV.

All of the listed items must be considered in measuring income.

Question 2A3-LS09

Topic: Profitability Analysis

In the last fiscal year, LMO Company had net sales of $7,000,000, a gross profit margin of 40%, and a net profit margin of 10%. What is its cost of goods sold?

- ☐ **a.** $4,200,000
- ☐ **b.** $6,300,000
- ☐ **c.** $2,800,000
- ☐ **d.** $700,000

Explanation: The correct answer is: **a.** $4,200,000.

Calculate gross profit by rearranging the next formula:

Gross Profit Margin = Gross Profit / Net Sales

Gross Profit = (Gross Profit Margin) (Net Sales)

Gross Profit = (40%) ($7,000,000) = $2,800,000

Calculate cost of goods sold by rearranging the next formula:

Gross Profit = Sales − Cost of Goods Sold

Cost of Goods Sold = Sales − Gross Profit

Cost of Goods Sold = $7,000,000 − $2,800,000 = $4,200,000

Question 2A3-LS10

Topic: Profitability Analysis

An increase in the gross profit margin for a merchandising firm indicates that the firm

- ☐ **a.** is increasing its revenues.
- ☐ **b.** is decreasing its fixed costs.
- ☐ **c.** is doing a better job of managing cost of sales.
- ☐ **d.** has been managing its quality control better, which results in fewer returns.

Explanation: The correct answer is: **c.** is doing a better job of managing cost of sales.

An increase in the gross profit margin indicates that the firm is doing a better job of managing cost of sales.

Question 2A3-LS11

Topic: Profitability Analysis

Earnings power is

- ☐ **a.** the company's ability to turn liabilities into income-generating activities.
- ☐ **b.** a forecasting tool that anticipates probable future conditions instead of making the assumption of a continued trend.
- ☐ **c.** a mathematical calculation based on past earnings that can absolutely predict future earnings.
- ☐ **d.** the best possible estimate of the average business earnings of a number of years.

Explanation: The correct answer is: **d.** the best possible estimate of the average business earnings of a number of years.

Earnings power is defined as the best possible estimate of the average business earnings that can be expected to be sustained in the future for a number of years, preferably over an entire business cycle. Earnings power is used as a forecasting tool but does not try to anticipate probable future conditions other than a continued trend.

Question 2A4-LS01

Topic: Special Issues

Which of the following are elements of earnings quality?

I. Management's discretion in choosing from among accepted accounting principles

II. Management compensation in relation to net earnings

III. The degree to which assets are maintained

IV. The effect of cyclical and other economic forces on the stability of earnings

☐ **a.** I, III, and IV only

☐ **b.** I and III only

☐ **c.** II and IV only

☐ **d.** I, II, III, and IV

Explanation: The correct answer is: **a.** I, III, and IV only.

The basic factors of earnings quality are management and accountants' discretion in choosing accounting principles, the degree to which maintenance of assets has been provided for, and the effect of cyclical and other economic forces on the stability of earnings.

Question 2A4-LS02

Topic: Special Issues

Which of the following statements is true?

☐ **a.** Economic profits are accounting profits minus explicit costs.

☐ **b.** Economic profits are accounting profits minus implicit costs.

☐ **c.** Accounting profits are economic profits minus implicit costs.

☐ **d.** Accounting profits are economic profits minus explicit costs.

Explanation: The correct answer is: **b.** Economic profits are accounting profits minus implicit costs.

Economic profits are the ability to make more than normal profits. Economic profits are calculated by subtracting implicit costs, such as opportunity costs, from accounting profits.

Question 2A4-LS03

Topic: Special Issues

Which of the following statements is true?

☐ **a.** Financial statements need not make adjustments for inflation, as earnings automatically reflect the higher prices.

☐ **b.** Financial statements generally make adjustments for inflation, so earnings may be clearly represented over time.

☐ **c.** Financial statements make adjustments for inflation every year and state the inflation rate for the year in the footnotes of the annual report.

☐ **d.** Financial statements generally do not make adjustments for inflation, so earnings may be significantly compounded over time.

Explanation: The correct answer is: **d.** Financial statements generally do not make adjustments for inflation, so earnings may be significantly compounded over time.

Question 2A4-LS04

Topic: Special Issues

A European company provides annual reports for U.S. investors purchasing ADRs of the company's stock in the United States. The company reports €1,500,000 net income. The exchange rate between the euro and the U.S. dollar is €1.19/$1. Which of the following statements is true?

- ☐ **a.** Annual statements sent to U.S. investors will show net income as €1,500,000.

- ☐ **b.** Annual statements sent to U.S. investors will show net income as $1,260,504.

- ☐ **c.** Annual statements sent to U.S. investors will show net income as $1,785,000.

- ☐ **d.** Annual statements sent to U.S. investors will show net income as $1,500,000.

Explanation: The correct answer is: **a.** Annual statements sent to U.S. investors will show net income as €1,500,000.

Financial statements generally do not make adjustments for foreign currency exchange rates, as this would show wild fluctuations due to the exchange rate rather than company performance.

Section B: Corporate Finance

Question 2B1-AT05

Topic: Risk and Return

Using the capital asset pricing model (CAPM), the required rate of return for a firm with a beta of 1.25 when the market return is 14% and the risk-free rate is 6% is

- ☐ **a.** 7.5%.
- ☐ **b.** 14.0%.
- ☐ **c.** 16.0%.
- ☐ **d.** 17.5%.

Explanation: The correct answer is: **c.** 16.0%.

The formula for the CAPM is:

$$K_e = R_f + \beta (K_m - R_f)$$

where:

K_e = required rate of return
R_f = risk-free rate (such as the return on U.S. Treasury bills or Treasury bonds)
β = beta coefficient for the company

K_m =   return on a market portfolio

K_e = $0.06 + (1.25)(0.14 - 0.06) = 0.06 + (1.25)(0.08)$
K_e = $0.06 + 0.10 = 0.16$, or 16%

Question 2B1-AT06

Topic: Risk and Return

The expected rate of return for the stock of Cornhusker Enterprises is 20%, with a standard deviation of 15%. The expected rate of return for the stock of Mustang Associates is 10%, with a standard deviation of 9%. The stock that would be considered riskier is

- ☐ **a.** Mustang, because the coefficient of variation is higher.
- ☐ **b.** Cornhusker, because the standard deviation is higher.
- ☐ **c.** Cornhusker, because the coefficient of variation is lower.
- ☐ **d.** Mustang, because the return is lower.

Explanation: The correct answer is: **a.** Mustang, because the coefficient of variation is higher.

The coefficient of variation can be used to measure relative risk. It is calculated by dividing the standard deviation by the expected return.

Coefficient of variation $= \sigma / \bar{R}$

where:

σ =   standard deviation
$\bar{R}$ =   expected return

Coefficient of variation for Mustang $= 0.09 / 0.1 = 0.9$
Coefficient of variation for Cornhusker $= 0.15 / 0.2 = 0.75$

Therefore, the stock of Mustang is riskier than the stock of Cornhusker, because its coefficient of variation is higher.

Question 2B2-LS04

Topic: Long-Term Financial Management

Which of the following statements about correlation and return variability **best** describes a portfolio with a limited number of stocks representing different industries?

- ☐ **a.** Low correlation and low portfolio return variability
- ☐ **b.** Low correlation and high portfolio return variability
- ☐ **c.** High correlation and high portfolio return variability
- ☐ **d.** High correlation and low portfolio return variability

Explanation: The correct answer is: **a.** Low correlation and low portfolio return variability.

Having fewer stocks in a portfolio representing different industries is more likely to show low correlation and low portfolio return variability. The probability that individual stocks in different industries move up and down in value at the same time or at the same rate is low.

Question 2B2-LS05

Topic: Long-Term Financial Management

If a firm's goal is to minimize portfolio risk, the **best** strategy would be to include

- ☐ **a.** investments with low betas and highly correlated returns.
- ☐ **b.** investments with high betas and low correlated returns.
- ☐ **c.** diversified investments with high betas.
- ☐ **d.** diversified investments with low betas.

Explanation: The correct answer is: **d.** diversified investments with low betas.

If the aim is to keep portfolio risk low, diversified investments having low betas should be included. Diversification reduces portfolio risk as long as the different investments are unlikely to all move in the same direction (i.e., they are not perfectly, positively correlated). Relative to beta measures, the higher the beta above 1.0, the greater the volatility in relation to market activity.

Question 2B2-CQ06

Topic: Long-Term Financial Management

Cox Company has sold 1,000 shares of $100 par, 8% preferred stock at an issue price of $92 per share. Stock issue costs were $5 per share. Cox pays taxes at the rate of 40%. What is Cox's cost of preferred stock capital?

- ☐ **a.** 8.00%
- ☐ **b.** 8.25%
- ☐ **c.** 8.70%
- ☐ **d.** 9.20%

Explanation: The correct answer is: **d.** 9.20%.

The cost of preferred stock capital is calculated as:

Cost of Preferred Stock Capital = (Preferred Stock Dividend per Share) / (Net Price of the Preferred Stock)

The dividend per share is calculated as:

Dividend per Share = (Dividend Rate) (Par Value of Stock)

Dividend per Share = (0.08) ($100) = $8 per Share

Cost of Preferred Stock Capital = $8 / ($92 − $5) = 9.20%

Question 2B2-CQ07

Topic: Long-Term Financial Management

Bull & Bear Investment Banking is working with the management of Clark Inc. in order to take the company public in an initial public offering. Selected financial information for Clark is as shown next.

Long-term debt (8% interest rate)	$10,000,000
Common equity:	
Par value ($1 per share)	3,000,000
Additional paid-in capital	24,000,000
Retained earnings	6,000,000
Total assets	55,000,000
Net income	3,750,000
Dividend (annual)	1,500,000

If public companies in Clark's industry are trading at 12 times earnings, what is the estimated value per share of Clark?

☐ **a.** $9.00

☐ **b.** $12.00

☐ **c.** $15.00

☐ **d.** $24.00

Explanation: The correct answer is: **c.** $15.00.

The earnings per share (EPS) for Clark is calculated as:

EPS = (Net Income − Preferred Stock Dividends) / (Weighted Average Number of Common Stock Shares Outstanding)

The number of shares outstanding is 3,000,000, which is derived by taking the $3,000,000 in par value common equity and dividing it by the $1 par value per share.

EPS = ($3,750,000 − $0) / (3,000,000 Shares) = $1.25 per Share

The estimated value per share of Clark stock can then be calculated as:

Estimated Value per Share = 12 ($1.25) = $15.00 per Share

Question 2B2-LS13

Topic: Long-Term Financial Management

A long-term call option to buy common stock directly from a corporation is a

☐ **a.** forward contract.

☐ **b.** warrant.

☐ **c.** convertible security.

☐ **d.** futures contract.

Explanation: The correct answer is: **b.** warrant.

By definition, a warrant is a long-term call option to buy common stock directly from a corporation. It gives bond or preferred stockholders the right to purchase shares of common stock at a given price.

Question 2B2-LS15

Topic: Long-Term Financial Management

An analyst observes a 15-year, 7% option-free bond with semiannual coupons. The required yield on this bond was 7%, but suddenly it drops to 6.5%. The price of this bond

- ☐ **a.** will increase.
- ☐ **b.** will decrease.
- ☐ **c.** will stay the same.
- ☐ **d.** cannot be determined without additional information.

Explanation: The correct answer is: **a.** will increase.

There is an inverse relationship between price and yield. If the required yield falls, the bond's price will rise, and vice versa.

Question 2B2-LS23

Topic: Long-Term Financial Management

What is the after-tax cost of debt for a 6% interest-bearing bond at an anticipated tax rate of 38%?

- ☐ **a.** 3.80%
- ☐ **b.** 3.72%
- ☐ **c.** 4.40%
- ☐ **d.** 6.00%

Explanation: The correct answer is: **b.** 3.72%.

The formula for determining the after-tax cost of debt is:

$$\text{After-Tax Cost of Debt} = k_d (1 - t)$$

$$\text{After-Tax Cost of Debt} = (0.06)(1 - 0.38) = .0372 = 3.72\%$$

Question 2B2-CQ09

Topic: Long-Term Financial Management

The Hatch Sausage Company is projecting an annual growth rate for the foreseeable future of 9%. The most recent dividend paid was $3.00 per share. New common stock can be issued at $36 per share. Using the constant growth model, what is the approximate cost of capital for retained earnings?

    ☐ **a.** 9.08%

    ☐ **b.** 17.33%

    ☐ **c.** 18.08%

    ☐ **d.** 19.88%

Explanation: The correct answer is: **c.** 18.08%.

The cost of capital for retained earnings, using the constant dividend growth model (Gordon's model), is calculated as:

Cost of Capital, Retained Earnings = (Next Dividend) / (Market Price) +
(Expected Dividend Growth Rate)

In this case, the next dividend is calculated by taking the current dividend of $3.00 per share and multiplying it by 1 plus the constant growth rate, as shown:

Value of Next Dividend = $3 (1 + 0.09) = $3.27

Therefore, the cost of capital for retained earnings can be calculated as:

Cost of Capital, Retained Earnings = ($3.27 / $36) + (0.09) = 0.0908
+ 0.09 = 0.1808, or 18.08%

Question 2B2-CQ10

Topic: Long-Term Financial Management

Angela Company's capital structure consists entirely of long-term debt and common equity. The cost of capital for each component is shown next.

Long-term debt	8%
Common equity	15%

Angela pays taxes at a rate of 40%. If Angela's weighted average cost of capital is 10.41%, what proportion of the company's capital structure is in the form of long-term debt?

    ☐ **a.** 34%

    ☐ **b.** 45%

    ☐ **c.** 55%

    ☐ **d.** 66%

Explanation: The correct answer is: **b.** 45%.

Angela's weighted average cost of capital (WACC) is given at 10.41%. The formula to calculate the WACC is:

WACC = (Weighted Cost of Debt, or w_i) (After-Tax Cost of Debt)
            + $(1 - w_i)$ (Cost of Common Equity)

where:

w_i = company's weighted cost (or portion) of debt

The after-tax cost of debt is calculated as:

After-Tax Cost of Debt = (1 − Tax Rate) (% Cost of Debt)
After-Tax Cost of Debt = (1 − 0.4) (0.08) = 0.6 (0.08) = 0.048, or 4.8%

This amount can then be substituted into the WACC formula and rearranged to solve for w_i as shown:

10.41% = 4.8 % (w_i) + $(1 - w_i)$ (15%)
10.41% = 4.8 % (w_i) + 15% − 15% (w_i)
            − 4.59% = −10.2% (w_i)
    w_i = − 4.59% / −10.2% = 45%

Question 2B2-CQ15

Topic: Long-Term Financial Management

Thomas Company's capital structure consists of 30% long-term debt, 25% preferred stock, and 45% common equity. The cost of capital for each component is shown next.

Long-term debt	8% before tax
Preferred stock	11%
Common equity	15%

If Thomas pays taxes at the rate of 40%, what is the company's after-tax weighted average cost of capital?

☐ **a.**   7.14%

☐ **b.**   9.84%

☐ **c.**   10.94%

☐ **d.**   11.90%

Explanation: The correct answer is: **c.** 10.94%.

The weighted average cost capital (WACC) is calculated as:

WACC = (Weight of Long-Term Debt) (After-Tax Cost of Long-Term Debt)
            + (Weight of Preferred Stock) (Cost of Preferred Stock) + (Weight of
            Common Equity) (Cost of Common Equity)

The after-tax cost of debt is calculated as:

After-Tax Cost of Debt = (1 − Tax Rate) (Before-Tax Cost of Debt)

After-Tax Cost of Debt = (1 − 0.4) (0.08) = (0.6) (0.08) = 0.048, or 4.8%

WACC = (0.3) (0.048) + (0.25) (0.11) + (0.45) (0.15) = 0.0144 + 0.0275
        + 0.0675 = 0.1094, or 10.94%

Question 2B3-AT13

Topic: Raising Capital

Arch Inc. has 200,000 shares of common stock outstanding. Net income for the recently ended fiscal year was $500,000, and the stock has a price/earnings ratio of 8. The board of directors has just declared a three-for-two stock split. For an investor who owns 100 shares of stock before the split, the approximate value (rounded to the nearest dollar) of the investment in Arch stock immediately after the split is

- ☐ **a.** $2,000
- ☐ **b.** $1,333
- ☐ **c.** $3,000
- ☐ **d.** $4,000

Explanation: The correct answer is: **a.** $2,000.

The stock split will not change the value of the firm, nor will it change the value of the investor's holding.

Original Stock Price = (P/E Ratio) (EPS)

where

EPS = Earnings per Share

EPS = Net Income / # Shares Common Stock Outstanding

EPS = $500,000 / 200,000 = $2.50

Original Stock Price = (8) ($2.50) = $20

Since the investment value does not change with the split, ($20) (100 shares) = $2,000.

After the split, the investor will have 3/2 more shares.

(100 Shares) (3/2) = 150 Shares

Each share will be worth: $2,000 / 150 shares = $13 1/3

Question 2B4-CQ08

Topic: Working Capital Management

Shown next are selected data from Fortune Company's most recent financial statements.

Marketable securities	$10,000
Accounts receivable	60,000
Inventory	25,000
Supplies	5,000
Accounts payable	40,000
Short-term debt payable	10,000
Accruals	5,000

What is Fortune's net working capital?

- ☐ **a.** $35,000
- ☐ **b.** $45,000
- ☐ **c.** $50,000
- ☐ **d.** $80,000

Explanation: The correct answer is: **b.** $45,000.

Net Working Capital = Current Assets − Current Liabilities

Current Assets = (Marketable Securities) + (Accounts Receivable)
                  + (Inventory) + (Supplies)

Current Assets = $10,000 + $60,000 + $25,000 + $5,000 = $100,000

Current Liabilities = (Accounts Payable) + (Short-Term Debt) + (Accruals)

Current Liabilities = $40,000 + $10,000 + $5,000 = $55,000

Net Working Capital = $100,000 − $55,000 = $45,000

Question 2B4-CQ10

Topic: Working Capital Management

The Rolling Stone Corporation, an entertainment ticketing service, is considering the next means of speeding cash flow for the corporation.

Lockbox system. A lockbox system would cost $25 per month for each of its 170 banks and would result in interest savings of $5,240 per month.

Drafts. Drafts would be used to pay for ticket refunds based on 4,000 refunds per month at a cost of $2.00 per draft, which would result in interest savings of $6,500 per month.

Bank float. Bank float would be used for the $1,000,000 in checks written each month. The bank would charge a 2% fee for this service, but the corporation will earn $22,000 in interest on the float.

Electronic transfer. Items over $25,000 would be transferred electronically; it is estimated that 700 items of this type would be made each month at a cost of $18 each, which would result in increased interest earnings of $14,000 per month.

Which of these methods of speeding cash flow should Rolling Stone Corporation adopt?

- ☐ **a.**   Lockbox and electronic transfer only
- ☐ **b.**   Bank float and electronic transfer only
- ☐ **c.**   Lockbox, drafts, and electronic transfer only
- ☐ **d.**   Lockbox, bank float, and electronic transfer only

Explanation: The correct answer is: **d.** lockbox, bank float, and electronic transfer only.

Rolling Stone Corporation should select the option with the greatest net benefit, which is calculated by subtracting associated costs from the benefits.

Net Benefit of Lockbox System = $5,240 − ($25) (170) = $5,240 − $4250 = $990

Net Benefit of Drafts = $6,500 − ($2) (4,000) = $6,500 − $8,000 = − $1,500

Net Benefit of Bank Float = $22,000 − ($1,000,000) (2%)
$$= $22,000 − $20,000 = $2,000$$

Net Benefit of Electronic Transfer = $14,000 − ($18) (700)
$$= $14,000 − $12,600 = $1,400$$

Adding up the net benefits of the different options:

Lockbox and Electronic Transfer Only: $990 + $1,400 = $2,390

Bank Float and Electronic Transfer Only: $2,000 + $1,400 = $3,400

Lockbox, Drafts, and Electronic Transfer Only: $990 − $1,500 + $1,400 = $890

Lockbox, Bank Float, and Electronic Transfer Only:
$990 + $2,000 + $1,400 = $4,390

Lockbox, Bank Float, and Electronic Transfer only have the highest net benefit of the four options listed.

Question 2B6-AT14

Topic: International Finance

A U.S.-based infant clothing company, Tiny Tot, is interested in importing fabric from China. Which of the following should Tiny Tot arrange first for the Chinese company to ship the merchandise?

- ☐ **a.**   Bill of lading
- ☐ **b.**   Time draft
- ☐ **c.**   Letter of credit
- ☐ **d.**   Sight draft

Explanation: The correct answer is: **c.** Letter of credit.

A letter of credit is sent from an importer's bank to an exporter. The letter states that the bank backs the importer's obligation to pay the exporter after the bank has received proper documentation that the trade has been completed as contracted.

Question 2B6-AT18

Topic: International Finance

An appreciation of the U.S. dollar against the Japanese yen would

- ☐ **a.** make U.S. goods more expensive to Japanese consumers.
- ☐ **b.** increase the translated earnings of U.S. subsidiaries domiciled in Japan.
- ☐ **c.** increase the cost of buying supplies for U.S. firms.
- ☐ **d.** make travel in Japan more expensive for U.S. citizens.

Explanation: The correct answer is: **a.** make U.S. goods more expensive to Japanese consumers.

An appreciation of the U.S. dollar against the Japanese yen means that it would take more Japanese yen to purchase U.S. products, thus making such purchases more expensive.

Question 2B6-AT19

Topic: International Finance

Technocrat Inc., located in Belgium, currently manufactures products at its domestic plant and exports them to the United States, since production is less expensive at home. The company is considering the possibility of setting up a plant in the United States. All of the following factors would encourage the company to consider direct foreign investment in the U.S. **except** the

- ☐ **a.** expectation of more stringent trade restrictions by the United States.
- ☐ **b.** depreciation of the U.S. dollar against Belgium's currency.
- ☐ **c.** changing demand for the company's exports to the United States due to exchange rate fluctuations.
- ☐ **d.** widening of the gap in production costs between locations in the United States and Belgium.

Explanation: The correct answer is: **d.** widening of the gap in production costs between locations in the United States and Belgium.

An increasing gap would favor production at home in Belgium because it would be even less expensive.

Section C: Decision Analysis

Question 2C1-CQ01
Topic: Cost/Volume/Profit Analysis

Following are the operating results of the two segments of Parklin Corporation.

	Segment A	Segment B	Total
Sales	$10,000	$15,000	$25,000
Variable costs of goods sold	4,000	8,500	12,500
Fixed costs of goods sold	1,500	2,500	4,000
Gross margin	4,500	4,000	8,500
Variable selling and administrative	2,000	3,000	5,000
Fixed selling and administrative	1,500	1,500	3,000
Operating income (loss)	$1,000	$(500)	$500

Variable costs of goods sold are directly related to the operating segments. Fixed costs of goods sold are allocated to each segment based on the number of employees. Fixed selling and administrative expenses are allocated equally. If Segment B is eliminated, $1,500 of fixed costs of goods sold would be eliminated. Assuming Segment B is closed, the effect on operating income would be

- ☐ **a.** an increase of $500.
- ☐ **b.** an increase of $2,000.
- ☐ **c.** a decrease of $2,000.
- ☐ **d.** a decrease of $2,500.

Explanation: The correct answer is: **c.** a decrease of $2,000.

If Segment B is closed, then Parklin would gain $13,000, which is calculated as shown:

Effect of Closing Segment B = ($1,500 in B's Fixed Cost of Goods Sold)
+ ($8,500 in B's Variable Cost of Goods Sold) +
($3,000 in B's Variable Selling and Administrative)
= $13,000

The closing would cause a reduction in sales of $15,000, resulting in a decrease in profits of $15,000 − $13,000 = $2,000.

Question 2C1-CQ02
Topic: Cost/Volume/Profit Analysis

Edwards Products has just developed a new product with a variable manufacturing cost of $30 per unit. The marketing director has identified three marketing approaches for this new product.

Approach X	Set a selling price of $36 and have the firm's sales staff sell the product at a 10% commission with no advertising program. Estimated annual sales would be 10,000 units.
Approach Y	Set a selling price of $38, have the firm's sales staff sell the product at a 10% commission, and back them up with a $30,000 advertising program. Estimated annual sales would be 12,000 units.
Approach Z	Rely on wholesalers to handle the product. Edwards would sell the new product to the wholesalers at $32 per unit and incur no selling expenses. Estimated annual sales would be 14,000 units.

Rank the three alternatives in order of net contribution, from highest to lowest.

- ☐ **a.** X, Y, Z
- ☐ **b.** Y, Z, X
- ☐ **c.** Z, X, Y
- ☐ **d.** Z, Y, X

Explanation: The correct answer is: **c.** Z, X, Y.

Contribution Margin = (Selling Price per Unit − Variable Costs per Unit) (Volume)

The contribution margin for Approach X is calculated as shown:

Contribution Margin, Approach X = [($36 − (0.1 Commission)
($36) − $30)] (10,000 units)

Contribution Margin, Approach X = ($2.40) (10,000) = $24,000

The contribution margin for Approach Y is calculated as shown:

Contribution Margin, Approach Y = [($38 − (0.1 Commission) ($38) − $30)]
(12,000 Units) − $30,000 Advertising

Contribution Margin, Approach Y = ($4.20) (12,000) − $30,000 = $20,400

The contribution margin for approach Z is calculated as shown:

Contribution Margin, Approach Z = ($32 − $30) (14,000 Units) = $28,000

Question 2C1-CQ04
Topic: Cost/Volume/Profit Analysis

Elgers Company produces valves for the plumbing industry. Elgers' per unit sales price and variable costs are as shown.

Sales price	$12
Variable costs	8

Elgers' practical plant capacity is 40,000 units. Its total fixed costs aggregate $48,000 and it has a 40% effective tax rate.

The maximum net profit that Elger can earn is

☐ **a.** $48,000.

☐ **b.** $67,200.

☐ **c.** $96,000.

☐ **d.** $112,000.

Explanation: The correct answer is: **b.** $67,200.

The maximum net profit that Elger can earn can be calculated as shown:

Maximum Net Profit = (1 − Tax Rate) (Sales − Variable Costs − Fixed Costs)

Maximum Net Profit = (1 − 0.4) [($12) (40,000) − ($8) (40,000) − $48,000]

Maximum Net Profit = (0.6) ($480,000 − $320,000 − $48,000)

Maximum Net Profit = (0.6) ($112,000) = $67,200

Question 2C1-CQ09

Topic: Cost/Volume/Profit Analysis

Cervine Corporation makes two types of motors for use in various products. Operating data and unit cost information for its products are presented next.

	Product A	Product B
Annual unit capacity	10,000	20,000
Annual unit demand	10,000	20,000
Selling price	$100	$80
Variable manufacturing cost	53	45
Fixed manufacturing cost	10	10
Variable selling and administrative	10	11
Fixed selling and administrative	5	4
Fixed other administrative	2	0
Unit operating profit	$20	$10
Machine hours per unit	2.0	1.5

Cervine has 40,000 productive machine hours available. The relevant contribution margins, per machine hour for each product, to be utilized in making a decision on product priorities for the coming year, are

	Product A	Product B
a.	$17.00	$14.00
b.	$18.50	$16.00
c.	$20.00	$10.00
d.	$37.00	$24.00

Explanation: The correct answer is: **b.** $18.50; $16.00.

Contribution per machine hour is calculated as shown:

Contribution per Machine Hour = (Unit Contribution Margin) / (Machine Hours per Unit)

Unit Contribution Margin (CMU) = Selling Price − Unit Variable Costs

Unit Variable Costs, Product A = ($53 + $10) = $63

CMU, Product A = ($100 − $63) = $37

Product A's Contribution per Machine Hour = $37 / 2 Hours = $18.50 per Hour

Unit Variable Costs, Product B = ($45 + $11) = $56

CMU, Product B = ($80 − $56) = $24

Product B's Contribution per Machine Hour = $24 / 1.5 Hours = $16.00 per Hour

Question 2C1-CQ10

Topic: Cost/Volume/Profit Analysis

Allred Company sells its single product for $30 per unit. The contribution margin ratio is 45%, and fixed costs are $10,000 per month. Allred has an effective income tax rate of 40%. If Allred sells 1,000 units in the current month, Allred's variable expenses would be

- ☐ **a.** $9,900.
- ☐ **b.** $12,000.
- ☐ **c.** $13,500.
- ☐ **d.** $16,500.

Explanation: The correct answer is: **d.** $16,500.

Variable expenses are calculated as shown:

Variable Expenses = (1 − Contribution Margin Ratio) (Sales Amount)

Sales Amount = ($30) (1,000 Units) = $30,000

Variable Expenses = (1 − 0.45) ($30,000)

Variable Expenses = (0.55) ($30,000) = $16,500

Question 2C1-CQ11

Topic: Cost/Volume/Profit Analysis

Phillips & Company produces educational software. Its unit cost structure, based on an anticipated production volume of 150,000 units, is:

Sales price	$160
Variable costs	60
Fixed costs	55

The marketing department has estimated sales for the coming year at 175,000 units, which is within the relevant range of Phillip's cost structure. Phillip's break-even volume (in units) and anticipated operating income for the coming year would amount to

- ☐ **a.** 82,500 units and $7,875,000 of operating income.
- ☐ **b.** 82,500 units and $9,250,000 of operating income.
- ☐ **c.** 96,250 units and $3,543,750 of operating income.
- ☐ **d.** 96,250 units and $7,875,000 of operating income.

Explanation: The correct answer is: **b.** 82,500 units and $9,250,000 of operating income. The break-even point in units is calculated as shown:

$$\text{Break-Even (Units)} = \text{(Total Fixed Costs)} / \text{(Unit Contribution Margin)}$$

Unit Contribution Margin = (Unit Sales Price − Unit Variable Costs)

Unit Contribution Margin = $160 − $60 = $100

Total Fixed Costs = (Fixed Cost per Unit) (Production Volume)

Total Fixed Costs = ($55) (150,000 Units) = $8,250,000

Break-Even Point (Units) = $8,250,000 / $100 = 82,500 Units

Operating Income = (Unit Contribution Margin) (Total Units) − Fixed Costs

Operating Income = ($100) (175,000 Units) − $8,250,000
$$= \$17,500,000 - \$8,250,000$$

Operating Income = $9,250,000

Question 2C1-CQ15

Topic: Cost/Volume/Profit Analysis

For the year just ended, Silverstone Company's sales revenue was $450,000. Silverstone's fixed costs were $120,000, and its variable costs amounted to $270,000. For the current year, sales are forecasted at $500,000. If the fixed costs do not change, Silverstone's operating profits this year will be

- ☐ **a.** $60,000.
- ☐ **b.** $80,000.
- ☐ **c.** $110,000.
- ☐ **d.** $200,000.

Explanation: The correct answer is: **b.** $80,000.

The operating profit is calculated as shown:

Operating Profit = (Contribution Margin Ratio) (Total Sales $) − Fixed Costs

Forecasted Sales, Current Year = $500,000

Contribution Margin Ratio, Year Just Ended = (Sales − Variable Costs) / (sales)

Contribution Margin Ratio, Year Just Ended = ($450,000 − $270,000) / ($450,000) = 0.4

Operating Profit = (0.4) ($500,000) − $120,000 = $200,000 − $120,000 = $80,000

Question 2C2-CQ01

Topic: Marginal Analysis

Williams makes $35,000 a year as an accounting clerk. He decides to quit his job to enter a one-year MBA program full-time. Assume Williams doesn't work in the summer or hold any part-time jobs. His tuition, books, living expenses, and fees total $25,000 a year. Given this information, the annual total economic cost of Williams's MBA studies is

- ☐ **a.** $10,000.
- ☐ **b.** $35,000.
- ☐ **c.** $25,000.
- ☐ **d.** $60,000.

Explanation: The correct answer is: **d.** $60,000.

The economic cost of pursuing the MBA program full time for one year is calculated by adding the $35,000 of forgone salary and the $25,000 of expenses together, which comes to $60,000 in total.

Question 2C2-CQ03

Topic: Marginal Analysis

Daily costs for Kelso Manufacturing include $1,000 of fixed costs and total variable costs, as shown:

Unit Output	10	11	12	13	14	15
Cost	$125	$250	$400	$525	$700	$825

The average total cost at an output level of 11 units is

- ☐ **a.** $113.64.
- ☐ **b.** $125.00.
- ☐ **c.** $215.91.
- ☐ **d.** $250.00.

Explanation: The correct answer is: **a.** $113.64.

The average cost per unit for 11 units is calculated by adding up the total costs (fixed and variable) for the 11 units and dividing that amount by 11:

Average Total Cost at an Output Level of 11 Units = ($1,000 + $250) / 11
$$= \$1,250 / 11 = \$113.64$$

Question 2C2-CQ04

Topic: Marginal Analysis

Harper Products' cost information for the normal range of output in a month is shown next.

Output in Units	Total Cost
20,000	$3,000,000
22,500	3,325,000
25,000	3,650,000

What is Harper's short-run marginal cost?

- ☐ **a.** $26
- ☐ **b.** $130
- ☐ **c.** $146
- ☐ **d.** $150

Explanation: The correct answer is: **b.** $130.

Marginal cost is the cost of the next unit produced. It is calculated by taking the change in costs and dividing it by the change in output (volume). Harper's marginal cost can be calculated as:

Marginal Cost = Change in Cost / Change in Volume

Marginal Cost = ($3,325,000 − $3,000,000) / (22,500 − 20,000)
               = $325,000 / 2,500 = $130

Question 2C2-CQ11

Topic: Marginal Analysis

Refrigerator Company manufactures ice makers for installation in refrigerators. The costs per unit, for 20,000 units of ice makers, are:

Direct materials	$7
Direct labor	12
Variable overhead	5
Fixed overhead	10
Total costs	$34

Cool Compartments Inc. has offered to sell 20,000 ice makers to Refrigerator Company for $28 per unit. If Refrigerator accepts Cool Compartments' offer, the plant would be idled and fixed overhead amounting to $6 per unit could be eliminated. The total relevant costs associated with the manufacture of ice makers amount to

- ☐ **a.** $480,000.
- ☐ **b.** $560,000.

  ☐ **c.** $600,000.

  ☐ **d.** $680,000.

Explanation: The correct answer is: **c.** $600,000.

  The total relevant costs associated with the manufacturing of ice makers are:

Total Relevant Costs = (Unit Variable Manufacturing Costs) (Number of Units) + (Any Avoidable Fixed Costs)

Unit Variable Manufacturing Costs = (Direct Materials + Direct Labor + Variable Overhead)

Unit Variable Manufacturing Costs = ($7 + $12 + $5) = $24

  Avoidable fixed costs are $6 per unit.

Therefore, the relevant costs to manufacture the ice makers
= ($24) (20,000 units) + ($6) (20,000 units).

Total Relevant Costs = $480,000 + $120,000 = $600,000

Question 2C2-CQ14

Topic: Marginal Analysis

Capital Company has decided to discontinue a product produced on a machine purchased four years ago at a cost of $70,000. The machine has a current book value of $30,000. Due to technologically improved machinery now available in the marketplace, the existing machine has no current salvage value. The company is reviewing the various aspects involved in the production of a new product. The engineering staff advised that the existing machine can be used to produce the new product. Other costs involved in the production of the new product will be materials of $20,000 and labor priced at $5,000.

  Ignoring income taxes, the costs relevant to the decision to produce or not to produce the new product would be

  ☐ **a.** $25,000.

  ☐ **b.** $30,000.

  ☐ **c.** $55,000.

  ☐ **d.** $95,000.

Explanation: The correct answer is: **a.** $25,000.

  The costs relevant to the decision to produce or not to produce the new product total $25,000 and are comprised of the $20,000 cost of materials and the $5,000 cost of labor. The costs associated with the old machine are irrelevant; they are sunk, historical costs.

Question 2C2-CQ15

Topic: Marginal Analysis

Current business segment operations for Whitman, a mass retailer, are presented next.

	Merchandise	Automotive	Restaurant	Total
Sales	$500,000	$400,000	$100,000	$1,000,000
Variable costs	300,000	200,000	70,000	570,000
Fixed costs	100,000	100,000	50,000	250,000
Operating income (loss)	$100,000	$100,000	$(20,000)	$180,000

Management is contemplating the discontinuance of the Restaurant segment since "it is losing money." If this segment is discontinued, $30,000 of its fixed costs will be eliminated. In addition, Merchandise and Automotive sales will decrease 5% from their current levels. What will Whitman's total contribution margin be if the Restaurant segment is discontinued?

☐ **a.** $160,000

☐ **b.** $220,000

☐ **c.** $367,650

☐ **d.** $380,000

Explanation: The correct answer is: **d.** $380,000.

Total contribution margin in dollars is calculated as shown:

Total Contribution Margin = Sales − Variable Costs

The total contribution margin for Whitman after discontinuing the Restaurant segment would be 95% of the Merchandise segment's current contribution, plus 95% of the Automotive segment's current contribution.

Total Contribution Margin, Whitman, after Discontinuing Restaurant Segment
= (0.95) ($500,000 − $300,000) + (0.95) ($400,000 − $200,000)
= $190,000 + $190,000 = $380,000

Question 2C2-CQ16

Topic: Marginal Analysis

Aril Industries is a multiproduct company that currently manufactures 30,000 units of Part 730 each month for use in production. The facilities being used to produce Part 730 have fixed monthly overhead costs of $150,000 and a theoretical capacity to produce 60,000 units per month. If Aril were to buy Part 730 from an outside supplier, the facilities would be idle and 40% of fixed costs would continue to be incurred. There are no alternative uses for the facilities. The variable production costs of Part 730 are $11 per unit. Fixed overhead is allocated based on planned production levels.

If Aril Industries continues to use 30,000 units of Part 730 each month, it would realize a net benefit by purchasing Part 730 from an outside supplier only if the supplier's unit price is less than

☐ **a.** $12.00.

☐ **b.** $12.50.

☐ **c.** $13.00.

☐ **d.** $14.00.

Explanation: The correct answer is: **d.** $14.00.

The appropriate purchase price would occur when the price for 30,000 units is equal to the variable manufacturing costs plus the avoidable fixed costs.

(P) (Units) = (Variable Manufacturing Costs) + (Avoidable Fixed Costs)

where:

P = purchase price
Units = 30,000
Variable Manufacturing Costs = ($11) (30,000 Units) = $330,000
Avoidable Fixed Costs = (0.6) ($150,000) = $90,000

(P) (30,000) = ($330,000) + ($90,000)
30,000 P = $420,000
P = $14.00

Question 2C3-CQ01

Topic: Pricing

A market research analyst determined the next market data for a commodity.

Price	Quantity Supplied	Quantity Demanded
$25	250	750
50	500	500
75	750	250
100	1,000	0

Based on this information, which one of the following statements is **correct**?

☐ **a.** At a price of $30, there will be excess demand.

☐ **b.** A market clearing price cannot be determined.

☐ **c.** At a price of $80, there will be insufficient supply.

☐ **d.** A market price of $50 cannot exist for very long.

Explanation: The correct answer is: **a.** At a price of $30, there will be excess demand.

The market clearing price of $50 occurs when supply equals demand (500 units). Any price less than $50 will create excess demand.

Question 2C3-CQ03

Topic: Pricing

An economic research firm performed extensive studies on the market for large-screen televisions (LSTs). Portions of the results are shown next.

Household Income	LST Sales (units)
$50,000	20,000
60,000	28,000
72,000	39,200
Price of LSTs	**LST Sales (units)**
$1,000	100,000
900	115,000
810	132,250

The income elasticity of demand for LSTs is

☐ **a.** 0.4.

☐ **b.** 1.5.

☐ **c.** 1.8.

☐ **d.** 2.5.

Explanation: The correct answer is: **c.** 1.8

Income elasticity of demand is defined as the percent change in quantity demanded (sales) given a percentage change in income. The percentage change in sales is calculated by taking the change in sales from 20,000 to 28,000 units, as shown:

% Change in Sales = (28,000 − 20,000) / 24,000 = 8,000 / 24,000 = 0.33

For that same change in sales units, the percentage change in income is calculated as:

% Change in Income = ($60,000 − $50,000) / $55,000
= $10,000 / $55,000 = 0.18

The income elasticity can then be calculated as shown:

Income Elasticity of Demand = % Change in Quantity Demanded
/ % Change in Income

Income Elasticity of Demand = 0.33 / 0.18 = 1.83

Note: These calculations are consistent with the CMA exam's use of the midpoint formula approach to calculate elasticity of demand, as explained in Section C, Topic 3.

Question 2C3-CQ04

Topic: Pricing

Jones Enterprises manufactures three products, A, B, and C. During the month of May, Jones's production, costs, and sales data were as shown.

	Products			
	A	**B**	**C**	**Totals**
Units of production	30,000	20,000	70,000	120,000
Joint production costs to split-off point				$480,000
Further processing costs	$–	$60,000	$140,000	
Unit sales price				
At split-off	3.75	5.50	10.25	
After further processing	–	8.00	12.50	

Based on this information, which one of the following alternatives should be recommended to Jones's management?

- **a.** Sell both Product B and Product C at the split-off point.
- **b.** Process Product B further but sell Product C at the split-off point.
- **c.** Process Product C further but sell Product B at the split-off point.
- **d.** Process both Products B and C further.

Explanation: The correct answer is: **c.** Process Product C further but sell Product B at the split-off point.

A product should be processed further if the change in the market price from processing exceeds the additional processing costs.

Product B can be sold at split-off for $5.50 (20,000) = $110,000.
Product B can be sold after further processing for $8(20,000) = $160,000.
The cost increase is $160,000 – $110,000 = $50,000.
$50,000 is less than the additional processing costs of $60,000.

Therefore, Product B should be sold at split-off.
Product C can be sold at split-off for $10.25 (70,000) = $717,500.
Product C can be sold after further processing for $12.50 (70,000) = $875,000.
The cost increase is $875,000 – $717,500 = $157,500.
$157,500 is greater than the additional processing costs of $140,000.
Based on this information, Product C should be processed further.

Question 2C3-CQ05

Topic: Pricing

Synergy Inc. produces a component that is popular in many refrigeration systems. Data on three of the five different models of this component are shown next.

	Model		
	A	**B**	**C**
Volume needed (units)	5,000	6,000	3,000
Manufacturing costs			
Variable direct costs	$10	$24	$20
Variable overhead	5	10	15
Fixed overhead	11	20	17
Total manufacturing costs	$26	$54	$52
Cost if purchased	$21	$42	$39

Synergy applies variable overhead on the basis of machine hours at the rate of $2.50 per hour. Models A and B are manufactured in the Freezer Department, which has a capacity of 28,000 machine processing hours. Which one of the following options should be recommended to Synergy's management?

☐ **a.** Purchase all three products in the quantities required.

☐ **b.** Manufacture all three products in the quantities required.

☐ **c.** The Freezer Department's manufacturing plan should include 5,000 units of Model A and 4,500 units of Model B.

☐ **d.** The Freezer Department's manufacturing plan should include 2,000 units of Model A and 6,000 units of Model B.

Explanation: The correct answer is: **c.** The Freezer Department's manufacturing plan should include 5,000 units of Model A and 4,500 units of Model B.

Synergy would want to maximize the contribution per machine hour, multiplied by the 28,000 machine hours available.

The contribution per machine hour for each product can be calculated as shown:

Contribution per Machine Hour = (Outside Price − Product's Unit Variable Costs) / (Number of Machine Hours Required to Make It)

Machine Hours Required to Make Any Model = Variable Overhead for That Model / ($2.50/hour)

Machine Hours Required to Make Model A = ($5) / ($2.50/hour) = 2 Hours

Machine Hours Required to Make Model B = ($10) / ($2.50/hour) = 4 Hours

Machine Hours Required to Make Model C = ($15) / ($2.50/hour) = 6 Hours

Contribution per Machine Hour, Model A = ($21 − $10 Variable Direct Costs −
$5 Variable Overhead) / (2 Hours)

Contribution per Machine Hour, Model A = $6 / 2 Hours = $3.00 per Machine Hour

Contribution per Machine Hour, Model B = ($42 − $24 Variable Direct Costs −
$10 Variable Overhead) / (4 Hours)

Contribution per Machine Hour, Model B = $8 / 4 Hours = $2.00 per Machine
Hour

Contribution per Machine Hour, Model C = ($39 − $20 Variable Direct Costs −
$15 Variable Overhead) / (6 Hours)

Contribution per Machine Hour, Model C = $4 / 6 Hours = $0.67 per Machine
Hour

Based on this information about contribution per machine hour, Synergy should:

First produce 5,000 units of Model A (the highest contribution margin per machine hour) using 5,000 (2) = 10,000 machine hours.

Then produce 4,500 units of Model B (the next highest contribution margin per machine hour) using 4,500 (4) = 18,000 machine hours.

The two models would use the entire capacity of 28,000 machine hours (10,000 + 18,000), so no additional products could be produced.

Question 2C3-CQ06

Topic: Pricing

Leader Industries is planning to introduce a new product, DMA. It is expected that 10,000 units of DMA will be sold. The full product cost per unit is $300. Invested capital for this product amounts to $20 million. Leader's target rate of return on investment is 20%. The markup percentage for this product, based on operating income as a percentage of full product cost, will be

☐ **a.** 42.9%.

☐ **b.** 57.1%.

☐ **c.** 133.3%.

☐ **d.** 233.7%.

Explanation: The correct answer is: **c.** 133.3%.

The price (*p*) of DMA is computed by using this formula:

$$(p - \text{Costs})(\text{Number of Units}) = (\text{Return on Investment \%}) (\text{Investment})$$

$$(p - \$300) (10,000) = [(0.2) (\$20,000,000)]$$

$$(p - \$300) = \$4,000,000 / 10,000$$

$$(p - \$300) = \$400$$

$$p = \$700$$

The markup percentage of full product cost = (Price − Cost) / (Cost).

Markup Percentage of Full Product Cost = ($700 − $300) / ($300)
$$= \$400 / \$300$$
$$= 1.333, \text{ or } 133.3\%.$$

Question 2C3-CQ08

Topic: Pricing

Almelo Manpower Inc. provides contracted bookkeeping services. Almelo has annual fixed costs of $100,000 and variable costs of $6 per hour. This year the company budgeted 50,000 hours of bookkeeping services. Almelo prices its services at full cost and uses a cost-plus pricing approach. The company developed a billing price of $9 per hour. The company's markup level would be

- ☐ **a.** 12.5%.
- ☐ **b.** 33.3%.
- ☐ **c.** 50.0%.
- ☐ **d.** 66.6%.

Explanation: The correct answer is: **a.** 12.5%.

The unit cost at 50,000 hours is:

Unit Cost at 50,000 Hours = (Fixed Costs / # Hours) + Variable Cost per Hour

Unit Cost at 50,000 hours = ($100,000 / 50,000) + $6 = $2 + $6 = $8 per Hour

Given the price of $9, the markup level on cost = (Price − Cost) / (Cost).

Markup Level on Cost = ($9 − $8) / ($8) = 1/8 = 0.125, or 12.5%

Question 2C3-CQ09

Topic: Pricing

Fennel Products is using cost-based pricing to determine the selling price for its new product based on the next information.

Annual volume	25,000 units
Fixed costs	$700,000 per year
Variable costs	$200 per unit
Plant investment	$3,000,000
Working capital	$1,000,000
Effective tax rate	40%

The target price that Fennell needs to set for the new product to achieve a 15% after-tax return on investment (ROI) would be

- ☐ **a.** $228.
- ☐ **b.** $238.
- ☐ **c.** $258.
- ☐ **d.** $268.

Explanation: The correct answer is: **d.** $268.

The target price (p) is computed by using this formula:

(Total Sales − Total Variable Costs − Total Fixed Costs) (1 − Tax Rate)
  = (Target ROI) (Investment)

Total Sales = (Volume) (Target Price) = (25,000) (p)

Total Variable Costs = (Volume) (Variable Cost per Unit)
      = (25,000) ($200) = $5,000,000

Total Fixed Costs = $700,000

Investment includes both plant and working capital = $3,000,000 + $1,000,000
             = $4,000,000.

$(25,000p − \$5,000,000 − \$700,000) (1 − 0.4) = (0.15) (\$4,000,000)$

$(25,000p − \$5,700,000) (0.6) = \$600,000$

$15,000p − \$3,420,000 = \$600,000$

$15,000p = \$4,020,000$

$p = \$268$

Section D: Risk Management

Question 2D!-AT06

Topic: Enterprise Risk

Which of the following is **not** an example of a form of political risk associated with foreign direct investment?

- ☐ **a.** Uncontrolled inflation
- ☐ **b.** Nationalization of factories
- ☐ **c.** Change in government regime
- ☐ **d.** Civil war

Explanation: The correct answer is: **a.** Uncontrolled inflation.

Uncontrolled inflation is an economic risk, not a political risk.

Question 2D1-AT17

Topic: Enterprise Risk

All of the following are valid reasons for expansion of international business by U.S. multinational corporations, **except** to

- ☐ **a.** secure new sources for raw materials.
- ☐ **b.** find additional areas where their products can be marketed successfully.
- ☐ **c.** protect their domestic market from competition from foreign manufacturers.
- ☐ **d.** minimize their costs of production.

Explanation: The correct answer is: **c.** protect their domestic market from competition from foreign manufacturers.

Protecting the domestic market from foreign competition is not a valid reason for expansion overseas; all the other options are valid.

Question 2D1-AT18

Topic: Enterprise Risk

Risk assessment is a process

- ☐ **a.** designed to identify potential events that may affect the entity.
- ☐ **b.** that establishes policies and procedures to accomplish internal control objectives.
- ☐ **c.** that identifies risk but does not include management's response to risk
- ☐ **d.** that assesses the quality of internal controls throughout the year.

Explanation: The correct answer is: **a.** designed to identify potential events that may affect the entity.

Risk assessment involves identifying all risks and vulnerabilities to which an organization is exposed.

Question 2D1-AT19

Topic: Enterprise Risk

Within a financial risk management context, the term *value at risk* (VaR) is defined as the

- ☐ **a.** maximum value a company can lose.
- ☐ **b.** worst possible outcome given the distribution of outcomes.
- ☐ **c.** most likely negative outcome.
- ☐ **d.** maximum loss within a certain time period at a given level of confidence.

Explanation: The correct answer is: **d.** maximum loss within a certain time period at a given level of confidence.

Value at risk is defined as the maximum loss within a given period of time and given a specified probability level (level of confidence).

Section E: Investment Decisions

Question 2E1-AT06

Topic: Capital Budgeting Process

In order to increase production capacity, Gunning Industries is considering replacing an existing production machine with a new technologically improved machine effective January 1. This information is being considered:

- The new machine would be purchased for $160,000 in cash. Shipping, installation, and testing would cost an additional $30,000.

- The new machine is expected to increase annual sales by 20,000 units at a sales price of $40 per unit. Incremental operating costs are comprised of $30 per unit in variable costs and total fixed costs of $40,000 per year.

- The investment in the new machine will require an immediate increase in working capital of $35,000.

- Gunning uses straight-line depreciation for financial reporting and tax reporting purposes. The new machine has an estimated useful life of five years and zero salvage value.

- Gunning is subject to a 40% corporate income tax rate.

Gunning uses the net present value method to analyze investments and will employ these factors and rates:

Period	Present Value of $1 at 10%	Present Value of an Ordinary Annuity of $1 at 10%
1	0.909	0.909
2	0.826	1.736
3	0.751	2.487
4	0.683	3.170
5	0.621	3.791

Gunning Industries' initial net cash outflow in a capital budgeting decision would be

- ☐ **a.** $160,000.
- ☐ **b.** $190,000.
- ☐ **c.** $225,000.
- ☐ **d.** $195,000.

Explanation: The correct answer is: **c.** $225,000.

Gunning's initial cash outflow at time zero is calculated as:

Initial Cash Outflow = (Initial Cost of New Machine) + (Shipping, Installation, and Testing Related to the New Machine) + Additional Working Capital Required

Initial Cash Outflow = $160,000 + $30,000 + $35,000 = $225,000

Question 2E1-AT07

Topic: Capital Budgeting Process

In order to increase production capacity, Gunning Industries is considering replacing an existing production machine with a new technologically improved machine effective January 1. Gunning Industries is considering this information:

- The new machine would be purchased for $160,000 in cash. Shipping, installation, and testing would cost an additional $30,000.

- The new machine is expected to increase annual sales by 20,000 units at a sales price of $40 per unit. Incremental operating costs are comprised of $30 per unit in variable costs and total fixed costs of $40,000 per year.

- The investment in the new machine will require an immediate increase in working capital of $35,000.

- Gunning uses straight-line depreciation for financial reporting and tax reporting purposes. The new machine has an estimated useful life of five years and zero salvage value.

- Gunning is subject to a 40% corporate income tax rate.

Gunning uses the net present value method to analyze investments and will employ these factors and rates:

Period	Present Value of $1 at 10%	Present Value of an Ordinary Annuity of $1 at 10%
1	0.909	0.909
2	0.826	1.736
3	0.751	2.487
4	0.683	3.170
5	0.621	3.791

Gunning Industries' discounted annual depreciation tax shield for the first year of operation would be:

- ☐ **a.** $13,817.
- ☐ **b.** $15,200.
- ☐ **c.** $20,725.
- ☐ **d.** $22,800.

Explanation: The correct answer is: **a.** $13,817.

The depreciation tax shield for a period is calculated by taking the depreciation for the period and multiplying it by the relevant tax rate.

Using straight-line depreciation, the annual depreciation charge is calculated as:

Annual Depreciation Charge, Straight-Line Depreciation
    = (Depreciable Base) / (Estimated Service Life)

For Gunning, the depreciable base will include the initial cost of the machine and the shipping, installation, and testing. Therefore, the depreciable base will be calculated as:

Depreciable Base = $160,000 + $30,000 = $190,000

Annual Depreciation Charge, Straight-Line Depreciation = ($160,000 + $30,000) / (5 years)

Annual Depreciation Charge, Straight-Line Depreciation = $190,000 / 5 Years = $38,000

The annual depreciation tax shield is calculated by taking the annual depreciation and multiplying it by the tax rate, as shown:

Annual Depreciation Tax Shield = (Annual Depreciation) (Tax Rate)
Annual Depreciation Tax Shield = ($38,000) (0.40) = $15,200

The discounted annual depreciation tax shield is calculated by taking the annual depreciation tax shield and discounting it by the appropriate present value of $1 factor, as shown:

Discounted Annual Depreciation Tax Shield
  = (Annual Depreciation Tax Shield) (Present Value of $1 Factor)

Present Value of $1 Factor for 10% at the End of Year 1 = 0.909

Discounted Annual Depreciation Tax Shield = ($15,200) (0.909) = $13,817

Question 2E1-AT08

Topic: Capital Budgeting Process

Which one of the following is **most** relevant to a manufacturing equipment replacement decision?

- ☐ **a.** Gain or loss on the disposal of the old equipment
- ☐ **b.** Original cost less depreciation of the old equipment
- ☐ **c.** A lump-sum write-off amount from the disposal of the old equipment
- ☐ **d.** Disposal price of the old equipment

Explanation: The correct answer is: **d.** disposal price of the old equipment.

Relevant costs and revenues include cash flows caused by the decision. The disposal price of the old equipment is a cash inflow that decreases the initial investment required for the replacement decision.

Question 2E2-CQ01

Topic: Discounted Cash Flow Analysis

Calvin Inc. is considering the purchase of a new state-of-art machine to replace its hand-operated machine. Calvin's effective tax rate is 40%, and its cost of capital is 12%. Data regarding the existing and new machines are presented next.

	Existing Machine	New Machine
Original cost	$50,000	$90,000
Installation costs	0	4,000
Freight and insurance	0	6,000
Expected end salvage value	0	0
Depreciation method	straight line	straight line
Expected useful life	10 years	5 years

The existing machine has been in service for seven years and could be sold currently for $25,000. Calvin expects to realize a before-tax annual reduction in labor costs of $30,000 if the new machine is purchased and placed in service.

If the new machine is purchased, the cash flows for the fifth year would amount to

- ☐ **a.** $18,000.
- ☐ **b.** $24,000.
- ☐ **c.** $26,000.
- ☐ **d.** $30,000.

Explanation: The correct answer is: **c.** $26,000.

The cash flow in year 5 of the project is calculated as shown:

Cash Flow, Year 5 = (Projected Savings − Depreciation Expense) (1 − Tax Rate) + Depreciation Expense

Annual Depreciation Expense = (Original Cost + Installation Costs + Freight And Insurance Costs) / Useful Life)

Annual Depreciation Expense = ($90,000 + $4,000 + $6,000) / 5 years = $20,000 per year

Cash Flow, Year 5 = ($30,000 − $20,000) (1 − 0.4) + $20,000 = $6,000 + $20,000

Cash Flow, Year 5 = $26,000

Question 2E2-CQ11

Topic: Discounted Cash Flow Analysis

For each of the next six years, Atlantic Motors anticipates net income of $10,000, straight-line tax depreciation of $20,000, a 40% tax rate, a discount rate of 10%, and cash sales of $100,000. The depreciable assets are all being acquired at the beginning of year 1 and will have a salvage value of zero at the end of six years.

The present value (PV) of the total depreciation tax savings would be:

- ☐ **a.** $8,000.
- ☐ **b.** $27,072.
- ☐ **c.** $34,840.
- ☐ **d.** $87,100.

Explanation: The correct answer is: **c.** $34,840.

The depreciation tax savings (or depreciation tax shield) is calculated by taking the after-tax PV of the annual depreciation charges.

Depreciation Tax Shield = (Tax Rate) (Depreciation Expense) (PV Annuity Factor)

Depreciation Tax Shield = (0.4) ($20,000) (4.355 PV Annuity, $i = 10$, $n = 6$)

Depreciation Tax Shield = (0.4) ($20,000) (4.355) = $34,840

Question 2E2-CQ14

Topic: Discounted Cash Flow Analysis

Fuller Industries is considering a $1 million investment in stamping equipment to produce a new product. The equipment is expected to last nine years, produce revenue of $700,000 per year, and have related cash expenses of $450,000 per year. At the end of the 9th year, the equipment is expected to have a salvage value of $100,000 and cost $50,000 to remove. The Internal Revenue Service categorizes this as 5-year Modified Accelerated Cost Recovery System (MACRS) property subject to the next depreciation rates.

Year	Rate
1	20.00%
2	32.00%
3	19.20%
4	11.52%
5	11.52%
6	5.76%

Fuller's effective income tax rate is 40% and Fuller expects, on an overall company basis, to continue to be profitable and have significant taxable income. If Fuller uses the net present value method to analyze investments, what is the expected net tax impact on cash flow in year 2 before discounting?

- ☐ **a.** Positive $28,000 impact
- ☐ **b.** $0 impact
- ☐ **c.** Negative $100,000 impact
- ☐ **d.** Negative $128,000 impact

Explanation: The correct answer is: **a.** Positive $28,000 impact.

The net tax impact in year 2 is calculated as shown:

Net Tax Impact, Year 2 = (Revenue − Cash Expenses − Depreciation) (Tax Rate)

Depreciation Expense, Year 2 = (Equipment Cost) (Year 2 MACRS rate)

Depreciation Expense, Year 2 = ($1,000,000) (0.32) = $320,000

Net Tax Impact, Year 2 = ($700,000 − $450,000 − $320,000) (0.4)

Net Tax Impact, Year 2 = −$28,000 (which is a reduction in taxes)

Question 2E2-CQ16

Topic: Discounted Cash Flow Analysis

AGC Company is considering an equipment upgrade. AGC uses discounted cash flow (DCF) analysis in evaluating capital investments and has an effective tax rate of 40%. Selected data developed by AGC are shown next.

	Existing Equipment	New Equipment
Original cost	$50,000	$95,000
Accumulated depreciation	45,000	–
Current market value	3,000	95,000
Accounts receivable	6,000	8,000
Accounts payable	2,100	2,500

Based on this information, what is the initial investment for a DCF analysis of this proposed upgrade?

- ☐ **a.** $92,400
- ☐ **b.** $92,800
- ☐ **c.** $95,800
- ☐ **d.** $96,200

Explanation: The correct answer is: **b.** $92,800.

The initial investment is calculated as:

Initial Investment = (Original Cost of Equipment) + (Increase in Accounts Receivable) − (Increase in Accounts Payable) − (Proceeds from Sale of Existing Equipment) + (Tax Effect of Disposal of Existing Equipment)

Increase in Accounts Receivable = ($8,000 − $6,000) = $2,000

Increase in Accounts Payable = ($2,500 − $2,100) = $400

Proceeds from Sale of Existing Equipment = $3,000 (given)

Net Book Value = Original Cost − Accumulated Depreciation

Net Book Value = $50,000 − $45,000 = $5,000

Tax Effect of Disposal of Existing Equipment = (Tax Rate) (Proceeds from Sale − Net Book Value)

Tax Effect of Disposal of Existing Equipment = (0.4) ($3,000 − $5,000) = −$800

Initial Investment = $95,000 + $2,000 − $400 − $3,000 − $800 = $92,800

Question 2E3-CQ01

Topic: Payback and Discounted Payback

Hobart Corporation evaluates capital projects using a variety of performance screens, including a hurdle rate of 16%, payback period of 3 years or less, and an accounting rate of return of 20% or more. Management is completing review of a project on the basis of these projections:

Capital investment	$200,000
Annual cash flows	$74,000
Straight-line depreciation	5 years
Terminal value	$20,000

The projected internal rate of return is 20%. Which one of the following alternatives reflects the appropriate conclusions for the indicated evaluative measures?

	Internal Rate of Return	Payback
a.	Accept	Reject
b.	Reject	Reject
c.	Accept	Accept
d.	Reject	Accept

Explanation: The correct answer is: **c.** Accept; Accept.

Since the project's internal rate of return (IRR) of 20% exceeds the hurdle rate of 16%, it should be accepted on that basis.

The project's payback = $200,000 / $74,000 = 2.7 years, which is less than the minimum 3 years required. Therefore, the project should be accepted based on payback.

Question 2E3-CQ02

Topic: Payback and Discounted Payback

Quint Company uses the payback method as part of its analysis of capital investments. One of its projects requires a $140,000 investment and has these projected before-tax cash flows:

Year 1	$60,000
Year 2	60,000
Year 3	60,000
Year 4	80,000
Year 5	80,000

Quint has an effective 40% tax rate. Based on these data, the after-tax payback period is

- ☐ **a.** 1.5.
- ☐ **b.** 2.3.

□ **c.**   3.4.

□ **d.**   3.7.

Explanation: The correct answer is: **d.** 3.7.

The payback is the length of time it takes to recover the initial investment.

After-Tax Cash Flow for Year 1 = $60,000 (1 − 40% Tax Rate)

After-Tax Cash Flow for Year 1 = $60,000 (0.6) = $36,000

After-Tax Cash Flow for Year 2 = $60,000 (1 − 40% Tax Rate)

After-Tax Cash Flow for Year 2 = $60,000 (0.6) = $36,000

After-Tax Cash Flow for Year 3 = $60,000 (1 − 40% Tax Rate)

After-Tax Cash Flow for Year 3 = $60,000 (0.6) = $36,000

After-Tax Cash Flows for Year 4 = $80,000 (1 − 40% Tax Rate)

After-Tax Cash Flows for Year 4 = $80,000 (0.6) = $48,000

After-Tax Cash Flows for Year 5 = $80,000 (1 − 40% Tax Rate)

After-Tax Cash Flows for Year 5 = $80,000 (0.6) = $48,000

By the end of year 3, Quint will recover $108,000 ($36,000 + $36,000 + $36,000) of the $140,000.

By the end of year 4, Quint will recover $156,000 ($36,000 + $36,000 + $36,000 + $48,000) of the $140,000.

Therefore, the payback occurs at some point between year 3 and year 4.

The payback can be calculated as:

Payback = 3 Years + [($140,000 − $108,000) / ($156,000 − $108,000)]

Payback = 3 Years + ($32 / $48) = 3 Years + 0.67 Years = 3.67 Years, which is approximately 3.7 years.

Question 2E3-CQ03

Topic: Payback and Discounted Payback

Foster Manufacturing is analyzing a capital investment project that is forecasted to produce the following cash flows and net income.

Year	After-Tax Cash Flow	Net Income
0	($20,000)	$0
1	6,000	2,000
2	6,000	2,000
3	8,000	2,000
4	8,000	2,000

The payback period of this project will be

- ☐ **a.** 2.5 years.
- ☐ **b.** 2.6 years.
- ☐ **c.** 3.0 years.
- ☐ **d.** 3.3 years.

Explanation: The correct answer is: **c.** 3.0 years.

The payback is the length of time it takes to recover the initial investment. The payback period is the amount of time it takes to have the initial investment equal to the future cash flows.

The investment will recover the initial investment of $20,000 in 3 years, as shown next.

Initial Investment = −$20,000

Sum of Cash Flows, Years 1, 2 and 3 = $6,000 + $6,000 + $8,000 = $20,000

At the end of year 3, the cash flows are equal to the initial investment

Question 2E3-LS02

Topic: Payback and Discounted Payback

Which of the following statements is **not** true of using the payback method in capital budgeting? The payback method

- ☐ **a.** provides a rough measure of project risk.
- ☐ **b.** takes into account the time value of money.
- ☐ **c.** does not distinguish between types of cash inflows.
- ☐ **d.** represents the break-even point for an investment.

Explanation: The correct answer is: **b.** takes into account the time value of money.

A disadvantage of the payback method is that it ignores the time value of money.

Question 2E4-CQ01

Topic: Risk Analysis in Capital Investment

Long Inc. is analyzing a $1 million investment in new equipment to produce a product with a $5 per unit margin. The equipment will last 5 years, be depreciated on a straight-line basis for tax purposes, and have no value at the end of its life. A study of unit sales produced these data:

Annual Unit Sales	Probability
80,000	0.10
85,000	0.20
90,000	0.30
95,000	0.20
100,000	0.10
110,000	0.10

If Long utilizes a 12% hurdle rate and is subject to a 40% effective income tax rate, the expected net present value of the project would be

- ☐ **a.** $261,750.
- ☐ **b.** $283,380.
- ☐ **c.** $297,800.
- ☐ **d.** $427,580.

Explanation: The correct answer is: **b.** $283,380.

To calculate the expected net present value (NPV) of the project, the first step is to calculate the expected annual sales, as shown:

Expected Annual Sales Volume = (Annual Sales Volume) (Associated Probability)

Expected Annual Sales Volume = (80,000) (0.1) + (85,000) (0.2) + (90,000) (0.3) + (95,000) (0.2) + (100,000) (0.1) + (110,000) (0.1)

Expected Annual Sales Volume = 8,000 + 17,000 + 27,000 + 19,000 + 10,000 + 11,000

Expected Annual Sales Volume = 92,000

Total Margin = (Sales) (Margin per Unit)

The expected margin per year would then be calculated as shown:

Expected Annual Margin = (92,000) ($5) = $460,000

The cash flow for each of the 5 years of the project is calculated as shown:

Cash Flow, Each Year = (Contribution Margin − Depreciation) (1 − Tax Rate) + Depreciation

Depreciation = $1,000,000 / 5 Years = $200,000 per Year

Cash Flow, Each Year = ($460,000 − $200,000) (1 − 0.4) + $200,000

Cash Flow, Each Year = $260,000 (0.6) + $200,000 = $156,000 + $200,000 = $356,000

The expected NPV of the project can now be calculated:

Expected NPV of Project = (Initial Investment) + (Estimated Annual Cash Flow)
(Present Value Factor of Annuity, $i = 12$, $n = 5$)

Expected NPV of Project = −$1,000,000 + ($356,000) (3.605) = $283,380

Question 2E4-CQ02

Topic: Risk Analysis in Capital Investment

Parker Industries is analyzing a $200,000 equipment investment to produce a new product for the next 5 years. A study of expected annual after-tax cash flows from the project produced these data:

Annual After-Tax Cash Flow	Probability
$45,000	0.10
50,000	0.20
55,000	0.30
60,000	0.20
65,000	0.10
70,000	0.10

If Parker utilizes a 14% hurdle rate, the probability of achieving a positive net present value is

- ☐ **a.** 20%.
- ☐ **b.** 30%.
- ☐ **c.** 40%.
- ☐ **d.** 60%.

Explanation: The correct answer is: **c.** 40%.

The annual after-tax cash flow required to generate a positive net present value (NPV) would be found by setting the NPV at 14% to 0.

The equation would be set up as shown next:

(Cash Flow) (3.433 Present Value Annuity, $i = 14$, $n = 5$) − $200,000 = 0

3.433 (Cash Flow) = $200,000

Cash Flow = $58,258 (which is almost $60,000)

The probability of having annual cash flows of $60,000 = 40% = (20% @ $60,000 + 10% @ $65,000 + 10% @ $70,000)

Question 2E4-LS03

Topic: Risk Analysis in Capital Investment

What is a primary caution when using a company's cost of capital as the discount rate to evaluate a capital project?

☐ **a.** Evaluation typically rejects high-risk projects.

☐ **b.** The cost of capital may need to be risk adjusted.

☐ **c.** Low-risk projects are favored.

☐ **d.** Opportunity costs can be distorted.

Explanation: The correct answer is: **b.** The cost of capital may need to be risk adjusted.

Many firms use their company's cost of capital as the yardstick to discount the cash flows on new investments. But in situations where new projects are more or less risky than is normal for the firm, use of the company rate can lead to erroneously accepting or rejecting a project.

Question 2E4-LS04

Topic: Risk Analysis in Capital Investment

Which type of real option would a firm be **most** likely to choose if there is a high probability that competitors can enter a market and capture profitable future cash flows?

☐ **a.** Adapt

☐ **b.** Abandon

☐ **c.** Postpone

☐ **d.** Expand

Explanation: The correct answer is: **a.** Adapt.

The ability of a firm to vary output or production methods in response to demand allows the firm to swap or exchange its output mix as demand changes. Given the myriad tumultuous and competitive market situations, companies often build flexibility into their manufacturing operations so they can respond quickly to any changes and produce the most valuable set of outputs.

Section E: Professional Ethics

Question 2F1-AT01

Topic: Ethical Considerations for Management Accounting and Financial Management

As management accountants progress in the profession, they often have the responsibility to supervise the work of less experienced workers. Which of the following is an ethical responsibility of the supervisor?

☐ **a.** Hire new workers who will fit in socially with existing staff.

☐ **b.** Maximize the profit or minimize the cost of the department.

☐ **c.** Ensure that workers handle confidential information appropriately.

☐ **d.** Encourage the workers to develop relations with customers.

Explanation: The correct answer is: **c.** Ensure that workers handle confidential information appropriately.

Per the *IMA Statement of Ethical Professional Practice,* a management accountant has the responsibility to keep information confidential except when disclosure is authorized or legally required. A management accountant also has the responsibility to inform all relevant parties regarding appropriate use of confidential information. This includes monitoring subordinates' activities to ensure compliance.

Question 2F1-AT02

Topic: Ethical Considerations for Management Accounting and Financial Management

Sam Smith has been offered a pair of tickets to the pro football team if Smith purchases a computerized inventory control system from a specific vendor. Which of the following steps should Smith take?

- ☐ **a.** Refuse any further conversations with the vendor.
- ☐ **b.** Review his company's policies on gifts from vendors.
- ☐ **c.** Sign the contract for the system if the price of the ticket is less than $50.
- ☐ **d.** Consult with the Audit Committee of the board of directors.

Explanation: The correct answer is: **b.** Review his company's policies on gifts from vendors.

According to the *IMA Statement of Ethical Professional Practice,* when faced with ethical issues, an individual should follow his or her organization's established policies on the resolution of such a conflict.

Question 2F1-AT03

Topic: Ethical Considerations for Management Accounting and Financial Management

John Moore was recently hired as assistant controller of a manufacturing company. The company controller, Nancy Kay, has forecasted a 16% increase in annual earnings. However, during the last quarter of the year, John estimates that the company will report only a 12% increase in earnings. When he reports this to Nancy, she tells him that meeting the numbers won't be a problem. She explains that there are several jobs in production that will finish after the end of the fiscal year, and she will record the associated revenue in the accounting system for the current year.

What is the first step that John Moore should take at this time?

- ☐ **a.** Notify the audit committee of the issue.
- ☐ **b.** Contact his lawyer to determine his rights.
- ☐ **c.** Discuss the issue with the chief financial officer of another company, who does not know any employees at John's company.
- ☐ **d.** Follow his organization's established policies regarding the resolution of this type of conflict.

Explanation: The correct answer is: **d.** Follow his organization's established policies regarding the resolution of this type of conflict.

Before taking any steps, John Moore should check to see if his organization has established policies regarding how to handle this type of conflict. If such policies exist, he should follow them.

Question 2F2-AT01

Topic: Ethical Considerations for the Organization

The Foreign Corrupt Practices Act is a U.S. law that prohibits U.S. companies from

- ☐ **a.** making "corrupt" payments to foreign officials for the purpose of obtaining or retaining business.

- ☐ **b.** making products in overseas markets that do not comply with the same safety and environmental regulations as for domestically produced products.

- ☐ **c.** exporting to countries that do not comply with U.S. human rights regulations.

- ☐ **d.** selling products for corrupt, unethical, or illegal purposes.

Explanation: The correct answer is: **a.** making "corrupt" payments to foreign officials for the purpose of obtaining or retaining business.

The 1977 Foreign Corrupt Practices Act is a U.S. law that forbids U.S. companies from obtaining contracts or business through the payment of bribes.

Question 2F2-AT02

Topic: Ethical Considerations for the Organization

Which of the following actions will most likely result in a successful foreign business venture in Islamic countries?

- ☐ **a.** Employ Islamic people.
- ☐ **b.** Behave in a manner that is consistent with Islamic ethics.
- ☐ **c.** Have property in an Islamic nation.
- ☐ **d.** Adhere to Islamic beliefs.

Explanation: The correct answer is: **b.** Behave in a manner that is consistent with Islamic ethics.

Successful operation by a company operating in a foreign country is a function of how well the company adapts to the host country's culture. Successful adaptation includes behaving in a manner that is consistent with the host country's ethics.

Time Value of Money Tables

Present Value of $1

Periods	1%	2%	3%	4%	5%	6%	7%	8%	9%	10%	11%	12%	13%	14%	15%	16%	18%	20%
1	0.990	0.980	0.971	0.962	0.952	0.943	0.935	0.926	0.917	0.909	0.901	0.893	0.885	0.877	0.870	0.862	0.847	0.833
2	0.980	0.961	0.943	0.925	0.907	0.890	0.873	0.857	0.842	0.826	0.812	0.797	0.783	0.769	0.756	0.743	0.718	0.694
3	0.971	0.942	0.915	0.889	0.864	0.840	0.816	0.794	0.772	0.751	0.731	0.712	0.693	0.675	0.658	0.641	0.609	0.579
4	0.961	0.924	0.888	0.855	0.823	0.792	0.763	0.735	0.708	0.683	0.659	0.636	0.613	0.592	0.572	0.552	0.516	0.482
5	0.951	0.906	0.863	0.822	0.784	0.747	0.713	0.681	0.650	0.621	0.593	0.567	0.543	0.519	0.497	0.476	0.437	0.402
6	0.942	0.888	0.837	0.790	0.746	0.705	0.666	0.630	0.596	0.564	0.535	0.507	0.480	0.456	0.432	0.410	0.370	0.335
7	0.933	0.871	0.813	0.760	0.711	0.665	0.623	0.583	0.547	0.513	0.482	0.452	0.425	0.400	0.376	0.354	0.314	0.279
8	0.923	0.853	0.789	0.731	0.677	0.627	0.582	0.540	0.502	0.467	0.434	0.404	0.376	0.351	0.327	0.305	0.266	0.233
9	0.914	0.837	0.766	0.703	0.645	0.592	0.544	0.500	0.460	0.424	0.391	0.361	0.333	0.308	0.284	0.263	0.225	0.194
10	0.905	0.820	0.744	0.676	0.614	0.558	0.508	0.463	0.422	0.386	0.352	0.322	0.295	0.270	0.247	0.227	0.191	0.162
11	0.896	0.804	0.722	0.650	0.585	0.527	0.475	0.429	0.388	0.350	0.317	0.287	0.261	0.237	0.215	0.195	0.162	0.135
12	0.887	0.788	0.701	0.625	0.557	0.497	0.444	0.397	0.356	0.319	0.286	0.257	0.231	0.208	0.187	0.168	0.137	0.112
13	0.879	0.773	0.681	0.601	0.530	0.469	0.415	0.368	0.326	0.290	0.258	0.229	0.204	0.182	0.163	0.145	0.116	0.093
14	0.870	0.758	0.661	0.577	0.505	0.442	0.388	0.340	0.299	0.263	0.232	0.205	0.181	0.160	0.141	0.125	0.099	0.078
15	0.861	0.743	0.642	0.555	0.481	0.417	0.362	0.315	0.275	0.239	0.209	0.183	0.160	0.140	0.123	0.108	0.084	0.065
16	0.853	0.728	0.623	0.534	0.458	0.394	0.339	0.292	0.252	0.218	0.188	0.163	0.141	0.123	0.107	0.093	0.071	0.054
18	0.836	0.700	0.587	0.494	0.416	0.350	0.296	0.250	0.212	0.180	0.153	0.130	0.111	0.095	0.081	0.069	0.051	0.038
20	0.820	0.673	0.554	0.456	0.377	0.312	0.258	0.215	0.178	0.149	0.124	0.104	0.087	0.073	0.061	0.051	0.037	0.026
22	0.803	0.647	0.522	0.422	0.342	0.278	0.226	0.184	0.150	0.123	0.101	0.083	0.070	0.056	0.046	0.038	0.026	0.018
24	0.788	0.622	0.492	0.390	0.310	0.247	0.197	0.158	0.126	0.102	0.082	0.066	0.053	0.043	0.035	0.028	0.019	0.013

Present Value of an Annuity

Periods	1%	2%	3%	4%	5%	6%	7%	8%	9%	10%	11%	12%	13%	14%	15%	16%	18%	20%
1	0.990	0.980	0.971	0.962	0.952	0.943	0.935	0.926	0.917	0.909	0.901	0.893	0.885	0.877	0.870	0.862	0.847	0.833
2	1.970	1.942	1.913	1.886	1.859	1.833	1.808	1.783	1.759	1.736	1.713	1.690	1.668	1.647	1.626	1.605	1.566	1.528
3	2.941	2.884	2.829	2.775	2.723	2.673	2.624	2.577	2.531	2.487	2.444	2.402	2.361	2.322	2.283	2.246	2.174	2.106
4	3.902	3.808	3.717	3.630	3.546	3.465	3.387	3.312	3.240	3.170	3.102	3.037	2.974	2.914	2.855	2.798	2.690	2.589
5	4.853	4.713	4.580	4.452	4.329	4.212	4.100	3.993	3.890	3.791	3.696	3.605	3.517	3.433	3.352	3.274	3.127	2.991
6	5.795	5.601	5.417	5.242	5.076	4.917	4.767	4.623	4.486	4.355	4.231	4.111	3.998	3.889	3.784	3.685	3.498	3.326
7	6.728	6.472	6.230	6.002	5.786	5.582	5.389	5.206	5.033	4.868	4.712	4.564	4.423	4.288	4.160	4.039	3.812	3.605
8	7.652	7.325	7.020	6.733	6.463	6.210	5.971	5.747	5.535	5.335	5.146	4.968	4.799	4.639	4.487	4.344	4.078	3.837
9	8.566	8.162	7.786	7.435	7.108	6.802	6.515	6.247	5.995	5.759	5.537	5.328	5.132	4.946	4.772	4.607	4.303	4.031
10	9.471	8.983	8.530	8.111	7.722	7.360	7.024	6.710	6.418	6.145	5.889	5.650	5.426	5.216	5.019	4.833	4.494	4.192
11	10.37	9.787	9.253	8.760	8.306	7.887	7.499	7.139	5.805	6.495	6.207	5.938	5.687	5.453	5.234	5.029	4.656	4.327
12	11.26	10.58	9.954	9.385	8.863	8.384	7.943	7.536	7.161	6.814	6.492	6.194	5.918	5.660	5.421	5.197	4.793	4.439
13	12.13	11.35	10.63	9.986	9.394	8.853	8.358	7.904	7.487	7.103	6.750	6.424	6.122	5.842	5.583	5.342	4.910	4.533
14	13.00	12.11	11.30	10.56	9.899	9.295	8.745	8.244	7.786	7.367	6.982	6.628	6.302	6.002	5.724	5.468	5.008	4.611
15	13.87	12.85	11.94	11.12	10.38	9.712	9.108	8.559	8.061	7.606	7.191	6.811	6.462	6.142	5.847	5.575	5.092	4.675
16	14.72	13.58	12.56	11.65	10.84	10.11	9.447	8.851	8.313	7.824	7.379	6.974	6.604	6.265	5.954	5.668	5.162	4.730
18	16.398	14.992	13.754	12.659	11.690	10.828	10.059	9.372	8.756	8.201	7.702	7.250	6.840	6.467	6.128	5.818	5.273	4.812
20	18.046	16.351	14.877	13.590	12.462	11.470	10.594	9.818	9.129	8.514	7.963	7.469	7.025	6.623	6.259	5.929	5.353	4.870
22	19.660	17.658	15.937	14.451	13.163	12.042	11.061	10.201	9.442	8.772	8.176	7.645	7.170	6.743	6.359	6.011	5.410	4.909
24	21.243	18.914	16.936	15.247	13.799	12.550	11.469	10.529	9.707	8.985	8.348	7.784	7.283	6.835	6.434	6.073	5.451	4.937
26	22.795	20.121	17.877	15.983	14.375	13.003	11.826	10.810	9.929	9.161	8.488	7.896	7.372	6.906	6.491	6.118	5.480	4.956
28	24.316	21.281	18.764	16.663	14.898	13.406	12.137	11.051	10.116	9.307	8.602	7.984	7.441	6.961	6.534	6.152	5.502	4.970
30	25.808	22.396	19.600	17.292	15.372	13.765	12.409	11.258	10.274	9.427	8.694	8.055	7.496	7.003	6.566	6.177	5.517	4.979
32	27.270	23.468	20.389	17.874	15.803	14.084	12.647	11.435	10.406	9.526	8.769	8.112	7.538	7.035	6.591	6.196	5.528	4.985
34	28.703	24.499	21.132	18.411	16.193	14.368	12.854	11.587	10.518	9.609	8.829	8.157	7.572	7.06	6.609	6.21	5.536	4.99
36	30.108	25.489	21.832	18.908	16.547	14.621	13.035	11.717	10.612	9.677	8.879	8.192	7.598	7.079	6.623	6.22	5.541	4.993
40	32.835	27.355	23.115	19.793	17.159	15.046	13.332	11.925	10.757	9.779	8.951	8.244	7.634	7.105	6.642	6.233	5.548	4.997

ICMA Learning Outcome Statements—Part 2

Revised January 2015
Source: Institute of Certified Management Accountants

Section A. Financial Statement Analysis (25%—Levels A, B, and C)

Part 2–Section A.1. Basic Financial Statement Analysis

a. for the balance sheet and income statement prepare and analyze common-size financial statements; i.e., calculate percentage of assets and sales, respectively; also called vertical analysis

b. for the balance sheet and income statement prepare a comparative financial statement horizontal analysis; i.e., calculate trend year over year for every item on the financial statement compared to base year

c. calculate the growth rate of individual line items on the balance sheet and income statement

Part 2–Section A.2. Financial Ratios

The candidate should be able to:

Liquidity

a. calculate and interpret the current ratio, the quick (acid-test) ratio, the cash ratio, the cash flow ratio, and the net working capital ratio

b. explain how changes in one or more of the elements of current assets, current liabilities, and/or unit sales can change the liquidity ratios and calculate that impact

c. demonstrate an understanding of the liquidity of current liabilities

Leverage

d. define solvency

e. define operating leverage and financial leverage

f. calculate degree of operating leverage and degree of financial leverage

g. demonstrate an understanding of the effect on the capital structure and solvency of a company with a change in the composition of debt vs. equity by calculating leverage ratios

h. calculate and interpret the financial leverage ratio, and determine the effect of a given change in capital structure on this ratio

i. calculate and interpret the following ratios: total debt to total capital, debt to equity, long-term debt to equity, and debt to total assets

j. define, calculate and interpret the following ratios: fixed charge coverage (earnings to fixed charges), interest coverage (times interest earned), and cash flow to fixed charges

k. discuss how capital structure decisions affect the risk profile of a firm

Activity

l. calculate and interpret accounts receivable turnover, inventory turnover and accounts payable turnover

m. calculate and interpret days sales outstanding in receivables, days sales in inventory, and days purchases in accounts payable

n. define and calculate the operating cycle and cash cycle of a firm

o. calculate and interpret total assets turnover and fixed asset turnover

Profitability

p. calculate and interpret gross profit margin percentage, operating profit margin percentage, net profit margin percentage, and earnings before interest, taxes, depreciation, and amortization (EBITDA) margin percentage

q. calculate and interpret return on assets (ROA) and return on equity (ROE)

Market

r. calculate and interpret the market/book ratio, the price/earnings ratio and price to EBITDA ratio

s. calculate and interpret book value per share

t. identify and explain the limitations of book value per share

u. calculate and interpret basic and diluted earnings per share

v. calculate and interpret earnings yield, dividend yield, dividend payout ratio and shareholder return

General

w. identify the limitations of ratio analysis

x. demonstrate a familiarity with the sources of financial information about public companies and industry ratio averages

y. evaluate the financial strength and performance of an entity based on multiple ratios

Part 2–Section A.3. Profitability analysis

a. demonstrate an understanding of the factors that contribute to inconsistent definitions of "equity," "assets" and "return" when using ROA and ROE

b. determine the effect on return on total assets of a change in one or more elements of the financial statements

c. identify factors to be considered in measuring income, including estimates, accounting methods, disclosure incentives, and the different needs of users

d. explain the importance of the source, stability, and trend of sales and revenue

e. demonstrate an understanding of the relationship between revenue and receivables and revenue and inventory

f. determine and analyze the effect on revenue of changes in revenue recognition and measurement methods

g. analyze cost of sales by calculating and interpreting the gross profit margin

h. distinguish between gross profit margin, operating profit margin and net profit margin and analyze the effects of changes in the components of each

i. define and perform a variation analysis (percentage change over time)

j. calculate and interpret sustainable equity growth

Part 2–Section A.4. Special issues

The candidate should be able to:

a. demonstrate an understanding of the impact of foreign exchange fluctuations
   1. identify and explain issues in the accounting for foreign operations (e.g., historical vs. current rate and the treatment of translation gains and losses)
   2. define functional currency
   3. calculate the financial ratio impact of a change in exchange rates
   4. discuss the possible impact on management and investor behavior of volatility in reported earnings

b. demonstrate an understanding of the impact of inflation on financial ratios and the reliability of financial ratios

c. define and explain off-balance sheet financing
   1. identify and describe the following forms of off-balance sheet financing: (i) leases; (ii) special purpose entities; (iii) sale of receivables; and (iv) joint ventures
   2. explain why companies use off-balance sheet financing
   3. calculate the impact of off-balance sheet financing on the debt to equity ratio

d. describe how to adjust financial statements for changes in accounting treatments (principles, estimates, and errors) and how these adjustments impact financial ratios

e. distinguish between book value and market value; and distinguish between accounting profit and economic profit

f. identify the determinants and indicators of earnings quality, and explain why they are important

Section B. Corporate Finance (20%—Levels A, B, and C)

Part 2–Section B.1. Risk and return

The candidate should be able to:

a. calculate rates of return
b. identify and demonstrate an understanding of systematic (market) risk and unsystematic (company) risk
c. identify and demonstrate an understanding of credit risk, foreign exchange risk, interest rate risk, market risk, industry risk and political risk
d. demonstrate an understanding of the relationship between risk and return
e. distinguish between individual security risk and portfolio risk
f. demonstrate an understanding of diversification
g. define beta and explain how a change in beta impacts a security's price
h. demonstrate an understanding of the Capital Asset Pricing Model (CAPM) and calculate the expected risk-adjusted returns using CAPM

Part 2–Section B.2. Long-term financial management

The candidate should be able to:

a. describe the term structure of interest rates, and explain why it changes over time
b. define and identify the characteristics of common stock and preferred stock
c. identify and describe the basic features of a bond such as maturity, par value, coupon rate, provisions for redeeming, conversion provisions, covenants, options granted to the issuer or investor, indentures, and restrictions
d. identify and evaluate debt issuance or refinancing strategies
e. value bonds, common stock, and preferred stock using discounted cash flow methods
f. demonstrate an understanding of duration as a measure of bond interest rate sensitivity
g. explain how income taxes impact financing decisions
h. define and demonstrate an understanding of derivatives and their uses
i. identify and describe the basic features of futures and forwards
j. distinguish a long position from a short position
k. define options and distinguish between a call and a put by identifying the characteristics of each
l. define exercise price, strike price, option premium and intrinsic value
m. demonstrate an understanding of the interrelationship of the variables that comprise the value of an option; e.g., relationship between exercise price and strike price, and value of a call
n. define swaps for interest rate and foreign currency
o. define and identify characteristics of other sources of long-term financing, such as leases, convertible securities, and warrants
p. demonstrate an understanding of the relationship among inflation, interest rates, and the prices of financial instruments

q. define the cost of capital and demonstrate an understanding of its applications in capital structure decisions

r. determine the weighted average (historical) cost of capital and the cost of its individual components

s. calculate the marginal cost of capital

t. explain the importance of using marginal cost as opposed to historical cost

u. demonstrate an understanding of the use of the cost of capital in capital investment decisions

v. demonstrate an understanding of how income taxes impact capital structure and capital investment decisions

w. use the constant growth dividend discount model to value stock and demonstrate an understanding of the two-stage dividend discount model

x. demonstrate an understanding of relative or comparable valuation methods, such as price/earnings (P/E) ratios, market/book ratios, and price/sales ratios

Part 2–Section B.3. Raising capital

The candidate should be able to:

a. identify the characteristics of the different types of financial markets and exchanges

b. demonstrate an understanding of the concept of market efficiency, including the strong form, semi-strong form, and weak form of market efficiency

c. describe the role of the credit rating agencies

d. demonstrate an understanding of the roles of investment banks, including underwriting, advice, and trading

e. define initial public offerings (IPOs)

f. define subsequent/secondary offerings

g. describe lease financing, explain its benefits and disadvantages, and calculate the net advantage to leasing using discounted cash flow concepts

h. define the different types of dividends, including cash dividends, stock dividends, and stock splits

i. identify and discuss the factors that influence the dividend policy of a firm

j. demonstrate an understanding of the dividend payment process for both common and preferred stock

k. define share repurchase and explain why a firm would repurchase its stock

l. define insider trading and explain why it is illegal

Part 2–Section B.4. Working capital management

The candidate should be able to:

Working capital

a. define working capital and identify its components

b. calculate net working capital

c. explain the benefit of short-term financial forecasts in the management of working capital

Cash

d. identify and describe factors influencing the levels of cash
e. identify and explain the three motives for holding cash
f. prepare forecasts of future cash flows
g. identify methods of speeding up cash collections
h. calculate the net benefit of a lockbox system
i. define concentration banking
j. demonstrate an understanding of compensating balances
k. identify methods of slowing down disbursements
l. demonstrate an understanding of disbursement float and overdraft systems

Marketable securities

m. identify and describe reasons for holding marketable securities
n. define the different types of marketable securities, including money market instruments, T-bills, treasury notes, treasury bonds, repurchase agreements, Federal agency securities, bankers' acceptances, commercial paper, negotiable CDs, Eurodollar CDs, and other marketable securities
o. evaluate the trade-offs among the variables in marketable security selections, including safety, marketability, yield, maturity, and taxability
p. demonstrate an understanding of the risk and return trade-off

Accounts receivable

q. identify the factors influencing the level of receivables
r. demonstrate an understanding of the impact of changes in credit terms or collection policies on accounts receivable, working capital and sales volume
s. define default risk
t. identify and explain the factors involved in determining an optimal credit policy

Inventory

u. define lead time and safety stock; identify reasons for carrying inventory and the factors influencing its level
v. identify and calculate the costs related to inventory, including carrying costs, ordering costs and shortage (stockout) costs
w. explain how a just-in-time (JIT) inventory management system helps manage inventory
x. identify the interaction between high inventory turnover and high gross margin (calculation not required)
y. demonstrate an understanding of economic order quantity (EOQ) and how a change in one variable would affect the EOQ (calculation not required)

Short-term credit and working capital cost management

z. demonstrate an understanding of how risk affects a firm's approach to its current asset financing policy (aggressive, conservative, etc.)

aa. identify and describe the different types of short-term credit, including trade credit, short-term bank loans, commercial paper, lines of credit, and bankers' acceptances

bb. estimate the annual cost and effective annual interest rate of not taking a cash discount

cc. calculate the effective annual interest rate of a bank loan with a compensating balance requirement and/or a commitment fee

dd. demonstrate an understanding of factoring accounts receivable and calculate the cost of factoring

ee. explain the maturity matching or hedging approach to financing

ff. demonstrate an understanding of the factors involved in managing the costs of working capital

General

gg. recommend a strategy for managing current assets that would fulfill a given objective

Part 2–Section B.5. Corporate restructuring

The candidate should be able to:

a. demonstrate an understanding of mergers, acquisitions, and leveraged buyouts

b. identify defenses against takeovers (e.g., golden parachute, leveraged recapitalization, poison pill (shareholders' rights plan), staggered board of directors, fair price, voting rights plan, white knight)

c. identify and describe divestiture concepts such as spin-offs, split-ups, equity carve-outs, and tracking stock

d. evaluate key factors in a company's financial situation and determine if a restructuring would be beneficial to the shareholders

e. validate possible synergies in targeted mergers and acquisitions

f. define bankruptcy

g. differentiate between reorganization and liquidation

h. value a business, a business segment, and a business combination using discounted cash flow method

i. evaluate a proposed business combination and make a recommendation based on both quantitative and qualitative considerations

Part 2–Section B.6. International finance

The candidate should be able to:

a. demonstrate an understanding of foreign currencies and how foreign currency affects the prices of goods and services

b. identify the variables that affect exchange rates

c. calculate whether a currency has depreciated or appreciated against another currency over a period of time, and evaluate the impact of the change

d. demonstrate how currency futures, currency swaps, and currency options can be used to manage exchange rate risk

e. calculate the net profit/loss of cross-border transactions, and evaluate the impact of this net profit/loss

f. recommend methods of managing exchange rate risk and calculate the net profit/loss of your strategy

g. identify and explain the benefits of international diversification

h. identify and explain common trade financing methods, including cross-border factoring, letters of credit, banker's acceptances, forfaiting, and countertrade

i. demonstrate an understanding of how transfer pricing affects effective world-wide tax rate

Section C. Decision Analysis (20%—Levels A, B, and C)

Part 2–Section C.1. Cost/volume/profit analysis

The candidate should be able to:

a. demonstrate an understanding of how cost/volume/profit (CVP) analysis (break-even analysis) is used to examine the behavior of total revenues, total costs, and operating income as changes occur in output levels, selling prices, variable costs per unit, or fixed costs

b. calculate operating income at different operating levels

c. differentiate between costs that are fixed and costs that are variable with respect to levels of output

d. explain why the classification of fixed vs. variable costs is affected by the time-frame being considered

e. calculate contribution margin per unit and total contribution margin

f. calculate the breakeven point in units and dollar sales to achieve targeted operating income or targeted net income

g. demonstrate an understanding of how changes in unit sales mix affect operating income in multiple-product situations

h. calculate multiple-product breakeven points given percentage share of sales and explain why there is no unique breakeven point in multiple-product situations

i. define, calculate and interpret margin of safety and margin of safety ratio

j. explain how sensitivity analysis can be used in CVP analysis when there is uncertainty about sales

k. analyze and recommend a course of action using CVP analysis

l. demonstrate an understanding of the impact of income taxes on CVP analysis

Part 2–Section C.2. Marginal analysis

The candidate should be able to:

a. identify and define relevant costs (incremental, marginal, or differential costs), sunk costs, avoidable costs, explicit and implicit costs, and relevant revenues
b. explain why sunk costs are not relevant in the decision-making process
c. demonstrate an understanding of and calculate opportunity costs
d. calculate relevant costs given a numerical scenario
e. define and calculate marginal cost and marginal revenue
f. identify and calculate total cost, average fixed cost, average variable cost, and average total cost
g. demonstrate proficiency in the use of marginal analysis for decisions such as (a) introducing a new product or changing output levels of existing products, (b) accepting or rejecting special orders, (c) making or buying a product or service, (d) selling a product or performing additional processes and selling a more value- added product, and (e) adding or dropping a segment
h. calculate the effect on operating income of a decision to accept or reject a special order when there is idle capacity and the order has no long-run implications
i. identify and describe qualitative factors in make-or-buy decisions, such as product quality and dependability of suppliers
j. calculate the effect on operating income of a make-or-buy decision
k. calculate the effects on operating income of a decision to sell or process further; and of a decision to drop or add a segment
l. identify the effects of changes in capacity on production decisions
m. demonstrate an understanding of the impact of income taxes on marginal analysis
n. recommend a course of action using marginal analysis

Part 2–Section C.3. Pricing

The candidate should be able to:

a. identify different pricing methodologies, including market comparables, cost-based, and value-based approaches
b. differentiate between a cost-based approach and a market-based approach to setting prices
c. calculate selling price using a cost-based approach
d. demonstrate an understanding of how the pricing of a product or service is affected by the demand for and supply of the product or service, as well as the market structure within which it operates
e. demonstrate an understanding of the impact of cartels on pricing
f. demonstrate an understanding of the short-run equilibrium price for the firm in (1) pure competition; (2) monopolistic competition; (3) oligopoly; and (4) monopoly using the concepts of marginal revenue and marginal cost

g. identify techniques used to set prices based on understanding customers' perceptions of value, competitors' technologies, products and costs

h. define and demonstrate an understanding of target pricing and target costing and identify the main steps in developing target prices and target costs

i. define value engineering

j. calculate the target operating income per unit and target cost per unit

k. define and distinguish between a value-added cost and a nonvalue-added cost

l. define the pricing technique of cost plus target rate of return

m. calculate the price elasticity of demand using the midpoint formula

n. define and explain elastic and inelastic demand

o. estimate total revenue given changes in prices and demand as well as elasticity

p. discuss how pricing decisions can differ in the short-run and in the long-run

q. define product life cycle and explain why pricing decisions might differ over the life of a product

r. evaluate and recommend pricing strategies under specific market conditions

Section D. Risk Management (10%—Levels A, B, and C)

Part 2–Section D.1. Enterprise risk

The candidate should be able to:

a. identify and explain the different types of risk, including business risk, hazard risks, financial risks, operational risks, and strategic risks

b. demonstrate an understanding of operational risk

c. define legal risk, compliance risk, and political risk

d. demonstrate an understanding of how volatility and time impact risk

e. define the concept of capital adequacy (i.e., solvency, liquidity, reserves, sufficient capital, etc.)

f. explain the use of probabilities in determining exposure to risk and calculate expected loss given a set of probabilities

g. define the concepts of unexpected loss and maximum possible loss (extreme or catastrophic loss)

h. identify strategies for risk response (or treatment), including actions to avoid, retain, reduce (mitigate), transfer (share), and exploit (accept) risks

i. define risk transfer (e.g., purchasing insurance, issuing debt)

j. demonstrate an understanding of the concept of residual risk and distinguish it from inherent risk

k. identify and explain the benefits of risk management

l. identify and describe the key steps in the risk management process

m. explain how attitude toward risk might affect the management of risk

n. demonstrate a general understanding of the use of liability/hazard insurance to mitigate risk (detailed knowledge not required)

o. identify methods of managing operational risk

    p. identify and explain financial risk management methods

    q. identify and explain qualitative risk assessment tools including risk identification, risk ranking, and risk maps

    r. identify and explain quantitative risk assessment tools including cash flow at risk, earnings at risk, earnings distributions, and earnings per share (EPS) distributions

    s. identify and explain Value at Risk (VaR) (calculations not required)

    t. define enterprise risk management (ERM) and identify and describe key objectives, components and benefits of an ERM program

    u. identify event identification techniques and provide examples of event identification within the context of an ERM approach

    v. explain the role of corporate governance, risk analytics, and portfolio management in an ERM program

    w. evaluate scenarios and recommend risk mitigation strategies

    x. prepare a cost-benefit analysis and demonstrate an understanding of its uses in risk assessment and decision making

    y. demonstrate an understanding of the COSO ERM conceptual framework

Section E. Investment Decisions (15%—Levels A, B, and C)

Part 2–Section E.1. Capital budgeting process

The candidate should be able to:

    a. define capital budgeting and identify the steps or stages undertaken in developing and implementing a capital budget for a project

    b. identify and calculate the relevant cash flows of a capital investment project on both a pretax and after-tax basis

    c. demonstrate an understanding of how income taxes affect cash flows

    d. distinguish between cash flows and accounting profits and discuss the relevance to capital budgeting of incremental cash flow, sunk cost, and opportunity cost

    e. explain the importance of changes in net working capital in capital budgeting

    f. discuss how the effects of inflation are reflected in capital budgeting analysis

    g. define hurdle rate

    h. identify and discuss qualitative considerations involved in the capital budgeting decision

    i. describe the role of the post-audit in the capital budgeting process

Part 2–Section E.2. Discounted cash flow analysis

The candidate should be able to:

    a. demonstrate an understanding of the two main discounted cash flow (DCF) methods, net present value (NPV) and internal rate of return (IRR)

   b. calculate NPV and IRR
   c. demonstrate an understanding of the decision criteria used in NPV and IRR analyses to determine acceptable projects
   d. compare NPV and IRR focusing on the relative advantages and disadvantages of each method, particularly with respect to independent versus mutually exclusive projects and the "multiple IRR problem"
   e. explain why NPV and IRR methods can produce conflicting rankings for capital projects if not applied properly
   f. identify assumptions of NPV and IRR
   g. evaluate and recommend project investments on the basis of DCF analysis

Part 2–Section E.3. Payback and discounted payback

The candidate should be able to:

   a. demonstrate an understanding of the payback and discounted payback methods
   b. identify the advantages and disadvantages of the payback and discounted payback methods
   c. calculate payback periods and discounted payback periods

Part 2–Section E.4. Risk analysis in capital investment

The candidate should be able to:

   a. identify alternative approaches to dealing with risk in capital budgeting
   b. distinguish among sensitivity analysis, scenario analysis, and Monte Carlo simulation as risk analysis techniques
   c. explain why a rate specifically adjusted for risk should be used when project cash flows are more or less risky than is normal for a firm
   d. explain how the value of a capital investment is increased if consideration is given to the possibility of adding on, speeding up, slowing up, or discontinuing early
   e. demonstrate an understanding of real options and identify examples of the different types of real options (calculations not required)

Section F. Professional Ethics (10%—Levels A, B, and C)

Ethics may be tested in conjunction with any topic area.

Part 2–Section F.1 Ethical considerations for management accounting and financial management professionals

Using the standards outlined in **IMA's** *Statement of Ethical Professional Practice*, the candidate should be able to:

  a. identify and describe the four overarching ethical principles

  b. evaluate a given business situation for its ethical implications

  c. identify and describe relevant standards that may have been violated in a given business situation and explain why the specific standards are applicable

  d. recommend a course of action for management accountants or financial managers to take when confronted with an ethical dilemma in the business environment

  e. evaluate and propose resolutions for ethical issues such as fraudulent reporting, manipulation of analyses, results, and budgets

Using the Fraud Triangle model, the candidate should be able to:

  f. identify the three components of the triangle

  g. use the model to explain how a management accounting and financial management professional can identify and manage the risk of fraud

Part 2–Section F.2. Ethical considerations for the organization

The candidate should be able to:

  a. identify the purpose of the U.S. Foreign Corrupt Practices Act

  b. identify the practices that the U.S Foreign Corrupt Practices Act prohibits, and explain how to apply this act to typical business situations

  c. apply relevant provisions of IMA's Statement on Management Accounting, "Values and Ethics: From Inception to Practice" to a business situation

  d. discuss corporate responsibility for ethical conduct

  e. explain why it is important for an organization to have a code of conduct

  f. demonstrate an understanding of the ways ethical values benefit an organization

  g. demonstrate an understanding of the differences between ethical and legal behavior

  h. demonstrate an understanding of role of "leadership by example" or "tone at the top" in determining an organization's ethical environment

  i. explain the importance of human capital to an organization in creating a climate where "doing the right thing" is expected (i.e., hiring the right people, providing them with training, and practicing consistent values-based leadership)

  j. explain how an organization's culture impacts its behavioral values

  k. explain the importance of an organization's core values in explaining its ethical behavior

  l. discuss the importance of employee training to maintaining an ethical organizational culture

  m. describe the following methods to monitor ethical compliance: human performance feedback loop and survey tools

  n. explain the importance of a whistleblowing framework (e.g., ethics helpline) to maintaining an ethical organizational culture

    o. identify the requirements of SOX Section 406—Code of Ethics for Senior Financial Officers

    p. discuss the issues organizations face in applying their values and ethical standards internationally

    q. demonstrate an understanding of the relationship between ethics and internal controls

Bibliography and References

American Institute of Certified Public Accountants, www.aicpa.org

Anderson, David R., Dennis J. Sweeney, Thomas A. Williams, Jeff Camm, and R. Kipp Martin. *Quantitative Methods for Business*, 11th ed. Mason, OH: South-Western, 2010.

Arens, Alvin A., Randal J. Elder, and Mark S. Beasley. *Auditing and Assurance Services: An Integrated Approach*, 13th ed. Upper Saddle River, NJ: Prentice-Hall, 2009.

Bergeron, Pierre G. *Finance: Essentials for the Successful Professional*. Independence, KY: Thomson Learning, 2002.

Bernstein, Leopold A., and John J. West. *Financial Statement Analysis: Theory, Application, and Interpretation*, 6th ed. Homewood, IL: Irwin, 1997.

Blocher, Edward J., David E. Stout, Paul E. Juras, and Gary Cokins. *Cost Management: A Strategic Emphasis*, 6th ed. New York: McGraw-Hill, 2013.

Bodnar, George H., and William S. Hopwood. *Accounting Information Systems*, 10th ed. Upper Saddle River, NJ: Prentice-Hall, 2010.

Brealey, Richard A., Stewart C. Myers, and Franklin Allen. *Principles of Corporate Finance*, 10th ed. New York: McGraw-Hill, 2011.

Brigham, Eugene F., and Michael C. Ehrhardt. *Financial Management: Theory and Practice*, 14th ed. Mason, OH: Cengage, 2013.

Campanella, Jack (ed.). *Principles of Quality Costs: Principles, Implementation, and Use*, 3rd ed. Milwaukee: ASQ Quality Press, 1999.

Committee of Sponsoring Organizations of the Treadway Commission (COSO), www.coso.org

Committee of Sponsoring Organizations of the Treadway Commission (COSO). *Enterprise Risk Management—Integrated Framework*. 2004.

Daniels, John D., Lee H. Radebaugh, and Daniel Sullivan. *International Business: Environments and Operations*, 14th ed. Upper Saddle River, NJ: Prentice-Hall, 2012.

Evans, Matt H. Course 11: The Balanced Scorecard, www.exinfm.com/training/pdfiles/course11r.pdf

Flesher, Dale. *Internal Auditing: Standards and Practices*. Altamonte Springs, FL: Institute of Internal Auditors, 1996.

Financial Accounting Standards Board, www.fasb.org

Financial Accounting Standards Board. *Statements of Financial Accounting Concepts*. Norwalk, CT: Author.

Forex Directory. "U.S. Dollar Charts," www.forexdirectory.net/chartsfx.html

Garrison, Ray H., Eric W. Noreen, and Peter Brewer. *Managerial Accounting*, 14th ed. Boston: McGraw-Hill/Irwin, 2011.

Gelinas, Ulric J. Jr., Richard B. Dull, and Patrick Wheeler. *Accounting Information Systems*, 9th ed. Cincinnati, OH: South-Western College Publishing, 2011.

Gibson, Charles H. *Financial Reporting and Analysis*, 13th ed. Mason, OH: South-Western Cengage Learning, 2013.

Goldratt, Elihayu M., and Jeff Cox. *The Goal: A Process of Ongoing Improvement*, 25th anniversary revised ed. Great Barrington, MA: North River Press, 2011.

Grant Thorton, LLP, www.grantthornton.ca

Greenstein, Marilyn, and Todd M. Feinman. *Electronic Commerce: Security, Risk Management, and Control.* Boston: McGraw-Hill Higher Education, 2000.

Hartgraves , A. L., and Wayne J. Morse. *Managerial Accounting*, 6th ed. Lombard, IL: Cambridge Business Publishers, 2012.

Hildebrand, David K., R. Lyman Ott, and J. Brian Gray. *Basic Statistical Ideas for Managers*, 2nd ed. Belmont, CA: Thomson Learning, 2005.

Hilton, Ronald W., Michael W. Maher, and Frank H. Selto. *Cost Management: Strategies for Business Decisions,* 4th ed. Boston: McGraw-Hill Irwin, 2007.

Horngren, Charles T., Srikant M. Datar, and Madhav Rajan. *Cost Accounting: A Managerial Emphasis*, 14th ed. Upper Saddle River, NJ: Prentice-Hall, 2012.

Hoyle, Joe B., Thomas F. Schaefer, and Timothy S. Doupnik. *Advanced Accounting,* 10th ed. Boston: McGraw-Hill Irwin, 2010.

Institute of Internal Auditors. "International Standards for the Professional Practice of Internal Auditing," https://na.theiia.org/standards-guidance/mandatory-guidance/Pages/Standards.aspx

Institute of Management Accountants, www.imanet.org

Institute of Management Accountants. *Enterprise Risk Management: Frameworks, Elements, and Integration.* Montvale, NJ: Author, 2006.

Institute of Management Accountants. *Enterprise Risk Management: Tools and Techniques for Effective Implementation.* Montvale, NJ: Author, 2007.

Institute of Management Accountants. *IMA Statement of Ethical Professional Practice.* Montvale, NJ: Author, 2005.

Institute of Management Accountants. *Managing Quality Improvements.* Montvale, NJ: Author, 1993.

Institute of Management Accountants. *Value and Ethics: From Inception to Practice.* Montvale, NJ: Author, 2008.

International Accounting Standards Board, www.ifrs.org

Investopedia.com, www.investopedia.com

Kaplan, Robert S., and David P. Norton. *The Balanced Scorecard: Translating Strategy into Action.* Boston: Harvard Business School Press, 1996.

Kaplan, Robert S., and David P. Norton. *The Strategy-Focused Organization: How Balanced Scorecard Companies Thrive in the New Business Environment.* Boston: Harvard Business School Press, 2001.

Kaplan, Robert S., and David P. Norton. "Using the Balanced Scorecard as a Strategic Management System." *Harvard Business Review* (January–February 1996).

Kieso, Donald E., Jerry J. Weygandt, and Terry D. Warfield. *Intermediate Accounting,* 14th ed. Hoboken, NJ: John Wiley & Sons, 2012.

Larsen, E. John. *Modern Advanced Accounting*, 10th ed. New York: McGraw-Hill, 2006.

Laudon, Kenneth C., and Jane P. Laudon. *Management Information Systems*, 11th ed. Upper Saddle River, NJ: Pearson Prentice Hall, 2010.

Mackenzie, Bruce, et al. *Interpretation and Application of International Financial Reporting Standards.* Hoboken, NJ: John Wiley & Sons, 2012.

McMillan, Edward J. *Not-for-Profit Budgeting and Financial Management.* Hoboken, NJ: John Wiley & Sons, 2010.

Moeller, Robert R. *COSO Enterprise Risk Management*, 2nd ed. Hoboken, NJ: John Wiley & Sons, 2011.

Moyer, R. Charles, James R. McGuigan, and Ramesh P. Rao. *Contemporary Financial Management*, 13th ed. Mason, OH: Cengage, 2014.

MSN Money. "Currency Exchange Rates," http://investing.money.msn.com/investments/exchange-rates/

Nicolai, Loren A., John D. Bazley, and Jefferson P. Jones. *Intermediate Accounting*, 11th ed. Mason, OH: Cengage, 2010.

Olve, Nils-Göran, and Anna Sjöstrand. *The Balanced Scorecard*, 2nd ed. Oxford, UK: Capstone, 2006.

Rosenberg, Jerry M. *The Essential Dictionary of International Trade*. New York: Barnes & Noble, 2004.

Sarbanes-Oxley, www.sarbanesoxleysimplified.com/sarbox/compact/htmlact/sec406.html

Sawyer, Lawrence B., Mortimer A. Dittenhofer, and Anne Graham (eds.). *Sawyer's Internal Auditing: The Practice of Modern Internal Auditing*, 5th ed. Altamonte Springs, FL: Institute of Internal Auditors, 2003.

Securities and Exchange Commission, www.sec.gov/rules/final/33-8177.htm

Shim, Jae K., and Joel G. Siegel. *Schaum's Outlines: Managerial Accounting*, 2nd ed. New York: McGraw-Hill, 2011.

Siegel, Joel G., Jae K. Shim, and Stephen W. Hartman. *Schaum's Quick Guide to Business Formulas: 201 Decision-Making Tools for Business, Finance, and Accounting Students*. New York: McGraw-Hill, 1998.

Simkin, Mark G., and Carolyn A. Strand Norman. Hoboken, NJ: John Wiley & Sons, 2011.

Simkin, Mark G., Jacob M. Rose, and Carolyn S. Norman. *Core Concepts of Accounting Information Systems*, 12th ed. Hoboken, NJ: John Wiley & Sons, 2012.

Stiglitz, Joseph E. *Globalization and Its Discontents*. New York: Norton, 2002.

Subramanyam, K. R., and John L. Wild. *Financial Statement Analysis*, 10th ed. New York: McGraw Hill, 2009.

U.S. Department of Justice. Foreign Corrupt Practices Act, Antibribery Provisions, www.usdoj.gov/criminal/fraud/fcpa/guide.pdf

U.S. Securities and Exchange Commission, www.sec.gov

Van Horne, James C., and John M. Wachowicz Jr. *Fundamentals of Financial Management*, 13th ed. Harlow, UK: Pearson Education

Warren, Carl S., James M. Reeve, and Jonathan Duchac. *Financial and Managerial Accounting*, 12th ed. Mason, OH: Cengage, 2013.

Wessels, Walter J. *Economics*, 5th ed. New York: Barron's, 2012.

XE.com, www.xe.com

Index

This index identifies the page on which a key term or concept is introduced in context. It is not meant as a comprehensive index of all references to that term or concept.